THE
CHAMPAGNE
GUIDE

For Linden Stelzer

MIRACLE CHILD OF A MIRACULOUS VINTAGE
22 SEPTEMBER 2008

Published in Australia by Wine Press 2019

Brisbane, Australia
www.tysonstelzer.com
stelzer@winepress.com.au

Distributed by Hardie Grant Books

A Cataloguing-in-Publication entry is available from the catalogue of the
National Library of Australia at www.nla.gov.au
The Champagne Guide 2020-2021
ISBN 978 0 9806400 7 6

Editor: Katri Hilden
Designer: Tyson Stelzer
Cover Designer: Tyson Stelzer
Photographer: Tyson Stelzer
Production Assistant: Jody Rolfe

Colour reproduction by ColourChiefs
Printed in China by 1010 Printing International Limited

Cover inspired by Krug Clos du Mesnil, Riedel Veritas Champagne Glass and The Magazine of Art, 1897

THE CHAMPAGNE GUIDE

2020-2021
EDITION VI

TYSON STELZER

Wine Press

The majestic grand cru slopes of Aÿ glisten under a dawn frost in the depths of winter 2015.

CONTENTS

The setting sun illuminates a blanket of snow over the grand cru of Oger in winter 2013.

Twilight on the commanding premier cru slopes of Cumières, summer 2011.

IN CRISIS

The first touch of late-summer dawn exposes a dense fog veiling Épernay and engulfing the Grande Vallée de la Marne like a floating ocean that laps the coastline of the Montagne de Reims. Unseasonal winds race down the Vallée, whipping up waves of mist and hurling them towards the thundering grand crus of the Montagne. Oblivious to the unfolding drama, the serene slopes of the Côte des Blancs break the dim line of the distant horizon. Perched high on the hillside, the abbey of the fabled outpost of Hautvillers stands as a sentinel, surveying lines of vines that make a hazy patchwork on the shoreline of mist below, never lifting its gaze from the churnings of the heavens and their mark on the earth. This ancient abbey has seen 1367 harvests. But never one like this.

All is quiet early on the morning of Monday 21 August 2017 in the final week of summer holidays. A lone driver descends the Montagne de Reims on the D951 and plunges into the ocean that was Épernay, visibly perturbed as he is confronted by the spectacle of dawn mist. Such dense fog is not unfamiliar here. But not in this crucial week so early in the season.

Louis Roederer chef de cave Jean-Baptiste Lécaillon is on a mission. This is not one of his regular tours to assess his vineyards, visit his growers, check that his press centres are ready for the ensuing onslaught, or even to meet with the regional authorities in Épernay. He's bound for the fabled crus of the Côte des Blancs to meet with three of the most influential grower-producers: Anselme Selosse (Jacques Selosse), Rodolphe Péters (Pierre Péters) and Didier Gimonnet (Pierre Gimonnet).

This meeting of four of the greatest minds in Champagne between the rows of vines will change the destiny of their year's labours and seal the fate of all of their harvests. Today they will make the most important decision of the year and decide the date of harvest of chardonnay.

Little do they know what is yet in store. Before the end of the week, 60 millimetres of rain will inundate the Montagne de Reims and Vallée de la Marne, drowning the vines and with them any last hope of rescuing the harvest. Vintage 2017 had already unleashed the perfect storm of severe frosts, record heat and torrential rain, inducing an outbreak of rot like Champagne had never seen. Jean-Baptiste Lécaillon would later join everyone in Champagne in declaring this far and away the toughest vintage of his career.

Champagne's climate is in crisis, to profound and unprecedented extremes in the past five vintages, and each for vastly disparate reasons (see page 27). The region that has been obliterated on the front line of centuries of wars, decimated by ever more tumultuous weather events and buffeted by economic and political crises could never have anticipated what August 2017 beheld.

And yet, impossibly and triumphantly, Champagne is emphatically in the best place today that it has ever been. Not in spite of the rising challenges it is facing on so many fronts, but because of them.

Across the sweep of history, it has been during the eras of prosperity that Champagne has become notoriously complacent in its viticulture, lazy in its winemaking and tiresomely fabricated in its marketing, for which it has been widely and rightly chastised.

And it has been from times of hardship that Champagne has made its greatest advances. Almost a century ago, it was ultimately out of the crisis of phylloxera that Champagne's appellation system was born. The string of vintages that followed the region's obliteration during World War II rank among some of the greatest of the century. And the global financial crisis of the past decade provided the much-needed impetus for Champagne to get its supply and demand balance in order and rethink the expansion of its appellation.

Champagne is in a very difficult place climatically, politically and economically right now. In response, its top players have never worked harder and have never been stronger. This decade, the region has entered a phase of fundamental change in the way its grapes are grown and sourced, the way its wines are made, how its companies are structured and even how and where its cuvées are sold.

Vintage 2017 was the wake-up call that Champagne had to have (see page 56). For decades, Champagne has been the laughing stock of responsible growers everywhere, notoriously piling on herbicides, fungicides, pesticides, fertilisers and even Parisian rubbish to shamelessly bolster its poor vines to ludicrous yields. The heroes of 2017 proved to be sustainably managed vines of respectable yields, setting a precedent that is inspiring otherwise reluctant growers to follow (see page 62).

In the market, global forces continue to buffet the region, and 2018 marked a milestone turning point for the balance of

Dawn mist rolls up the slopes of Mutigny at the end of harvest 2014.

champagne sales. A depressed French market collided with Brexit and, for the first time in history, not only did champagne exports exceed French sales, but exports to countries outside the European Union exceeded those within. Highly dependent upon the domestic market, grower-producers were the hardest hit.

These challenges of erratic harvests and global economies are fundamentally changing the balance within Champagne, driving growers to sell all their fruit, some to relinquish their status and become négociants, and others to sell up altogether (see page 68).

At the same time, the economies of champagne production are in a rapid state of flux as grape and vineyard prices spiral. The region with the highest cost of production in the wine world continues to churn out the most affordable wines of the luxury world, but is this sustainable (see page 74)?

It's crunch time in Champagne, as climatic, political and economic upheaval fundamentally and dramatically transforms the champagne landscape. I have been privileged to go deeper behind the scenes in Champagne than ever over the past two years, with more long visits and conversations on and off the record, not with the authorities, but with the houses, growers and coopératives working fanatically on the front lines of the vineyards, the cellars and the marketplace to make champagne what it is today.

And that is a very different place to what it was 20 years ago, or even five years ago. The dynamic on the ground in Champagne is ever more complex and changing rapidly. I feel a deeper weight of responsibility than ever to communicate this in the detail that it deserves, and this is why this edition is more than double the size of any before it.

In spite of the challenges facing Champagne today, the ultimate measure must always be the quality of the wine in the glass. For Champagne's top houses, who rigorously uphold fanatical attention to the finest detail in their vines and their wines, while maintaining an adaptable dexterity in the wake of the frenzy of change around them, this quality has never been higher than it is today (pages 15–19).

But this is not universal, and the disparity between those houses, growers and coopératives who have made changes and those who haven't is becoming an ever more gaping chasm. Those whose energy and focus remain stuck on art installations, spraying from podiums, coating bottles in metallic bling and even building rockets, have been left behind in the dark ages by houses whose obsession is set on improving vineyards, production and ultimately what's inside the bottle.

Quality, not quantity, must be upheld as the resolute priority. Some are concerned that champagne is losing market share. 'Once upon a time we were one-third of global sparkling wines, and now we are just four or five percent,' points out Jean-Hervé Chiquet (Jacquesson). 'But Champagne needs to have a smaller market share! Does it matter that Domaine de la Romanée Conti has a tiny market share? If you are the best, you don't care about being the biggest.'

At a time when sparkling regions the world over are rallying to craft ever more refined alternatives, Champagne must raise its game by upholding its quality, and marketing its only true point of difference: terroir.

'There are some houses who are adamant that we must promote ourselves like Prosecco, but I am convinced that Champagne must remain premium and promote the uniqueness of its terroirs,' urges Vitalie Taittinger.

However, the Comité Champagne, the region's official promotional and regulatory body, has a different priority. 'The Comité Champagne does not want us to talk about the detail because they are concerned we are complicating champagne,' reveals Antoine Malassagne (AR Lenoble). 'People are no longer buying champagne just because it's champagne.' The complexity of Champagne's terroir is second only to Burgundy, and its complicated production is second to none, and herein lie its fundamental points of difference that deserve to be front and centre. 'The Syndicat Général des Vignerons spent €4 million on a promotion that says nothing of the vineyards or what makes champagne distinctive or special,' bemoans Sophie Déthune (Paul Déthune).

'It is very important to promote what makes Champagne unique,' emphasises Laurent d'Harcourt (Pol Roger). 'We have two key competitive advantages: bad weather and bad soil!'

For Lécaillon, 'The magic of champagne belongs to the climate.' Even in the toughest vintage of his career.

As the fog lifts on that misty summer morning in August 2017, Lécaillon farewells his three grower friends. 'We are survivors,' he declares. 'So we have to be resilient. It is hard to grow anything here. And yet in spite of all this, we make the wines of celebration, of life and of resilience.'

THE CHAMPAGNE GUIDE

BIENVENUE!

WELCOME TO THE SIXTH EDITION OF THE CHAMPAGNE GUIDE

There's a dazzling world of champagne to be discovered. Never has a greater variety of styles, wider diversity of brands or more exquisite quality emerged from the source of the finest fizz on earth. Champagne offers more options than ever to add sparkle to your occasion, your cuisine and your mood. It's a thrilling chase to find just the right bottle, but it can be a daunting task, too. This book dares to present the most up-to-date picture of Champagne, to get under the surface of this vast and complex place to uncover the character of every cuvée and take the guesswork out of your next bottle of bubbles.

Champagne is fast on the move, and never have there been more groundbreaking developments, telling conversations, gripping stories, thrilling new discoveries and breathtaking cuvées to be shared. This is why this book is more than double the size of every edition to date.

Every year, 4159 champagne growers, 395 houses, and 42 coopératives lob some 302 million bottles into the world. This Guide is purposely not an onerous overview of them all, but rather a behind-the-scenes introduction to the very best, the most important and the most interesting.

It is an enchanting journey to get under the surface and discover the grand plethora of fascinating elements that shape the intricate personality of a bottle of champagne: its house style, vintage, grape varieties, reserve wines, winemaking techniques, chef de cave preferences, maturation time, dosage, time since disgorgement and, of course, the terroir of the vineyards themselves.

In the following pages, you'll discover not just what these things mean but, most importantly, how they smell, taste and feel in 834 champagnes from 139 of the top houses, all of which have been tasted recently, providing an up-to-date snapshot of champagnes just as you'll find them this year.

UP-TO-THE-MOMENT GUIDE

Time is everything in the development of champagne, and the landscape of the wines on the shelves is changing rapidly. An up-to-the-minute guide to the champagnes to drink this year is just as critical as it is for any other wine, and this is why this book is very different to every other champagne guide.

Every review is new. Since my last edition, new vintages have landed and non-vintages have rolled on to new blends. On occasions when last year's vintage is still current, I've retasted the wine and written an all-new assessment. I'm amazed yet again how quickly some have blossomed, and others have wilted.

Champagne is the most intricately complex of all wines to craft, and hence to assess. Every batch is different, according to how long it has relied upon the sustaining presence of lees prior to disgorgement, how long it has evolved post-disgorgement, the composition of the blend and the dosage for that disgorgement, not to mention how it has travelled. Even non-vintage blends change every vintage as an ever more temperamental mother nature foils even the most skilful blenders. This presents a dilemma in communicating meaningful guidance on each cuvée, and I have again earnestly sought to retaste as many times as possible, in some cases on as many as six different occasions.

This has all led me to a bold step which I believe to be unprecedented in champagne publishing – inclusion not only of disgorgement date, base vintage and location of tasting, but also of different scores for the same cuvée when these details change. A complex undertaking, but I'm convinced there's no other way to fairly interpret champagne for its markets across the globe.

I remain fiercely independent and have always completely distanced myself from champagne sales and distribution. There are some in champagne communication who align themselves only with growers, and others whose allegiances are tied exclusively with large houses. To me, both extremes fly in the face of the fabric of modern champagne and of all the structures and relationships that define it. Every player is granted voice in the following pages, purposely not equally, but as each is due merit.

This book is in every way my most courageous yet. Not because I have ever held back on honest assessments and frank ratings, but because space has not always permitted inclusion of the lesser houses and poorer cuvées. This year, they are almost all here, in their stark, unadorned and at times rustic authenticity, if not to encourage you to avoid them, then at least to highlight the great houses in their proper context. I've updated all 123 champagne producers, dropped a few lesser estates and added 32 new players. Even a massive 584 pages is insufficient to include everything, so 16 houses and scores for 20 cuvées that didn't make the cut are featured in the index (page 571).

A new era in champagne has arrived, and there has never been a better time to raise a glass to discover the intricate personality of the most celebrated beverage on earth. Get ready to sparkle.

The village of Le Mesnil-sur-Oger surrounds the fabled Clos du Mesnil.

USING THIS GUIDE

*C*hasing *the best fizz that money can buy? Bienvenue! Your glass is about to froth over. You'll be astounded at what champagne has to offer if you know what to look for this year, and the following pages will guarantee you don't miss a thing.*

My best-of lists and index by score provide instant access to all the highlights, and page references so you can get up to speed on the full story. A detailed glossary (pages 580–583) demystifies champagne language, a fully updated vintage guide (pages 27–35) gives an up-to-the-minute assessment of how the past 23 vintages are tracking today, and maps of the region are the most detailed in print (pages 40–53). As always, there are updates on where champagne is grown (page 39), how it is made (pages 54–55), and how to open, serve and cellar it (pages 78–79). To guarantee you are up to date with the very latest in Champagne, I've added all-new chapters on how to crack bottle codes to decipher disgorgement dates (pages 22–26), Champagne's response to climate change (pages 56–61), the move to sustainability (pages 62–67), the threats to the existence of grower producers (pages 68–73), the future of champagne prices (page 74) and champagne faults (pages 75–76).

WHAT DO MY SCORES MEAN?

Points are a quick way to highlight the best champagnes in each category. There is much controversy surrounding wine scores. It is of course a travesty to reduce the grand complexities of champagne to a single number, but I persist in doing so because many readers find this useful in honing in on the best cuvées of the year. As always, my descriptions, back story and technical details on each cuvée are infinitely more informative than scores, and more detailed than ever this year.

I persevere with the international 100 point system, not because I endorse it, but simply because it is universally understood. Broadly, anything less than 85 is faulty, less than 90 is sound but unexciting, and 91 is where all the real fun begins. A 94 point champagne has impeccable purity and immaculate balance – a gold medal in a wine show. Beyond, it's not greater concentration of flavour, more obvious fruit or more clever winemaking tricks that set it apart. True greatness is declared by something more profound: the inimitable stamp of place – 'terroir' to the French, articulated most eloquently in length of finish and palate texture. Persistence of aftertaste and depth of mineral character set apart the very finest champagnes.

100 The pinnacle of character, balance and persistence. This year, just 0.7% of champagnes tasted scored 100 points. Only two are currently available. Sadly, both are ear-splittingly expensive.

99 Almost perfection (20 on the 20 point scale). Just over 1% of champagnes tasted.

98 An exceedingly rare calibre of world-class distinction. Less than 3% of champagnes tasted. The prestige cuvées of the top houses tend to rule this territory.

97 More than exceptional. Less than 4% of champagnes tasted. Look out for one $$$ cuvée in the stratosphere this year.

96 Exceptional. Top gold or trophy standard in a wine show (19/20); less than 8% of champagnes tasted. There's something for everyone here this year, including eight $$ cuvées.

95 Offering an edge that pushes beyond excellent; less than 10% of champagnes tasted. Look out for 12 $$ cuvées.

94 Excellent champagne that I love. Gold medal in a wine show (18.5/20). Less than 14% of champagnes tasted.

93 Almost excellent; 13% of champagnes tasted.

92 A very good wine that characterises its place and variety; less than 10% of champagnes tasted. Look out for one $ cuvée.

91 Better than good, offering an edge of distinction. Silver medal (17/20); 9% of champagnes tasted. With 600 champagnes at 91 or above this year, why drink anything less?

90 A good wine that I like; 7% of champagnes tasted. Only buy if it's cheap.

89 Better than sound and almost good; just over 7% of champagnes tasted.

88 Sound. Worth buying if it's cheap. Bronze medal standard (15.5/20); less than 4% of champagnes tasted.

87 Almost sound; less than 4% of champagnes tasted.

86 Simple and ordinary; less than 2% of champagnes tasted.

85 Ordinary and boring, though without notable faults (14/20); less than 2% of champagnes tasted.

84 Borderline faulty. Just 1.5% of champagnes tasted.

83 Faulty. Caution! Less than 1% of champagnes tasted.

82 Distinctly faulty (12/20).

81 Exceedingly faulty. Keep a safe distance.

80 Horrid. You've been warned.

See page 571 for a full index of cuvées by score.

PRICE

Whether you're on the hunt for a bargain or a decadent splurge, this guide will help you find the right bottle in no time. Each cuvée is price-coded to indicate what you can expect to pay in an average retail store. Champagne is one of the most readily discounted wines on the shelves, so shop around and you're sure to find the big brands on special. Back-vintage champagnes not currently available are listed without indication of price, featured throughout the guide to provide an insight into the potential of the most age-worthy cuvées. This year there are fewer $ cuvées in the market than ever, as Champagne continues to raise quality, elevate its entry cuvées, and increasingly do away with its bottom-shelf supermarket labels. They were never worth drinking, anyway.

	Euros (France)	Great British Pounds	US Dollars	Australian Dollars	Hong Kong Dollars	Singapore Dollars
$	<€25	<£30	<$50	<$60	<$400	<$80
$$	€25–50	£30–50	$50–80	$60–100	$400–550	$80–140
$$$	€51–65	£51–65	$81–100	$101–150	$551–650	$141–160
$$$$	€66–140	£66–130	$101–200	$151–300	$651–1100	$161–250
$$$$$	>€140	>£130	>$200	>$300	>$1100	>$250

ON THE HOUSE

The Best Champagnes of the Year lists on the following pages highlight the most important wines in this book. These are the finest fizzes that money can buy this year, the most reliable bargains, the most pristine big blends, the most sought-after growers, the most sublime rosés, the most brilliant blanc de blancs, the most balanced low-dosage champagnes, and the upper reaches of the stratosphere of prestige.

The Champagne Guide 2020–2021 Hall of Honour is the most rigorous and up-to-the-minute shortlist in existence of the finest houses of the year. To win a coveted place is the highest endorsement a house can receive. Reputation, history, museum wines, branding, marketing, rhetoric and past performance count for nothing if the wines you can buy don't live up to expectation. A house is only as worthy as its current cuvées, so this ranking is built purely, exclusively and definitively on the cuvées on the shelves this year.

A high ranking requires the highest level of excellence at every level: entry non-vintage, vintage and prestige cuvées. Roughly, to rate 10 out of 10, the entry non-vintage cuvée of the house would typically score 95/100, vintage cuvées around 96, and prestige cuvées 97. To attain 5 out of 10, these drop to 91, 93 and 94 respectively.

This is by definition categorically not an all-inclusive list in which every child wins a prize; 5/10 is not a pass mark. Less than half – just 68 of the 139 houses tasted – made the cut this year, which means that achieving a coveted place in this list even at 5/10 is strong endorsement. To qualify, the entry cuvée of the house needs to achieve a score at least equivalent to a silver medal in a wine show. There is a prudent saying in Champagne that if you make a good brut NV, you are a good house. The entry-level cuvées that comprise the majority of the house's production bear a strong weighting in its rating.

Underperforming houses do not deserve your attention nor mine, so unless a house scores at least 5 out of 10, it does not score at all.

Now in its sixth edition, inclusion in my Hall of Honour is highly aspirational. Chef de caves and house principals ask me what they need to do to achieve a higher ranking, and express disappointment when they don't achieve it.

These ratings are by their nature highly controversial. As Champagne house styles increasingly diversify, it is ever more challenging to reduce their grand complexities to a single number. I encourage you to use these only as a guide to quickly home in on the very best houses. Bollinger and Krug are deserving of special mention for maintaining the highest rating of 10/10 in all six revisions, and Philipponnat for ascending two tiers this year.

HALL OF HONOUR

THE CHAMPAGNE GUIDE
· 2020–2021 ·

The Best Champagnes of the Year

🍂 Under $ 🍂

Lanson Black Label Brut NV
$ • 92 points • page 348

Baron-Fuenté Millésime Brut 2008
$ • 91 points • page 113

**De Saint Gall Blanc de Blancs
Premier Cru NV**
$ • 91 points • page 184

**Dérot-Delugny Cuvée des Fondateurs
Pinot Gris Brut NV**
$ • 91 points • page 197

🍂 Under $$ 🍂

Bollinger Special Cuvée Brut NV
$$ • 96 points • page 144

**Camille Savès Grand Cru
Cuvée Prestige Bouzy NV**
$$ • 96 points • page 160

Deutz Brut Millésimé 2013
$$ • 96 points • page 201

Lanson Gold Label Brut Vintage 2008
$$ • 96 points • page 352

**Marc Hébrart Mes Favorites
Vieilles Vignes NV**
$$ • 96 points • page 404

Billecart-Salmon Brut Réserve NV
$$ • 95 points • page 130

Louis Roederer Brut Premier NV
$$ • 95 points • page 387

**Philipponnat Blanc de Noirs
Extra Brut 2012**
$$ • 95 points • page 456

Philipponnat Royale Réserve Brut NV
$$ • 95 points • page 455

André Clouet Millésime Brut 2009
$$ • 94 points • page 95

Bérêche & Fils Brut Réserve NV
$$ • 94 points • page 119

Bruno Paillard Premier Cuvée NV
$$ • 94 points • page 156

**Camille Savès Premier Cru
Carte Blanche NV**
$$ • 94 points • page 160

Eric Rodez Blanc de Noirs Ambonnay NV
$$ • 94 points • page 249

Gatinois Aÿ Grand Cru Brut Réserve NV
$$ • 94 points • page 266

Jacquesson Cuvée 742 Extra Brut NV
$$ • 94 points • page 310

**Le Brun Servenay Grand Cru
Melodie en C Brut NV**
$$ • 94 points • page 371

Le Brun Servenay Odalie Brut NV
$$ • 94 points • page 371

Leclerc Briant Brut Réserve NV
$$ • 94 points • page 377

**Marc Hébrart Sélection
Brut Premier Cru NV**
$$ • 94 points • page 403

Philipponnat Royal Réserve Non Dose NV
$$ • 94 points • page 455

Pol Roger Brut Réserve NV
$$ • 94 points • page 486

Tarlant Zero Brut Nature NV
$$ • 94 points • page 525

**Veuve Clicquot Extra Brut
Extra Old 2 NV**
$$ • 94 points • page 548

🍂 Under $$$ 🍂

Billecart-Salmon Vintage 2008
$$$ • 97 points • page 132

Charles Heidsieck Brut Réserve NV
$$$ • 96 points • page 175

**Eric Rodez Cuvée des Grands Vintages
Ambonnay Grand Cru Brut NV**
$$$ • 96 points • page 249

**Philipponnat 1522 Grand Cru
Extra-Brut 2008**
$$$ • 96 points • page 457

**André Clouet Dream Collection
Vintage 2008**
$$$ • 95 points • page 96

Billecart-Salmon Vintage 2007
$$$ • 95 points • page 133

Devaux D Millésimé 2008
$$$ • 95 points • page 208

**Dumangin J Fils Le Vintage
Extra-Brut 2004**
$$$ • 95 points • page 225

**Egly-Ouriet Les Vignes de Vrigny
Premier Cru Brut NV**
$$$ • 95 points • page 239

**Gaston Chiquet Or
Premier Cru Brut 2008**
$$$ • 95 points • page 264

**Lallier Millésime Grand Cru
Brut 2008**
$$$ • 95 points • page 345

Marc Hébrart Special Club 2014
$$$ • 95 points • page 404

Pol Roger Vintage Brut 2012
$$$ • 95 points • page 487

**Taittinger Prélude Grand Crus
Brut NV**
$$$ • 95 points • page 518

**Vilmart & Cie Grand Cellier
Brut Premier Cru NV**
$$$ • 95 points • page 564

Alfred Gratien Brut Millésime 2005
$$$ • 94 points • page 92

Alfred Gratien Cuvée 565 NV
$$$ • 94 points • page 90

**De Sousa Mychorize Grand Cru
Extra Brut NV**
$$$ • 94 points • page 189

**Duménil Special Club
Premier Cru 2012**
$$$ • 94 points • page 229

**Eric Rodez Dosage Zéro
Ambonnay NV**
$$$ • 94 points • page 249

**Geoffroy Volupte Brut Premier Cru
Millésimé 2004**
$$$ • 94 points • page 271

**Laurenti Grande Cuvée
Tradition NV**
$$$ • 94 points • page 362

**Laurent-Perrier Millésimé
Brut 2007**
$$$ • 94 points • page 365

Louis Roederer Brut Vintage 2012
$$$ • 94 points • page 388

Mumm RSRV Cuvée 4.5 Brut NV
$$$ • 94 points • page 420

Nicolas Maillart Premier Cru 2012
$$$ • 94 points • page 427

Palmer & Co Vintage 2012
$$$ • 94 points • page 433

Paul Bara Special Club 2009
$$$ • 94 points • page 440

Pol Roger Vintage Brut 2009
$$$ • 94 points • page 488

**Roger Brun Grand Cru
Cuvée Des Sires Millésime 2013**
$$$ • 94 points • page 503

The Best Blanc de Blancs Champagnes of the Year $$–$$$

Rosé de saignée tank sample at Veuve Fourny, harvest 2017.

The Best Rosé Champagnes
of the Year $$–$$$

Deutz Brut Rosé Millésimé 2013
$$ • 96 points • page 202

Bollinger Rosé Brut NV
$$$ • 96 points • page 145

Louis Roederer Rosé 2013
$$$ • 96 points • page 391

Alfred Gratien Brut Rosé NV
$$ • 95 points • page 90

J.L. Vergnon Rosémotion
Grand Cru Extra Brut NV
$$ • 95 points • page 301

Lallier Grand Rosé Brut Grand Cru NV
$$ • 95 points • page 345

Billecart-Salmon Rosé Brut NV
$$$ • 95 points • page 132

Gosset Grand Rosé Brut NV
$$$ • 95 points • page 277

Pierre Péters Cuvée Rosé
for Albane Brut NV
$$$ • 95 points • page 474

Veuve Fourny & Fils Rosé
Les Rougemonts Extra Brut
Premier Cru NV
$$$ • 95 points • page 559

Veuve Fourny & Fils Rosé Vinothèque
Vertus Premier Cru MV12
Extra Brut NV
$$$ • 95 points • page 559

André Clouet Rosé No 3 Brut NV
$$ • 94 points • page 94

Camille Savès Grand Cru
Cuvée Rosé Bouzy NV
$$ • 94 points • page 161

Devaux D Rosé NV
$$ • 94 points • page 208

Diebolt-Vallois Brut Rosé NV
$$ • 94 points • page 210

Dumangin J Fils Le Rosé Extra Brut NV
$$ • 94 points • page 225

J. Lassalle Rosé Premier Cru Brut NV
$$ • 94 points • page 293

Le Brun Servenay
Juste Rosé Brut NV
$$ • 94 points • page 372

Marc Hébrart Brut Rosé
Premier Cru NV
$$ • 94 points • page 403

Nicolas Maillart
Rosé Grand Cru NV
$$ • 94 points • page 426

Paul Bara Grand Rosé Brut NV
$$ • 94 points • page 439

Philipponnat Royale Réserve
Rosé Brut NV
$$ • 94 points • page 455

Delamotte Brut Rosé NV
$$$ • 94 points • page 193

Laurent-Perrier
Cuvée Rosé Brut NV
$$$ • 94 points • page 365

Veuve Clicquot Vintage Rosé 2012
$$$ • 94 points • page 549

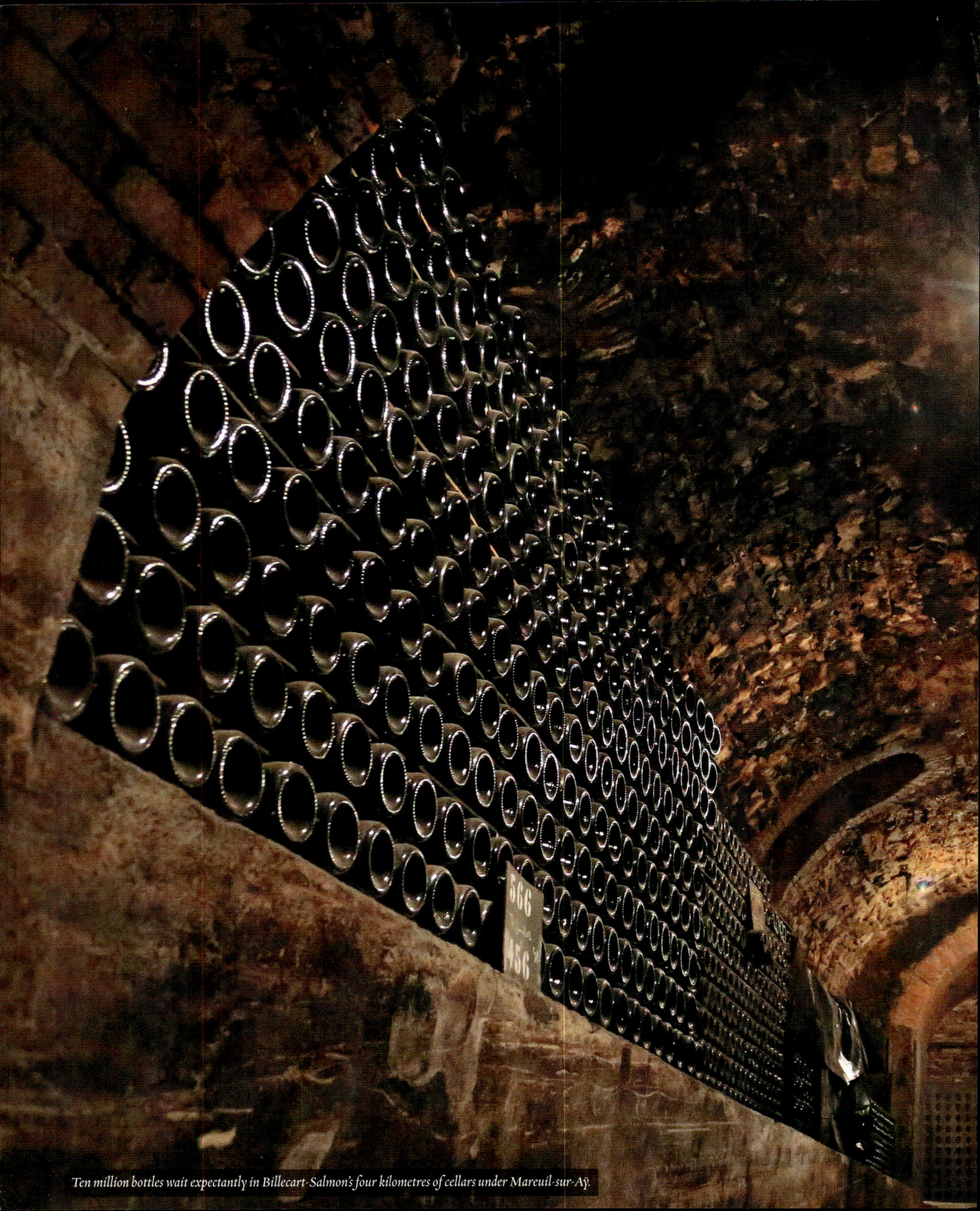

Ten million bottles wait expectantly in Billecart-Salmon's four kilometres of cellars under Mareuil-sur-Aÿ.

vintage, advancing ripeness, with good results. Rodolphe Péters (Pierre Péters) now ranks it alongside 2008 as his favoured vintage of recent decades, 'with an electric character and vibrations like we have not seen since 2008', and suggests the highlights of the season will trump the best of 2012, although 2012 will be better on average. For Benoît Gouez (Moët & Chandon), 'On paper, 2013 was as good as 2012 for chardonnay and pinot noir in the grand and premier crus.'

Severe July hailstorms battered some 3000 hectares, with more than 300 hectares completely destroyed, particularly around Épernay and the Côte des Blancs, where 10–20% of the grand cru crop was lost. Later-ripening villages were delayed by high yields, afflicted by rain in September and a cold, windy October. It was not until well into that month that ripeness was achieved, with stringent selection required to avoid rot. This proved a particularly challenging year in the western Marne and Côte des Bar, though the Grande Vallée de la Marne and Côte des Blancs were superb. Such were the acidities that Louis Roederer put a record number of parcels through malolactic fermentation.

Most 2013 cuvées are yet to be released. To date, the greatest are Deutz Brut Millésime, Deutz Brut Rosé Millésime and Louis Roederer Rosé.

2012 • 8/10

A stark reminder that blanket generalisations are grossly inadequate in Champagne's grand diversity. I visited and tasted the *vins clairs* in early 2013 and was amazed at their scintillating acidity, expressive concentration, entrancing purity and classic refinement, yet surprised by the polarising reports about the vintage.

Superlatives rolled: 'The vintage of my career' (Dumangin), 'amazing' (Veuve Clicquot), 'very, very good' (Jacquesson), 'perfect balance' (Mumm), 'spectacular, one of the three classic vintages so far this century' (Louis Roederer), 'very similar to 2002' (Taittinger), 'better than 2002 or 2008' (Pierre Gimonnet), 'better than 1996' (Vilmart), 'challenging yet beautiful' (Devaux), 'just fantastic, wow!' (Billecart-Salmon).

Then this: 'One of the toughest seasons I can recall in 25 years' (Larmandier-Bernier), 'challenging' (Dom Pérignon), 'very difficult' (Piper Heidsieck), 'tough' (Pierre Péters), 'every challenge that can happen in Champagne' (Moët & Chandon). 'For a good vintage in Champagne, we do not want a good summer,' clarifies Didier Gimonnet. 'The grapes must suffer!'

Record rainfall between March and July made diligence in controlling rot paramount, a nightmare for some organic and biodynamic growers. While a few of the most fanatical growers reported bumper yields, most lost one-third of their crop. A cool summer upheld dizzying acidity, while perfect conditions from mid-August produced a long harvest of generous sugar ripeness of 10.2 or even 10.7 degrees potential, so ripe that some growers saw no need to chaptalise.

Those who waited and picked ripe were rewarded, and there will be many spectacularly concentrated, acid-driven, long-lived

vintage cuvées made this season. Gilles Dumangin considers 2012 to be '2002 with the potential of 1996'. Rodolphe Péters (Pierre Péters) agrees. 'With such structure and generosity, it will age forever,' he suggests. Though there are notable exceptions: Ruinart did not see the stamina in chardonnay to produce a Dom Ruinart in 2012, and Krug will not release a vintage cuvée, instead keeping its small crop in reserve.

The greatest 2012 vintage champagnes released to date are Agrapart & Fils Minéral Blanc de Blancs Extra Brut, Deutz Hommage à William Deutz Meurtet Pinot Noir Parcelle D'Aÿ Brut, Deutz Hommage à William Deutz La Côte Glacière Pinot Noir Parcelle D'Aÿ Brut, Deutz Rosé Brut, Egly-Ouriet Grand Cru Ambonnay Rouge, J. Lassalle Special Club Rosé, Pierre Gimonnet & Fils Special Club Chouilly Grand Cru Extra Brut, Pierre Gimonnet & Fils Special Club Cramant Grand Cru Extra Brut, Pierre Gimonnet & Fils Special Club Grands Terroirs de Chardonnay, Pierre Péters Les Chétillons Cuvée Special Blanc de Blancs Brut, Pierre Péters Cuvée Millésime L'Esprit Blanc de Blancs, Pierre Péters Montjolys Cuvée Spéciale Blanc de Blancs Brut and Pol Roger Blanc de Blancs Brut, with many, many more still to come.

2011 • 2/10

A dismal vintage summed up succinctly by Charles Philipponnat as 'shitty', marked by underripeness, dilution and widespread rot. I visited at the height of summer in mid-July, and for two weeks there was not one day of sunshine to ripen the harvest. Misty mornings made way for sullen, grey days, frequently sodden with downpours. Summer was otherwise hot, furnishing a short growing cycle and grapes devoid of complexity, intensity and

Sézanne, harvest 2014

character. In spite of a lack of ripeness, the threat of rot, particularly in the black grapes, during a rain-interrupted harvest, prompted the CIVC to announce some of the earliest harvest dates in history, with some villages beginning on 19 August. Haunted by the all too recent memory of rampant rot in 2010, a hurried harvest of underripe fruit ensued.

Growers prayed for warmth, and late summer delivered so spectacularly that by 24 August maturation ceased altogether as vines shut down in oppressive heat. Moët & Chandon sent 400 pickers home for four days, but even this was insufficient for maturation, concentration or complexity to come. The daring few who made the gamble to hold off until September were rewarded with cool nights and dry winds to evaporate the botrytis, and this proved to be the secret to the best wines of this dismal season.

For all the inconsistencies of 2011, Dominique Demarville (Veuve Clicquot) upholds the season as evidence Champagne is still capable of producing strong acidity. Very few vintage wines were produced. 'For me, 2011 should not exist as a vintage cuvée,' decreed Benoît Gouez (Moët & Chandon). Non-vintage cuvées based on 2011 were marked by dusty, dry, mushroomy rot, its impact exacerbated by the weakness of 2010, hampering any hopes of resurrecting non-vintage cuvées with generous reserves.

Harvested in September, Pierre Péters Les Chétillons Cuvée Special Blanc de Blancs is the top 2011 vintage cuvée released to date, though still only scoring 94 points.

2010 • 3/10

A challenging season, with ripe fruit marred by dilution, low acidity and rampant rot. A hot, dry summer ended abruptly in a mid-August deluge, prompting a devastating outburst of botrytis across the Marne. 'There was such a fog of dry rot in the air I couldn't see the guys throwing the grapes into the press!' one Montagne de Reims grower revealed. Sorting was paramount, and some houses elected to keep less than their appellation allowance. This proved to put a timely damper on production after the global financial crisis significantly dented champagne sales in 2009.

The vintage is likened to 2005 by Dom Pérignon's new chef de cave Vincent Chaperon for its concentration and phenolics. By contrast, Dominique Demarville picked early at Veuve Clicquot and values the wines as reserves for their higher acidities.

The greatest 2010 vintage champagnes released to date are Bollinger Vieilles Vignes Françaises Blanc de Noirs, Deutz Hommage à William Deutz Parcelles d'Aÿ Brut, Diebolt-Vallois Fleur de Passion and Pierre Gimonnet & Fils Special Club Grands Terroirs de Chardonnay.

2009 • 6/10

Dry, hot continental weather produced a sunny, ripe vintage of rounded exuberance, clean and appealing right away, without the acidity to age, making 2009 the antithesis of the tense, enduring 2008. While this vintage will forever lurk in the shadow of its predecessor, it is a season with some surprises. 'An excellent vintage!' found Jacquesson's Jean-Hervé Chiquet, who likens 2008/2009 with 1988/1989. 'For me, the best 1989s today are among the best wines of the region!' For Didier Gimonnet of Pierre Gimonnet, 2009 was one of the best of the decade after 2002. However, relatively few vintage wines were made, as much in response to the global financial crisis as the pedigree of the season.

The greatest 2009 vintage champagnes today are Deutz Amour de Deutz Brut Millésime, Deutz Amour de Deutz Rosé Millésime Brut, Deutz Cuvée William Deutz Brut Millésime, Deutz Brut Rosé, Dom Pérignon, Egly-Ouriet Grand Cru Millésime, Eric Rodez Les Fournettes Ambonnay Pinot Noir, Louis Roederer Cristal, Louis Roederer Cristal Rosé, Jacquesson Dizy Terres Rouges Rosé Extra Brut, Louis Roederer Cristal Rosé and Pierre Péters Cuvée Spéciale Blanc de Blancs Les Chétillons.

2008 • 10/10

A vintage of classic finesse, crystalline purity, tightly clenched acidity, impeccable concentration and monumental longevity, 2008 is the essence of champagne. It will be decades before the full distinction of this transcendental season becomes truly apparent, but I am now resolutely convinced that it will eclipse even 1996 and every season since. There is no more exquisite recipe for champagne than a wet spring, a cool, not particularly sunny, yet dry, summer, followed by idyllic, bright days and cool nights, lingering gloriously for the entire duration of harvest. The result was textbook ripeness of 9.6–9.8 degrees potential, and heightened acidities of 8.5–8.6g/L. To Jean-Pierre Vazart (Vazart-Coquart), 2008 is 1996 with balance. Even many lesser growers and houses produced admirable results in this near-perfect vintage, while the flagship cuvées of the top houses will endure for half a century.

My palate memory is not sufficiently deep to find a vintage that is its equal. Some have suggested even 1928. 'This is the most classic Champagne vintage,' says Jean-Baptiste Lécaillon (Louis Roederer). 'If we were to be drinking champagne 50 years ago, this is the style that we would have been drinking.'

You can't go wrong with 2008 under any good name, and there are far too many to list, but my favourites right now are Billecart-Salmon Vintage Extra Brut, Bollinger La Grande Année, Deutz Amour de Deutz Brut, Deutz Amour de Deutz Rosé Brut, Deutz William Deutz Brut, Dom Pérignon, J.L. Vergnon Résonance Millésime Grand Cru Blanc de Blancs Extra Brut, Jacquesson Dizy Corne Bautray Extra Brut Récolte, Jacquesson Vauzelle Terme Récolte, Louis Roederer Cristal, Louis Roederer Cristal Rosé, Philipponnat Mareuil-sur-Aÿ Premier Cru Extra Brut, Pierre Gimonnet & Fils Special Club Millésime de Collection Blanc de Blancs, Pierre Gimonnet & Fils Millésime de Collection Extra Brut en magnum, Pol Roger Cuvée Sir Winston Churchill, Robert Moncuit Les Chétillons Blanc de Blancs Grand Cru, Taittinger Comtes de Champagne, Veuve Clicquot La Grande Dame and Veuve Clicquot La Grande Dame Brut Rosé, with many more stunners yet to be released.

2007 • 7/10

A vintage of delicacy and finesse, with endurance, if not concentration, terroir expression or distinctive character. A warm winter made for an early season, retarded by a wet, cold and rot-inducing summer. Harvest was saved by a north wind and sunny days from mid-August, furnishing adequate maturity while upholding good acid levels. This proved to be a highly variable vintage from one village to the next, largely dependent upon picking date, vineyard care and sorting regime. Following the warm, sunny style of 2006, the elegance of 2007 is sometimes compared to that of 1997 following 1996. To Richard Geoffroy (Dom Pérignon), '2007 was slight – it never happened!' Those who harvested later were rewarded with better expression and character.

The greatest 2007 vintage champagnes today are Billecart-Salmon Cuvée Elisabeth Salmon Brut Rosé, Bollinger La Grande Année, Bollinger La Grande Année Rosé, Deutz Amour de Deutz Brut, Deutz Cuvée William Deutz Brut Millésime, Egly-Ouriet Grand Cru Millésime, Exception Blanche Blanc de Blancs, Gosset Celebris Vintage, Gosset Celebris Rosé Extra Brut, Louis Roederer Cristal, Louis Roederer Cristal Rosé, Philipponnat Clos de Goisses Juste Rosé Extra Brut, Pierre Péters Cuvée Spéciale Blanc de Blancs Les Chétillons, Ruinart Dom Ruinart Blanc de Blancs Brut Salon Cuvée S Les Mesnil Blanc de Blancs Brut and Taittinger Comtes de Champagne.

2006 • 6/10

A soft, fruity, approachable vintage, without particularly distinct acid structure, peaking early, and some cuvées are already beginning to decline. A warm June, record hot July, cold, rainy August and sunny September produced ripe, clean fruit of 10.2 average degrees potential and low acidity of just 7g/L, 15–20% below Champagne's average acid levels. Benoît Gouez (Moët & Chandon) says 2006 is about 'amplitude, volume and expansive mouthfeel', likening it to 1999. To Didier Gimonnet, it has the structure and 'clumsy richness' of 2005 and the minerality of 2004.

The greatest 2006s today are Billecart-Salmon Cuvée Louis Blanc de Blancs Brut, Billecart-Salmon Cuvée Nicolas François, Bollinger Vieilles Vignes Françaises, Charles Heidsieck Millésime Vintage Brut, Charles Heidsieck Millésime Vintage Rosé, Deutz Amour de Deutz Brut, Deutz Amour de Deutz Rosé Brut, Egly-Ouriet Grand Cru Millésime, Dom Pérignon, Dom Pérignon Rosé, Emmanuel Brochet Extra Brut Premier Cru Millésime, Louis Roederer Cristal, Paul Bara Special Club Rosé, Pierre Gimonnet & Fils Millésime de Collection Vieilles Vignes de Chardonnay Extra Brut en magnum, Pierre Péters Cuvée Spéciale Blanc de Blancs Les Chétillons, Pol Roger Sir Winston Churchill, Ruinart Dom Ruinart Blanc de Blancs Brut, Salon Cuvée S Les Mesnil Blanc de Blancs Brut, Taittinger Comtes de Champagne Blanc de Blancs and Veuve Clicquot La Grande Dame, with more yet to be released.

2005 • 5/10

A hot, tricky season of overripe character and dry phenolic grip, lacking freshness and elegance, with most cuvées already at their peak. Extremes of heat spikes alternating with heavy rainfall triggered mildew attacks in July, though a cool August and mild September prompted an elongated harvest. Ultimately, a mature vintage of 9.8% degrees potential, with some pinot noir and meunier afflicted by botrytis. The vintage recorded the highest concentration of phenolics in Champagne history, which Cyril Brun (Charles Heidsieck) goes so far as to equate with the legendary, enduring harvests of 1928 and 1947.

The greatest 2005 vintage champagnes today are Bollinger La Grande Année, Bollinger La Grande Année Rosé, Jacquesson Avize Champ Caïn Récolte Extra Brut, Jacquesson Aÿ Vauzelle Terme Récolte Extra Brut, Jacquesson Dizy Corne Bautray Récolte Extra Brut, Pierre Gimonnet & Fils Millésime de Collection Blanc de Blancs, Pierre Gimonnet & Fils Special Club Blanc de Blancs, Pierre Péters Cuvée Spéciale Blanc de Blancs Les Chétillons, Taittinger Comtes de Champagne and Taittinger Comtes de Champagne Rosé.

2004 • 8/10

A magnificent vintage of fine aromatic profile, lightness, finesse, energy, mineral definition and terroir expression. Record high yields took everyone by surprise in producing champagnes of beauty and stamina. With energy in the vines in reserve after the tiny 2003 season, the enormous 2004 harvest was evidence that you can make great champagne from high yields, provided the vines are in balance. A warm, sunny July was followed by a cool, wet August, but the crucial first three weeks of September were idyllically sunny and dry, producing properly ripe fruit of well-structured acidity. 'One would expect that high yields would mean less minerality, but in 2004 we had both, testimony to the extraordinary terroir of Champagne!' exclaims Didier Gimonnet.

The greatest 2004s today are Billecart-Salmon Blanc de Blancs Brut, Bollinger R.D. Extra Brut, Charles Heidsieck Blanc des Millénaires, De Sousa Cuvée des Caudalies Grand Cru Millésime Brut, Dom Pérignon, Krug Clos du Mesnil, Krug Vintage, Louis Roederer Cristal Rosé, Mailly Grand Cru Exception Blanche Blanc de Blancs Brut, Perrier-Joüet Belle Epoque Blanc de Blancs, Pierre Péters Cuvée Spéciale Blanc de Blancs Les Chétillons, Pol Roger Cuvée Sir Winston Churchill, Ruinart Dom Ruinart, Salon Cuvée S Blanc de Blancs, Taittinger Comtes de Champagne Blanc de Blancs, Veuve Clicquot La Grande Dame Brut, Veuve Clicquot La Grande Dame Rosé.

2003 • 2/10

A calamitous vintage of pronounced concentration, overripe flavour profile, low acidity and hard phenolic bitterness that leaves most cuvées finishing astringent, coarse, dry and short. The most devastating April frosts in 70 years decimated 43% of the crop, hitting Côte des Blancs chardonnay hardest, wiping

out 90% of Avize and Le Mesnil-sur-Oger; in early June, violent hailstorms battered the Montagne de Reims and Vallée de la Marne. Summer was the hottest to ever hit Champagne, with a sweltering August averaging 10°C above the norm, shrivelling grapes like raisins, prompting the earliest start to harvest since 1822. Of what little fruit remained in the Marne, opulent, over-ripe pinot noir and meunier boasted high sugar levels and low acidity. 'The perfect description of a nightmare,' in the words of Cyril Brun (Charles Heidsieck). Dom Pérignon registered the lowest acidity it has ever recorded. Says Richard Geoffroy, '2003 is border territory for Champagne, as border as it can be'. This is not a vintage for the cellar, and most are now well past their prime. Krug is the grand exception that proves the rule, testimony to stringent selection and tiny production.

The greatest 2003 vintage champagnes today are Dom Pérignon Rosé, Gosset Cuvée Celebris Rosé Extra Brut, Krug Clos du Mesnil, Krug Vintage and Le Brun-Servenay Cuvée Chardonnay Brut Millésime Vielles Vignes.

2002 • 9/10

A benchmark harvest that balances finesse, power and structure like no other in Champagne's recent history. The best wines possess decades of potential. A well-mannered season of continental climatic influence, with perfect harvest conditions from 10 September of dry, sunny days fostering ripe fruit intensity, and cool nights maintaining acidities a fraction below average. 'The 2002 was revenge for the challenging 2001, with nature giving everything that it withheld!' exclaims Régis Camus (Piper-Heidsieck). Didier Gimonnet considers it the greatest vintage since 1990, 'exemplifying the ultimate balance between elegance, concentration and freshness, nearly the best wine we could obtain'.

It's impossible to list all the greatest 2002 vintage champagnes, but the very best today are Billecart-Salmon Cuvée Elisabeth Salmon Brut Rosé, Billecart-Salmon Cuvée Nicolas François Billecart, Bollinger R.D. Extra Brut, Dom Pérignon, Gosset Celebris, Jacquesson Aÿ Vauzelle Terme Recolte Brut, Krug Clos du Mesnil, Krug Vintage, Louis Roederer Cristal, Louis Roederer Cristal Rosé, Pierre Péters Cuvée Spéciale Blanc de Blancs Les Chétillons, Piper-Heidsieck Rare Millésime, Pol Roger Cuvée Sir Winston Churchill and Taittinger Comtes de Champagne Blanc de Blancs.

2001 • 1/10

Olivier Krug rates 2001 as Champagne's worst vintage in two decades. A dire season of incessant rain from early in the season all the way through to harvest, with particularly violent rain and hail from the latter part of July destroying 800 hectares across 55 communes. A cold September was accompanied by torrential rain and less sun than Champagne had seen in 45 years, cementing the fate of the season, diluting the wines and producing low ripeness of just 8.5 degrees potential. Virtually no vintage wines were produced.

2000 • 7/10

A warm, voluptuously ripe year of deep colour and rich fruit well suited to early drinking, with many cuvées now a deep yellow hue and quickly reaching the end of their peak. Dubbed *gourmandise orageuse* ('stormy indulgence') by Krug, 2000 was a tumultuous season delivering some of the most destructive hailstorms ever to lash Champagne, with 2900 hectares completely devastated across 114 communes. Warm, dry conditions arrived in August, after a hot June and cold July, and held out throughout harvest, producing abundant, large grapes, blessed with above-average levels of sugar (9.8 degrees potential), slightly lower than average acidities, and very little disease.

The greatest 2000 vintage champagnes today are Billecart-Salmon Cuvée Nicolas François Billecart, Billecart-Salmon Cuvée Elisabeth Salmon Brut Rosé, Bollinger La Grande Année, Dom Pérignon P2, Dom Pérignon Rosé, Duval-Leroy Femme de Champagne, Krug Clos d'Ambonnay, Krug Clos du Mesnil, Krug Vintage, Pierre Péters Cuvée Spéciale Blanc de Blancs Les Chétillons, Pol Roger Cuvée Sir Winston Churchill, Taittinger Comtes de Champagne Blanc de Blancs and Veuve Fourny & Fils Clos Faubourg Notre-Dame Blanc de Blancs Extra Brut Vertus Premier Cru.

1999 • 6/10

A fruity, soft season lacking acid drive, with most cuvées now past their prime; a warm vintage of continental climatic influence, recording Champagne's hottest summer since 1959 (though 2003 trumped it), and higher than usual rainfall. Harvest started optimistically, but hopes were diluted by heavy, persistent rain. The result was a vintage of high maturity and low malic acidity (just 6.5g/L total acidity), likened to 1989 by Jean-Baptiste Lécaillon.

The greatest 1999s today are Billecart-Salmon Blanc de Blancs Brut, Billecart-Salmon Le Clos Sainte-Hilaire, Bollinger La Grande Année Rosé, Delamotte Collection Blanc de Blancs, Larmandier-Bernier Special Club, Pol Roger Cuvée Sir Winston Churchill, Salon Cuvée S Blanc de Blancs, and Taittinger Comtes de Champagne Blanc de Blancs.

1998 • 7/10

The most enduring cuvées of 1998 retain elegant freshness amidst the expressive presence of the season, though lesser cuvées are now tired and heavy. Evidence that it is ultimately the weather at harvest that bears the strongest influence on the calibre of the vintage, 1998 followed a dismal progression of a wet, rot-inducing July, debilitating August heatwave, and rain storms in early September. It was not until mid-September that the weather finally delivered warm, dry conditions for harvest. Balanced ripeness of 9.8 degrees potential and strong acid levels of 9.8g/L came as the first surprise; the unwavering stamina of the best cuvées of the season the second.

The greatest 1998 vintage champagnes today are Billecart-Salmon Cuvée Nicolas François Billecart, Billecart-Salmon

Grande Cuvée, Billecart-Salmon Le Clos Saint-Hilaire, Dom Pérignon P2, Gosset Cuvée Celebris Extra Brut Vintage, Gosset Cuvée Celebris Rosé Brut, Krug Clos du Mesnil, Krug Clos d'Ambonnay, Krug Vintage, Louis Roederer Blanc de Blancs, Piper-Heidsieck Rare Millesime, Pol Roger Cuvée Sir Winston Churchill, Taittinger Comtes de Champagne Blanc de Blancs, and Veuve Clicquot La Grande Dame Brut.

1997 • 4/10

The least vintage of the latter years of that century, 1997 was a ripe, rounded, accessible season, forever lost between the memory of 1996 and 1998. A tough lead-up to harvest saw 1997 plagued by frost, hail, uneven set and rot, producing the lowest yields since 1985. A hot July and very warm August were finally rescued by a bone-dry harvest, producing a high 10.2% degrees potential, and surprisingly good acidities for such ripeness. Salon registered acidity on equal par with 1996, infusing freshness and brightness.

Few vintage wines were released; most are now well past their peak. The most notable exceptions are Jacquesson Avize Dégorgement Tardif Extra Brut, Salon Cuvée S Blanc de Blancs, and Pierre Péters Cuvée Spéciale Blanc de Blancs Les Chétillons.

1996 • 10/10

One of Champagne's most enduring, spectacular and lauded vintages, with both acidity and ripeness in extreme proportions, rendering its wines unbalanced in their youth. They are only beginning to find their poise after two decades, and the best will effortlessly endure for a lifetime. This vintage has gone down in history as the perfect 10/10 season of 10 degrees potential alcohol and 10g/L acidity – to this day the highest acidity ever recorded for Dom Pérignon. A less than ideal summer alternating between rain and intense heat was followed by rain until 20 September, then clear, sunny days, cool nights, and a strong north wind. This wind proved the key to the vintage, not only evaporating the threat of rot but, crucially, dehydrating the grapes and concentrating sugar and acidity to levels not seen since 1928. Quickly hailed among the greatest vintages of all time, some have since raised reservations, as some cuvées matured in flavour before their intense acidities softened. The benefit of hindsight has led many top chef de caves including Jean-Baptiste Lécaillon (Louis Roederer) and Dominique Demarville (Veuve Clicquot) to now admit they picked a week too early, to beat the botrytis, and that they would have made even greater wines again with higher ripeness and lower acidity. No such fear for the finest cuvées, the best of which are only now coming into their own, with glorious years of potential stretching before them.

The greatest 1996 vintage champagnes today are Billecart-Salmon Cuvée Nicolas François Billecart, Billecart-Salmon Grande Cuvée, Bollinger R.D. Extra Brut, Dom Pérignon Oeno-thèque, Dom Pérignon P2, Dom Pérignon P2 Rosé, Duval-Leroy Femme de Champagne, René Geoffroy Cuvée Autrefois, Henriot La Cuvée des Enchanteleurs, Krug Vintage, Larmandier-

Bouzy, harvest 2014

Bernier Special Club, Louis Roederer Brut Rosé, Pierre Péters Cuvée Spéciale Blanc de Blancs Les Chétillons, Pol Roger Cuvée Sir Winston Churchill, Salon Cuvée S Blanc de Blancs, and Taittinger Comtes de Champagne Rosé.

1995 • 8/10

A vintage of elegant opulence, refined power and classic endurance, marvellously evidenced in a set of cuvées that attained a lofty magnificence at 20 years of age, and will hold their lofty plateau for many years yet. Long forgotten in the shadow of 1996, 1995 is more classic and arguably more consistent, if less showy. This was Champagne's finest season since 1990, with a hot, dry summer accelerating maturity, and a sunny, late harvest furnishing good ripeness of 9.2% degrees potential and normal acidity. In 2014 Didier Gimonnet hosted a tasting with the French press to ascertain the best vintage of the 1990s. After 1990 was deemed too rich and 1996 too acidic, the winner was 1995.

The greatest 1995 vintage champagnes today are Billecart-Salmon Cuvée Nicolas François Billecart, Charles Heidsieck Blanc des Millénaires, Dom Pérignon P2 Rosé, Jacquesson Dégorgement Tardif Extra Brut Millésime, Krug Vintage, Louis Roederer Cristal Vinothèque, and Salon Cuvée S Blanc de Blancs.

Dawn frost in Aÿ, winter 2015

The winter snowfall of 2013 transforms the magnificent slopes of Aÿ.

DOWN TO EARTH

*O*n a small range of hills rising less than impressively from a chalk plain 145 kilometres north-east of Paris lies a patchwork of 33,868 hectares of 278,000 plots of vines that is Champagne. Too exposed to wind and rain and not sufficiently blessed by the sun, there is no chance of ripening grapes on the flatter land here. And yet this place sends a shiver down my spine every time I come close. By some miracle, its gentle hillsides produce fruits that thousands of winegrowers around the globe strive desperately to emulate, yet none have equalled.

'Only in wine does the ungrateful chalk pour out its golden tears,' penned Colette in 1932. Chalk blesses champagne with minerality, texture and mouthfeel.

Austere and impoverished soft white chalk is Champagne's secret, a remnant of a 90 million-year-old seabed. Its true blessing is espoused not only in cool, damp 17-century-old cellars, but especially in the vineyards, bestowing its fruits with crystalline minerality, freshness and endurance, reflecting and storing heat and retaining moisture – a perfectly regulated vine humidifier.

Champagne comprises 319 villages spanning five departments: the Marne (most importantly the Montagne de Reims, Côte des Blancs and Vallée de la Marne), the Côte des Bar (Aube), the Aisne, the Haute-Marne and the Seine-et-Marne.

THE MONTAGNE DE REIMS
The Montagne de Reims is no mountain – more a wooded hillock, rising to an unimpressive 180 metres above the surrounding plains and just 275 metres above sea level. Yet even this elevation is sufficient to orientate some of Champagne's mightiest vineyards. The vines of the Montagne de Reims follow the slope of a hillside topped with dense forest, in a backward 'C' formation from Villers-Allerand on the northern slopes, reaching a crescendo in the thundering grand crus of Bouzy and Ambonnay in the south. These stand alongside Verzenay as the Montagne de Reims' finest villages. Pinot noir is king of these chalky sites, and nowhere in Champagne produces its equal. There are also substantial plantings of meunier, and chardonnay is on the rise.

The 'Petite Montagne' is a north-western extension of the Montagne de Reims, extending north of Reims itself, nurturing Champagne's most northerly vineyards on soils of sand and clay, well suited to meunier.

CÔTE DES BLANCS
Chardonnay is left largely to the Côte des Blancs, 96% of which is planted to the variety, the remainder largely pinot noir in the commune of Vertus in the south. Chardonnay loves wet seasons and the hydrating nourishment of chalk.

With dramatic slopes, warmer days and thinner topsoils making chalk more accessible than anywhere in the region, the Côte des Blancs produces Champagne's most regular fruit, and most reliable, exhilarating and mineral-infused wines. This is why many are sold unblended as blanc de blancs. These are among Champagne's most searingly structured and long-lived wines. There is perhaps no village in Champagne that stands alone as confidently as Le Mesnil-sur-Oger, though Cramant, Avize, Chouilly, Oger and the premier cru of Vertus command great respect.

VALLÉE DE LA MARNE
More than half of the Vallée de la Marne is planted to meunier, although pinot noir plantings are on the increase. The south-facing sites of Aÿ and Mareuil-sur-Aÿ towards its eastern end rival the great grand crus of the Montagne de Reims. Its cooler western reaches of clay, sand and chalk soils are exclusively the territory of meunier, easier to grow and ripen on a variety of soils than pinot noir and chardonnay.

CÔTE DE SÉZANNE
The Côte de Sézanne is a little way south of the Côte des Blancs in the Marne and shares the same south-east orientation and dominance of chardonnay. Its soils are heavier and its wines more rustic.

CÔTE DES BAR
More than 100 kilometres south-east of the Côte des Blancs, the outpost of the Aube (Côte des Bar) is closer to Burgundy than to Reims. Pinot noir is the principal grape here, comprising four-fifths of the region's plantings, producing vigorous and more rustic wines. Planted largely during the late 1980s, vine maturity is now in step with the rest of the region, and the Aube has enjoyed significant increases in quality in recent years. Its finest villages are Celles-sur-Ource, Urville and Les Riceys, Champagne's largest village and one of its most important sources of red wine for rosé.

ATLAS DE LA FRANCE VINICOLE L. LARMAT

Les vins de Champagne

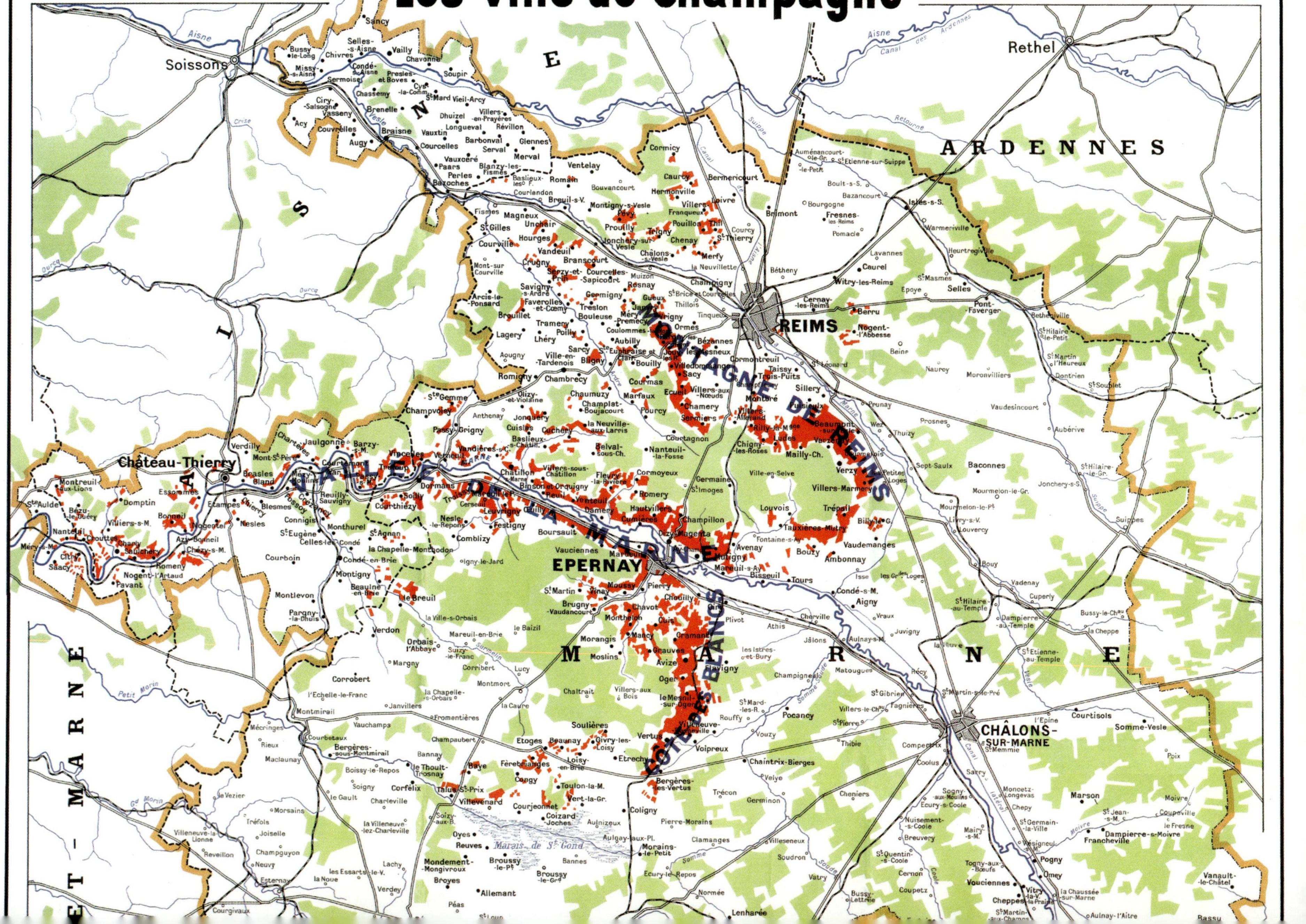

ARDENNES
AISNE
MARNE
SEINE-ET-MARNE
MONTAGNE DE REIMS
VALLÉE DE LA MARNE
CÔTE DES BLANCS
Reims
Epernay
Châlons-sur-Marne
Château-Thierry
Soissons
Rethel
Marais de St Gond

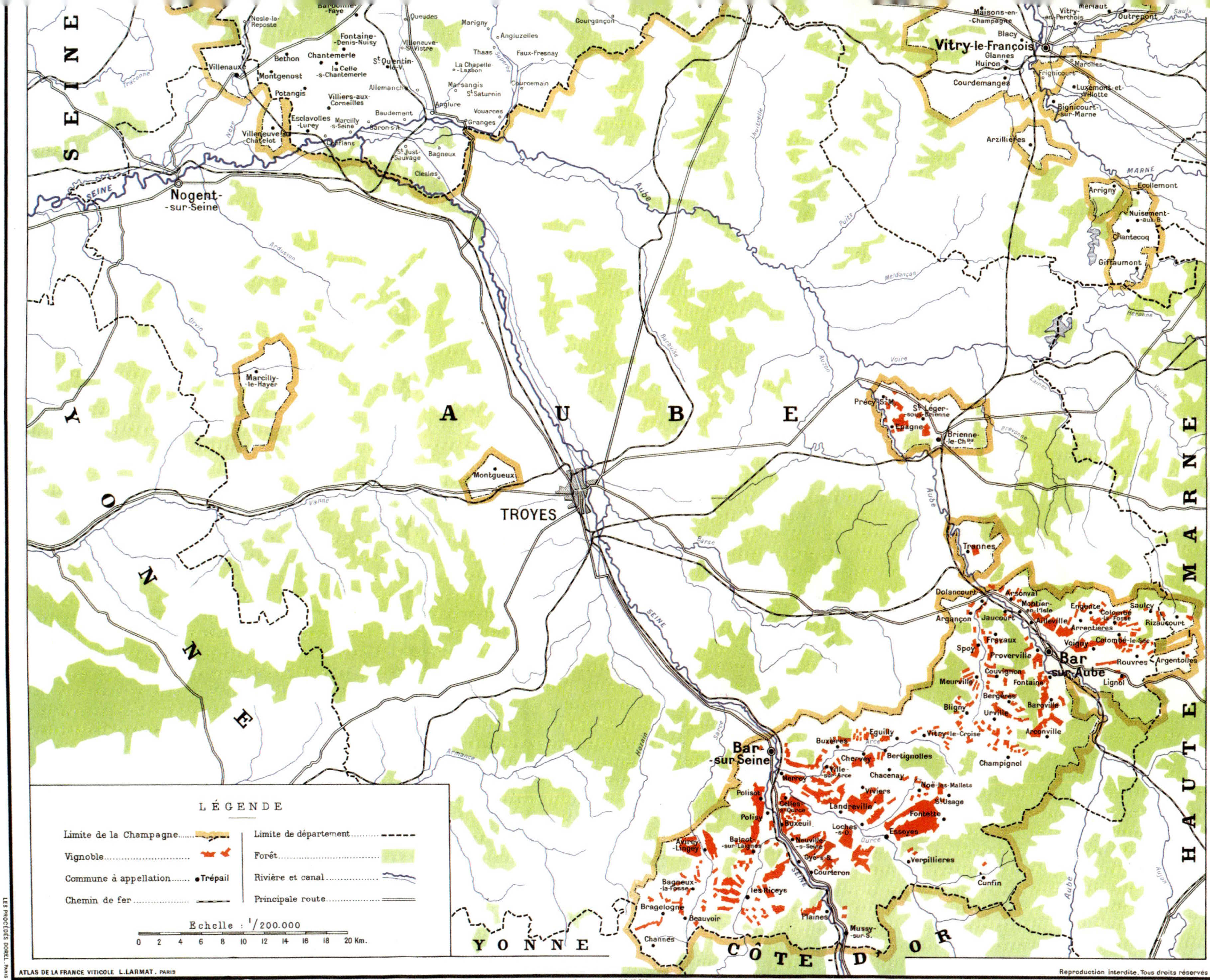

HAUTE MARNE

CÔTE-D'OR

YONNE

SEINE

AUBE

TROYES

Bar-sur-Aube

Bar-sur-Seine

Vitry-le-François

Nogent-sur-Seine

Brienne-le-Chateau

Montgueux

Marcilly-le-Hayer

LÉGENDE

Limite de la Champagne	‒ ‒ ‒ ‒
Vignoble	
Commune à appellation	● Trépail
Chemin de fer	
Limite de département	‒ ‒ ‒ ‒
Forêt	
Rivière et canal	
Principale route	

Echelle : 1/200.000

0 2 4 6 8 10 12 14 16 18 20 Km.

ATLAS DE LA FRANCE VINICOLE L. LARMAT

"Les vins de Champagne"

LA CÔTE DES BLANCS

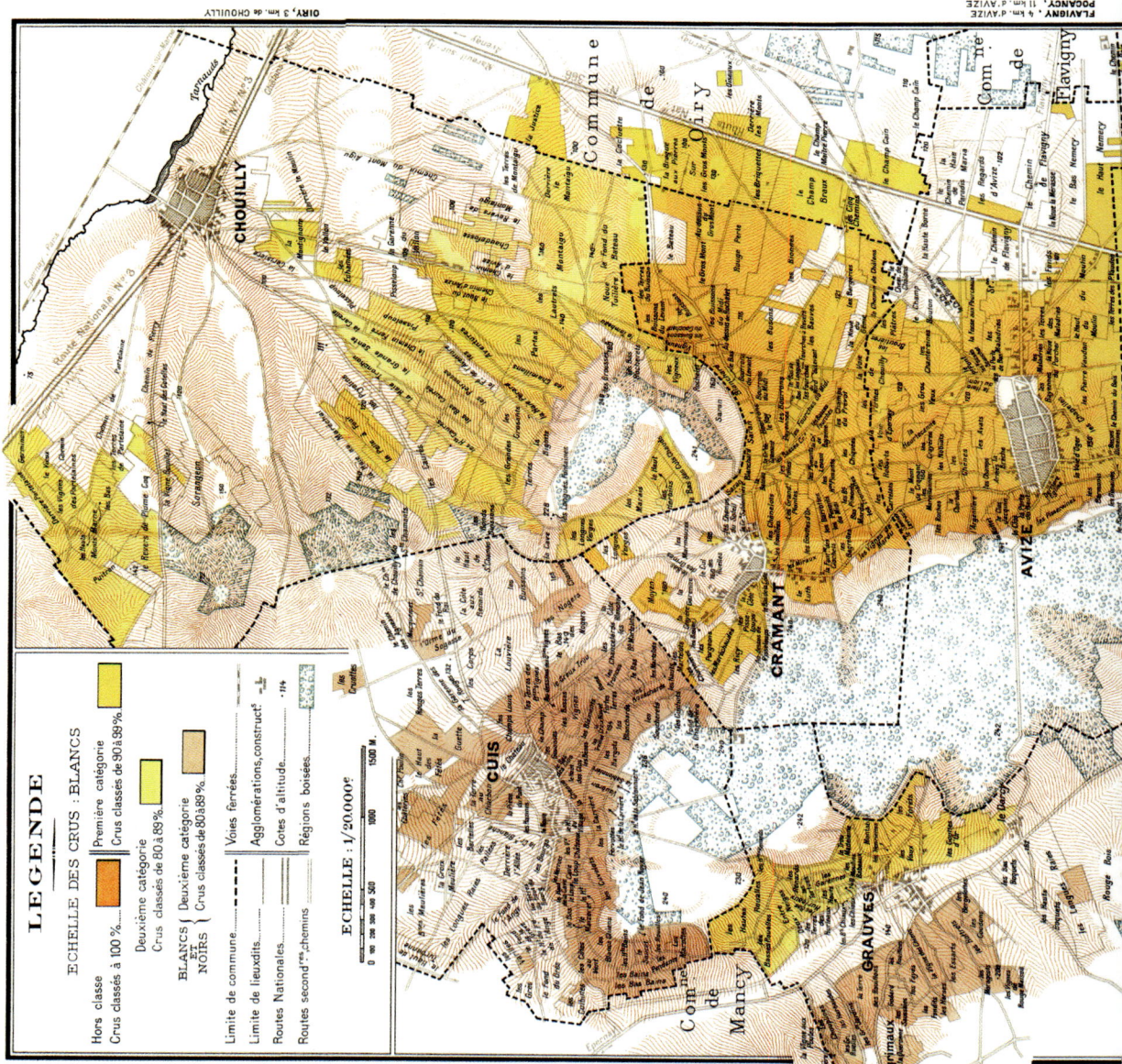

CHOUILLY

CUIS

CRAMANT

AVIZE

GRAUVES

Montgrimaux

Commune de Oiry

Commune de Mancy

LÉGENDE

ECHELLE DES CRUS : BLANCS

Hors classe — Crus classés à 100 %.

Première catégorie — Crus classés de 90 à 99 %

Deuxième catégorie — Crus classés de 80 à 89 %

BLANCS ET NOIRS { Deuxième catégorie — Crus classés de 80 à 89 %

Limite de commune
Limite de lieuxdits
Routes Nationales
Routes second'res chemins

Voies ferrées
Agglomérations, construct'
Cotes d'altitude. ·114
Régions boisées.

ECHELLE : 1/20.000e

0 100 200 300 400 500   1000   1500 M.

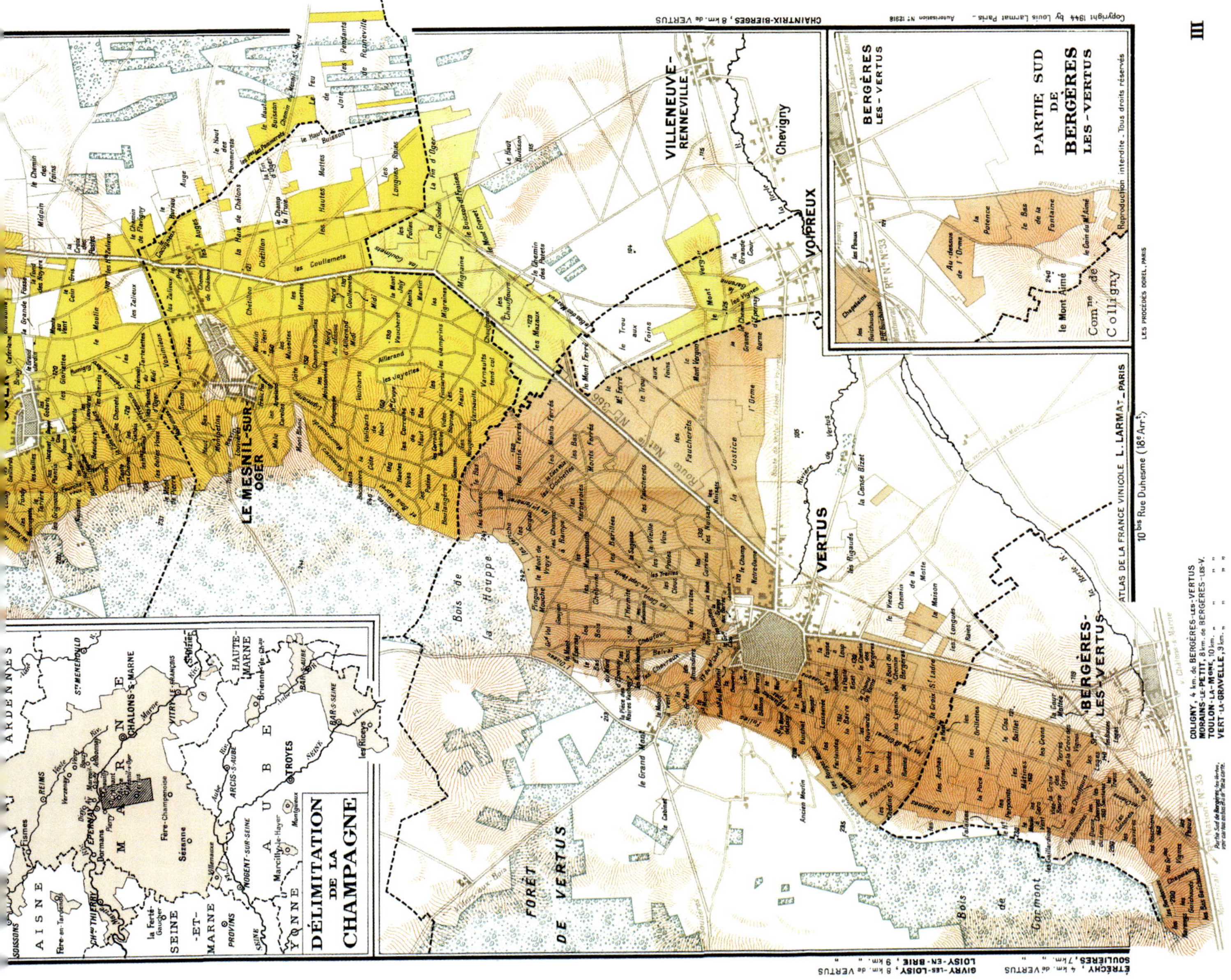

CHAINTRIX-BIERGES, 8 km. de VERTUS

PARTIE SUD
DE
BERGÈRES
LES-VERTUS

BERGÈRES
LES-VERTUS

VOIPREUX

VILLENEUVE-
RENNEVILLE

Chevigny

la Potence

le Mont Aimé

Com. de Coligny

LES PROCÉDÉS DOREL, PARIS

Reproduction interdite - Tous droits réservés

LE MESNIL-SUR-OGER

Bois de Houppe

VERTUS

BERGÈRES-
LES-VERTUS

FORÊT DE VERTUS

Bois de Dormont

DÉLIMITATION
DE LA
CHAMPAGNE

ARDENNES
AISNE
SOISSONS
Fère-en-Tardenois
MARNE
REIMS
CHALONS-S-MARNE
VITRY-le-Fçois
STE-MENEHOULD
HAUTE-MARNE
St-DIZIER
BAR-le-DUC
SEINE-ET-MARNE
PROVINS
MARCILLY-le-Hayer
SÉZANNE
NOGENT-SUR-SEINE
AUBE
ARCIS-S-AUBE
TROYES
BAR-SUR-SEINE
BAR-SUR-AUBE
YONNE

ÉTRÉCHY, 4 km. de VERTUS
GIVRY-LES-LOISY, 8 km. de VERTUS
LOISY-EN-BRIE, 9 km. "
SOULIÈRES, 7 km. "

COLIGNY, 4 km. de BERGÈRES-LES-VERTUS
MORAINS-LE-PETIT, 8 km. de BERGÈRES-LES-V.
TOULON-LA-MARNE, 10 km. "
VERT-LA-GRAVELLE, 3 km. "

ATLAS DE LA FRANCE VINICOLE L. LARMAT – PARIS
10 bis Rue Duhesme (18e Arrt.)

Morning fog settles over the grand cru of Avize as harvest 2014 draws to a close.

"Les vins de Champagne" M...

Cne de Romain

Courlandon

Montigny-sur-Vesle

Pévy

Breuil-s-Vesle

les Venteaux

Prouilly

Trigny

la Vesle

Jonchery s.-Vesle

Châlons

Unchair

Hourges

Muizon

Vendeuil

Branscourt

Sapicourt

Crugny

Courcelles-Sapicourt

Rosnay

Gu

Serzy-et-Prin

Savigny-sur-Ardre

Germigny

Janvry

Faverolles-et-Coëmy

Treslon

Méry

Prin

Coulomme

Brouillet

Tramery

Bouleuse

Méry-Prémecy

Coëmy

Peuzennes

Aubilly

Clairizet

Lhéry

Poilly

Ste Euphraise-et-Clairizet

Sarcy

Lagery

Bouilly

Bligny

Onréz

VILLE-EN-TARDENOIS

Chambrecy

Chaumuzy

Romigny

Cou

DÉPARTt DE L'AISNE

Cuitron

Marfaux

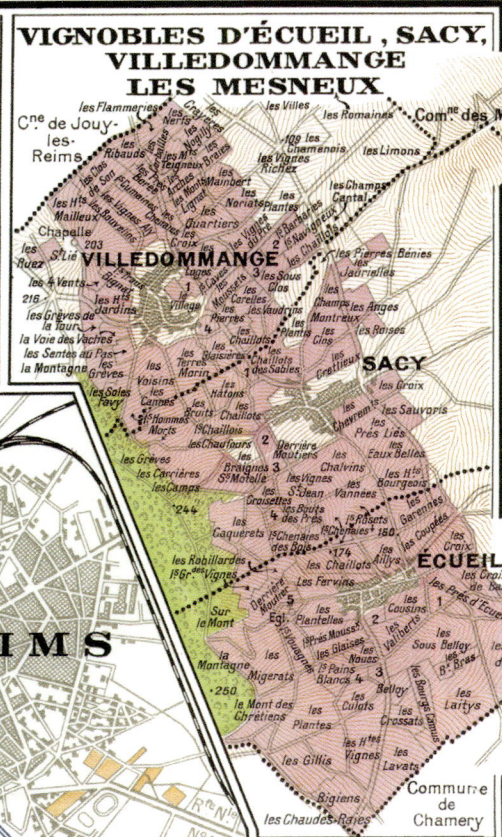

ÉCHELLE DES CRUS

Deuxième catégorie
Crus classés de 80 à 88 %....

Troisième catégorie
Crus classés de 70 à 78 %.....

Quatrième catégorie
Crus classés de 60 à 68 %..

Cinquième catégorie
Crus classés de 50 à 58 %

VIGNOBLES D'ÉCUEIL, SACY, VILLEDOMMANGE LES MESNEUX

REIMS

NOMENCLATURE DES LIEUX-DITS INDIQUÉS PAR UN CHIFFRE DANS CHAQUE COMMUNE RESPECTIVE.

VILLEDOMMANGE
Les Fortes Maisons...........1
Les Quarterons............2
Les Ravillons..........3
Les Masures.........4

SACY
Fosse Evrard...........1
Les Terres Josselet......2
L'Echafaud........3
Les Grands Prés......4

ÉCUEIL
Les Blanches Vignes........1
Ami la Ville.........2
La Fontaine Belloy......3
Les Groseillières.........4
Le Cimetière 5

LÉGENDE

Limite de commune..............
Limite de lieuxdits..............
Voie ferrée..............
Route nationale..............
Route secondaire..............

Chemin, sentier..............
Canal..............
Agglomération..............
Région boisée..............
Cote d'altitude..............·215

ÉCHELLE 1:50.000ᵉ

0   1   2   3   4   5 km.

Reproduction interdite _ Tous droits réservés

IV

"Les vins de Champagne"

ATLAS DE LA I

MONTAGNE DE REIMS

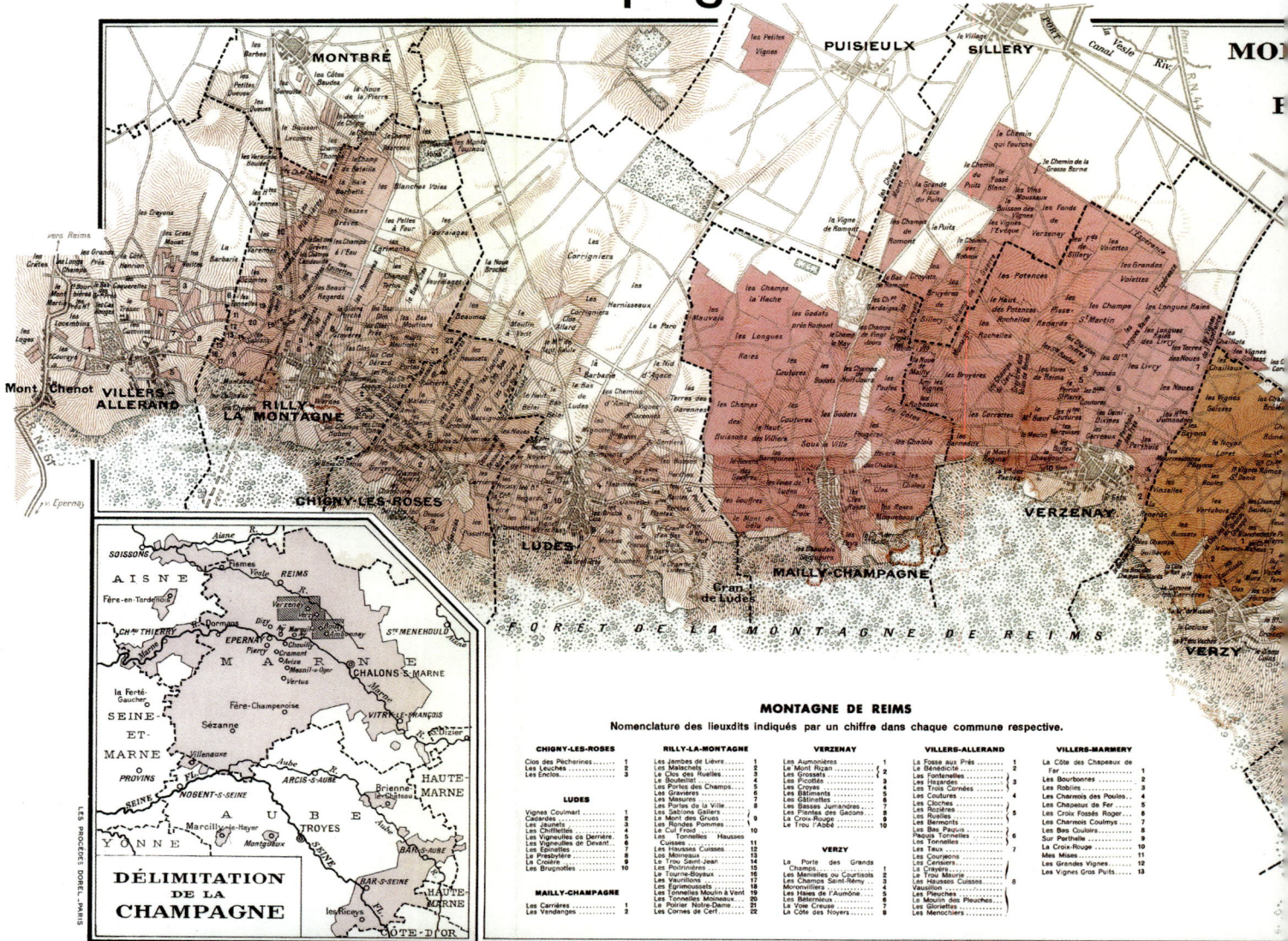

Nomenclature des lieuxdits indiqués par un chiffre dans chaque commune respective.

CHIGNY-LES-ROSES

Clos des Pécherines	1
Les Leuches	2
Les Enclos	3

LUDES

Vignes Coulmart	1
Cadardes	2
Les Jaunets	3
Les Chifflettes	4
Les Vigneulles de Derrière	5
Les Vigneulles de Devant	6
Les Epinettes	7
Le Presbytère	8
La Croière	9
Les Brugnottes	10

MAILLY-CHAMPAGNE

Les Carrières	1
Les Vendanges	2

RILLY-LA-MONTAGNE

Les Jambes de Lièvre	1
Les Malachets	2
Le Clos des Ruelles	3
Le Boutellat	4
Les Portes des Champs	5
Les Gravières	6
Les Masures	7
Les Portes de la Ville	8
Les Sablons Galiers	9
Le Mont des Grues	
Les Rondes Pommes	10
Le Cul Froid	
Les Tonnelles Hausses	
Cuisses	11
Les Hausses Cuisses	12
Les Moineaux	13
Le Trou Saint-Jean	14
Les Poitrinières	15
Le Tourne-Boyaux	16
Les Vaurillons	17
Les Egrimoussets	18
Les Tonnelles Moulin à Vent	19
Les Tonnelles Moineaux	20
Le Poirier Notre-Dame	21
Les Cornes de Cerf	22

VERZENAY

Les Aumonières	1
Le Mont Rizan	2
Les Grossets	
Les Picottes	3
Les Croyas	
Les Bâtiments	4
Les Gâtinettes	5
Les Basses Jumandres	6
Les Plantes des Gacons	7
La Croix-Rouge	9
Le Trou l'Abbé	10

VERZY

Le Porte des Grands	
Champs	1
Les Menielles ou Courtisols	2
Les Champs Saint-Rémy	3
Moronvilliers	4
Les Haies de l'Aumône	5
Les Bétemieux	6
La Voie Creuse	7
La Côte des Noyers	8

VILLERS-ALLERAND

La Fosse aux Prés	1
Le Bénédicite	2
Les Fontenelles	
Les Hazardes	3
Les Trois Cornées	
Les Coutures	4
Les Cloches	
Les Rozières	5
Les Ruelles	
Les Bermonts	
Les Bas Paquis	6
Paquis Tonnelles	
Les Tonnelles	
Les Taux	7
Les Courjeons	
Les Cerisiers	
La Crayère	
Le Trou Meurie	
Les Hausses Cuisses	8
Vausillon	
Les Pleuches	
Le Moulin des Pleuches	
Les Gloriettes	
Les Menochiers	

VILLERS-MARMERY

La Côte des Chapeaux de Fer	1
Les Bourbonnes	2
Les Roblins	3
Les Charmois des Poulns	4
Les Chapeaux de Fer	5
Les Croix Fossés Roger	6
Les Charmois Coulmys	7
Les Bas Couloirs	8
Sur Parthelle	9
La Croix-Rouge	10
Mes Mises	11
Les Grandes Vignes	12
Les Vignes Gros Puits	13

DÉLIMITATION DE LA CHAMPAGNE

ATLAS DE LA FRANCE VINICOLE L. LARMAT _ PARIS   10bis Rue Duhesme (18e Arrt)

Bouzy, harvest 2014

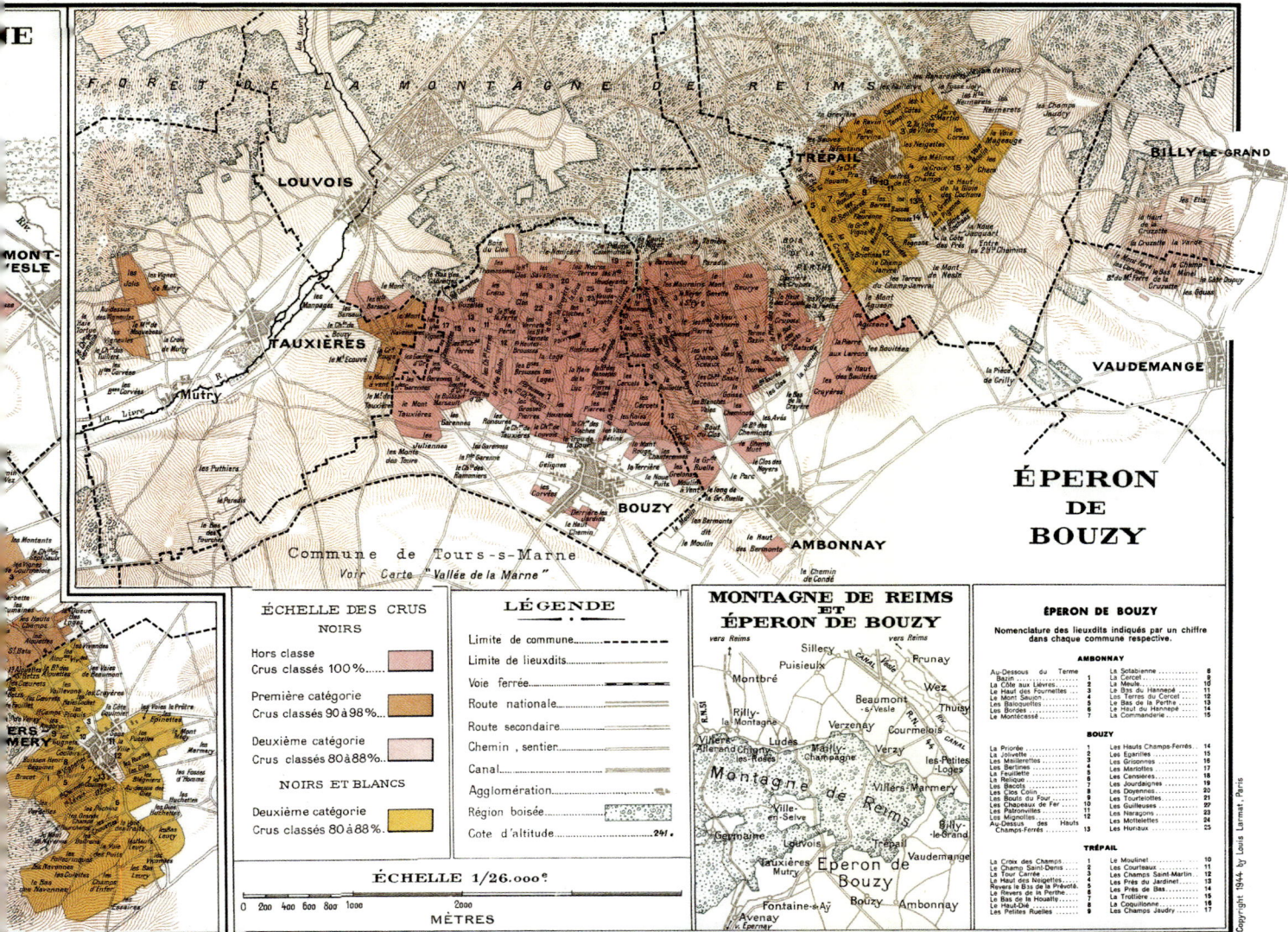

FORÊT DE LA MONTAGNE DE REIMS

LOUVOIS

TRÉPAIL

BILLY-LE-GRAND

MONT-'ESLE

TAUXIÈRES

Mutry

VAUDEMANGE

BOUZY

AMBONNAY

ÉPERON
DE
BOUZY

Commune de Tours-s-Marne
Voir Carte "Vallée de la Marne"

ÉCHELLE DES CRUS

NOIRS

Hors classe
Crus classés 100 %...

Première catégorie
Crus classés 90 à 98 %..

Deuxième catégorie
Crus classés 80 à 88 %..

NOIRS ET BLANCS

Deuxième catégorie
Crus classés 80 à 88 %.

LÉGENDE

Limite de commune.............
Limite de lieuxdits.............
Voie ferrée.............
Route nationale.............
Route secondaire.............
Chemin , sentier.............
Canal.............
Agglomération.............
Région boisée.............
Cote d'altitude.............241.

ÉCHELLE 1/26.000e

0 200 400 600 800 1000   2000
MÈTRES

MONTAGNE DE REIMS et ÉPERON DE BOUZY

vers Reims   vers Reims

Silley   Prunay
Puisieulx
Montbré   Wez
Beaumont   Thuisy
-s-Vesle
Rilly- Verzenay   Courmelois
la-Montagne
Villers- Ludes   Mailly-   Verzy
Allemand Chigny   Champagne   les-Petites
les-Rosés   -Loges
Montagne de Reims   Villers-Marmery
Ville-   Billy-
eri-Selve   -le-Grand
Germaine   Louvois   Trépail
Tauxières   Éperon de   Vaudemange
Mutry   Bouzy
Fontaine-s-Aÿ   Bouzy   Ambonnay
Avenay
v. Epernay

ÉPERON DE BOUZY

Nomenclature des lieuxdits indiqués par un chiffre
dans chaque commune respective.

AMBONNAY

Au-Dessous du Terme Bazin	1	La Sotabienne	8
La Côte aux Lièvres	2	La Cercel	9
Le Haut des Fournettes	3	La Meule	10
Le Mont Saujon	4	Le Bas du Hannené	11
Les Baroquelles	5	Les Terres du Cercel	12
Les Bordes	6	Le Bas de la Perthe	13
Le Montécossé	7	Le Haut du Hannené	14
		La Commanderie	15

BOUZY

La Priorée	1	Les Hauts Champs-Ferrés	14
La Jolivette	2	Les Egarilles	15
Les Maillerettes	3	Les Grisonnes	16
Les Bertines	4	Les Mariottes	17
La Feuillette	5	Les Censières	18
La Relique	6	Les Jourdaignes	19
Les Bacols	7	Les Doyennes	20
Les Clos Colin	8	Les Tourteiottes	21
Les Bouts du Four	9	Les Guilleuses	22
Les Chapeaux de Fer	10	Les Naragons	23
Les Patronvilles	11	Les Mottelettes	24
Les Mignolles	12	Les Huriaux	25
Au-Dessus des Hauts Champs-Ferrés	13		

TRÉPAIL

La Croix des Champs	1	Le Moulinet	10
Le Champ Saint-Denis	2	Les Courteaux	11
La Tour Carrée	3	Les Champs Saint-Martin	12
Le Haut des Neigettes	4	Les Prés du Jardinet	13
Revers le Bas de la Prévoté	5	Les Prés de Bas	14
Le Revers de la Perthe	6	La Trottière	15
Le Bas de la Houalle	7	La Coquillonne	16
Le Haut-Dié	8	Les Champs Jaudry	17
Les Petites Ruelles	9		

"Les vins de Champagne"

ATLAS D[...]

Com.ne de Cormoyeux

BOIS DU ROI

FLEURY-LA-RIVIÈRE

ROMERY

HAUTVILLERS

Montorgueil

.263

Éolienne

VILLERS-SOUS-CHATILLON

BOIS ST-MARC

CUMIÈRES

Tincourt

Arty

DAMERY

REUIL-SUR-MARNE

VENTEUIL

Echelle

Canal latéral à la Marne

MARNE RIV.

Canal latéral

vers Château-Thierry et Paris

la Gare

Château Villemengeois

la Chaussée

R.te Nat. N°3

MAR[...]

ŒUILLY

Montvoisin

Villesaint

la Chaussée

FORÊT D'ÉPERNAY

BOURSAULT

VAUCIENNES

MOUSSY

Com.ne de Vinay

Nomenclature des lieuxdits indiqués par un chiffre dans chaque commune respective.

AVENAY
La Gloire	1
Les Cornes	2
Les Thomailles	3
Le Chateud	4
Le Devant du Fond Bonnet	5
Bec-de-Coq	6
Saint-Martin	7
La Côte des Perches	8
Le Fond	9
Le Derrière du Feuilly	10
La Perrière	11
Le Trou des Féteux	12
Mont-de-Fer	13
La Côte de Chignon	14
La Folie	15
Haut-des-Bonnet	16
Carreau	17
Lambinet	18

CHAMPILLON
Demoiselles	1
Placardes	2
Champ Bigot	3
Basses-Genèves	4
Genèvre-Viciardes	5
Revvers du Midi	6
Clos Saint-Thierry	7
Bauties-d'Argent	8
Baudevins	9
Gouttes-d'Or	10
Hauts-Olives	11
Le Four à Chaux	12
Bois Communaux	13
Trou-Gessez	14
Chaufours	15

AY – CHAMPAGNE
Croteau-Côtelette	1
Le Fond de Vaurepvner	2
Vauregnier-Villers	3
Croteau-Villers	4
Chêne-Vigny	5
La Loge aux Vigniers	6
Côte Pelle	7
La Vigne aux Brebis	8
La Range aux Pierres	9
Devant Cochlerel	10
La Côte Vernaul	11
Blanc Fossé	12
La Voie aux Vaches	13
Champ Margot	14
La Croix	15
La Tartallotte	16
Le Haut-Baron	17
Le Bas-Baron	18

CUMIÈRES
Le Revers des Chalmonts	1
Le Chalmont du Bois	2
Les Grenieres	3
Les Jarretelles	4
Le Haut du Bois des Jotes	5
Les Pithoses	6
Le Clos	7
Les Ligneres	8
Les Longues Violles	9
Les Chèvres Pierreuses	10
Les Plantes Françaises	11
Les Bussettes	12
Chapelon	13
Les Rolennes	14
Les Ravigonnes	15
Flamme Chien	16

HAUTVILLERS
Le Pigmien	1
La Lignée	2
Les Cadettes	3
Les Tatarts l'Abbé	4
Les Côtes aux Renards	5

CHAMPILLON (continued columns)
Le Haut-des-Crayères	19
Chatbut	20
Le Clos	21
Trouaille	22
Boulevard de l'Est	23
Vauzelle Terme	24

(middle column)
Le Clos Sainte-Hélène	17
Les Jessonne	18
Les Rueilles	19
Les Duras Peines	20
Belle Maux	21
Madelonne	22
Les Prés Avoines	23
Le Grain d'Argent	24
Montgolfs	25
La Demoiselle	26
La Leyrière	27
Les Crayeres	28
Les Treilles-Monet	29
Les Linettes	31
Les Chevria	32
Les Barremonts	33

DIZY-MAGENTA
Le Haut de Rouge-Chausse	1
Grimpe-Chat du Couchant	2
Grimpe-Chat du Midi	3
Hautsé-Bride	4
Le Haut de Souchienne	5
La Pierre	6
Les Terres de Conscience	7
Le Bout de Moguebouteilles	8
Sur du Pourceaux	9
Conscience	10
Braus	11
Fondgrand	12
Les Terres du Crayon	13
Longues Raies	14

MAREUIL-SUR-AY
Florion	1
Le Poisson	2
Purget-Caillet	3
Garveaux	4
Cuvron	5

Les Basses Coyères	6
Derrière les Murs	7
Le Cugnot	8
Le Pri-Godet	9
Baccovas	10
Les Esbarts	11
La Cisopine	12
La Fôllarne du Gros-Buisson	13
Ruelle aux Vaches	14
La Crapaudiere	15
Les Cohommes	16
Les Tullaux	17
Terres Rouges	18
Le Grain d'Argent	19
Les Anges	20
Les Missères	21
Le Sabot	22
Le Trésor	23
Les Terres de Vorivats	24
Les Terres des Garennes	25
Cosarde	26
Houppe-Dondaine	27
Les Bornes Blanches	28
Clos Saint-Pierre	29
Les Beurry-du-Chemin-Creux	30
Le Bourot	31
Les Hautes-Montécuelles	32
La Grange à Dizy	33
Les Terres de la Cure	34
Les Noëls Crémonts	35
Au-dessous des Sablons	36

(far right column)
Vauleron-Paunet	7
Champ Bernard	8
Migremime	9
Capinel-Flammé	10
Bello-Faget	11
La Remissonne	12
Sur la Carrière	13
Les Faubourgs d'Enfer	14
Brotreuil	15
Les Vignes aux Champs	16
La Fosse Arzillers	17
Les Cohues	18
Beguine	19
Tournofftie	20
La Croix Trubert	21
Les Champs Bouverds	22
Les Quartiers Pointus	23
La Sente des Demoins	24

MUTIGNY
Mainberlin	1
Les Huriaux	2
Les Clos	3
La Pâture aux Oies	4
Garvaux	5
La Vielle-Tuillorie	6
Beugnard	7
Les Ponnées	8
Les Blancs-Chiens	9
Les Soussens	10
La Côte de Mai	11

PIERRY
Les Maries-Malottes	1
La Marguefterie	2
Canfbet	3
Les Digues	4
Les Bas-Bordels	5
Le Monboras	6
Les Grandes Voies	7

Atlas de la France Vinicole – L. LARMAT – Paris
10bis Rue Duhesme (18e Arr.t)

DÉLIMITATION DE LA CHAMPAGNE

(Regional location map: ARDENNES, AISNE, MARNE, SEINE-ET-MARNE, HAUTE-MARNE, AUBE, YONNE — with REIMS, ÉPERNAY, CHALONS-S-MARNE, TROYES, etc.)

Épernay, harvest 2014

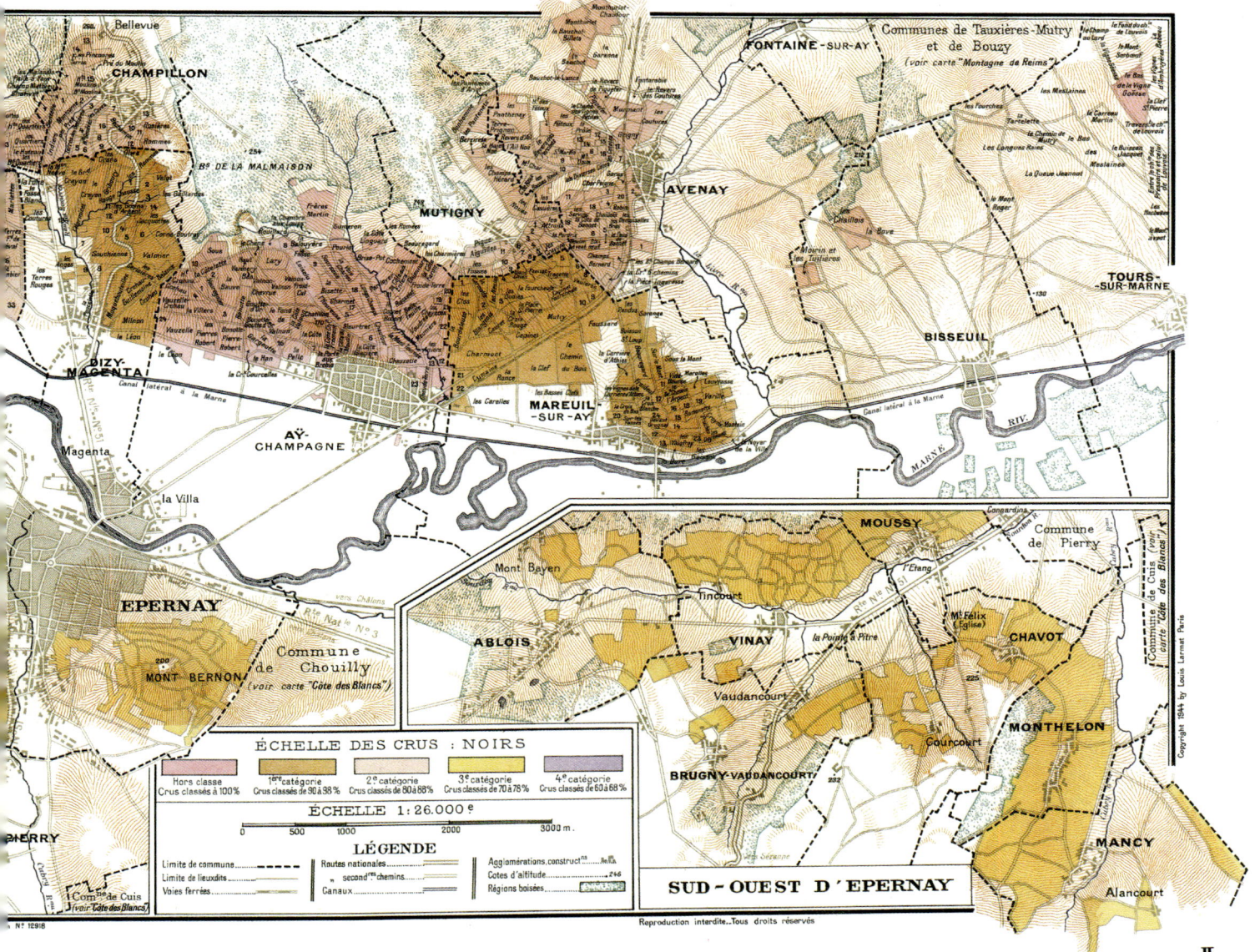

FRANCE VINICOLE L. LARMAT

VALLÉE DE LA MARNE

ÉCHELLE DES CRUS : NOIRS

Hors classe Crus classés à 100%	1ère catégorie Crus classés de 90 à 98%	2e catégorie Crus classés de 80 à 88%	3e catégorie Crus classés de 70 à 78%	4e catégorie Crus classés de 60 à 68%

ÉCHELLE 1:26.000e

0   500   1000   2000   3000 m.

LÉGENDE

Limite de commune .... Routes nationales .... Agglomérations, construct.ᵒⁿˢ
Limite de lieuxdits .... „ second.ᵗᵉˢ chemins .... Cotes d'altitude 246
Voies ferrées .... Canaux .... Régions boisées ....

SUD-OUEST D'EPERNAY

Reproduction interdite..Tous droits réservés

II

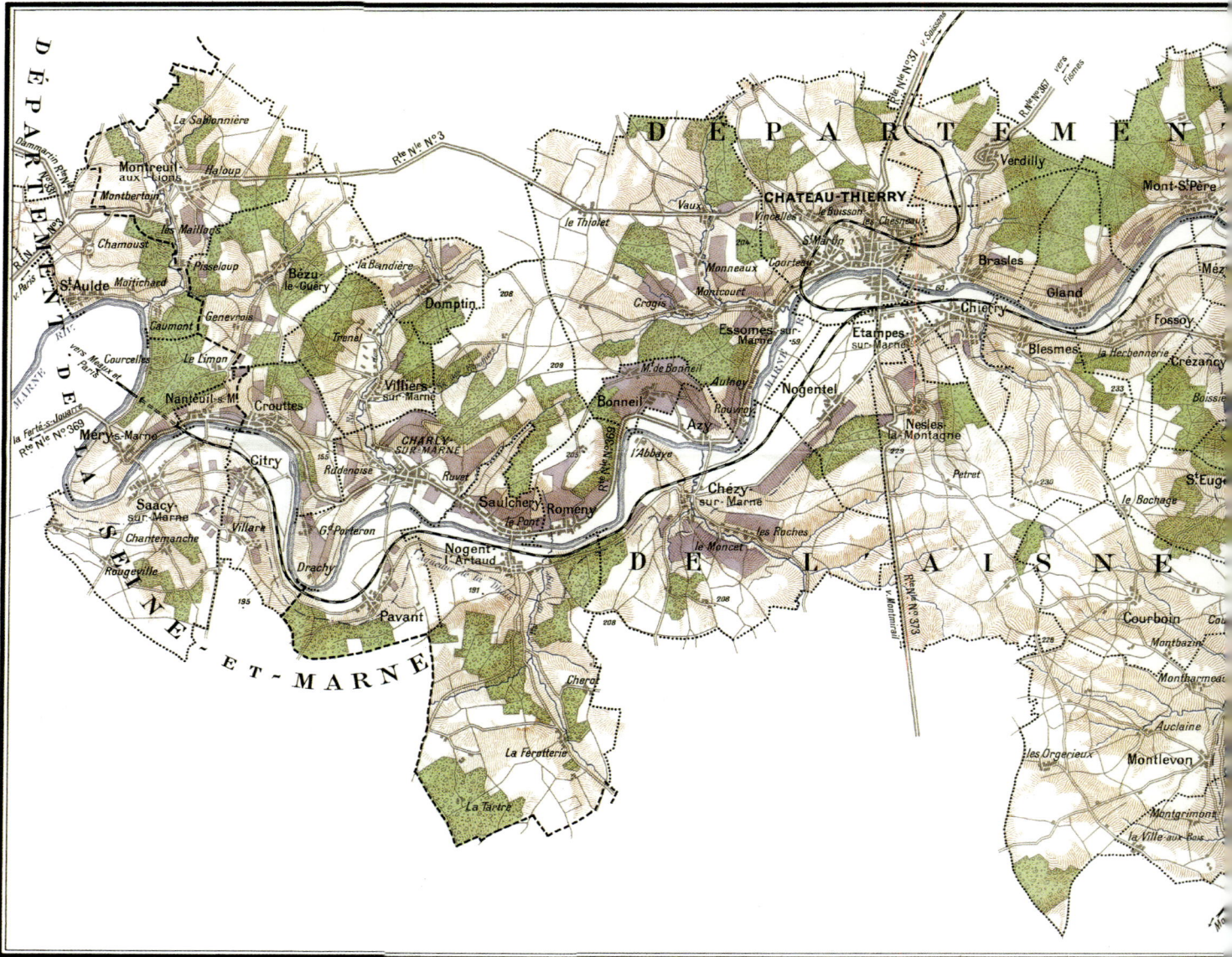

Châtillon-sur-Marne, summer 2014

NICOLE L. LARMAT

VALLÉE DE LA MARNE ET L'AISNE

AISNE

vers Reims

Commune de Romigny

Ste Gemme

la Défense

Colletterie

les Rosiers

R.N. No 380

Olizy-et-Violaine

Champvoisy

La Chapelle-Huxley

Passy-Grigny

Anthenay

Violaine

Jonquery

Boujacourt

FORÊT

Grigny

l'Hérolle

Pareuil

Trotte

la Maquerelle

Champlat-et-Boujacourt

DÉPARTEMENT

La Neuville-aux-Larris

DE

Barzy-sur-Marne

Marcilly

la Malmaison

Cuisles

Guchery

Paradis

Varennes

Rosay

RIS

Vincelles

Verneuil

Ht Verneuil

Vandières-sous-Chatillon

Melleray

Menicourt

Orcourt

La Charmoise

Belval-sous-Chatillon

Treloup

Courcelles

Chassins

Bas Verneuil

Montigny

Basllieux-sous-Chatillon

La Fortelle

Passy-sur-Marne

R.N. No3

MARNE

Reuilly-Sauvigny

Vassieux

CHATILLON-SUR-MARNE

Binson-Orquigny

Grand-Pré

DORMANS

DE

Villers-sous-Chatillon

Montorgueil

Sauvigny

Vassy

Troissy

Mareuil le Port

Port-à-Binson

Reuil-sur-Marne

Tincourt

Fleury-la-Rivière

Courthiézy

Chavenay

Bauquigny

LA

R.N. No3

Venteuil

Raday

Soilly

Champaillet

Gerseuil

Leuvrigny

Œuilly

l'Echelle

vers Epernay

Arty

Les Coqs

MARNE

Arty

St Agnan

Mantlevan

Chézy

Nesles-le-Repons

le Vivier

Festigny les Hameaux le Mesnil-le-Huttier

Montvoisin

Commune de Boursault

DAMERY

Saconnet

la Chapelle-Monthodon

Comblizy

la Rue

Chêne-la-Reine

Evry

Clairefontaine

Mt Mergey

Neuville

Beaurepaire

Monchevret

les Glapieds

Bauline-en-Brie

ARDENNES

SOISSONS

Aisne

L'Huis

AISNE

Fismes

REIMS

St MENEHOULD

3e Fontaine

le Mancets

le Bordet

Ch THIERRY

Dormans

Bligy

Verzenay

Terpy

EPERNAY

Ambonnay

Le Breuil

Piero

Chouilly

CHALONS-s-MARNE

Violaine

Avize

Mesnil-s-Oge

Vertus

Fransauges

Fère-Champenoise

VITRY-LE-FRANÇOIS

R. St Dizier

MARNE

Verdon

la Ferté-Gaucher

Sézanne

Villenauxe

SEINE-ET-MARNE

PROVINS

Aube

HAUTE-MARNE

Courbevin

SEINE

NOGENT-S-SEINE

ARCIS-s-AUBE

Brienne-le-Château

Marcilly-le-Hayer

Montgueux

AUBE

TROYES

BAR-SUR-AUBE

YONNE

Ph.

BAR-SUR-SEINE

HAUTE-MARNE

les Riceys

ÉCHELLE DES CRUS

3e Catégorie
Crus classés 70 à 78 %.

5e Catégorie
Crus classés 50 à 58 %.

4e Catégorie
Crus classés 60 à 68 %.

6e Catégorie
Moins de 50 %.

LÉGENDE

Limite de département .... _ _ _

Chemin, sentier ....

Limite de commune ....

Canal ....

Voie ferrée ....

Agglomération .... %a%

Route nationale ....

Cote d'altitude .... •214

Route secondaire ....

Région boisée ....

ÉCHELLE 1/62.000e

0   1   2   3   4   5   6   7.km.

Reproduction interdite _ Tous droits réservés

DÉLIMITATION DE LA CHAMPAGNE

ATLAS DE LA FRANCE VINICOLE L. LARMAT

"Les vins de Champagne"

VIGNOBLES DU BAR-SÉQUANAIS ET DU BAR-SUR-AUBOIS

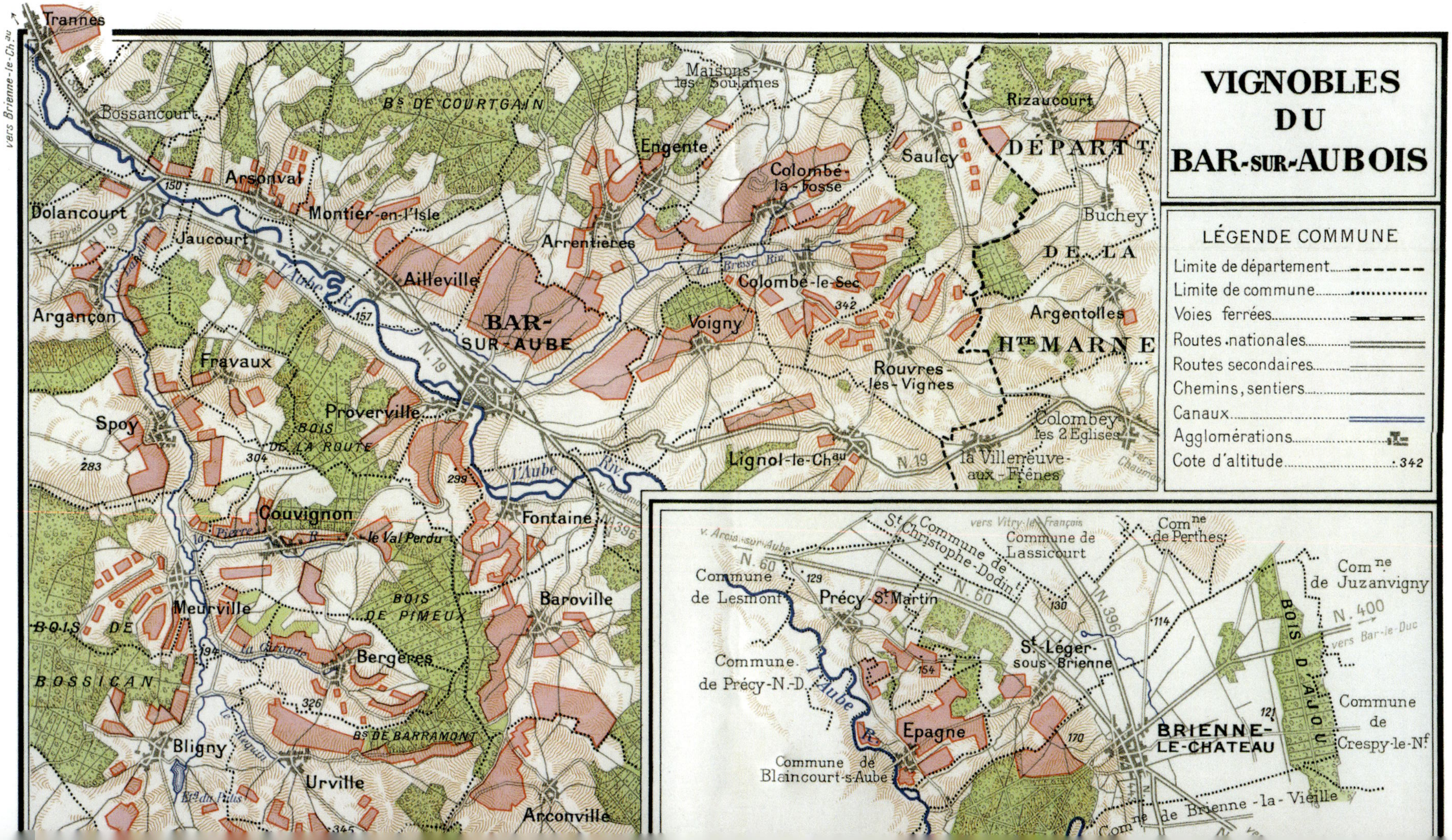

VIGNOBLES DU BAR-SUR-AUBOIS

LÉGENDE COMMUNE

Limite de département	—··—··—
Limite de commune	··········
Voies ferrées	▬▬▬
Routes nationales	———
Routes secondaires	———
Chemins, sentiers	········
Canaux	══════
Agglomérations	▪▪
Cote d'altitude	·342

VIGNOBLES
DU BAR-SÉQUANAIS

VI

LÉGENDE COMMUNE (Suite)

Vignobles..........

Bois..........

Nota.- Seules les communes en caractères gras
ont droit à l'appellation "Champagne"

ÉCHELLE

0   1   2   3   4   5   6 Km.

ENSEMBLE
du BAR-SÉQUANAIS et du BAR-sur-AUBOIS
Appellation "Champagne"

HAUTE-MARNE

AUBE

CÔTE-D'OR

YONNE

TROYES

Cunfin à 7 km 500 de Verpillières
2 Ha 5 de vigne

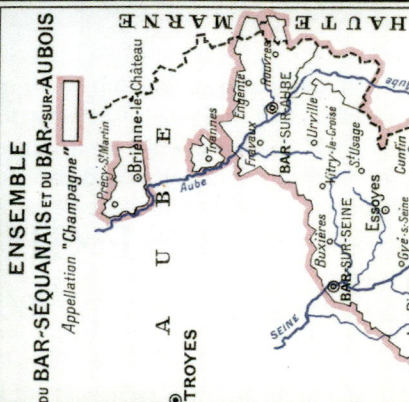

ATLAS DE LA FRANCE VINICOLE. L. LARMAT. PARIS. 10 bis Rue Duhesme 18e

Autorisation N° 12918.

LES PROCÉDÉS DOREL - PARIS

Aÿ basks in the glow of the setting sun on a midsummer's eve in 2017.

GREEN CHAMPAGNE

THE QUICKENING MARCH TO SUSTAINABLE VINEYARDS

No French wine region has been revolutionised over the past two decades as dramatically as Champagne. And no appellation has needed it more desperately. For decades, Champagne has been the laughing stock of responsible growers everywhere, notoriously piling on herbicides, fungicides, pesticides, fertilisers and even Parisian rubbish to shamelessly bolster its poor vines to ludicrous yields. But the slow march to change is gathering momentum on the hillsides of Champagne, and in the past two years it has intensified like never before. Though not as you might expect.

In the silent dormancy of winter, the skeletons of naked vines reveal the stark disparity of soil treatments, even from afar. From the upstairs terrace of his home above his Larmandier-Bernier cellars at the southern end of the Côte des Blancs, Pierre Larmandier showed me a panoramic view of the hillside of Vertus. 'Ten years ago, we could look out and it was only our vineyards that appeared green in winter, thanks to grasses cultivated in the mid-rows, but now there are more and more,' he points out excitedly.

It's a spectacular visual manifestation of a slow yet steady transformation in the mindset of Champagne growers. Just 17 years ago, Larmandier and Anselme Selosse (Jacques Selosse) expressed interest in purchasing a vineyard in Vertus, and the agent was surprised that both showed such interest in the way the vines had been tended, without the use of herbicides, having never seen buyers interested in this before.

Selosse and Larmandier were instrumental among a small band of like-minded growers, the radical pioneers who inspired a generation of Champenois to embrace responsible viticulture. Their story is well familiar, and rightfully celebrated. Now a new chapter is unfolding, with an unexpected and dramatic twist.

Later on the same day, I found myself bumping through the hallowed ground of Le Mesnil-sur-Oger on the edge of Vertus in the big truck of Larmandier's neighbour, organic leader Pascal Doquet. A stark and surprising reality begins to emerge as he points out the green vineyards: Louis Roederer, Taittinger, Moët & Chandon. 'The large houses are planting grasses in the mid-rows, ploughing and taking better care of the vines than the small growers,' he reveals.

The romanticised aura of growers as the heroes who are saving Champagne from the industrialised menace of the houses has long been the rhetoric of the wine world. Not only is this a fundamentally flawed and simplistic misconception, the truth today is that precisely the opposite is playing out between the vines.

Nobody understands this better than Doquet, president of Champagne's organic body, *Association des Champagnes Biologiques*. It was a sign of the evolution of the mindset of the region that Doquet was elected a board member of the *Syndicat Général des Vignerons* in 2018. 'It was significant for them to have an organic grower in this position!' he exclaims.

'The big houses are in contact with the customers and have to show a better and greener technique in response to public expectation,' he points out. 'Growers who are selling their grapes don't have to show customers what they are doing in the vineyards.'

The truth in Champagne today is that the leaders in sustainability in the vines and the wines, those whose vineyards set the pace in thwarting chemical intervention and who inspire, encourage, cajole and incentivise their partners to take up the challenge and step into a new millennium of responsibility are, with a small number of notably famous exceptions, not by and large the growers themselves, but the houses and cooperatives, even and most notably some of the biggest players of all.

Louis Roederer and Veuve Clicquot have forged forward as the new leaders of Champagne's eco-revolution. 'The change in the vineyards in the last decade has been unbelievable!' enthuses Dominique Demarville (Veuve Clicquot). 'The growers were the pioneers, and now the big houses have done great things in our own vineyards.'

THE BIG DILEMMA OF YIELDS

While it took famous growers to lead the charge towards more environmentally friendly practices, if this were to ever gain widespread traction, it had to be the big houses who took it up. For Champagne, sustainability is more than just doing the right thing for the vineyards, the workers, the planet and the customers – an eco-friendly approach shakes the very core of the fabric of the champagne model, not only in how the grapes are grown but, tellingly and crucially, in how the growers are paid.

Pascal Doquet inspects the pruning in Le Mesnil-sur-Oger in winter 2019.

Champagne's antiquated and grossly simplistic classification system has long dictated that growers are remunerated on nothing more than volume and cru, with a blatant disregard for quality. No wonder yields have spiralled in recent decades, reaching an average of nearly 100 hectolitres (hL) per hectare in the first decade of the new millennium, from less than 60hL over the 30 years prior. In the enormous 2018 vintage, there were reports of as much as 250hL per hectare on the southern Côte des Blancs.

'The problem with Champagne is that every grower considers the maximum yield permitted by the appellation to be an economic minimum,' Jean-Hervé Chiquet (Jacquesson) admits. 'About 90% of growers harvest the maximum permitted by the appellation, plus whatever remains on the vines.' For the full story on excessive yields, see *Has the Bubble Burst?* in the 2014–2015 edition of this Guide.

In 2018 the maximum permitted yield was 10.8 tonnes per hectare, plus an additional 4.7 tonnes for reserves, hence 15.5 tonnes in total. This equates to a maximum pressing of 98,800 litres per hectare, or 98.8hL, which breaks down to just under 80hL of cuvée and 19hL of tailles. Across the entire appellation, Champagne is currently averaging around 75hL per hectare. 'In Vertus, you are considered a bad grower if you do not produce 100hL/hectare,' reveals Larmandier,

who limits his yields to 60–70hL. 'People produce too much in the Côte des Blancs, and the big houses just buy everything.'

This creates a dilemma around sustainability, because herbicides, fungicides and chemical fertilisers bolster yields, while grasses cultivated in mid-rows create competition and diminish yields. 'You lose in quantity but you win in quality,' explains Jean-Baptiste Lécaillon, who manages Champagne's biggest biodynamic vineyard at Louis Roederer. 'It's all about the discussion between quality and quantity. This has been the debate for 300 years.'

THE WAKE-UP CALL OF 2017

With no incentive to boost quality at the expense of quantity (and hence return), it was going to take a dramatic wake-up call for growers and houses to get off the downward spiral of chemical warfare that has ravaged the landscape of Champagne vineyards since the 1970s. That wake-up call came in 2017.

'I was worse than stressed, I was disorientated by the harvest of 2017,' discloses Hervé Dantan (Lanson). 'It was the most complicated harvest I have ever faced. What happened at the end of August was terrible – a deluge of rain followed by very warm

days, accelerating the onset of botrytis, and we lost an enormous amount of fruit. It was a revelation that we have to change something in the vineyards in Champagne. We saw it in 2005 and 2011, but we did nothing then. And now we must respond. With global warming, we will have to face harvests like 2017 again in the near future. We always have rain in Champagne, but the difference now is that 30 years ago, it came during harvest in October, when it was too cold for botrytis, but now it's warmer so botrytis takes off. We need to change our viticulture in order to be ready.'

The big lesson of 2017 came in the startling disparity between traditional and sustainable viticulture. In a vintage that unleashed botrytis and mildew like Champagne has never seen, it was the vineyards that survived unscathed that were the surprise exceptions.

'In 2017 the estate vineyards of Veuve Clicquot and Louis Roederer had zero botrytis – zero,' reveals Demarville. The same phenomenon was observed in sustainable vineyards across the region. There are four factors at play here. An absence of herbicides and competition from grasses in the mid-rows not only builds resilience in the vines to resist botrytis, but also lowers susceptibility by decreasing vigour and yields. Further, grasses in the mid-rows push the roots deeper into the chalk, crucial for heightening mineral expression in the wines, and also for diminishing uptake of water during downpours. Finally, the grasses absorb the water before it reaches the roots of the vines.

HOUSES TAKE THE LEAD

Dantan noted that all of his sustainable growers had better results than those practising chemical viticulture in 2017. He immediately took action, establishing a new department within Lanson, under which growers can obtain sustainable certification, and committing to paying a higher price for their grapes. 'We are working very hard to engage our growers in sustainable viticulture,' he says. 'As a big brand, we have a role to work alongside our growers and demonstrate that the future of Champagne is about being more ecological.' Still in its early days, the program has had a good response, and he hopes he might have all growers signed up within five years. The harsh economic truth is that when sustainability might save their yields, growers are interested.

'In quality and sustainability, the Champagne region is changing very, very fast,' observes Olivier Krug. 'But the difficulty is still those growers who supply grapes and don't produce their own wines. If you inherited half a hectare from your grandmother and you are working in a car factory, you just want your vineyard for revenue, so it is very challenging for me to ask you to change the way you work.'

In response, Krug has joined Lanson and many of Champagne's top houses in handling the paperwork, audits and costs of sustainable certification for its growers. 'We do the administrative stuff, so they can concentrate on their field,' explains Krug senior winemaker Julie Cavil, who works closely alongside growers and already has 20% certified. At Veuve Clicquot, Demarville has appointed a team of three dedicated exclusively to helping their growers with sustainability, but admits it might take a decade to get everyone on board. 'The champagne region is on the move, and all the serious houses are doing this: Bollinger, Louis Roederer, Moët, Laurent-Perrier, Nicolas Feuillatte, Mailly Grand Cru,' he says. 'When I studied winemaking in Avize 30 years ago, viticulture was all about chemicals, but now they are explaining to the next generation that you must protect biodiversity and be careful with the planet, so I am very confident for the future of this region.'

CERTIFIABLE

Despite the region's best efforts, Champagne's erratic climate makes practising a fully certified biodynamic or even organic regime a nail-biting pursuit. The biggest menace in this wet and humid place is disease, a challenge to manage organically or biodynamically, without the fallback of systematic fungicide sprays. Like many houses and growers, Billecart-Salmon adopts organic and biodynamic practices without seeking certification, so as to uphold the flexibility to intervene when rot sets in. 'A lot of biodynamic vineyards yielded zero in 2016 and 2017,' points out Antoine Roland-Billecart. Anselme Selosse is Champagne's champion of intuitive winegrowing, rigorously biodynamic, yet emphatically non-prescriptive, so as to respond to save his crop when he needs to. 'A production system which does not allow you to produce is not a production system at all,' he proposes.

Of Champagne's 33,868 hectares, just over 2% (700 hectares) are certified organic, of which one-fifth are owned by Louis Roederer. 'There is a big fight on in organics,' says Lécaillon. 'Consumers want organic but growers don't. You need a high level of technical attention to be organic, and it's not possible for everybody, especially on a large scale. It's demanding and costly, and without the knowledge or the money, you are better to be inorganic.'

For this reason, the region established sustainable certification as an option to go 'halfway to organics', as Lécaillon puts it. In 2001, the French Ministry of Agriculture developed Haute Valeur Environmentale (HVE), and in 2014 the Comité Champagne launched Viticulture Durable en Champagne (VDC). Both certifications are roughly similar and require minimum standards in chemical inputs and biodiversity less rigorous than organics. Eradication of herbicides is widely agreed to be the most important first step in vineyard improvement, yet VDC still permits full use of herbicides on up to half of the vineyard area. Meanwhile, all of Champagne's top houses and growers have already fully eradicated herbicides in their own vineyards. Nonetheless, HVE and VDC are a good interim step, though far from sufficiently rigorous to be an adequate end point in themselves.

The Comité Champagne aspires to completely eradicate herbicides by 2025, and has already made some progress toward this goal. Twenty percent of Champagne vineyards have been certified HVE or VDC, with a goal of 100% by 2030. The region halved its use of nitrogen fertilisers in the first 15 years of this century. Pests rank third after disease and weeds among the

woes afflicting Champagne vineyards, and pesticides have now been almost completely eradicated, thanks to pheromone sexual confusion techniques.

THE COPPER SULPHATE CRISIS

Disease is Champagne's most deadly menace, and its most elusive. 'We need to have products that are very efficient with mildew,' emphasises Demarville, 'or we can lose the crop in 24 hours.' Without chemical intervention, he estimates that he would have lost 50–70% of his crop to the rains in May 2018.

Copper sulphate is currently the only alternative to chemical fungicides to control mildew permitted under organic and bio-dynamic certification, yet itself remains controversial, as debate continues over whether there is a cumulative effect of toxicity in the soil. And it has just become more controversial still.

In January 2019, the European Commission lowered the limit for copper sulphate application under organics from its current cap of 6kg per hectare per year over a five-year average, to just 4kg per hectare per year spread over seven years.

'There is a concern that this regulation will lead some organic growers to give up their certification,' says Doquet, who has gone in on behalf of the growers to 'fight' with the Commission. Between 2012 and 2017, almost two-thirds of organic growers in Champagne used more than 4kg per hectare per year.

In the village of Mareuil-sur-Aÿ, Laurent Bénard (Bénard Pitois) used 6kg in the challenging 2012 and 2016 seasons. 'With the change of climate the storms damage the fruit, the temperature is high and it's humid, so we are in danger!' he exclaims. 'And it is even worse in the Aube and the Vallée de la Marne, where it rains more!' Even those who use less are unhappy. 'We have been using 3–4kg of copper in our vineyards for 100 years and there is no toxicity, so it is a nasty decision to kick us!' says Lécaillon.

There are murmurs that the EU is ultimately planning to forbid use of copper sulphate in vineyards altogether. 'If we are not allowed to use copper sulphate we cannot be organic in Champagne,' says Jean-Hervé Chiquet (Jacquesson), who has organic certification for one-third of his vineyards.

Intensive research is currently underway to develop a new organic product to replace copper sulphate, or even new grape varieties resistant to mildew. Demarville hopes that within 10 years Champagne will be able to eradicate chemical treatment of not only mildew, but also oïdium and botrytis. For now, fighting disease without resorting to chemical fungicides is a dilemma with no simple solution.

BACK TO THE OLD WAY

Champagne's march back to a more sustainable way promises the possibility of great improvements in quality, as the deep history of the region attests.

'Champagne was organic for three centuries,' Lécaillon reminds us. 'Champagne in the 1950s was made by peasants who were proud of their work and doing their best for their soils that they were giving to their children. It has only had chemicals since the 1960s. A century ago, the yields were very low and the wines were very concentrated. We developed our biodynamic conversion to go back to the levels of balance we used to have in the 1950s and 1960s. The best champagnes ever produced were made between 1945 and 1970. And my target in 20 years is to come back to this. Biodynamics and organics are not a goal in themselves, but a tool to take us back to the golden age of champagne!'

It's illegal to leave grapes unpicked, but so extreme were the yields of 2018 that many growers took the risk, as this vineyard in Hautvillers in January 2019 attests.

At the northern end of the Côte des Blancs, Cramant is one of chardonnay's most powerful and enduring grand crus.

HAS THE GROWER BUBBLE BURST?

IS THIS THE BEGINNING OF THE END OF THE GROWER PRODUCER?

Forces are at play that threaten the survival of Champagne's grower producers. Global economies, erratic harvests, incentives from négociants and even the French taxation system itself are driving growers to sell all their fruit, some to relinquish their status and become négociants, and others to sell up altogether. Are our beloved champagne growers on a path to extinction?

The rise of the grower producer has revolutionised this generation in Champagne. Recent decades have seen the little guy step forward to demonstrate that top champagne is no longer the exclusive realm of the big players. Champagne is not just oceanic blends from everywhere, but single crus and individual vineyards, tended, crafted, matured and presented lovingly to the world by the same pair of hands.

And, oh, how we have celebrated. Champagne's grower producers are the darlings of sommeliers and hip bars the world over; the prize of the most fanatical champagne purists. Top growers like Egly-Ouriet and Jacques Selosse have realised prestige prices. Rightly or wrongly, the 'RM' (Récoltant-Manipulant) insignia on labels has become a status symbol over 'NM' (Négociant-Manipulant). And the négociants have taken notice, inspired into more sustainable viticultural practices, more creative vinification and the creation of specialist cuvées to capture the detail of single crus and vineyards. It's been a heyday for champagne. But all this is changing.

DEVASTATING DECLINE

'Champagne is going to be a very different place in the next decade,' I was recently told by one small grower and négociant struggling to sustain his family business in a highly respected premier cru on the Montagne de Reims. 'It will not be possible for many of the small brands to survive.'

Already many have given up. In 2018, 112 grower producers followed a growing trend and closed down production. In 2008, growers sold 78.5 million bottles, almost one-quarter of all champagne production. A decade later, grower sales declined to just 54.9 million bottles, merely 18% of champagne sales by volume and less than 15% by value. This represents a devastating drop of more than 30%. Over the same time, sales by champagne houses grew a little and coopératives declined by more than 7% as Champagne continued its march towards a steadily increasing house dominance.

Global forces continue to fuel this trend, and 2018 marked a milestone turning point for the balance of champagne sales. For the first time in history, not only did champagne exports exceed French sales, but exports to countries outside the European Union exceeded those within (excluding France). Fifteen years ago, exports represented barely more than one-third of the region's production. This trend will only increase. 'I believe that in 20 years Champagne will sell only 35–40% of its production in France and 60–65% in export markets,' forecasts Veuve Clicquot chef de cave Dominique Demarville. 'And this is going to change the balance inside Champagne. The producers are going to change.'

The changing balance in champagne sales is hitting growers much harder than houses and coopératives. Of Champagne's 15,800 growers, 4159 sold their own champagnes in 2018, but only 1269 exported their cuvées outside of France, and just 829 outside of Europe. More than two-thirds of champagne growers rely exclusively on domestic sales, and more than four-fifths entirely on European countries.

'Every year, we are losing sales to the big houses,' reveals Nicolas Chiquet of respected grower-producer Gaston Chiquet in the village of Dizy. He is fortunate to be among the minority with global distribution. 'Outside of France we have less competition, and we have distribution through agents who are passionate about pushing growers. But in France we are alone, it is more difficult, and we have to work harder.'

Growers sold more than 47 million bottles, 86% of their production, in France in 2018. This left exports at just 7.4 million bottles, more than 60% of which (4.5 million) were destined for other European Union countries. The rest of the world shared less than 3 million grower bottles, compared with more than 71 million bottles from houses and close to 5 million from coopératives.

'In mature markets like the US, there was once a time when growers equated to top quality in the minds of consumers,

journalists and sommeliers, so they imported something like 400 or 500 different growers,' points out leading grower Rodolphe Péters (Pierre Péters). 'And then they realised that it's not because it's a grower that it's good, so now they are back to 350 growers.'

ENTER THE NÉGOCIANTS

'The problem is that the French market is tough and very competitive,' says Maxime Toubart, Président of Champagne's winegrower's union, the *Syndicat Général des Vignerons de la Champagne*. 'Vineyards are increasingly dependent on the houses to sell their stocks, because they have the means to sell the bottles in distant markets at high prices. So they can afford to pay a lot for the grapes.'

Champagne pays its growers the highest grape price in the world, an average of more than €7 per kilogram, and more than €8 in top grand crus, and rising annually – more than 80% up on the price 15 years ago. In the dismal 2017 harvest, Champagne's largest player, Louis Vuitton–Moët Hennessy, shocked everyone by offering its growers a premium of 6–7% on the price of grapes, and in some crus as much as 15%, inflating prices across the region. The only grower-producers able to sustain these rising costs are those able to pass on price increases in export markets. Yet champagne remains one of the most price-sensitive luxuries.

Even the big players are troubled. 'This is a problem for us, as we need to follow the price rise, but we cannot increase our ex-cellar price,' reveals Lanson chef de cave Hervé Dantan. 'We expect the price of grapes to continue to rise for the next four or five years, and some brands are going to die. The next five years are going to be very important, and the balance between houses, growers and coopératives is going to change.'

This scenario coincides with the retirement of many of the founders who produced their own grower champagnes for the first time. As the next generation takes over, many are recognising that strong grape prices and high demand for quality fruit presents a more stable and compelling opportunity to focus back on selling to négociants. 'It's so easy to sell grapes at the moment that I am afraid that some growers will give up,' says Dantan. 'Growers who don't manage to sell good volumes of their own wines will be completely fed up and sell more to négociants.'

At a time when Champagne's large houses are seeking to increase production, they are eager to actively engage growers to shore up supply. 'I have been working on the relationship between growers and champagne houses for 20 years, and something is changing now,' says Demarville. His engagement and support has fostered loyal growers, and he believes the balance in Champagne will change, and more and more small growers will stop bottling.

'We are creating a new generation of growers who don't necessarily want to sell bottles, but who want to be top growers and sell their fruit to the leading houses,' he says. 'In the next 10 years, 35% of growers will retire, and most will lease or sell their vines to other growers.'

THE STORMS OF CLIMATE CHANGE

This critical reconciliation in grower champagnes has been amplified not only by economic forces but by the harrowing extremes of climate change. The vagaries of Champagne's marginal climate and the diversity of its microclimates have long dictated a wine style dependent upon blending multiple vintages, varieties and crus. Ever more dramatic extremes are taking their toll, and yields suffered bitterly in 2016 and even more in 2017.

'A small grower in one village has nothing to compensate for difficult weather,' said Benoît Gouez, chef de cave of Moët & Chandon. 'Grower wines are very good, and I have friends among many of them, but by nature the quality of champagne is uneven. The more grapes you can access, the more you can be consistent.'

Champagne's average grower now owns less than 0.7 hectares. In a good harvest, this would facilitate production of just 7000 bottles. Larger growers are naturally more likely to bottle their own champagnes, but the average production of Champagne's 4159 growers is a mere 13,200 bottles.

As vineyards are increasingly divided through inheritance, owners are forced to seek employment elsewhere. 'We have observed that with the new generation, sometimes they have lost the soul of a vigneron,' admits Charles Heidsieck chef de cave Cyril Brun. 'They lose involvement with the technical side of viticulture, not so important in an easy harvest, but critical in vintages like 2018.'

TOP GROWERS ARE BECOMING NÉGOCIANTS

Jérôme Prévost is one of Champagne's most celebrated growers, producing just 13,000 bottles from a 2.2 hectare vineyard he inherited from his grandmother in 1987. Although his wines are in high demand and sell for respectable prices worldwide, such a small production is insufficient to sustain his livelihood. In 2017, frost wiped out 80% of his harvest, and he relinquished his récoltant-manipulant credentials to be reincarnated as a négociant-manipulant in order to purchase fruit and grow production, to the collective gasp of the hip sommelier world.

This is a trend followed by an increasing band of Champagne's most celebrated growers, including Diebolt-Vallois and J.L. Vergnon, though not all for the same reason. The acclaimed 9.5 hectare estate of Bérêche et Fils recently joined the négociant world, to open up the flexibility not only to buy from growers but, surprisingly, to purchase more vineyards. 'We wanted to buy a 0.3 hectare plot in Mailly-Champagne, but as a récoltant the authorities only permitted us to buy half because they said we were too big,' explains co-owner and chef de cave Raphaël Bérêche. The change has opened the way for him to purchase small parcels from growers in other villages to make a new range of single-vineyard cuvées. In the village of Bouzy, famed grower André Clouet has likewise become a négociant to create new cuvées from fruit exchanged with growers in other villages.

Jérôme Prévost relinquished his récoltant-manipulant status to source fruit when frost wiped out his harvest in 2017.

THE THREAT OF INHERITANCE TAX

For the De Sousa family in the fabled grand cru of Avize, the decision to become a négociant came for a very different reason. As third-generation grower Erick De Sousa prepares to pass the estate on to his three children, a threat has arisen more crippling than global economics and climate change.

France boasts one of the highest levels of inheritance tax in the world, and children are stung with 45% tax on assets worth more than €1.8 million. A generation ago it was possible to pay off inheritance tax in a single harvest. Today, the average Champagne vineyard is valued at more than €1.5 million per hectare, ranking Champagne as the highest-value appellation viticultural land on earth, and its top Côte des Blancs grand crus are now fetching up to €3 million per hectare.

De Sousa owns 11 hectares of almost exclusively Côte des Blancs grand crus to produce 100,000 bottles, and at any time holds 250,000 bottles in its cellar. This little family estate must be worth well in excess of €30 million. It would take a lifetime to pay off the tax on such an inheritance.

'In France we say that the inheritance tax is a stupid law!' exclaims Erick's daughter Charlotte. 'If the parents pass away and haven't prepared for this, then the children say it's a poison gift and they're forced to sell the vineyards to big companies.'

And hence the more than slightly ironic twist of switching from récoltant to négociant to uphold the business in the family name. 'We changed to a négociant in 2013 to pass on the domaine to us three children,' explains Charlotte. French taxation is more kind in the inheritance of a company than vineyard land. Erick and his wife Michelle now own the vineyard, and their children the company, 'so we effectively buy the grapes from ourselves'. By definition, this makes them a négociant.

As in Burgundy, France's heavy inheritance taxes make it increasingly unviable for Champagne's top vineyards to remain in family hands as récoltants. Though there are other ways. In Vertus, the Larmandier family (Larmandier-Bernier) has been able to avoid inheritance tax by passing on a portion of their 18 hectares of vineyards to their children every 10 years, and then renting them back.

THE LINES ARE BLURRING

In an age when champagne markets religiously celebrate récoltant-manipulant status, relinquishments such as these are testimony to the reality that in Champagne itself, there is no such segregation between récoltants and négociants, and its very suggestion is vigorously dismissed by both sides.

'We need to change this stupid, simplistic view of the market!' exclaims chef de cave Jean-Baptiste Lécaillon, who blends Louis

Roederer's vintage cuvées exclusively from estate sources. 'There are some growers who are more négociants than growers, and some négociants who are more growers than négociants.' The very designation of récoltant and négociant in Champagne has become so convoluted that it has diminished to virtually complete meaninglessness, and this is why I have never published it in any edition of this Guide. The lines are blurring as négociants increasingly purchase vineyards, growers source from many villages rather than just their own, and coopératives focus more and more on selling their own brands.

'Champagne has moved on,' says Olivier Krug. 'I grew up with this idea that Champagne was about the growers and the maisons, but today I feel closer to many of the growers than I do to the houses.'

LAST MAN STANDING

We are now at a critical juncture in the evolution of the Champagne grower-producer. The years to come will see an increasing reconciliation of growers. While many smaller and lesser estates will return to selling their fruit to négociants, Dominique Demarville predicts that the top growers like Egly-Ouriet will grow and increase.

'In the past it was very easy for small producers to sell champagne, but today a lot have trouble finding their place in the market,' says Champagne's top grower, Francis Egly (Egly-Ouriet) in Ambonnay, whose rising production of exceptional cuvées is in very strong demand. 'The new generation of champagne lovers expect very good quality from small producers, and those who make mediocre quality will find it increasingly difficult to sell their production.'

In the same village, Sophie Déthune (Paul Déthune) goes so far as to suggest that 'today we are 4000 independent grower-producers, and I think in five years we will just be 150'.

Jacquesson's Jean-Hervé Chiquet proposes that in the grower world there is a 'super top ten', and beyond that just a few dozen who are successful today. 'I will be generous and say there are 150 great growers, but there are more than 4000 making wine the way the laboratory tells them to make it, and the quality is very low,' he suggests. 'But Champagne is the fastest moving wine region in France. Things are changing now, and you have to adapt.'

Rodolphe Péters puts an even smaller number on it. 'Very few growers are succeeding and fewer and fewer are producing,' he discloses. 'There are very, very few growers with a strong demand, probably no more than fifty. And another 200 who are less successful. And so there are really only 250 growers selling worldwide.'

It would be no catastrophe for Champagne's lesser growers to redirect their fruit to the négociant houses. And there is no doubt that the very best growers, well established and well loved across the champagne world, will continue, against all odds, to strengthen their rightful place among the great wine estates of the world.

Chardonnay grapes arrive at the press at De Sousa during harvest 2014.

The tranquil slopes of Le Mesnil-sur-Oger slumber during the bitterly cold winter of 2013

WHY IS CHAMPAGNE SO CHEAP?

*T*he writing is on the cellar wall. Vineyard prices are up more than five-fold in 25 years. Grape prices are up 80% in 15 years. Champagne has the highest cost of production in the wine world. Yet the price of a bottle of champagne has risen less than 15% in the past decade. Champagne cannot remain the outright bargain of the fine wine world forever.

Did you know that Champagne pays its growers the highest grape price in the world, averaging more than €7 per kilogram, and rising annually, more than 80% up on 15 years ago? It takes 1.3 kilograms of grapes to make a bottle of champagne, not to mention a production process more complex, labour-intensive and time-consuming than any other in the wine world. Besides fortified, champagne is the only wine style matured to its prime prior to release. Champagne currently has almost 1.5 billion bottles stockpiled, which will remain in waiting for an average of more than 4.5 years.

The average Champagne vineyard is now valued at more than €1.5 million per hectare, ranking Champagne as the highest-value appellation viticultural land on earth, 60 times the value of an average Bordeaux vineyard! Champagne also ranks as the fastest inflating value of France's wine appellations, with the price of vineyards growing by 3.4% per annum over the past decade, and more than five-fold in the past 25 years. Champagne's top Côte des Blancs grand crus are now fetching up to €3 million per hectare.

And Champagne's cost of production is rising for another reason. The harrowing extremes of climate change are taking their toll, and the region has suffered bitterly in recent vintages. The 2016 season saw catastrophic climatic events that decimated yields by almost one-quarter, and 2017 was even worse, written off by many growers as their most challenging vintage ever. Meanwhile, as Champagne slowly but increasingly turns to sustainable viticulture, vineyard management costs increase as yields decrease, further multiplying spiralling costs.

'Over the next 10 years, the price of champagne will grow a little more than in the past, because of the cost of producing sustainable grapes,' forecasts Veuve Clicquot chef de cave, Dominique Demarville. He postulates that champagne might inflate by 20–30%, but adds that his La Grande Dame prestige cuvée will never be the price of First Growth Bordeaux or Grand Cru Burgundy.

In 2017, Champagne's largest player, Louis-Vuitton–Moët Hennessy, maker of Moët & Chandon, Mercier, Dom Pérignon, Veuve Clicquot, Ruinart and Krug, offered its growers a premium of 6–7% on the price of grapes, inflating prices across the region.

The only houses able to sustain these rising costs are those able to pass on price increases in export markets. Yet as sales within Europe continue to decline, champagne remains one of the most price-sensitive luxuries in growing markets outside of Europe. Big-brand discounting accounted for the majority of growth in key markets in recent years. Champagne is caught in the squeeze between the most expensive (and rising) cost of materials and production in the wine world, and the most price-competitive and frequently discounted premium wine category on the shelves.

In the midst of all this, Champagne remains the outright bargain of the luxury wine world, with prestige champagne ranking far and away as the most affordable and most accessible of all flagship global benchmark wines. When was the last time you found a mature First Growth Bordeaux or Grand Cru Burgundy for the same price as Krug Grand Cuvée, Louis Roederer Cristal or Veuve Clicquot La Grande Dame?

In 1904, Moët & Chandon Carte Bleue sold for the same price as Château Latour, Château Margaux and Château Haut-Brion. A 30-year-old Château Lafite was just double the price of a bottle of Louis Roederer, Mumm Cordon Rouge or Veuve Clicquot. Today, these Bordeaux icons are 20 times the price. Champagne does not rank even once among the top 20 most expensive wines in the world.

Champagne is the envy of the wine world, the universal and inimitable symbol of celebration. It accounts for 20% of French wine sales, from just 4% of the country's vineyards.

When I recently hosted an intimate group of champagne lovers for a special week of visits during harvest in the region, they arrived sceptical about the high price of champagne. After experiencing vineyards, cellars and cuveries of the top houses and growers across the region, they witnessed just what went into its production, and left astounded by its value.

Can champagne maintain its bargain prices? It can, and it will, but only until the moment demand hits a record high in the coming years. Following crashes in the French and UK markets, Champagne sales in 2018 hit their lowest point since the post-GFC crisis of 2009, yet prices are on the rise and 2018 posted record turnover for the region. For the first time in history, exports exceeded French sales.

'The price of champagne is going to increase, because there is more pressure on supply and demand,' declares Dom Pérignon chef de cave Vincent Chaperon. Now is the time to buy up.

FIZZERS

CORKED, OXIDISED AND LIGHTSTRUCK

The inconsistent condition in which champagne reaches its markets is the single most significant factor impeding its quality today — bigger than global warming, chemical viticulture, overcropping, rot and depressed sales in traditional markets. I've had countless conversations and written a great deal on corked, oxidised and lightstruck champagnes over the past decade, and there is still much more that needs to be done.

Champagne can no longer simply trade off its name to hold the affections of its markets, if ever it could. Consumers have never been more discerning, and sparkling wine regions the world over have never produced finer wines. The one and only way in which Champagne can assert its superiority and its price is by an absolute and uncompromised insistence on remaining the best. And to do so it must be the most consistent. As a luxury product, champagne cannot afford to continue to abuse the faith of its customers with the levels of inconsistency in cork taint, oxidation and to a lesser extent lightstruck that have plagued its bottles for decades. In recent times, great advances in technology and initiative have taken every element of champagne viticulture and vinification to hitherto unknown levels of sophistication, consistency and quality, and it is a travesty that this can be completely undone by the final little element in the process, for which simple solutions are readily and affordably available.

CORKED

Across my tastings for this Guide, I've encountered 27 bottles sealed by natural cork destroyed by cork taint (3.8%); see full list on the next page. Imparted randomly by natural corks, cork taint gives a mouldy, 'wet cardboard' or 'wet dog' character to champagne. It suppresses fruit and shortens the length of finish. In its most subtle form, it may simply have a slight dulling effect on the bouquet and palate.

Champagne has certainly made progress towards solving its cork taint crisis, and I now consistently see half the level of taint that I observed five years ago. But even one corked bottle is still too many, especially with taint-free technology readily at hand.

Houses that have made a serious commitment to addressing cork taint have demonstrated that it is indeed possible to eradicate this sinister threat. Thirty percent of the 1072 champagnes I tasted were sealed with Mytik DIAM, a micro-agglomerate closure moulded from granulated fragments of cork which have been treated to extract cork taint and some 150 other molecules that might produce 'off' characters. I have never seen cork taint in any DIAM-sealed wine.

For houses that uphold an attachment to natural corks there appears to be no reliable remedy. 'Cork suppliers are well aware of batches afflicted with higher levels of taint and mix these through good batches to maintain acceptable averages,' I was informed by a former head of the CIVC Research & Development unit, and longstanding chef de cave for several significant houses. 'Most houses use 1.5% cork taint as the threshold for rejecting a batch of corks, but the lower the rate demanded, the better the corks supplied.'

Louis Roederer is one of the most rigorous houses, testing 460 corks in every batch of 100,000. This is repeated for 200 batches every year, and sometimes a batch is tested twice. If a single tainted cork is found, the entire batch is rejected. The company rejects one batch in three. I have historically found Louis Roederer to have a very low incidence of cork taint, but its record was let down by two corked bottles this year. Of all the corked bottles I encountered in my tastings, more than half hailed from just six houses — though, to be fair, some did open many more cuvées and vintages than others.

Cork company Amorim told me almost 15 years ago that it had solved cork taint. Three years ago, the company introduced NDtech corks guaranteed to be free of detectable TCA, at a not inconsiderable price. It was only in July 2019 that the company announced that NDtech would be introduced for sparkling corks. I know of two bottles of an icon Australian still wine with a price tag of more than AUD$1000 that have been cork tainted by NDtech corks. On the evidence to date, TCA-free natural cork is nothing more than a hoax and will remain so until such time as the cork industry gets serious about solving this problem rather than investing in unsuccessful bandaid solutions and marketing stunts.

Charles Heidsieck chef de cave Cyril Brun recently attended a vertical tasting at another house in which five out of six bottles

were cork tainted. If you encounter a cork-tainted bottle, always take it back and request a replacement.

OXIDISED

Champagne is the most fragile of all wine styles, and particularly susceptible to degradation in contact with oxygen. Oxidation shows itself in champagne as premature development, flattening fruit expression, contributing characters of burnt orange or vinegar, and drying out the finish. It can occur before a champagne is bottled, at disgorgement, or after it is shipped, losing freshness from sealing faults, poor transportation, bad storage conditions or simply sitting on the shelf too long. This is random oxidation (the next bottle opened is sound), by comparison with oxidation inherent to the batch or the cuvée.

Champagne's oxidation predicament is aggravated on two fronts. Winemakers use sulphur dioxide as a preservative to protect wine from oxidation, and there is an alarming trend among some Champagne growers to reduce or even eliminate its use. At the same time, increasing use of oak barrels provides more opportunity for oxygen contact during base wine ageing. Long barrel ageing with a low-sulphur regime is the most dangerous mix, exemplified most dramatically and famously by Jacques Selosse.

In my tastings for this Guide, I encountered random oxidation in 12 cuvées (just over 1%), equally prevalent in DIAM as in natural cork. This is a vast improvement on more than 6.5% five years ago. Together with cork taint, this brings the strike rate on natural corks to almost 5% and on DIAMs to just over 1%.

Everyone in Champagne knows that a crown seal is the most reliable closure, as more than a billion bottles in tirage attest, but sadly the region bans its use in the market, apparently based on perceived consumer reaction. Perhaps the market should make this decision, not the gatekeepers.

LIGHTSTRUCK

There is another factor that plagues champagne freshness. Did you know that if you leave a bottle in the light it might taste like onions, garlic or cabbage?

'Lightstruck' is the menacing effect of degradation of wine exposed to ultraviolet light from fluorescent lamps and, worse, sunlight. There is no wine more susceptible to lightstruck than champagne in clear glass bottles, diminishing citrus aromas and producing reductive characters such as sulphur, corn, gherkin, bacon, gunsmoke or burnt rubber.

Lightstruck can even deteriorate champagne in your glass. One afternoon in the middle of winter in Brisbane, Moët & Chandon chef de cave Benoît Gouez poured me a glass of his 2006 Vintage on a sunny upstairs balcony. In just five minutes it was lightstruck and he immediately summonsed a repour.

Keep your bottles in the dark, and if they come in a box, cellophane or bag, keep them covered until they're opened. As always, return any bottle that's out of condition.

CORKED

27 of 735 bottles tasted under natural cork were cork tainted (3.7%)

BOLLINGER SPECIAL CUVÉE BRUT NV
CATTIER CLOS DU MOULIN BRUT PREMIER CRU NV
CHARLES HEIDSIECK MILLÉSIME VINTAGE ROSÉ 2005 (2 CORKED)
DOM PÉRIGNON P2 1998
DUVAL-LEROY FEMME DE CHAMPAGNE 1996
EGLY-OURIET GRAND CRU MILLÉSIME 2007
FRANCK BONVILLE BLANC DE BLANCS GRAND CRU BRUT VINTAGE 2012
GEOFFROY LES HOUTRANTS COMPLANTÉS NV
HENRIOT BRUT MILLÉSIME 2008
HENRIOT BRUT ROSÉ NV
LANSON PÈRE ET FILS BRUT NV
LOUIS ROEDERER BRUT VINTAGE 2012
LOUIS ROEDERER CRISTAL 2002
PIERRE PAILLARD LA GRANDE RÉCOLTE
BOUZY GRAND CRU MILLÉSIME EXTRA BRUT 2006
PIPER-HEIDSIECK SUBLIME DEMI-SEC NV
POL ROGER PURE EXTRA BRUT NV
POL ROGER ROSÉ BRUT 2009
TAITTINGER BRUT MILLÉSIMÉ 2012
TAITTINGER COMTES DE CHAMPAGNE BLANC DE BLANCS 2005
TAITTINGER NOCTURNE SEC NV
THIÉNOT BLANC DE BLANCS NV
VADIN-PLATEAU BOIS DES JOTS PREMIER CRU DOSAGE ZERO 2013
VEUVE CLICQUOT LA GRANDE DAME 1989
VEUVE CLICQUOT LA GRANDE DAME 2006 (2 BOTTLES CORKED)
VEUVE CLICQUOT LA GRANDE DAME BRUT ROSÉ 2008

RANDOM OXIDATION – NATURAL CORK

8 of 735 bottles tasted under natural cork were randomly oxidised (1.1%)

COMTES DE DAMPIERRE FAMILY RÉSERVE
BLANC DE BLANCS GRAND CRU BRUT 2007
LE BRUN DE NEUVILLE LADY DE N CUVÉE CLOVIS BRUT NV
LOMBARD BRUT NATURE GRAND CRU MILLÉSIME 2008
ANDRÉ CLOUET DREAM COLLECTION VINTAGE 2002
BOLLINGER LA GRANDE ANNÉE 2007
BOLLINGER R.D. EXTRA BRUT 2004 (2 BOTTLES OXIDISED)
DELAMOTTE BLANC DE BLANCS 2008

RANDOM OXIDATION – DIAM

4 of 337 bottles tasted under DIAM were randomly oxidised (1.2%)

MOËT & CHANDON ROSÉ IMPÉRIAL NV
PERRIER-JOUËT BELLE EPOQUE BLANC DE BLANCS 2006
PIERRE GIMONNET & FILS ROSÉ DE BLANCS 1ER CRU NV
VEUVE FOURNY & FILS ROSÉ VINOTHÈQUE
VERTUS PREMIER CRU MV12 EXTRA BRUT NV

Dizy, harvest 2014

AWASH WITH BUBBLES

HOW TO SERVE CHAMPAGNE

CHAMPAGNE GLASSES

Using decent glassware is essential for fully appreciating wine, and all the more for champagne.

How important? 'We worked with wine glass company Riedel for more than a year to develop a glass which was ideal for Krug Grande Cuvée,' Olivier Krug told me. 'They proposed 26 glasses and I would take them home to try with my wife until very late at night!' He created the hashtag #noflutes and likens drinking Krug out of a flute to going to a concert with ear plugs.

The more I visit and taste with the Champenois, the more I appreciate the way a large glass draws a champagne out of itself. Champagne holds its bead longest in an elongated glass, but don't select one so narrow that you can't get your nose in to appreciate the bouquet. 'It's not just about the bubbles. Champagne is a wine, not just scenery!' says Duval-Leroy Sales Manager Michel Brismontier, who serves champagne in normal wine glasses rather than flutes.

The Champenois prefer slightly wider glasses than typical champagne flutes, to allow their finest cuvées sufficient space to open out. Think closer to a fine white wine glass than a flute. All good glasses curve in slightly at the top. The finer the glass, the easier they are to hold, the better they look at the table, and the less the champagne will warm up when you pour it. Cut, engraved or coloured glasses make it harder to appreciate the wine's appearance.

The glass I use most often now is the Riedel Veritas Champagne Glass. That's its profile in the geometric pattern on the cover! There are now many beautiful champagne glasses readily available. The best are very fine, with a bowl of white wine glass proportions that draws down into the stem sufficiently to produce a focused stream of bubbles. They'll set you back as much as a bottle of non-vintage champagne (each!), making for an expensive but worthy investment in champagne enjoyment.

For value for money, if a little less elegant, the Luigi Bormioli Magnifico Flute is a good alternative. If you can't find these, grab a medium-sized white wine glass over a champagne flute for any serious bottle of fizz.

The traditional flat champagne 'coupe' glasses are now practically unheard of in Champagne, except in historical ceremony. They are inferior because their large surface area evaporates both bead and aroma rapidly. The wide, flanged rim also spills the wine to the sides of the tongue, where sensitivity to acidity is heightened.

It's paramount that there is not the slightest residue of detergent in the glass, as this will instantly destroy the mousse (bubbles) and the taste. Always wash only under warm water without detergent. If you need to deal with lipstick residue, a quick wipe with a dry tissue will do the trick. Polish with a microfibre towel, supporting the bowl. Never dry a glass by holding the base and twisting the bowl, as this may snap the stem.

SERVING TEMPERATURE

'The temperature of service is very important,' emphasises Oliver Krug, who admits to being obsessed with the quality of service. 'We may work for 10 or 20 years to create Grande Cuvée, ship it in the best refrigerated container, and then you might be served the first Krug of your life in a stupid flute as cold as ice, and you miss 99% of the pleasure and the message!'

Antoine Roland-Billecart (Billecart-Salmon) says wine is like a human being in the cold. 'Put yourself out in the snow and you won't show anything either, you'll be all covered up!' he says. 'Three degrees breaks everything in champagne. It should be served at cellar temperature, and never below 8°C.' Cellar temperature for the Champenois means 10°C.

Champagne is often served much too cold. Poured at fridge temperature, it will taste flavourless and acidic. The only exceptions are particularly sweet styles, which are best toned down with a stern chill. In general, the finer the wine, the warmer I tend to serve it. The Champenois suggest 8–10°C for non-vintage and rosé styles, and 10–12°C for vintage and prestige wines. When poured in a room at 20°C, a champagne at 10°C will typically warm by 3°C.

If you're pulling a bottle out of a climate-controlled cellar, it will need to be cooled a little further, so pop it in the fridge for half an hour. If it's at room temperature to start with, 3–4 hours in the fridge or 15 minutes in an ice bucket might be in order. On a warm day, serve champagne a touch cooler, as it will soon warm up. I serve champagne from an ice box with one freezer brick, as this will usually hold the right temperature for several hours.

Seal an unfinished bottle with a decent champagne stopper. The best have a plug that forms a tight seal with the top of the bottle, and a single metal swing clip to lock it to the neck. Avina brand stoppers also work a treat. Kept cold, these hold pressure for weeks.

AGE AND CELLARING

Twenty-year-old champagne is one of my favourite indulgences, and a top vintage wine or prestige cuvée will comfortably go the distance. Generally, aim to drink vintage champagnes between eight and 15 years after vintage, and non-vintage wines within five years. Most entry-level NVs have little to gain from bottle ageing, but exceptions are noted throughout this guide. Late-disgorged vintages are held on lees in the cellar and can improve over many decades.

Late-disgorged champagne is generally best consumed within a few years of disgorgement, as it doesn't tend to cellar confidently post-disgorgement. 'Disgorgement is a shock for a wine, like a human going into surgery,' explains Antoine Roland-Billecart. 'When you're young, you recover much better. When an old champagne is disgorged, it may oxidise.' This is why Billecart disgorges its museum stock at the same time as its standard releases. Different houses have different philosophies, and there are always exceptions. One of the most profound champagnes I've ever tasted was Bollinger 1914 disgorged in 1969. After more than half a century on lees and almost as long on cork, it was so youthful I guessed it was late 1970s!

Champagne spends the first years of its life in a dark, humid, chalk cellar under Champagne at a constant temperature of 8–10°C, so it will get a rude shock if it's thrust into a warmer environment. Champagne is highly fussy when it comes to proper cellaring conditions and, unless you live somewhere particularly cold, if you don't have a climate-controlled cellar, err on the side of caution and drink it within a few years.

Champagne in clear glass bottles is remarkably light sensitive, so keep it in the dark at all times. If it comes in a box, bag or cellophane wrap, keep it covered until you serve it.

HOW TO OPEN A BOTTLE OF FIZZ

Opening a champagne bottle is pretty easy, but some people make such a fuss about it that they end up stuffing it up altogether. There are a few basic points to grasp before spraying your friends with fizz.

First, ensure that nobody has shaken the bottle before you get hold of it (not funny!). Always have a target glass nearby to pour the first gush into, but not too close (I once inadvertently shot the bowl clean off one of those expensive Riedels with a stray cork!). Check the firing range for chandeliers and unsuspecting passers-by and re-aim if necessary.

Remove the capsule using the pull-tab, if it has one. Hold the bottle at 45 degrees and remove the cage with six half-turns of the wire, keeping your thumb firmly over the end of the cork, in case it attempts to fire out of the bottle. I prefer to loosen the cage and leave it on the cork, which can assist with grip.

Twist the bottle (not the cork) slowly and ease the cork out gently. If you encounter a stubborn, young cork, use a clean tea towel to improve your grip. When the cork is almost out, tilt it sideways to release the gas slowly. It should make a gentle hiss, not an ostentatious pop. This is important, as it maintains the maximum bead (bubbles) in the wine and reduces the risk of a dramatic gush.

I don't 'sabrage' bottles of champagne, for the same reason that I don't spray them over my friends like I've just won the grand prix! It's disrespectful of the wine and of your guests. Knocking the top off a champagne bottle with a sabre, knife or any blunt object shocks the wine more than just popping the cork, and you're likely to lose some in a vigorous gush. Or, worse, the whole bottle could explode all over you in a shower of bubbles and shards of glass (Google it!). A sabraged bottle is a risk to drink as it can contain splinters of glass. If you are to engage in such frivolous antics, by all means do it with a cheap bottle of fizz from somewhere else and, for goodness' sake, don't waste a great bottle of champagne.

HOW TO POUR CHAMPAGNE

Check that the wine tastes right, then pour half a glass for each drinker, topping them up after the 'mousse' has subsided. A glass of champagne contains around a million bubbles, and you can save tens of thousands by pouring down the wall of a tilted glass – I always do. Sparkling wine is the only style where you can break the rule of never more than half-filling a glass, but do leave sufficient room for your nose so you can appreciate the bouquet!

Always hold a champagne glass by its base or stem, to avoid warming the wine in your hand. This will also reduce the likelihood of any aromas on your hands interfering with its delicate bouquet.

The Champenois sometimes recommend decanting champagne. This does offer some advantages in encouraging older or more robust champagnes to open up, but I have never been successful without losing most of the bubbles.

Great champagnes deserve decent glasses.

Moët's Montaigu Lodge surveys a whitewashed Chouilly in the depths of winter 2013.

AGRAPART & FILS

(A-gra-pah e Feess)

(7/10)

57 Avenue Jean Jaurès 51190 Avize
www.champagne-agrapart.com

CHAMPAGNE
AGRAPART & Fils

AVIZE - GRAND CRU

'If we have good grapes we have good wines,' is Pascal Agrapart's refreshing philosophy. While many others rigidly pursue regimes in the vineyard and winery because that's the way it's always been done, or is the latest fad, the ethos and practice of Agrapart are quite the antithesis. This fanatical Avize grower upholds practices not far from organics or biodynamics, yet has never sought certification under either, preferring to maintain the freedom to listen sensitively to the rhythm of the seasons and respond to the benefit of his vines. His restless pursuit of a detailed expression of place is articulated in the purity and deeply crystalline mineral expression of his wines.

In Champagne it is a rare claim to be the fourth generation to produce champagne from one's own vineyards. Yet Pascal and brother Fabrice Agrapart do so not with a staid reliance on the ways of their forebears, but with a progressive and at times courageous sense of spontaneity.

Inspired by Burgundy to make wines of character true to their place, Agrapart upholds terroir as being more important than variety. Chardonnay comprises 95% of 12 hectares of enviable estate plantings, mainly in the grand crus of Avize, Oger, Cramant and Oiry, divided across 70 plots of vines of an impressive average age of 40 years – some more than 65 years.

'Champagne has the same soils as Burgundy,' Pascal reveals. 'Three different parcels just 500 metres apart in the same village have very different terroirs and make very different wines.'

Every effort is focused on encouraging the roots of his old vines deep into the mother rock to draw out the mineral character of each site. Vineyard management is painstakingly eco-friendly, with no chemical pesticides or herbicides used. Vineyards are ploughed to break up surface roots, aerate the soil and maintain microbial life, while organic fertilisers, compost and manure are adapted according to soil analyses.

'For me it is very important not to have compacting of the soils or to use chemicals, so the old vine roots can go deeper and extract more minerality,' Pascal explains. 'The microbial action is essential to extract the minerality.'

When I first met him six years ago, Pascal Agrapart explained that '25% of the wine is made by the soil and 25% by the climate and the sun', though recently he has promoted the soil to 75%. 'Some growers say when you have good weather you can make good wine, but for me it's more important to have good terroir,' he maintains.

Nonetheless, he points out that the microclimates are very different in each of his parcels, posing a greater challenge to an organic regime than would a single site.

'I don't want to have certification because I want to be able to plough the soil when I can, and use chemicals when I need to,' he says. The disease threat of the wet 2012 vintage necessitated chemical treatments.

Agrapart works his 1959 vines in his 'La Fosse' vineyard in Avize only by hand and horse, and he's more down-to-earth about this than anyone else I've met in Champagne. 'There is no compacting of the soil, and perhaps there is more oxygen and microbial life, and perhaps the roots go deeper, and perhaps there

is more minerality in the wine. Perhaps, perhaps! Perhaps it is better – and perhaps it's just sentimental!'

Old vines provide natural regulation of yields, and he does not green harvest. 'My grandfather said, "Pascal, if the vines produce the grapes, you take the grapes!"' Yields are refreshingly well below the regional average of 100 hectolitres per hectare. 'We can achieve a good balance of acidity and maturity in chardonnay between 50 and 70hL/ha. If it is under 50 it is no better than 60, but if it is above 70 it is very bad!'

Each winemaking element is designed to preserve the detail of the vineyard. Sensitive, intelligent use of large, old oak for vinification and ageing of finer parcels for vintage wines and non-vintage reserves are not for woody flavour, but oxidation – for Agrapart, 'oxidation is not the enemy of wine'. He buys five-year-old barrels from Burgundy and the Loire and maintains them until they're very old. Larger 600-litre demi-muids are favoured, for a higher ratio of wine to wood.

No ferments are inoculated, instead favouring wild yeasts from the vineyards to further draw out the character of each site. Full malolactic fermentation is encouraged, for stability, balance and evolution of the wine, which he suggests removes the need for sterile filtration and high levels of sulphur dioxide preservative. The results are usually clean and precise.

The energy of Agrapart's grand cru chardonnay vineyards and the endurance infused through barrel fermentation make these very long-lived cuvées that appreciate extended lees ageing prior to release. Ageing a minimum of three years for non-vintage and seven for vintage cuvées necessitates a stock of 360,000 bottles to sustain an annual production of 90,000. This is a significant production for hand-riddling, but the hands-on approach of the estate is maintained.

Most of Agrapart's seven cuvées are blanc de blancs, with a little pinot in his entry wine, and a single-field blend of six grape varieties. Low dosages are used throughout, which he suggests reduces the importance of ageing the wine between disgorgement and release. While disgorgement dates aren't printed on back labels, they're easy to decode from the cork. The number is the year of disgorgement, and the letter is the month (A for January, B for February, and so on).

Agrapart's wines are characterful, deeply mineral expressions of the great, enduring terroirs of the Côte des Blancs, given articulate voice through diligent attention to detail.

My most recent visit was Pascal's first opening of his 2012 releases. 'I am very happy!' he concluded. 'They exemplify the style of Agrapart: fresh, precise and elegant, with distinctive vineyard character and bitter almond structure. This is my signature.'

These are long-enduring cuvées of an exceptional custodian of remarkable terroirs.

AGRAPART & FILS 7 CRUS NV $$

92 points • 2015 BASE VINTAGE • DISGORGED JULY 2018 • TASTED IN CHAMPAGNE

90% chardonnay, 10% pinot from the 7 crus of Avize, Oger, Cramant, Oiry, Avenay-Val-d'Or, Coligny and Vauciennes; 40% 2014 chardonnay from reserves; young vines of 20–40 years of age; full malolactic fermentation; 7g/L dosage

For Pascal, 2015 was a good vintage but not the best – difficult in June and July, but with good maturity from a sunny August and September.

Agrapart's entry cuvée is glorious testament to the ability of his vineyards to tap minerality that brings freshness even in a vintage as generous as 2015 – an admirable achievement for younger vines from lesser sites. This is a ripe and approachable 7 Crus in a rich, fruity and immediate style, that Pascal aptly considers 'a wine to drink with friends'. It's a beautifully pure and fresh introduction of ripe pear, even hints of mandarin and fig, concluding with nicely balanced dosage. Just when you think the fruit is going to make it simple and round, its chalk minerality and acidity kick in on the end, running long and fresh, furnishing focus and refinement.

AGRAPART & FILS TERROIRS GRAND CRU BLANC DE BLANCS EXTRA BRUT NV $$$

95 points • 2014 BASE VINTAGE • TASTED IN CHAMPAGNE

100% chardonnay from 20-50-year-old vines in Avize, Oger, Cramant and Oiry; 40% 2014; 60% 2013 reserves aged in barrel for 6 months; 5g/L dosage

A seamlessly crafted blanc de blancs that walks a confident tightrope between wonderful fruit presence, focused acid line and heightened mineral character, singing with the freshness of apple and lemon fruit. Deeply embedded in grand cru chalk soils, the minerality of these older vines shines brilliantly in fine chalk structure, soft, salty and frothy. In line, length and most of all inimitable Côte des Blancs chalk minerality, this is a beautifully crafted and terroir-infused cuvée, and hands-down the greatest Terroirs since the stunning 2010/2009 blend.

PASCAL AGRAPART COMPLANTÉE EXTRA BRUT À AVIZE GRAND CRU NV $$$

91 points • 2015 BASE VINTAGE • TASTED IN CHAMPAGNE

Single-site Avize; field blend of chardonnay, pinot, meunier, arbane, petit meslier and pinot blanc; planted in 2002 and 2003 (hence 12-year-old vines here); vinified entirely in barriques; 2014 reserves; 5g/L dosage

To Pascal Agrapart, 'the terroir is very important, perhaps more important than the *cépage*'. His aspiration is for this cuvée to express the character of the Côte des Blancs, not of the grapes. He builds a structure that is more than just acidity and sugar, with an almond-like bitterness that he upholds as important for precision.

As complex as its ingredients and recipe anticipate, this is a multi-layered blend, encompassing the full sweep of its six varieties in exotic star fruit, persimmon and grapefruit, set against the subtle undercurrent of toastiness and texture infused by barrel fermentation. With vine age, Complantée is becoming more coherent and less gangly than its early years, though still not yet showing the persistence, line and chalk mineral depth of Agrapart's older vines. Nonetheless, the presence of fine, gentle chalk minerality is unmistakable and its acid balance is accurate. A good Complantée.

AGRAPART & FILS MINÉRAL BLANC DE BLANCS EXTRA BRUT 2012 $$$$

96 points • DISGORGED ON THE SPOT • TASTED IN CHAMPAGNE

As always, an equal blend of two nearby parcels, Les Bionnes in Cramant and Le Champ Bouton in Avize, both with the same very thin soil over chalk; Cramant vinified in old oak barrels, Avize in tank; tasted with no dosage, the final blend will have 3g/L dosage

Pascal Agrapart describes 2012 as a very good vintage of stable weather and a harvest at the beginning of September that produced a good equilibrium of sugar and acidity, with no botrytis.

Mineral it is, boring deep into the hard white chalk very close to the surface of these two plots. The 2012 is a glorious return to the high notes of the brilliant 2008, a vintage that glistens with bright, stark high-noon sunlight. It brings an exacting precision and tightly coiled focus that make for a particularly chiselled Minéral of outstanding tension and heightened chalk mineral presence, fine, salty and frothing. Pristine, youthful definition of apple and grapefruit linger long on a honed palate. It will benefit from plenty of time to open up post-disgorgement and promises to be a long-lived Minéral, set to go down as one of the greats. True to its mandate, the presence of pronounced minerality is epic, churning with the ocean that laid down its chalk foundations more than 70 million years ago.

Pascal Agrapart Avizoise Robarts Gros Yeux à Avize Grand Cru Extra Brut Blanc de Blancs 2012 $$$$

95 points • Disgorged on the spot • Tasted in Champagne

Previously Avizoise, its name recently updated to include its two parcels on the best slopes of Avize, Robarts and Gros Yeux, sharing the same profile of deep, clay-rich topsoil over chalk; vines 50–60 years of age; fully vinified in old oak barrels; aged on lees under natural cork; tasted with no dosage, the final blend will have 3g/L dosage

Just 600–800 metres from the parcels that comprise Minéral, here the soils are deep clay over chalk, expressing a very different personality of frothy, salty chalk texture that contrasts the creamy mouthfeel of full barrel fermentation. This makes for a rich blanc de blancs, counterpointed by bitter grapefruit pith that sits comfortably within its generosity, backed with the roast nuts and toast of full barrel vinification. For all of its magnitude, there is exacting Agrapart focus here, defined by fine chalk minerality that marks out a finish of profound persistence. A credit to a great season, this is a captivating and characterful Avizoise that seamlessly, if daringly, unites grand expression of soil with the strong presence of its maker's method.

Pascal Agrapart Vénus Fosse aux Pourceaux à Avize Grand Cru Brut Nature Blanc de Blancs 2012 $$$$$

95 points • Disgorged on the spot • Tasted in Champagne

Formerly labelled 'Vénus' (after his horse), now also named according to its single-site Fosse aux Pourceaux of just 0.6 hectares just behind the house, planted on profoundly chalky soil in 1959 and tended only by hand and horse; vinified exclusively in old oak barrels; full malolactic fermentation; aged on lees under cork; zero dosage

'Solely worked by man and by horse, perhaps there is more oxygen in the soil, perhaps the roots go deeper, perhaps there is more minerality – but most of all, this is good terroir,' sums up Pascal Agrapart in his refreshingly frank manner.

He describes the minerality of Vénus as reminiscent of the chalk dust from the blackboard when he was at school. Breathe deep: the intensity of the chalk minerality of this cuvée is something to behold. The story here is all about the soil, and its pronounced mineral expression in the wine: frothy, salty, elegant and coiled. It focuses the pinpoint precision of understated lemon, grapefruit and nashi pear, drawing out a finish of profound persistence. Delightfully composed, it contrasts incisive precision with a creamy bead and well-defined acidity, fully ripe yet tense and pronounced. Full barrel fermentation brings notes of toasted almonds and a texture that somehow elevates the salt mineral mood of the village, like the high notes of the strings of an orchestra are propelled by rumbling depths of percussion and horns. A cuvée of textural precision and grand mineral persistence, this is an intellectual style, far from a mosh pit encounter, rather a philharmonic experience of the highest order.

Pascal Agrapart Exp. 14 Brut Nature à Avize Grand Cru Blanc de Blancs NV $$$$$

93 points • 2014 base vintage with a little 2015 • Tasted in Champagne

Previously 'Experience', now Exp. 14 to denote the 2014 vintage, blended with a smaller proportion of 2015; old Avize vines, a blend of equal parts of the parcels comprising Avizoise and Minéral; wild fermented for both primary and secondary ferments; vinified in 600L demi-muid; no additives (including no chaptalisation, liqueur de tirage or liqueur d'expédition); full malolactic fermentation; trialled since 2003 and commercially in 2007, 2012 and 2014; no dosage

Made without any additives, Pascal refers to Exp. 14 as his 'ultimate natural champagne challenge'. This is not an aspiration that many in Champagne have the tenacity to attempt, let alone the skill to pull off, yet if there is one shining example in the region to prove the merits of this daring pursuit, this is surely it. It's a fruity, exotic and characterful style of star fruit notes accenting the precision of long-lingering grapefruit and lemon and just a subtle note of charcuterie. Acidity works in tandem with bitter grapefruit-pith structure and the signature, saline chalk minerality of Avize. It's engaging and complex, with surprising energy to age.

ALEXANDRE BONNET

(A-lex-ond Boh-nay)

138 Rue du Géneral de Gaulle 10340 Les Riceys
www.alexandrebonnet.com

Champagne
Alexandre Bonnet
Vins Fins de Champagne
LES RICEYS

Famed for pinot noir increasingly prized by many of Champagne's top houses, Les Riceys borders Burgundy in the far south of the Côte des Bar and holds the title of Champagne's largest cru. Alexandre Bonnet is one of the biggest domains in the village, a small house boasting an enviable 45 hectares, mostly in Les Riceys and a few of its neighbouring villages. The house upholds a rightful focus on pinot noir, comprising 100% of every cuvée, besides a little chardonnay in its entry label and a blanc de blancs blend of chardonnay and pinot blanc. The family has been growing grapes here since 1934, though the brand was only established in 1970. For its relatively short history, it is privileged to a longstanding team: Director-General François Lange has been with the house 43 years, oenologist Alain Pailley 35 years and vineyard manager Didier Mele 20 years. Its best cuvées are its young, fruity and friendly blanc de noirs, celebrating the succulent mood of Les Riceys pinot, marked by ample honeyed dosage.

ALEXANDRE BONNET GRANDE RÉSERVE BRUT NV $$

89 points • TASTED IN AUSTRALIA

20% Les Riceys chardonnay, 80% Côte des Bar pinot; 40% reserves; average vine age 25 years; 9g/L dosage; cork

Celebrating the fruity and spicy exuberance of Côte des Bar pinot noir, this is a cuvée of crunchy golden-delicious apple generosity, honeyed richness and the gingernut biscuit complexity of bottle age. A bite of apple skin bitterness and tangy lemon acidity on the finish are met by honeyed dosage.

Alexandre Bonnet Harmonie de Blancs Brut NV $$

89 points • Tasted in Australia
87 points • 2014 base vintage • Tasted in Australia

50% Les Riceys chardonnay; 50% pinot blanc; average vine age 25 years; 9g/L dosage; cork

In its latest disgorgement of undeclared base vintage, this is a flattering blend of pinot blanc and chardonnay, built around crunchy apple, nashi pear, ripe fig and the signature spice of Les Riceys. Notes of fennel integrate harmoniously with lemon juice acidity and the toasty, roast nut appeal of lees age. A touch of phenolic bite on the finish is juxtaposed by the creamy texture of lees age and the sweetness of honeyed dosage. The 2014 base is a fruity style of tropical pinot blanc exoticism and candied dosage.

Alexandre Bonnet Blanc de Noirs Brut NV $$

90 points • Tasted in Australia
90 points • 51% 2014, with 16% 2013, 8% 2012, 13% 2011, 12% 2009 reserves • Tasted in Australia

100% pinot, sourced mainly from estate vines in Les Riceys; average vine age 25 years; 45% reserves; 8g/L dosage; cork

On the border of Burgundy, Les Riceys is home to a particularly succulent, generous and spicy expression of pinot noir, and this fleshy and rounded cuvée celebrates it unashamedly. Rich layers of glossy red cherries, mirabelle plums, dried nectarines and wild strawberries are underlined by mixed spice, balanced acidity and honeyed dosage. The result is a friendly and soft party style of fruit integrity and persistence.

Alexandre Bonnet Perle Rosée Brut NV $$

89 points • Tasted in Australia
89 points • 2014 base vintage • Tasted in Australia

100% pinot; Les Riceys; average vine age 25 years; 9g/L dosage; cork

Crunchy and refreshing in its most recently disgorged guise, this is a young and fruity cuvée of pretty, pale salmon hue and flavours of wild strawberries, red apples, red cherries and notes of white pepper. Subtle, fine tannins are well managed and meld seamlessly with soft acidity and slightly candied dosage on a short, sweet finish.

Les Riceys

Alfred Gratien

(Al-fre Gra-shah)

(7/10)

30 Rue Maurice Cerveaux 51201 Épernay
www.alfredgratien.com

Crafting seamlessly integrated cuvées exclusively in oak barrels with absolutely no reliance on malolactic fermentation calls for tenacity and talent in equal measure, and in this art the small house of Alfred Gratien in Épernay stands alongside Vilmart (page 562) as the greatest of them all. Nicolas Jaeger is the fourth generation of his family to step up to this challenge since the house was founded in 1864. When it comes to wielding the shining sabre of malic acidity, Nicolas possesses Jedi-like prowess. After 15 years of significant development and investment, his cuvées have never looked more confident. Alfred Gratien convincingly epitomises its aspiration of maturity with freshness, triumphantly juxtaposing deep-set complexity and creamy texture with radiant acidity and sheer joy.

Alfred Gratien was acquired by the Henkell & Co group in 2004, retaining its own small holdings of just four hectares of vineyards and sourcing from 65 growers within 35 kilometres of Épernay. This furnishes a small production of 300,000 bottles annually.

The house enjoys a long history of making wines of complexity. Its cuvées are crafted in a rigorously classical way, with the first fermentation and at least six months of ageing taking place exclusively in 1000 small 228-litre neutral barriques, of 12 years average age. Barrels are maintained for 20–25 years, and between 30 and 50 are renewed each year, previously used at least four times at La Chablisienne in Chablis.

The house considers its barrels a key to its relationship with its growers, allowing it to keep every plot separate. Every barrel is labelled with the name of the village and the grower, and each grower is invited to come to taste their own wines every second year.

Fermentation and maturation in small barrels builds texture, complexity and integration, but the goal for Jaeger is not oak flavour. Wines are kept on lees in barrel for at least six months prior to blending, because he suspects the lees capture some of the wood flavours. Reserve wines are stored in large oak barrels.

Fermentation in small barrels also provides flexibility in challenging vintages like 2017. 'We are lucky fermenting in small barrels because we separate all the wine,' explains Jaeger. 'If I have a problem, I have a small problem. But if you ferment in big tanks, if you have a problem you have a *big* problem!'

Henkell & Co invested considerably in the house, building a new cuverie for blending of the young wines. At just 9°C, its cellars are some of the coldest in Champagne. This is too cold for the second fermentation to kick off in the presence of such high levels of malic acidity, so bottles are first held in the barrel hall for two weeks. It

then takes 70–80 days to complete the second fermentation in the cellar below. The house maintains a considerable stock of 1.5 million bottles, since long ageing is important for softening malic acidity.

The house recently invested in air-conditioning and humidifying its old barrel cellar, to facilitate cool fermentation at 12°C, to reduce losses to evaporation from 7% to 4%, and to reduce the frequency of topping barrels from fortnightly to every three weeks. Cooling also makes for fresher wines and lower levels of sulphur dioxide preservative.

Malolactic fermentation is systematically avoided, to ensure that cuvées retain their original character, maintaining freshness as they age and preserving the aroma of the grapes and the land from which they came. 'My philosophy is always to try to uphold freshness in every cuvée,' Jaeger emphasises. 'Blocking malolactic fermentation is vital to achieving this.' He attributes longevity both to malic acidity and oak tannins.

Barrel fermentation without malolactic is no trivial balancing act, though Alfred Gratien pulls it off with more than a little accomplishment, and never as seamlessly or triumphantly as in the current set of cuvées.

Since he took over in 2007 after his father retired, having worked with him since 1990 from the age of 18, the new owners have wisely left the house in Nicolas' hands. 'We work within the Henkell group, but we are a family company,' he explains. 'My wife works in the office and we buy grapes from my uncle.'

Henkell & Co joined forces with the Spanish giant Freixenet Group in mid-2018 to become the biggest sparkling group in the world. The merger unites the house with Freixenet-owned Henri Abelé (page 281) and Nicolas Jaeger now oversees production for both brands.

If the cuvées since Nicolas' tenure began are any indication, the house is in talented hands. All the more laudable because production has doubled in the past 14 years, with a target to reach the capacity of the facility of 400,000–450,000 bottles by 2020.

Chardonnay is the theme of the house, blessed by great sources in the finest crus of the Côte des Blancs. In concert with malic acidity, chardonnay's incisive focus brings a zingy freshness to the deeply complex Gratien style, softened gently by barrel fermentation and impressive lengths of bottle age. Current non-vintage releases have enjoyed five years on lees in bottle, and vintage cuvées more than eight. Vintage wines are aged under natural cork, which Jaeger claims assists in preventing oxidation and enhancing tertiary aromas, complexity and firmness. He tastes every bottle as it is disgorged and rejects 1% to cork taint and 2% to leakage or other variation.

The first two digits of the labelling code on the neck foil are the year of disgorgement, and the next three digits are the day of that year. For instance, L18264 is the 264th day of 2018.

Alfred Gratien's processes are labour-intensive, and every bottle is touched at least ten times during production. While recent investment has brought progress in its modern facilities, the processes remain rigorously classical.

'When I taste vintages from our library collection, I feel the philosophy of my grandfather and my father, and I try to uphold these in my wines,' Nicolas reflects. 'We have changed nothing. We have worked in oak for many, many years and we have never had malolactic fermentation. The methods are the same, and this is very important for me. This is my baby.'

'I think I am lucky,' he concludes humbly. 'I am sure you can make a good wine if this is your policy. It is expensive – you pay more for good grapes, oak barrels are a lot of work, and hand-made wines are labour-intensive, but you can make a good wine if your boss gives you the possibility.'

With full barrel vinification and no malolactic fermentation, these are captivating and long-ageing champagnes of fine, creamy bead, lively acid line and expertly managed, barrel-matured complexity.

Alfred Gratien boasts 1000 barrels, ranking it third after Krug and Bollinger for the most barrels in Champagne.

ALFRED GRATIEN BRUT NV $$

89 points • 70% 2013 BASE • 49% CHARDONNAY, 23% PINOT, 28% MEUNIER • TASTED IN CHAMPAGNE
93 points • 70% 2012 BASE VINTAGE • 56% CHARDONNAY, 20% PINOT, 24% MEUNIER • DISGORGED
15 MAY 2018 • TASTED IN AUSTRALIA

Perpetual reserve solera commenced in 1997, stored in tank, with two-thirds taken each year to become one-third of this cuvée; 9g/L dosage from a solera of Cuvée Paradis of 65% chardonnay and 35% pinot with cane sugar; cork

There is quite some skill entwined into this cuvée. The recipe is something to behold, and its execution in the 2012 base is exemplary. It is quite a feat to evenly and compellingly harmonise the biscuity complexity of barrel fermentation not only with the deep character of a 15-year-old solera, but also with a bright flash of malic acidity. This base is particularly complex, layered with freshly roasted chestnuts, ginger cake, dried peach, even a hint of freshly roasted coffee. It is at once creamy and luscious and at the same time vibrant and cut – that magical interplay of barrel fermentation and malic acidity that nobody achieves quite like Alfred Gratien. Sea salt chalk minerality is impressively prominent, in no way overwhelmed by its grand complexity. It carries its full grandeur long into the finish, evenly and beautifully uniting body, cut and drive. The 2013 base is surprisingly disappointing, a biscuity style of dusty, dry-extract grip and bitter phenolic bite that interrupt apple and pear fruit.

ALFRED GRATIEN BRUT ROSÉ NV $$

95 points • 56% CHARDONNAY, 23% PINOT, 21% MEUNIER • DISGORGED 2 OCT 2018 • TASTED IN AUS
95 points • 54% CHARDONNAY, 28% PINOT, 18% MEUNIER • 2014 BASE • TASTED IN CHAMPAGNE

Brut NV blended with 12% pinot noir red wine from the meticulous Hervé Savès (Camille Savès, page 159) in Bouzy; the percentage of red wine varies from 8% to 12% according to the year; 8g/L dosage; cork

The Gratien house style is particularly flattering to rosé, and this pretty, bright medium salmon-pink-tinted style is alive, full and more precise than ever, with layers of crunchy and vibrant red cherry, raspberry, wild strawberry and tangy pomegranate fruit accented with rose hip and pink pepper. The textural synergy that defines the house is no easy balancing act, calmly uniting the creamy, silky texture of barrel fermentation, the fine mouthfeel of exactingly managed tannins, the magnificently fine and salty chalk mineral definition of great terroirs, and the enlivening cut of malic acidity. Barrel and bottle age contribute subtle savoury allure of roast chestnuts and dried nectarines, eloquently supporting and never competing with bright red fruits focus. A rosé of freshness and poise, with impeccably composed malic acidity streaming out long on the finish. As magnificent as ever.

ALFRED GRATIEN CUVÉE 565 NV $$$

94 points • DISGORGED 5 JUNE 2018 • TASTED IN AUSTRALIA

65% chardonnay, 35% pinot; 6 years on lees; 5 consecutive vintages 2007 to 2011 as a perpetual reserve; according to the back label 565 is '5 consecutive vintage years united in one blend, 6 years of ageing on lees, to delight the 5 senses'; no liqueur added during disgorging; cork

Cuvée 565 takes the depth and complexity of Gratien's solera system to another level after six years on lees, another testimony to the juggling act that this house has masterfully accomplished. It leads out with the pineapple and golden delicious apple of ripe fruit (confidently led by a two-thirds majority of chardonnay), layering it richly with broad brush strokes of fruit mince spice, dried peach, honey, even coffee and high-cocoa dark chocolate. Long barrel age has lent savoury, charcuterie complexity, though this is well toned behind its fruity, spicy exuberance. Malic acidity keeps this maelstrom tightly in check, lending tension, drive and endurance to an impressively long and salty chalk mineral finish. A richly generous cuvée for main course fare and winter contemplation.

Alfred Gratien Brut Nature NV $$

91 points • 2011 base vintage • Tasted in Champagne

Brut NV aged longer on lees; around 40% reserves; created by demand from Parisian and Japanese sommeliers; with no malolactic fermentation, it is only made in the warmer years; zero dosage

By Jaeger's own admission, 2011 was a difficult year in Champagne, yet he has managed confidently the daring challenge of oak fermentation without malolactic or dosage. True to its recipe, this is a savoury and tense style of firm structure, searing acidity and a crunchy profile. Oak fermentation brings spice and serves to gently soften its austere texture. A well-crafted cuvée, but this is no party fizz and must be reserved strictly for champagne die-hards.

Alfred Gratien Grand Cru Blanc de Blancs Brut 2012 $$$

94 points • Disgorged 5 June 2018 • Tasted in Australia

100% chardonnay; majority Avize and Cramant; 8g/L dosage; cork

'In the 1960s, my grandfather always made a blend of one barrel of Le Mesnil-sur-Oger and one of Cramant for drinking with friends, never sold. This inspired my father to create a blanc de blancs in the same way, with more crus.' – Nicolas Jaeger

The crystalline sea salt minerality of especially Avize and Cramant shines in the glittering 2012 vintage with radiance and brilliance, contrasting the deeply complex and moody succulence of Alfred Gratien. Ripe fruit reminiscent of fig, juicy white peach and dried nectarine is framed in the spicy complexity and creamy mouthfeel of barrel fermentation. Malic acidity tucks neatly into this interplay, drawing out a finish of grand persistence and focused line. A touch of phenolic grit on the end is well accommodated by the generosity of the style and its balanced dosage. The great 2012 season is flattering indeed for Alfred Gratien, harmonising the union between the magnitude of the house and the tension of distinguished grand crus of the Côte des Blancs.

Alfred Gratien Grand Cru Blanc de Blancs Brut 2009 $$$

94 points • Tasted in Champagne

100% chardonnay, mostly Avize and Cramant, with Le Mesnil-sur-Oger, Chouilly and Oger

The rich and succulent white fruits and pear of 2009 contrast a flourish of bright malic acidity and the fine, salty chalk minerality of the A-list of Côte des Blancs grand crus. The result is compelling and enduring, with the complex spice and the creamy texture and tannin touch of barrel fermentation supporting the purity of lemon, grapefruit, pear and apple. It holds with excellent length and line.

Alfred Gratien Cuvée Paradis 2009 $$$$

93 points • Tasted in Champagne

65% chardonnay from Le Mesnil-sur-Oger, Avize, Chouilly, Oger, Cramant, Bouzy, Vertus and Villers-Marmery, 35% pinot from Rilly-la-Montagne, Ludes, Cumières, Ambonnay and Bouzy; no meunier in Paradis since 2006

A seamlessly composed blend that achieves freshness in the rounded 2009 season, thanks to the sustaining tension of malic acidity. A pure fruit profile of lemon, white nectarine and pear unite harmoniously with the brioche, honey and vanilla cream of lees age. A little phenolic grip and oak tannin texture on the finish sit comfortably enough within this style of complexity and flesh. The harmony and heightened tension of the marvellous 2008 was always going to be a tough act to follow, but this is a good result for a warm vintage, and one to enjoy while the 2008 mellows.

Alfred Gratien Brut Millésimé 2005 $$$

94 points • Disgorged 24 July 2018 • Tasted in Australia and Champagne

70% chardonnay, 15% pinot, 15% meunier; aged on lees under cork; 8.5g/L dosage; cork

A bright glow to a medium straw-yellow hue proclaims the energy and endurance with which Alfred Gratien has sustained the powerful and ripe 2005 vintage. This is a cuvée of considerable presence and heightened character, finding a larger-than-life harmony of its own as every element elevates every other in stature and presence. Chardonnay assumes a commanding lead, evolving from preserved lemon and succulent stone fruits to green olive and fruit mince spice, even the green asparagus notes true to the uneven ripeness of 2005, energised by frothing sea salt minerality, charged with magnificent malic acidity. The grand crus of the Côte des Blancs assert their commanding and glorious presence, laying out a finish at once poised and linear and at the same time monumentally persistent. The dry-extract grip and coffee bean dryness that are characteristic of 2005 are present here, but find a comfortable place in the midst of its bold proportions, creamy, oak-derived mouthfeel and structural precision. This grip unites with malic acidity and sea salt freshness to promise a grand future for another decade and beyond. Alfred Gratien proves its merit thanks to its confidence in the lesser seasons, and herein lies another triumph.

Alfred Gratien Cuvée Paradis Brut Rosé 2007 $$$$

95 points • Disgorged 25 September 2018 • Tasted in Australia

63% chardonnay, 37% pinot; 8g/L dosage; cork

A pale salmon copper hue announces a complex and crafted rosé of structural endurance. The juxtaposition of elegant, spicy wild strawberry fruit and anise, the complexity of lees age, the toasty, coffee bean allure of barrel fermentation and the sabre of malic acidity sit apart here more distinctly than in any other cuvée in the current Gratien line. Yet for all of its fragmentation, no detail dominates, each proclaiming the potential for grand longevity unusual in the refined 2007 season. Sea salt chalk minerality meets finely handled tannins and subtle phenolic grip with confidence, streaming long and strong into a finish vividly enlivened by the noble malic acidity of 2007. Such is its structural assurance that it demands protein fare, which it will consume effortlessly. Its conclusion is a revelation – unwavering, undeviating, enduring. Patience for at least another decade is mandatory.

Alfred Gratien 1975

95 points • Tasted in Champagne

72% chardonnay, 14% pinot, 14% meunier; less than 20 bottles remaining; made by Nicolas' grandfather and disgorged around 1980

With a glowing yellow golden hue and very little bead remaining, this is a grand old bottle, glorious testimony to the endurance of the house and one of the great vintages of the 1970s. Its stamina is all the more profound since this bottle was shipped to the UK and back in 1979. Today, it still upholds the complexity of dried nectarine, pineapple and loquat fruit amidst the complexity of tertiary nuances of sweet pipe smoke, green olives and toast. It holds with magnificent confidence, persistence and poise, showing no signs of tiring any time soon.

ANDRÉ CLOUET

(On-dray Cloo-ay)

7/10

8 RUE GAMBETTA 51150 BOUZY
www.andreclouet.com

CHAMPAGNE
ANDRÉ CLOUET

DEPUIS 1741

Bouzy and Ambonnay are the epicentre of pinot noir in Champagne, and the Clouet family is the privileged custodian of eight hectares of estate vines in the best middle slopes of both villages. These are rich and concentrated expressions of pinot, wines of deep complexity, multifaceted interest and engaging character, yet with remarkable restraint and sense of control. Tasting after tasting confirm my impression that this relatively unknown and fast-ascending house ranks high among Champagne's finest practitioners of pinot noir — and represents one of the best value of all.

When I first met flamboyant young chef de cave Jean-François Clouet, he didn't show me through his winery or cellars, didn't walk me through rows of vines, or even pour his champagnes. He took me to the top of the vineyards, on the edge of the forest overlooking Bouzy, and recounted the remarkable sweep of history that had played out in view of this place over two millennia: Attila the Hun, the Battle of the Catalaunian Fields, the birth of the monarchy, the crusades, the Templars, Marie Antoinette. Then he showed me original documents of his village in his family archives, and took me to another part of town to recount another branch of history. 'To understand Champagne you need to understand its political history,' he said.

For Clouet's family, that history began here in 1492, and his family still resides in the house his ancestors built in Bouzy in 1741. Today, 278 harvests on, he still uses the cellar they dug under the house for storing wine, one of the oldest in the region. 'My family was making wine in Champagne at the same time Dom Pérignon was starring!' he exclaims. This history lives on, not only in the spectacular labels designed by Jean-François' great-grandfather in 1911 (harking back to the family's printer heritage, making books for the king since 1491), but in a traditional approach in the vineyards. 'I like the idea of the work of human hands in pruning, performing the same actions as my grandfather and even the Romans, who planted vines here 2000 years ago.'

Jean-François is deeply rooted in the heritage of his village, one of Champagne's key historic places, and the leading role of his ancestors. He still possesses his family's request for a deed for the purchase of land in Champagne by their ancestors in 1689, and a letter from the 1820s requesting an order of rosé to be sent to Paris — just a few years after the widow Clicquot was believed to have invented blended rosé in the same village.

André Clouet was Jean-François' grandfather, and passed away when he was very young. His grandson carries on the legacy, upholding his family's traditions and adding his own creative daring and distinctly modern approach.

One of the living rock stars of Champagne, Jean-François choreographs every element of his business with his inimitable flair and accomplishment, from the vineyards to the design of the labels, even the evocative words and images on his achingly cool (and hilariously crazy!) new website.

Every time I see him he has an exciting new cuvée to share, and another ambitious idea to announce.

In 2011 he created 'Clouet world', a substantial logistics facility for disgorgement, remuage and bottling on land he inherited just outside the village. He recently showed me plans to extend it into an astonishing visitor centre.

Jean-François is a courageous visionary and an ebullient creative with the nous to bring his dreams to completion and the humility to gather around him the talent to make it happen. When his close friend Cyril Brun was still employed by Veuve Clicquot, he engaged him as a consultant for his winemaking. One of the greatest winemakers in the region, Cyril helped Jean-François take his wines to the next level.

He also has what very few growers possess in Champagne: the drive and flair to market his cuvées in all five continents, and the larger-than-life personality to propel an incredible growth trajectory.

And grow it has. Like many of Champagne's top growers, expansion can only be achieved through purchasing grapes. He now purchases from some 60 hectares of growers in addition to his own vineyards to furnish an incredible production of around 600,000 bottles annually.

And not only buying grapes but wines, too. 'Growers on the Côte des Blancs make a national sport of finding red wine for rosé on the Montagne de Reims, and I prefer to swap than to sell – so I amassed a cellar of Côte des Blancs chardonnay.' Not wanting to change the style of his existing cuvées by blending, he instead conceived a new range, which he dubbed 'Dream Vintage', of between 2000 and 4000 bottles of blanc de blancs each season. The fruit he sources is not always of the same calibre as that of his own prized vineyards, but his core cuvées have not suffered to date.

It is his goal that some day none of his champagnes will have any dosage, an ideal that he rightly describes as revolutionary.

'Not to be snobby or arrogant, but I have a real sense that a zero-dosage wine from a single village can really showcase the pedigree of the village,' he suggests. 'You have to be an extremely good winemaker to make zero-dosage champagne.' And if anyone can do it anywhere, Jean-François can in Bouzy and Ambonnay. To this end, for some years he has experimented with using Sauternes barriques from Château Doisy Daëne for alcoholic fermentation. 'It gives the illusion of the wine being sweet, when it is not sweet at all!' he claims. The result, to my astonishment, is quite magnificent.

When Clouet began working on the estate over a decade ago, he took note of those embarking on organic and biodynamic regimes. 'Biodynamics and organics look good on paper,' he says, 'but my idea is that it is simply important to take care of the ground by hand without the use of herbicides.' Stringent sorting during harvest maintains freshness and purity in his cuvées.

Clouet's focus remains resolutely on pinot noir, which comprises 100% of every cuvée except his Dream Vintage cuvées and Millésime, a 50/50 blend of pinot noir and chardonnay. 'I am frustrated with the idea of blending from everywhere!' he exclaims. 'I love pure pinot noir! No make-up and no compromise!'

Clouet is as fascinated by the geological history of his soils as he is with the political history of his village, and makes it his goal to express the minerality of pure chalk in his wines. 'Fantastic minerality and low dosage are important for good pinot noir,' he claims. His cuvées receive low dosages of 6g/L.

As seriously as he takes his responsibilities, Clouet doesn't take himself too seriously. 'Champagne is always for flirting!' he grins. And he likens his wines to independent films. 'I love Hollywood movies, but sometimes I want to watch something independent. Winemaking in Champagne is the same,' he says. 'One is not better than the other. Dom Pérignon and Pol Roger are fantastic, with all the action of James Bond in *Skyfall*, but sometimes I have a taste for something else.'

His champagnes offer that something else, without the Hollywood budget, yet with pyrotechnics all of their own.

ANDRÉ CLOUET ROSÉ NO 3 BRUT NV $$

94 points • 2015 BASE VINTAGE • TASTED IN CHAMPAGNE
94 points • 2012 BASE VINTAGE • TASTED IN CHAMPAGNE

100% Bouzy and Ambonnay pinot; 50% reserves from a solera of 10 vintages; blended with 10-15% red wine from the four best lieux-dits of the estate in Bouzy, ideally yielding 7000-8000kg/ha; macerated on skins for 2 weeks, with tannin removed

'Ten percent of the blend is from my blood!' declares Jean-François, crediting Cyril Brun for teaching him that rosé is 'a sublimation of pinot noir'. His 'Clouet No 3' was inspired by Coco Chanel, the number introduced to denote the style, recognising that the colour is different each year, with the number 3 representing a light, elegant apéritif style. He tried to make a fuller style in the ripe 2015 vintage, but the restraint of the result held it at No 3. Elegance and freshness are his goals for rosé, avoiding what he describes as the 'full, rustic and heavy' styles of the past.

Clouet's 2015 base rosé epitomises elegance and focus, while flamboyantly celebrating the generous raspberries, red cherries and pomegranates of Bouzy. The depth and presence of the village are sensitively toned by the lively, bright acidity and fresh precision of the house. Structure is fine and confident, driven by the chalk minerality of the village, working seamlessly in concert with finely executed tannin texture. It finishes with great length, vibrancy and elegance, with lingering poise and detail of exquisite red berry fruits. An engaging and enticingly priced rosé of primary integrity and pretty medium salmon crimson hue. The 2012 base carries an identically elegant mood.

André Clouet Rosé No 5 Brut NV $$

94 points • Tasted in Champagne

As for Rosé No 3

Boasting a full ruby hue, No 5 is notably deeper than No 3 in both appearance and flavour. As flamboyant and exuberant as its maker himself, it brims with wild strawberries, raspberries and morello cherries, encapsulating that wonderful talent of great pinot to build and rise triumphantly on the finish. For all of its generosity, it never deviates from the control and precision of the house, focused by bright acidity and the omnipresent chalk minerality that underscores this legendary village. A great expression of the freshness, mineral airiness and presence of Bouzy pinot noir.

André Clouet The V6 Experience by André Clouet NV $$

92 points • Tasted in Champagne

100% pinot; 80% 2012, 20% solera of 2008, 2005, 2004 and 2002; aged 72 months on lees; zero dosage here but released with 5g/L dosage based on a liqueur of barrel-aged chardonnay and refined sugar

Jean-François describes pinot noir as entering a phase he dubs 'The Whirlwind' in its sixth year of maturation. The rest of his inspiration is impossible to put into words, but clicking on 'Cuvée Design Specification' on his website will put you on the right trajectory. For the exuberance of Bouzy pinot noir and not inconsiderable age, the freshness packed into this cuvée is something to behold. Grapefruit tang meets crunchy red apple fruit, contrasting the generosity and spice of the village and the tension of zero dosage. Get on board.

André Clouet Millésime Brut 2009 $$

94 points • Tasted in Champagne

50% pinot, 50% chardonnay from Bouzy and Ambonnay

A beautifully fresh and lively take on a rich vintage in a powerful village, this is a cuvée that transcribes its presence with the vivacity and purity of Clouet. I first tasted it in its coiled, pre-release youth four years ago, and proclaimed that it promised great things in times to come. That time has now come, and it has admirably upheld its primary fruit focus of crunchy lemon, pink grapefruit, precision of white cherry and exuberance of blood orange. Youthful fruit remains the theme, but with subtle nuances of almond and creamy texture from lees age. A vintage to drink right away – while the 2008 rests.

André Clouet Dream Collection Vintage 2009 $$$

93 points • Tasted in Champagne

100% chardonnay; 80% Bouzy, 20% Le Mesnil-sur-Oger; Dream Vintage was conceived to showcase fruit from swaps with other growers; 2000–4000 bottles each vintage

This is a wonderfully elegant Dream Vintage, transcending its warm season and the rich mood of Bouzy. It is pale in colour and refreshingly fruitful, with lime, lemon and nashi pear, finishing with lively acidity. Prominent, fine-chalk minerality is heightened by a dash of Le Mesnil-sur-Oger. A vintage that Jean-François enjoys drinking in spring and summer, hence its pale lime livery.

André Clouet Dream Collection Vintage 2008 $$$

95 points • Tasted in Champagne en magnum

100% chardonnay; 80% Le Mesnil-sur-Oger, 20% Bouzy; no oak; 8g/L dosage

Sourced from a grower as a swap for pinot noir, the union of Le Mesnil-sur-Oger and Bouzy chardonnay is perhaps an unlikely marriage, but it works to delightful effect. The tension, minerality and presence of Le Mesnil is bolstered by the body and richness of Bouzy, softening the mineral tension of the village and the scintillating acid cut that defines 2008. Layered with spice, grapefruit and white peach of effortless poise, it propels upward with epic length and seamless line.

André Clouet Dream Collection Vintage 2005 $$$

90 points • Tasted in Champagne en magnum

100% chardonnay; no oak

Jean-François prefers his 2005 Dream Collection to 2008. Both accurately articulate the mood of their contrasting seasons, the 2005 already a golden yellow hue and brimming with luscious golden delicious apple and pineapple fruit, true to this warm vintage. It's a spicy and rich style and it relies on this generosity in order to carry the dry phenolic grip and coffee and cocoa notes of the season.

André Clouet Dream Collection Vintage 2002 $$$

92 points • Tasted in Champagne

100% chardonnay

A vintage that contrasts body with tension better than perhaps any other in recent decades, 2002 has ascended to the height of its trajectory here. Now boasting a medium to full yellow-gold hue, it's layered with luscious fruit evoking recollections of white peach, pineapple and golden delicous apple that flows into mixed spice and vanilla custard. Tertiary nuances have begun to waft to the surface in suggestions of pipe smoke and baked apple, concluding with a long finish of dry textured crunch. One bottle showed premature development of toffee and burnt-orange oxidation (88 points).

André Clouet Le Clos 2008 $$$$$

96 points • Tasted in Champagne en magnum

100% pinot noir; single vineyard; only released in magnums; harvested 10 days earlier than the rest of the village, thanks to the microclimate of the Clos; zero dosage

The Clouet Clos between the house and the cuverie on the lower edge of Bouzy is not the family's finest terroir, lacking the pronounced chalk mineral definition characteristic to their hillside sites, and it takes an exceptional season to infuse it with the confidence to stand alone. The tense 2008 vintage delivered that season, with a captivating poise and introverted reticence containing grand complexity now beginning to burst out. Deep and luscious plums, black cherries and violets declare the depth, body and impact of Bouzy, rising to the rhythm of an exceptional season, abounding with a cornucopia of gingernut biscuits, anise, glacé orange, fig, mixed spice, baked white peach, golden fruit cake and roast almonds. Tense, focused 2008 acidity draws out the finish long and true, coaxing out a pronounced, fine chalk mineral texture of glittering, crystalline definition. It's attained its glorious pinnacle, and will sustain it confidently for some years to come.

ANDRÉ CLOUET LE CLOS 2009 $$$$$

94 points • DISGORGED ON THE SPOT IN JANUARY 2019 • TASTED IN CHAMPAGNE

As for Le Clos 2008

Amplified in magnitude four-fold, the universes of generosity of site, village, vintage and variety align with metronomic precision in this young-disgorged style. For all of the exuberance that its bright, full straw-yellow hue anticipates, it delivers impressive accuracy and generosity of white peach and lingering spice. Well-balanced acidity and the soft, fine chalk minerality of the vineyard preserve admirable focus and poise.

ANDRÉ CLOUET VERSAILLES DIAMANT COTEAUX CHAMPENOIS 2015

95 points • TASTED IN CHAMPAGNE ON THREE VISITS

100% Bouzy chardonnay; single vineyard; two barrels; 500 bottles

'Bouzy was the wine of the king, so I want to recreate the story of the wines that were served for the coronations, capturing the exuberance and glamour of Versailles, with freshness!' – Jean-François Clouet

Singly the finest Coteaux Champenois blanc I have ever tasted, a cuvée that exemplifies the exuberance and tension of a warm Champagne terroir, presenting the presence of Bouzy chardonnay with exacting precision and poise. Lemon, lime and white peach fruit flow with grace and grand persistence, accented by magnificent nectarine exoticism and rounded eloquently by the vanilla of classy French oak. Inimitable fine chalk mineral definition and taut, profound Champagne acid line provide tension to the finish without any suggestion of austerity. It would sit confidently alongside a respectable premier cru white Burgundy from a good domaine. It will be exceedingly long-lived, and will appreciate some time to soften and for oak and acidity to integrate, having hardly moved in the nine months between my three tastings.

ANDRÉ CLOUET VERSAILLES RUBY COTEAUX CHAMPENOIS 2015

93 points • TASTED IN CHAMPAGNE ON THREE VISITS

100% Bouzy pinot noir; single vineyard

2015 was the warmest year Jean-François has ever seen in Bouzy, the perfect opportunity for his Coteaux Champenois debut. It evolved magnificently across three tastings spanning nine months, into an elegantly understated style of Chambolle-esque fragrance. Vibrant red cherry fruits, beetroot, pink pepper and musk morph into deeper allusions of blackberry, black cherry and fruit mince spice that showcase the presence and depth of Bouzy. Vibrant, focused Champagne acidity, firm, fine tannins and fine chalk minerality define a refreshingly lighter style with a very long future stretching out before it.

ANDRÉ CLOUET 1994

93 points • DISGORGED ON DAY OF VISIT IN JAN 2019 • TASTED IN CHAMPAGNE

50% chardonnay, 50% pinot; Jean-François' first vintage; zero dosage

At a full 25 years of age, this is a wonderful surprise for a lesser vintage! The exuberance of Bouzy has evolved into a complex style of characterful presence, with pineapple and grapefruit notes, subtle brioche complexity, and tertiary allusions of warm hearth and green olive. On first opening, it was let down a little by a firm and dry finish, but all was resolved with time in the glass. Within an hour, pinot noir rose magnificently to blossom into a spicy style, drawing out a long finish.

ANDRÉ HEUCQ

(On-dray Erk)

---

9 RUE EUGÈNE MOUSSÉ 51700 CUISLES
www.champagne-heucq.com

CHAMPAGNE
ANDRÉ HEUCQ
NATURE ● TERROIR

Midway between Reims and Château-Thierry and 6 kilometres north of the river Marne, the tiny village of Cuisles is unique for its green illite clay soils and low rainfall. Here, four generations of the Heucq family have adopted an increasingly attentive and sustainable approach in their family vineyards and winery. The path to conversion to biodynamic viticulture fulfils an aim to reactivate microbial life in the soil to enhance terroir expression, and coincides with the construction of a new ecological cuverie with natural ventilation, collection of rainwater and self-sufficiency in solar electricity. Unusual in Champagne, the same facility also serves to house all the pickers, who are trained to be particularly discerning in what they harvest. Meunier is naturally the focus in this part of the world, though chardonnay and pinot play a significant role in most cuvées, too. Vinification is refreshingly intuitive, with each parcel fermented and aged separately in stainless steel tanks or used oak barrels from Meursault to suit, and malolactic fermentation encouraged or blocked selectively. Cuvées are aged long and dosages are low. Informative back labels declare crus, cépage and time on lees. For such a small estate, its huge portfolio of no fewer than 20 cuvées must be one of the most diverse in Champagne, with many labels comprising fewer than 1000 bottles. The finest cuvées of André Heucq epitomise just what can be achieved in lesser terroirs with sufficient determination and focus.

ANDRÉ HEUCQ HÉRITAGE BLANC DE MEUNIER EXTRA BRUT NV $$

91 points • 2013 BASE VINTAGE • DISGORGED 26 JULY 2018 • TASTED IN AUSTRALIA

100% meunier; Cuisles, Châtillon-sur-Marne, Serzy-et-Prin and Mareuil-le-Port; average vine age 30 years; 40% 2012 reserves; fermented in tanks; full malolactic fermentation; aged 48 months on lees; 4g/L dosage; cork; 20,000 bottles

The spicy red berry fruits of meunier are on grand display here, brimming flamboyantly with raspberries and wild strawberries, underscored confidently with sarsaparilla, fruit mince spice, fruit cake and boiled sweets – not from dosage but from ripe, expressive fruit. For its flamboyant start, it concludes abrupt and dry, lacking in carry and drive. An expressive take on meunier.

André Heucq Héritage Blanc de Meunier Brut Nature NV $$

90 points • 2013 base vintage • Disgorged 26 July 2018 • Tasted in Australia

As for the Extra Brut, but with zero dosage; cork

The same cuvée without dosage emphasises the profound effect of even a touch of dosage, and without its calming and lifting effect, the dry austerity of the finish is more pronounced, as is its fine, salty chalk minerality. Its varietal fruits and spice are the victims of this tussle, sadly subdued.

André Heucq Héritage Assemblage NV $$

89 points • 2012 base vintage • Disgorged 26 July 2018 • Tasted in Australia

40% chardonnay, 30% pinot, 30% meunier; Cuisles and Baslieux-sous-Châtillon; average vine age 30 years; 43% 2011 reserves; vinified in 70% stainless steel (with malolactic fermentation) and 30% oak (without malolactic); aged 5 years on lees; 6g/L dosage; cork; 10,000 bottles

A complex style that showcases the spicy character of the Vallée de la Marne and heightens it with partial oak fermentation, while upholding tension with retention of some malic acidity. Five years on lees has built creamy texture and seamless integration. A little oxidation lets it down on the finish, concluding dry with some vinegary astringency, lacking in fruit definition and freshness.

André Heucq Héritage Rosé de Meunier – Phase 1 2014 $$

92 points • Disgorged 26 July 2018 • Tasted in Australia

100% meunier; 100% 2014, though not labelled as a vintage; Cuisles, from the vineyard parcel Le Bout de la Ville; average vine age 50 years; aged 3 years on lees; saignée of 24 hours maceration; fermented and aged in tanks; no malolactic fermentation; 6g/L dosage; cork; 3400 bottles

A full day's maceration makes for a deeply coloured saignée of full, bright crimson pink hue in a characterful and expressive style that ripples with fresh raspberries, wild strawberries and red gala apples. Meunier is on full parade here, in its luscious, fruity flamboyance, even with an air of musk. For such a maceration, tannins have been masterfully handled, super fine and supportive, yet never firm nor bitter. It doesn't carry a lot of complexity, persistence or endurance, but that's not what it's about; this is an unashamedly primary and youthful style, wonderfully complete and ready to drink right away – and it's none the less for it.

André Heucq Héritage Rosé de Meunier – Phase 2 2014 $$

92 points • Disgorged 26 July 2018 • Tasted in Australia

30% chardonnay, 70% meunier; Cuisles, from the vineyard parcel Le Bout de la Ville; average vine age 50 years; from the same terroir as the Phase 1, but here an assemblage rosé with red wine of meunier; again 100% 2014, but not labelled as such; fermented in tank; aged 3 years on lees; 6g/L dosage; cork; 3400 bottles

The ultimate masterclass in rosé production, and indeed the first I've ever tasted to showcase the vast contrast between the saignée and the blending methods with fruit from the same terroirs (albeit with the addition of chardonnay here). The proportion of red wine is not declared, but it must be considerable as the colour is a vivid, medium crimson pink. A gorgeously fragrant and precocious rosé that dances with rose petal fragrance, strawberry ice cream and poached red cherry fruit, accented with cracked pink pepper and Campari. A gorgeous core of red fruit flamboyance drives long through the finish, masterfully supported by super-fine tannin texture. A gorgeous rosé to drink right away.

ANDRÉ HEUCQ HÉRITAGE MILLÉSIME 2012 $$$

93 points • DISGORGED 26 JULY 2018 • TASTED IN AUSTRALIA

50% chardonnay, 30% pinot, 20% meunier; Cuisles, from the vineyard parcels Le Bout de la Ville and La Sablonnière; 50% stainless steel (with malolactic fermentation) and 50% oak (without malolactic); aged 5 years on lees; 4g/L dosage; cork; 2500 bottles

A beautifully fresh and characterful 2012 that expresses the spicy personality of Cuisles. It brims with strawberry yoghurt, fresh raspberries, vanilla cream and brioche, seamlessly uniting the vibrant pop of crunchy, fresh berry fruits with the silky, creamy allure of five years on lees. Partial oak fermentation and partial malolactic have been masterfully played to create a harmonious and enticing style. It holds with outstanding line and length. Proof of just what can be achieved in lesser terroirs with sufficient determination and focus.

Festigny, summer 2014

APOLLONIS

(A-pol-lo-neess)

---

13 Rue de Bel Air 51700 Festigny
www.champagneapollonis.com

APOLLONIS
CHAMPAGNE
Michel Loriot

Wth speakers mounted atop poles, Michel Loriot plays classical music to his vines, his barrels and his bottles. Three generations of his family were members of the village band, and music is in Loriot's blood. For a decade now, it's also been in his wines. His ancestors have been growing grapes since 1675 and were the first to build a press house in his village of Festigny in the Vallée de la Marne in 1903. Twelve generations on, the brand changed from Michel Loriot (a common name here) to Apollonis in 2015. This small grower produces 30,000 bottles annually from less than three hectares of estate vines spanning 20 plots in the village. Meunier is the resounding theme (80% of plantings), supplemented with chardonnay (18%) and just 2% pinot. The majority of the estate's vineyards surround the dramatic hill overlooking the village, planted on steep slopes in marl-rich clay over chalk. Festigny contrasts good exposure to the sun with particularly chalky soils for the Vallée de la Marne. Using only natural fertilisers and no herbicides for more than a decade, Loriot has received High Environmental Value certification. His single-vineyard old-vine meunier shines in great seasons, though unfortunately some other cuvées are marked by underripeness and oxidation. Full details and disgorgement dates are printed on back labels.

APOLLONIS AUTHENTIC MEUNIER BRUT — BLANC DE NOIRS NV $

83 points • 2015 BASE VINTAGE • DISGORGED JULY 2018 • TASTED IN AUSTRALIA

100% meunier; a selection of vineyards in Festigny on clay-rich marl and limestone over wet chalk; reserve wine from solera; aged 2 years on lees; 9g/L dosage; DIAM

The phenolic grip of 2015 unites with notes of green pea underripeness to produce a callow style of dusty, dry-extract grip and grainy, phenolic coarseness, marked by gherkin-like notes of oxidative development.

APOLLONIS THÉODORINE BRUT ROSÉ NV $

85 points • 2012 BASE VINTAGE • DISGORGED AUGUST 2018 • TASTED IN AUSTRALIA

50% chardonnay, 20% pinot, 30% meunier; including 10% pinot noir red wine; a selection of vineyards in Festigny on clay-rich marl and limestone over wet chalk; 2011 reserves; aged 3 years on lees; 9g/L dosage; DIAM

A savoury rosé of pale copper-salmon hue and vegetal character meeting notes of charcuterie, lacking primary fruit character and freshness. It concludes short and callow.

APOLLONIS MONODIE MEUNIER VIEILLES VIGNES EXTRA-BRUT 2008 $$

93 points • DISGORGED AUGUST 2018 • TASTED IN AUSTRALIA

100% meunier from three plots on a single, south-facing lieu-dit ('l'Arpent' in Festigny), planted on grey marl over wet chalk by Michel's grandfather in 1942 (hence 66 years of age); aged 9 years 9 months on lees; ; 5g/L dosage; DIAM

The generosity of old-vine Festigny meunier is a dynamic foil to the tension of the energetic 2008 season, igniting an exciting style of bright medium straw hue. Meunier's personality is well articulated in layers of fig, mixed spice, baked apple and gently evolved strawberry fruit, while age has built white fruit cake and brioche complexity. The 2008 season infuses its charge in lemon accents and a spine of confident acid cut, accentuating salt minerality and softened gently by the creamy texture of time. It concludes long and focused, promising grand potential over the coming decade.

The cellars of AR Lenoble in Damery.

AR Lenoble

(A.R. Ler-nob-ler)

(6/10)

35–37 Rue Paul Douce 51480 Damery
www.champagne-arlenoble.com

A·R LENOBLE
Champagne

'The two important things for making great champagne are the quality of your grapes and the size of your stock,' declares Antoine Malassagne, who is richly blessed with both. With his sister Anne, he is the fourth generation to manage the family cellars and vineyards of the Graser-Malassagne family. The 18 hectares of the small house of Lenoble transcend its position in the centre of the village of Damery, in the middle of the Vallée de la Marne, thanks to a majority of holdings of a glorious 10 hectares in the core of the Côte des Blancs grand cru of Chouilly. The chardonnay from these vines defines Lenoble's finest cuvées, supplemented with pinot noir from six hectares of estate vineyards in Bisseuil (on the Marne between Mareuil-sur-Aÿ and Tours-sur-Marne), and just two hectares of meunier in Damery. The remainder of its needs, including all meunier, is sourced from Damery growers. For an annual production of 400,000 bottles, Lenoble's cellar stock of 1.5 million is sizeable, furnishing long ageing of three to four years for non-vintage cuvées, and six or more for vintage wines. True to its name, a noble approach in the vines and the cellar produces well-composed and tantalisingly affordable cuvées that exemplify Malassagne's philosophy of 'full body with elegance', showcasing most of all the strength, structure, definition and opulence of Chouilly.

Lenoble was established in 18th century cellars in Damery almost a century ago. When Antoine Malassagne returned to the family company in 1996, he was unimpressed with traditional techniques and set about improving practices in the vineyards and winery in 1998. 'I am starting to see the results of our efforts in the past three or four vintages,' he told me when we first met in 2015.

A natural approach in the vineyards has seen the elimination of herbicides and pesticides, ploughing to control weeds and aerate the soil, use of organic manure, and cultivation of grasses in the mid-rows of some sites to moderate yields and increase ripeness. 'I am nearly organic but not quite, as I am concerned about using copper sulphate to combat mildew,' says Malassagne, a qualified chemical engineer. For these initiatives, Lenoble was the second in Champagne after Bollinger to receive High Environmental Value certification.

Malassagne's philosophy of making champagne is to vinify it like still wine. The winery was rebuilt in 2008 and maintains three wooden presses between 30 and 45 years of age. All parcels are vinified separately, with the best from the finest seasons fermented in small Burgundy barrels for oxidative character. 'Champagne is a very delicate wine, and the barrel needs to support the wine rather than dominating,' he emphasises. For the most part, his cuvées reflect sensitive use of oak, generally with no more than one-third of any blend vinified in barrels, though a foray into 100% small-barrel fermentation in 225-litre Burgundy barrels is bold and at times dominating.

'I like buying new barrels, as you know what you're getting,' explains Malassagne. To reduce new oak character, the first year's fermentation is sold for distillation – a costly and time-consuming process. Nine brand-new 5000-litre foudres have been acquired in recent years for fermenting and ageing reserves for 4–5 months post-fermentation. 'I buy more and more big barrels, because they impart less oaky flavour than small barrels and produce clear, clean wines of finesse and complexity.'

Malassagne is frank in volunteering that he made a mistake when he started out by ageing wines in barriques for some years, resulting in oxidised wines. In order to obtain autolytic ageing on lees and slow oxidative evolution that he can't achieve in tank, he's been bottling reserves in magnums under 1.5 atmospheres of pressure and sealing these with corks since 2010.

Climate change has fundamentally turned on its head the way he views the role of reserve wines. 'In the past, reserves were about adding complexity and depth to a blend, but after four of the earliest harvests in history this century, acidity levels are much lower than they used to be, and we are now talking about how we can use reserves to enhance freshness,' says Malassagne. Using reserves to build freshness rather than complexity is a new mindset for Champagne, and a progressive change of thinking.

Lenoble adapts vinification to suit the harvest, with malolactic fermentation used selectively, according to the season and the parcel, and not at all in reserve wines. 'It's difficult to find a balance between finesse and intensity,' Malassagne admits. 'Twenty years ago I always did malolactic, but champagne must have freshness, and with earlier harvests and lower acidities I now need to adapt and partially block malolactic' – using none at all in 2017.

'I loved 2017 because it was very complex and very hard,' he reveals. 'I like when it is hard because when you make more effort you can really see the difference. I refused some grapes in 2017 in Damery, though this was not the first time I have done this. And the grower was really furious! If the fruit isn't properly sorted you can taste and smell the mushroom in the *vins clairs*.'

Malassagne is not afraid to go the extra mile to get it right, and he has an impressive portfolio of wines to show for it. He possesses the tenacity to boldly try new things, and the humility to admit when he gets it wrong. Driven by a scientific mind, he is constantly experimenting to refine the details and improve his wines, rather than following trends. He has trialled wild yeasts, bâtonnage and Hungarian oak, though is not convinced of any.

Dosage is very low – no more than 5g/L, and more often just 3g/L. Back labels are particularly informative, detailing base vintage, reserves and vinification.

Malassagne doesn't produce the same non-vintage wines each vintage, and has recently adopted the admirable initiative of introducing the base vintage in the name of each cuvée. 'The idea is not to make the same wine every year, but to make *better* wine every year. I try to improve and make the best wines I can,' he explains. 'Generation after generation, we try to improve vinification and practices in the vines.'

AR Lenoble Intense 'Mag 14' NV $$

92 points • 2014 base vintage • Tasted in Champagne

25% Chouilly chardonnay, 30% Bisseuil pinot, 45% Damery meunier; 40% perpetual reserve dating from 2010; 25% vinified in wood; new proprietary bottle with embossed neck and base; 5g/L dosage

Since the 2010 harvest, reserve magnums have been bottled under 1.5 atmospheres of pressure and sealed with corks to achieve autolytic ageing on lees and slow oxidative evolution not possible in tanks. No easy process, since it's tricky to disgorge at this low pressure. These magnums have been blended with reserves aged in foudres, barriques and stainless steel vats to form a perpetual reserve. Every year, part of the blend of this cuvée is kept in magnums as the perpetual reserve. Mag 14 is the first release, based on the 2014 vintage. Mag 15 will be next, and so on. Mag 14 Brut Nature and Mag 14 Rosé will also follow.

The first of the exciting new Mag era is an impeccably crafted cuvée of integrity and poise that reflect its noble fruit sources, boasting a complexity commensurate with its super-detailed and labour-intensive reserve regime. Medium straw hue. A core of crunchy red apple and grapefruit is surrounded by a universe of barrel and reserve depth in nuances of biscuit, spice, brioche and toast, flowing seamlessly into a line of focused acidity that lingers long and true. Fine phenolic grip sits comfortably within the complexity of the style.

AR Lenoble Brut Nature Dosage Zero NV $$

91 points • 2013 base vintage • Tasted in Champagne

30% Chouilly chardonnay, 35% Bisseuil pinot, 35% Damery meunier; 30% reserves; 25% vinified in wood; the same cuvée as Intense, with another year on lees, made in this way since 1999, before it was trendy; zero dosage

A Brut Nature made on the same base as the Brut never seems to work, but there are exceptions to prove the rule and this is one, perhaps because Intense has such low dosage to start with. Tension and freshness of citrus zest and beurre bosc pear meet the biscuit complexity of long lees age. The dryness of zero dosage is calmed by the depth and texture afforded by barrel vinification and long lees age.

AR Lenoble Grand Cru Blanc de Blancs Chouilly 'Mag 14' NV $$

91 points • 2014 base vintage • Disgorged early 2018 • Tasted in Champagne

100% Chouilly chardonnay; 40% reserves; 25% vinified in wood; 5g/L dosage

The classic exuberance and ripe opulence of Chouilly are on grand parade in a full and unabashed explosion of glowing white peach, fig, even pineapple and mandarin, pulled into line obediently by the fresh focus of lemon and grapefruit. Gentle phenolic grip builds structure, working in elegant tandem with bright acidity and subtle dosage. The toasty complexity and subtle charcuterie of lees age and oak fermentation add layered complexity to a long and complex conclusion.

AR Lenoble Rosé Terroirs Chouilly-Bisseuil NV $$

91 points • 2012 base vintage • Tasted in Champagne

88% Chouilly chardonnay, 12% Bisseuil pinot red wine; 35% reserves; 20% vinified in oak; 3g/L dosage

Lenoble's pinot noir and meunier are too rich to stand alone as a rosé, so the house tactically calls upon the structure and fresh acid drive of its Chouilly chardonnay to take a confident lead. This release has maintained the medium copper salmon hue of when I first tasted it two years ago, though its momentary fanfare of tangelo, candied strawberry, red cherry and musk have now vaporised, making way for a characterful and savoury style of creamy mouthfeel and tomato complexity over a core of wild strawberries with a hint of balsamic. Chardonnay upholds its decisive lead in grapefruit focus articulated through the discreetly handled texture of a glimpse of oak. It concludes elegant, focused and fine, thanks to the tension and fine chalk mineral structure of Chouilly.

AR Lenoble Grand Cru Blanc de Blancs Chouilly Vintage 2008 $$$

94 points • Tasted in Champagne

100% Chouilly chardonnay; 10% vinified in wood; 3g/L dosage

The tension and definition of the energetic 2008 vintage is endearing in the opulent village of Chouilly, and Antoine Malassagne has sensitively matched the elegance of the vintage with a subtle 10% oak vinification and an even lighter dosage than when I first tasted it four years ago. Such is the stamina of the season that this cuvée did not evolve one iota in its first two years, and has only now grown into a deep yet still bright straw hue and expanded in generosity and complexity, building charcuterie and biscuit character. It upholds the succulent exuberance of Chouilly, propelled by the energy and dynamism of this brilliant season, driven by a wonderful line of glistening acidity and the pronounced, frothing salt mineral texture of the northern Côte des Blancs, elongating a finish of magnificent line, impeccable balance and enduring persistence.

AR Lenoble Premier Cru Blanc de Noirs Bisseuil Vintage 2012 $$$

93 points • Tasted in Champagne

100% Bisseuil pinot; 35% vinified in oak; partial malolactic fermentation; 3g/L dosage

Malassagne's goal here is distinctiveness, richness and opulence, and so there's a little more oak vinification than in his blanc de blancs cuvées. In the past, oak presence has at times jostled with the elegant and gentle fruit profile of Bisseuil, but here it integrates seamlessly and harmoniously, in spite of a higher proportion of oak vinification than in the past, testimony to his growing expertise in barrel management. The presence of Bisseuil pinot noir juxtaposes the tension of 2012, creating a style that leads out with confident red berry and wild strawberry fruit, and concludes focused and tense, thanks to the energising effect of upholding some malic acidity. The result is a bright and engaging blanc de noirs.

AR Lenoble Cuvée Gentilhomme Grand Cru Blanc de Blancs Chouilly Vintage 2009 $$$$

92 points • Tasted in Champagne

100% Chouilly chardonnay; 100% vinified in small oak barrels for the first time; partial malolactic fermentation; 3g/L dosage

A glowing, bright medium-straw hue has evolved toward yellow over the two years since its release. It contrasts the exuberance of succulent Chouilly grilled pineapple and grapefruit in the rich 2009 season with a tart malic acid core. Full oak vinification lends coffee bean character, firmness and fine tannin structure, disrupting Lenoble's hitherto impeccable record of sensitive use of oak. It consequently lacks something of the dignified refinement that this cuvée has exuded in the past, a powerful cuvée that collides lemon zest tension with firm acidity and prominent oak. That said, time has helped it to subsume its oak, and it achieves its accord with poise and harmony, thanks to the tension of malic acidity and the prominent, fine, omnipresent chalk minerality of Chouilly, drawing out a long and accurate finish. It will benefit from at least another five years to continue its evolution of integration.

AR Lenoble Les Aventures Grand Cru Blanc de Blancs Chouilly NV $$$$

93 points • 2006 base vintage • Tasted in Champagne

Single-vineyard Chouilly Les Aventures from a half-hectare plot; 40% 2002 reserves; 22% vinified in oak; 3g/L dosage; just 2000 bottles released each year

Blended only from seasons released as vintages in their own right, the philosophy of 'The Adventures of Lenoble' is to showcase just what a small terroir in Chouilly can achieve in top years. Quite a quest it is, engineered and structured with a scaffold of Chouilly tension, amplified by barrel fermentation. Never has it looked finer, and this blend has softened and toned magnificently over some five years since its release. The assurance with which the generous white fruits of Chouilly have upheld their stamina is a surprise even from its evolution of two years ago, and the confidence with which its 2002 reserves have stepped forward in the blend is something to behold. Malassagne believes 2002 to uphold greater potential even than 2008. Heightened by long age on tirage under cork, its tense, coiled acidity is now calm and integrated, and the soft creaminess of oak fermentation more generous and textural than ever. Wood work has likewise toned in flavour, evolving to a place of calm, spicy, charcuterie complexity. The salty chalk minerality of Chouilly remains transfixed, upholding exacting poise, enduring persistence and characterful definition. This is a powerful and formidable experience for the adventurous, yet is never heavy nor broad, promising a journey that will linger for some years still. It's main-course ready, and deserves large glasses.

Armand de Brignac

(Ah-mon de Brin-yak)

---

6 Rue Dom Pérignon 51500 Chigny-les-Roses
www.armanddebrignac.com

ARMAND DE BRIGNAC
CHAMPAGNE

When the house of Cattier set out to make the most expensive champagne in the world in 2000, they could not have dreamed of the exposure it would receive. In what Cattier describes as 'a great miracle', US hip-hop sensation Shawn Carter (Jay Z) discovered the wine in New York shortly after its release in 2006. To Cattier's 'great surprise' and delight, Jay Z immediately featured it in his new video clip. On the day of the clip's release, Armand de Brignac's US distributor received more than 700 requests for the champagne. A decade later, the company cannot keep up with demand, with a little more than 100,000 bottles sold in 110 countries annually, and Jay Z is the proud owner of the brand. 'We have only 12 years of sales so far, and from the beginning we could not have imagined that we would have such success!' beams Jean-Jacques Cattier.

The striking gold, silver, pink and emerald-clad livery and glam pewter Ace of Spades branding are among Champagne's most lux designs of the modern era. But is the wine inside worth the hype and not inconsiderable price?

The focus of Armand de Brignac is said to be pinot noir and meunier, though the lead cuvée (Brut Gold) comprises 40% each of pinot noir and chardonnay. There are now five cuvées, with Brut Gold representing close to 85% of production, Rosé 10%, Blanc de Blancs 5%, Blanc de Noirs 2.5% and Demi Sec 2.3%. Blanc de Blancs and Blanc de Noirs are always the standouts, assuming you can find them (and afford them!). An increasing proportion of both have been laid down in the cellar, prompted by demand.

The aspiration of the house is to give pleasure, without being too complicated or complex. Each cuvée is a young, fruity, non-vintage blend of three harvests, to contrast with Cattier's older Clos du Moulin, the inspiration for the three-vintage recipe. *Liqueur de dosage* is aged for a full year, mostly in new Argonne oak barrels to add a little touch of the complexity and spice of wood to the blends, and to distinguish from Cattier, which uses no oak. Armand de Brignac is made by Cattier alongside its own

cuvées in its home of Chigny-les-Roses, 150-year-old cellars in neighbouring village Rilly-la-Montagne and a 3600 square metre warehouse in Reims (largely to facilitate the space required for a big production of large-format bottles, according to Jean-Jacques Cattier). The house created what is believed to be Champagne's biggest bottle. Dubbed the 'Titan', its 45 kilogram, 37.5-litre bulk holds 50 standard bottles. The first is yet to be opened (assuming it can be lifted!).

Underneath its Rilly facility, Armand de Brignac's gloriously glam and spectacularly lit display of shiny bottles resides in some of Champagne's deepest cellars, no less than 136 steps below the street. The premises were bought by the Cattier family 17 years ago and progressively rebuilt, though in contrast to the show-piece cellars, the production facilities are still quite rustic. Work is underway, and when I visited in 2016, old epoxy resin-lined concrete tanks were being replaced with temperature-controlled stainless steel, important for temperature stability, particularly for malolactic fermentation.

The decision to allocate a wine to Armand de Brignac or to Cattier is made not in the vineyards but based on the fermented

Armand de Brignac's cellar in Rilly-la-Montagne.

wines in tank prior to blending. 'The best for Armand de Brignac, of course,' explains Jean-Jacques. When I questioned the impact of this on the quality of Cattier, he reasoned it away on the basis that Cattier produces eight times the volume of Armand de Brignac.

'We don't have any rules for how we blend Armand de Brignac,' Jean-Jacques reveals. 'The goal is to be flexible.' There is thus no focus on particular crus, with souring adjusted according to which terroirs perform best in that year. Fruit is sourced from Cattier's estate vineyards in the premier cru villages of the northern slopes of the Montagne de Reims, particularly Rilly-la-Montagne, Chigny-les-Roses and Ludes, supplemented with growers from across the Marne, including the villages of Avize, Verzenay and Bouzy, with a desire to increase supplies from the Côte des Blancs and Aÿ. Unclassified villages comprise about 10% of the mix.

Cuvées are aged on lees for four or five years, up from three years for Brut Gold in the past, though the goal is not for long ageing. There is no aspiration to make a vintage cuvée, though this must surely be tempting for a brand of such aspiration and success.

Dosages are higher than they need to be, which Jean-Jacques justifies on the basis that the target audience is a young demographic seeking young and fresh champagnes, and this style demands sweetness to soften it.

In October 2018, chef de cave since 2014 Émilien Boutillat took up a position at Piper-Heidsieck. Alexandre Cattier stepped up to greater responsibility for winemaking alongside his father, Jean-Jacques, who describes himself as a 'retired oenologist', though he remains active in tasting and blending alongside Alexandre.

The philosophy and recipe are sound, though on paper there's nothing to distinguish Armand de Brignac from the entry NV blends of many houses. Like them, the current release is based on the 2012 vintage. But does that glam bottle justify ten times the price?

As an insightful chef de cave of another small house suggested, 'Armand de Brignac is a fantastic marketing coup, but the wine could be anything from anywhere. But champagne needs that as much as it needs Francis Egly and Anselme Selosse.'

ARMAND DE BRIGNAC BRUT GOLD NV $$$$$

89 points • 2012 BASE VINTAGE • TASTED IN CHAMPAGNE EN MAGNUM

40% chardonnay, 40% pinot, 20% meunier; 2010 and 2009 reserves; 9g/L dosage; 85,000 bottles

A cuvée that unites gentle apple and pear fruit with the subtle brioche of lees age, concluding with gentle phenolic grip and more honeyed dosage than it needs. The house showed me the same blend from magnum as it poured for me from bottle two years earlier, and I had hoped that it might have held up better in magnum. But the aspiration is not to age, and even in magnum its fruit has already begun to diminish, causing its finish to contract. The result is a simple champagne in a clean, non-vintage style, finishing short and simple. It's otherwise evenly balanced and well made, albeit young and straightforward for its price.

Armand de Brignac Rosé NV $$$$$

91 points • 2012 base vintage • Tasted in Champagne en magnum

10% chardonnay, 50% pinot, 40% meunier; 2010 and 2009 reserves; 17% red wine from Cattier's vineyards in Chigny-les-Roses, Verzenay, Verzy and Mailly-Champagne, made both in-house and by growers; 8.5g/L dosage

Meeting its aspiration of approachability without being too complicated, this is a rosé that showcases the presence and structure of pinot and meunier. The same blend in magnum as the house poured for me in bottle two years ago, it has now deepened to a full crimson hue while accurately upholding its red cherry and strawberry fruits, accented with the savoury complexity of tamarillo and the subtle nutty complexity of lees age. Time has not toned its tussle between candied, honeyed dosage and the phenolic grip of considerable tannin structure. Tangy acidity comes to the rescue on a short and simple finish. A rosé for pink protein dishes to tone its tannins.

Armand de Brignac Blanc de Blancs NV $$$$$

94 points • 2008 base vintage • Disgorged mid-2018 • Tasted in Champagne en magnum

100% chardonnay; around 50/50 Montagne de Reims and Côte des Blancs; 2006 and 2005 reserves; aged 8 years on lees; less than 1000 bottles produced, and this was one of the last of 500 magnums; 6g/L dosage

The 2009 base Blanc de Blancs was my favourite Armand de Brignac cuvée until the release of the glorious 2008 base. Regrettably, there is no way to tell which you're buying (assuming you can find a bottle of this rare cuvée). The union of Côte des Blancs and Montagne de Reims brings vibrant crunch and supple body in equal measure. Grilled-toast reduction adds layers of complexity to a core of white peach, preserved lemon and spice. Lees age has built layers of honey biscuits and candied almonds. Six grams represents the lowest dosage in the range, and it's spot on for the lively acidity of 2008. The finish holds good persistence, structured with fine salt minerality and balanced acidity.

Armand de Brignac Blanc de Noirs Assemblage One NV $$$$$

93 points • 2009 base vintage • Disgorged 2015 • Tasted in Champagne

100% Montagne de Reims pinot noir; 2008 and 2006 reserves; only 53 bottles left of a total production of 3000; 8g/L dosage

It's refreshing to note a renaming of this cuvée in the wake of the release of the second blend, and the recognition that it's stylistically distinct; the house describes Assemblage Two as less fruity and more herbal. I first tasted Assemblage One two years ago, before it was named as such. I liked it then and it's the one cuvée in the range from the same blend that I like even more now. The restrained mood of northern Montagne de Reims pinot has fully transformed, its pale straw hue graduating to a full straw with gold tints, and its crunchy red apple and pear stepping up to nothing short of deep black fruits of plums, mirabelles, cherries, blackberries, even plum liqueur, crème de cassis and plum jam. It's layered with mixed spice, anise and sarsaparilla, even high-cocoa dark chocolate, personifying the full depth and character of this beguiling grape. The finish is full and rich, yet for all of its proportions it upholds freshness and poise, carrying with excellent length and balanced acidity and dosage.

Armand de Brignac Demi-Sec NV $$$$$

89 points • 2012 base vintage • Tasted in Champagne

40% chardonnay, 40% pinot, 20% meunier; 2010 and 2009 reserves; an older blend of Gold with 33g/L dosage

Claimed to be the only prestige demi-sec, this is Brut Gold with more than three times the sugar, and it certainly shows. Boiled sweets and honey collide with bruised apple and grilled pineapple in a confected style of jelly fruits and mixed spice. Already a full straw hue with gold tints, a deep colour for its age, it concludes short and simple with a little phenolic grip.

AYALA

(Eye-yah-lah)

---

2 BOULEVARD DU NORD 51160 AŸ
www.champagne-ayala.fr

Big changes are at hand at Ayala, returning to the grand scale of its glory days of a century ago as sales have mushroomed a massive two-and-a-half times in just a decade. A youthful enthusiasm is breathing through the grand, historic premises of Château d'Aÿ. The house that had been left sleeping until it was purchased by Bollinger in 2005 is now wide awake, and its elegant, chardonnay-charged cuvées have been refreshed.

In 2011, Ayala assistant chef de cave and former Bollinger quality manager Caroline Latrive was appointed chef de cave at the age of 36. A year later, former Bollinger chief administrative officer, Hadrien Mouflard, was appointed managing director of Ayala at the age of 32. In the meantime, the production facilities of the house were modernised in 2007 with the purchase of new, small 25–100hL temperature-controlled vats.

'For me, it is a big change,' Mouflard explained when I visited. 'We need to capitalise on 150 years of great heritage and history of the house and to translate this into a contemporary style and feel, with the energy and the freedom to innovate.' This means reinventing the house with new packaging and a wine style to differentiate it from Bollinger and other houses.

Labels were changed to stately black, the style of the house a century ago, but the big changes at Ayala go much deeper, boring to the core of the house style. 'Our objective was not to change the style but to make it more precise,' Latrive outlined.

To distinguish it from the pinot-dominant style of Bollinger, the percentage of chardonnay in the key wine of the house, Ayala Brut Majeur, was raised from 25–30% to more than 40%. In an attempt to emphasise freshness, elegance and balance, average dosage levels were lowered from 11g/L of sweetness to just 7g/L.

And, again in contrast to its stablemate, every cuvée is vinified in stainless steel tanks, in a quest for minerality, purity of fruit expression and freshness.

'Elegance, purity, freshness and precision are our goals,' Latrive states succinctly. 'It is important for us to have a style that complements Bollinger, though not completely different.' To achieve this, she believes that a focus on every step of vinification is crucial.

'I am looking for an equilibrium, and to use black grapes to improve the expression of chardonnay,' she explains. 'Pinot noir for structure, though not exclusively grand cru, as I don't need a very powerful expression.' She favours villages like Les Riceys for their fruity expression and elegance without strong structure.

Ayala sources from more than 50 growers and some 100 hectares. Its own holdings comprise 20 hectares (predominantly in the Vallée de la Marne, one hectare in Chouilly and a tiny plot in Le Mesnil-sur-Oger), having grown from less than five hectares in recent years, though such small holdings are somewhat misleading, as it continues to access fruit from the original 40 hectares retained by its previous owners. It is also in the fortunate position of sharing vineyard sources with Bollinger – an easy share, thanks to Ayala's strong reliance on chardonnay.

Ayala is a medium-sized house on a tremendous growth trajectory, exploding from annual sales of 400,000 bottles in 2007 and 600,000 in 2012 to just over 1 million in 2017, three years ahead of its 2020 target to equal its production of a century ago. At the same time, the range was streamlined from nine cuvées to six. Going forward, its aspiration is not to grow further in size, but in value. 'It is so important for us to improve and continue our evolution,' states Latrive, who is experimenting with such options as egg fermenters.

The big question for Ayala now is how to raise quality in the aftermath of such frenetic growth. Brut Majeur has always wobbled a little from one release to the next, dependent upon its seasons, and it has dipped a little at more than double the volume today of what it was a decade ago.

Ayala's growth has been furnished primarily through increasing its grower partners, and it aspires to add an additional 3–5 hectares of chardonnay to its supply each year. 'It would have been much more difficult to source more grapes alone than it has been with Bollinger,' Mouflard discloses. 'It is difficult to source grand cru pinot, and especially chardonnay.'

There are currently between 3 and 4 million bottles in its 2.5 kilometres of cellars, 25 metres under Aÿ, where non-vintage wines spend 30 months on lees, vintage wines six years, and prestige wines up to ten. Perle d'Ayala wines are aged under natural cork, said to produce a wine more resilient to the effects of oxygen during ageing. As with Bollinger, this necessitates hand disgorgement, and every bottle must be checked for taint. All wines undergo full malolactic fermentation. Everything is done on site at Ayala, all the way to shipping the bottles, by a small team of 20, of average age under 35.

The house constructed a new cuverie in 2007, boasting 100 small tanks to permit vinification of separate parcels. In November 2017 it completed an extension, including another 30 thermoregulated tanks to facilitate increased production, with a total capacity today of 1.2 million bottles. It proved to be fortuitously timed for the record-volume 2018 harvest.

Ayala's long history with dry wines began in 1870, just a decade after the house was founded, with the release of a champagne of 22g/L residual (in a market of typically 100–150g/L). The house claims to have produced the first zero-dosage champagne (in contention with Perrier-Jouët). However, Ayala's success with this style is uncontested, with its Brut Nature Zero Dosage finding tremendous popularity by the glass in London.

Ayala's noble practice of printing the disgorgement date on the back of each bottle gives us all a chance to identify a fresh disgorgement – an opportunity precious few champagne houses deliver. Its new website boasts particularly informative data sheets for every cuvée.

AYALA BRUT MAJEUR NV $$

90 points • 2014 BASE VINTAGE • TASTED IN CHAMPAGNE
90 points • 2013 BASE VINTAGE • DISGORGED SEPTEMBER 2017 • TASTED IN AUSTRALIA

40% chardonnay, 40% pinot, 20% meunier; 100 ferments from 60 villages; 25% reserves from the two years prior; full malolactic fermentation; aged 3 years on lees; 7g/L dosage; 84,000 bottles

True to its aspiration of elegance, this is a clean and fresh Ayala bathed in white fruits of apple, pear and grapefruit, accented with the brioche and biscuity complexity of three years lees age. It culminates in a finish defined by the focused elegance of chardonnay, with a little bitter almond firmness from dry extract lending a touch of grip. Dosage is well integrated, making for a fresh and lively apéritif style, showcasing the fine, salty chalk minerality of the Côte des Blancs.

AYALA BRUT NATURE NV $$

90 points • 2012 BASE • DISGORGED APRIL 2016 • TASTED IN CHAMPAGNE AND AUSTRALIA

40% chardonnay, 40% pinot, 20% meunier; 2011 and 2010 reserves; Brut Majeur with at least one more year on lees, but more often two; aged four years on lees; zero dosage

I tend to prefer the low-dosage Brut Majeur to the no-dosage incarnation, which often shows less freshness, particularly accentuated in this older disgorgement after three years on lees and more than two years on cork. It's predictably a particularly toasty style by virtue of its maturity, laced with ginger, spice and almost smoky complexity. Grapefruit, lemon and crunchy pear uphold their focus and tension, particularly in the bottle tasted at the house. It's a dry and taut and tightly coiled style with some phenolic bitter grip on a structured finish of focused acidity and heightened chalk minerality.

Ayala Rosé Majeur Brut NV $$

89 points • 2014 base vintage • Tasted in Champagne

50% chardonnay, 40% pinot, 10% meunier; 25% 2012 and 2013 reserves; 6% red wine made by Bollinger; 7g/L dosage; a little under 100,000 bottles

Latrive's ambition is a rosé for summer, not autumn or winter — a wine of freshness, lightness and chalk texture, not vinous or tannic, with the minerality and character of chardonnay, 'a very white expression of red fruits'. She achieves her elegant aspiration in a gorgeous, bright salmon-pink hue, subtle apple and pear fruit and notes of pomegranate. Its refined purity is marked by a biscuity, dry-extract note than lends astringency to the finish.

Ayala Le Blanc de Blancs 2012 $$$

92 points • Disgorged February 2018 • Tasted in Champagne

100% Côte des Blancs chardonnay from Le Mesnil-sur-Oger, Chouilly and Cramant; a selection of the best villages each season; only made in the best years; aged 5 years on lees; classy new bottle and label; 6g/L dosage

I was privileged to be one of the first to taste Latrive's first Blanc de Blancs Vintage as chef de cave, considered by managing director Hadrian Mouflard to be the flagship of the new Ayala. Latrive's favourite cuvée is a focused and tense style in its newly disgorged state, energised by the pizzazz of lime and lemon fruit, with a linear and straight palate of fine chalk minerality that epitomises three of the Côte des Blancs' great grand crus. It opens with a hint of grilled-toast reduction, notes of white pepper and even a hint of grass. A taut style that will benefit from time in the cellar to open, expand and blossom.

Ayala Blanc de Blancs 2010 $$$

93 points • Disgorged January 2017 • Tasted in Champagne and Australia

100% Côte des Blancs chardonnay from Chouilly for diversity of expression, Cramant for minerality, Oiry for chalk minerality and elegant white fruits, and Vertus for floral and vegetal complexity; aged 6–7 years on lees; 6g/L dosage

The aspiration of this cuvée is to tell the story of the great vintages on the Côte des Blancs, and the crus change each season accordingly. The generosity of four of the more expensive crus of the Côte des Blancs is well focused by the elegance of Ayala in this season of good acid presence. It's a pretty and elegant style that captures the refined mood of the house in pear, apple, lemon and grapefruit, even a note of succulent depth of mirabelle plums. Beautiful struck-flint and grilled-toast reductive complexity and a hint of vanilla nougat add subtle character to its elegant fruit. Six years on lees has built gentle toasted brioche and roast almond complexity, and a creamy, silky texture. Finely structured, salty chalk minerality and subtle phenolic grip work together harmoniously with low dosage, holding an even finish of focus and poise. A pretty and refined result for 2010. I tasted it on three separate occasions and it continues to improve with time on cork. Latrive rejected one bottle (lightstruck).

Ayala Cuvée Perle d'Ayala Brut Millésimé 2006 $$$$

93 points • Tasted in Champagne

80% chardonnay, 20% pinot; Avize, Chouilly and Oger chardonnay and Aÿ pinot noir; aged on cork; hand riddled; only made in the best years; just a few thousand bottles produced

Ayala's flagship is a classic expression of the powerful 2006 season, interpreted through the voice of four legendary grand crus. Generous vanilla cream heralds a style of succulent white peach fruit and layers of biscuity complexity. The generosity of the year and the complexity of bottle age rise in unison on a long and silky palate, making for a vintage ready to delight right away.

BARON-FUENTÉ

(Bah-roh Foo-en-teh)

---

21 AVENUE FERNAND DROUET 02310 CHARLY-SUR-MARNE
https://baronfuente.com

CHAMPAGNE
BARON-FUENTÉ

The Baron family has owned vineyards in Charly-sur-Marne in the western Vallée de la Marne beyond Château-Thierry since the 17th century. Vineyard holdings have expanded over the past half century to an impressive family estate of 38 hectares in the surrounding villages, supplemented by purchased fruit to service an extensive portfolio of 14 labels. Meunier is naturally the focus here, although chardonnay also plays a strong role in most blends. To uphold freshness, fermentation takes place at 16°C in thermoregulated stainless steel tanks, and malolactic fermentation is run to completion. Non-vintage cuvées are aged three years on lees and vintage cuvées up to seven, making for a stock of 5 million bottles in climate-controlled warehouses.

BARON-FUENTE MILLÉSIME BRUT 2008 $

91 points • TASTED IN CHAMPAGNE

45% chardonnay, 15% pinot, 40% meunier; Charly-sur-Marne; aged 7 years on lees

A contrast between the strawberry fruits of Vallée de la Marne meunier, the tension of vibrant 2008 acidity and the toasty complexity of seven years lees age, this is a complex vintage champagne ready to drink now. Acid and dosage find even balance on a long finish.

BEAU JOIE

(Boh Zhowha)

6 RUE DE LA CÔTÉ LEGRIS 51200 ÉPERNAY
www.beaujoiechampagne.com

Clad in the USA with patented armour of 100% recycled copper, Beau Joie is the brand of Toast Spirits LLC in Las Vegas. An annual production claimed to be 1 million bottles is made by Charles Ellner in Épernay, sourced from 70% estate vines and 30% purchased fruit, mostly from the Vallée de la Marne and Sézanne. The asking prices are not inconsiderable, though hard acidity, underripeness and unhealthy fruit mar the style.

BEAU JOIE SPECIAL CUVÉE BRUT NV $$$$

85 points • TASTED IN AUSTRALIA

40% chardonnay, 60% pinot; 4 years on lees; zero dosage

Underripe notes of green coffee bean make for a tense and dry style, with the earthy notes of unclean fruit amplified by zero dosage. It's dusty and biscuity, with hard acidity.

BEAU JOIE SPECIAL CUVÉE BRUT ROSÉ NV $$$$

87 points • TASTED IN AUSTRALIA

50% chardonnay, 50% pinot; 3 years on lees; fermented in stainless steel; 3.8g/L dosage

A bright, medium salmon hue and aromas and flavours of strawberries herald a fruity rosé of tense, firm acidity and bitter tannin grip. It's assertive, short and surprisingly candied for a low dosage of 3.8g/L.

BEAU JOIE SPECIAL CUVÉE SUGAR KING DEMI-SEC NV $$$$

83 points • TASTED IN AUSTRALIA

30% chardonnay, 50% pinot, 20% meunier; fermented in stainless steel; aged 4 years on lees; 33g/L dosage

A grubby, dusty and earthy style of candied sweetness, hard phenolic grip and a short finish, lacking in fruit hygiene and integrity. The name says it all, really.

BENOÎT LAHAYE

(Bur-nwah La-ay)

---

33 RUE JEANNE D'ARC 51150 BOUZY

A BOUZY

BENOÎT LAHAYE
CHAMPAGNE
GRAND CRU

*O*nly the most daring and fastidious growers practise a certified biodynamic regime in a climate as erratic as Champagne's. Benoît Lahaye is among the more thoughtful of these, an advocate of natural winegrowing from the beginning. His champagnes are a testimony to ripe fruit and intuitive practice in the vineyard and cuverie: powerful, exuberant and characterful wines of creamy mouthfeel, yet never heavy.

After taking responsibility for the family estate in 1993, Benoît ceased systematic herbicides the very next year and progressively introduced cover crops to encourage competition and prevent erosion. He achieved full organic certification in 2007, and biodynamic in 2010, but didn't stop there, attempting to reduce soil compaction by introducing his Burgundy horse, named Tamise, to work the vines. He thanks such techniques for higher ripeness and natural acid retention.

In the heart of the pinot noir epicentre of Bouzy, Lahaye's 4.8-hectare estate is planted to 88% pinot noir: three hectares in Bouzy, one next door in Ambonnay, and tiny parcels in Tauxières-Mutry and Vertus. Vine age is impressive, infusing a fantastic mineral expression in his cuvées, even as young *vins clairs*. A ripe style produced by full maturity in the vineyard is his aspiration, and he notes that everyone in Vertus except Pierre Larmandier and Pascal Doquet finish harvest before he begins. It has only been since 1996 that Lahaye has bottled his own champagnes, today producing just 50,000 bottles annually.

Lahaye's natural, minimalist, intuitive approach extends to the cellar. Since 2012, all base wines have been fermented in 205-litre barriques of between new and 15 years of age, though he emphasises that his is not an oxidative style, preferring to leave oxidative development to occur in the bottle. He is experimenting with new small tanks, 200-litre egg fermenters for red wines, and has been pleased with 300-litre Tuscan amphorae for enhancing fruit and mineral expression in rosé.

Natural yeasts are used for every ferment, with malolactic fermentation blocked or allowed, according to the parcel and the season. Vintage wines are aged under cork or crown seal, with corks favoured for more structured seasons, and crown seals for more expansive vintages. Lahaye has progressively decreased dosage, with Brut NV released as both Brut and Brut Nature.

'I prefer to work in the vineyard, so I am automating the cellar as much as I can, to make more time to work in the vines,' he told me. This hasn't always been smooth: he lost 500 bottles, almost one-third of the production, of an old-vine cuvée, when the basket was dropped by his new gyropalette. He built a new cellar for barrels in 2013, with an air pump for natural cooling, and installed a new automatic disgorgement machine in 2015.

Lahaye has used full malolactic fermentation since 2008 to enhance complexity and permit the reduction of sulphur as a preservative. Some parcels are made without sulphur in the right seasons. His attention to detail extends to his labels, with disgorgement date, dosage and assemblage on the back of every cuvée.

Benoît Lahaye Blanc de Noirs Extra Brut NV $$

92 points • Disgorged November 2017 • Tasted in Champagne

100% pinot noir, 80% Bouzy and 20% Tauxières-Mutry for mineral strictness; vines planted in 1960, 1980 and 1990; 80% fermented in oak barrels; at least 24 months on lees; 5g/L dosage; 8000 bottles

The exuberance of Bouzy glows in a full straw hue with a not insubstantial hint of blush. Lahaye's aspiration here is richness and minerality, and the wine delivers on both fronts emphatically. It oozes with red cherries, red berry compote and fruit cake, accented with a more savoury mood in this disgorgement, hinting at walnut and even a note of mustard seed. Such fleshy exuberance commands structural support, which it offers abundantly in vibrant acid line, finely textured minerality and excellent length. This is a distinctive, characterful and crafted blanc de noirs that proclaims the magnitude of Bouzy without the heaviness that this village can sometimes exude.

Benoît Lahaye and his vineyard worker, Tamise

BÉRÊCHE & FILS

(Bair-aysh e Feess)

7/10

LE CRAON DE LUDES 51500 LUDES
https://bereche.com

GRAND VIN DE CHAMPAGNE

Bérêche & Fils

PROPRIÉTAIRES DE VIGNES

Young brothers Raphaël and Vincent Bérêche exemplify an enthusiastic and talented new generation that is transforming some of Champagne's smaller, longstanding estates. Working alongside their father, Jean-Pierre, the brothers represent the fifth generation of the family to grow and make champagnes with a very real sense of purity and craftsmanship. They are rightly celebrated among the leading minds of Champagne's young generation, and their extensive range of current cuvées is proof of their talent. Theirs are intelligent and perceptive minds, not afraid to change and adapt, reflected resoundingly in an ever more refined house style.

While many would uphold organic or biodynamic certification as the holy grail of viticulture, Champagne's tumultuous climate makes such ideals in many sites infeasible at best. After many visits to Bérêche's cellars on the edge of the forest above Craon de Ludes, I have been left with the overwhelming impression that if there is any philosophy in force in the vines and wines of Bérêche it is one of intuitive sensitivity, agile adaptability and good sense.

'We take a bit of this and a bit of that,' Raphaël declares unassumingly. 'We work in an organic way, but if there is too much rain in July and disease breaks out, we use a systemic chemical and then continue with our organic approach.' He's the first to admit Champagne is a difficult place to attempt to control everything, particularly in an estate as far-flung as this.

Since 1950, Bérêche's holdings have grown from just 2.5 hectares in Ludes to a total of 9.5 hectares, predominantly in Ludes, Ormes west of Reims, extending as far as Mareuil-le-Port in the Vallée de la Marne, and little holdings in nearby Mailly-Champagne, and Trépail in the eastern Montagne de Reims.

Raphaël emphasises the importance of managing all the vines themselves, to control yields. A modest production of 85,000 bottles from 9.5 hectares of mature vines averaging 38 years of age reflects particularly low yields. 'One problem of Champagne is that the yields are sometimes too high,' he admits. His brother Vincent has managed the vineyards since 2008, achieving balanced vines and fully mature fruit by maintaining yields of just 60–65hL/hectare – less than two-thirds the regional average. 'If we have higher yields, we need to put more products on the vines and there is a greater risk of disease,' Raphaël explains. 'It's like me: if I ate at [nearby Michelin-starred restaurant] Le Grand Cerf every day I would die in two weeks!'

Bérêche encourages balance in his vines through spontaneous grass grown in the mid-rows. Herbicide use has been eliminated since Raphaël began in 2004. He believes this is the most important treatment to avoid, for the sake of the pH and acidity of the finished wines.

Biodynamics has been trialled since 2007 on a three-hectare plot in front of the house, as a test for the whole estate, but Raphaël admits that it's easier to manage nearby than 36 kilometres away in Mareuil-le-Port. 'We are just nine people and 9.5 hectares, so it's very important that we don't lose our crop!' he says.

Bérêche's simple and natural approach in the vineyard carries into the cellar, where labour-intensive, traditional techniques are favoured, from pressing and first fermentation to disgorgement. The brothers visit the vineyards three or four times to choose the right moment to harvest, and pickers are paid by the hour, not by the kilogram, to encourage stringent selection. Everything is pressed at the estate in Craon de Ludes. When I visited one Sunday morning two-thirds of the way through vintage 2014, I found Raphaël had been working until 2am and was at the press again by 7.30. He is hard-working, reflective and intuitive in responding to the seasons. While long, slow, natural primary fermentations are the goal, if the ferments run too long, they are energised with commercial yeasts. He likes the idea of yeasts from the domaine and the grape, but admits they're really derived from the cellar and barrels.

Fermentation is equally divided between oak barrels and small stainless steel tanks, which have replaced old enamel-lined concrete tanks. Slightly larger and older 300-litre Burgundy barrels are preferred to Champagne's traditional 205-litre barrels, as their more subtle influence on the wine maintains fruit precision. Vinification in barrels has increased to 80%.

Bérêche purchased white Burgundy barrels from Pierre-Yves Colin-Morey in Chassagne in the past, but saw too much influence of Chasssagne, so now buys new barrels and seasons them by fermenting tailles in the first year. Red wine barrels are sourced from Domaine de la Romanée-Conti, no less.

Wines are matured for extended periods in both barrels and tanks prior to bottling. Ageing on lees with a little bâtonnage allows the wines to become slightly reductive, providing protection from oxidation, even with only very small additions of sulphur dioxide. A low-sulphur regime is a priority, with small additions to maintain freshness only on the press and after fermentation, and none at bottling or disgorgement. Bérêche prizes low pH, dissolved carbon dioxide gas and sugar in the dosage ahead of sulphur dioxide for preserving freshness. This seems to work most of the time, although funky barrel notes do appear in some cuvées. To his credit, Raphaël has recognised when sulphur levels are too low and corrected in subsequent releases.

Even with such low sulphur levels, Bérêche has no trouble blocking malolactic fermentation in around 70% of his ferments, thanks to very cold (8°C) cellars at the top of Craon de Ludes. 'Historically, Champagne did not have malolactic fermentation,' Raphaël points out. 'This was only introduced in the 1980s, to make it easier to drink, and to reduce the time in the cellar.' But for him malolactic is not a key question. 'The terroir is strong and my focus is on terroir definition.'

Bérêche is working to increase the time each cuvée is aged, with extended cellar space under the house to increase capacity for reserve wines. With the exception of the entry Brut NV and Extra Brut NV, all cuvées are aged on cork instead of crown seal, to increase oxygen interaction and produce a softer, creamier bead and a more open, characterful and complex wine, with a more logical coherence of nose and palate.

Cork ageing necessitates hand disgorgement, and it takes two people to taste and disgorge 1200 bottles a day. A traditional *liqueur d'expédition* is used in place of grape concentrate, at very low levels of dosage, so as to faithfully preserve tension and minerality in the wines. Raphaël highlights that even 2–3g/L of dosage is important for ageing, and does not regard his Extra Brut NV as a style to age for more than five years. Back labels of all cuvées are impressively informative, disclosing dosage, disgorgement date and base vintage. A very classy website discloses more detail again. The number of bottles produced has recently been added to the front label of each cuvée.

Bérêche relinquished its Récoltant-Manipulant status in favour of Négociant-Manipulant, so as to open up the opportunity to purchase more vineyards and buy from growers. 'We wanted to buy a 0.3 hectare plot in Mailly-Champagne, but the authorities only permitted us to buy half because they said we were too big,' Raphaël explains. Champagne's counterintuitive regulations strike again! Their NM status has opened up the opportunity to selectively purchase single-vineyard fruit for new cuvées (not to adapt existing blends) as well as tiny quantities of mature champagnes *sur latte* from top terroirs to sell under their Raphaël et Vincent Bérêche label. In the first year, they assessed 30 different champagnes in this way and selected three, for which they managed disgorgement and dosage. This fleeting pursuit was short-lived, and they have recently discontinued buying *sur latte,* to focus on crafting their own wines from their five villages of estate vines and growers in Rilly-la-Montagne, Ambonnay, Aÿ and Cramant. This is as it should be. Rilly-la-Montagne has been released as its own single-site cuvée, with Mailly-Champagne, Ambonnay, Aÿ and ultimately Cramant to follow. If the calibre of Rilly is any indication, Bérêche's négociant wines are worthy of attention, and I await the arrival of his grand crus with great anticipation. 'I am very lucky to have access to four of the best grand crus, and I don't want more than this,' he discloses. His aim is to release a vintage cuvée from each in every year, pending hail and frost.

In an age when champagne markets religiously celebrate Récoltant-Manipulant status, such relinquishment, like that of De Sousa, Jérôme Prévost and André Clouet at around the same time, is testimony to the higher esteem in which this is upheld outside of Champagne than it is within. Like their approach in the vineyard and the cellar, Raphaël and Vincent are driven to change and adapt for the betterment of their cuvées, rather than subscribing to dogmatic regimes.

The wines of Bérêche are vinous champagnes of dry complexity. Even as young vins clairs, they are generously expressive of both ripe fruit intensity and the mineral signature of their sites. Raphaël and Vincent have succeeded in progressively toning the assertive temperament of malic acidity, barrel fermentation and low dosage, making for champagnes that continue to keep fanatics enthralled.

BÉRÊCHE & FILS BRUT RÉSERVE NV $$

94 points • 2015 BASE VINTAGE • DISGORGED OCTOBER 2017 • TASTED IN CHAMPAGNE

35% chardonnay, 30% pinot, 35% meunier; 35% reserves; half premier crus; average vine age 40+ years; fermented in barrels and small tanks; 10% tailles aged for 2 years before blending to reduce vegetal notes and austerity; aged on lees 24–36 months; 65,000 bottles, 2500 magnums, 300 jéroboams; 7g/L dosage

Bérêche admits that this is his most difficult wine to make, with an aspiration of richness, finesse, chalk minerality, creamy texture and a clean, bright finish. He is working on its refinement though focusing on the date of picking, increasing vinification in barrel, and aiming to age on lees as long as his special cuvées. The result is brilliantly characterful for the lead cuvée of the house, and to sustain such consistency and impeccable fruit integrity even with a majority of barrel fermentation is a feat few estates as small as this can pull off. The current release is more extroverted and flamboyant than ever, thanks to the ripe and expressive 2015 base vintage springing to life in a full straw hue with a salmon tint, overflowing into a palate brimming with orange rind, strawberry hull and layers of spice. It holds excellent persistence, fullness and presence, while lingering very long with well-focused malic acidity, underlined by the almond notes of at least two years lees age. A characterful and crafted wine of presence, poise and class that rises to the character and complexity of a powerful season, yet at every moment upholding seamless cohesion.

BÉRÊCHE & FILS RIVE GAUCHE 2014 $$$

89 points • DISGORGED NOVEMBER 2017 • TASTED IN CHAMPAGNE

100% Mareuil-le-Port meunier, formerly one parcel and now two (though production volume has only increased 10%); planted in 1969 on cold soil with north exposure, hence it holds freshness; 100% vinified in 350-litre barrels of between 1 and 6 years of age; aged 3 years on lees; no malolactic fermentation; 3g/L dosage; 4197 bottles

More than one-third of Bérêche's estate holdings reside in chardonnay and meunier 36 kilometres from the house in Mareuil-le-Port on the left bank (*rive gauche*) of the Vallée de la Marne. Its limestone clay soils are expressed in salty mineral texture, heightened by the taut focus of malic acidity drawing out a finish of excellent persistence. Regrettably, oak dominates its balance much more in 2014 than it ever has before, with toasty woody flavours, charcuterie barrel fermentation notes and the firm, splintery grip of oak tannins.

BÉRÊCHE & FILS LES BEAUX REGARDS LUDES PREMIER CRU 2014 $$$

90 points • DISGORGED JANUARY 2018 • TASTED IN CHAMPAGNE

100% Ludes chardonnay; formerly single parcel, now two on chalky soils close to the village; average vine age 50 years; picked ripe at 11–11.3 baumé; fermented in oak barrels; aged 3 years on lees under cork; no malolactic fermentation; 3g/L dosage; 3950 bottles

This cuvée is always a jousting contest between tense, tart, zesty lemon and grapefruit and the charcuterie and spice of barrel fermentation, impaled by the structure of high-tensile malic acidity and pronounced, fine chalk minerality. Fruit ripeness is the key for this tussle, bringing ripe balance to its malic cut and rich character of loquat and nashi pear. Give it some years to find its place.

BÉRÊCHE & FILS CAMPANIA REMENSIS ROSÉ 2014 $$$

93 points • DISGORGED MARCH 2018 • TASTED IN CHAMPAGNE

30% chardonnay, 60% pinot, 5% meunier, 5% Coteaux Champenois rouge 2014; single-parcel Les Montées in Ormes on the Petite Montagne de Reims on more sandy soils; fermented in oak barrels; aged 3 years on lees; 5650 bottles; 3g/L dosage

This is a very restrained rosé, more about lovely texture and structure than it is about fragrance, with a creaminess amplified by barrel fermentation and ageing on lees under cork. Raphaël is critical of saignée rosé for its heaviness, instead crafting this as a blend with a very small addition of 5% red wine. Its colour is a pretty pale salmon hue, much paler than in the past, likely a credit to his method of blending in black glasses to judge the addition of red wine on nose and palate rather than colour. The result is a rosé of elegance, poise and focused strawberry hull and white cherry fruit. Raphaël suggests its lingering personality of pinot's red cherry fruits is reinforced by ageing under cork. Tight, bright malic acidity and low dosage are impressive in their ability to accentuate the subtle chalky mineral texture of Ormes.

BÉRÊCHE & FILS RILLY-LA-MONTAGNE 2014 $$$$

93 points • DISGORGED MARCH 2018 • TASTED IN CHAMPAGNE

100% pinot from single-site Les Sablons, atop the hill in Rilly-la-Montagne, with east exposure and very stony soil with a touch of sand, silex and stone; picked at full ripeness of 11.3 baumé; vinified in oak barrels; no malolactic fermentation; aged 3 years on lees; 3g/L dosage

This cuvée makes a grand statement of the calibre of Bérêche's négociant wines and bodes great things for the arrival of his grand crus in years to come. Rilly-la-Montagne's predominantly north-facing slopes are home to delicate pinot noir, but this second release from a trusted grower in this premier cru captures an unusual presence and definition of pinot, perhaps thanks to its easterly exposure. A beautiful display of red apple, strawberry hull and spice is underlined by the lovely, fine chalk mineral presence of the northern slopes of the Montagne de Reims. Malic acidity infuses vibrancy, lift and endurance, and will appreciate time to soften. A cuvée of character and poise.

BÉRÊCHE & FILS LE CRAN LUDES PREMIER CRU 2010 $$$$

95 points • DISGORGED DECEMBER 2017 • TASTED IN CHAMPAGNE

50% chardonnay, 50% pinot from two plots on very thin soils over chalk on the crest of Ludes, the pinot facing east and the chardonnay facing west to catch the afternoon sun; planted 1965-1969 by Raphaël and Vincent's grandfather; vinified in barrels; no malolactic fermentation; aged on lees 8 years; 3g/L dosage; 3870 bottles, 245 magnums

Bérêche has been refining the ripeness, oak and sulphur of this cuvée for seven vintages. The scintillating 2008 proved his efforts – his finest work yet – and the great 2010 confirms it, evidence of the heights of his terroirs and his methods even in a lesser season (though he discloses that he loves this classic vintage). A truly great 2010 by any measure, uniting the morello cherries and strawberry hull of pinot noir with the pear and lemon of chardonnay, bolstering the accord with the toasty complexity and creamy texture of long lees age. The chalk minerality tapped by these old vines on thin soils melds harmoniously with pronounced malic acidity on the finish. Such proximity to the chalk produces the lowest pH (highest acidity) in the winery. For all of its tension, the ripe fruit aspiration of the house creates wonderful presence and confidence which lingers very long. Patience.

BERNARD REMY

(Behr-nah Reh-mee)

19 RUE DES AUGES 51120 ALLEMANT
www.champagnebernardremy.com

Bernard Remy is a small house in Allemant on the edge of Sézanne, which is a central location from which to source from the far-flung extremes of Champagne in all directions: locally from the Sézannais, chardonnay north from the Côte des Blancs and east from Vitry-le-François, pinot noir south from the Aube and meunier north from the Vallée de la Marne. Since Bernard Remy bought his first vines in 1968, the house has grown to 11 hectares of estate vines, supplemented with fruit sourced from growers. Bernard built his winery in 1983 and expanded to meet growing production in 1990, 1997 and 2008, when his son Rudy took command of the house. Their cuvées are simple, rustic and sweet.

BERNARD REMY CARTE BLANCHE NV $

83 points • TASTED IN AUSTRALIA

35% chardonnay, 60% pinot, 5% meunier from Allemant; aged 2 years on lees; no oak; 10g/L dosage; DIAM

Built around pinot noir from Allemant in the Sézanne, this is a style of apple and pear fruit, sadly troubled by the mushroom notes of unhealthy fruit, rendering the finish coarse and bitter. A high dosage adds candied sweetness, without resolving its tribulations.

BERNARD REMY BLANC DE BLANCS BRUT NV $$

89 points • TASTED IN AUSTRALIA

100% chardonnay; aged 3 years on lees; no oak; 10g/L dosage; DIAM

A synergy between the apple and pear of chardonnay, the grainy, firm mineral structure of the Sézanne and more biscuity, brioche complexity than one might expect for three years lees age. It accents this interplay with a well-gauged struck-flint edge of reductive complexity. Dosage of 10g/L is a touch more than it needs, rendering the finish a little candied. The result is an engaging, characterful and accurate expression of Sézanne chardonnay, if a little rustic.

BERNARD REMY GRAND CRU NV $$

90 points • TASTED IN AUSTRALIA

100% chardonnay from Le Mesnil-sur-Oger; aged 5 years on lees; no oak; 10g/L dosage; DIAM

The fine, chalk minerality of Le Mesnil-sur-Oger is a profound contrast to the grainy structure of Sézanne in Bernard Remy's other cuvées. There is class and finesse here, backed by the creamy texture and vanilla custard and ginger cake complexity of five years of lees age, sadly disrupted by a heavy-handed 10g/L dosage, which renders the finish sugary and simplistic.

Épernay, summer 2014

Besserat de Bellefon

(Bess-rah der Bell-foh)

22 Rue Maurice Cerveaux 51200 Épernay
www.besseratdebellefon.com

CHAMPAGNE
BESSERAT DE BELLEFON
1843

A medium-sized house in Épernay under the banner of the Lanson-BCC group, Besserat de Bellefon produces 1.3 million bottles annually from 25 hectares of estate vineyards situated mainly in the Vallée de la Marne, substantially supplemented with supply from some 100 growers. The house style is distinctive in a lower pressure of 4.5 atmospheres (compared with 6 in most champagnes), but more importantly in a complete absence of malolactic fermentation in all cuvées. The softening effect of age is consequently important, with non-vintage cuvées aged for a minimum of three years and vintage cuvées at least five years, though even this is insufficient to tame the hard malic acidity that marks the house style. This makes non-vintage blends challenging, but confidently balances warm seasons like 2006. Cédric Thiébault has been with the house since 1999 and immediately introduced DIAM across the range when he became cellar master in 2006. Disgorgement dates are printed on back labels.

BESSERAT DE BELLEFON BLEU BRUT NV $$

85 points • 2014 BASE VINTAGE • DISGORGED JULY 2018 • TASTED IN AUSTRALIA

35% chardonnay, 20% pinot, 45% meunier; around 40 crus including Le Mesnil-sur-Oger, Avize, Vertus, Bisseuil, Mareuil-sur-Aÿ, Grauves, Louvois, Cumières, Damery, Neuilly, Venteuil and Boursault; 30% solera reserves; 9g/L dosage; DIAM

Besserat's names and labels have been stripped back to racing spec, complete with nautical accents, and Bleu Brut replaces Cuvée des Moines. The style of Besserat's non-vintage entry point remains unchanged, a cuvée of power and tension, with considerable bottle-age secondary complexity of roast hazelnuts and toast. There is an underripe astringency to the 2014 base release, lending a grassy edge to the black cherry depth of meunier. Unfortunately its bitter, burnt toffee and hazelnut development has progressed well into oxidative degradation of varnishy character, quashing fruit expression. This clashes with a taut finish of firm malic acidity, engulfing dosage and concluding tense and dry, lacking fruit presence, freshness and integrity.

BESSERAT DE BELLEFON BRUT ROSÉ NV $$

86 points • 2014 BASE VINTAGE • DISGORGED FEBRUARY 2018 • TASTED IN AUSTRALIA

30% chardonnay, 30% pinot, 40% meunier; around 40 crus including Le Mesnil-sur-Oger, Avize, Vertus, Bisseuil, Mareuil-sur-Aÿ, Grauves, Louvois, Cumières, Damery, Neuilly, Venteuil, Boursault, Bouzy, Vincelles, Les Riceys; 5% reserves; 9g/L dosage; DIAM

A copper tint to a medium salmon hue announces a rosé that contrasts tangy morello cherry fruits with the signature sabre of searing Besserat malic acidity, and a developed note of olive tapenade and onion (which is perhaps a consequence of reduction, or perhaps of lightstruck in its clear bottle?).

BESSERAT DE BELLEFON BLANC DE BLANCS NV $$$

84 points • DISGORGED JUNE 2018 • TASTED IN AUSTRALIA

100% chardonnay from Le Mesnil-sur-Oger, Avize, Oger, Oiry, Chouilly, Cramant; 100% 2014, though not labelled as a vintage; 9g/L dosage; DIAM

2014 was not the easiest season on the Côte des Blancs, and this cuvée shows its mark in green, underripe astringency of tinned asparagus, colliding awkwardly with tense malic acidity and a touch of phenolic bitterness.

BESSERAT DE BELLEFON BLANC DE NOIRS NV $$$

90 points • DISGORGED DECEMBER 2017 • TASTED IN AUSTRALIA

100% pinot from Bouzy, Ambonnay, Verzy, Mailly; 100% 2012, though not labelled as a vintage; 6g/L dosage; DIAM

A full straw hue declares a rich and powerful blanc de noirs, brimming with the luscious presence of grand cru pinot in waves of berry compote, roast figs and dried nectarines. Lees age has introduced grand depth of roast nuts and toffee, which jostle with the stark cut of malic acidity. It holds impressive length, and its fruit and secondary complexity have found a comfortable equilibrium, which its malic sadly threatens to unsettle.

BESSERAT DE BELLEFON EXTRA BRUT NV $$$

89 points • DISGORGED OCTOBER 2015 • TASTED IN AUSTRALIA

56% chardonnay, 44% pinot; Grauves, Cuis, Cumières, Bisseuil, Tauxières, Tours-sur-Marne, Bouzy; 100% 2007, though not labelled as a vintage; 3.5g/L dosage; DIAM

There is regrettably no hint of its 12 years of maturity on the label, but this cuvée boldly declares its age in a full yellow hue with gold tints and a bouquet and palate ricocheting with grand depth of complexity. Exuberant grilled pineapple, loquats and preserved lemons lead out, wrapped in honey, layers of mixed spice and freshly baked pâtisserie. Almost four years post-disgorgement, the finish is dry and marked by a little phenolic bitterness, amplified by the searing malic acidity of the house, which has not yet found its place of calm, even at this age. Structurally, it is but a juvenile, yet its fruit is already drying out on the finish and has failed to last the distance.

Besserat de Bellefon BB 1843 MV $$$$$

85 points • 2009 base vintage • Disgorged December 2015 • Tasted in Australia

45% chardonnay, 45% pinot, 10% meunier; Oger, Chouilly, Cramant, Cumières, Festigny, Ambonnay, Mailly, Mareuil-sur-Aÿ; 50% 2008 reserves; aged one year in oak; 5g/L dosage; DIAM

The BB cuvée was launched in 2013 to commemorate the 170th anniversary of the house. At a full decade of age (including 3.5 years on cork), it's a tense and awkward style that impales green olive development with bracing malic acidity and underripe allusions of lime. The result is awkward and challenging.

Besserat de Bellefon BB1843 Brigitte Bardot NV $$$$$

86 points • Disgorged June 2018 • Tasted in Australia

56% chardonnay, 44% pinot; Le Mesnil-sur-Oger, Bisseuil, Grauves, Cumières, Mailly, Mareuil-sur-Aÿ; solera; 19g/L dosage; DIAM

A generous dose of sugar certainly tones the malic acid cut of Besserat, but it lacks the fruit integrity and expression to properly support this bold acid–sugar balancing act. The result is short and firm, with a disjoint feeling that gives the sensation that it's been manufactured rather than grown or crafted. The question of why it commands such a lofty price remains elusive.

Épernay, winter 2015

BILLECART-SALMON

(Bill-khah Sal-moh)

10/10

40 RUE CARNOT 51160 MAREUIL-SUR-AŸ
www.champagne-billecart.fr

CHAMPAGNE
**BILLECART
SALMON**

The art of crafting elegant, graceful champagne requires the most exacting skill. Sweetness, richness and breadth cover all manner of sins in champagne, but a wine in its unadorned, raw nakedness reveals even the slightest blemish for all to see. The mark of Billecart is made not by the heavy footfall of concentration, power and presence, but rather by the fairy touch of delicacy and crystal-clear fidelity. Every one of its dozen cuvées articulately speaks the house philosophy of 'respecting the integrity of the fruit, freshness and acidity'. Billecart has long held a coveted position among the top ten houses of Champagne, and confidently again this year upholds its mantle as the most elegant of them all.

On the surface, there appears little to distinguish the fruit sources of this medium-sized house in Mareuil-sur-Aÿ. Vineyard holdings are small, servicing a 2.4 million bottle annual production with just 20 hectares of estate vines (in Mareuil-sur-Aÿ and Chouilly) and more than 300 hectares of purchased fruit managed by 185 growers. How does Billecart maintain such transcendental standards in each of its cuvées?

Antoine Roland-Billecart, who manages the house with his brother François, answers this question with a refreshingly frank honesty. 'We are not very focused on marketing,' he begins in impeccable English. 'Vinification is the key for us, and all the rest is bullshit.'

Its elegant delicacy places Billecart dizzyingly high among Champagne's finest houses, but also infuses its cuvées with an inherent fragility, rendering them particularly vulnerable to imperfections in closure, transportation or storage. Without disgorgement dates indicated on bottles, it's difficult to ascertain the age of non-vintage cuvées, but be sure to ask for fresh stock that hasn't lingered on retail shelves.

Billecart's vintage wines can be coiled up tight in their youth and appreciate plenty of time to open up in large glasses.

Over many hours of visits and intensive tastings with Antoine and cellar master François Domi and their team over the past decade, an enlightening picture emerges, illuminating some 12 spheres that account for the astounding performance of Billecart-Salmon.

LONGSTANDING FAMILY MANAGEMENT
Although not exclusively owned by the family, Billecart has been under family management since it was founded in 1818. The family still lives on site, and there is a long-visioned continuity at play. In January 2019, Mathieu Roland-Billecart, seventh generation of the family, replaced his cousin François Roland-Billecart as CEO. François took the place on the board of his father Jean, now 96.

'We are very lucky that my father still joins us for every tasting,' Antoine reflects. 'He began working in wine when he was 16 and has over 70 harvests in his memory. His experience of terroir is so great that he can comment on the effect of every parcel in a blend and challenge us to consider what a wine will be like in 20 years. "This

sample won't last, and in 15 years you're going to cry!" he tells us. He has such experience that he can feel a vintage by smelling and tasting the musts, building the blend in his mind before we even taste it.'

HANDS-ON VINEYARD MANAGEMENT

'It's easy to work for a company that is searching for quality as the goal across the whole process,' François Domi says. Starting with the fruit. 'The best grapes on the best terroirs are expensive, but this is our priority.' A team of 40 local pickers is paid by the hour rather than by the kilogram to be particularly selective in the most sensitive vineyards.

Billecart's production has trebled in the past 20 years, and since that time the house has set about acquiring vineyards centred around Mareuil-sur-Aÿ and Chouilly. In 2004, the family sold a 45% share in the firm, and in so doing secured access to an additional 80 hectares of grand cru fruit.

'In seeking new growers, we are only interested in grand crus,' Antoine reveals. 'Twenty years ago we were knocking on growers' doors, but now they are knocking on ours.'

Today, the company also manages 100 hectares (and rising) under lease arrangement, taking full control, from pruning to harvest. 'This is very important,' explains Antoine, 'because it enables us to conduct the vineyard the way we want, yielding 70hL/hectare rather than 85–90, ensuring consistent ripeness and balanced concentration and acidity.'

Billecart's policy is to harvest early. 'We focus on acidity, not on alcohol,' explains Antoine, 'so we don't wait for the authorities to give the green light to start harvest!' Even with its mandate to harvest early, the house performs no chaptalisation and adds no acid: 'We work with what the grapes give us.' Ten degrees potential alcohol and 10g/L acidity is upheld as the ideal balance.

In vineyards under company control, there has been a return to a more natural way of growing vines and promoting soil health through 'Viticulture Durable en Champagne' certification, by eliminating pesticides and herbicides, and using only natural fungicides. All growers are encouraged to grow grasses in the mid-rows to limit yields. A generational approach to farming, rather than a full biodynamic regime, is the aspiration, though Clos Saint-Hilaire has been worked biodynamically for 14 years, and other estate vineyards are working towards the same regime, with five hectares of vineyards beginning biodynamic trials in 2020.

'But even in attempting biodynamics, we will keep the flexibility to intervene if required,' Antoine explains. 'The problem in Champagne is that we are the most northerly of French vineyards, which means we are very highly sensitive to oidium and mildew. And a lot of biodynamic vineyards yielded zero in 2016 and 2017, and that is not economically sustainable. The most important thing is to harvest a certain quantity of grapes.'

PARCEL SELECTION

Even at a modest 70hL/hectare, Billecart's output is tiny for an estate sourcing from 320 hectares. Antoine considers the flexibility of sourcing grapes from 185 growers to be strategic, permitting vinification of 140% of production every year, with

Le Clos Saint-Hilaire

lesser parcels sold as still wines, or declassified to Billecart's second label, Charles-le-Bel. In the disastrous 2017 harvest, a record 250,000 litres of wine was written off and sent for distillation, equivalent to one-third of the year's reserves.

'It's great to own your own vineyards, but the opportunity to be selective is something fantastic!' Antoine exclaims. Production is currently at 2.5 million bottles for Billecart (up from 1.7 million five years ago) plus 300,000 for Charles-le-Bel, with total capacity of 3 million, though with no immediate aspiration to grow further.

METICULOUS PRODUCTION REGIME

The precision of Billecart is proclaimed in a squeaky-clean winery, even during my visits at the height of vintage. 'Welcome to my kitchen!' Antoine announces as we enter the cuverie, pointing out the Brittany granite floor 'because it is very hygienic'. Each element of its meticulous production is geared towards capturing every nuance in the fruit. Billecart presses half the fruit it purchases and uses a pneumatic press for larger parcels, because it's more gentle than the traditional press. One hundred 40hL tanks and some 450 barrels maintain individual control over every one of 280 parcels. Billecart constructed a new press house in 2019, with small presses to further increase the capacity for parcel-by-parcel vinification. In 2017, a new 1.5 million litre winery was commissioned in Oiry to facilitate increasing production.

'We have to be very precise, increasing quality by being overly selective, keeping what we want and getting rid of what we don't want to keep,' explains Antoine. A massive new blending tank was commissioned in 2009 to lower the risk of oxidation and increase the consistency of the blends.

COLD SETTLING AND COOL FERMENTS

Perhaps Billecart's most revolutionary technique is its practice of double débourbage. After the standard clarification process to settle out solids, the juice is settled a second time at 3–4°C for at least 48 hours without use of enzymes. The house pioneered this technique in 1952, inspired by the brothers' maternal grandfather's experience in brewing beer. At this temperature, the coarser lees are removed without risk of oxidation, delivering pristine juice for fermentation. The process is expensive and time-consuming. 'Most of our colleagues thought we were crazy!' admits Antoine.

With increasingly warm harvests, the house is the first in Champagne to build, in 2019, a cold room to chill the grapes, with the capacity to cool 40–45 tonnes of fruit to 5°C overnight. All the grapes picked in the afternoon will be ready for cold pressing at 5am the following morning. 'Instead of chilling the musts, we will chill the grapes!' exclaims Antoine. 'We have done trials, and overnight chilling makes a big difference in acid retention in the grapes.'

The juice is then brought up to just 12–13°C (never more than 14°C) for the primary fermentation. Antoine has growers and houses tell him it's impossible for yeast to work at this temperature. At 13°C, cultured yeasts from the natural yeasts of nearby villages take 3–5 weeks, and sometimes 6 weeks, to complete fermentation (compared with just 15 days normally). Such cool, long ferments are crucial for retaining greater freshness and delicacy than a standard champagne ferment of 1 week at 20°C, particularly in a warm vintage like 2015.

Parcels then stay on lees in tank for six months, crucial for development of personality, structure and aroma. 'Our dream would be to have wine on lees in tank for years to build more structure!' Antoine says. Bâtonnage is performed in tanks post-fermentation.

SELECTIVE MALOLACTIC

Traditionally, all parcels for non-vintage blends have passed through malolactic fermentation, but for vintage wines this is dependent upon the season. In 2016 malolactic was blocked in two-thirds of the harvest, and in the warm 2018 vintage, in all parcels except some key pinot noir grand crus. For Antoine, 'respecting the style of the vintage is more important than anything else', and winemaking is adapted each year to suit. Such intuitive flexibility is a strong key to Billecart's rock-solid consistency in the wake of Champagne's tumultuous and changing environment.

Malolactic fermentation is blocked in barrels because there is a high acid conception in barrel fermentation. 'It's easier to block in tank, but advantageous to do it the hard way!' he outlines.

INCREASING USE OF OAK

When Antoine comes to work every day he asks himself what can be done to improve vinification within the house style. As a devotee of Krug Clos du Mesnil – he openly volunteers the inaugural vintage as his favourite blanc de blancs of all time – it's no surprise Billecart has increased the use of oak barrels for fermentation since 1995.

'When we first made Clos Sainte-Hilaire in 1995, we had no barrels, so just before harvest I drove a big truck to Olivier Leflaive in Meursault and brought back 25 barrels!' Antoine recounts. Fifty barrels in that year became 80 in 1997. A new barrel room now houses 500 barrels and two new large oak foudres, ranking Billecart fourth for barrels in Champagne, after Krug, Bollinger and Alfred Gratien. In 2018, the house added a spectacular new facility housing 29 new 80hL thermoregulated oak foudres for vinification.

Old barrels, having seen six or seven vintages in Burgundy, are used for the fermentation of all grand cru fruit, and bâtonnage is conducted weekly, according to taste. Barrels currently range from five to 15 years of age, though recent experimentation with oak sources has revealed that Stockinger oak from old forests in Austria has such low tannin that they are even able to ferment in new barrels. Selection of the right growths has been identified as the key to elegant oak expression. The goal at Billecart, as always, is to encourage subtle complexity rather than overt character. 'Just to add some spice and aroma,' as Antoine puts it.

LOW DOSAGE

Antoine considers a decrease in dosage over the past decade as crucial in allowing the fruit to show its full character. 'It is like make-up,' he proposes. 'You don't need it if there is no problem, and you want to show the real character of the wines.' Dosage

Antoine Roland-Billecart shows off his spectacular new foudre cellar.

levels are low: typically 8g/L in non-vintage wines, and around just 4g/L in vintage wines ('Extra Brut'). Any more sweetness might play havoc with such delicate styles.

DIFFERENT LIQUEUR FOR EACH DOSAGE

The final nuance comes at disgorgement: every cuvée has a different liqueur at Billecart. François Domi conducts many tastings with different dosages, from wines aged in barrel and those in tank, to determine which best suits each wine. A different liqueur and different dosage is used for every disgorgement, so completely different liqueurs can be chosen for the start, the middle and the end of a cuvée, typically starting with pinot and slightly higher dosage, and ending with chardonnay and lower dosage.

LONG AGEING

Billecart's non-vintage wines are aged for 3–4 years, and its millésime collection a minimum 8–10 years and sometimes much longer – Clos Saint-Hilaire 2002 was released in January 2019. Brut Réserve NV is now released after 32 months in the cellar (up from 24 months), with a goal to reach 40 months by 2022 (though this necessitates decreasing sales allocations). Such long maturation necessitates a continuous stock of 10 million bottles in Billecart's four kilometres of cellars under Mareuil-sur-Aÿ.

Billecart holds a deep collection of reserves, with at least one-third of every harvest kept in reserve, held on lees at 9°C. In addition, one-third of Brut Reserve NV is kept as reserve for the next blend. 'This is a key for consistency,' Antoine emphasises. The precision and freshness of the Billecart house style is all the more compelling in the context of such deep reserves and long ageing.

SUPERIOR CLOSURE

Finally, and crucially, all non-vintage wines except blanc de blancs have been sealed with DIAM cork since 2006. DIAM is not perfect, but it is demonstrably and consistently superior to natural cork. Billecart's Australian agent reported an immediate drop in returned bottles as soon as DIAM was introduced. Billecart has been trialling ageing of vintage wines under DIAM for more than a decade. I look forward to the day when Billecart's top wines are entrusted to a reliable closure.

THE GENIUS OF FRANÇOIS DOMI

Alongside the enthusiastic energy of Antoine Roland-Billecart, François Domi is the quietly spoken and reflective genius. He started in the lab at Billecart as an oenologist 30 years ago and describes himself today as part of the furniture. His unassuming manner means his name is never listed among Champagne's rock stars, but his greatest hits of the past two decades surely place him at the top of the charts.

In 2018, François retired as chef de cave, succeeded by Florent Nys, his capable protégé since 2005.

Billecart-Salmon Brut Réserve NV $$

94 points • 2015 BASE VINTAGE • DISGORGED 5 JUNE 2018 • 30% CHARDONNAY, 30% PINOT, 40% MEUNIER • TASTED IN AUSTRALIA

95 points • 2014 BASE VINTAGE • 38% 2013 CHARDONNAY, 20% 2012 PINOT, 42% 2014 MEUNIER • TASTED IN CHAMPAGNE

Pinot from the Montagne de Reims and the Grande Vallée de la Marne, meunier from the Vallée de la Marne and the southern slopes of Épernay; 86% grand cru, with an aim to grow to 90%; vinified in stainless steel tanks; 50-60% reserves; full malolactic fermentation; aged 32 months on lees (with a goal to reach 40 months by 2022); 8g/L dosage; dosage liqueur of 2008 chardonnay; DIAM; 1.5 million bottles (60% of production)

Billecart's enchanting Brut Réserve upholds its aspiration of lofty freshness and elegance, even in the presence of impressive levels of reserve wines, now generously more than 50% of the blend, and impressive lees age, now 32 months. This cuvée is a captivating contradiction, dressing one of Champagne's higher representations of meunier in one of the most delicate and graceful of attires.

The generous 2015 base vintage sets the stage for an especially rich Brut Réserve, leading out with the succulent strawberries, crunchy red gala apples and mixed spice of meunier and the lemon zest of chardonnay. For all of the flamboyance of the season, it upholds classic Billecart control, in a dazzling display of elegant, soft, salty, crystalline chalk minerality and understated, fragrant elegance. Lees age furnishes more impressive depth than ever of brioche, toasted almonds and gingernut biscuits, without for a moment dipping its gaze from purity and definition, concluding with fresh, bright acidity, well-integrated dosage, gentle phenolic balance, good persistence and fine chalk mineral drive. An outstanding 2015 base. The 2014 base is even more elegant and refined, magnificently backward and poised for such deep reserves and long maturation. With more fruit definition and personality than ever, it sings with wild strawberries and blood oranges, a complete champagne with every molecule of detail in the right place.

Billecart-Salmon Extra Brut NV $$

93 points • 2014 BASE VINTAGE • DISGORGED 13 FEBRUARY 2018 • TASTED IN AUSTRALIA

30% chardonnay, 30% pinot from the Montagne de Reims and the Grande Vallée de la Marne, 40% meunier from the Vallée de la Marne and the southern slopes of Épernay; 50-60% reserves; vinified in stainless steel tanks; full malolactic fermentation; aged 40 months on lees; zero dosage; DIAM

The precision of Billecart lends itself well to this style, making for one of the most refined zero-dosage champagnes, built on the same base as Brut Réserve – but crucially, not simply a zero-dosage version of the same. It's older, with an extra year on lees – 'not so it has more fat', explains Antoine, 'but so it is more rounded, with less angles'. Its age is crucial for building silky texture in this otherwise strict and abrupt style. The liqueur in the dosage is different, too, with 5mL of reserve wines contributing volume, structure and persistence.

Age has layered considerable depth of complexity in roast hazelnuts, buttered toast, nougat and toasted brioche, preserved in a brittle shell of bone-shaking purity and citrus minerality, with excellent focus and drive of vibrant lemon juice, grapefruit and crunchy pear energising a long finish. Zero dosage makes for a firm finish which would benefit from even the slightest touch of sweetness.

Billecart-Salmon Demi-Sec NV $$

91 points • 2014 BASE VINTAGE • DISGORGED 4 DECEMBER 2018 • TASTED IN AUSTRALIA

30% chardonnay, 30% pinot from the Montagne de Reims and the Grande Vallée de la Marne, 40% meunier from the Vallée de la Marne and the southern slopes of Épernay; 50-60% reserves; vinified in stainless steel tanks; partial malolactic fermentation; aged 30 months on lees; 40g/L dosage; DIAM

Again one of the better-crafted sweet champagnes on the shelves this year; the same base as Brut Réserve charges it with the acidity and poise to handle its honeyed sweetness. This transforms the clean fruit precision that defines Billecart into apple chews, lemon drops and glacé pears. Its sweet finish is well toned by balanced acidity, fine, gentle phenolic bite and gentle salt minerality. The 2014 base is back to the clean purity that sets this house apart. Well executed.

BILLECART-SALMON BLANC DE BLANCS GRAND CRU BRUT NV $$$

95 points • 2013 BASE VINTAGE • DISGORGED 26 JUNE 2018 • 4 YEARS ON LEES • 8G/L DOSAGE • 50,000 BOTTLES • TASTED IN AUSTRALIA

96 points • 2012 BASE VINTAGE • 2011 AND 2010 RESERVES • 5 YEARS ON LEES • 5.5G/L DOSAGE • 55,000 BOTTLES • TASTED IN CHAMPAGNE

94 points • 75% 2011 BASE • 5 YEARS ON LEES • 80,000 BOTTLES • TASTED IN CHAMPAGNE

A blend of Avize for structure and fruit, Chouilly for depth and salty chalk minerality, Cramant for florals and acidity, and Le Mesnil-sur-Oger for definition and structure; 33-40% reserves; vinified in stainless steel tanks; partial malolactic fermentation; DIAM

'In your dreams,' responded Jean Roland-Billecart when his son Antoine proposed a non-vintage blanc de blancs. 'We don't have sufficient quantity of chardonnay, but if you find the grapes to produce it, go ahead.' And find them he did. Not just anywhere, but in the five grand crus of the Côte des Blancs, and in 1997 Billecart made its first non-vintage blanc de blancs.

Oh my, how Billecart's Blanc de Blancs is back on form in the 2012 and 2013 vintages, after the challenges of 2011! The 2013 is an arresting rendition, a magnificent accord of white citrus, dainty white flowers and white stone fruits meeting the gentle pâtisserie, butter, vanilla and nougat of five years of maturity. It morphs seamlessly an enticing style at once focused, honed and refreshing and at the same time creamy, silky, soft and textural, energised by lively, energetic acidity and the brilliantly crystalline sparkle of salty grand cru minerality. It coasts unwavering and alluring, an impeccably crafted cuvée of pinpoint precision that embodies the captivating juxtaposition of refined elegance and characterful confidence that epitomises the modern Billecart. Outstanding.

The 2012 base enjoyed another year on lees to tone the high acidity of this great season, and to give the fruit time to express itself. A sensationally pure and beach-fresh expression of the Côte des Blancs grand crus, fantastically mineral and precise, with magnificent, frothing, heightened chalk powder texture perfectly integrating with a laser line of acidity. It captures its Avize core with exacting precision and desperate purity as radiant as high-noon daylight.

The 2011 base is an impressive result for a tough season, an exotic style of tight grapefruit and lemon, with great integrity, persistence and pronounced salt mineral definition.

BILLECART-SALMON BRUT SOUS BOIS NV $$$

92 points • 2011 BASE VINTAGE • DISGORGED 5 APRIL 2018 • TASTED IN AUSTRALIA

33% premier and grand cru chardonnay from the Côte des Blancs, 33% premier and grand cru pinot from the Montagne de Reims, especially Aÿ and Mareuil-sur-Aÿ, 33% meunier from the right bank of the Vallée de la Marne; 30-35% reserves; vinified and aged in oak casks at low temperature; partial malolactic fermentation; aged 6-7 years on lees; 7g/L dosage

Its bold, swirling label is no more, and Sous Bois has pulled into line with Billecart's elegant new livery, yet the style remains even more bold than ever in the 2011 base vintage. 'With the diversity of Champagne's regions and the rise of growers, it's increasingly important for us to produce more interesting, small-production wines,' points out Antoine. *Sous bois* is literally 'under wood', inspired by oak-fermented parcels destined for Billecart's top cuvées. Its aspiration is to uphold the mandate of Billecart in freshness, tightness and elegance.

The savoury grip of 2011 is well massaged by the generous richness of the style, and oak fermentation is unashamedly the lead act here. Idealistically, method should never trump terroir or season, but when vintage presents so little worthy of showcasing, this is the ideal. An epic, swirling current of impressive magnitude and richness sweeps up deep strokes of caramel, honey, crème brûlée and roast nuts, all holding long on the finish amidst impressive line of tangy lemon juice acidity and fine chalk minerality. It's silky, creamy, buttery and unashamedly bold, a sure victory for a dismal season. Don't serve it too cold, and be sure to present it in large glasses.

BILLECART-SALMON BRUT ROSÉ NV $$$

93 points • 2015 BASE VINTAGE • DISGORGED 29 AUGUST 2018 • TASTED IN AUSTRALIA
94 points • 2014 BASE VINTAGE • TASTED IN CHAMPAGNE
95 points • 2013 BASE VINTAGE • TASTED IN CHAMPAGNE

40% chardonnay, 30% pinot from the Montagne de Reims and the Grande Vallée de la Marne, 30% meunier from the Vallée de la Marne and the southern slopes of Épernay; less than 8% red wine; 40% reserves; vinified in stainless steel tanks; full malolactic fermentation; aged 36 months on lees; 9g/L dosage; DIAM

Some 20% of Billecart's production is rosé (400,000 bottles), claimed to be the biggest proportion of rosé among Champagne's larger houses (though Moët may have just caught up). The house now dedicates 15 hectares in Mareuil-sur-Aÿ and Ambonnay to red wine for rosé. The utter restraint of the house places delicate rosés very close to its heart, dubbed internally 'champagne rosé' rather than 'rosé champagne'. Antoine recounts a tasting in which he poured the wine into black glasses for sommeliers. Not one identified it as a rosé. 'When my grandfather began producing rosés in the early 1960s, most thought it a fanciful, artificial wine that lacked purity,' he recalls. 'He persevered, convinced it would have its place. Those sceptics are now making their own!'

The generous 2015 season has emphasised the more structured and savoury side to this delicate label, upholding its pale salmon hue and rose petal and strawberry personality, accenting it with notes of red apple skin and firm beurre bosc pear. The ripeness of 2015 lends a little bite to the finish, though its tannin texture remains as elegantly fine and eloquently controlled as ever, testimony to the skill of the house in crafting super-fine red wine. This cuvée has attained that wonderful place where lees age contributes great texture and mouthfeel, without diminishing purity or freshness. Eminently persistent, it carries with grace and poise amidst fine chalk mineral texture, taut acid focus and a fine, creamy bead. Enjoy it in its ravishing youth.

The 2014 base captures the season in a beautifully fresh, elegant and lively style of rose petal, liquorice and pink grapefruit, even redcurrants in time, culminating in a long-lingering, fine chalk mineral finish. Even as the oldest, the 2013 base is the most delightfully refined, fresh and chalk mineral of them all.

BILLECART-SALMON VINTAGE 2008 $$$

97 points • DISGORGED JUNE 2018 • TASTED IN CHAMPAGNE

12% chardonnay, 88% pinot from Verzy, Verzenay, Mareuil-sur-Aÿ, Aÿ (for structure) and Ambonnay (for delicacy); 20% of the pinot fermented in barrels; 3.2g/L dosage; less than 100,000 bottles

Extra Brut Vintage was conceived in 2004, a good vintage but without the structure required for the Nicolas François label. Hence it was effectively declassified and released as Extra Brut Vintage. Both labels were produced in 2006, 2007 and 2008. To distinguish it from Nicolas François, the Extra Brut blend comprises more Verzy, Verzenay and Trépail, though its ultimate aspiration is to show the personality of Mareuil-sur-Aÿ. The first blend in 2004 boasted 70% pinot noir, which has progressively evolved to 88% – almost blanc de noirs!

Categorically the finest Extra Brut ever conceived, this is a cuvée of laser line and immortal structure that rejoices in the lightning energy of 2008 and the exacting precision engineering that is Billecart. A glowing, medium straw hue is a dazzling prelude to its scintillating purity and drive, cut with magnificent acid line and high-tensile chalk structure. The distinguished, north-east facing slopes of Verzy and Verzenay take a delightfully fragrant and pure lead, presenting white cherry and strawberry hull that ring out in clear peals like church bells. Age has done nothing to evolve its pitch-perfect high notes, lending just the most subtle nuance of fresh almond. A cuvée to age for another 20 years at least – and it will live effortlessly for 50. In sheer, breathtaking purity, monumental chalk minerality, endless longevity – not to mention ludicrous affordability – Extra Brut 2008 is one of the champagne buys of the decade.

BILLECART-SALMON VINTAGE 2007 $$$

95 points • TASTED IN CHAMPAGNE AND AUSTRALIA

25% chardonnay from Avize, Cramant, Le Mesnil-sur-Oger, Oger, Chouilly and Vertus, 75% pinot from the Montagne de Reims and the Grande Vallée de la Marne, especially Mareuil-sur-Aÿ and Aÿ; vinified in stainless steel tanks and 5% in oak barrels; partial malolactic; aged 8–9 years on lees; 3g/L dosage; DIAM

The juxtaposition of the understated yet expansive mood of 2007 lends itself eloquently to the restrained style of Billecart in its pinot-led vintage cuvée, providing a compelling counterpoint to the generosity of the 2006 and the tension of 2008. A core of red cherry and red apple fruit is accented with the lemon and grapefruit tang of the Côte des Blancs and the vivacious energy of malic acidity. The rising complexity of roast almond, toast and mixed spice are more reflective of bottle age than of a 5% component vinified in oak, now displaying more development than in the early phase of its release cycle. It's still charged with plenty of malic energy to propel it along, sustained by the omnipresent support of salty chalk minerality.

BILLECART-SALMON CUVÉE LOUIS BLANC DE BLANCS BRUT 2006 $$$$$

96 points • TASTED IN CHAMPAGNE AND AUSTRALIA

Le Mesnil-sur-Oger (les Coullemets and Chétillon), Avize (les Pierres Vaudon), Cramant and Chouilly (Mont Aigu); 5% vinified in oak barrels (Le Mesnil); partial malolactic fermentation; aged 10 years on lees; 4g/L dosage; cork

The quartet of Le Mesnil, Avize, Cramant and Chouilly unite their structure, endurance and stamina in the generous presence of 2006 in a Louis of power and determination. The vintage declares its richness in a core of spicy white peach, white nectarine, fig, honey, preserved lemon and apple, coasting with outstanding presence and unerring line. Its body is amplified by the elegant brioche, shortbread, vanilla, toasted coconut, hazelnut and mixed spice of a touch of barrel fermentation in concert with a decade of lees age. Malic acidity heightens tension on a long finish that glitters with a spectacular fanfare of pronounced, salty, grand cru minerality. It declares its true greatness in its spectacular finish, gliding unwavering, undeterred, uncompromising, on a mirror sea of crystalline minerality. This is a Billecart of main-course proportions, engineered with a rigid chassis that upholds focus and consummate control.

BILLECART-SALMON CUVÉE ELISABETH SALMON BRUT ROSÉ 2007 $$$$$

97 points • DISGORGED LATE 2017 • TASTED IN CHAMPAGNE AND AUSTRALIA

50% Avize and Chouilly chardonnay, 50% Mareuil-sur-Aÿ, Ambonnay and Mailly-Champagne (for silkiness in this cool vintage) pinot; 8% pinot noir red wine, from old-vine 'Valofroy', south-facing Mareuil-sur-Aÿ, because it is more structured; 5% vinified in oak casks; 35% malolactic fermentation; aged 10 years on lees; 6g/L dosage; cork

The tightrope balance of long-aged rosé is one of Champagne's most noble arts, and the restrained style of Billecart is energised with tension by the cool, edgy mood of 2007. It faithfully and resoundingly meets the aspiration for this cuvée of silkiness over complexity. With a medium salmon copper hue, white cherries and wild strawberry hull meet the depth of black plum fruit, evolving in time to the full depth of blackcurrants, with an ever-present savoury edge of tamarillo, even subtle mint and fresh sage. Upholding two-thirds of its malic acidity lends cut and drive to a very long finish, frothing with pronounced, salty chalk minerality and the harmonious grip of fine tannin bite. In impeccable line, enduring length and grand determination, this is a stunningly confident Billecart with the structural engineering to consummately support protein fare. Its frame will appreciate further time in the cellar to soften, with the promise to evolve into a compelling, savoury and deeply complex style in its grand old age. And yet its primary purity is flattering right away, so dip in whenever you fancy. One of the great 2007s.

BILLECART-SALMON CUVÉE NICOLAS FRANÇOIS BRUT 2006 $$$$$

95 points • TASTED IN CHAMPAGNE AND AUSTRALIA

40% Côte des Blancs chardonnay, 60% pinot from Aÿ, Mailly-Champagne and Rilly-la-Montagne; 10% vinified in oak barrels (15% of pinot and 5% of chardonnay); partial malolactic fermentation; aged 10 years on lees; 6g/L dosage; cork; 60,000 bottles

A powerful Nicolas François that ricochets with the ripe 2006 vintage. The rich generosity and fast-evolving mood of this generous season is heightened by the toasty, spicy complexity of a little oak vinification, lending subtle, savoury smoked charcuterie notes to a core of rich grilled pineapple, fig and mirabelle plum. Age has layered its personality in wild honey, vanilla nougat, gingernut biscuits, butter, cream and bees wax. This is a Billecart of medium straw hue, even a copper tint, juxtaposing the tension of malic acidity with the bite of warm-season phenolic grip in concert with partial barrel ferment structure, making for a tussle that leaves a little dry astringency to its very long finish. It has the generosity and polish to flatter and entice nonetheless, holding outstanding line amidst frothy salt minerality. Such a rigid and consummately engineered frame promises great endurance, and it begs for time to soften and calm. Acknowledging that the vintage was 'not as exceptional', the house took the noble step of dropping the price by 10€.

BILLECART-SALMON CUVÉE NICOLAS FRANÇOIS BRUT 2002 $$$$$

99 points • DISGORGED IN 2016 • TASTED IN CHAMPAGNE

40% chardonnay from Chouilly, Cramant and Avize, 60% pinot from Mareuil-sur-Aÿ, Aÿ, Ambonnay and a little from Verzenay and Verzy; 20% vinified in old oak barrels; partial malolactic fermentation; aged almost 13 years on lees; 4g/L dosage; 50,000 bottles

Some champagnes volunteer their life story within seconds of first introduction, like overworked movie trailers that leave you fully convinced you've seen the film. Others churn in your consciousness for days, slowly unravelling their story long after the credits have rolled. NFB 2002 has played out a captivating script since my first dramatic encounter in mid-2013. Six years on, it just keeps on opening to reveal ever more magnificent complexity, yet at every moment clinging to impeccable elegance, coiled focus of malic acid tension and exhilarating chalk mineral texture. Even now at 17 years of age, it continues to evolve at giant sea turtle pace, upholding brilliant primary definition as pinot noir begins to rise and blossom in layers of red fruits and spice, contrasting very subtle, graceful evolution of nougat, butter, honey, roast almonds and toast, promising decades of potential yet. As always, the greatness of Billecart is proclaimed not by impact or power, but by slowly rising complexity, astonishing chalk mineral presence of mouth-enveloping texture and a revelation of stunning persistence. Minerality cascades in ultra-fine detail, to the point of silkiness, yet simultaneously poised and confident. Delightful grace and intricate craftsmanship proclaim one of the great Billecarts of the modern era, a champagne with many characters and subplots to reveal, to be enjoyed slowly in the presence of the most intimate company – and ideally not for at least another decade. It will continue to enthral for many decades yet.

BILLECART-SALMON LE CLOS SAINT-HILAIRE BRUT 2002 $$$$$

98 points • Disgorged early 2018 • Tasted in Champagne

1 hectare clos in Mareuil-sur-Aÿ on silty-clayish-limestone 7 metres above chalk; planted exclusively to pinot noir since 1964 and managed biodynamically since 2003, though not certified; yielding a minuscule 40–45hL/hectare, less than one bottle per vine; harvested in two passes at full ripeness; two cuvées vinified in situ; entirely slow fermented and aged on lees 5–6 months in 15-year-old oak barrels; no malolactic fermentation; no filtration; aged on lees at least 10 years, but here more like 15 years; zero dosage; less than 4000 bottles

Le Clos Saint-Hilaire has no right to its profound echelon. It is but a premier cru, although this is more a reflection on the inadequacies of an oversimplified cru system. More significantly, in soil (deeper and less chalky than, for instance, the Clos des Goisses at the other end of the village), and in aspect (due east, far from the sought-after south-facing orientation), it has no claims to greatness. It is but a near flat expanse beside the press house in the village. The genius of François Domi and the painstaking attention to detail of Billecart play a dramatic role. I could not name another wine at this level, anywhere in the world, of which the same could be said.

Alongside Krug Clos d'Ambonnay, Billecart Le Clos Saint-Hilaire is the king of blanc de noirs. It was conceived as Antoine and François Roland-Billecart stood on the wall of the clos late one night during harvest in 1995. With plenty of red wine in stock for rosé, they decided they could afford to put this pinot noir in the cellar for a decade to see how it looked on its own. With no barrels in the house, Antoine drove a big truck to Olivier Leflaive in Meursault just before vintage, returned with 25 barrels, and Le Clos Saint-Hilaire was born.

Le Clos Saint-Hilaire's fifth release is a towering masterpiece, the definition of blanc de noirs and exacting Clos Saint-Hilaire, a larger than life cuvée of full yellow-gold hue with a blush tint. It epitomises 2002, the vintage that delivered heightened acidity and expansive dimensions like no other. Every detail is magnified to another level, finding intense poise and balance in its towering heights somewhere in the stratosphere. Its light dims to a soft-focus twilight of dark mystery, revealing deep tones of black cherry, plum, blood orange, fresh fig and then glorious layers of crème brûlée, gingernut biscuits and fruit mince spice. The profound salt mineral clarity of the site meets the very fine texture of bitter tannin grip that provides tension and bite to the finish. Brilliant malic acidity pierces its darkness like pinpoint starlight illuminating a soft landscape of understated yet deeply penetrating and mouth-engulfing mineral texture. To stand in this place and behold Le Clos Saint-Hilaire is a time-stopping experience that will stir the depths of your soul. Give it at least another 10 years to find its calm. Its twilight won't fade for decades.

BILLECART-SALMON LE CLOS SAINT-HILAIRE BRUT 1999 $$$$$

95 points • Tasted in Australia

As above; 6750 bottles

François Domi describes 1999 as opposite in personality to 1998. I was privileged to be the first outside of the house to taste it, and on pouring he exclaimed with a cheeky smile, 'Le rosé de Saint-Hilaire!' – such is its deep hue, now a full copper. It's not the towering masterpiece of the profound mineral clarity and freshness of the 1998 or the 2002, rather it's true to its power and depth in encapsulating a warm season at now a full 20 years of age. Le Clos Saint-Hilaire has attained monumental proportions in the generous 1999 vintage. It's spicy and oxidative in style (though not oxidised), with a deep well of black cherries encircled in flavours from the far-flung extremes of burnt orange and plum pudding. Twenty years of maturity have piled on fruit mince spice and immense exotic spice. In the midst of the swirling maelstrom, the energy, drive and control that full malic acidity brings to the finish are admirable, accented by the inimitable fine chalk minerality of its site, upholding grand integrity and terrific persistence. The tertiary development, dry structure and bitter phenolic grip that marked the bottle I tasted two years ago were not disruptive here. On this bottle's performance, it will hold its own for a good few years yet.

BOIZEL

(Bwah-zel)

—

46 Avenue de Champagne 51200 Épernay
www.boizel.com

ÉPERNAY · FRANCE

CHAMPAGNE
BOIZEL

MAISON FONDÉE EN 1834

Young brothers Florent and Lionel Roques-Boizel are the sixth generation to head Boizel, respectively appointed Chairman and Deputy Managing Director of the house in 2018. Seven hectares of estate vineyards are complemented with long-term contracts with growers in about 50 villages, boosted in 1994 after an injection of funds when the house joined the Lanson-BCC group. Boizel's clean, fruity style is achieved through fermentation in stainless steel vats at 18°C, full malolactic fermentation, and long ageing of non-vintage cuvées of at least three years. Vintage wines are aged five to seven years, after a small proportion of vinification in barrel. Production facilities have recently been updated, with the installation of a new cellar of large foudres and small stainless steel tanks to increase single-parcel vinification, 'allowing us to further refine our assemblages towards ever greater precision, purity and character,' says Florent. Boizel's current set of cuvées regrettably teeter on the brink of underripeness, which is not a trait I've ever seen in the house in the past. Back labels declare the blend and disgorgement date.

BOIZEL BRUT RÉSERVE NV $$

84 points · 2014 BASE VINTAGE · DISGORGED JUNE 2018 · TASTED IN AUSTRALIA

30% chardonnay from Mailly-Champagne, Cuis and Nogent-l'Abbesse, 55% pinot from Mailly-Champagne, Venteuil and Pierry, 15% meunier from Vandières, Châtillon-sur-Marne and Mont-Saint-Père; 30% reserves; aged 3 years on lees; no oak; 8g/L dosage; cork

This is an uncharacteristically awkward and challenging release for Boizel, suffering dramatically in the wake of the difficult 2014 season. It is plagued by underripeness and dry rot, rendering it dusty and astringent with green capsicum notes, devoid of the bright citrus purity that flattered the 2012 base.

Boizel Ultime Extra-Brut NV $$$

85 points • 2010 base vintage • Disgorged June 2017 • Tasted in Australia

37% chardonnay from Avize, Oger and Le Mesnil-Sur-Oger, 50% pinot from Mailly-Champagne, Pierry and Chavot, 13% meunier from Passy-Grigny, Vandières and Cumières; aged 6-8 years on lees; on oak; zero dosage; cork

Ultime spends double the length of time on lees of Boizel's other NVs, rendering a medium to full straw hue and bitter almond complexity. Zero dosage amplifies the astringency of the finish, making for a wine of searing acid tension and bitter grip. Crunchy crab apple and grapefruit zest hold long aftertaste. Not one for the uninitiated.

Boizel Blanc de Blancs NV $$$

90 points • 2013 base vintage • Disgorged May 2018 • Tasted in Australia

100% chardonnay from Cramant, Le Mesnil-Sur-Oger, Vertus and Chouilly; 40% reserves; aged 4 years on lees; no oak; 8g/L dosage; cork

Blessed by the refreshing 2013 harvest, this is a bright celebration of four of the great crus of the Côte des Blancs. The zest of lemon and lime are accented with characters of apple chews and even a hint of fennel. A creamy bead supports vibrant acid line, fine salt minerality, with candied dosage sitting a little disjoint on the finish. A bright, lively, pure and crystalline expression of Boizel.

Boizel Blanc de Noirs NV $$$

90 points • 2014 base vintage • Disgorged November 2018 • Tasted in Australia

100% pinot from Mareuil-sur-Aÿ, Les Riceys, Cumières and Mailly-Champagne; 30% reserves; aged 3 years on lees; no oak; 8g/L dosage; cork

This is a spicy blanc de noirs that expresses the crunch and understated personality of four of Champagne's second-tier pinot noir crus — villages of structure and character, if not the presence or drive of the top grand crus. The challenging 2014 season lends its own *al dente* guise here, with crunchy acidity and slightly underripe red apple notes riding the edge of ripeness. It lands just within the right side, lending appealing pink pepper and pomegranate crunch that distinguish the style from the juicy red fruits of more generous crus. Dosage is in balance, though sits just a little candied and disjoint on the finish.

Boizel Rosé NV $$$

85 points • 2014 base vintage • Disgorged May 2018 • Tasted in Australia

20% chardonnay from Vertus, Chouilly and Nogent-l'Abbesse, 50% pinot from Cumières and Les Riceys, 30% meunier from Ferebrianges, Troissy and Châtillon-sur-Marne; 8% pinot red wine; 20% reserves; aged 3 years on lees; no oak; 8g/L dosage; cork

Boizel's delicate rosé style of pretty, medium salmon hue is sadly plagued by the challenging 2014 vintage, making for a firm and austere style, inflicted with dusty, mushroomy impurity and green capsicum underripeness.

Boizel Grand Vintage 2008 $$$

93 points • Disgorged November 2017 • Tasted in Australia

50% chardonnay from Oger, Le Mesnil-sur-Oger, Avize and Vertus, 50% pinot from Mailly-Champagne, Bisseuil and Chigny-les-Roses; aged 8 years on lees; no oak; 4g/L dosage; cork

Boizel has established an impressive standard in its vintage cuvée, and the great 2008 season confidently upholds the tradition – though with the emphatic proviso that it needs considerably more time to come into its own. Some in Champagne criticise this vintage for lack of ripeness, and this cuvée runs this precarious knife edge. Uniting four of the region's great chardonnay crus with three of its prettier and more restrained and vibrant pinot crus makes for a searingly structured style. Pretty red fruits of pomegranate and morello cherry are underlined by mixed spice and the beginnings of toasty complexity. It holds impressive persistence and line, and only screams out for time.

Boizel Joyau de France Chardonnay 2007 $$$$

89 points • Disgorged September 2016 • Tasted in Australia

100% chardonnay from Avize, Le Mesnil-sur-Oger, Oger and Vertus; aged 8 years on lees; no oak; 6g/L dosage; cork

Boizel's current set of cuvées teeter on the brink of underripeness, here expressed as austere acidity, *al dente* phenolic grip and a savoury, sappy undercurrent. Eight years on lees has softened its edges, lending a creaminess to its structure and an almond-meal character to its profile. Preserved lemon is the predominant theme, with apparent lime underripeness. It has the acid drive and persistence to improve for many years yet, though will never push beyond its edgy austerity.

Boizel Joyau de France 2004 $$$$

91 points • Disgorged June 2017 • Tasted in Australia

40% chardonnay from Avize, Vertus, Oger and Le Mesnil-sur-Oger, 60% pinot from Mailly-Champagne, Vertus, Pierry and Cumières; aged 13 years on lees; 15% vinified in oak; 3g/L dosage; cork

At a full 15 years of age, this cuvée upholds a vibrant, medium straw hue, though expresses the full amplitude of its maturity in a flavour and aroma profile of considerable breadth and depth. It reverberates with fruit mince spice, candied citrus rind, crème caramel and preserved lemon, amplified in its toasty allure thanks to 15% oak vinification. Such glowing richness is juxtaposed with firm, fine, bitter phenolic grip and tense acidity on the cusp of ripeness, conspiring to a not inconsiderable impact that challenges the finish, heightened by low dosage.

Boizel Joyau de France Rosé 2007 $$$$

93 points • Disgorged June 2017 • Tasted in Australia

38% chardonnay from Oger, Avize and Le Mesnil-sur-Oger, 62% pinot from Mailly-Champagne, Vertus and Cumières; 10% red wine; aged 9 years on lees; no oak; 4g/L dosage; cork

With a pale salmon copper hue, this is a cuvée that juxtaposes structural drive with the complexity of maturity. It's at once tense and lively, cut with vibrant acidity and salty chalk minerality, yet at the same time deeply contemplative in its layers of fruit mince spice, gingernut biscuits and nougat. It's fine-boned and structured, led by the morello cherry and cracked pink pepper personality of pinot from three of Champagne's more restrained crus. It upholds the structural tension to further age confidently, though its flavour profile has already attained a comfortable evolution of development.

BOLL & CIE

(Bohl e See)

———

9 RUE ANDRÉ PINGAT 51065 REIMS
www.boll-cie.com

BOLL&C IE
CHAMPAGNE

The small Reims-based grower of Boll & Cie was established in 1853 and revived in recent years to craft a little portfolio of just three cuvées (as well as ratafia of unfermetned grape juice fortified with brandy spirit) using only the first press, low sulphur and low dosage. Its Extra Brut NV and Grand Cru vintage cuvées are 100% chardonnay and its Rosé 100% pinot. Uniting a small set of disparate villages across the region, these are compellingly composed cuvées, though marked by a little phenolic bitterness.

BOLL & CIE BLANC DE BLANCS EXTRA BRUT NV $$

91 points • TASTED IN AUSTRALIA

100% chardonnay from Montgueux, Vindey and Le Mesnil-sur-Oger; 5 years on lees; 7g/L dosage

A compellingly composed style that unites the three disparate villages of Montgueux, Vindey (Sézanne) and Le Mesnil-sur-Oger. Apple, citrus and white stone fruit characters are layered with the biscuity, honeyed complexity of five years on lees, concluding with a little dry, grainy extract and grapefruit bitterness, though with the persistence, generosity and fruit integrity to handle it.

BOLL & CIE BLANC DE BLANCS GRAND CRU VINTAGE EXTRA BRUT 2010 $$$

92 points • TASTED IN AUSTRALIA

100% chardonnay from Oger and Le Mensil-sur-Oger exclusively; 5 years on lees; 5.8g/L dosage

Noble fruit sources stand tall even in a challenging season. Apple and pear fruit are layered with the spice and honey of lees age, concluding with grapefruit bitterness. Its grand cru foundation provides fruit integrity, concentration and persistence that win out on the finish.

BOLLINGER

(Boh-lahn-zhay)

10/10

20 BOULEVARD DU MARÉCHAL DE LATTRE DE TASSIGNY 51160 AŸ
www.champagne-bollinger.com

CHAMPAGNE
BOLLINGER
MAISON FONDÉE EN 1829

It's another world at Bollinger. Take everything you know about large champagne houses, the way champagne tastes, the way it's fermented, the way it's aged, even the ownership of the vineyards and the companies, and brace yourself for a very different story at Bollinger. I've met with the good Bollinger folk countless times over the past decade in Australia and in their illustrious maison in Aÿ, and on every occasion I have been astounded by the pace of change. If Bollinger wasn't your style ten years ago, come hither! There's never been a better time to bask in the glory of this legendary house. These are ravishing champagnes that now rank high among the very best of the region. James Bond, you've finally got it right.

The Bollinger house style has long been a love-or-hate champagne, once maligned for the aldehydes that can develop as a result of oxidation during barrel ageing. Oxidation during fermentation is positive, but prior to fermentation it suppresses fruit, and post-fermentation it dulls the wine. The priority now is to suppress oxidation, creating fresher and less aldehydic wines, an imperative that the house balances delicately with its mandate of using as little sulphur dioxide preservative as possible. Exacting attention to the finer details has transformed Bollinger over the past decade, lifting its wines to the cleanest, most precise, least aldehydic it has ever made.

The house appointed Gilles Descôtes as chef de cave following the surprise resignation of Mathieu Kauffmann in early 2013. After almost a decade of experience on Bollinger's tasting panel, overseeing the estate vineyards, managing grower relations and taking charge of production in 2012, Descôtes was a natural choice. While some questioned his appointment, the house was rightfully proud to introduce a chef de cave with a background in viticulture rather than oenology. The calibre of the cuvées under his tenure is testimony to their astute decision.

Descôtes brings a deeply analytical and attentively focused approach to Bollinger, and has worked intensively with his team

to courageously trail countless new initiatives in the vineyards, winery and cellars to progressively refine the intricate detail of Bollinger to a degree I have witnessed in no other house besides Jean-Baptiste Lécaillon's revolutionary regime at Louis Roederer. 'It is all about being more precise at Bollinger, but also about having fun with the team!' Descôtes grins.

The monumental stature of Bollinger's cuvées derives from several key facets: estate-grown vineyards, centred around Aÿ; blends built on pinot noir, barrel fermentation, deep reserves, long lees maturation and ageing under cork. There are eleven features that set it apart among champagne houses, beginning in the vineyards.

ESTATE VINEYARDS

Bollinger is a champagne of cathedral proportions: towering, impacting and magnificent. Its weight derives foremost from estate-grown pinot noir. 'We have pinot noir in our blood,' says Descôtes. 'We are nicknamed "The Burgundy house"!' Every cuvée has a minimum of 60% pinot noir, and an impressive 68% of the grapes come from estate vineyards. (The only other house boasting such proportions is Louis Roederer.) Centred around Aÿ, Champagne's pinot noir epicentre, Bollinger's mighty

180 hectares comprise 85% grand cru and premier cru vineyards spanning seven villages in the Marne – pinot noir predominantly from 20 glorious hectares in Aÿ, the surrounding villages of Tauxières-Mutry, Avenay-val-d'Or and Louvois, and Verzenay on the north-east edge of the Montagne de Reims; chardonnay from Cuis in the Côte des Blancs; and meunier from Champvoisy in the Vallée de la Marne. Aÿ and Verzenay together comprise more than half of Bollinger's own vineyards. 'We liken ourselves more with champagne growers than houses, since our vineyards are such an important part of our house,' Descôtes declares. Bollinger allocates 500 man hours per hectare each year to manage its vineyards, compared with 380 on average across the region.

The house has grown production from 2.5 to 3 million bottles in recent years, though always upholding at least 60% of supply from estate vineyards, and has expanded holdings by 16 hectares over the past two years alone. This is no trivial pursuit. For instance, one hectare of grand cru purchased in 2015 cost €1.5 million. 'We aspire to grow a bit in volume and a bit in price,' former president Jérôme Philipon told me in 2017, before he was promoted within the group and succeeded by Charles-Armand de Belenet later that year. 'Our long-term plan in 10–15 years is to be able to supply 3.5 million bottles.'

The policy of the house is to only buy grapes that it can assess visually. It thus only sources from the Marne, and favours Aÿ and the nearby villages of Louvois, Mareuil-sur-Aÿ, Verzy and Verzenay, though the great Côte des Blancs crus of Le Mesnil-sur-Oger, Cramant, Oger and especially Avize and Cuis are also important. Aÿ is at the core of every Bollinger blend, with its opulence foiled by the elegance of Verzenay, which ranks second. Bouzy holds a special place, too. The house is also privileged to strong holdings in nearby Tauxières-Mutry and Avenay-Val-d'Or.

Grape maturity is pushed a little further at Bollinger through careful choice of harvest date, a blessing the house attributes to vineyard ownership. When I visited on the second-last day of harvest 2014, Bollinger's red wines for rosé had only just started fermenting, while most at Veuve Clicquot had already finished. Bollinger's balance of fruit is sourced from winegrowers who have worked with the house for many generations (every one of 120 parcels is vinified separately at Bollinger; there is no purchase of *vins sur lattes*). This accounts for the consistency, depth and complexity in Bollinger's wines.

The house is experimenting with organics in a few of its plots, though doesn't aspire to seeking certification, having found sustainable viticulture better for the environment than certified organics. 'I don't care about being organic, but I am very interested in what is happening in the soils and in the ferments,' Descôtes reveals.

NEW PRESS HOUSE AND CELLARS

Bollinger's philosophy of vinification is to express the fruit and the terroir rather than characters of fermentation or yeast. To reduce pre-ferment oxidation, a new press centre was constructed in neighbouring Mareuil-sur-Aÿ, within line of sight of the maison in Aÿ, in time for the 2003 vintage. All of the grapes of estate vineyards are now pressed by the house. In Mareuil, eight-tonne pneumatic presses work 24/7 to press 200 tonnes daily. Every grape variety, every cru and sometimes even individual growers are kept separate.

Bollinger's cellars under Aÿ

To facilitate long ageing, no tailles are used in Bollinger's cuvées.

In 2013, Bollinger doubled its red wine processing capacity in response to increasing demand for rosé. Since 2005, the house has produced all of its own red wine from tiny yields of just 30hL/hectare. When I visited during harvest 2014, I was impressed by a stringent team of eight, fanatically working the sorting table as tiny grapes for red wines arrived at the press centre.

The house recently commissioned new cellars in Mareuil, not to increase capacity, but to consolidate the entire production process in Mareuil and Aÿ. With tiny microtanks and a small-scale bottling plant to produce trial batches, the new facilities have been engineered with the flexibility to facilitate what Descôtes describes as his 'experimental focus'.

BARREL FERMENTATION

Bollinger uses only the cuvée (the first and best pressing) and ferments under temperature control in both stainless steel tanks and oak barrels. Use of barrels for fermentation and ageing is a key element in reinforcing Bollinger's house style, and Descôtes goes to great lengths to retain freshness and fruit purity through diligent barrel cleaning and cellar hygiene. Every barrel is tasted post-fermentation and again before blending.

The magnitude of this task becomes apparent after witnessing more than 3300 Burgundy barrels of 228-litre capacity stacked long and high, row after row, plus 208 barrels of 400-litre capacity, made by Bollinger in 1903, and some recently acquired new 350–400L 'pipes'. The house has grown its barrel stocks from 2500 in 2005 to more than 3500 today. To increase consistency, old barrels of at least five years of age are purchased annually from Bollinger-owned Burgundy négociant Chanson and maintained until they are 35–40 years old (and some until they are 80), by the last in-house cooper in Champagne. Bollinger's vintage wines are 100% barrel fermented, as are all of its reserve wines, and any other parcels with sufficient acidity to handle 6–7 months in barrel. La Grande Année components are matured in barrels until April or May of the year following harvest. The latest blend of Special Cuvée based on the 2018 vintage now includes 15% of oak-fermented components.

Comparing vins clairs (fermented still base wines) fermented in stainless steel and oak is enlightening, the barrel-fermented samples in no way woody (thanks to the age of Bollinger's barrels), but better integrated, more textured, more complex and better balanced. Bollinger considers barrels an insurance policy for the wine, providing controlled oxidation, and drawing out the longevity of Grande Année to 20 years and beyond.

FAMILY OWNERSHIP

Bollinger is the largest independent champagne house after Louis Roederer, owned and run completely by members of the Bollinger family. This provides the freedom to uphold practices, such as later harvesting and longer ageing under cork, that might be considered infeasible under a large owner.

LONGER AGEING

Bollinger keeps its cuvées on lees for long periods: a minimum of three years and an average of 3.5 years for non-vintages (until recently 2.5 years), and eight years or longer for Grande Année (previously six). This is considered crucial for producing small bubbles and very fine, velvety textures. The aspiration is to extend Special Cuvée to a minimum of 3.5 years, but this necessitates holding stock back, a challenge for a brand in strong demand globally. La Grande Année is aged seven years on lees, and the house is currently holding back stock to extend R.D. to 14 years.

More than 12 million bottles are held in storage in Bollinger's 5.5 kilometres of cellars over four levels under Aÿ, plus an additional 750,000 reserve magnums (and growing) of grand and premier cru pinot noir and chardonnay, fermented in barrels, bottled with natural corks and kept for between five and 15 years, or longer. To preserve freshness, reserves are aged in oak barrels for just two months after the completion of malolactic fermentation, before they are bottled in magnums. There is a desire to increase production, but only at the very slow rate of 5000 bottles per year, so as to uphold quality. To sell one more bottle in five years' time, the house needs to put five more bottles in the cellar now.

Infused with the resilience of barrel maturation, Bollinger's white cuvées possess propensity for great longevity (but its rosés are best drunk as youthful as possible). Her Majesty the Queen of England cellars her Special Cuvée for 10 years, and reportedly did not pop the 2001 disgorgement until 2010!

DEEP RESERVES

Bollinger's Special Cuvée is blessed with astonishing depth of reserves, up from 40% a decade ago to 60% today, unrivalled by any other house besides Krug itself. The most recent blend comprises less than 40% of 2018 and an enormous 60%+ of reserve wines – the majority from 2017, along with eight older vintages, the oldest from reserve magnums. The small percentage of older reserves are considered crucial for maintaining consistency in this blend of a massive total of 400 wines in all.

AGEING UNDER CORK

Bollinger upholds that ageing its reserve wines in magnum on natural cork rather than crown seal affords more complexity, a practice followed by a small number of growers and small houses, but no other sizeable house. Six grams of sugar is added for a *prise de mousse* (carbonic fermentation) to produce a light sparkle of two atmospheres to retain fresh flavour and aroma in these reserve magnums, dubbed 'aromatic bombs' by the house.

Only 1% of champagne is aged under cork, and it's not hard to see why: it necessitates riddling and disgorgement by hand, not to mention wastage to cork taint. In 2018, it took a team of 10 workers three weeks to open 85,000 reserve magnums by hand for Special Cuvée and Rosé – a tedious and expensive process to check every bottle for cork taint, not simply by nosing the bottle but by tasting. Workers are instructed not to wear perfume on

Bollinger matures its reserves in 750,000 magnums.

disgorgement days, and not to front up at all if they have a cold. The house reports a rejection rate to cork taint of less than half of 1%, but admits that even this is too much.

'Eradicating this cork-taint risk would make a big change in our work!' exclaims Descôtes. Since he commenced, he has sensibly tiraged all reserve magnums and most bottles of La Grande Année under 'technological' corks such as DIAM. However, all cuvées are still disgorged with natural corks. 'Jerôme Philipon was adamant that we would never sell under DIAM, because they are considered aesthetically inferior, but with a new president, we will see!' discloses Descôtes.

Sixty corks from every batch are tested, not only for cork taint but for density. 'Corks tend to vary from 8g to 10g, and this difference in density makes a huge difference to oxidation and hence longevity,' explains Descôtes, who is experimenting with corks of different densities and talking with cork producers in the hope of securing corks of higher density.

'Technological corks like DIAM are much more consistent,' he says. 'We have been trialling them since 2007, and comparing wines under both closures today. The only difference we see is that we have no cork taint under technological corks.'

It's not only Special Cuvée that's produced using a labour-intensive process at Bollinger. Vintage wines are hand disgorged, with every bottle tasted at disgorgement, and non-vintage rosé is hand riddled. Asked about the practice of ageing under cork, Christian Pol Roger allegedly replied: 'It's a great idea, but we are not as crazy as they are at Bollinger!'

MALOLACTIC FERMENTATION

In the past, malolactic fermentation occurred haphazardly, only in those barrels and tanks that happened to progress naturally. In pursuit of greater consistency, malolactic bacteria are now introduced to ensure systematic completion of malolactic fermentation.

ONE BLEND

All 2 million bottles of Special Cuvée are tiraged at once in a single blend in February, to maintain the consistency of each blend. To further promote freshness, Bollinger disgorges three times a year, with each disgorgement from the same original blend, yet subtly different, due to a different length of time on lees. Bottles are aged on lees at least three years, and on average 3.5 years.

Disappointingly, disgorgement dates are not stamped on non-vintage bottles, although they are on the vintage wines, and regrettably the house now declines to volunteer disgorgement dates and base and reserve vintages when asked. This is a pity, especially for a cuvée blessed with such incredible depth of reserves. Labelling occurs shortly after disgorgement, so the labelling date provides a good indication. The first two digits of the labelling code on the neck of Special Cuvée and Rosé are the year, and the next three digits are the number of the day of that year, so L1802201 means the 22nd day of 2018.

The letter on the cork is the month of disgorgement and the number is the year, so 6I is September 2016.

MODERN FACILITIES

To further reduce post-ferment oxidation, in 2012 Bollinger installed one of Champagne's most modern disgorgement lines. A computerised system checks for defects in the seal of cork-sealed bottles, and rejects 3–4%. (If only it could detect cork taint, too!) When I visited, a cart was stacked 10 high with rejects destined to be used as liqueur for dosage.

Since 2013, Bollinger has introduced a system of 'jetting' at disgorgement. A tiny droplet of water is sprayed to foam the wine and push out oxygen. Internal trials have revealed this process to greatly diminish oxidation during disgorgement. Bollinger does not use special dosage liqueur to tweak its cuvées, rather instead simply mixing white cane sugar with the wine that is being dosed. Bottling facilities were updated in 2005, 2008 and again in 2012, this time in preparation for a new bottle design.

NEW BOTTLE

In 2012, Bollinger launched its gloriously refined '1846' bottle with a wider base, narrower neck and elegant curves, based on an original champagne bottle found in the Bollinger cellars dated 1846. The benefits are more than just aesthetic. With a neck three millimetres narrower, the new bottle has a neck cross-sectional area 20% smaller than the last, which slows the oxygen exchange, better for ageing. This neck is also said to take up 40–50% less oxygen during disgorgement. La Grande Année boasts this glorious new bottle from the recent release of the stunning 2008. With the previous four vintages in the cellar and the market pessimistic in the wake of the GFC, no La Grande Année Rosé was made in 2008.

This year I have again been greatly disconcerted to encounter random oxidation in bottles of Bollinger. At a dinner I hosted with International Sales Manager Guy de Rivoire in Brisbane, his local sales manager and I rejected one bottle in eight of La Grande Année 2007, three in ten of La Grande Année Rosé 2007 and two in nine of R.D. 2004. Subsequent bottles from the same shipment were on form. I also recently encountered two oxidised bottles of R.D. 2004 at different tastings in Australia and Champagne, and cork taint in one bottle of Special Cuvée. In all, I tasted 16 bottles of R.D. 2004 on six separate occasions in researching this book, and one-quarter of these, four bottles, were rejected as out of condition. And three in 12 bottles of LGA Rosé 2007 – one-quarter again. This is an appalling strike rate, and no one-off, replicating the inconsistency I observed last year in La Grande Année 2007, 2005 and R.D. 2002. It's certainly encouraging to see Bollinger's initiatives in reducing oxidation and use of DIAM, but long ageing dictates that it will take time for the effects of these measures to filter through to its wines in the market. As always, request a replacement if you encounter a bottle out of condition.

For a champagne of breadth, depth and grandeur, and one that is readily available and affordable, Bollinger is in a world of its own. It's no surprise the house is setting new sales records in value and volume and cannot keep up with demand, imposing allocations in every market. Coteaux Champenois aside, my lowest score on any of the dozen Bollinger cuvées I've rated this year is 96 points, a record no other house besides Krug itself could claim.

BOLLINGER SPECIAL CUVÉE BRUT NV

96 points • 2013 BASE • DISGORGED JUNE 2017 • TASTED IN CHAMPAGNE AND AUSTRALIA

25% chardonnay, 60% pinot, 15% meunier; more than 300 crus; more than 85% grand cru and premier cru; 15% fermented in old oak barrels; aged 3–4 years on lees; 8g/L dosage; 90% of production, more than 2.5 million bottles

The complexity and richness of Special Cuvée is unparalleled among the entry non-vintage blends of every champagne house, short of ascending to the mesosphere of Krug. Its grand recipe explains why, built on incredible depth of 50–60% reserves. The house declines to volunteer the reserve composition of each release, which is disappointing and counterintuitive, being one of its strongest points of difference. As an indication, the most recent blend laid in the cellar comprises less than 40% of 2018 and an enormous 60%+ of reserves – the majority from 2017, with eight older vintages, the oldest from reserve magnums. A massive total of 400 wines in all. The 2013 base boasts more than 50% reserves.

This is the finest Special Cuvée since the stunning 2008 base five years ago – and it just might top that monumental wine! Triumphant complexity is a given at Bollinger, but it's dynamic freshness and vitality that really set apart the very best releases. Its exceptional refinement and pristine articulation of the gorgeous red cherry personality of pinot noir take it to another level, epitomising the character, freshness and chalk mineral definition of this beguiling grape more eloquently than ever before. It resonates with all of the exceptional depth of pinot noir treated to deep reserves, in a universe of complexity, spanning light years of black cherries, red apples, pears, figs and a panoply of spice. Layers of character emerge from the woodwork, reverberating with Bollinger's signature notes of ginger, toasted brioche, mixed spice, roast nuts and honey. For all this, it upholds achingly pristine brightness of lemon zest and grapefruit, at every moment freshened and enlivened by the prominent chalk minerality of its fabled terroirs, culminating in a masterful crescendo of fine, frothing, salt and iodine-infused minerality. More refined and multifaceted than ever, Special Cuvée remains one of the finest entry NVs on the planet. Readily available and affordable, I recommend it more often than any other. One bottle was cork tainted.

Bollinger Rosé Brut NV $$$

96 points • Disgorged January 2018 • Tasted in Champagne and Australia

24% chardonnay, 62% pinot, 14% meunier; more than 85% grand cru and premier cru; 5–6% red wine; 7–8g/L dosage

Bollinger Rosé NV has doubled in volume since its much-celebrated introduction in 2008, though it still represents just 250,000 bottles, merely one-tenth of Special Cuvée. The blend is now slightly different to Special Cuvée, to which is added pinot noir red wine from the grand cru villages of Verzenay (predominantly) and Aÿ, which has been made with one-third of whole bunches since 2015, with a long pre-ferment maceration, before maturing in barrel for 12 months. The house prides itself on its red wine, and such is its strength, concentration, depth of colour and robust tannin structure that a tiny 5–6% is all that is required. Like Special Cuvée, it is matured 3–4 years on lees. While the proportion of reserves in Special Cuvée have increased from 40% to 60% over the past decade, reserves for Rosé Brut have been held stable to maintain freshness.

This is a breathtaking rosé, full-bodied in every way, with magnificent stature, spellbinding purity and impeccable poise. Greater elegance is the aspiration, and it meets the brief with effortless grace and a gorgeous medium-salmon hue. Pinot noir communicates its characterful poise in very pretty red cherry, and wild strawberry fruit, transposed on a background of classic Bollinger complexity of mixed spice, even subtle suggestions of coffee bean and dark chocolate. It's all intricately laced together with fine-tuned acidity, a creamy bead and subtle tannin texture, illuminated brilliantly by glittering chalk minerality, carrying the finish with delightful persistence and effortless poise. A rosé that delivers that great paradox of vibrant liveliness and profound depth.

Bollinger La Grande Année 2008 $$$$

98 points • Disgorged June 2018 • Tasted in Australia

29% chardonnay, 71% pinot; from 18 crus, mainly Aÿ and Verzenay for pinot and Le Mesnil-sur-Oger and Cramant for chardonnay; fermented entirely in barrels; aged 9 years on cork; '1846' bottle for the first time; the front label now declares Elevé en fûts, remué & dégorgé à la main ('Aged in barrels, riddled and disgorged by hand'); 8g/L dosage; cork

The greatest cuvées do not unveil their true grandeur in seconds or even minutes, and I tasted La Grande Année 2008 six times over two days. At the end of a week of tasting more than 70 cuvées, this was the last wine standing and the only one I chose to return to. The remarkable blossoming of its captivating pinot noir presence is testimony not only to its grandeur but its remarkable longevity. The unleashing of La Grande Année from the greatest vintage in decades comes with tremendous anticipation, not least in that it is the first in the glorious new, narrow-necked '1846' bottle. For all the opulent splendour and vast amplitude that is Bollinger, its hue is a bright, medium straw. The detailed precision of this season presents the space and focus for every element to be laid out with clarity and detail never before visible in a young Bollinger, amplifying its complexity to hitherto unfathomable heights, all the while juxtaposing this with newfound poise and energy. Exceedingly youthful, even by the enduring standards of 2008, it confidently presents the bold presence of pinot noir from the Montagne de Reims' southern slopes in layers of red cherries, blackberries, satsuma plums and mixed spice, brightened by the crunch of preserved lemon of chardonnay. All the exuberant character of barrel fermentation is on display more visibly than ever, layered in high-cocoa dark chocolate, freshly ground coffee beans, ginger, candied citrus rind and spices of all kinds. Nine years on lees has heightened its creaminess and contributed layers of crème caramel and roast hazelnuts. The acid line of this classic season brings a focus, tension, energy and drive to the finish that promises an exceedingly long life, confidently supported by the frothing salt minerality of thundering grand cru proportions, the commanding voice of four of the most profound sparkling crus on earth. Twelve hours after opening, the precise red cherry fruits of pinot noir rose to a resounding presence that utterly trumped all influence of oak and maturity, empowered by scintillating chalk minerality and the laser acidity of 2008. In length and line, this will go down as one of the greatest Bollingers of the modern era. Even at more than a decade of age, it is not nearly ready to be unleashed yet, and demands at least as long again before daring to approach. The house considered not releasing it, but rather holding the full production back for release as R.D. Instead they held back 30–40 percent rather than the usual 10 percent. My advice is to buy as much as you can find the instant it lands, and cellar it as long as you can possibly keep your hands off it.

BOLLINGER LA GRANDE ANNÉE BRUT 2007 $$$$

97 points • DISGORGED OCTOBER 2017, NOVEMBER 2017 AND JANUARY 2018 • TASTED IN CHAMPAGNE AND AUSTRALIA

30% chardonnay, 70% pinot; a blend of 14 crus; chardonnay mainly from Cramant, Oger and Avize, pinot mainly from Aÿ and Verzenay; 91% grand cru, 9% premier cru; entirely fermented and matured 6-7 months in oak barrels; aged under natural cork 9.5 years on lees; 7g/L dosage

Gilles Descôtes describes 2007 as a very difficult vintage in which they took a risk and picked late. It paid off, and the wines looked good in barrel, so they declared the vintage. Twelve years on, this is the resounding evidence that they made the right decision. The best La Grande Année since 2002 has held every molecule of freshness of its release two years ago. Radiating through a glowing, bright, full straw-yellow hue, this is a succulent and enticing LGA that contrasts the tension of 2007 with the reverberating depth of Aÿ pinot noir and all the structure and fanfare of small-barrel fermentation. Layers of spice are packed around a magnificent core of pronounced black and red cherry fruit, fig, even radiant yellow pineapple, before exploding into a universe of all that we love of Bollinger: Christmas cake, fruit mince spice, ginger and roast nuts. The depth and character of pinot noir build incrementally on the palate to profound proportions, while the creamy and silky effect of barrel fermentation caresses fine chalk minerality, flowing seamlessly into a very long, full and captivating finish of dark chocolate. Charged with ebullient freshness, effortless drive and magnificent mineral complexity, it promises to live long and strong. Of 11 bottles tasted, one was oxidised.

BOLLINGER LA GRANDE ANNÉE BRUT 2005 $$$$

96 points • DISGORGED FEBRUARY 2016 • TASTED IN AUSTRALIA

30% chardonnay, 70% pinot; a blend of 13 crus; chardonnay mainly from Avize, Chouilly and Le Mesnil-sur-Oger; pinot mainly from Aÿ and Verzenay; 95% grand cru, 5% premier cru; entirely fermented and matured in oak barrels; aged under natural cork 10 years on lees; 6g/L dosage

The powerful 2005 season captures the full magnificence of Bollinger exuberance, with a fruit integrity rarely seen in this bold vintage. Blossoming incrementally to even greater voluptuous succulence since its release, it has never looked finer than it does today. A grand celebration of pinot noir at full throttle, it glows with mirabelle plums, figs and red apples, oozing with ripe peach and resonating with the depth of black cherries, before launching into a firmament of Bollinger complexity in golden fruit cake, spice, pâtisserie and roast nuts. The depth and body of Bollinger confidently step up to the grip of the season, and maturity has toned its phenolic structure with more flesh, silkiness, drive and persistence than ever, giving voice to its balanced acidity and fine chalk minerality. The vintage to drink while 2007 and 2008 rest.

BOLLINGER LA GRANDE ANNÉE ROSÉ 2007 $$$$

97 points • DISGORGED NOVEMBER 2016 • TASTED IN CHAMPAGNE

28% chardonnay, 72% pinot; a blend of 14 crus; chardonnay mainly from Avize, Cramant and Oger; pinot mainly from Aÿ and Verzenay; 5% still red wine from La Côte aux Enfants; 92% grand cru, 8% premier cru; entirely fermented and matured in oak barrels; aged under natural cork 8.5 years on lees; 7g/L dosage

The 2007 vintage was a challenging one in which to produce great red wine in Champagne, and this result is testimony both to the standards of La Côte aux Enfants and the expertise of the house in crafting red wine for rosé. LGA Rosé is LGA with a tiny inclusion of red wine from the same vintage. The effect is profound, beckoning from its radiant, medium copper-salmon gown with exuberant, flamboyant and extroverted appeal. Its purity of red cherry fruits and violet fragrance has begun to dim as its secondary universe steps to the fore in great complexity of golden fruit cake, fruit mince spice, butter, even hints of toasted coconut and vanilla custard. The fine tannin grip of its youth has faded into a silky smooth, creamy structure, laced with fine chalk minerality, lingering long and seamless with refined, understated red cherry purity. Three in 12 bottles tasted were oxidised.

BOLLINGER R.D. EXTRA BRUT 2004 $$$$$

97 points • DISGORGED 21 FEBRUARY 2018 • TASTED IN CHAMPAGNE
97 points • DISGORGED 21 FEBRUARY 2018 • TASTED IN AUSTRALIA
98 points • DISGORGED NOVEMBER 2017 • TASTED IN AUSTRALIA EN MAGNUM

34% chardonnay, 66% pinot; 88% grand crus, 12% premier crus; fermented entirely in oak barrels; the 25th R.D. since 1952; aged 13 years on lees; 3g/L dosage; less than 1% of production

In the mid-1960s, journalists asked Madame Bollinger when she would release a prestige cuvée. She told them, 'Never, because all of my wines are prestige – but I will show you how well my wines age!' She had 1952 and 1953 disgorged in 1967, hence recently disgorged ('Récemment Dégorgé') – and R.D. was born. Confusingly, it's not necessarily 'recently disgorged' today, but a vintage of La Grande Année aged longer on its lees and with lower dosage. Each vintage of La Grande Année is sold over 2–3 years, and at the end of this time it is assessed for its potential be kept as an R.D. release. If it then doesn't look right when the time for release comes around, it is repurposed as reserves. Depending upon where you catch R.D. in its release cycle, it may be blessed with but a few more years on lees than LGA, which makes double the price difficult to swallow. My advice is always to buy the top vintages of LGA like 2008 and cellar them carefully yourself. The house has recognised this dilemma and is working to hold R.D. longer on lees. The aspiration is to increase Special Cuvée to 3.5 years on lees, maintain La Grande Année at 7 years and extend R.D. to 14 years. This necessitates holding stock back, and with the bold (and correct) decision not to release R.D. 2005, there will be no R.D. released in 2019 or 2020. A larger than usual proportion of the eternally enduring and spectacular 2008 has been held back for release as R.D. Released only a few months after it is disgorged, the house recommends drinking R.D. in the year after disgorgement.

September was warm and sunny in Champagne in 2004, and Bollinger waited until the end of the month to achieve more ripeness than many, making this vintage a powerful release for the house. I liked it in La Grande Année guise five years ago, and I like it even more in its encore as R.D. The freshest bottles still uphold a brilliant straw hue, while others have evolved to full, golden yellow. This is a deeply spicy and generous Bollinger, celebrating the personality of ripe pinot noir in rich white peach and grilled pineapple notes, set to an undercurrent that swirls and tosses with pipe smoke, truffles, dried peach, wild honey and Bollinger's signature notes of ginger, crystalline orange, dark chocolate, crème brûlée and fruit mince spice. For such a maelstrom, it preserves profound freshness and preserved lemon vitality, with a long finish of bright energy and salty chalk mineral tension, heightened to a dizzying, airy stratosphere more vibrant in bottles tasted in Champagne than in Australia. The best capture the dynamic endurance of this great season, and transcend the magnitude of Bollinger with astonishing endurance and coiled tension. None more so than in magnum, with an astonishingly unique personality of its own, a fragrant air of white lilies, lemon, struck-flint reduction and wonderful crunchy white peaches and pears. A stunning R.D. with an airiness and luminosity transposed on the reverberating depth of Bollinger, echoing on a finish that hovers in motionless silence for minutes. Four in 16 bottles tasted were oxidised.

BOLLINGER R.D. EXTRA BRUT 2002 $$$$$

98 points • DISGORGED 17 MAY 2017 • TASTED IN AUSTRALIA

40% chardonnay, 60% pinot; a blend of 16 grand crus and 7 premier crus; aged 14 years on lees; 3.5g/L dosage

The 2002 was an exhilarating LGA of driving energy and a razor edge of structure that barely evolved across the years of its release cycle. It naturally makes for a brilliant and enduring R.D. that is maturing every bit as slowly and magnificently as we had hoped. It holds a brilliance of light through its now full yellow-gold hue, upholding youthful dynamism and focus, still reflecting brilliant lemon freshness and wonderful tension. Projecting all the exuberance of pinot noir's red cherry and plum fruits, it strikes a wonderful interplay with the mixed spice of barrel fermentation and the integration of 17 years of age, creating creamy depth amidst tightly honed focus. The rising depth of powerful maturity billows with all the layers of brioche, toffee, dark chocolate, dried peach and crystallised orange that we love from Bollinger, concluding in epic line and persistence that promise many years of stamina yet.

BOLLINGER R.D. EXTRA BRUT 1996

100 points • DISGORGED NOVEMBER 2017 • TASTED IN AUSTRALIA
96 points • DISGORGED MAY 2012 • TASTED IN AUSTRALIA

30% chardonnay, 70% pinot

In an exercise to demonstrate the profound impact of disgorgement date, Bollinger presented the same R.D. after both 15 and 20 years on lees. The younger disgorgement is charged with stunning energy and vitality, upholding a primary lemon vivacity that drives the finish with remarkable precision and stamina. True to the heightened energy of its great season, it soars with profound line and length and astonishing focus. Twenty-two years of age has enveloped it in gorgeous complexity of exotic spice, fresh truffles, wild honey and sautéed mushrooms. Even now, it is still not yet at its glorious peak, and will effortlessly live another 20 years. And more. An older disgorgement was more toasty and tertiary, sadly foiled by a touch of cork wood flavour.

BOLLINGER R.D. EXTRA BRUT 1988

98 points • DISGORGED SEPTEMBER 2003 • TASTED IN AUSTRALIA EN MAGNUM

28% chardonnay, 72% pinot

1988 is my favourite vintage of the 1980s, apparently charged with searing acidity in its youth, which has secured its enduring longevity. After 15 years on lees and the same time on cork, this is a brilliant Bollinger in which glowing yellow fruits and layers of toast are zapped with the exceptional acid drive of the season, flowing gracefully into a finish layered with alluring complexity of subtle tertiary character, in allusions of truffle and wisps of sweet pipe smoke.

BOLLINGER LA GRANDE ANNÉE 1985

99 points • TASTED IN CHAMPAGNE

35% chardonnay, 65% pinot

From a year of extremes, in which one-third of Champagne's vines died in a bitterly cold winter, this is a triumphant La Grande Année. Boasting a glowing, golden-yellow hue, it resonates with magnificent layers of truffles, pipe smoke, grilled pineapple and crème brûlée, and yet preserves delightful freshness, energetic grapefruit crunch and sensational poise, even at a full third of a century of age. In commanding and enduring line, length and sheer, jubilant confidence, this is epic Bollinger, and one of the greatest 1985s I have ever tasted.

BOLLINGER LA CÔTE AUX ENFANTS COTEAUX CHAMPENOIS AŸ ROUGE 2013 $$$$

91 points • TASTED IN AUSTRALIA

100% pinot from the 4-hectare estate vineyard La Côte aux Enfants on a steep, south-facing slope in Aÿ; farmed organically since 2009; vinified and aged 8 months in small oak barrels; cork

Bollinger is unique among the larger champagne houses to market a Coteaux Champenois still wine (at least until the advent of recent balmy vintages in Champagne – watch this space!). La Côte aux Enfants is impeccably focused and refined in 2013, a complex pinot noir red wine of spicy berry fruits, white pepper, even a hint of ginger, framed in beautifully fine yet confident Bollinger tannins. It's a dry and tense style of excellent line and length, sustained by firm, fine-ground tannins, melding coherently with chalk minerality. As always, the high-tensile mood of Coteaux Champenois begs for a long spell in the cellar.

Bollinger Vieilles Vignes Françaises Blanc de Noirs 2010 $$$$$

96 points • Disgorged September 2018 • Tasted in Champagne

100% pinot; usually 2000–2500 bottles, but a very low crop of just 1400 bottles in 2010; 4g/L dosage

Vieilles Vignes Française is one of Champagne's rarest, most legendary and most distinctive cuvées. It is the product of two tiny plots, Clos Saint-Jacques and Chaudes Terres, together just 0.36 hectares, adjacent to the house within Aÿ, maintained in memory of the way champagne was grown pre-phylloxera: non-grafted and non-trelissed, in the traditional 'en foule' (without order) layering system, worked entirely by hand and sometimes by horse. Dense planting and severe pruning reduces yields by as much as one-third, producing particularly ripe and concentrated juice. It's always the first vineyard that Bollinger harvests, and usually a special dispensation must be requested to harvest before picking is officially open. The aim is to harvest at 11 or 11.5 degrees potential, not over 12 or 13, to create a cuvée of power with personality and yet balance, freshness and approachable drinkability.

The first Vieilles Vignes Françaises since 2007, this is a young release for VVF, launched before the 2009 and 2008. I was privileged to join the winemaking team for the dosage trial, tasting 2g/L, 4g/L, 6g/L and 8g/L blind. Every time I experience such an exercise, I am staggered by the profound impact that such small differences in dosage makes, even on a wine as commanding as VVF; 4g/L was their choice (and mine). The sheer confidence of VVF is enrapturing, abounding with the inimitable presence of its unique sites and unusual method. It declares its presence in a full yellow hue, red Burgundy-like expansiveness and a peacock's-tail flourish of theatrical proportions. In volume and sheer persistence it takes champagne to an altogether higher plateau, layered with magnificent complexity of golden delicious apples, golden syrup and ginger, abounding in layers of generosity unexpected at such a young age: truffles, pipe smoke and exotic spice. Its ripeness brings a gentle phenolic texture, which has been expertly controlled, meshing in comfortably with pronounced, fine salt minerality. A VVF of profound strength, if not the fitness of the great seasons.

Sorting pinot noir for red wine during harvest 2014.

Bouché Père & Fils

(Bouh-shay Pehr e Feess)

—

10 Rue du Général de Gaulle 51530 Pierry
www.champagne-bouche.fr

CHAMPAGNE
BOUCHÉ
— Père & Fils —

Fourth generation oenologist Nicolas Bouché aspires to produce 'fine, subtle and elegant champagnes'. His little house in Pierry just south of Épernay sources from 30 hectares of vineyards, spanning nine villages including Pierry, Chouilly, Verzenay, Verzy and Tauxières-Mutry, boasting vines of 30 years of average age, and some more than 60 years. Cuvées are aged between four and ten years on lees in chalk cellars dug 10 metres under the house in Pierry in 1897.

BOUCHÉ PÈRE & FILS BLANC DE BLANCS NV $$

84 points • 2013 BASE VINTAGE • DISGORGED FEBRUARY 2018 • TASTED IN AUSTRALIA

100% chardonnay from Chouilly, Pierry and Barbonne-Fayel; 2012 reserves; 10% new oak; 8g/L dosage; DIAM

A firm and savoury blanc de blancs that amplifies dusty fruit with a touch of new oak. The result is astringent, grainy and phenolic.

BOUCHÉ PÈRE & FILS CUVÉE SAPHIR NV $$$

85 points • 2005 BASE VINTAGE • DISGORGED FEBRUARY 2018 • TASTED IN AUSTRALIA

75% chardonnay, 20% pinot, 5% meunier from Pierry and Épernay; 2002 and 2004 reserves; 30% new oak; 8g/L dosage; DIAM

So unique is a mature flagship cuvée in a clear bottle that I mistook it for a rosé in the dim lighting of my cellar. In the stark light of day, it's a full straw hue. The idiosyncratic chardonnay of 2005 takes the lead in this blend, with a green edge of inconsistent ripeness in this awkward season, lending overt notes of green capsicum and tinned peas. Age has built toasty complexity. It holds 30% new oak surprisingly effortlessly, though the structural dominance of the grainy phenolic bite of 2005 is unavoidable on a firm finish.

BOURGEOIS-DIAZ

(Bohr-zhwah Dee-az)

—

43 GRANDE RUE, 02310 CROUTTES-SUR-MARNE
www.bourgeois-diaz.com

CHAMPAGNE

BD

BOURGEOIS-DIAZ

It is no simple feat to practise biodynamics across 30 parcels, let alone in the wet, western reaches of the Vallée de la Marne. On the northern banks of the Marne, the village of Crouttes-sur-Marne lies far west of Château-Thierry, precisely midway between Reims and Paris. Here, fourth-generation vigneron Jérôme Bourgeois-Diaz farms 6.5 hectares of vines certified biodynamic since 2015, after six years in conversion. Meunier represents 3.5 hectares, pinot two hectares and chardonnay one hectare, with vines averaging 35 years of age, spread across his village and the neighbouring villages of Nanteuil-sur-Marne and Villiers-Saint-Denis. All vineyard work is performed by hand, with no herbicides, pesticides or synthetic fertilisers. Each parcel is wild-fermented separately in stainless steel tanks or old oak barrels, with no chaptalisation or synthetic sulphur dioxide preservative. His cuvées express the personality of western Marne meunier with low dosage, though at times rustic and funky.

BOURGEOIS-DIAZ CUVÉE 3C TROIS CÉPAGES NV $$

88 points • 2014 BASE VINTAGE • DISGORGED 26 JULY 2017 • TASTED IN AUSTRALIA

17% chardonnay, 28% pinot, 55% meunier; 40% 2013 reserves; 35% vinified in oak barrels; 2g/L dosage; 19,880 bottles; cork

From the far western reaches of the Vallée de la Marne, this is a complex cuvée of medium straw salmon-blush hue. It ripples with the mixed spice of meunier, accented with hints of charcuterie. It concludes short and hard, lacking freshness, fruit expression and carry.

BOURGEOIS-DIAZ CUVÉE N BLANC DE NOIRS NV $$$

87 points • 2014 BASE VINTAGE • DISGORGED 2 JUNE 2017 • TASTED IN AUSTRALIA

63% pinot from Les Biens Aimées planted in the 1960s in Nanteuil-sur-Marne, 37% meunier from Crouttes-sur-Marne; 45% vinified in oak barrels; zero dosage; 4212 bottles; cork

Pinot noir and meunier unite in a spicy and characterful style, true to the mood of the western Marne. Barrel vinification lends charcuterie complexity. It lacks vibrancy, fruit expression and persistence, finishing bitter and callow.

Bourgeois-Diaz Cuvée M 100% Meunier NV $$$

90 points • 2014 base vintage • Disgorged 22 November 2016 and 2 June 2017 • Tasted in Australia

100% meunier from Villiers-Saint-Denis; average vine age 40 years; 35% fermented in oak barrels, zero dosage; 4154 bottles; cork

Mature-vine meunier defines a spicy and characterful style that contrasts the savoury complexity of partial barrel fermentation with the tang of vibrant 2014 acidity. With a full straw hue and a subtle blush tint, this is a spicy style of baked apple, nutmeg, vanilla and honey, finishing firm with dry extract and a little phenolic grip that would appreciate a touch of dosage to tone its finish. Oak use is well handled, balanced acidity is well married with low dosage, and lees age has built subtle pâtisserie notes which carry with good persistence. A characterful expression of the secondary personality of meunier.

Église Saint-Brice d'Aÿ dates from the 1400s.

BRIMONCOURT

(Brih-mon-cour)

84 BOULEVARD CHARLES DE GAULLE, 51160 AŸ
www.brimoncourt.com

BRIMONCOURT
CHAMPAGNE

Brimoncourt was born in 2008 when Reims-born New York lawyer Alexandre Cornot came to the rescue of Champagne's oldest label print house. He ultimately bought the 1883 premises in Aÿ, complete with old machines and 8000 printing blocks still on their shelves. The family who owned the Brimoncourt brand agreed to sell it, and Alexandre embarked upon its revival. Gathering a young team around him, he called on his grower and cooperative friends, sourcing chardonnay from the Côte des Blancs and Sézanne, and pinot and a little meunier for rosé from the Montagne de Reims and Vallée de la Marne. He employed François Huré (from Huré Frères in Ludes) as oenologist and they produced their first harvest in 2009. The focus of the brand is on the elegance of chardonnay fermented in stainless steel tanks and aged long on lees, showcased in a range of non-vintage blends to date, with a 2009 blanc de blancs vintage cuvée yet to be released. The house has grown quickly to more than 150,000 bottles, with an aspiration of 300–400,000. The house style is marked by phenolic bitterness.

BRIMONCOURT BRUT RÉGENCE NV $$

88 points • 2014 BASE VINTAGE • DISGORGED JANUARY 2018 • TASTED IN AUSTRALIA

80% chardonnay, 20% pinot from Hautvillers, Avenay-Val-d'Or, Cuis and Vertus; fermented in stainless steel tanks; aged 3 years on lees; 6.1g/L dosage; cork; 80% of production

Regarded by the house as its flagship, this is a bright and crunchy style that celebrates chardonnay in a palate accented with lemon, grapefruit, nashi pear and star fruit. Three years on lees has infused layers of brioche and almond nougat. It concludes with bitter, grainy phenolic bite.

BRIMONCOURT BLANC DE BLANCS NV $$

86 points • 2013 BASE VINTAGE • DISGORGED JANUARY 2018 • TASTED IN AUSTRALIA

100% chardonnay from Avize, Vertus, Oger, Grauves, Mesnil-sur-Oger, Villers-Marmery, Cuis and Chouilly; aged 4 years on lees; fermented in stainless steel tanks; 7.1g/L dosage; cork

Four years lees age has built a biscuity style, upholding the salty definition of the Côte des Blancs. A dusty overlay of imperfect fruit quashes the vibrancy and precision that is expected from great crus in the strong 2013 season. It concludes with phenolic bite and dry astringency.

BRIMONCOURT BRUT ROSÉ NV $$

88 points • 2013 BASE VINTAGE • DISGORGED DECEMBER 2017 • TASTED IN AUSTRALIA

35% chardonnay, 40% pinot, 25% meunier from Villers-Marmery, Vertus, Avenay-Val-d'Or, Mailly, Hautvillers, Rilly-la-Montagne, Ludes, Ville-Dommange, Oger, Avize, Grauves and Chouilly; 17% still red wine from Aÿ; fermented in stainless steel tanks; aged 4 years on lees; 8g/L dosage; cork

Rosé has been Brimoncourt's most balanced cuvée since the inception of this young house, and 17% represents a generous inclusion of red wine, making for a cuvée of medium crimson hue and brimming with red cherry, red apple and strawberry fruit. It's a clean, balanced and fruit-focused style. Firm, bitter phenolic bite marks the finish.

BRIMONCOURT EXTRA BRUT NV $$$

84 points • 2012 BASE VINTAGE • DISGORGED DECEMBER 2017 • TASTED IN AUSTRALIA

80% chardonnay, 20% pinot from Aÿ, Bouzy, Ambonnay, Cramant, Oger, Le Mesnil-sur-Oger; fermented in stainless steel tanks; aged 5 years on lees; 1.9g/L dosage; cork

The contrast of ripe and underripe fruit lends notes of fresh asparagus and honey, concluding with lemony acidity and bitter roast hazelnut complexity. The bite of phenolic bitterness is pronounced and renders the finish astringent.

The majestic slopes of Aÿ, summer 2018

BRUNO PAILLARD

(Broo-no Peye-yarh)

7/10

AVENUE DE CHAMPAGNE 51100 REIMS
www.champagnebrunopaillard.com

Champagne

BRUNO PAILLARD

Reims-France

When Lanson-BCC director and former CIVC communications chair and Appellation Committee president Bruno Paillard set out to establish his own champagne brand in 1981, he sold his Jaguar to finance the operation. 'It takes three generations to create a house,' he says. 'But there are some advantages starting three centuries after everyone else!' Almost four decades on, his finely crafted cuvées are evidence of just what can be achieved with sufficient connections and determination… and one Jaguar.

It's no simple thing to establish a champagne house, and when Paillard set out he had no land, no stock, no vineyards and no right to even purchase fruit. What he did have was a great network and considerable knowledge. Back then, a regulation banned any upstart from purchasing fruit, so, instead, he sourced wines from earlier vintages to establish his brand and gain purchasing rights.

A generation later, Paillard crafts a stable production of around 400,000 bottles annually – 'small enough to hand-craft, but large enough to make the hard decisions and to be selective!' he says. The freedom to be selective is fundamental for Paillard, and he sets the rare and noble precedent of selling half the fruit he presses, all of his second pressings, and anything else that doesn't meet the standard for his blends.

Paillard has assembled an enviable cache of estate vines since 1994, with each selection curated according to its potential in his blends. Sourcing spans more than 40 villages, with 105 plots across 34 hectares of estate vines in 17 villages (including an enviable 12 hectares of grand crus) supplying an impressive 50–60% of requirements. Chardonnay is sourced exclusively from the Côte des Blancs, pinot from the Montagne de Reims and Les Riceys in

the Aube, and meunier from the Montagne de Reims and the south-facing slopes of the eastern reaches of the Vallée de la Marne.

Vineyards are ploughed to encourage deep roots and worked with no herbicides or pesticides, calling for a vineyard worker for every two hectares, rather than the average three hectares. Paillard says it takes 5–8 years to get the results he wants. 'A lot of people thought we were crazy to work this way!' he admits. 'Most of the vineyards we purchase are not in a good position, so we need to work very hard and be brutal to encourage the roots to go deep. We have had plots with 10–15% mortality, and some up to 40%, and it's impossible to guess before we start. It's a bit of hard love!'

Paillard built his winemaking facility next door to Piper-Heidsieck in Bezannes on the outskirts of Reims in 1990, and expanded its capacity in 2000. In 2018 he commissioned a new press centre with a smaller press and gravity flow to 12 small settling tanks to permit more precise, parcel-by-parcel vinification. Temperature-controlled settling tanks were a response to warmer harvests.

Every parcel is vinified separately in 96 tanks and 400 old oak barrels purchased after three vintages, and kept for eight or

nine. A further 100 barrels hold reserve wines. Just one-fifth of all base wines are fermented and matured in barrels, so as not to dominate the blends, with the exception of his Nec Plus Ultra cuvée, which is entirely barrel fermented.

Malolactic fermentation is carried to completion in 80–90% of ferments. Late bottling dictates that every barrel goes through malolactic, while tanks can be blocked by temperature control. 'As harvests continue to warm, we may evolve this in the coming years,' explains Alice Paillard, who ably assists her father in taking responsibility for sales and marketing of the house. 'To maintain energy, balance and finesse, if we need to increase the malic acidity we will. Everything needs to change for everything to stay the same!'

In 1985, Paillard established a reserve solera which today comprises between 25% and 51% of each of his multi-vintage cuvées (as he prefers to call them). Testimony to his skill, his reserve is impeccably managed and fresh, bringing texture and complexity to his blends, while never imposing heaviness or tertiary complexity; 35% of the previous year's blend is added as reserve. All cuvées are aged long, with Brut NV and Rosé enjoying three years on lees, Blanc de Blancs four, Vintage eight and Nec Plus Ultra 11–12. Every cuvée is extra brut, with low dosages of between 3g/L and 6g/L.

Progressive from the outset, Paillard led the way in using a gyropalette in Champagne, and was the first in the region to publish the disgorgement date on every bottle (and every carton) – more than controversial when he set out in 1983. Today, his website is super informative.

Paillard is an influential and respected figure in Champagne, volunteering 10–20% of his time to responsibilities to support the region, and is currently Commandeur of the Order des Coteaux de Champagne

BRUNO PAILLARD PREMIÈRE CUVÉE NV $$

94 points • 2013 BASE VINTAGE • DISGORGED OCTOBER 2017 • TASTED IN CHAMPAGNE

33% chardonnay from the Côte des Blancs and Étoges, 45% pinot from the Montagne de Reims and from Les Riceys (not always in the blend but especially in cooler years), 22% meunier from the north of the Montagne de Reims and the first 15km of the Vallée de la Marne, from Hautvillers to Festigny; 35 villages; only the first pressing; 20% fermented in old barrels; reserve solera dating from 1985, including 35% of the previous year's blend; aged 3 years on lees; 5g/L dosage

Bruno Paillard describes his entry cuvée as 'a synthesis of the three varieties, an assemblage in the noble sense of the term'. It's a wonderfully jubilant wine that celebrates the fleshy personality of pinot first and foremost in wonderful red cherry and strawberry fruits, bringing tension with the citrus zest of chardonnay. The whole accord is given wonderful brioche and bitter almond complexity and creamy texture thanks to a portion of barrel fermentation, three years lees age and not least very deep and sensitively deployed reserves. In time, hints of marzipan emanate. It concludes long and linear, with beautifully fine chalk minerality. A benchmark Bruno Paillard and testimony to both a wonderful base vintage and the exacting craft of this small house.

BRUNO PAILLARD DOSAGE ZÉRO NV $$$

89 points • DISGORGED FEBRUARY 2018 • TASTED IN AUSTRALIA

106 parcels from more than 30 crus; a large proportion of reserves, vinified in wood; aged 3 years on lees; zero dosage; cork

A bold inclusion of substantial wood-vinified reserves makes for a chewy and firm Zéro that contrasts charcuterie complexity with the vanilla-custard creaminess of age. It's at once soft and spicy and at the same time tangy and edgy, with complex notes of quince and orange zest. Its bitter edge, tannin grip and acid tension make for a fearsome finish, which would appreciate a little dosage to soften. Not for the timid.

BRUNO PAILLARD ROSÉ PREMIÈRE CUVÉE NV $$$

93 points • 2013 BASE VINTAGE • DISGORGED OCTOBER 2017 • TASTED IN CHAMPAGNE

80-85% pinot, 15-20% chardonnay from the northern Côte des Blancs; typically less than 5% pinot noir red wine; only the first press; 35% reserve solera back to 1985; 5g/L dosage

Bruno Paillard considers the role that a touch of northern Côte des Blancs chardonnay play in his rosé to be like that of a classic ruby ring, surrounded by diamonds to bring light to the ruby. The aspiration of his rosé is to showcase the delicacy and fragility of pinot — more delicate than chardonnay, with thin skins, requiring a very precise harvest-timing decision, and the longest in the cellar before it opens up to be ready to taste.

With a pretty pale-salmon hue, this is a rosé of real definition, alive with pomegranate, pink grapefruit and strawberry hull, fresh and fruity and yet exactingly focused, drawn out by excellent, vibrant acidity, fine chalk minerality and fine-ground tannin structure. It handles this tannin impeccably, without falling into astringency or bitterness, uniting comfortably with the salty umami character of the chalk on a long and bright finish. The creamy texture of three years lees age has unified everything harmoniously.

BRUNO PAILLARD BLANC DE BLANCS GRAND CRU NV $$$

95 points • 2011 BASE VINTAGE • DISGORGED SEPTEMBER 2016 • TASTED IN CHAMPAGNE

40% Le Mesnil-sur-Oger, 40% Oger and 20% Avize, Cramant and Chouilly; 40% reserve solera back to 1985; aged 4 years on lees; clear bottle in biodegradable cellophane wrap; aged 4 years on lees; 5g/L dosage

A wisp of grilled-bread reduction heralds a style of beautiful fruit intensity, wonderful acid tension and heightened, super-fine, salty chalk minerality, an exacting articulation of the ancient geology of the five most legendary grand crus of the Côte des Blancs. Boasting wonderful line and length, the focus and tension of its drive is impeccably softened by the silky, creamy structure of long lees age. Its deep reserves are strategically yet gently played to craft a delightfully effortless blanc de blancs that utterly transcends its challenging base year.

BRUNO PAILLARD BLANC DE BLANCS EXTRA BRUT 2006 $$$$

93 points • DISGORGED JULY 2015 • TASTED IN CHAMPAGNE

Grand crus of the Côte des Blancs and Vertus; aged 8 years on lees; 4g/L dosage

Bruno Paillard describes 2006 as *volupté* (voluptuous), an abundant vintage which required severe grape selection, and in which chardonnay was the clear winner. He has faithfully captured the generous, velvety, silky, buttery mood of the harvest in a grand and rich display of bright, medium straw hue and succulent white peach and juicy pear. Age both on and off lees has blessed it with vanilla and almond nougat, accented with gentle, creamy palate softness and fine mineral grip. A well-composed cuvée, ready to drink now.

BRUNO PAILLARD ASSEMBLAGE BRUT 2008 $$$$

96 points • DISGORGED JUNE 2015 • TASTED IN CHAMPAGNE

42% chardonnay, 42% pinot, 16% meunier from 10 crus; aged 6 years on lees and 3 years on cork; 5g/L dosage

A vintage that combines maturity with vivacious energy, Bruno likes 2008 'because the character of the vintage was a good match for our style'. True to the Peter Pan endurance of this stunning season, the same disgorgement I reviewed two years ago is looking even more magnificent today. I predicted at the time that 'it needs at least another few years before approaching and will happily live for a decade and beyond', and it has followed this trajectory in slow motion, so I would still hold off for another few years. The tension of 2008 plays to exacting effect in the precise yet generous style of Bruno Paillard. Its heightened acidity drives a taut structure that contrasts subtle biscuit, toasted brioche and almond nougat development of six years on lees. Testimony to grand fruit sources, a core of strawberry and lemon fruit translates bright energy, enduring structure, and well articulating prominent, fine, salty chalk mineral mouthfeel. A cuvée that sings with the stamina of the season in pitch-perfect high notes sustained with sensational line and persistence.

BRUNO PAILLARD N.P.U. NEC PLUS ULTRA 2002 $$$$$

95 points • DISGORGED SEPTEMBER 2014 • TASTED IN CHAMPAGNE

50% chardonnay, 50% pinot from Oger, Le Mesnil-sur-Oger, Chouilly, Verzenay, Mailly and Bouzy; fermented and matured 10 months exclusively in 28 small old oak barrels; 3g/L dosage; aged 11 years on lees; 6200 bottles

Literally 'ultimate', N.P.U. is 'a very different plant in the B.P. solar system', suggests Alice Paillard. 'It's not intended to be the best wine, but a cuvée that we push to the extreme.' She qualifies this by adding that 'liveliness is more the focus here than complexity and richness' (though its age and method, and not least the exuberant magnitude of the results, strongly suggest the opposite). The idea is to create this cuvée only in the greatest vintages, and 2002 is the sixth since 1990 (including 2003, which was released in 2016).

In the wake of the expansive proportions of the 1999 and 2003 releases, I wondered to what extent the magnitude of N.P.U. was the philosophy of the cuvée compared with the volume of the season. Herein lies the answer, because even the poised 2002 vintage presents great amplitude here. It delivers this with silky structure, cuddly allure and wonderful focus and integrity. With a medium yellow hue and tints of gold, this is a powerful and ripe 2002 of bold, golden fruit cake, grilled pineapple and dried peach, layered with the brioche, honey and nougat of maturity. A hint of balsamic is characteristic of the style. It holds this grand fanfare with great persistence, succulent on the front, flowing into a finish with some dry grip defining the structure as much as its chalk minerality and well-integrated acidity. It holds long and strong.

CAMILLE SAVÈS

(Cah-mill Sah-ves)

7/10

4 RUE DE CONDÉ BP 22 51150 BOUZY
www.champagne-saves.com

S

Eugène Savès began estate-bottling champagne in Bouzy in 1910 and his 1880 press still stands proudly in front of the press house. Today, fourth-generation grower and Harley rider Hervé Savès riddles bottles for an hour every morning before carefully tending 10 hectares of family vineyards across 25 plots on the famed Montagne de Reims terroirs of Bouzy, Ambonnay, Tours-sur-Marne and Tauxières-Mutry.

Every time I visit Savès I am impressed by the spotless order of his facilities, which are climate-controlled to 10–12°C. 'The precision of the vinification and cleanliness of the cellar are important for sustaining the minerality of our terroirs,' he outlines. For the same reason, Savès has fully blocked malolactic fermentation in all of his cuvées except Coteaux Champenois since 1982 (his cool cellar temperature ensures malolactic doesn't kick off spontaneously). 'This respects the wine and you can feel the terroir and minerality.' He points out that many other good growers in Bouzy are now also blocking malolactic, prompted by warmer vintages due to global warming. 'I would like to conserve the acidity and freshness,' he says.

Mature pinot noir (85%) and chardonnay (15%) vines are managed naturally with respect for the soil, with crop-thinning to balance yields and emphasise site character. Savès cultivates the soil and propagates grasses in the mid-rows. No insecticides or herbicides are used, though a synthetic fungicide prohibits a fully organic approach.

Wines are fermented and aged cool in climate-controlled, small stainless steel tanks and oak barrels. New stainless steel tanks replaced his old enamel-lined tanks in 2015, and in 2018 he installed a new Coquard press. In tasting reserves with Savès, I am impressed with the freshness, liveliness and fruit presence of his wines and the very elegant influence of oak barrels. He is impressed with the effect of oak vinification for his Blanc de Blancs, Blanc de Noirs, single-vineyard cuvées and *liqueur de dosage*, and has been increasing his stocks of barrels and foudres. All barrels are purchased new and seasoned by fermenting tailles for the first two years. Reserves are held in barrel until the next harvest.

All ten of his cuvées spend at least four years on lees. All are built exclusively on Bouzy, except his entry Carte Blanche, a blend of his four villages. An annual production of about 85,000 bottles includes a still pinot noir from old Bouzy vines. Red wine is a specialty for Savès and he makes the rouge for Alfred Gratien's impressive Cuvée Paradis Rosé (see page 92).

Savès' attention to detail is exacting, right down to hand riddling his vintage and single-vineyard cuvées and laser etching disgorgement dates on every bottle. New front labels are very smart, and refreshed back labels boast disgorgement dates for export markets. His informative new website features tech sheets for every cuvée.

When I commended him on his cuvées, he humbly credited Bouzy and Ambonnay. His precise approach and mineral attentiveness is the perfect foil for his bold terroirs, producing impeccably crafted champagnes of confident, intense, pinot-led character, honed by malic acidity. They represent excellent value.

CAMILLE SAVÈS PREMIER CRU CARTE BLANCHE NV $$

94 points • 2012 BASE VINTAGE • DISGORGED 20 NOVEMBER 2017 • TASTED IN CHAMPAGNE

25% chardonnay from Tauxières-Mutry, 75% pinot from Bouzy, Ambonnay and Tours-sur-Marne; 20 plots; average vine age 35 years; vinified and aged 7 months in stainless steel tanks; 40% 2011 reserves; no malolactic fermentation; 9g/L dosage

Hervé Savès calls Bouzy 'the Chambertin of Champagne', and to temper its strength and dominance he adds a touch of chardonnay to his entry blend. He describes 2012 as a very beautiful vintage, and the precision of his style and the personality of Bouzy and its neighbours sings right from his very first cuvée. This is a focused expression of some of Champagne's most powerful and celebrated villages, alive with flamboyant red cherries and strawberries, underlined by pink grapefruit tang. It's got it all – persistence, purity, freshness, energy and beautifully fine chalk minerality. The finest since the stunning 2008 base, a magnificent celebration of pinot noir from some of its most fabled crus. Wow, what a start!

CAMILLE SAVÈS GRAND CRU CARTE D'OR BOUZY NV $$

91 points • 2011 BASE VINTAGE • DISGORGED 26 NOVEMBER 2016 • TASTED IN CHAMPAGNE

25% chardonnay, 75% pinot; 12 plots in Bouzy; vinified and aged 7 months in stainless steel tanks; 2010 reserves; no malolactic fermentation; 8g/L dosage

A blend of Bouzy pinot and chardonnay. Savès explains that Bouzy has more chardonnay on the flat near the village, since there is just 10 centimetres of soil before the chalk here. There is more pinot on the slope, where there is more clay. This cuvée is also produced as an Extra Brut with 4g/L dosage.

Sourcing exclusively from one village provides little insurance against the tough seasons, and while Savès' exacting approach has drawn some wonderful single-vineyard and vintage cuvées from the troubled 2011 season, my suspicion is that holding off for his 2012 base Carte d'Or will pay dividends. Nonetheless, the dark cherry, plum and spice personality of Bouzy pinot noir resonates with great depth here. It lingers with deep black fruits and finishes with just a little of the dusty extract of the 2011 vintage. Still, it's a credit to Savès for extracting such class and depth from two challenging seasons.

CAMILLE SAVÈS GRAND CRU CUVÉE PRESTIGE BOUZY NV $$

96 points • 2012 BASE VINTAGE • DISGORGED 18 FEBRUARY 2016 • TASTED IN CHAMPAGNE

65% chardonnay, 35% pinot; 100% Bouzy; vinified and aged 7 months in stainless steel tanks; 25% 2011 reserves fermented and aged in oak barrels; no malolactic fermentation; aged 4-5 years on lees; 8g/L dosage; 10% of production, around 8500 bottles

To capture the expansive complexity and grand cru proportions of Bouzy with definition, finesse and energy calls for exacting skill, exemplified by Hervé Saves and nowhere more pronounced than in his Prestige. Evidence that there's more to Bouzy than just pinot noir, this is a cuvée led by grand cru chardonnay of very distinct character to the Côte des Blancs. It assumes its lead to compelling effect, with ripe nectarine and pineapple supported by the strawberry and black cherry fruit of pinot noir. Fine, scintillating, crystalline chalk minerality unites effortlessly with bright malic acidity to define a finish of focus and poise that lingers undeterred for minutes. The 2012 base is every bit as lofty as the sensational 2008, and that says a lot. Benchmark Bouzy, this is a stunning tribute to Savès' hallowed terroirs and acute attention to detail, one of the finest cuvées for its price on the shelves this year.

CAMILLE SAVÈS GRAND CRU CUVÉE ROSÉ BOUZY NV $$

94 points • 2013 BASE VINTAGE • DISGORGED 15 MAY 2017 • TASTED IN CHAMPAGNE

60% chardonnay, 28% pinot white wine, 12% Bouzy rouge; 2012 reserves; vinified and aged 7 months in stainless steel tanks; no malolactic fermentation; 8g/L dosage; 15% of production, around 13,000 bottles

The definition of malic acidity and Savès' restraint make Bouzy rosé a naturally elegant hit, surprisingly but intelligently led by chardonnay. Savès' deeply coloured red wine infuses a medium salmon hue. True to his craft, the result is characterful and precise, singing with the red fruits of deep Bouzy rouge, while beautifully toned by its chardonnay lead. Succulent red cherry, wild strawberry, raspberry fruit and even notes of anise unite with pink grapefruit freshness, energised by malic acidity that heightens prominent chalk mineral brightness, blending in beautifully with finely managed tannin structure. A fabulous rosé from a red wine master, it's no surprise it represents an impressive 15% of production.

CAMILLE SAVÈS GRAND CRU LE MONT DES TOURS BLANC DE BLANCS BOUZY NV $$$

94 points • 2011 BASE VINTAGE • DISGORGED 19 MARCH 2017 • TASTED IN CHAMPAGNE

100% chardonnay; single vineyard of 0.37 hectares on just 10cm of soil above chalk at the bottom of the slope west of Bouzy; 35-year-old vines are not very vigorous, hence small production; fermented and aged for 7 months in barrels; aged on lees in bottle 3–4 years; 10% 2010 reserves; no malolactic fermentation; 4g/L dosage

The generosity of Bouzy reverberates in chardonnay equally as it does in pinot noir, brimming with mirabelle plums, pineapple, golden fruit cake and fruit mince spice. Holding with great line and length, the finish is defined by the vibrancy of malic acidity and the pronounced chalk minerality of the thin soils on the flat of Bouzy. Its integrity is testimony to Savès' attentiveness to the date of harvest in the hot 2011 season, a stunning result for these two tough vintages.

CAMILLE SAVÈS GRAND CRU LES LOGES BLANC DE NOIRS BOUZY NV $$$$

94 points • 2011 BASE VINTAGE • DISGORGED 15 MAY 2017 • TASTED IN CHAMPAGNE

100% pinot; single vineyard of 0.47 hectares of vines almost 40 years of age in the middle of the slope in the heart of Bouzy; fermented and aged for 7 months in barrels; aged on lees in bottle 3–4 years; 10% 2010 reserves; no malolactic fermentation; 4g/L dosage

Boasting a medium straw hue with a blush tint, the deep black fruits of Bouzy resonate in notes of satsuma plum, liquorice and plum liqueur, masterfully toned by malic acidity and the gentle tannin grip of oak fermentation, building its dark chocolate and roasted coffee bean allure. With freshness, poise and precision so seldom seen in 2011 (or 2010, for that matter), it lingers with wonderful integrity, focused line and exacting chalk mineral precision.

Camille Savès Grand Cru Bouzy 2011 $$$

93 points • Disgorged 15 January 2017 • Tasted in Champagne

20% chardonnay, 80% pinot; 100% mid-slope Bouzy vines over 35 years of age; vinified and aged 7 months in stainless steel tanks; no malolactic fermentation; 7g/L dosage

Hervé Savès has drawn a vintage cuvée of rare integrity from the tumultuous and hot 2011 season, testimony to his attentiveness to the date of harvest and very strict selection. It leads out confidently with deep and powerful satsuma plum and black cherry fruits, accented boldly with notes of fruit mince spice and dark fruit cake, even plum liqueur. Oak heightens notes of coffee, dark chocolate and well-managed dry extract, while the focus remains resolutely on extroverted presence of bright, crunchy, dark fruits. Vibrant malic acid line is well supported by the chalk minerality of Bouzy, holding precision and composure long on the finish. A standout 2011.

Camille Savès Cuvée Anaïs Jolicoeur Brut Grand Cru Bouzy 2012 $$$$

95 points • Disgorged 15 May 2017 • Tasted in Champagne

10% chardonnay, 90% pinot; 5 plots in the heart of Bouzy: Les Cercets, Les Pierres, Le Bas de la Haie de la Lue, Les Loges and La Poivresse; fermented and aged for 7 months in barrels; aged on lees in bottle 3-4 years; no malolactic fermentation; 7g/L dosage

Barrel fermentation and maturation to tone the tense malic acidity of 2012 would seem a natural fit for pinot noir of the concentration of Bouzy, but the balance is a delicate one, and a result as impeccably crafted as this is testimony to the talent and sensitivity of Hervé Savès. The first release of his flagship since the thrilling 2008, this is a vintage in which the magnitude and magnificence of Bouzy attain soaring heights, reverberating with deep satsuma plum and black cherry fruit, bolstered by firm, fine tannin structure. The dark chocolate and dark roasted coffee beans of oak fermentation sit calm and acquiescent in the background. For its bold frame and deep wells of complexity, it remains beautifully poised, thanks to the freshness of malic acidity, carrying the finish very long, linear and tense. A cuvée of magnificent body and chiselled magnitude. Named after Hervé's great-grandmother, wife of the founder, Camille Savès. She would be proud.

Camille Savès Coteaux Champenois Grand Cru Bouzy Rouge 2011 $$

91 points • Tasted in Champagne

Savès' three best Bouzy vineyards: La Poivresse, Le Nonicart and Les Loges, two high on the slope and one in the heart of the slope of 65-year-old vines; green harvested in July to 7-8 tonnes per hectare; 10-15% whole bunches; aged 10 months in barrel; bottled 2-3 years after harvest, following full natural malolactic fermentation

Hervé Savès makes a good Bouzy rouge, even in a season as tough as 2011. It's laced with white pepper, set against a backdrop of red cherry and blackberry fruit, beautifully fragranced with violet aromas. Black and red cherry fruit lay out a finish of excellent presence, depth and lingering line. Vibrant acidity and fine, firm tannins both scream out for many years to integrate and soften.

Canard-Duchêne

(Cah-nah Dew-shen)

61 Rue Edmond-Canard 51500 Ludes
www.canard-duchene.fr

CHAMPAGNE
Canard-Duchêne
MAISON FONDÉE EN 1868
FRANCE

'I make wine first, and then I make sparkling wine with bubbles,' says Laurent Fédou, chef de cave of Canard-Duchêne since the house was acquired from LVMH in 2003 by entrepreneur Alain Thiénot (see page 528). 'That was the black history of the company, as LVMH was not interested in Canard-Duchêne,' Fédou reflects, 'so Thiénot charged me to "make the wine so people are proud to drink it". And we slowly cleaned up the house and changed the style to become more modern and young.' Over the past 15 years, Canard-Duchêne has doubled production to 4 million bottles and continues to grow slowly. The brand has traditionally been an inexpensive champagne, and remains relatively affordable. These are largely simple, fruity champagnes._

From its home in the village of Ludes on the northern slopes of the Montagne de Reims, Canard-Duchêne claims to be the only négociant house located in the vineyards (though a list of others would contest this). 'Pinot noir is the fingerprint of the house,' declares Fédou, 'and we are located in the Montagne de Reims near the growers.'

The company is privileged to 45 hectares of vineyards, supplemented substantially from some 350 hectares owned by growers, many of whom the house has sourced from for 10–15 years. The diversity of its sourcing spans 60 communes in Ludes, the Vallée de la Marne, Côte des Blancs, Sézanne, and a significant proportion from the Aube.

Fédou has slowly increased the representation of pinot noir in the blends, and most of all in his Cuvée Léonie range, which he describes as 'a rich, rounded and fruity style focused on pinot noir'. Once only a French supermarket brand, Fédou introduced Cuvée Léonie to realise Canard-Duchêne's aspiration to be a global brand with a focus on restaurants, airlines and boutique hotels. The Cuvée Léonie range now represent 1 million bottles, one-quarter of the production of the house.

Fédou's aspiration is to pick ripe grapes. Every cuvée goes through full malolactic fermentation. With the advent of warmer vintages, he experimented with blocking malolactic, but found that this changed the style of the house, and instead prefers to use components from higher-acid villages in his blends.

In addition to the Léonie range, Fédou has been responsible for developing Canard-Duchêne's Charles VII and Parcelle 181 organic wine, a statement of the house's commitment to sustainability.

Canard-Duchêne Brut NV $$

83 points • Tasted in Australia

20% chardonnay, 40% pinot, 40% meunier; 20% reserves; 9g/L dosage; cork

A cuvée led by pinot noir and meunier, true to the style of the house. This is regrettably a particularly dusty and mushroomy release, with marked dry rot in the fruit imposing an astringent, grubby, bitter and truncated palate.

Canard-Duchêne Rosé NV $$

84 points • Tasted in Australia

30% chardonnay, 30% pinot, 40% meunier; 10% pinot noir red wine; 8g/L dosage; DIAM

With a medium salmon hue, this is a rosé of crab apple bite and tart redcurrant crunch. Its phenolic bitterness is overwhelming, quashing its subtle, tangy red fruit presence.

Canard-Duchêne Cuvée Léonie Brut NV $$

85 points • Tasted in Australia

20% chardonnay, 50% pinot, 30% meunier; 25% reserves; aged 3 years on lees; 8g/L dosage; DIAM

Devoid of the bright fruitiness that has defined this cuvée in the past, this is a developed style, marked by the burnt toffee and spice notes of oxidation. Primary fruits have been quashed, leaving dry, bitter phenolic grip to dominate a short finish. A second bottle was identical.

Canard-Duchêne Cuvée Léonie Brut Rosé NV $$

88 points • Tasted in Australia

30% chardonnay, 30% pinot, 40% meunier; 25% pinot noir vinified in red reserves; 3 years on lees; certified vegan; dedicated to the founder of the house; 8g/L dosage; DIAM

25% pinot noir red wine is a monumental proportion and infuses a bright, medium-salmon hue, much more subtle than expected for such a strong inclusion. The palate is likewise subtle in its red fruits influence, a cuvée of pomegranate, strawberry hull and cracked pink pepper. Red wine tannins lend bitter grip to the finish, though nonetheless finely structured. A clean, fresh and lively style in which bright acidity is well balanced by integrated dosage.

Canard-Duchêne Parcelle 181 Extra Brut $$

88 points • Tasted in Australia

40% chardonnay, 30% pinot, 30% meunier; from the 7-hectare Parcelle 181 in Verneuil, plus 5 hectares in Villers-Marmery, Moussy, Villenauxe-la-Grande and Épernay; certified organic; chardonnay fermented in oak; aged 3 years on lees; less than 6g/L dosage; DIAM

Parcelle 181 presents a contrast between crunchy red apple, bitter grapefruit and the brioche and freshly buttered toast of lees age. A fresh and clean style of focused acidity and low dosage, the finish is marked by grainy, bitter phenolic grip.

Canard-Duchêne Millésime Vintage 2012 $$

90 points • Tasted in Australia

40% chardonnay, 46% pinot, 14% meunier; Ambonnay, Chouilly, Verzy and Avenay-Val-d'Or; aged at least 4 years on lees; 8g/L dosage; cork

True to the brightness and balance of the 2012 season, this is a strong vintage release for Canard, built around crunchy red apple and zesty grapefruit, underscored by the almond-meal complexity and creamy texture of four years of lees age. The bright lemon tang of the season carries long through the palate, with some grainy, pear-skin like phenolic bitterness on the close.

Canard-Duchêne Charles VII Blanc de Blancs Brut NV $$

87 points • Tasted in Australia

100% chardonnay; 25–30% reserves; aged 4 years on lees; 6g/L dosage; DIAM

This is a concentrated and characterful release for Charles VII, and its bright, medium-straw hue does little to anticipate the impact to follow, filled with preserved lemon and golden delicious apple, even grilled pineapple and fruit mince spice. A touch of volatility and burnt-orange oxidation makes for a developed style displaying some dryness and degradation on a firm finish, suggesting premature oxidation. A second bottle was identical.

Canard-Duchêne Charles VII Blanc de Noirs Brut NV $$

86 points • Tasted in Australia

70% pinot, 30% meunier; 20% reserves; aged 4 years on lees; 9g/L dosage; DIAM

An especially secondary release for Charles VII, this is a cuvée that presents a medium straw hue amidst layered complexity of brioche, roasted almonds and buttered toast. It leads out with subtle golden delicious apple, lemon and pear fruit, which unfortunately dissipates rapidly, trumped by grainy apple-skin bitterness that renders the finish callow, dry and short.

Canard-Duchêne Cuvée V Vintage 2010

91 points • Tasted in Australia en magnum

30% chardonnay from Avize and Chouilly, 60% pinot from Ambonnay and Aÿ, 10% meunier; to mark the 150th anniversary of the house (founded 1868); 6g/L dosage; 7000 magnums; DIAM

Fédou refers to this as a 'free-style cuvée, as we had no restraints, and aimed to make the best that we could'. He suggests 'V' stands for Victor Canard, the founder of the company. And for victory, vintage and vineyards! With a medium straw hue, this is a cuvée that upholds crunchy brightness in a magnum of nine years of age. Accurate to the signature of the house, pinot noir takes the lead in spicy red apple notes, contrasting the nashi pear and grapefruit tension of chardonnay, and even a note of fennel. Lees age has layered notes of biscuity brioche, lemon meringue and vanilla nougat, concluding with well-integrated dosage. It holds good persistence, though the grainy, phenolic, dry grip of 2010 lends an astringency to a slightly muted finish. Nonetheless, one of the most precise cuvées I've tasted from Canard-Duchêne, though the difficult 2010 season is a surprising choice of vintage for a cuvée that aspires to be the best the house could make.

CATTIER

(Ca-tiay)

6 Rue Dom Pérignon 51500 Chigny-les-Roses
www.cattier.com

CHAMPAGNE

CATTIER

Every summer, roses burst into colour along the streets and premier cru vineyards of the romantic village of Chigny-les-Roses, on the northern slopes of the Montagne de Reims. The family-owned house of Cattier is the most famous in the village, a small négociant with an annual production of 800,000 bottles spanning an extensive portfolio that captures the bright, clean, fruity elegance of the northern Montagne de Reims. Its non-vintage cuvées are the freshest I've seen them in some years, an impressive achievement because they're now matured for longer, too.

The Cattier family has long had its roots in the vines, owning vineyards in Chigny-les-Roses since 1625, and selling its own wines since 1918. It now tends 33 hectares of mainly premier cru vineyards, mostly in Chigny-les-Roses and nearby Ludes, Rilly-la-Montagne and Taissy, half planted to pinot noir, and the remainder equally to chardonnay and meunier. Vineyards are managed with an environmentally sustainable philosophy, supplying around one-third of the needs of the house, and supplemented with grapes from across Champagne, particularly from the Montagne and chardonnay from the Côte des Blancs.

Cattier's production reached a little over a million bottles prior to the economic crisis. The launch of Armand de Brignac (see page 107) in 2006 was timely, proving to be quite a boost to the company's profile.

Allocation of cuvées is made to each house prior to blending. 'The best for Armand de Brignac, of course,' highlights head of the house and winemaker, Jean-Jacques Cattier. He upholds that the growth of Armand de Brignac to a production of 100,000 bottles has not had a derogatory impact on the standard of Cattier.

In fact, it appears that something of the opposite effect may be playing out at Cattier. My most recent tastings have observed a newfound optimism in the style, coinciding with stylish new bottles and smart new labels. The family's resounding success with Armand de Brignac (not to mention the injection of funds and resources to go with it) now seems to be rubbing off on the mother ship.

Jean-Jacques retired and handed over responsibility to his son Alexandre in 2011, though still remains actively involved in the tastings, which he describes as the nicest part of the job. In October 2018, chef de cave since 2014 Émilien Boutillat took up a position at Piper-Heidsieck, so Alexandre has stepped up to taking full responsibility for winemaking.

A stock of 2.5 million bottles for both houses is matured in some of the region's deepest cellars in their 150-year-old facility purchased by Jean-Jacques' father in the 1960s in neighbouring Rilly-la-Montagne. A total of 2 kilometres of cellars in Chigny and Rilly have capacity for 5 million bottles, and while they are far from full, the space is supplemented with a 3600m² warehouse in Reims.

Cattier's Clos du Moulin cuvées exemplify the character and elegance of the northern Montagne.

Cattier's cellars under Rilly-la-Montagne are among the deepest in Champagne.

CATTIER BRUT PREMIER CRU NV $$

90 points • DISGORGED NOVEMBER 2018 • TASTED IN AUSTRALIA

25% chardonnay, 35% pinot, 40% meunier; aged 4 years on lees; 9g/L dosage; cork

A bright, clean and fruity style with a medium straw hue, celebrating the meunier and pinot of the northern Montagne de Reims. It unites red apple, pear and grapefruit with the gingernut biscuit notes of four years lees age and a touch of dry, phenolic grip. A full dosage of 9g/L provides a honeyed balance to its zesty northern acidity, and helps in countering its phenolic firmness. It holds good persistence on a bright finish accented by fine salt minerality. In its smart new bottle and elegant label, this is the finest I've seen Cattier's entry cuvée in at least five years, making for a value-for-money apéritif.

Cattier Brut Blanc de Blancs Premier Cru NV $$

91 points • **Disgorged September 2018** • **Tasted in Australia**

100% chardonnay; aged 4 years on lees; 9g/L dosage; cork

Cattier has ascended beautifully in the past few years to the freshest, cleanest and brightest I've ever seen it – a very impressive achievement as its non-vintage cuvées are now aged longer than ever (four years on lees). Its mood is now a more accurate reflection than ever of the bright elegance of the northern Montagne de Reims. Its blanc de blancs is a pretty, delicate, primary apéritif style that unites fresh lemon and crunchy nashi pear with only the most subtle reflections of development in almond meal nuances. Dosage finds an even harmony with bright acidity, fine chalk minerality and gentle phenolic structure. A light and refreshing style with a short finish.

Cattier Brut Millésime Premier Cru 2009 $$

89 points • **Disgorged October 2017** • **Tasted in Australia**

33% chardonnay, 33% pinot, 33% meunier; 7g/L dosage; cork

The rich and ripe 2009 season is articulated in developed fruit characters of red apple, pear and grapefruit. Seven years lees age has accumulated layers of biscuits, almonds and ginger. The phenolic bite of this warm vintage makes for a firm finish of grainy texture, beginning to tire and dry out. A vintage quickly fading.

Cattier Clos du Moulin Brut Premier Cru NV $$$$

93 points • **2008 base vintage** • **Disgorged November 2018** • **Tasted in Australia**

50% chardonnay, 50% pinot; 96 months on lees; from a single 2.2-hectare site on a gentle, windy ridge at the bottom of the village of Ludes, owned by the house since 1951; always a blend of three vintages; 40% 2007 and 10% 2006 reserves (declared on the back label); aged 6.5 years on lees; 6g/L dosage; 17,933 bottles; cork

Clos du Moulin remains the most famous and most engaging cuvée of Cattier. With another two years on lees since I tasted this blend for the previous edition of this guide, its medium straw hue has darkened a fraction and its primary assemblage of white citrus, wild strawberry, red cherry fruits, pink pepper and struck-flint reductive edge have begun to dim as the toast and brioche of bottle age have arisen. It holds its line, thanks to the tension of the 2008 vintage cutting through the finish, honed and angular, with chalk minerality and soft phenolic grip uniting to compelling effect. An elegantly understated style, refined and fine, an excellent expression of the restraint of the northern Montagne de Reims, true to the refined pinot and chardonnay of Ludes. Drink now. One bottle was mildly cork tainted.

Cattier Clos du Moulin Rosé Brut Premier Cru NV $$$$

91 points • **2009 base vintage** • **Disgorged 25 September 2018** • **Tasted in Australia**

50% chardonnay, 50% pinot; 2008 and 2007 reserves (declared on back label); aged 8 years on lees; vineyard as above; 6g/L dosage; 3325 bottles; cork

Carrying the mood of the warmer 2009 vintage, this release is a stark contrast to the bright freshness of the spectacular 2008 base before it. With a copper tint to its full salmon hue, this is a more savoury style, built around a core of red apple and strawberry fruits, accented with tomato and smoky paprika. The dry phenolic grip of 2009 makes for a firm, dry, grainy and short finish. The gentle acidity of ripe fruit melds seamlessly with nicely balanced dosage.

CHARLES DE CAZANOVE

(Shahl deh Cah-za-nohv)

---

8 PLACE DE LA RÉPUBLIQUE 51100 REIMS

www.champagnedecazanove.com

CHAMPAGNE

Charles
de Cazanove

Founded in Avize in 1811, Charles de Cazanove was the victim of a succession of buyouts in the latter half of the 20th century, ultimately landing as a key brand of the G.H. Martel group in 2004. With an annual production of more than 3 million bottles, the house represents a key brand across French supermarkets. Vinified mostly in stainless steel vats, with a little use of oak barrels, its inexpensive cuvées are young, fruity, sweet and simple.

CHARLES DE CAZANOVE BRUT TRADITION PÈRE & FILS TÊTE DE CUVÉE NV $

87 points • 2014 BASE VINTAGE • TASTED IN AUSTRALIA

20% chardonnay, 40% pinot, 40% meunier; Montagne de Reims; 20% reserves; aged 2 years on lees; 10g/L dosage; DIAM

A young, simple and fruit-focused style that contrasts ripe and underripe fruit in tropical fruit and even banana ripeness with firm, raw acid grip and rustic structure. Juvenile acidity and dosage reminiscent of green-apple chews unite to create a sweet and sour effect on a short and simple finish.

CHARLES DE CAZANOVE TRADITION PÈRE & FILS BRUT ROSÉ NV $$

88 points • 2014 BASE VINTAGE • TASTED IN AUSTRALIA

20% chardonnay, 40% pinot, 20% meunier; 15% red wine; Montagne de Reims; 20% reserves; aged 2 years on lees; 10g/L dosage; DIAM

A savoury cuvée of medium crimson hue, exacting a rhubarb and subtle tomato character, accented with strawberry hull tang, sadly devoid of perfume and fruit vibrancy. Full dosage tones a fine tannin grip and raw acidity on a short finish.

CHARLES DE CAZANOVE BRUT TRADITION PÈRE & FILS MILLÉSIME 2007 $$

89 points • TASTED IN AUSTRALIA

59% chardonnay, 26% pinot, 15% meunier; 9 years on lees; 10g/L dosage; DIAM

A ripe and fleshy style for 2007; nine years on lees has built a buttery, creamy, biscuity mood that unites stewed nectarines with notes of golden fruit cake. Full dosage is deployed tactically to counter an edgy bitterness to the finish.

Aÿ chardonnay, harvest 2014

CHARLES DUFOUR

(Shahl Dew-for)

---

6 RUE DE LA CROIX MALOT 10110 LANDREVILLE

www.bullesdecomptoir.fr

CHAMPAGNE

Charles Dufour

À LANDREVILLE

The young Charles Dufour cultivates six hectares of vines organically in Landreville and neighbouring Essoyes and Celles-sur-Ource in the Aube, planted to 60% pinot noir, 30% chardonnay and 10% pinot blanc. He makes his seven cuvées 'naturally', as he puts it — wild fermented, unfined, unfiltered, with no added sulphur, and low dosages under 6g/L and mostly under 4g/L. Regrettably, his low-sulphur regime in concert with long ageing (most of his cuvées are aged in Burgundy barrels and foudres on lees for 12 months) puts his wines at considerable risk of brettanomyces infection, though not all are affected.

CHARLES DUFOUR LE CHAMP DU CLOS BLANC DE BLANCS PINOT BLANC LR14 NV $$$$

86 points • 2014 BASE VINTAGE • DISGORGED 11 JULY 2017 • TASTED IN AUSTRALIA

Landreville; fermented and aged in barrels; unfiltered, unfined, wild yeast, no added sulphur

A lactic style of medium straw hue, inflicted with the charcuterie and boiled sausage notes of brettanomyces, rendering the finish dry, and accentuating the firm graininess of its pronounced phenolic grip. The acidity is tart and firm, lingering with lemon-butter character.

CHARLES DUFOUR BLANC GOURMAND COTEAUX CHAMPENOIS 2010 $$

90 points • TASTED IN AUSTRALIA

100% pinot blanc; Landreville; fermented and aged in barrels; unfiltered, unfined, wild yeast, no added sulphur; cork

The exotic mood of pinot blanc is preserved after nine years, with notes of star fruit, apple and grapefruit. Champagne acidity upholds its lively tang amidst the texture of bottle age. Wild fermentation has brought suggestions of charcuterie and spice. It holds good line and length; a pinot blanc of surprising integrity and endurance.

CHARLES HEIDSIECK

(Shahl E-dseek)

10/10

12 ALLÉE DU VIGNOBLE 51000 REIMS
www.charlesheidsieck.com

CHAMPAGNE

CHARLES HEIDSIECK

Maison fondée à Reims en 1851

Among the greatest of all champagne houses there is no common recipe for success, and the rise and rise of Charles Heidsieck over the past decades, and in particular the last eight years, has been defined by an especially unique and turbulent journey. There are three champagne houses named Heidsieck, all from families once related, and Charles is the smallest and the best of them. With an annual production of 1 million bottles, Charles Heidsieck is made alongside the larger Piper-Heidsieck, and it is this unique coexistence that has springboarded Charles to its current heights. But, more than this, the house has been privileged to a lineage of particularly dynamic and remarkably talented chef de caves since 1976, and a current director as charismatic and sharp as any in the region. Together, they have ushered in an era of monumental change, initiating dramatic developments that are shaking the very core of this dynamic and exciting house. The new Charles Heidsieck is built on deep, autumnal complexity, juxtaposed with vibrant energy and astonishing poise. Its cuvées have never looked more sublime.

Charles and Piper-Heidsieck have admirably upheld distinctly unique styles, thanks to their insightful and talented chef de cave, Régis Camus, who has focused the vision of both houses since 1994. 'We cannot make Charles without Piper,' he reveals. 'There is a brotherhood of the two. The magic is to arrange their coexistence.'

Camus distinguishes Charles by likening its mood to late summer and early autumn, describing its floral spectrum in tones of aromatic flowers, dried flowers and leaves. 'Charles is more about generosity and fleshy expression of late summer fruits, like biting into a peach and having the juice run down your face,' he says. 'It evokes dates, cream and a toasty register of warm brioche just out of the oven, or a crusty Parisian baguette.' This is a contemplative, mature, darker champagne style for cooler weather.

The late Daniel Thibault was the visionary mastermind behind Charles Heidsieck from 1976 until his untimely passing in 2002. In its heyday in 1985, the production of the house reached 4.5 million bottles, more than that of Veuve Clicquot at the time.

The global financial crisis hit Piper and Charles Heidsieck hard, throwing the company into some €240 million of debt, and forcing it to lay off a quarter of its staff. Owner Rémy Cointreau sold the brand to French fashion-led luxury company Société Européenne de Participations Industrielles (EPI) in early 2011. President Christopher Descours named Régis Camus as one of the key reasons the company committed to the purchase.

The dynamic and sharp Stephen Leroux was brought on as director of Charles Heidsieck in early 2013. 'We are recuperating after many

Charles Heidsieck chef de cave Cyril Brun

years in which Rémy Cointreau were not focusing at all on Charles Heidsieck, so we disappeared from many markets,' he admits. In the year of his appointment, sales hit rock bottom of just 210,000 bottles. 'We could have gone bust!'

With the relaunch of Charles Heidsieck in 2012, Thierry Roset was appointed chef de cave under Camus, after 25 years with the house. He had already refined the style by honing its sourcing from 120 villages to the 60 finest crus, with a particular focus on Ambonnay for pinot noir, Oger for chardonnay and Verneuil for meunier, three strong villages which Camus dubs 'the three pillars of Charles'. Roset simultaneously increased the average age of reserve wines for Brut Réserve NV from an already considerable eight years to an incredible 10 years – monumental figures for a blend comprising a high 40% of reserves.

Leroux describes the effect of Roset's vision. 'When I joined Charles, I expected this to produce an even more powerful cuvée,' he admits. 'But the longer ageing of reserves gives more complexity and more depth, and honing the selection of crus makes the wines cleaner, fresher and more precise. The intensity of the old Charles was enormous, but the wines could be a bit weighty. The new Charles is powerful but not heavy.'

Roset passed away tragically and suddenly at the end of harvest 2014, and the talented, insightful and articulate Cyril Brun was appointed as his successor. After 15 years overseeing wine development and communication at Veuve Clicquot, Brun was well qualified to define

the next chapter of Heidsieck, and his appointment was something of a dream come true.

'When I first became a winemaker, I applied at my two favourite wineries, Veuve Clicquot and Charles Heidsieck,' he reflects. 'And Clicquot got in first!'

In 2015, his very first vintage at Charles, Brun surprised many by not making a vintage champagne from a season he himself described as 'very good' and Camus as 'a vintage more in the Charles style than the Piper style', instead electing to build the reserve stocks, as he did again in 2016, following the legacy of the house. 'My predecessors made no 2004 or 2002 vintage wines, and upheld their philosophy of building great reserves,' he reflects.

Brun's deeply intuitive approach gives him the confidence to craft his cuvées with sensitivity, responding instinctively to the vagaries of the seasons with creativity and dexterity. 'I tend to trust my palate more than I trust an Excel spreadsheet!' he exclaims. This is particularly pertinent in Champagne's impetuous and changing climate. 'We would have got it wrong if we made wines in the rich and ripe 2018 vintage by copying the recipe for a standard year,' he reveals. He instead harvested early and ran much cooler ferments to sustain freshness.

In preparing for warmer vintages, Brun suggests that Champagne needs to be more precise with viticulture and open to different clones, different varieties and different vineyard locations. And to be adaptable

in vinification. 'Not just zero or one, yes or no. It does not have to be everything or nothing with malolactic fermentation and with oak,' he suggests. 'We need to be globally more flexible in everything we do. The Champenois can be perceived to be quite arrogant, but we need to have our two feet on the ground to redefine what is champagne.'

Brun has a long-term vision for the house. 'We are rebuilding to get Charles on track and we need excellent reserve wines for the future,' he explains. 'The reserves are the fundamentals of our non-vintage wines.' The generosity of the Charles style relies not only on extended lees age but on its deep reserve stocks, stored on fine lees in stainless steel tanks at 15–16°C to retain freshness.

Charles Heidsieck has an aspiration to grow its sales to 2 million bottles in the next 7–10 years. 'At 2 million, we can be premium and on-trade, but after 2 million you have to do business with the mass retailers,' Leroux explains. In anticipation, production was stepped up to 1.5 million bottles in 2016 and 2017. In 2018, the house bottled 1.6 million bottles of Brut Réserve alone. 'That's more than the 2008, 2010 and 2012 base releases put together!' Brun discloses – a tremendous growth trajectory since the house hit rock bottom in 2013.

'Within the supply of the two houses, we have room to manoeuvre to achieve this growth in Charles,' Leroux explains. Just 5% of production is currently sourced from a total of 60 hectares across both houses, with the balance provided by some 400 growers. Grape supply has been in double-digit growth for the past three harvests. 'Every year we ask Christopher Descours if we can buy more grapes and more expensive grapes, and in 2018 we purchased everything we could find!' Brun divulges.

The house is also looking to acquire more of its own vineyards, and one or two hectares have been added each year since Descours purchased the company, and he has empowered his team to be active in acquiring more. 'He gave me his mobile number the week I started and said, "If you need a fast decision on purchasing vineyards or anything else, call me,"' Brun reveals.

The growth of the house has been exclusively in its non-vintage cuvées, with no increase in sales in its Millésime or Rosé Millésime, and in fact Blanc des Millénnaires outsells both put together. 'A friend told me our vintage cuvées don't sell so well because our NV is too good!' Brun confides. He aspires to ultimately double Blanc des Millénnaires' current production of 75,000 bottles.

The house is blessed with reserve stocks to sustain the growth of its non-vintage blends. 'We are sitting on a treasure of reserve wines!' Brun exclaims. Charles Heidsieck's dismal sales under its previous owners dictated a backlog and hence long ageing of its recent releases, with Brut Réserve blessed with as long as seven or eight years on lees, unsustainable with increasing volumes today. The ambition for the future is freshness. 'The market is looking for fresher styles of champagne, and we will not be able to maintain seven or eight years of lees age, so we now need to prepare for shorter ageing time, and we are doing everything we can to anticipate this,' he says. The aim is to maintain Brut Réserve on lees for four years, without destroying the fleshy and opulent style of Charles. A high proportion of reserves will be upheld, and oak barrels will be introduced to add complexity, spice and, most of all, texture.

To this end, Brun has purchased 500 barrels over the past three years. For all of its complexity and depth, the Charles Heidsieck style has always relied exclusively on stainless steel tanks for fermentation and ageing. For Brun, oak must be very well managed. 'The oak I like is the oak you cannot detect,' he explains. 'More to play with textures rather than flavours, through micro-oxygenation, with more impact on the palate than the nose – though most in Champagne are doing the opposite.' The 2018 base for his Blanc de Blancs NV will include 10% of components aged in barrel.

Markets are responding to the rise and rise of Charles Heidsieck, posting 20–30% annual sales growth, even in the wake of a recent price increase. 'Charles is no longer a sleeping beauty, it is a beauty!' Cyril beams. 'In the next two to three years we will have duly repositioned the brand, the wines and the volumes, and we will be out of the danger zone – which will have taken 15 years from the first purchase of the new owner. We are currently still recovering the glory days of Charles!'

Another of Brun's visions is to bring back Champagne Charlie, the famous flagship of the house, discontinued in 1985. 'When we have a great vintage, I will put it aside as a Charlie,' he says. He plans to uphold the historical Charlie philosophy of no rules, sometimes pinot dominant and sometimes chardonnay. 'We will take our time and do it properly.' In the meantime, look out for the impending release of the first Charles Heidsieck Coteaux Champenois Blanc!

A broad sweep of 10–11g/L dosage across the range may seem heavy-handed in these days of low dosage across champagne. While there has been a small decrease from 11 to 10g/L since 2005, lower dosage is not the aspiration.

'Many people have brainwashed consumers into thinking "the lower the dosage, the better the champagne", but this is not the case,' points out Brun. 'Sugar is not the enemy of champagne. When you have a style like Charles that lies long in the cellar, with deep, rich expression, sugar is on your side. Some people think we are crazy with 11g/L as very few houses use this level of dosage. But the more aged reserves you use, the more you need dosage to amplify the profile of the reserves. This was a point I wanted to challenge when I joined the winery, so I trialled dosages from 7g/L to 11g/L – and every time, 11g/L was right!'

In another statement of consistency and quality, the house is in the process of moving exclusively to 'technological' corks like DIAMs, currently used across 80% of its non-vintage cuvées. This initiative can't come too soon; Brun opened for me two cork-tainted bottles in a row of his Rosé Millésime 2005. 'I was at a champagne tasting recently and five out of six bottles were corked in a vertical tasting from one house,' he discloses.

In addition to sporting smart new front labels, Charles Heidsieck's back labels are now some of the most informative among champagne houses, detailing bottling and disgorgement years (with the quarter of the year in which it was disgorged recently added), proportion of reserve wines, and number of crus in the blend. The base vintage can be easily ascertained as the year before the bottling date.

With Brun's appointment completing a talented and dedicated team, I am quietly excited by the pace of progress at Charles Heidsieck. This year, its deeply contemplative yet thrillingly engaging cuvées again confidently uphold their rank among the finest in all of Champagne.

CHARLES HEIDSIECK BRUT RÉSERVE NV $$$

95 points • 2012 BASE VINTAGE • DISGORGED JUNE 2018 • TASTED IN CHAMPAGNE
94 points • 2010 BASE VINTAGE • DISGORGED EARLY 2018 • TASTED IN CHAMPAGNE AND AUSTRALIA
96 points • 2008 BASE VINTAGE • DISGORGED 2014 • TASTED IN CHAMPAGNE

40% chardonnay, 40% pinot, 20% meunier; 60 crus; 40% reserves of 50% chardonnay and 50% pinot; reserves average 10 years of age)and some up to 20 years of age) at the time of blending; fermented in stainless steel tanks, cru by cru, variety by variety; 11g/L dosage; technological cork; 80% of the sales of the house

The delectable Charles Heidsieck mood is nothing short of winter-time generosity, full-straw hue, mellow autumn-leaf character, contemplative appeal, waxy, creamy, fleshy, toasty and brimming with juicy stone fruits, fig, pear and crunchy red apples. It declares its magnificent age and deep reserves in rumbling maturity of dried peach, coffee, cocoa, nougat, pâtisserie, deep mixed spice, even pipe smoke, molten wax and truffles... you get the idea (the grand complexity of Charles always evokes the longest lists of flavour comparisons in my notes). Fragrance, freshness and vitality are preserved in crunchy grapefruit and lemon, which linger with brilliant line and length on a finish underscored by the structural depth of pronounced, fine, soft, salt minerality. The 2012 is a particularly refined base vintage of poise and confidence that define a triumphant and worthy Charles. The complexity of recipe and depth of mood of this generous cuvée counter the grip of the challenging 2010 season in a dynamic and compelling style. The 2008 remains the greatest of them all, billowingly complex, at once silky and creamy and yet blessed with the brilliant radiance that defines 2008. A prestige cuvée disguised behind an affordable label. Quintessential Charles.

CHARLES HEIDSIECK ROSÉ RÉSERVE NV $$$$

95 points • 2012 BASE VINTAGE • DISGORGED OCTOBER 2017 • TASTED IN CHAMPAGNE AND AUSTRALIA
96 points • 2008 BASE VINTAGE • DISGORGED 2016 • TASTED IN CHAMPAGNE

35% chardonnay, 40% pinot, 25% meunier; 60 crus; 20% reserves of 50% chardonnay and 50% pinot; reserves average 5 years of age; 5-6% red wines from Les Riceys; fermented in stainless steel tanks, cru by cru, variety by variety; 11g/L dosage; cork; just 4% of the sales of the house

For Cyril Brun, Les Riceys produces the ideal red wine for Charles Heidsieck Rosé, soft and fruity, never angular or aggressive, respectful of the base wines and deeper in colour than the red wines of the north of Champagne. The result is a medium salmon-copper hue, though colour is not the focus here. The gloriously splendid complexity of lees age in concert with rich reserves rises on the palate, resonating with wonderful allure of roast chestnuts, baked apples, dried fruits of all kinds, anise, exotic spice, truffle, honey and freshly baked pâtisserie, laced with delightful wisps of pipe smoke, yet presented with dynamism and definition. The 2012 base is of course fresher than the 2008 before it, presenting precise red cherry, wild strawberry, raspberry, red apple and berry compote fragranced with rose petals, and underlined by the structural assurance of firm, fine tannins that fuse effortlessly with the expansive sea of generosity that is Charles. Salt chalk minerality hovers with magnificent line and length. The 2008 base still soars with focus, precision, freshness and breathtaking red fruit purity. Outstanding.

CHARLES HEIDSIECK BLANC DE BLANCS NV $$$

95 points • 2012 BASE VINTAGE • DISGORGED MAY 2017 AND 2018 • TASTED IN CHAMPAGNE AND AUSTRALIA

100% chardonnay, half Oger and Vertus, half Villers-Marmery, Trépail, Vaudemange, Montgueux; 25% reserve wines averaging 5 years or age; fermented in stainless steel vats, cru by cru; 10g/L dosage; technological cork; 60,000 bottles

The first release of the modern reincarnation of Charles Heidsieck Blanc de Blancs NV, first made in the 1970s and discontinued after about five vintages with the launch of Champagne Charlie when Remy Cointreau took ownership. The house has a deep history producing Blanc de Blancs Vintage since at least 1947, and there was a Charles Heidsieck Le Mesnil 1906.

In the shadow of the majesty of the legendary Blanc des Millénaires, there was great expectation surrounding the unveiling of a non-vintage blanc de blancs in the noble Charles family, and the result has resoundingly stepped up to the expectation. The brief for Charles' new Blanc de Blancs was a purposeful and distinct juxtaposition to the mandate of Blanc des Millénaires. By stark contrast to the Côte des Blancs endurance of BdM, this is a complex union between the most generous crus of the Côte (50% Oger and Vertus), the equal balance from the east-facing villages of the Montagne de Reims and the outposts of Montgueux and the Sézanne. The stark contrast of this cuvée leads out from the outset in a hue of full straw, yet bright and radiant. Projecting the unmistakable, definitive DNA of Charles, it's layered in deep allusions of truffle, vanilla bean, baked apple, ripe pear, butter croissant, a complex interplay of spice, even a suggestion of warm hearth, incense and wax unexpected in a cuvée that does not depend upon old reserves. In the midst of the signature deep and contemplative mood of the house, it sings with the pure lemon high notes of chardonnay, the vivacity of youthful 2012 acidity, and the grainy, glittering, frothing salt chalk mineral structure of Oger, the eastern Montagne de Reims and Montgueux – crus quite distinct in their geography, yet sharing a commonality in the grainy grip of their mineral structure. A one-quarter dose of the challenging 2011 season is well deployed to build structure, tension and grip. A masterfully assembled blanc de blancs of rolling persistence and a worthy addition to the hallowed halls of Charles.

CHARLES HEIDSIECK MILLÉSIME VINTAGE BRUT 2006 $$$$

95 points • DISGORGED 2017 • TASTED IN CHAMPAGNE AND AUSTRALIA

40% chardonnay, 60% pinot; 11 grand and premier crus; fermented in stainless steel tanks, cru by cru, variety by variety; 10g/L dosage; technological cork; 40,000 bottles

A full yet bright-yellow hue with a gold tint heralds the succulent generosity of Charles and the exuberant, exotic richness of 2006, yet with definition and poise. A glorious assemblage of golden grilled pineapple, juicy white peach, fig, tarte tatin, toffee, warm honey, brioche, truffles, vanilla, candied almonds, roast chestnuts, nutmeg, cinnamon, even hints of pipe smoke and high-cocoa dark chocolate – definitive, flamboyant and luscious Charles! The firm, fine phenolic grip of this warm season is well set against its juicy creaminess, melding seamlessly with pronounced chalk mineral grit (of Oger and Vertus in particular), boasting a structure that would obliterate any mortal cuvée. It holds magnificent line, length, poise and integrity, even in the midst of such proportions and not inconsiderable structure. A fantastic 2006 to drink now and over the next few years.

CHARLES HEIDSIECK MILLÉSIME VINTAGE BRUT 2005

93 points • TASTED IN CHAMPAGNE

40% chardonnay, 60% pinot noir; with a strong base of Ambonnay, then Verzy, Verzenay, Bouzy, Avize, Oger, Cramant, Vertus, Mailly and Vindey; 10g/L dosage

The first release since 2000, 2005 is a bold vintage to choose for this cuvée, and it's not shy on muscle, nor the wood spice notes, almond-skin grip, drying phenolic texture and firm, chewy structure that defines the season. Cyril Brun reveals that this vintage had the highest concentration of phenolics since they started measuring them, and 'if I had a choice, I would bet on high phenolics over high acidity for ageability'. Had he been with the company at the time, he would have held off the release of this vintage until after the 2006, and even now he believes it's far from its peak. Heidsieck has conjured a flattering take on this season, cunningly using creaminess, golden layers of ripe yellow summer fruits, pineapple and honeyed dosage to counter its drying mouthfeel. The volume of the vintage and its pinot noir lead are well contrasted with a note of fennel and a decade of maturity, defining the aged complexity of coffee, mocha and the classic autumn-leaf allure of the house. Boasting a medium gold robe, this is a bold Charles of exuberance and commanding structure.

CHARLES HEIDSIECK MILLÉSIME VINTAGE ROSÉ 2006

97 points • TASTED IN CHAMPAGNE

37% chardonnay from Oger, Le Mesnil-sur-Oger, Cramant and Vertus, 63% pinot from Avenay, Louvois, Tauxières, Ambonnay and Aÿ, including 8% pinot noir red wine, half from Bouzy, Ambonnay, Verzenay and Hautvillers and half Les Riceys; fermented in stainless steel tanks, cru by cru, variety by variety; 10g/L dosage; just 6% of the sales of the house

One of Cyril Brun's first decisions on joining the company was to release this vintage before the 2005 (which he recalls brought some strange looks – 'Who is that new guy doing crazy things?!'). I loved it on that first release and I adore it even more now, its pinot core having burst through its surface in a display of breathtaking red cherries, wild strawberries, even cassis, at once fresh, flamboyant and vivacious, and at the same time complex and contemplative. The elegant freshness and freeze-frame evolution of its early life have held transfixed, melting effortlessly into a vortex of deeply evocative Charles spice, ginger and brioche, all the while projecting beautifully refined acid structure and stunning chalk mineral freshness. A delightful Rosé for long conversations on cool nights.

CHARLES HEIDSIECK MILLÉSIME VINTAGE ROSÉ 2005 $$$$

92 points • DISGORGED 2017 • TASTED IN AUSTRALIA

37% chardonnay from Oger, Le Mesnil-sur-Oger, Cramant and Vertus, 63% pinot from Avenay-Val-d'Or, Louvois, Tauxières, Ambonnay and Aÿ, 8% red wine, half from Bouzy and half from Les Riceys; fermented in stainless steel tanks, cru by cru, variety by variety; 10g/L dosage; cork; released after the 2006

With a medium salmon-copper hue, this is a deeply savoury rosé, true to the firm grip and bold structure of 2005. Notes of underripeness representative of the season project through in tamarillo, tomato leaf and capsicum allusions, contrasting sour morello cherries. Its structural grip of firm, coarse phenolic dryness and tannin has appreciated additional time on lees to settle, though remains astringent, contrasting tangy acidity. The magnitude of Charles reverberates in layers of exotic pipe smoke and truffles, its generous proportions holding this tussle with integrity, but even this proves insufficient, and ultimately the challenges of the season have the final say. Two bottles in a row opened at the house were mildly cork tainted.

CHARLES HEIDSIECK BLANC DES MILLÉNAIRES 2004 $$$$$

98 points • TASTED IN CHAMPAGNE AND AUSTRALIA

100% chardonnay; 20% each of Cramant, Avize, Oger, Le Mesnil-sur-Oger and Vertus, as always; aged 11 years on lees; fermented in stainless steel tanks, cru by cru; full malolactic fermentation; 9g/L dosage, the first Charles below 10g/L; 65-70,000 bottles

Just the fifth Blanc de Millénaires since 1983, parading a gloriously bright yet full straw-yellow hue, this is another enthralling release brimming with all of the ravishing exuberance that is Charles Heidsieck. Glorious sweet pipe smoke, molten wax, nougat, golden fruit cake, glacé peach, quince and truffles well up in a magical torrent, while the honed definition and coiled tension of the great 2004 season shines like a beacon, illuminating with great focus the pristine cut of lemon and apple fruit. In texture it is an ethereal sensation, at once silky, creamy, luscious and extravagantly rich, yet at every moment defined by the focus of 2004 acidity, washing with a magnificent sea of fine chalk mineral texture that inscribes the signature of the greatest crus of the Côte des Blancs. With epic determination, drive and brilliance, this is a worthy follow-on to the sublime 1995, and will, like it, blossom and grow triumphantly in the decades to come.

CHARLES HEIDSIECK BLANC DES MILLÉNAIRES 1995 $$$$$

98 points • TASTED IN CHAMPAGNE

20% each of Cramant, Avize, Oger, Le Mesnil-sur-Oger and Vertus; stored in Charles Heidsieck's crayères at 11°C and disgorged successively for an incredible release cycle now spanning 12 years; 10g/L dosage

The oldest currently available champagne in all four of the last editions of this guide has returned for one final encore! With each passing year, it evolves and unravels to reveal a little more of its remarkable personality, and the house discloses a little more of its incredible story. 'I knew Daniel Thibault well,' reveals Cyril Brun, 'and he took the chance to make the vintage of a lifetime. He was asked by the President to make a small amount because times were tough. But when he made Blanc des Millénaires 1995 he could tell that the potential was enormous, and it would be at its best from 15 or 20 years. So he would have thought, "F#$%, I'll make more so that it will be at its best when it is finally enjoyed!"'

And so, 17 years after his passing, boasting almost a quarter-century of maturity, Thibault's gift lives on. Before he himself passed away in 2014, Thierry Roset declared that he would probably never again be able to make another wine like this. Interestingly, he did make a small batch of 1996, but it did not meet expectation and was sold off to an airline some years ago. The 1995 is an enigma, a grand testimony to the eternal Peter Pan endurance of the greatest crus of the Côte des Blancs, and it will live for decades yet. Its medium-straw hue is shot with a brightness that eludes its age, the freshest bottles upholding green tints, and there's still yellow fruit crunch and citrus-zest freshness here, rumbling in tones of impeccable, soft chalk minerality. It's spicier and richer than ever, its voice deepening into grand middle age, taking on the understated, magical allure of maturity in rising depth of molten wax, sweet pipe smoke, truffles and warm hearth. For all of its glorious maturity and silken magnificence, it has retained dizzying vivacity, framed in epic salt minerality and vibrant acidity nothing short of mindblowing at such age. After an epic 12 years in the market, the house has now finally stopped its release. Yet the story of this fabled cuvée is not yet over, for the remainder will be held for re-release, perhaps in another 10 years. Who knows what might yet be in store in the decades to come?

CHARLES HEIDSIECK BLANC DES MILLÉNAIRES 1983

96 points • TASTED IN CHAMPAGNE

The first Blanc des Millénaires, and Cyril Brun suggests it is probably still the best; disgorged early 1999 as one of 2000 bottles released for the new millennium

A fraction more advanced than the previous bottle I tasted two years ago, this cuvée has evolved to a full copper hue and glorious maturity, ricocheting with such exuberant exoticism of orange rind, crème brûlée, mocha, fruit mince spice, ginger and apricot jam, surrounding a jubilant core of glacé apricot, billowing with all the smoky, tertiary fascination of more than 30 years in the bowels of the earth. After 10 years on lees and more than 20 years on cork, it retains the utmost integrity and life, holding its confidence effortlessly on a finish of outstanding persistence.

CHARLES HEIDSIECK MIS EN CAVE 1990 NV

95 points • 1989 BASE VINTAGE • DISGORGED AROUND 1996 • TASTED IN CHAMPAGNE EN MAGNUM

40% chardonnay, 40% pinot, a little less than 20% meunier; original disgorgement; 14g/L dosage

Mis en Cave was one of my very first favourite champagnes when I first fell in love with the region in the late 1990s. The legendary Daniel Thibault was decades ahead of his time when he emblazoned the front label of his entry non-vintage cuvée with the year it was laid in the cellar (*mis en cave*). Hence the base year is one year prior. The market wasn't ready for it then, but now it seems every self-respecting house is communicating the changing editions of its non-vintage releases. It's astonishing that the entry non-vintage cuvée of any house could uphold such integrity at a full 30 years of age, let alone based on a vintage of such warmth and phenolic structure as 1989. Cyril Brun's message here is crystal clear, bringing this magnum to the surface from the depths of the crayères in mid-September 2018, at the height of another harvest built on warm phenolics. This gloriously mature Mis en Cave is wrapped in a medium-yellow gold robe, enveloped in complex, rich, ripe layers evoking fig, grilled pineapple, persimmon, golden delicious apple, glacé pear, apricot, wild honey and mixed spice. It carries the persona of the season in fine phenolic grip not out of place for such bountiful lusciousness.

Charles Heidsieck's third-century Roman crayères

COLLET

(Coh-lay)

14 BOULEVARD PASTEUR 51160 AŸ
www.champagne-collet.com

CHAMPAGNE
COLLET
AŸ - FRANCE
DEPUIS 1921

Collet sits alongside Jacquart and Montaudon as the brands of Champagne's longest-standing and third largest cooperative, Coopérative Générale des Vignerons. The group has enjoyed considerable development in recent years, with a new headquarters built in its home town of Aÿ, and a new production facility constructed in Oger in 2004 and significantly expanded in 2011, to a capacity of 27 million bottles. The cooperative sources from 162 villages, of which 100 are utilised in the Collet blends. A production of 500,000 bottles makes Collet less than one-fifth the size of Jacquart, and its distribution consequently focuses more towards restaurants than supermarkets. These are generally long-aged cuvées of fruit integrity, though at times lacking polish.

COLLET BRUT ART DÉCO PREMIER CRU NV $$

89 points • 2012 BASE VINTAGE • DISGORGED 18 JULY 2018 • TASTED IN AUSTRALIA

40% chardonnay, 40% pinot, 20% meunier; seven grand crus, 13 premier crus; no oak; 8g/L dosage; DIAM

A fresh and lively cuvée based on the vibrant 2012 season, upholding a bright, pale straw hue. It's a crunchy style in which chardonnay assumes a confident lead, built around apple and pear fruit, with pinot lending subtle strawberry-hull notes in the background. It concludes dry and a little bitter as a consequence of grainy phenolic grip.

COLLET EXTRA BRUT PREMIER CRU NV $$

87 points • 2012 BASE VINTAGE • DISGORGED 17 APRIL 2018 • TASTED IN AUSTRALIA

40% chardonnay, 40% pinot, 20% meunier; seven grand crus, 13 premier crus; no oak; 3g/L dosage; DIAM

Art Déco without the safety net of dosage, this is a masterclass in the profound difference between 8g/L and 3g/L: a difference equating to just a quarter of a teaspoon of sugar in a cup of coffee. The result here is tense, firm and astringently dry. The biscuity complexity and creamy texture of five years on lees certainly helps, but this is not a cuvée for the uninitiated.

COLLET BLANC DE BLANCS PREMIER CRU NV $$$

88 points • 2013 BASE VINTAGE • DISGORGED 28 MAY 2018 • TASTED IN AUSTRALIA

100% chardonnay; Avize, Chouilly, Oger, Villers-Marmery, Trépail and Vaudemange; no oak; 7g/L dosage; DIAM

The tension of chardonnay's acid backbone contrasts the roast nut and toast complexity of four years of lees age, though the two have not yet found a harmonious synergy. A little phenolic bitterness on the finish is more than the softening effect of well-integrated dosage can resolve.

COLLET BLANC DE NOIRS PREMIER CRU NV $$$

91 points • 2014 BASE VINTAGE • DISGORGED 25 MAY 2018 • TASTED IN AUSTRALIA

85% pinot, 15% meunier; five grand crus and five premier crus; no oak; 8g/L dosage; DIAM

A bright and crunchy blanc de noirs that presents an elegant style, muted on the nose but delivering pretty vibrancy of morello cherry, redcurrant and strawberry hull on the palate. It's tangy and bright, with a vibrant finish energised by morello cherry acidity. Dosage is well played and harmoniously integrated.

COLLET BRUT ROSÉ NV $$$

87 points • 2012 BASE VINTAGE • DISGORGED 27 JUNE 2018 • TASTED IN AUSTRALIA

40% chardonnay, 50% pinot, 10% meunier; 20 different villages; no oak; 10g/L dosage; DIAM

Unashamedly rosé, this is a cuvée of medium crimson hue and no lack of firm, fine tannin grip. Flavours of tamarillo and strawberry define a style both savoury and fruity. A strong dosage of 10g/L is the highest of the range, evidently an attempt to soften the tannin blow, but instead the accord renders it both firm and sweet.

COLLET MILLÉSIME 2008 $$$$

94 points • DISGORGED 28 MAY 2018 • TASTED IN AUSTRALIA

40% chardonnay, 50% pinot, 10% meunier; 10 villages in premier and grand crus; no oak; 8g/L dosage; cork

Collet's synergy of mostly chardonnay and pinot noir in its vintage cuvée makes for a style of enduring tension and refreshing purity, virtues the scintillating 2008 season serves only to magnify. Pinot noir leaps forth in its characterful yet understated perfume of precise red cherry, wild strawberry and rose petal, backed emphatically by the lemon tension of chardonnay. A full nine years on lees has allowed this great season to unravel in slow motion, lending but subtle nuances of almond and gently harmonious texture as the only clues to its maturity. It promises to continue to improve for at least another decade yet.

COMTES DE DAMPIERRE

(Com-t deh Dom-pee-air)

3 PLACE BOISSEAU 51140 CHENAY
www.dampierre.com

Comtes de Dampierre
CHAMPAGNE

The charismatic aristocrat Count Audoin de Dampierre established his eponymous house in 1986 from his home in Chenay in the Massif de Saint-Thierry north-west of Reims. His family has resided in the village for 700 years, and his château is now home to his classic car collection – his other passion alongside champagne. With no vineyards in his name, he upholds the choice of vignerons as his first priority, followed by the know-how of blending and ageing. Sourcing is focused exclusively on chardonnay hailing from the grand and premier cru villages of the Côte des Blancs and pinot noir from the premier crus of the Montagne de Reims, with no use of meunier. Dampierre upholds personal involvement throughout production, which is handled under contract by the cooperatives in Bouzy and Avize. Chardonnay is the focus of the house, led by four blanc de blancs cuvées, the best of which is his Family Réserve, showcasing the long-aged power of Côte des Blancs grand crus.

COMTES DE DAMPIERRE GRANDE CUVÉE BRUT NV $$

91 points • 2013 BASE VINTAGE • DISGORGED OCTOBER 2017 • TASTED IN AUSTRALIA

100% Vertus chardonnay; 2011 reserves; aged 3.5 years on lees; 6g/L dosage; cork

The exoticism of Vertus in notes of pineapple, star fruit and baked apple and clove is well poised by lemon and grapefruit brightness, underlined by prominent secondary complexity of spicy gingerbread and the creamy texture of lees age. It concludes with good persistence and smooth, friendly appeal.

Meunier in Coulommes-la-Montagne at the end of harvest 2018

COMTES DE DAMPIERRE CUVÉE DES AMBASSADEURS BLANC DE BLANCS EXTRA BRUT GRAND CRU NV $$$

87 points • 2011 BASE VINTAGE • DISGORGED 25 MARCH 2015 • TASTED IN AUSTRALIA

100% Le Mesnil-sur-Oger chardonnay; 10% 2008, 2009 and 2010 reserves; aged 3 years on lees; 3.5g/L dosage; DIAM

After a good spell on lees and as long on cork, this is a toasty and secondary style of biscuity, honeyed, ginger complexity. The dusty, dry phenolic grip, green capsicum notes and tense underripe acidity of 2011 contrast with its creamy development, concluding dry, grainy and tense.

COMTES DE DAMPIERRE FAMILY RÉSERVE BLANC DE BLANCS GRAND CRU BRUT 2007 $$$$

93 points • DISGORGED EARLY 2015 • TASTED IN AUSTRALIA

100% chardonnay; 50% Oger, 40% Le Mesnil-sur-Oger, 10% Cramant; parcels vinified separately, with 77% completing malolactic fermentation; aged 7 years on lees; 8g/L dosage; cork

With a medium straw hue, this is a great marriage of the complexity of lees and cork age and the generosity of distinguished crus of the Côte des Blancs. The layered, spicy apple, ripe pear and lemon fruit of chardonnay is evolving into preserved lemon, with the generosity of Oger contrasting the tension of Mesnil and Cramant. At 12 years of age, it's loaded with spicy, toasty, honeyed, biscuity complexity, concluding with good persistence, upholding decent line and length, well supported by salty chalk minerality. A generous and characterful cuvée, in the right place to drink now. One bottle showed some burnt-orange oxidation which dried out and contracted the finish.

De Saint Gall

(UNION CHAMPAGNE)

(Der Sahn Gahl)

7 RUE PASTEUR 51190 AVIZE
www.union-champagne.fr

DE SAINT-GALL

CHAMPAGNE

De Saint Gall is the brand of the Union Champagne cooperative, an enormous conglomerate of 14 member cooperatives of more than 2000 member growers controlling 1366 hectares of champagne vineyards. Close to half of these are located in grand cru villages, encompassing half the surface of the Côte des Blancs and many of the great pinot villages of the southern Montagne de Reims, and close to half in premier crus. The cooperative operates from substantial facilities in Avize (updated in 2013 to state-of-the-art, Starship Enterprise levels) and Vertus and a (relatively) smaller site in Oger, where it produces the equivalent of 12 million bottles annually. Reserves are held in both stainless steel tanks and large oak foudres. The majority of production is sold to other houses, including highly sought after components of such cuvées as Taittinger Comtes de Champagne, Laurent-Perrier Grand Siècle and Dom Pérignon, and a sizeable number of bottles to member growers. Since 1984, the Union has marketed its own brand in De Saint Gall, steadily growing to a production of some 2.2 million bottles, which can represent good value in an at times reductive style.

DE SAINT GALL BLANC DE BLANCS PREMIER CRU NV $

91 points • 2013 BASE VINTAGE • DISGORGED 8 OCTOBER 2018 • TASTED IN AUSTRALIA

100% chardonnay; Côte des Blancs; no oak; 100% steel tank; 8g/L dosage; DIAM

A delightfully affordable expression of the purity and vivacity of the premier crus of the Côte des Blancs in the refreshingly lively 2013 harvest. Lemon, grapefruit and beurre bosc pear are framed in the subtle almond meal and vanilla nougat of four years of lees age. It concludes with nicely poised acid cut, evenly integrated dosage and a subtle crunch of phenolic bitterness. A classy blend for De Saint Gall, and one of the most precise blanc de blancs on the market at this price.

DE SAINT GALL LE ROSÉ PREMIER CRU NV $$

84 points • 2013 BASE VINTAGE • DISGORGED 8 JUNE 2018 • TASTED IN AUSTRALIA

59% chardonnay, 25% pinot; 16% red wine; Côte des Blancs and Montagne de Reims; no oak; 9g/L dosage; DIAM

A savoury and reductive style plagued with the onion and garlic notes of lightstruck degradation – a perpetual hazard in a clear, unprotected bottle. This strips any sense of fruit definition and appeal, rendering the finish short, callow, coarse and austere. A second bottle was identical.

DE SOUSA

(De Soo-za)

(7/10)

12 PLACE LÉON BOURGEOIS 51190 AVIZE
www.champagnedesousa.com

CHAMPAGNE

De Sousa

à Avize

Un Champagne de Précision

If you could write the perfect recipe for the greatest champagnes it might read something like this: a tiny grower based in Avize in the exact centre of the grand crus of the Côte des Blancs, sourcing chardonnay from estate vineyards on the finest slopes of the grand crus of Avize, Oger, Cramant and Le Mesnil-sur-Oger, and pinot noir and meunier from the grand crus of Aÿ and Ambonnay. Vines would be very old and painstakingly tended biodynamically by an experienced artisan, fanatical about drawing every detail of character and minerality from every site. Crop levels and dosage would be low, oak would be used generously when the fruit called for it and sparingly when it did not, blending would be performed from a deep pool of reserve wines, cuvées would mature long on their lees in cold cellars, and bottling and disgorgement dates and dosages would be printed on every bottle. Welcome to the wonderful world of De Sousa.

On paper, this might be the finest recipe in all of Champagne. But do the wines live up to it?

I first met third-generation head of the house Erick de Sousa over the gigantic French oak table in his tasting room in the heart of Avize. 'My job is to maximise the minerality in the vines,' he commenced, and everything from this point served to demonstrate his vision — every cuvée opened, every vineyard technique expounded, every cellar procedure demonstrated.

Over 30 years, Erick has refined the best of traditional thinking and progressive methods to revitalise, transform and grow the estate to become one of the finest on the Côte des Blancs. Production has increased to 100–110,000 bottles annually and vineyard holdings have grown to 42 plots spanning 10 hectares, including 2.5 hectares of coveted old vines in Avize, Cramant and Oger. The family also has small holdings in the premier crus of Épernay and Grauves, from Erick's wife Michelle's side of the family.

With the exception of his entry Brut Tradition, every vineyard source is grand cru, with 70% of vines over 40 years of age and a significant percentage 50–60 years old. Some planted by his grandfather are more than 80 years old. 'I must give my wine the minerality that can only come from old vines,' he emphasises.

The roots of these old vines plunge deep into the soil, even as far as 35–40 metres into the chalk, he suggests. Here they extract the salts and trace elements that are fundamental to the structure of these wines. 'Minerality comes from the chalk,' he says. And his wines sing with crystal clear mineral fidelity.

Old vines have a natural moderating effect on yields, which generally average just 60hL from 8000 vines per hectare, 25–30% less than the average of the appellation. Such yields provide greater concentration and permit him to harvest only when the grapes have attained full ripeness. 'I want to maintain the maturity in the sugar level at harvest, but not too high, so as to keep a balance of acidity and minerality,' he explains. 'High maturity at harvest provides opulence, while minerality maintains freshness.'

I have always admired De Sousa's aspiration to achieve full ripeness, though over the past five years the house style has evolved to a notably riper, more fleshy and more exotic mood, especially since the 2011 harvest. This was his first harvest after full biodynamic certification was granted, though I see no apparent cause-and-effect relationship here. This has obviously coincided with increasingly warmer seasons in Champagne, but 2006 and 2009 were warm, too, and vintage and non-vintage cuvées based on those seasons showed greater vitality than more recent warm years. It is well worth seeking out cuvées based on the most energetic vintages like 2008.

In his own words, Erick de Sousa 'lives in the rhythm of the vines' and regards his work in the vineyards as the key to the quality of the grapes. Respect for the vine and the earth is paramount, and he spent a decade prior to 2010 converting the domaine to biodynamic viticulture. Biodynamics for him is about equipping his old vines to capture minerality, 'to encourage the vine to draw deeply the trace elements specific to each terroir and provide different characteristics to each cuvée.' The soil is ploughed for ventilation and to restore microbial life, and in some vineyards even with the family's recently acquired horse.

'By focusing on the vineyards, making the wine is easy,' he smiles. 'Like in the kitchen, if the ingredients are fresh from the beginning, the quality is there.'

To increase production, de Sousa purchased new cellars on the opposite side of the village square in 2004 for his négociant label, Zoémie de Sousa. With walls at least half a metre thick, the stable temperature is ideal for ageing wines. When he showed me through, I was surprised by the small scale of production. His enamelled tanks are tiny; he owns one foudre for ageing red wine, a small wooden vat for red wine fermentation, and little 225-litre barrels made from oak harvested in Avize and from a cooper friend in Burgundy.

Fruit from vines older than 50 years is fermented in small oak barrels, with regular bâtonnage to enhance depth and breadth. He has used about 15% new barrels for his top cuvées, and increased the proportion slightly since 2004. Such is his sensitive and masterful use of barrels that fruit flavours always take precedence over oak flavours, and texture is enhanced, amplifying minerality and definition. Chaptalisation is performed when necessary, the first fermentation is initiated with natural yeasts, and sulphur dioxide is used sparingly.

All wines have traditionally passed through malolactic fermentation, but in the low-acid 2018 season, the decision was not to inoculate any barrels that didn't naturally go through malolactic. 'With a warming climate, we might not always complete the malolactic anymore,' Erick reveals.

Narrow and atmospheric, the 200-year-old cellars under the house run 800 metres directly beneath the square in the middle of the village. A stable temperature of 10°C is ideal for long ageing. Here, the old method of *poignettage* is practised, in which autolytic flavours are enhanced by shaking the bottles by hand to stir up the lees. Bottles are also riddled by hand.

De Sousa's profound prestige Cuvée des Caudalies' claim to uniqueness is not so much that it is a prestige cuvée of non-vintage blend, but just how this blend is assembled. Sourced from chardonnay vines exceeding 50 years of age in Avize, Oger, Le Mesnil-sur-Oger and Cramant, and vinified in small barrels with no chaptalisation, it is blended as a solera of reserve wines that currently spans the 18 harvests from 1995 to 2012. Cuvée des Caudalies is also released as an ultra-complex vintage wine and a mesmerising rosé. De Sousa's substantial and diverse portfolio now boasts ten cuvées, which the family admits is a bit complicated, but upholds their mandate to maintain the specificity of their sites and blends.

Erick is ably assisted by his wife Michelle, and increasingly by his three children, Charlotte, who oversees exports, Valentin, who works alongside his father in the vineyard, and Julie, who manages the technical side and works with their horse in the vines. Erick and Michelle plan to transition their work into the hands of their children over the coming decade.

To this end the family recently made the bold decision to convert De Sousa from Récoltant-Manipulant to Négociant-Manipulant. Not, as some other growers have done, to facilitate purchasing grapes or vineyards, but for an altogether different reason – the more than slightly ironic mandate of upholding the business in the family name.

France's antiquated inheritance tax is one of the highest in the world, slamming children with a 45% tax on their parents' assets. A generation ago, it was possible to pay off inheritance tax in a single harvest, but today, owning ten hectares of grand cru vineyards (fetching €3 million per hectare), not to mention more than 250,000 bottles in the cellar, it would take the De Sousa children a lifetime to pay off the tax. 'In France we say that the inheritance tax is a stupid law!' exclaims Charlotte. 'If the parents pass away and haven't prepared for this, then the children say it's a poison gift and they're forced to sell the vineyards to big companies. We changed to a négociant to pass on the domaine to us three children.'

French taxation is more kind in the inheritance of a company than vineyard land. Erick and Michelle now own the vineyard, and their children the company, 'so we effectively buy the grapes from ourselves'. By definition, this makes them a Négociant-Manipulant.

In an age in which Récoltants are vigorously celebrated in champagne markets the world over, what has been the response?

'Since Zoémie de Sousa was introduced as a négociant label 15 years ago and De Sousa made the change six years ago, nobody has asked,' Charlotte reveals. 'Nobody noticed. And the mentality is changing that people will accept growers as négociants. It is not true that "négociant" in Champagne means that you are making a big volume. With more growers becoming négociants, it is better understood by consumers.'

This change has also opened up the opportunity for the family to purchase grapes. 'With three children deriving their livelihood from the company, we need to increase production a little, perhaps by one-third,'

Cramant chardonnay, harvest 2014

says Charlotte. 'We feel that to be successful, we need to be a little bigger. We are now locked, as it's impossible to buy vineyards today, as they are rare to find and expensive. It's easier for us to buy grapes than vineyards.' Though this is not so simple for a certified biodynamic producer.

'We have tried to find organic grower partners,' explains Charlotte, 'but growers are worried that they will produce less grapes and hence less income with organics, even though there is no difference in yields compared with conventional viticulture. So we work hard to find people prepared to take the small risk and become organic, and we pay for their certification.'

It takes three years until organic certification is granted, so in order to uphold the De Sousa brand as organic, the family will introduce a new label for fruit from grower partners still in transition. The possibility of inclusion in De Sousa will be considered when certification permits. They have decided to phase out their Zoémie de Sousa label, perceiving that trading under two brands has confused the market. 'People thought it was the second wine and hence inferior,' Charlotte suggests.

In addition to disgorgement dates, back labels disclose the bottling date, which is a useful insight as the base vintage of NV cuvées is always the year prior.

De Sousa has risen to a rightful place among Champagne's great family estates under Erick's visionary guidance over the past quarter century. Theirs are masterfully grown and crafted wines, every one of which is brilliantly mineral, profoundly exact and beautifully fresh. At the end of a long tasting and vigorous conversation over that massive oak table, I once told Erick as much.

'It's all about mature vines with roots that go deep into the soil,' he replies with unassuming humility.

And it must also have a little to do with what is indeed one of the finest recipes in Champagne.

De Sousa Brut Tradition NV $$

91 points • 2015 base vintage • Disgorged July 2018 • Tasted in Champagne

50% chardonnay, 40% pinot, 10% meunier; Vallée de la Marne, Côte des Blancs and Épernay surrounds; average vine age 25-30 years; 20% reserves; stainless steel tank fermentation; 7g/L dosage

De Sousa's entry cuvée is a soft, approachable and appealing apéritif style of pleasant balance, without trying to be particularly mineral, complex or profound. Its fruit focus unites the red apple and red cherry of pinot noir with the citrus crunch of chardonnay and the ginger-cake complexity of lees age.

De Sousa Grand Cru Réserve Brut Blanc de Blancs NV $$

92 points • 2015 BASE VINTAGE • DISGORGED 3 JULY 2018 • TASTED IN CHAMPAGNE
95 points • 2008 BASE VINTAGE • DISGORGED 14 NOVEMBER 2017 • TASTED IN CHAMPAGNE

100% chardonnay from Cramant, Avize, Oger, Le Mesnil-sur-Oger and Chouilly; average vine age 43 years; vinified in stainless steel tanks; 30% reserves; 7g/L dosage, and considering 5g/L for the next disgorgement

De Sousa's mandate here is focused minerality and freshness. In concert with the heightened fruit presence of ripe chardonnay, this makes for an exciting blanc de blancs that captures the mood of the house and the grandeur of its terroirs. Beurre bosc pear and apple declare fruit ripeness, well harmonised with soft acidity and gentle salt mineral presence. Lees age contributes gingernut biscuit complexity, while dosage lends a honeyed note to the finish. The suggestion of the house to lower dosage to 5g/L makes good sense, particularly in the context of the rich 2015 season. It's an elegant style for this ripe harvest, concluding long and enticing.

On its first release four years ago, I declared the 2008 base 'a breathtakingly refined De Sousa, the very definition of chardonnay from the heart of its finest terroirs'. It has returned quite unexpectedly for a rousing encore, after the house fortuitously discovered an undisgorged pallet and a half in the cellar that it had set aside and forgotten! They are now presenting it with a dosage of 3g/L alongside the current release as evidence of how slowly and spectacularly this cuvée can age. They didn't reveal the base vintage and I guessed 2012, such was its desperate freshness! The dainty lemon blossom and anise of its youth have now morphed magnificently into toasty, spicy complexity, laced with butter, vanilla and roast nuts. Its delightfully silky mouthfeel has been heightened by 8.5 years on lees, to a lofty place more creamy than ever, while its mineral impact has remained transfixed, a revelation of frothing, sea-surf chalk of impeccable definition. I predicted that it would age magnificently and yet again, on current performance, there's no stopping it.

De Sousa Brut Rosé NV $$

88 points • 2015 BASE VINTAGE • DISGORGED 10 OCTOBER 2017 • TASTED IN CHAMPAGNE

92% chardonnay from Grauves, 8% pinot noir red wine from Aÿ, made by the house, destemmed and macerated in its own vat, before ageing 1 year in barrel; average vine age 25-30 years; fermented in stainless steel tanks; 20% reserves; 7g/L dosage

De Sousa's aspiration for rosé is to express the freshness of chardonnay, sourced entirely from the premier cru of Grauves, over the hill behind Avize. Now at the end of its release cycle, this bottle unfortunately misses the mark of its target. More than 15 months after disgorgement, it has lost its aromatic lift and fruit freshness, instead dusty and savoury with notes of tomato and macerated strawberries. Nonetheless, it upholds the fine, salty chalk mineral definition of Grauves.

De Sousa 3A Aÿ Avize Ambonnay Grand Cru Extra Brut NV $$$

92 points • 2014 BASE VINTAGE • DISGORGED 12 JANUARY 2018 • TASTED IN CHAMPAGNE

50% Avize chardonnay, 25% Aÿ pinot, 25% Ambonnay pinot, all co-fermented, half in barrels, half in tanks; average vine age 25-30 years; 20% reserves; 5g/L dosage

The trend in Champagne is towards keeping parcels separate to increase definition, but De Sousa has boldly co-fermented to created a profoundly seamless union of chardonnay and pinot noir from three of Champagne's most distinctive villages. At once crunchy and succulent, it's led by the red apple fruit of pinot noir and the grapefruit tang of chardonnay, with biscuity character and creamy texture contributed by lees age. The mood of 3A swings dramatically according to its base vintage, and 2014 lacks the purity and poise of 2012 and 2013, instead concluding with some coffee bean and dusty dryness, reflecting its lesser season. The salty minerality and harmonious acid balance of Avize triumph, lingering long on the finish.

De Sousa Mycorhize Grand Cru Extra Brut NV $$$

94 points • 2014 base vintage • Disgorged 1 July 2018 • Tasted in Champagne

100% chardonnay from the lieu-dit Les Hauts Nemery of 2 hectares in Avize; average vine age of over 60 years; wild fermented entirely in 225 barrels, 5% new; aged long in barrel for micro-oxygenation; 25% perpetual reserve; 3g/L dosage; 1212 bottles

Mycorrhizae is a micro fungus living on plant roots that metabolises the soil and helps the vines to ingest minerality. By only ploughing these vineyards by horse, the theory is that soil compaction is reduced and hence the roots achieve not only greater penetration, but increased oxygenation, which, in concert with elimination of chemical treatments, enhances mycorrhizal life. The family hopes that in time this will bring greater mineral character in their wines.

The result already exemplifies the science to dramatic effect as the mineral, saline, iodine definition of Avize is accentuated in De Sousa's exacting regime. True to its mantra it is deeply salt mineral in texture, the roots of these old vines boring deep into the ancient chalk, balancing the body and succulence of white peach and white nectarine and the spicy crunch of white grapefruit. The toasty complexity and spicy presence of barrel fermentation meets the body and presence of old-vine Avize chardonnay, held in well-harmonised balance in spite of its proportions, thanks to a finish of dynamic acidity. A cuvée of unique character, great presence, and enduring persistence, this is the finest Mycorhize from De Sousa yet.

De Sousa Cuvée Umami Grand Cru 2009 $$$$

95 points • Disgorged April 2018 • Tasted in Champagne

60% chardonnay from Avize, and a little from Oger and Le Mesnil-sur-Oger; 40% pinot noir from Aÿ and Ambonnay; average vine age of over 60 years; vinified entirely in new and old barrels; 4.5g/L dosage; 7000 bottles and 1000 magnums to be released over 10 years, with only 500 bottles allocated each year

De Sousa associates the Japanese concept of 'umami' with the mouthfeel of salinity and sappiness derived from the chalk soils of the Côte des Blancs, drawn out by biodynamic viticulture. Coming from anyone else, I would dismiss such umami aspirations as a trite, contrived marketing line, but the texture, frothing sea salt minerality and even salty, maritime-air bouquet of this first release are an irrefutable testimony to the successful execution of an ambitious brief. Few estates in the world have the terroirs and the expertise to embody umami as emphatically as this. The umami character of glutamic acid in the lees is enhanced through bâtonnage (stirring) three or four times in barrel and poignettage (shaking) in bottle to stir up the lees. The 2009 was chosen for this first release for its strength, roundness and power, and it has arisen majestically in depth and stature over the four years since its launch, building great layers of complexity, fleshy depth and creamy, silky appeal, while shedding nothing of its salty, iodine umami. The ripe-fruit body of the season is morphing into a spicy and honeyed mood that unites the fleshy body of pinot noir with the crunch of chardonnay, all encased in a brittle mineral shell. A cuvée of great personality and breathtaking line and length, presenting a captivating point of difference within the De Sousa style.

De Sousa Cuvée des Caudalies Blanc de Blancs Extra Brut Grand Cru NV $$$$

94 points • 2013 base vintage • Disgorged October 2018 • Tasted in Champagne

100% chardonnay; average vine age of more than 60 years; 100% vinified in small oak barrels; 50% reserves from a solera of every vintage from 1995; matured 5 years on lees; 5g/L dosage

Caudalies is De Sousa's pinnacle and definitive range, with a mandate to showcase the house's aspirations of minerality, strength and balance. I tasted the Caudalies solera for the first time during the 2014 harvest and was stunned at its complexity. Five years on, it reverberates with more depth than ever, reflecting the multifaceted depth of its ever-ageing solera. The result is a powerfully complex cuvée of presence and intrigue, a stroll through an autumnal landscape of spicy red apple, golden leaves and butter on toast. Tertiary nuances of charcuterie are beginning to appear along the way for the first time, but the great 2013 season upholds integrity and freshness in a pale, bright-straw hue and crunchy grapefruit purity. Dosage and acidity are well integrated, leaving the structural stage clear for the main act: the ever-present, heightened, dancing spectacle of chalk minerality.

De Sousa Cuvée des Caudalies Brut Rosé NV $$$$

95 points • 2011 base vintage • Disgorged 6 April 2018 • Tasted in Champagne

90% chardonnay from Avize, Oger and Le Mesnil-sur-Oger, 10% Aÿ pinot red wine matured in oak casks for 1 year; average vine age of over 60 years; 100% vinified in small oak barrels; no reserves; 3g/L dosage

Such is the powerful colour, pure fruit and delicate structure of De Sousa's red wine that a 10% dose transforms a pristine blanc de blancs into a characterful and multifaceted savoury rosé, more deeply spicy and complex than ever. Relentless beauty of haunting plum liqueur and fruit mince spice hover in suspension amidst the barrel fermentation nuances of charcuterie. Pinot noir brings body and succulence, intricately entwined and perfectly integrated with the deep-set chalk of De Sousa, concluding with wonderfully persistent, frothy salt minerality of exceptional line and length. With no reserves to lean on, this is a graceful triumph for 2011.

De Sousa Cuvée des Caudalies Grand Cru Millésime Extra Brut 2010 $$$$$

94 points • Disgorged 27 January 2010 • Tasted in Champagne

100% chardonnay from Avize and Oger; average vine age of more than 60 years; 100% vinified and aged 10 months in barrels; 4g/L dosage

De Sousa's first year of being certified as biodynamic happened to be a warm season that has yielded a powerful, rich and rounded cuvée of medium straw hue. The white peach and grapefruit of ripe chardonnay unites with the fruit mince spice and subtle charcuterie of barrel fermentation. The result is creamy, succulent and seamless, structured by harmonious acidity and the gentle grip of fine, salty chalk minerality. It concludes with excellent line and length. Ready to drink now, it will hold for a couple of years yet.

De Sousa Cuvée des Caudalies Grand Cru Millésime Extra Brut 2008 $$$$$

96 points • Disgorged February 2016 • Tasted in Champagne

As above; aged 6.5 years on lees; 4.5g/L dosage; 5000 bottles; half sold and half held as an oenothèque for re-release

Erick De Sousa describes 2008 as a fantastic and perfect season, and bottled 5000 bottles of this cuvée rather than the usual 2000. This is a ripe and exuberant take on such a tense year, a wine of grand stature and proportions, evolving in freeze-frame slow motion since its release two years ago. It upholds its succulent old-vine fruit and zesty grapefruit freshness, while morphing to a place of layered fruit mince spice, candied orange rind, even an unexpected hint of cherry liqueur. The toasty complexity of barrel fermentation is lifted by the evolution of lees age. This is a blanc de blancs of tremendous dimension, juxtaposed consummately with the tension and focus of pure 2008 acidity, the high-tensile definition of Oger and, most especially, Avize, and an all-consuming shower of epic, cascading, salty chalk minerality as embracing as a dousing in an icy waterfall, dissolving fruit and oak perfectly in a finish of crystalline mineral definition.

Delamotte

(Deh-la-mot)

6/10

5–7 Rue de la Brèche d'Oger 51190 Le Mesnil-sur-Oger
www.salondelamotte.com

CHAMPAGNE
DELAMOTTE
Le Mesnil sur Oger depuis 1760

Delamotte is effectively the second label of Salon (page 511), though the house prefers to call them 'sister houses'. It has been Salon's neighbour for over a century, and celebrates its 260th birthday this year. The two joined forces in 1988, and the following year were bought by Laurent-Perrier, which handles the winemaking for both brands. 'Delamotte has long been in the shadow of Salon, but we are now very proud of Delamotte,' declares Salon Delamotte president Didier Depond. And he has good reason to be, because the initiatives he's put in place have set this exciting house on the rise.

Delamotte produces 800,000 bottles annually from 35 hectares of its own vineyards, largely in Le Mesnil-sur-Oger, and a similar volume of purchased fruit. Chardonnay is sourced principally from the grand crus of Le Mesnil-sur-Oger, Oger, Avize and Cramant, and pinot noir for its Brut NV and Rosé primarily from Bouzy, Ambonnay and Tours-sur-Marne. While Delamotte has shared production with Laurent-Perrier under Michel Fauconnet for more than 30 years in the house's substantial facility in Tours-sur-Marne, the vineyard resources of the house are distinct.

Delamotte also receives all the leftovers from Salon, and in years when Salon doesn't declare (two in five, to date), the entire Salon harvest is dedicated to Delamotte Blanc de Blancs NV (not the vintage, so as to avoid the perception of a declassified Salon). All the fruit of the Jardin de Salon went to Delamotte until the 2012 vintage, as it was replanted in 2003 and the average vine age for Salon is 35–40 years. For other parcels, the ultimate destiny of each tank (there are no barrels here) is quickly determined post-fermentation, since Delamotte undergoes malolactic fermentation while Salon does not.

Delamotte has been riding a steep growth curve for the past couple of decades, more than trebling its output from 250,000 bottles, spurred by strong demand across Asia. Depond discloses that he could increase production to 1 million bottles, but this is not his aspiration.

His vision, instead, is to make Delamotte the reference house for blanc de blancs. Since Salon is blanc de blancs, it's no surprise that Delamotte's blanc de blancs cuvées are its soaring highlights. 'My dream is to produce only blanc de blancs, but it is impossible!' Depond exclaims.

When he commenced with the house in 1997, he streamlined the portfolio from seven to four cuvées. 'It was a nonsense!' he exclaims. 'Everyone wants to create new cuvées in Champagne now, but I prefer to be focused on just four.

Depond has no interest in following the Champagne trends to make zero dosage or oak-fermented cuvées. 'Zero dosage is like a recipe without salt,' he proclaims. 'And the taste of wood is nonsense in champagne. For me, champagne is about freshness and elegance.'

In tune with this vision, he has been proactive in changing the balance of production of Delamotte, astutely reducing the volume of Brut NV, which represented the majority of the output of the house in 1997, and today just 50% of production. He has also been successful in gradually shifting the blend of this cuvée over more than a decade, in tune with his philosophy, from equal thirds of pinot noir, chardonnay and meunier when he commenced with the house, to 55% grand cru chardonnay, pinot noir from Bouzy, Ambonnay and Tours-sur-Marne, and just 10% meunier today, with the hope of ultimately fading the meunier out altogether in years to come.

Disgorgement dates can be decoded from cork codes. The letter is the trimester and the year is inverted, so A61 denotes the first trimester of 2016.

Delamotte Brut NV $$

88 points • 2014 base vintage • Disgorged February 2018 • Tasted in Australia
89 points • 80% 2013 base vintage • Tasted in Champagne

55% chardonnay from Oger, Avize and Le Mesnil-sur-Oger, 35% pinot from Bouzy, Ambonnay and Tours-sur-Marne, 10% meunier from Vallée de la Marne; 20% reserves from the preceding six years; aged 3 years on lees; 8g/L dosage; cork; half of the production of the house, roughly 400,000 bottles

The progress made in both the rise of chardonnay in this blend and its laudable vineyard sources over the past decade have created a cuvée ever more in tune with the blanc de blancs theme of the house. The 2014 base has given birth to a zesty apéritif style of lemon, grapefruit, red apple and pear, lively and primary, with underripe notes of fennel and subtle almond-meal nuances of lees development only just beginning. Lively acid presence is met by well-integrated dosage, though marked by a dusty, dry, tilled-earth phenolic bite to the finish. The 2013 base, upheld by the house as a fantastic vintage for chardonnay, contrasts the salty minerality of the grand crus of the Côte des Blancs with the gentle fruit harmony of chardonnay and pinot, marked by the bitter bite of grapefruit and the firmness of phenolic grip.

Delamotte Blanc de Blancs NV $$$

94 points • 2013 base vintage • Disgorged April 2018 • Tasted in Australia
94 points • 2012 base vintage • Tasted in Champagne

Le Mesnil-sur-Oger, Oger and Avize; 7g/L dosage; 10% reserves; aged 4 years on lees; cork; 280,000 bottles

Delamotte Blanc de Blancs is stunning in the great base vintages, but unfortunately it isn't possible to ascertain this pre-purchase, as there's some detective work required in removing the foil, decoding the disgorgement date from the cork and working backwards. Delamotte has captured the flattering and energetic mood of the 2013 base vintage in a compelling and enticing rendition of its NV blanc de blancs. The characteristic struck-flint reduction of the style makes way for crunchy lemon, fresh grapefruit and spicy white nectarine, set against a rising torrent of brioche and nougat. It confidently projects the majesty of its grand cru origins in great fruit presence, lively acid tension and, most of all, the spectacular, fine, frothing chalk mineral structure of Le Mesnil-sur-Oger, concluding with fantastic harmony and persistence. The 2012 base presents gently creamy finesse with poised assurance and approachable grace.

Delamotte Brut Rosé NV $$$

91 points • 2013 base vintage • Tasted in Champagne
94 points • 2012 base vintage • Tasted in Champagne
89 points • 2012 base vintage • Disgorged April 2016 • Tasted in Australia

Co-maceration of 20% chardonnay mostly from Le Mesnil-sur-Oger and 80% pinot from Bouzy, Ambonnay and Tours-sur-Marne; similar saignée process as Laurent-Perrier; aged 3 years on lees; 8g/L dosage; cork; small production of 35,000 bottles, so as not to compete with Laurent-Perrier

The personality of southern Montagne de Reims pinot noir and the dexterity of Michel Fauconnet with maceration rosé are both on display here in a style designed as a simple and fresh union of the structure of pinot noir and the delicacy and femininity of chardonnay. It was first created by Fauconnet's predecessor Alain Terrier, who set out to make a rosé of cassis character. The 2013 is refreshingly and unusually elegant for a maceration rosé, a tangy and characterful expression of pinot noir, tweaked with the tension of chardonnay. Boasting a medium salmon-copper hue, the strawberry hull and red apple fruit of pinot are focused by the bright acidity and fine chalk minerality of chardonnay, concluding with gentle tannin grip. Subtle, almost savoury notes of cracked pink pepper and rhubarb accent a lively finish. The 2012 base shone with a radiant medium salmon hue and spectacular finesse and restraint of pretty red berry fruits on release at the house, but sadly quickly faded to a copper tint and savoury characters of sun-dried tomato and paprika, its diminishing fruit definition amplifying the grip and dry texture of firm, fine tannin structure.

Delamotte Blanc de Blancs 2008 $$$$

95 points • Disgorged early 2018 & September 2018 • Tasted in Champagne and Australia

All six Côte des Blancs grand crus for the first time; 60% Le Mesnil-sur-Oger, Oger and Avize, 40% Cramant, Oiry and Chouilly; aged 9 years on lees (the longest yet, usually 7 years); 6.5g/L dosage; cork; 60,000 bottles (usually 90-95,000)

In the hallowed, towering shadow of Salon, Delamotte vintage has ascended to great heights over recent releases, and the scintillating 2008 season has predictably given birth to the finest yet. Capturing the essence of this stunning harvest, this is a cuvée of brilliant purity and promise, projecting a radiant, luminescent straw-green hue. It leads out with a touch of reductive complexity of grilled toast, underlining concentrated preserved lemon and pear fruit. Nine years on lees has brought a creamy texture and not inconsiderable layers of toasted lemon meringue, brioche, vanilla cream, marzipan and dried pear. The fine, frothing salt minerality of all six grand crus of the Côte des Blancs is sensational, exciting and all-consuming, marking out a long, frothing and focused finish of great energy and precise 2008 acid drive, promising a magnificently enduring future. One bottle showed gherkin and vinegar-like oxidation. The next from the same shipment was sublime.

Delamotte Collection Blanc de Blancs 1999 $$$$$

95 points • Disgorged 2017 and early 2018 • Tasted in Champagne

Aged 19 years on lees; 5g/L dosage

Boasting a bright, full straw hue and wonderful freshness, this is a cuvée that transcends the ripeness of its season and looks but half its age. After a full 20 years, it's attained a beautiful place in its maturity, upholding primary poise in the grand presence of rising secondary and tertiary maturity. It rejoices in the exuberant succulence of a warm harvest, layered with juicy, fleshy peach and nectarine, even glacé pineapple. Fresher bottles still uphold primary apple and citrus fruit, amidst the glowing complexity of wild honey, pipe smoke, mixed spice, even white pepper and mint. A 1999 of confidence, harmony and joy.

DELAVENNE PÈRE & FILS

(Deh-la-ven Pear e Feess)

5/10

6 Rue de Tours-sur-Marne 51150 Bouzy
www.champagne-delavenne.fr

CHAMPAGNE
DELAVENNE Père & Fils
RÉCOLTANTS · MANIPULANTS
BOUZY

Bouzy, Ambonnay and Cramant are a formidable trilogy of crus in which the Delavenne family is privileged to estate holdings exclusively of pinot noir and chardonnay. In these days of ever-warmer harvests, pushing fruit ripeness to impressive levels in such bold terroirs is no easy juggling act, a balance that this little family estate maintains masterfully with gently integrated malic acidity and the pronounced, salty chalk minerality of its lauded sites. Marcel Delavenne began making champagne in Bouzy in 1920, and today his great-grandson Jean-Louis works alongside his father Jean-Christophe to uphold an integrated viticultural approach, shunning pesticides and moving towards organic practices wherever possible. Their cuvées are wild fermented in stainless steel tanks, with malolactic fermentation completely blocked to uphold freshness. The ripeness of the house style and the complexity and confidence of its terroirs do not call for deep reserves, and hence non-vintage cuvées comprise just 20% of the previous harvest. Bottling occurs in July, followed by ageing in the family's natural chalk cellars. Cork codes are six digits, the first two indicating the base vintage, the next two the month of disgorgement and the final two the year of disgorgement. Delavenne's cuvées present a captivating juxtaposition of the allure of ripe fruit from powerful terroirs, energised by malic acidity and fantastic chalk minerality.

DELAVENNE PÈRE & FILS GRAND CRU BRUT TRADITION NV $$

93 points • 2013 base vintage • Disgorged December 2016 • Tasted in Australia

40% chardonnay, 60% pinot; estate Bouzy and Ambonnay vineyards; 20% 2012 reserves; wild fermented in stainless steel tanks; no malolactic fermentation; aged 29 months on lees; 9g/L dosage

The rich, exuberant mood of Bouzy and Ambonnay is captured to compelling effect by Delavenne right from its youngest cuvée, a flamboyant, rich and ripe fanfare of succulent black and red fruits, fruit mince spice, mixed spice and ginger. This little estate pushes fruit ripeness to impressive levels and tensions it masterfully with gently integrated malic acidity and the pronounced, salty chalk minerality of its lauded terroirs. Lees age has built layers of toasty, biscuity complexity and wonderfully harmonious, seamless creaminess that holds a very long finish. The result is a fleshy and full style of main-course confidence and magnificent freshness.

Bouzy, harvest 2014

Delavenne Père & Fils Grand Cru Brut Réserve NV $$

92 points • 2012 base vintage • Disgorged November 2016 • Tasted in Australia

40% chardonnay, 60% pinot; estate Bouzy vineyards halfway up the slope; 20% 2011 reserves; wild fermented in stainless steel; no malolactic fermentation; 8.4g/L dosage

The beautifully rounded fruit allure of ripe Bouzy pinot noir shines in spicy, expansive and rich black fruits of all kinds, contrasting the citrus counterpoint of chardonnay. Malic acidity is played to compelling effect, bright, fresh and taut, yet well integrated, marvellously underscored by the prominent, salty chalk minerality of Bouzy. More than three years on lees has brought seamless integration and coaxed out subtle biscuity complexity, lingering long on an excellent finish of succulent, ripe fruit enticement.

Delavenne Père & Fils Grand Cru Brut Nature NV $$

89 points • 2011 base vintage • Disgorged November 2016 • Tasted in Australia

40% chardonnay, 60% pinot; 100% estate Bouzy; 20% 2010 reserves; aged 4 years on lees; wild fermented in stainless steel tanks; no malolactic fermentation; zero dosage

There is quite some power of estate pinot noir, here well countered by the refinement of chardonnay and the cut of malic acidity. Black cherry fruits and layers of mixed spice and fruit mince spice mark out a characterful style of lees age texture and biscuity complexity. The dusty dryness of imperfect fruit marked by the challenging 2011 season, and to a lesser extent the difficult 2010 vintage, makes for a coarse finish, with no dosage to save it. Nonetheless, a good effort under the circumstances.

Delavenne Père & Fils Grand Cru Blanc de Blancs NV $$

91 points • 2013 base vintage • Disgorged May 2017 • Tasted in Australia

100% Cramant chardonnay; aged 3 years on lees; no malolactic fermentation; 7.8g/L dosage

The thundering generosity of ripe Cramant chardonnay ripples in waves of pineapple, white peach, fig and even the tropical exuberance of paw paw of magnificent amplitude and expansive breadth, held in check by the fine, salty chalk minerality of this legendary terroir and gentle malic acidity. This is a ripe style of main-course scale that holds itself with confident enthusiasm and lingering persistence. Inimitable Cramant of slightly larger than life proportions.

Delavenne Père & Fils Grand Cru Brut Rosé NV $$

92 points • 2013 base vintage • Disgorged May 2017 • Tasted in Australia

40% chardonnay, 43% pinot, 17% Bouzy Rouge; estate Bouzy vineyards; aged 3 years on lees; wild fermented in stainless steel; no malolactic fermentation; 9g/L dosage

True to the Delavenne style, this is a rosé of considerable amplitude, thanks to a generous 17 percent of Bouzy Rouge. A medium crimson hue with a subtle copper tint heralds a rosé rippling with red fruits of all kinds, accented with savoury notes of tomato and crushed pink pepper. Glorious Bouzy breadth and depth are freshened masterfully by focused malic acidity and the pronounced chalk minerality of Bouzy. Firm, fine tannin structure is well managed and makes for a rosé of the structural confidence to partner with pink meats.

Delavenne Père & Fils Coteaux Champenois Bouzy Rouge Pinot Noir 2015

88 points • Tasted in Australia

100% estate Bouzy pinot from the family's best parcels; destemmed and crushed manually

A Bouzy Rouge of impressive colour, boasting a medium red purple hue. It's a tense style that screams out for considerable bottle age to tone its angular edges. Firm, fine tannins, taut acidity and oak conspire to create an austere finish of dry firmness. One hopes that in time it might build flesh and generosity, but that might take decades, if it ever comes to fruition.

DÉROT-DELUGNY

(Deh-roh Der-loo-nee)

15–21 GRANDE RUE 02310 CROUTTES-SUR-MARNE
www.champagne-derot-delugny.com

CHAMPAGNE
Dérot — DD — Delugny
Fondé en 1929

Since 1929, the Dérot and Delugny families were the first to produce champagne in their village of Crouttes-sur-Marne in the western Vallée de la Marne, midway between Reims and Paris. Today, the great-grandson of the founders, Laurent, assists his father François in the vineyards and the winery, while his sister, Claire, oversees marketing and administration. Twelve hectares in their village and its surrounds are tended sustainably with natural fertilisers and grasses in the mid-rows, certified both 'High Environmental Value' and 'Sustainable Viticulture in Champagne'. Meunier is king in these western reaches, supplemented with plantings of pinot, chardonnay and even pinot gris, which produces an unusual and more than respectable cuvée flying solo.

DÉROT-DELUGNY CUVÉE DES FONDATEURS PINOT GRIS BRUT NV $

91 points • 2014 BASE VINTAGE • TASTED IN AUSTRALIA

2013 reserves; vinified in stainless steel and oak; 7g/L dosage

As impressive as it is unique, nobly articulating the voice of terroir above the din of variety, this is a young style that showcases classy winemaking, juxtaposing the tension of bright acidity with the fine, firm grip of the telltale phenolic structure of gris. Exotic varietal hallmarks of blood orange and white nectarine are tensioned with a flash of lemon and refreshing chalk minerality. It upholds a fine, creamy bead and a finish lingering with line and length.

DEUTZ

(Derts)

8/10

6 RUE JEANSON 51160 AŸ
www.champagne-deutz.com

FONDÉ EN 1838

Champagne
DEUTZ
AY- FRANCE

*F*abrice, you are crazy!' came the response when Deutz president Fabrice Rosset joined the house in 1996 and set a mandate to grow sales from 576,000 bottles to 1.5 million in just six years. 'As long as I could find the grapes, I could do it,' he reflects. 'And not only did we do it, we exceeded it!' Deutz continued to grow like a mad thing, more than tripling production to more than 2 million bottles every year from 2004 to 2008, dipping only slightly in response to the global recession and reaching 2.4 million bottles today (and 2.65 million in the generous 2018 harvest). For such a breathtaking pace of expansion, the standards it has maintained are not only admirable, they're downright remarkable. Its entry non-vintage cuvée is built on more generous inclusions of reserves than ever, vintage cuvées are the most sublime the house has created, and an all-new tier of prestige takes the top end to soaring new heights. There isn't one wine out of place in this line of crisp, pure champagnes, impeccably crafted in a style of elegant finesse.

Deutz is still setting a cracking pace. The main press house in Aÿ was razed in 2010 and two new layers of cellars dug underneath. An investment of some €20 million was made in the cuverie alone, with a completely new press house erected just in time for vintage 2011, with new four- and eight-tonne presses, a new bottling line and increased capacity for reserve wines. These extensions increased cellar capacity from 8 million to 11.5 million bottles, and Deutz is now bottling its annual production target of 2.5 million bottles, having secured the grape supply to sustain it.

Owned by the Rouzaud family (Louis Roederer) since 1993, the house has maintained autonymity in its fruit sourcing, production and distribution. It lays claim to just 42 of now more than 200 hectares from which it sources fruit, all in grand and premier cru villages in the Marne. Chardonnay and pinot noir are the focus for Deutz, with meunier comprising just 5% of its fruit. 'We are looking for vineyards to buy, but the availability of good vineyards is not high,' reveals Rosset, still very much the dynamic powerhouse behind the house. Most of the supply increase in recent years has come from purchased fruit. 'There is as much rivalry and fighting upstream in searching for good grapes as there is downstream in our markets!' he discloses. To reward quality, growers are paid based not only on the standard of their terroir, but the quality of grapes delivered. Growers are hearing of Deutz's reputation and calling the company to offer

Three kilometres of Deutz cellars extend 65 metres below its vineyard behind Aÿ.

their grapes. 'This is the highest compliment we could be paid!' exclaims Rosset.

Can the house continue to maintain quality while following such a steep trajectory of growth? 'It is crucial that we maintain the same quality of supplies,' chef de cave Michel Davesne emphasises. The intention is to uphold the same suppliers, continuing to source from within 35 kilometres of Aÿ and using only the first pressings. He is confident the investments in the new winery and cellars will only aid the pursuit of quality.

Assuming the house can maintain reliable supply channels, Deutz will be well equipped to uphold its production target. Recently modernised disgorgement and warehousing facilities are already in operation, and 10 million bottles wait in anticipation for between three and 12 or more years in three kilometres of cellars extending into the hill, up to 65 metres deep beneath the vineyard behind Aÿ. In all, Deutz has invested €30 million in its modernisation since it was purchased by the Rouzaud family.

With sustainable agriculture a priority, Deutz is trialling organics and even biodynamics in its plot immediately above the winery. Chemical pesticides have been abandoned, and grasses cultivated in the mid-rows of some plots to avoid the use of herbicides and reduce yields. Pruning techniques and green harvests have also been adopted to reduce yields to slightly below the average. Pickers are paid by the hour rather than by the kilogram, so as to promote a more rigorous selection. This can double the cost of picking in difficult years like 2017.

Rosset spends much of his time during harvest visiting press houses and growers, and he personally joins the winemaking team at every blending session throughout the year, tasting every vat. Most batches of tailles are discarded, but even these are tasted four times, to ascertain which to sell. 'We must uphold our integrity and standards by selling off any parcel not up to standard,' he emphasises. When I visited during blending tastings in February 2016, Rosset and his team had already identified 776hL to sell off (from a total production of 17,000hL). It is such exacting attention to detail that defines the purity and precision of the house.

Even in its young *vins clairs*, the clean, crisp, fresh, pristine focus of the house is abundantly clear. Deutz preserves the purity of its fruit through fermentation plot by plot in 350 stainless steel tanks (no barrels, apart from five for *liqueur d'expédition*, introduced in the austere 2011 vintage), temperature controlled to 16–17°C. Malolactic fermentation is encouraged systematically. Non-vintage wines are aged for two and a half years on lees, and are rested in the cellar for a further six months post-disgorgement. Dosages of around 9g/L are well matched to the graceful style of the house.

The disgorgement date is the last five digits of the lot code printed clearly on the neck foil. The last two digits are the year and the preceding three digits are the day of that year. So 15018 is the 150th day of 2018.

In vintages not up to standard, the prestige cuvées of William Deutz and Amour de Deutz are sacrificed to provide fruit resources to maintain the calibre of the non-vintage cuvées of the house. 'No way are we going to make Brut Classic with the leftovers!' Rosset exclaims.

Elegant rosé is a particular specialty of Deutz, at all three tiers of non-vintage, vintage and prestige, though it represents just seven percent of the total production of the house.

'The key to Deutz is elegance,' expounds Rosset. 'The Deutz style is made on refinement and harmony – this is the quintessence of champagne.' Then he checks himself and grins warmly. 'I am exaggerating!'

But he's right. In its classic, eloquently labelled bottles, Deutz has upheld its air of consistently refreshing, pure lemon sunshine.

Deutz Brut Classic NV $$

92 points • 2014 base vintage • Disgorged October 2017 • Tasted in Champagne and Australia

Roughly 33% chardonnay, 33% pinot, 33% meunier; 100 wines from 20-30 crus across the Marne; 45% reserves from 2013 and 2012; aged 2.5 years on lees; 8g/L dosage; cork; around 1.8 million bottles

Brut Classic is the barometer of Deutz, representing 80% of the volume of production, and the house gives it first priority. Even in the wake of steady growth, it remains as pure and true as ever, with a consistency built on a generous 45% of young reserves (more than the usual 20–40%). Consequently, this release steps beyond the classic realm of Deutz of quintessential, refreshing apéritif, presenting a full, fleshy and rich style in which reserves support the weaker 2014 base. The red apple signature of the label remains the hallmark, verging on baked apple, fleshy plum and rich layers of spice, even fruit mince spice. Pinot upholds a confident lead, fleshy and fuller than ever, with chardonnay cutting in on the finish to bring tension and acid drive. The complexity of bottle age makes it ready to drink right away, rich in nuances of nougat, brioche and honey. It finishes full and long, with well-integrated dosage, gentle bite and soft chalk minerality finding seamless balance. There is presence and flesh here, more than expected in the vivacious and subtle style that defines the signature of Deutz, yet no less confident for it.

Deutz Brut Rosé NV $$

91 points • 2014 base vintage • Disgorged July 2018 • Tasted in Australia

Roughly 10% chardonnay, 90% pinot; Montagne de Reims and Côte d'Aÿ; 8% pinot noir red wine from old vines in Meurtet in Aÿ; aged 3 years on lees; 8.5g/L dosage; cork

The pure, fresh style of Deutz is perfectly suited to elegant and restrained rosé, and the house is unusual in producing the style at three different levels. Right from the start, the entry cuvée is a gorgeous, bright, medium salmon hue. Deep nuances of black cherry and cherry kernel contrast fleshy poached strawberries, meeting dusty notes of dried spice and dried rose petal. Far from the graceful mood of the 2012 base, this is more reticent and more savoury than the usual bright, lifted guise of this cuvée, structured with firm yet super-fine phenolic grip and fine, salty chalk minerality. It upholds its integrity and confidence on a long finish of impressive red berry fruit integrity. A second bottle was identical.

Deutz Blanc de Blancs Brut 2013 $$$

95 points • Disgorged September 2018 • Tasted in Champagne and Australia

100% chardonnay; 37% Avize, 33% Oger, 12% Le Mesnil-sur-Oger, 6% Épernay, 6% Villers-Marmery, 6% Villeneuve-Renneville; aged 4.5 years on lees; 7.5g/L dosage; cork

The tension and precision of 2013 in concert with the pinpoint accuracy of Deutz, led by the structural drive of Avize, makes for a blanc de blancs of radiant freshness and electric energy. Deutz has met this honed focus with magnificent fruit presence, leading out with precise wild lemon and granny smith apple and then flowing into rich and expansive white peach and fig, even fresh apple pie – beautifully elegant fruit purity that perfectly synergises ripe intensity with tense freshness. Lees age has brought subtle almond nougat and Parisienne baguette complexity. The chalk minerality of Avize defines a magnificent undercurrent of salty, fresh texture that washes through a very long stream of crystalline, sparkling structure, drawing out a finish of gliding persistence, undeviating line and delightful poise. Brilliant blanc de blancs.

Deutz Brut Millésimé 2014 $$

93 points • Disgorged June 2018 • Tasted in Champagne

Chardonnay from the Côte des Blancs, pinot from Aÿ, Mareuil-sur-Aÿ, Bouzy and Ambonnay, meunier from Pierry; aged 3 years on lees

After all the glories of 2012 and especially 2013, 2014 presented a more challenging season for Deutz. I tasted this vintage pre-release and it was certainly in a tightly coiled guise in this state. This is a crunchy and lively vintage of red apple and pear fruit, accented with grapefruit tang, holding good body and balance, supported by fine salt mineral structure. A good result for the vintage, but buy the 2012 or 2013 instead.

Deutz Brut Millésimé 2013 $$

96 points • Disgorged January 2018 • Tasted in Australia

33% chardonnay from Villeneuve-Renneville and Villers-Marmery, 63% pinot noir from Aÿ, Bouzy and Verzenay, 4% meunier from Venteuil; aged 4 years on lees; 8g/L dosage; cork

Pinot noir that's larger and lighter than life, with desperate purity and epic precision, this vintage is the essence of Deutz and testimony to both the depth of the vineyard resources and the blending mastery of this grand estate. A dazzling showpiece and exuberant celebration of all there is to love about pinot in all of its radiant glory, it intricately marries the rumbling black cherry, anise and sarsaparilla of Bouzy and Ambonnay with the white cherry freshness, euphoric morello cherry tangy energy and fine-ground pink pepper of Aÿ and Verzenay. It's charged with an epic undercurrent of heightened, super-fine, frothing chalk minerality that captures the core of the finest grand crus of the Montagne de Reims, amplifying it with chardonnay from Villeneuve near Vertus. It's magnificent from start to finish, holding every pristine detail in suspended animation on a finish that just does not seem to end, never glitching or hesitating for a nanosecond. The epitome of Deutz vintage, a profound demonstration of the accomplishment of all this house has achieved in recent decades. This is the embodiment of all there is to adore about Deutz, and the finest vintage cuvée yet to emerge from the hallowed halls of this gracefully distinguished house.

Deutz Brut Millésimé 2012 $$

95 points • Disgorged September 2017 • Tasted in Champagne and Australia

29% chardonnay from Le Mesnil-sur-Oger, 67% pinot from Aÿ, Bouzy and Ambonnay, 4% meunier from Leuvrigny; aged 4.5 years on lees; 8.5g/L dosage; cork

The elegance of Deutz in concert with the purity and succulence of the most revered grand crus of the Montagne de Reims creates a style that delivers presence with restraint. Pinot noir takes a confident lead in crunchy gala apple, fleshy red cherries, fresh strawberries and layers of mixed spice, eloquently brightened and propelled by the chardonnay of Le Mesnil-sur-Oger. The roasted almond and nougat of lees age unites seamlessly with glossy fruit exuberance, the fine-boned acidity of 2012, soft chalk minerality and seamlessly integrated dosage. A gorgeous and enticing style of enduring persistence and irresistible beauty.

DEUTZ BRUT ROSÉ MILLÉSIMÉ 2013 $$

96 points • DISGORGED OCTOBER 2017 • TASTED IN AUSTRALIA

21% chardonnay from Avize, 79% pinot from Aÿ, Bouzy, Verzenay and Ambonnay; 8% pinot noir red wine from old vines in La Pelle in Aÿ and Cumaine and Charmont in Mareuil-sur-Aÿ; aged 3.5 years on lees; 8.5g/L dosage; cork

The parade of vintages of Deutz Rosé is like a ravishing catwalk line-up of elegant splendour, and the latest outfit is every bit as drop-dead gorgeous as the dazzling 2012. Dressed in a medium-pale salmon silk ball gown, it's a rousing celebration of pinot noir from Champagne's four greatest crus in all its glossy red cherry and strawberry succulence, yet transcended with a remarkable, long-legged gracefulness. With a delicate touch of just 8% old-vine red wine, the rosé wizardry of the talented Deutz outfit is exemplified in tannins of invisible finesse, furnishing a palate of silky, slippery seamlessness. It culminates in a long train of bright acidity and fine, soft-chalk mineral lace, illuminated by a radiant flashbulb of Avize chardonnay. Transfixing, adorable and downright delicious, just stand back and watch it turn heads and win hearts.

DEUTZ DEMI-SEC 2012 $$$

92 points • TASTED IN CHAMPAGNE

The same base as Brut Vintage; 29% chardonnay from Le Mesnil-sur-Oger, 67% pinot from Aÿ, Bouzy and Ambonnay, 4% meunier from Leuvrigny; 35g/L dosage

A demi-sec vintage of such age is a rare thing (Philipponnat is the only other one I know), and all the more unusual to find such clean purity, freshness and persistence – but no surprise for Deutz! This is a fresh and fruity style of stone fruit character, clean balance and integrity. As impressive as ever, though the 2012 Brut shows much greater finesse and poise in its standard, low-dosage rendition.

DEUTZ CUVÉE WILLIAM DEUTZ BRUT MILLÉSIME 2009 $$$$

95 points • DISGORGED JUNE 2018 • TASTED IN AUSTRALIA
96 points • DISGORGED JUNE 2018 • TASTED IN CHAMPAGNE

29% chardonnay from Avize, Chouilly and Villers-Marmery, 67% pinot from Aÿ, Verzenay, Bouzy and Ambonnay, 4% meunier from Pierry; aged 8 years on lees; 6.5g/L dosage; cork; released before the 2008

A wonderful expression of the exuberant personality of 2009, captured with the refinement and attentive focus that define Deutz. It brims with flamboyant ripeness of grilled pineapple, ripe fig and succulent pear proportions, contrasting with grapefruit bite and even a suggestion of fennel crunch. Lees age has brought notes of vanilla-candied almonds. The ripe phenolics of 2009 have been well managed, though define the grip and structure as emphatically as its fine chalk minerality and ripe yet tangy acid line. A cuvée of impressive persistence, personality and presence... just not a patch on the 2008 (coming next!). Bottles tasted in Champagne show a little more refinement, poise and lemon freshness.

Deutz Cuvée William Deutz Brut Millésime 2007 $$$$

95 points • Disgorged January 2017 • Tasted in Australia
96 points • Disgorged January 2017 • Tasted in Champagne

Roughly 30% chardonnay, mostly from Avize and a little from Villers-Marmery; 65% pinot, mostly from Aÿ, Verzenay, Bouzy and Ambonnay; 5% meunier, mostly from Pierry; aged 9 years on lees; 8.5g/L dosage; cork

A beautifully bright, pale straw hue for 12 years of age, this is a cuvée that rejoices in the grilled toast of reduction in concert with the buttered-toast allure of long lees age. Within the tempered and contemplative mood of Deutz, there is exuberance here, as vanilla custard melds with flamboyant complexity of orange rind, apricot tart, honey, white fruit cake and persimmon. The fleshy shape of pinot noir defines its generous succulence, with the creamy silkiness of long lees age, while vibrant acid line and fine, salty chalk minerality draw out a long and focused finish. This is a subtly complex and full style, within the ever elegant mood that is William Deutz. Bottles tasted in Champagne show a little more focused lemon and apple freshness.

Deutz Amour de Deutz Brut Millésime 2009 $$$$

96 points • Disgorged May 2018 • Tasted in Australia
97 points • Disgorged May 2018 • Tasted in Champagne

49% Avize, 40% Le Mesnil-sur-Oger, 6% Villers-Marmery, 5% Villeneuve-Renneville; aged 8 years on lees; 8g/L dosage; cork

A cuvée that ripples with the generous enticement of lees age, layered with toasted coconut, vanilla marshmallow and almond nougat. There is a wonderful overtone of lifted, wispy, struck flint and grilled toast reduction. A core of ripe fruit of pear, apple, white peach and grapefruit typifies this warm season in the great grand crus of the Côte des Blancs, led by the thundering refinement of Avize and Le Mesnil-sur-Oger, polished by the eloquent finesse that defines Deutz. It lingers with outstanding line and length, supported by soft, salty minerality and perfectly harmonised acidity and dosage. Tasted in Champagne, its delightful elegance transcends the ripe breadth of the season.

Deutz Amour de Deutz Rosé Millésime Brut 2009 $$$$

97 points • Disgorged May 2018 • Tasted in Australia

43% chardonnay from Avize, Le Mesnil-sur-Oger, Chouilly and Villers-Marmery, 57% pinot from Aÿ, Verzenay, Ambonnay and Bouzy; aged 8 years on lees; 8g/L dosage

A grand successor to the dashing 2008, this is a cuvée that singly exemplifies the mastery of Deutz in creating rosé of graceful refinement, even in a season of bold extremes. A gloriously delightful pale salmon hue heralds a subtle style of strawberry hull and pomegranate crunch, white cherry subtlety, tamarillo complexity, even a wisp of sweet pipe smoke. True to its season and the delicate touch of the house, this is a cuvée that declares its mood more in savoury refinement than fruity flamboyance, underscored by the fine salt minerality of the A-list of Montagne de Reims and Côte des Blancs grand crus. The phenolics of its warm season are honed with graceful Deutz finesse, seamlessly melding with chalk minerality, furnishing definition and structure without any suggestion of bitterness or firmness. Triumphant.

Deutz Hommage à William Deutz La Côte Glacière Pinot Noir Parcelle d'Aÿ Brut 2012 $$$$

97 points • Disgorged July 2018 • Tasted in Champagne and Australia

New cuvée; 100% pinot; Aÿ La Côte Glacière, a steep, south-facing slope of low-yielding, 50-year-old vines, directly above the cellar in Aÿ; aged 5 years on lees; 6.5g/L dosage

A profound statement of the impact of aspect in Champagne's finest crus, Côte Glacière is but a stone's throw from Meurtet (read on), yet its steep, south-facing slope transports it a world away from the focus of easterly exposure. A full straw with a blush tint, this is a ravishing celebration of pinot noir, brimming with succulent red cherries, mirabelle plums, tangy berry compote and violet fragrance. Serve it in dark glasses and you'd swear it's a rosé, right down to fine tannin grip (not from red wine here, but from the phenolics of this sun-catching site). Its luscious ripeness brings a creamy allure to its mouthfeel, delightfully underscored by the ever-freshening and omnipresent influence of inimitable Aÿ chalk. For its sensational presence it upholds beautifully coiled precision, unwavering line and effortless persistence.

Deutz Hommage à William Deutz Meurtet Pinot Noir Parcelle d'Aÿ Brut 2012 $$$$

98 points • Disgorged July 2018 • Tasted in Champagne and Australia

New cuvée; 100% pinot; Meurtet in Aÿ, purchased by William Deutz in 1838, the year of the founding of the house, an east south-east facing slope of 25-year-old vines, just 200 metres from Côte Glacière, sharing the same thin clay above belemnite chalk, yet distinct in altitude, slope and exposure; aged 5 years on lees; 7.5g/L dosage; cork

A daring and glorious new venture for Deutz, and a grand statement of the pinnacle of the vineyard resources of this distinguished house. This is an enigma, at once reverberating with the depth and colour of pinot noir in a full straw hue with a blush tint, and yet singing with the elegant restraint that is Deutz. It is in this tension that it captures the regal personality that defines Aÿ, at once deeply succulent and simultaneously lighter than air. A luscious core of the most gloriously precise red cherry fruit is graced with juicy mirabelle plum, layered with mixed spice and fragranced with delicate rose petals. Its gorgeous fruit core is infused seamlessly with the subtle almond nougat of five years of lees age. A finish of impeccably focused line and undeviating length rides on a magnificent sea of chalk minerality of super-fine structure, the very voice of Aÿ itself. Drink it as you would the finest rosé.

Deutz Hommage à William Deutz Parcelles d'Aÿ Brut 2010

97 points • Disgorged March 2018 • Tasted in Champagne and Australia

New cuvée in celebration of the 180th anniversary of the house; 100% Aÿ pinot; 52% Meurtet, 48% Côte Glacière (see above); aged 7 years on lees; 8.5g/L dosage; cork; 6000 bottles

It takes a bold house to launch an inaugural flagship in a harvest that even it describes as 'difficult', and this is not a house afraid to pull the pin even at this level – Amour de Deutz Rosé 2005 never saw the light of day, from a vintage most would rank well ahead of 2010. A mix-up in the cellar in 2010 saw the two plots of Meurtet and Côte Glacière blended, though there is absolutely nothing lost in this union. With a full straw and even hints of gold and blush, this is a cuvée that proclaims all the majesty and glory of Aÿ pinot noir. It reverberates with deep, succulent and expansive black and red cherry fruits of the most exacting beauty, even satsuma plum and nuances of sarsaparilla, pink pepper and the crunch of greengage plum. In mouth-filling, glorious fruit fullness, this is quintessential blanc de noirs of the highest level. Yet it presents all this with a rose petal and musk freshness, lightness and vitality that only Aÿ can create, like bursting a segment of pink grapefruit between your teeth. It encapsulates the exacting precision that defines Deutz, with every detail of its rumbling depths and soaring heights preserved in high fidelity on a long finish sustained by very fine chalk minerality. A glorious triumph of 2010 that will one day go down as a benchmark of the season – but don't wait until then, drink it right away, in its glorious prime.

DEVAUX

(Deh-voh)

6/10

DOMAINE DE VILLENEUVE, 10110 BAR-SUR-SEINE
www.champagne-devaux.fr

1846

Devaux

CHAMPAGNE
VEUVE A.DEVAUX

Champagne Devaux is the label of the large Union Auboise cooperative based in Bar-sur-Seine in the heart of the Champagne outpost of Côte des Bar. Owned by more than 800 growers, with some 1400 hectares under vine, the cooperative is the largest grower in the region and sells a substantial quantity of juice to other houses. Its headquarters are located in the country, on the banks of the Seine, where the soil is too moist for subterranean storage, so air-conditioned, industrial warehousing is employed. The house no longer likes to talk about its relationship with the Union Auboise, which is perplexing because herein lies not only its identity and its history, but indeed its greatest asset and point of difference in its depth of grower relations, access to extensive vineyard resources and its stringent selection and declassification capability. The house is progressive and innovative, and its value-for-money champagnes are well made, living up to its aspiration of flagship Côte des Bar cuvées of long-aged pinot noir and chardonnay with no tailles, showcasing the fruit power and definition of the region.

The Union Auboise dedicates just 100 hectares to the production of Devaux, and even this is more than 1.5 times the requirement for producing 650,000 bottles each year. Twenty percent of volume is lost through avoidance of tailles in the blends. Chef de cave Michel Parisot visits every vineyard prior to harvest to decide which will be rejected.

More than 25 years at Devaux have blessed Parisot with a keen insight into the diversity of terroirs across the many valleys of the large region of the Aube. He compares some with the soils of Chablis, and others with those of Burgundy – which comes as no surprise, with many of his vineyards closer to both than the Côte des Blancs.

'We are not about comparing the Côte des Bar with the Côte des Blancs,' he emphasises. 'We have vineyards in both, and we focus on the diversity of Champagne in its villages, landscapes and finished products.'

Pinot noir rules in the Côte des Bar, and leads most of Parisot's cuvées, but chardonnay is increasing in the region, showing particular promise in Urville, and finding representation in the wines accordingly. Since 1987, Devaux has turned its attention more resolutely towards the Aube, focusing on pinot noir and chardonnay, removing meunier from its cuvées.

Parisot works closely with his many growers, though a team of six full-time liaison officers is required to help them better manage their vineyards.

'We decided some years ago that we want to have a large representation of organic vines, and we tell our growers that this is how they should manage their vineyards,' Parisot reports. Devaux performs extensive experimental work, investigating different techniques in its vineyards.

Growers are paid a premium for fruit destined for the premium D de Devaux range, which currently represents an impressive 40%

of the brand. This represents a doubling in production of D de Devaux since 1999. There is an aspiration to increase this to 50%, and to slowly grow production by 5% every year, a conservative target given the vineyard resources at Devaux's disposal.

The house is equally progressive in vinification, creating a vast array of different parcels from every vintage. Parisot compares his philosophy to that of a perfumer, creating different flavours to assemble a blend of great complexity. 'The first work is in the vineyard; the second is to create many different possibilities for fermentation and vinification, so as to produce a large palette of flavours,' he says.

This defines an interesting and unusual house style that encompasses a bit of everything – tank fermentation, barrel fermentation, large barrels and small, bâtonnage, full malolactic, no malolactic, even reserve soleras back to 1995. With 500 tanks and barrels of all sizes at his disposal, the permutations for Parisot's experimentation are vast. In the rare and privileged position of selling an enormous 95% of every harvest to other houses, he is afforded the luxury of keeping only those ferments that suit his blends.

Malolactic fermentation is completed for the Devaux range, and carried out or blocked for D de Devaux, according to the parcel and the year. Parisot likes the complexity of blending with the two so much that he will sometimes split parcels and allow part to go through malolactic fermentation.

The D de Devaux wines are fermented in oak barrels, and large stocks of reserve wines are kept in large oak tuns of 3000–7000-litre capacity for up to three years. This allows the opportunity for slow, natural oxidation. 'I don't like oxidative wines, I like well-developed wines,' Parisot emphasises. 'A good champagne should have just the beginning of oxidation flavours, but always maintain its freshness.' To further preserve freshness, malolactic fermentation is blocked on all oak-fermented parcels.

A small percentage of reserves are fermented in small barrels and matured on lees with weekly bâtonnage for four months.

After extensive trials, Parisot was surprised to discover that 300-litre barrels produce finer and more elegant wines than 600-litre demi-muids.

Parisot's latest pursuit has been in pioneering the use of local oak from the Côte des Bar, motivated by an imperative to improve the company's carbon footprint. He is working with the University of France to compare oak from the Côte des Bar, Montagne de Reims and Argonne, but it's still early days and he admits he is yet to identify any differences in flavour. 'We would like to determine whether a certain forest suits a particular parcel of pinot noir or chardonnay, but it will take us many years, and maybe we will find that the place of origin doesn't matter!' he admits. His latest pursuit has been in trialling new Burgundian toasting techniques, favouring long toasting at low temperature to achieve an elegant result.

A focus on raising quality since 1987 has seen a trend towards increasing use of reserve wines, an impressive increase in bottle age of non-vintage cuvées from two years to between three and five, and a progressive decrease in dosage to under 10g/L. Each of three or four different disgorgements for each cuvée receives a different dosage, generally 7–9g/L. Unique metal neck labels declare admirable durations of lees age in the D de Devaux range.

A number of cuvées are sealed under DIAM closures and Parisot is delighted. 'We have only had two complaints in four years regarding the look of these closures,' he says. Unfortunately, the D de Devaux range is still consigned to natural cork, but Parisot believes he's close to convincing the company's president to move the entire range across to DIAM.

Since 2014, disgorgement dates have been laser etched clearly into every bottle. The last digit of the bottling code is the base year, so, for instance, LYD15 is 2015 base.

Parisot's innovative and progressive spirit continues to drive advancement at Devaux. 'It is always possible to improve,' he maintains. 'We can't sit on our reputation. We must always look for ways to improve.'

Devaux Grande Réserve NV $$

92 points • 2014 base vintage • Disgorged 15 October 2018 • Tasted in Australia

Majority Côte des Bar pinot noir, the balance chardonnay; alcoholic fermentation in stainless steel vats followed by malolactic fermentation; roughly 20% reserves partially aged in oak foudres; 3 years on lees; 8g/L dosage; DIAM

Devaux's entry point continues to set a cracking pace for the house, and this is another enticing rendition of this impeccably assembled blend, showcasing the inviting lusciousness and definition of the Côte des Bar at an affordable price. Pinot noir is the perpetual theme of this blend, more vibrant and crunchy than ever this year in a guise of pomegranate, morello cherry and wild strawberry, backed with a flash of fresh lemon acidity. It's supported by all the fanfare of long lees age in layers of vanilla custard, gingernut biscuits and a hint of golden fruit cake, impeccably enlivened with a vibrant acid backbone, soft minerality and just the right level of phenolic bite to bring poise, tang and focus to the finish – the perfect foil for the succulence of the Côte des Bar. As ever, it's well made and great value.

Devaux Coeur des Bar Blanc de Noirs Brut NV $$

91 points • 2015 BASE VINTAGE • DISGORGED 16 OCTOBER 2018 • TASTED IN AUSTRALIA

100% Côte des Bar pinot; alcoholic fermentation in stainless steel vats followed by malolactic fermentation; roughly 20% reserves partially aged in oak foudres; aged 2.5 years on lees; 8g/L dosage; DIAM

Pinot noir has long been the backbone of Devaux, making a blanc de noirs an obvious addition to the line-up. This is the first time I've seen it, and it's been worth the wait, a flamboyant celebration of Côte des Bar pinot! A cuvée of full straw hue with a blush tint, it brims with wild strawberry, red cherry liqueur, raspberry and crunchy red apple fruit, layers of mixed spice and the gentle pâtisserie complexity of lees age. It holds brightness and succulence, contrasting confidently yet sensitively with the dry apple-skin phenolic grip of ripe pinot noir. There's value and character here, albeit a little rustic, without the persistence or refinement of the D de Devaux tier.

Devaux Cuvée Rosée NV $$

90 points • 2013 BASE VINTAGE • DISGORGED 11 DECEMBER 2017 • TASTED IN AUSTRALIA

20% Montgueux and Vitry-le-François chardonnay, 80% Côte des Bar pinot, including 10% red wine and 5% saignée skin-contact juice from Les Riceys; alcoholic fermentation in stainless steel vats, followed by malolactic fermentation; 20-25% reserves partially aged in oak foudres; aged 3.5 years on lees; 8g/L dosage; DIAM

The aim here is for an easy-drinking, fruity rosé, with colour infused by the addition of both red wine and maceration skin-contact rosé from Les Riceys. This is the deepest and fullest I've seen this cuvée, celebrating Côte des Bar pinot in a medium salmon hue and luscious layers of soft strawberry and royal gala apple fruit, even a subtle nuance of paprika. A touch of dry apple-skin tannin brings grip and definition to the finish.

Devaux Cuvée D NV $$

93 points • 2010 BASE VINTAGE • DISGORGED 12 JUNE 2018 • TASTED IN AUSTRALIA

45% chardonnay from Côte des Blancs, Montgueux and Côte des Bar, 55% pinot from Côte des Bar; alcoholic fermentation largely in stainless steel vats and partly in 300-litre wood barrels; partial malolactic fermentation; at least 35% reserves, aged mostly in oak foudres; aged 7 years on lees; 8g/L dosage; cork

A captivating celebration of the spicy, luscious generosity of Aube pinot, enlivened with largely Côte des Blancs chardonnay, the deep complexity of rich reserves aged long in large oak casks, polished with extended bottle age, all the while upholding vibrancy and the energetic tang of partial malolactic fermentation. Michel Parisot has maintained a reserve solera in large oak tuns since 2002, showcasing the complexity of maturity that can be built in a solera, while upholding wonderful purity, freshness and finesse. As these reserves have matured, they now contribute an alluring tertiary nuance of pipe smoke to the blend for the first time. For its age, ever greater depth of reserves and its confident pinot noir lead, it still presents a bright medium-straw hue and primary freshness of crunchy red apple, lemon juice and all the flavours of wild strawberries and baked figs. Gentle malic acidity brings vibrancy to its succulence, streaming into a long finish defined by the creamy and fine, mouth-filling texture of five years of lees age, making for a finish of effortlessly harmonious persistence. A showcase for the intelligent winemaking of this underrated outfit in top form.

Devaux Ultra D NV $$

92 points • 2010 base vintage • Disgorged 18 January 2018 • Tasted in Australia

45% chardonnay from Côte des Blancs, Montgueux and Côte des Bar, 55% pinot from Côte des Bar; alcoholic fermentation largely in stainless steel vats and partly in 300-litre wood barrels; partial malolactic fermentation; at least 35% reserves, aged mostly in oak foudres; aged 7 years on lees; 3g/L dosage; cork

To its credit, Devaux studiously avoids a zero-dosage cuvée, instead favouring a dosage of 3g/L to provide better balance and persistence. The result is a more taut, metallic and coiled expression of Cuvée D, accenting lemon zest and chalk mineral structure on a firmer, tenser finish. Long lees age brings compelling layers of biscuity complexity. The crunchy red apple fruit of the Aube springs forth in abundance, though the dry bitterness of phenolic structure is likewise elevated, albeit moderated by the creaminess of lees age. A touch more dosage and refinement makes for a more relaxed style than the searing tension of the past, though still a case for the foils of a dry style from a base built for a normal dosage.

Devaux D Rosé NV $$

94 points • 2012 base vintage • Disgorged 12 June 2018 • Tasted in Australia

45% chardonnay from Côte des Blancs, 55% pinot from Côte des Bar, including 10% red wine; alcoholic fermentation in stainless steel vats; partial malolactic fermentation; dosage liqueur aged in oak foudres; aged 5 years on lees; 6g/L dosage; cork

The mandate here is a light and fresh apéritif style, so much so that it does not rely on any reserves, though it is still only labelled as a non-vintage cuvée in spite of five years of lees age. In execution, this release is more colourful, more characterful and more dynamic than ever, an excitingly primary and alluringly fruity style that belies its age. A medium salmon hue launches into a style that contrasts the juicy succulence of wild strawberries, black cherries and raspberries with the fragrance of musk and the crunch of pomegranate and pink lady apple, framing the whole, glorious affair in beautifully fine chalk mineral texture that holds the finish long and linear. More than five years on lees has built wonderfully seamless integration and a fine and creamy bead, without diminishing its beautifully primary focus and refined purity. A fragrant, flamboyant and delightfully crafted Devaux Rosé.

Devaux D Millésimé 2008 $$$

95 points • Disgorged 4 July 2016 • Tasted in Australia

52% chardonnay from Côte des Blancs, 48% pinot from Côte des Bar; fermented in stainless steel tanks; full malolactic fermentation; aged 7 years on lees; dosage liqueur aged in oak foudres; 8g/L dosage

The cuddly generosity of Côte des Bar pinot noir is the perfect foil for the tension of Côte des Blancs chardonnay in the magnificently high-strung 2008 season. The result is a fine-tuned accord between the red cherry and juicy peach fruit of pinot, the citrus attack of chardonnay, the energy of lively 2008 malic acidity and the toasty, spicy, brioche enticement of now more than seven years on lees. Another year on lees since I first tasted it two years ago has done nothing to unsettle its vibrant, pale straw hue, and has only increased its creamy texture and deeply spicy, vanilla-touched complexity, without losing one iota of definition, freshness or purity. It finishes with fine, creamy texture, well-composed, subtle salt minerality and captivating appeal. A stunning Devaux with many years before it yet!

DIEBOLT-VALLOIS

(Dee-boh Val-wah)

(6/10)

84 RUE NEUVE 51530 CRAMANT
www.diebolt-vallois

CHAMPAGNE
Diebolt-Vallois

In the grand tapestry of Champagne vineyards, the great crus are well celebrated, but prime placement within the village is perhaps the most important yet under-recognised privilege. In this the Diebolt-Vallois family is particularly blessed. The marriage of Jacques Diebolt and Nadia Vallois in 1960 marked the union of his old family vineyards, largely on the prized, steep, east-south-east facing slopes in the southern part of Cramant, with significant holdings that her family had cultivated since the 1400s, very close to Cramant in Cuis. Smaller holdings are located in Chouilly, Le Mesnil-sur-Oger, Épernay (in a plot of all three varieties just 20 metres from Chouilly), a little meunier from Marfaux in the Vallée de la Marne, and in the Aube. 'Cramant, Chouilly and Le Mesnil-sur-Oger are all very different, and it is great to have the chance to mix the three big diamonds!' exclaims their daughter Isabelle Diebolt, who is increasingly taking responsibility for the estate, alongside her brother, Arnaud. Blanc de blancs are the showpiece of the terroirs of the northern Côte des Blancs, and the Diebolt family is masterful in uniting the radiant creaminess of Cramant with the body of Chouilly and the strict minerality of Le Mesnil-sur-Oger, illuminated with the pinpoint clarity of Cuis.

When Pol Roger managing director Laurent d'Harcourt graciously welcomed me to shadow him for a day at the height of vintage 2014, our first visit was to the Diebolt family in Cramant, such was the importance of this grower to Pol Roger at the time. 'Monsieur Diebolt is a king of ageing blanc de blancs!' d'Harcourt exclaimed. The winery is pristine, and that day I saw some of the cleanest fruit I've seen going into any press in Champagne.

The family astutely manages its 14 hectares using grasses in the mid-rows and minimal treatments. Jacques and Nadia's daughter, Isabelle, spent the whole day of my visit with the pickers, continually checking quality and ensuring they were cutting out any rot.

A similar attentiveness is applied in the winery, where Isabelle and her brother Arnaud assist their father. 'We control everything from the land through the whole process, pressing and vinifying every parcel ourselves,' Isabelle told me. 'Every plot in Cramant is different, and we focus on the terroirs of our vineyards, so we use small tanks, barrels (purchased from Burgundy after four vintages)

and large oak vats to keep every parcel separate.' Fermentation temperature is carefully controlled at a cool 17.5°C. Wood is reserved for vintage cuvées, with the exception of some reserves for Blanc de Blancs Prestige from Cramant, Chouilly and Le Mesnil-sur-Oger. These are stored in a 'méthode perpetuelle' system of every vintage back to vintage 2009 in three 40hL foudres of more than 10 years of age to mature slowly in a deep, cool cellar 14 metres underground, 'to uphold energy, body and richness'. The purity of the house is elegantly set off by low dosages of around 6–8g/L.

The house currently produces 160,000 bottles, vintage pending, and has increased its vineyard holdings in the hotly contested grand crus of Cramant, Chouilly and Le Mesnil-sur-Oger, hoping to increase production of its top cuvées. So as to facilitate sourcing from Nadia's paternal estate, the house is now a négociant-manipulant. They no longer supply Pol Roger, instead focusing exclusively on crafting their precise and enduring blanc de blancs, which remain on restricted allocation globally.

Diebolt-Vallois Tradition Brut NV $$

92 points • 2014 base vintage • Disgorged June 2018 • Tasted in Champagne

50% chardonnay, mostly from Cramant and Cuis, 40% pinot, 10% meunier; 6g/L dosage; about 20,000 bottles

True to the spirit of the house, chardonnay has been elevated to the lead variety and its entry cuvée has ascended accordingly. It's a spicy and fruity style that unites the red apples and strawberry hull of pinot with the grapefruit and pear of chardonnay, even some elegantly exotic notes of pink grapefruit and spice. Low dosage is well matched to integrated acidity on a finish of purity and persistence.

Diebolt-Vallois Brut Rosé NV $$

94 points • Tasted in Champagne

44% chardonnay, 40% pinot, 8% meunier; Tradition Brut with 8% Bouzy Rouge purchased from Delavenne (page 194), described by Isabelle Diebolt as 'more or less a cousin'; 7g/L dosage; 8000 bottles

Faithful to the elegant mood of the house, this rosé of pretty, bright salmon-pink hue is alive with the pure fruit definition and youthful precociousness of raspberry, strawberry hull and red cherry. Thanks to the sensitivity of the Delavenne family in crafting elegantly structured Bouzy rouge, tannins are fine and supportive, providing space for the eloquent expression of the fine chalk minerality of the Côte des Blancs. This makes for a delightfully elegant rosé of fresh, primary delicacy that marries the chardonnay signature of the house with the pretty red-fruit purity of Bouzy.

Diebolt-Vallois Blanc de Blancs NV $$

90 points • 2015 base vintage • Disgorged September 2018 • Tasted in Champagne

Cramant and Cuis in roughly equal proportions; fermented in stainless steel; 2014 reserves; 5g/L dosage; 60,000 bottles

Fermented entirely in stainless steel tanks, the brief of this popular cuvée is a super fresh, transparent expression of the purity of chardonnay and the terroirs of Cramant and Cuis, which Isabelle Diebolt describes as 'strict in personality and sharp like iron'. It meets the brief in a tense, crunchy and quite firm style. The body of Cramant is expressed in beurre bosc pear fruit, while the generosity of the 2015 harvest lends its ripe phenolic mark of dry grip and firm, dusty dryness. It's honed and structured, celebrating the firm salt minerality of its crus.

Diebolt-Vallois Blanc de Blancs Prestige NV $$

96 points • 2015 base vintage • Disgorged June 2018 • Tasted in Champagne

Cramant, Chouilly and Le Mesnil-sur-Oger; reserves stored in a 'méthode perpetuelle' system of every vintage back to vintage 2009 in three 40hL foudres of more than 10 years of age to mature slowly in a deep, cool cellar 14 metres underground, 'to uphold energy, body and richness'; 5g/L dosage

The creaminess of Cramant is the signature of this cuvée, likened by Isabelle Diebolt to butter and brioche. The result more than transcends its warm 2015 vintage base, a wonderful contrast between the depth of deep reserves and the tension and crunch of northern Côte des Blancs chardonnay. It froths and churns with outstanding fine chalk minerality, seamlessly integrating with grapefruit, lemon and apple. Its effortless juxtaposition of freshness, tension and deep-set concentration is profound, concluding with breathtaking freshness, seamless line, enduring length and the utmost integrity.

DIEBOLT-VALLOIS MILLÉSIMÉ 2011 $$

93 points • **DISGORGED SEPTEMBER 2018** • **TASTED IN CHAMPAGNE**

60% Cuis, 40% Chouilly, Épernay and young vines of Cramant; fermented entirely in stainless steel; aged 6.5 years on lees; 5g/L dosage; 11,000 bottles

Isabelle Diebolt describes 2011 as a very good vintage in the Côte des Blancs, in spite of its tribulations in the Montagne de Reims and Vallée de la Marne. This cuvée backs her assessment, a blanc de blancs of deep power and complexity. All the gingernut biscuit and brioche character of long lees age supports powerful fruit presence of white peach, fig and layers of fruit mince spice. Its body and breadth are held in tension thanks to the fine chalk minerality of Cuis and Chouilly, concluding with great line and length. An impressive 2011, ready to drink now.

DIEBOLT-VALLOIS FLEUR DE PASSION 2010 $$$$

96 points • **TASTED IN CHAMPAGNE**

Cramant old vines of 65–80 years of age in the family's four plots (five in more recent vintages) and especially Les Buzons; entirely fermented and aged 6 months in small oak barrels; no malolactic fermentation; unfiltered; aged 8 years on lees; 5g/L dosage; just 5000 bottles

Isabelle Diebolt describes 2010 as a 'romantic vintage of body and depth, to drink with food like scallops', comparing its creaminess, body and structure to 2006, in stark contrast to the apéritif strictness of 2008. The family didn't release Fleur de Passion in 2009, finding insufficient acidity in the *vins clairs* to age for 8–10 years, though now admits they may have got this wrong. They certainly didn't make the same mistake in 2010, instead conjuring a benchmark cuvée from this tricky season. Projecting a bright straw hue with a brilliant green tint, this is a delightfully alluring style that melds the creamy texture of Cramant with the soothing influence of barrel fermentation. Deep-set complexity wells up in a torrent of spice, vanilla custard and brioche, propelling the succulence of ripe fruit in mirabelle and juicy white peach, even an exotic hint of nectarine. Old vines infuse an effortless seamlessness and sensational line and length, with the brightness of malic acidity wonderfully integrated with generous fruit integrity, underlined by the signature, profound, fine salty chalk minerality that sets Cramant among chardonnay's most revered terroirs. A benchmark 2010 and a cuvée to drink now, with potential for the next few years.

DOM PÉRIGNON

(Dom Pe-ri-ngon)

8/10

20 AVENUE DE CHAMPAGNE 51200 ÉPERNAY
www.domperignon.com

Dom Pérignon

Dom Pérignon is the prestige cuvée of Moët & Chandon, but so distinct are the production, style and sheer class of the wines that the two brands are best considered completely autonomous. The two are made in the same premises in Épernay, and some facilities are shared, but the winemaking teams are distinct. Of Moët's colossal resource of 1180 hectares of estate vineyards, some are designated as Moët, others Dom Pérignon, and the rest are vinified by Dom Pérignon and allocated at the time of blending. 'The Dom' is a wine of tension, power and long-ageing endurance, the king of the most readily available and perpetually discounted prestige cuvées.

Dom Pérignon has been the vision of the talented and insightful Richard Geoffroy, dedicated to this cuvée from 1990 until 2019, and who also oversaw the entire production of Moët & Chandon ('piloting the cruise liner!'). The man who deserves much of the credit for the rise of one of Champagne's most famous and celebrated brands of the modern age carries his responsibility with unassuming humility. When I congratulated him on this, he praised the positive energy of his team and the extensive resources at his disposal. 'I must be the most privileged winemaker in the world!' he grinned.

Geoffroy worked painstakingly to draw out the best wines he could in each season, while juggling the politics of big business and a frenetic travel schedule to introduce his wines to the world. While deeply embedded in the history and tradition of Champagne, he steered this sizeable house with a courageous sense of daring (more on this later), and there is no doubt he is one of the great minds of modern Champagne.

On 1 January 2019, Geoffroy handed over the responsibility for Champagne's most significant prestige brand to his offsider of 13 years, the talented and articulate Vincent Chaperon.

Alongside Louis Roederer Cristal, Dom Pérignon was the very first of champagne's prestige cuvées, introduced in the mid-1930s with the 1921 vintage. There are only two wines: a vintage and a vintage rosé, traditionally produced less than one year in two, released after a minimum of seven years' bottle ageing on lees, and again selectively in later life recently renamed, less than romantically, Dom Pérignon P2 and P3 (formerly 'Oenothèque'). There are no non-vintage wines. Every vintage is harvested and vinified, and the decision is made at the blending table as to whether the wine will be made and released, or the entire vintage sold off.

Dom Pérignon's production remains a closely guarded secret and rumours abound in Champagne, with some putting annual sales at 3.5 million bottles, and others suggesting as many as 8 million each vintage. Sources close to the company have quietly suggested that it is between 5–6 million. If this is true, Dom Pérignon might approach the scale of every other prestige champagne put together, since the region's prestige sales totalled just 14.5 million bottles in 2018. This places it at some 20 times the scale of champagne's other most famous prestige cuvée, Louis Roederer Cristal. The official company line is that Dom Pérignon represents very much

less than this, divulging only that it's more than Krug's 600,000 bottles. There is a desire to increase production, but opportunities to increase estate holdings are extremely limited. 'I would love to have more grand cru vineyards!' Geoffroy exclaimed. 'We're already making as much as we can.'

And making much more than 20 years ago. The big question for Dom Pérignon today lies in its ability to uphold prestige standards as its scale spirals to hitherto unknown heights. The answer remains elusive, at least until today's harvests are unveiled in a decade. For now, 2008 demonstrates that the arresting endurance and mythical complexity of the great vintages of the 1990s remain alive and well. The lesser seasons today tell a very different story (stay tuned).

VAST VINEYARD RESOURCES

Dom Pérignon is based on a core of five grand cru villages of pinot noir: Aÿ, Ambonnay, Bouzy, Verzenay and Mailly-Champagne; and four of chardonnay: Le Mesnil-sur-Oger, Avize, Cramant and Chouilly, in which the company owns 'huge' resources. In all, there are about 20 villages in the blend, including the premier crus of Hautvillers and Vertus. Every plot used for Dom Pérignon is on pure chalk. Estate vineyards in 14 of Champagne's 17 grand crus are called upon, and fruit is sometimes purchased from two of the others, but over the past decade more than 98% has come from estate sources, including the oldest vines of the premier cru of Hautvillers, the historical and spiritual home of Dom Pérignon.

The key to Dom Pérignon's sourcing is the vast diversity of vineyards at its disposal. Historically, particular sites have been dedicated to each Moët Hennessy house, and Dom Pérignon has had first choice. 'There are core grand crus for Dom Pérignon and we have a privilege to access the fruit sources of the other houses as we desire,' Geoffroy divulged. He was afforded 'tremendous latitude' to change the plots and take the very best that a given year had to offer. Blending is fundamental to Dom Pérignon, and Geoffroy upheld that this is more important than ever in vintage champagne. 'If there is one house able to make vineyard-specific wine styles, surely it is Dom Pérignon – we own more vineyards than anyone else in every grand cru,' he pointed out. 'If anyone is capable of making Le Mesnil, it is Dom Pérignon! But I want to use Le Mesnil in the blend.'

The Dom Pérignon house style is about a tension between chardonnay and pinot noir, in a blend of roughly 50/50, though it can drift to 60/40 in either direction, according to the season. Chardonnay is the limiting ingredient in production, and in the current time of short supply, Geoffroy and Chaperon have been pleased to have the security of a majority of estate vineyards and a single contract with a 'top cooperative'.

'We grow our vines in a more vigorous way than a lot of people in Champagne, because this is what we want for the juices in our reductive style,' explains Chaperon. 'You can easily recognise our vineyard signature; it is a very complex relationship that has a huge impact on phenolics. The more vigorous you are, the less phenolics you will have in your grapes.'

The precise moment of harvest is given the utmost attention, and the grapes are tasted twice every day. The window of picking is short – 'in 2008 it was vegetal on Monday and too ripe on Tuesday!' Geoffroy used pH over acid, flavour and sugar as the most important indicator of properly ripe fruit. Waiting for sugar ripeness doesn't work in the wildly fluctuating vintages of current times. 'Ten degrees of sugar ripeness in 2003 was not like 10 degrees in 2004!' he pointed out.

Work is underway to redefine vineyard plots using observation tools such as aerial surveying, and to separately vinify each plot to further hone the detail of each parcel. Trials have also been conducted into an acceptable distance for fruit to be trucked between vineyard and press house, finding that a distance exceeding 15–20 kilometres can be problematic. Dom Pérignon is not afraid of some oxidation prior to fermentation in order to reduce phenolics in the juice, but this needs to be carefully controlled, according to the maturity of the grapes and their phenolic content.

REDUCTIVE WINEMAKING

'We are very dedicated to the fruit and the vineyards, but fermentation is just as important,' Geoffroy declared. Wines are fermented exclusively in stainless steel tanks, using a cultured house yeast strain, with sulphite added at the press to kill off indigenous wild yeasts. 'I love the idea of the yeast emptying into the wine to bring an added dimension; the organic meeting the mineral,' Geoffroy said. The wine is judiciously protected from oxidation post-fermentation. 'Our vision is to age our wine in a reductive way, as too much oxidation kills champagne's complexity, making it fat and heavy.'

In 2017, the company commenced a five-year program to completely upgrade its Épernay facility and bring it up to the same level of sophistication as Moët & Chandon's state-of-the art winery at Mont Aigu (page 406). 'In driving Formula One, you need more technologies and more monitoring to be driving at 500km/h, and in winemaking we need the same,' Chaperon suggests, in reference to ever-finer monitoring of vineyards and ferments. 'The impact is huge. We need more information in the vines and the vineyard, in the pressing and the fermentation. In Champagne we must be the charismatic leaders in the sparkling world. And at Dom Pérignon we are the spiritual leaders and we must be ready to open the door to a new era.'

Malolactic fermentation is run to completion using a culture co-inoculated with the primary fermentation, upheld as a key to achieving freshness as the wines build complexity and texture through long ageing. If vintages continue to warm, malolactic may be blocked in some parcels to maintain balance.

There is no rule for the dosage level in Dom Pérignon, which is determined through trials of different reserve wines and varying levels of sugar and sulphur dioxide six months prior to release. The dosage sweetness has diminished from 10g/L in 1996 to less than 7g/L today. 'Perhaps the maturity of the grapes is higher, or perhaps we're doing different things in the making?' postulates Chaperon.

The decision to release a wine is made at the point of blending. 'Even in the lousiest years we go to the final blend with no preconceived ideas,' Geoffroy said. 'Since Dom Pérignon has been Dom Pérignon we have always harvested a vintage every year.'

The key to Dom Pérignon lies in blending to achieve 'a state of completeness', a perfect balance of white and black grapes. 'Harmony is so intense!' was Geoffroy's line. 'It's like playing tennis. If you're not experienced you try to make it up with power, but if you have the right swing, it's effortless. You can forget about power and deliver intensity. When you hit it right, you hear it because the sound of the ball is different. You hear the pop! That's my quest. Dom Pérignon is about the pop.'

DOM PÉRIGNON ROSÉ

First released in 1959, Dom Pérignon Rosé represents just a few percent of the blanc volume, and typically sells for close to twice the price. There is an attempt to make rosé in every vintage, but it is only made in seasons in which phenolics are in balance, and is typically released every second year. Over the past 20 years the focus has increasingly been on pinot noir, displaying a riper fruit profile than the blanc, since the pinot noir for the red wine for blending is picked riper, with more aromatics and more jammy character. 'The challenge is to balance this to maintain delicacy in the wine,' Chaperon explains. 'It's a highly bodied wine that needs to maintain an equilibrium between authority and seduction.' Since 2000, the mandate has been to make a more substantial rosé style. 'Burgundy is all the rage and the market is looking for a more substantial style,' Geoffroy explained.

The house has been experimenting with villages for red wines for rosé, with Hautvillers, Bouzy and especially Aÿ looking the most promising, and select plots in Verzenay and Verzy in warm seasons. 'Bouzy can very quickly turn overripe and too heavy for Dom Pérignon,' Chaperon reveals. 'We try to find the moment when it is pristine and citrusy, before it turns too jammy. We have 10 hectares on pure chalk, exposed to the south in Hautvillers that are fantastic for red wine, more gentle and delicate, with raspberry character that contrasts the darker blackcurrant and spice of Aÿ. When we combine these three villages, and sometimes a little Verzenay, it brings the complexity and versatility that we need.'

The thundering power of Dom Pérignon Rosé is built on one of Champagne's strongest inclusions of red wine (30% in 2004, 27% in 2005 and 24% in 2006), up from 17–20% in the past, and this will diminish in subsequent releases. The red wine facility was renewed in 2006, and the way in which red wines were selected was changed, facilitating a reduction in their inclusion from this point onwards.

THE NEW DOM PÉRIGNON

Prior to 1990, Dom Pérignon released 29 vintages in 70 years – one release every two and a half years. Since Geoffroy commenced in 1990, the frequency has almost doubled, to 15 vintages in 20 seasons. This has recently increased further still. Since 1997, so far only 2001 and 2007 have not been released. This is the first time in its almost century-long history that Dom Pérignon has released 10 out of 12 vintages. 'My dream is to make Dom Pérignon every year,' Geoffroy revealed. 'I am a physician; my commitment is to bring vintages to life.'

Conspiracy theories abound, but he thanked an improvement in Champagne vintages for this trend. 'I have often been asked about global warming, and I am embarrassed to say that so far it has been for the better in Champagne!' he exclaimed. 'Good crop sizes, more consistent yields, good consistency of quality, good levels of ripeness, lower acids and more rounded wines, which I'm very excited about.' Chaperon adds that they can make Dom Pérignon in difficult vintages like 2017, provided they have sufficient levels of concentration and maturity.

Geoffroy admitted he was not able to make Dom Pérignon every year. 'But if you cross global warming with smart viticulture and more precision in the winemaking, the only question is the volume of the blend.' In the difficult 2005 vintage, he released a smaller volume and suggested that in the most challenging years, a release might represent one-quarter or even one-eighth of a large vintage such as 2004.

It was bewildering that Dom Pérignon released a full production volume of the controversial 2003 vintage, a difficult and atypical season, when the hottest summer to ever hit Champagne was recorded. Geoffroy admitted that '2003 is high in phenolics, it's the key to the vintage'. The hard bitterness that this brings is my biggest concern with this vintage. He revealed it had the lowest acidity he's ever recorded, and then made an unexpected announcement: 'I take it as it is. It's not about the style of Dom Pérignon, it's about the vintage. I am sick of the word "style". There is no style. Dom Pérignon is pushing the idea of vintage more than anything else.'

There's something noble and inherently authentic in this statement, something perhaps more Burgundian than it is Champenois: a wholesome celebration of the voice of the elements over the force of the hand of man. Yet in a climate as tumultuous and increasingly erratic as Champagne's, there is something deeply disturbing in this statement, too. It changes the game for Dom Pérignon.

The Dom Pérignon that we know and love has never been all about the vintage. Chaperon explained to me long ago that 'Dom Pérignon is about creating a balance between the style of the vintage and the style of the house, and we are able to drive the vintage in the direction of our style by selecting the finest sites in each season. Whether we release a vintage is more a question of style than of quality.'

'Style' hasn't always been a dirty word for Dom Pérignon. Until recently, if the style of the vintage hadn't met the style of Dom Pérignon, it was never released. And there will always be Champagne vintages unworthy of standing alone. But it seems something changed in 2003. Geoffroy admitted that '2003 is border territory for Champagne, as border as it can be. We took the risk, a technical risk. Frankly, we never lacked confidence, but we had to push harder.'

The 2003 Dom Pérignon was no one-off. Geoffroy alluded to a fundamental shift in the philosophy of the house. 'Some

Hautvillers, spiritual home of Dom Pérignon

future vintages will be more than you might expect from Dom Pérignon, very much on the ripe side' he warned. No doubt 2005 and especially 2009 were fresh in his mind at the time. 'In the past, Dom Pérignon has been very gentle and very accessible. But the decade of the 2000s is more about pushing the style. We are pushing the factor of vintage, covering a much broader span of scope than anything in the past, making wine in the character of the vintage by playing with the ripeness. We are not playing on the safe side as much as we used to, and as much as other champagne makers are, which implies that there is an element of risk. This is doing very good things for the brand, and I will keep taking the risks because it is the only way to keep the brand alive.'

Vincent Chaperon continues the legacy. 'It is a new universe at Dom Pérignon,' he declares, 'exploring new frontiers, while trying to remain true to the DNA of Dom Pérignon. The last decade was a great opportunity to expand this universe. Our aim is not to have an archetype that is Dom Pérignon, but to open up vintages and to embrace the diversity that is Champagne.'

Are we entering an era in which the consumer must exercise greater discretion in selecting vintages of Dom Pérignon? If 2003 suggested that we are, 2005 confirmed it and 2009 cemented it.

'Analytically, 2003 had the lowest acidity ever,' Chaperon recalls. 'Freshness, vibrancy and tension are more important to Dom Pérignon than acidity, and we have more levers to achieve tension than acidity – we have minerality, phenolics, bitterness and aromatics. In 2009, when the aromatics were particularly ripe, generous and mature, we had to play with other dimensions like phenolics to maintain freshness.'

THE PLENITUDES P1, P2 AND P3
Geoffroy spoke of three ages of peak maturity in Dom Pérignon's life, the first after 7–10 years (the standard release, formerly released at seven years of age and now nine or ten, the 'first plenitude,' dubbed P1), a second at 12–20 years (now P2, formerly 'Oenothèque') and a third at 35–40 years (P3, the 'plenitude of complexity').

Dom Pérignon makes these mature vintages available through an extremely limited library of releases, representing just 1–2% of only the most age-worthy vintages, and typically at double the price of the first release.

P1 and P2 are each disgorged as a single batch, and surprisingly not necessarily soon before release (1998 P2 was disgorged five years before release), but P3 tends to be disgorged progressively according to demand. P2 is released in vintage order and P3 in any order, as each vintage is ready. P2 and P3 are a testament to the remarkable battery pack of energy and vitality contained within the lees in a bottle of champagne, capable of sustaining a bottle for a lifetime. If a vintage is not deemed worthy of a P2 and P3 release, it is never released, even as P1. If it then didn't develop satisfactorily for P2 and P3, the theory is that they would not be re-released, though it hasn't happened yet.

P2 and P3 are based on the same wine as the standard release, sealed from the outset with a cork and cellared on lees for an extended time. Bottles are kept upside down so the lees settle inside the cork and impede oxygen ingress. Surprisingly, trials have found crown caps less reliable than corks beyond 10 years, perhaps due to phenolics and antioxidants leaching from the cork. 'After 10 years a cork is so superior to crown cap,' Geoffroy believed. 'There is a wonderful chemistry, which would be very difficult to reproduce with a different closure.'

The cork seal necessitates manual disgorgement of P2 and P3 releases, and each bottle is checked for cork taint as it is disgorged. 'On tirage you have an added effect from the first and second cork,' he explained. 'You may not detect any problem from the first cork, but after you insert the second cork it may become noticeable.' Further, as in any wine style, long-ageing under natural corks creates bottle variation, and no two P2s and P3s are alike, adding an element of risk to a significant outlay. The house reports more variation due to oxidation and reduction than to cork taint, but I still encounter dreaded cork taint in the market. Of 36 bottles of Dom Pérignon Vintage, P2 and Rosé that I opened for a dinner recently, one bottle of P2 1998 and one Rosé 2004 were cork tainted.

Dom Pérignon's best buy is always its standard blanc.

Dom Pérignon Vintage Brut 2009 $$$$

92 points • Disgorged 2017 • Tasted in Champagne and Australia

50% chardonnay, 50% pinot; 17 grand crus plus Hautvillers; cork

2009 was a vintage of very ripe aromatic maturity, which concerned the house more than its relatively low acidity. In response, parcels were selected with restraint and lower ripeness and maturity, so as to uphold freshness and liveliness, particularly in pinot noir. In its firm phenolic structure, Vincent Chaperon groups 2009 with 2003 and especially 2005. For him, phenolics were a key to maintaining freshness in this season.

A powerful, robust and broad-shouldered Dom of bombastic proportions, this is a cuvée of pale, bright straw hue that unashamedly flaunts a generous fruit spectrum true to the warm 2009 season of golden delicious apple, ripe pear, grapefruit pith, lemon zest and spice, contrasting with the buttery, biscuity, brioche, roast hazelnut and cream complexity of seven years on lees. This warm and phenolic season accentuates the ground coffee and classically reductive struck-flint notes that typify Dom Pérignon. Its creamy structure and mouth-filling breadth go some way towards smoothing its firm, grainy, bitter phenolic grip, though it concludes with dry bitterness. It holds reasonable length, rippling layers of chalk minerality and no shortage of presence. A vintage of main-course proportions, ready to drink now.

Dom Pérignon Vintage Brut 2008 $$$$

97 points • Tasted in Champagne

50% chardonnay, 50% pinot; released after 2009 (the first ever released out of chronological order)

After a grey, rainiy, old-fashioned Champagne summer, Vincent Chaperon describes the reappearance of the sun in September as 'the Champagne miracle' that gave birth to this classic year. 'The challenge for Dom Pérignon was to reinterpret a classic,' he explains, 'to try to give a certain level of depth, of volume, of richness to a vintage which is so much about tension and precison.'

Paler in colour than 2009 and any other Dom Pérignon in this decade right now, this is a vintage that the house lists alongside 2004 as the classic vintages of the decade. It launches with tremendous velocity, ricocheting with the crunch of grapefruit and the bitterness of preserved lemon and red apple. The rumbling exuberance of a decade in the deep in concert with the blending mastery of the house builds deeply layered complexity of brioche, ginger, Parisian baguette, mocha and coffee bean, contrasting with the gunpowder reduction of the Dom Pérignon style. The cut of citrus freshness of 2008 defines a finish of energy and drive, supported by finely structured phenolic grip. It hovers with exceptional line and length, energised and driven by the omnipresent, amplified acidity of this great season. A Dom Pérignon of the most profound potential.

Dom Pérignon

Dom Pérignon Vintage Brut 2006 $$$$

95 points • Tasted in Champagne and Australia

45% chardonnay, 55% pinot; 6g/L dosage

For me, this vintage has always sat at the crossroads of the Dom Pérignon 2000s, with more finesse than the warm 2003, 2005 and 2009, yet without the full tension and finesse of the great 2002, 2004 or 2008. The inherent magnitude and generosity of the house are bolstered in no small measure by this warm season of scorching July and summery September, though it holds the acid line and focus to maintain its poise. The red apple and grapefruit of its youth hold their integrity, layered with coffee bean, mocha and even dark chocolate. This is a silky and creamy Dom Pérignon that upholds balance, texture, accurate line and excellent persistence amidst the fine, bitter phenolic aftermath of the vintage. Immediately and unmistakably Dom, there is an extroverted confidence to 2006 which charges it with a larger-than-life, room-filling personality, toned with just the right level of acidity to keep the finish admirably determined and well defined. This is a Dom that will stand out and turn heads, though not forever – a vintage at its finest in the short to medium term.

Dom Pérignon Vintage Brut 2005 $$$$

94 points • Tasted in Champagne

60-62% chardonnay, perhaps the highest ever; 38-40% pinot noir; a quarter of the production of 2004

When he first introduced it to me in 2015, Richard Geoffroy said 2005 was the ripest vintage he had seen, as ripe as Burgundy or Bordeaux; '2005 is on the edge. It was not an easy vintage.' Acidity was low, and botrytis called for rigorous sorting. Building in colour to a medium straw yellow today, this is a vintage that has held its confidence and stature, celebrating the exuberance of the season in exotic notes of orange rind, apricot and fruit mince spice. Blessed by long lees age, creamy vanilla and exotic spice linger very long on the finish. The bitter phenolic grip and green notes characteristic to the season are reflected in some bitter greengage plum notes, held in place thanks to the generous succulence of the style. Its tension will appreciate more years of maturity yet in order to soften.

Dom Pérignon Vintage Brut 2004

97 points • Tasted in Champagne

48% chardonnay, 52% pinot noir

I've long been captivated by the aura of understated intensity and dramatic, high-voltage tension that radiates from Dom Pérignon 2004, and this recent encounter reaffirms the marvellous endurance of this vintage. At a full 15 years of age, it seems to transcend the very passage of time itself, projecting breathtaking purity, focus and energy that sustain it as one of the greatest Dom Pérignons of the decade. There is still crunch and definition here of fresh lemons and grapefruits, set against a backdrop of Parisian baguette, ginger and orange rind. A heightened, brittle core of chalk mineral texture defines a finish of persistence, precision and grace. A vintage of poise and confidence, promising a grand future indeed.

DOM PÉRIGNON VINTAGE BRUT 2003

93 points • TASTED IN CHAMPAGNE

40% chardonnay, 60% pinot noir

Dom Pérignon 2003 wears the battle scars of its challenging season, parading the exuberance of pinot noir that survived the hottest summer to ever hit Champagne, producing a hard phenolic bitterness that has always troubled me. To its credit, the voluptuous exuberance of this vintage has risen with another couple of years in bottle. Vincent Chaperon explains that this vintage is maturing slower than those around it due to the protective nature of its phenolic structure. Now a full straw hue with a copper tint, this is a Dom Pérignon evolving to a place of secondary depth of buttered toast, roast brazil nut, ground coffee, milk chocolate and ginger cake. The grip of bitter phenolic structure inherent to this warm season provides definition and frame to a long and full finish, and have appreciated the integrating effect of time. The result is a more creamy mouthfeel, beginning to soften its chewy structure and subsume its bitterness, building persistence, though it still has some way to go. While 2003 remains one of the lesser Dom Pérignons, it's the best I've ever seen it today, more forgiving now than it was on release, and will continue to hold on for quite some years yet – and that I never expected.

DOM PÉRIGNON VINTAGE BRUT 2002

98 points • TASTED IN CHAMPAGNE

Released as P2 from mid-2019

2002 represents a particularly ripe vintage for Dom Pérignon, yet every successive encounter demonstrates its remarkably slow evolution. Now a glowing, radiant yellow hue, this is a cuvée that rejoices in the succulent exuberance of the season and the structural integrity to uphold it. A universe of complexity glows in the gentle warmth of maturity in white peach, honey, glacé pineapple, brioche and vanilla custard. It contrasts intoxicating complexity with poised confidence, upholding outstanding line and length, sustained by tangy, integrated acidity and finely structured texture. It holds its head high – one of the greatest of its decade, a benchmark Dom, magnificent now, with many years stretching marvellously before it.

DOM PÉRIGNON P2 BRUT 2000 $$$$$

96 points • TASTED IN CHAMPAGNE AND AUSTRALIA

50% chardonnay, 50% pinot; 18 grand crus plus Hautvillers

The full might and majesty of the generous 2000 season are transposed upon the inimitable Dom style to compelling effect, and this bottle presents it with particularly articulate definition and structure. With a full, bright straw hue, it is at once fully secondary in its evolution, deeply buttery, reverberating with coffee beans, cocoa, bitter roast almonds, warm Parisian baguette, vanilla custard, honey, golden fruit cake, even tertiary suggestions of green olives. And yet it is simultaneously vibrant, fresh, bright and energetic in its bitter grapefruit and tangy preserved lemon, all suspended in rigid order thanks to a firm chassis of Dom Pérignon phenolic grip and bitter bite. It has upheld the rounded, buttery, silky, golden burnt-butter, grilled pineapple and mirabelle plum allure that defines 2000. Line and length are enduring and accurate, sustained by balanced, integrated acidity and phenolic tension. It unashamedly proclaims its inimitable house style with warm-season confidence, but begs for many more years yet to build silky softness and melted butter charm.

THE CHAMPAGNE GUIDE

Dom Pérignon P2 Brut 1998 $$$$$

99 points • TASTED IN CHAMPAGNE

50% chardonnay, 50% pinot; 6.5g/L dosage

Four years on from its first heralded release, P2 1998 has not dipped its gaze one iota, ascending to the finest I have ever seen it, at a full 21 years of age. The seamless harmony that this vintage has attained as P2 is something to behold, evenly juxtaposing the lemon and white peach of its youth with the transfixing complexity of toasted brioche and vanilla nougat of long age. It upholds sensational determination, energy and poise thanks to well-defined acidity that grips a finish of profound line and length. At once creamy, silky, tangy and crunchy, this is a benchmark 1998 that somehow only seems to get better and better. In sheer line and persistence, it's a Dom Pérignon of the highest order. Four years ago I announced that it had attained an incredible plateau, with plenty of life to ascend higher still. Gosh, it has, and it's in no hurry to move on. Of six bottles that I opened for a dinner, one was corked.

Dom Pérignon P2 Brut 1996 $$$$$

99 points • TASTED IN CHAMPAGNE

50% pinot noir, 50% chardonnay; same disgorgement as the original Oenothèque release but with new label; first release was 10g/L dosage, P2 6g/L

Dom Pérignon P2 1996 is one of the greatest Doms of all, ranking among the greatest champagnes of all. At this age, every bottle is different, and the most vivacious and energetic have not evolved one iota from the perfect bottle I tasted in 2013 and 2015; the rest are but one point behind. P2 1996 is almost completely devoid of time evolution, and only now, after a glorious 23 years, is it finally beginning to evolve into its tertiary era, yet still singing with energy, drive and acid tension, clinging to the vibrant preserved lemon of its youth with aching precision. Layers of green olive, pipe smoke, bitter almond and the most pristine roast chestnuts conceivable are emerging, while preserving the struck-flint reductive stamp of the house. Its mineral texture is an epiphany, dancing with fairy lightness on a stage of solid chalk, slowly becoming ever more creamy as lees-derived texture inflates. There is a brightness and energy here that will sustain it seemingly forever, charging line and length of stunning confidence, hovering immovable for minutes. Dom Pérignon absolutely, finally and resoundingly silences the question on the lips of critics and connoisseurs for the past two decades: will this bizarre and inimitable season of dehydrated concentration and low ripeness ever find balance between its intoxicating power and its searing acidity? It will and, my goodness, it has. And it will live for a lifetime.

Dom Pérignon P3 Brut 1990

100 points • TASTED IN CHAMPAGNE

Richard Geoffroy describes his first vintage as 'defining everything about Dom Pérignon: the harmony, the integration, the opulence, the ...' And then he runs out of words and waves his arms like he is about to take to flight. 'And all the more so with extra age.' After almost three decades, this is a 1990 that has attained that glorious place where every universe of complexity intersects with profound balance and integrity. Radiating a glowing golden-yellow hue, primary fruit has evolved to glacé peach, grilled pineapple and preserved lemon, even a suggestion of peppermint, perfectly massaged by almond nougat, brioche and layers of mixed spice, subtly evolving to a place of incense, pipe smoke and dark chocolate. The energy and poise that it upholds are earth-shattering in the presence of such complexity, a grand paradox of creamy and silky meets chalky, mineral and focused. In sheer line and length it is effortless, enduring, undeviating. The greatest bottle of 1990 Dom Pérignon I have ever tasted, arresting as much by its sheer freshness as its mythical complexity.

Dom Pérignon Rosé Brut 2006 $$$$$

96 points • Tasted in Champagne

35% chardonnay, 65% pinot, including 24% red wine

At 24%, this represents one of the highest doses of pinot noir red wine in a blended champagne rosé, though a little down on the two preceding releases. In line with Geoffroy's mandate to create a more substantial style, it also has less chardonnay in the blend. Boasting a full crimson copper hue, this is a rosé that captures all the exuberance of pinot noir, rippling with morello cherry, strawberry and orange rind, set against a deep, dark backdrop of fruit mince spice, even hints of sweet pipe smoke. It upholds outstanding line and length, sustained by balanced acidity and finely structured tannins. There is a great tension on the finish between bitter orange rind and generous red fruits, making for a stunning rosé that utterly transcends its season.

Dom Pérignon Rosé Brut 2005 $$$$$

95 points • Tasted in Champagne and Australia

45% chardonnay, 55% pinot, including 27% pinot red wine

Vincent Chaperon describes 2005 as 'particularly Burgundian', boasting pinot noir that leaps out of the glass, hence a slightly smaller inclusion of red wine was warranted than in the vintages around it. Richard Geoffroy was so happy with the quality of red wine in this harvest that he decreased the volume of Dom Pérignon blanc in order to uphold the volume of rosé in the wake of stringent fruit sorting following rain close to harvest. A generous proportion of red wine stains this cuvée a full salmon crimson hue. The palate launches with pink pepper, red cherry and strawberry fruits in a vibrant burst more pink and red than purple, glittering and sparkling through a finish built around the grainy phenolic structure of 2005 and a tannin grip and tension akin to young red Burgundy. Intensely spicy, this is a cuvée that unites the tension and tang of its season in greengage plum and bitter orange, wrapped in the age-induced complexity of vanilla bean, coffee bean and dark chocolate. It builds in length with time in the glass, concluding persistent and complex.

Dom Pérignon Rosé Brut 2003 $$$$$

96 points • Tasted in Champagne

30% chardonnay, 70% pinot; 20% pinot noir red wine from Aÿ, Bouzy and Hautvillers

If Dom Pérignon Vintage 2003 was evidence of the ability of this phenolic season to improve with age, its rosé sibling proves just how dramatic this transformation can be. To Richard Geoffroy, this is a vintage of gravitas and depth, and there's no denying either. It upholds a full crimson copper hue, an impossibly deeper colour than any other on this page, even with a smaller dose of red wine than the more recent vintages. It's a grand expression of 2003, still projecting primary fruit at a grand 16 years of age, layered with black cherries and wild strawberries, while age has heightened high-cocoa dark chocolate and fruit mince spice notes. The grip of this ripe vintage holds its fruit exuberance in form, with fine, bitter tension that melds well with gracefully evolving red fruits, concluding long and characterful. Massive glasses are in order; Geoffroy serves it in Riedel Oregon Pinot Noir glasses.

DOM PÉRIGNON P2 ROSÉ BRUT 1996 $$$$$

97 points • TASTED IN CHAMPAGNE

38% chardonnay, 62% pinot; 18% pinot noir red wine

Dom Pérignon rosé takes longer to hit its straps than the blanc, and hence 1996 is only just being released as P2 now, rejoicing in a glorious 23 years of maturity. Flaunting a full crimson salmon hue, this is a rosé of tension and bite that define the endurance and athletic form of this inimitable and hallowed season. It upholds the acid drive of tangy morello cherry fruit, transposed against a drying backdrop of high-cocoa dark chocolate and the tertiary evolution of green olives, culminating in a spectacular conclusion of outstanding line and length. I never expected Dom Pérignon to come forth with one of the finest rosés on the shelves this year, but here it is.

Hautvillers, harvest 2014

DRAPPIER

(Drah-piay)

RUE DES VIGNES 10200 URVILLE
www.champagne-drappier.com

CHAMPAGNE
DRAPPIER

DOMAINE À URVILLE DEPUIS 1808
CAVES À REIMS · FRANCE

The medium-sized, family-owned house of Drappier makes lively, fruity wines from 53 hectares of estate vineyards in and around Urville in the Côte des Bar, planted to 70% pinot noir. Fruit is also sourced from a further 40 hectares, notably chardonnay from Cramant and Chouilly, and pinot noir from Bouzy and Ambonnay. Georges Drappier was the first to plant pinot noir extensively here in the early 1900s, and today Michel Drappier is the seventh generation to grow grapes, using minimal intervention and organic practices, though organic certification is not sought. Fermentation takes place partly in large oak casks, and liqueurs d'expédition are aged in oak casks and large foudres for more than a decade. Use of the lowest levels of sulphur dioxide is a mixed blessing, as this can make for darker colours and premature biscuity flavours. These are not champagnes to hang on to, but a production scale of 1.5 million bottles annually makes for enticing value for money across its finer offerings.

DRAPPIER BLANC DE QUATRE BLANCS BRUT NV $$$

88 points • TASTED IN AUSTRALIA

25% arbane, 25% petit meslier, 25% pinot blanc, 25% chardonnay; aged at least 3 years on lees; very low sulphur; unfiltered; full natural malolactic fermentation; 4.2g/L dosage

A fruity, youthful, exotic and complex wine that celebrates the full fanfare of its four varieties in all manner of tropical fruits and exotic spice, supported by tangy acidity and gentle phenolic grip.

DUMANGIN J. FILS

(Dew-mohn-zhan J. Feess)

6/10

3 RUE DE RILLY 51500 CHIGNY-LES-ROSES
www.champagne-dumangin.com

CHAMPAGNE
DUMANGIN
J. Fils

'The secret to making great wine is attention to the fine details at every stage' is the mantra of Gilles Dumangin. The fifth-generation chef de cave must be the hardest worker in Chigny-les-Roses. When I visited late one Sunday afternoon in July, he'd been at the bottling machine since 4am, as he had been every morning for the previous two weeks. The week before, his air-conditioner had died, then his brine chiller, then his labelling machine. He fixed all three himself. A self-confessed control freak, Gilles works 20–22 hours every day during harvest. And he loves it.

Such fanaticism defines every stage of production at Dumangin J. Fils. 'My wife spent one harvest with me and declared, "You are in love with your presses! You do not leave them for a moment!"' Gilles recounts. And he doesn't disagree. His old Coquards are 'the Rolls Royce' of champagne presses. 'The week and a half of harvest is a lovely time. I listen to my presses the whole time. I know them so well that if anything sounds different, I know something is wrong. If you can't press well, you can't make good champagne.'

I spent a day shadowing Gilles in the middle of harvest 2014 and I have not seen more focused attention to detail anywhere in Champagne. There was a subtle change in the sound of the press and he stopped mid-sentence and jumped to its attention.

These are handmade champagnes, and a production of just 150,000 bottles permits every step in the process to be performed manually by Gilles and his small team, including riddling (by transfer between pallets). Every parcel is kept separate, thanks to tiny tanks, some not much larger than a bar fridge. 'A house this size would normally have 20 tanks,' Gilles points out. 'I have 80.'

Based in the romantic little village of Chigny-les-Roses, on the northern slopes of the Montagne de Reims, in the old school building that Gilles's grandfather converted, the estate sources from 15 hectares in this and the surrounding villages. Gilles owns a little more than three hectares of his own vines; he purchases from his parents' two hectares of vineyards and a further nine hectares from growers with long-term contracts.

Irrespective of ownership, Gilles's principles for the management of the vines are consistent across all of his sources. 'I work mostly organically when I can, but I will save my harvest when I have to.' He interacts with each of the vineyards in the same way, monitoring the vines during the year, going into the rows to determine the optimal time for harvest, and supporting his own managers throughout the year in the same manner as he supports his growers. He is therefore technically a négociant-manipulant, but very much with the approach of a dedicated récoltant-manipulant. 'Would I produce better wines if I grew all the grapes myself?' he asks. 'No. I'd do everything the same way.'

This is pinot country, and both pinot and meunier feature heavily in the Dumangin style. Chardonnay finds its place, too, and the local quality is impressive, as his expressive single-vineyard, single-vintage blanc de blancs attests. Meunier is more important here than it is in most champagne houses. 'This is the grape that makes champagne what it is, providing its fruit and its easy-drinking style,' says Gilles, whose entry Grande Réserve NV contains an impressive 50% of the variety.

Gilles is obsessive about preserving fruit in optimal condition. In 2008 he terminated some contracts with growers of inferior vineyards, and signed up other vineyards to bring all of his sources to within seven kilometres of his beloved old Coquard presses. 'They're so gentle,' he says, 'that the pips stay on the skins and the seeds remain inside!' The second-press cut is used only in Brut 17 and Grande Réserve.

Gilles pioneered 18-kilogram picking crates rather than the usual 50-kilogram crates, so as not to crush the fruit at the bottom. When fruit arrives it never spends more than five minutes in the sun before he brings it into his air-conditioned press room. He personally presses every grape. 'I don't believe you can make very good wine if you don't press your own grapes,' he upholds.

Capturing the grace of the northern Montagne de Reims, Dumangin is a rosé specialist, and production is on the rise; it is now his key cuvée, representing an impressive 50% of production. Testimony to his attention to quality, he made the difficult and noble decision to sell his entire production of 2011 base Le Rosé NV *sur lattes*, as it was 'too earthy', afflicted by its challenging season. He has a beautiful vintage rosé in the cellar, with the delightful inaugural 2012 cued for release in a few years' time.

Non-vintage cuvées rely on deep stocks of reserve wines, with a full year's production volume in reserve, and Grande Réserve and Extra Brut cuvées each boast a whopping 60%. In every vintage 40% is kept in reserve. Since his growing production of non-vintage rosé doesn't call for large reserves, an ever-increasing proportion of reserves are available for Cuvée 17, now also 60%. All cuvées have traditionally undergone full malolactic fermentation, but such was the acid and sugar balance of his 2012 fruit that he blocked malolactic fermentation in some parcels for the first time, necessitating rigorous cleaning and sanitisation in the winery. He has continued to block malolactic in order to preserve freshness since, and has been very pleased with the results. He also started trialling barrel fermentation in 2012.

'I was worried when I started blocking malolactic that I would need to increase dosage, but I have continued to decrease dosage!' he exclaims. 'However, I do de-acidify, which is necessary for the high acidities of the northern Montagne.'

For the past 15 years, Gilles has invested all his income back into his stocks, and now boasts an incredible six years' supply in storage.

Moving forward, he aspires to streamline the focus of his portfolio to just four cuvées: La Cuvée 17, Extra Brut NV, Rosé Vintage and a vintage cuvée named 'Aegidius', the first of which will be a particularly enduring cuvée from 2012.

To preserve the elegance of the terroirs of the northern Montagne, Gilles disgorges every shipment of non-vintage wine to order, and seals every bottle with a DIAM cork. 'In my trials, the wines keep fresher under DIAM.' The dosage of every shipment is tweaked from its usual 10g/L sugar to suit. As length of time on lees has increased, dosages have been progressively lowered across the range over recent years. 'From my tests, the wines stay fresher if they're disgorged just prior to shipment,' Gilles says. It's different for the vintage wines, which he finds hold their freshness best if disgorged 3–4 years after bottling.

For champagnes disgorged to order, back labels are impressively informative, disclosing disgorgement date, blend and dosage. Each disgorgement now receives a unique QR code to provide a great depth of information, including disgorgement date, blend, reserve wines, vineyards, food matches, reviews and importer's details.

Gilles's painstaking attention to detail shines in every bottle. I have been following his champagnes for more than 13 years now, and they are cleaner, fresher, more precise and more focused than ever. As a result, they effortlessly handle lower dosage than before, and all but Cuvée 17 are Extra Brut. These rank high among the best-value small-producer champagnes.

DUMANGIN J. FILS LA CUVÉE 17 BRUT NV $$

92 points • 2013 BASE VINTAGE • DISGORGED 15 FEBRUARY 2018 • TASTED IN CHAMPAGNE

40% chardonnay, 25% pinot, 25% meunier (previously one-third of each); 60% reserves (previously 43%); 50% malolactic fermentation (previously 100%); aged 4 years on lees; 8.8g/L dosage

La Cuvée 17 is on the rise, with more chardonnay and more reserves than ever, and with partial malolactic (for the second time) it's looking fresher and more precise than ever. A beautifully refined apéritif and a cracking entry cuvée, it unites lemon zest and red apple with the complexity of toast and biscuits of four years lees age. Its malic acidity enlivens the finish, serving to draw out its persistence and heighten the chalk mineral texture of the northern slopes of the Montagne de Reims. A wonderful Cuvée 17 of balance, poise and fantastic value for money.

DUMANGIN J. FILS LE ROSÉ EXTRA BRUT NV $$

94 points • 2010 BASE VINTAGE WITH 2008 RED WINE • DISGORGED 12 APRIL 2018 • TASTED IN CHAMPAGNE

54% chardonnay, 46% pinot, from one vineyard in Taissy and one in Rilly-la-Montagne; 2008 meunier red wine; 100% malolactic fermentation; 4.4g/L dosage; 50% of production

Gilles used his 2008 red wine in four releases of Le Rosé, increasing the proportion every year as it dropped colour with age, and this is the last. In spite of its growing popularity, Gilles has resolved not to increase production of this cuvée, so as not to unbalance his other cuvées. His rosé is a reflection of his precision, one of Champagne's most finely crafted and elegant rosés at a refreshingly affordable price. Red wine from meunier is unusual in Champagne, yet his is well suited to his elegant rosé style, creating a pretty medium-salmon hue, neatly supported by the finesse of chardonnay and the fragrance of pinot noir. The result is classic Dumangin and definitive northern Montagne, a beautifully graceful and refined rosé of delicate strawberry hull and red cherry fruit, striking a seamless accord between effortless acidity, fine chalk minerality and perfectly integrated dosage. An incredible seven years on lees has brought creaminess to its texture without in any way compromising exacting purity. As picture-perfect and refined as ever.

DUMANGIN J. FILS LE VINTAGE 2006 $$$

89 points • DISGORGED 2 FEBRUARY 2018 • TASTED IN CHAMPAGNE

54% chardonnay, 46% pinot; 100% malolactic fermentation; 5g/L dosage

Dumangin's vintage cuvées have always tended to mature slowly and gracefully, though 2005 developed faster than 2004, and 2006 faster again. Gilles likens it with the development of 2003, and suspects this is typical of the northern Montagne de Reims in this season, as his 2006 Blanc de Blancs also developed quickly. The rounded generosity of the vintage makes for a gentle and soft style of medium straw hue, characterised by roast nuts, honey and spice. Well into its secondary evolution, it's showing some oxidative golden syrup notes that contract the persistence of the finish. In these days of ever warmer vintages, Gilles' mandate since 2012 to block malolactic fermentation seems astute.

DUMANGIN J. FILS LE VINTAGE EXTRA-BRUT 2004 $$$

95 points • DISGORGED EARLY 2017 • TASTED IN CHAMPAGNE

54% chardonnay, 46% pinot noir; liqueur aged in oak barrels 1-2 years; zero dosage; 15,000 bottles

Dumangin made a cracking 2004. I have been following its curve of evolution avidly over the past four years, and never has it looked finer than this. Such was the yield in this vintage that he produced three times the usual volume of this cuvée, the final release of which was disgorged with zero dosage after a glorious 12 years on lees. Testimony to his precision and to the stamina of the season, at a full 15 years of age it still upholds a medium straw-yellow hue and beautiful poise of yellow fruits and citrus. Time has ushered in layers of brioche and vanilla. It concludes long, focused and enticing, sustained by well-integrated, refreshing acidity and the fine chalk minerality of the northern Montagne de Reims.

Dumangin J. Fils Le Vintage Extra-Brut 2002

93 points • Disgorged 3 January 2018 • Tasted in Champagne en magnum

54% chardonnay, 46% pinot; 2g/L dosage

I have not tasted this cuvée since my very first meeting with Gilles in 2010, when I reviewed it for the inaugural edition of this Guide. It's doubled in age since then, and upheld its full integrity in glorious magnums, gaining some classic magnum struck-flint and grilled toast reduction. Still a bright, medium straw hue, the generosity of 2002 glows in mirabelle plums, white nectarines and figs, while the tension of the season holds its succulence in check with grapefruit and fennel notes, and the excellent acid drive and fine chalk minerality of the northern Montagne de Reims. It lingers long and confident.

Dumangin J. Fils Achille Blanc de Pinot Meunier Brut Nature 2000 $$$$

89 points • Disgorged 5 April 2018 • Tasted in Champagne

100% meunier from Carizets vineyard on clay soils in Chigny-les-Roses; wood aged 18 months; bottle aged 16 years; zero dosage; DIAM

Gilles's trio of single-vineyard, single-varietal, single-vintage champagnes make for a fascinating comparison, and his inaugural vintage will soon make way for his 2002 release. Meunier has predictably evolved more rapidly than chardonnay and pinot noir in the generous 2000 season, and this cuvée has always been the least of the trio, progressively tiring over the past five years. It now radiates a full yellow hue with gold tints, a powerful, rich and exuberant cuvée of grilled pineapple and golden delicious apple fruit, layered with fruit mince and mixed spice. Some bruised apple development leaves the finish a little tired and dry.

Dumangin J. Fils Firmin Blanc de Chardonnay Brut Nature 2000 $$$$

91 points • Disgorged 5 April 2018 • Tasted in Champagne

100% chardonnay from Monthouzons vineyard in Taissy; wood aged 18 months; bottle aged 16 years; zero dosage; DIAM

The toasty influence of barrels in concert with extended lees age lends layers of complexity and spice that ride over a core of chardonnay that captures both the exuberance of 2000 and the refreshing refinement of the northern Montagne de Reims. Now a full yellow hue, the golden delicious apple, preserved lemon and yellow summer fruits of its youth have evolved into a lingering spectrum of billowing fruit mince spice, hovering long on the finish.

Dumangin J. Fils Hippolyte Blanc de Pinot Noir Brut Nature 2000 $$$$

93 points • Disgorged 5 April 2018 • Tasted in Champagne

100% pinot from Cornes de Cerf vineyard in Rilly-la-Montagne; wood aged 18 months; bottle aged 16 years; zero dosage; DIAM

Hippolyte has stepped forward as the best, freshest and most confident of Dumangin's trilogy, still the palest and brightest in colour at almost two decades of age, testimony to the presence and endurance of pinot on the elegant slopes of the northern Montagne de Reims. Boasting a full yellow hue, primary red fruits are evolving into layers of creamy texture, mixed spice and toasted brioche, trailing long on a finish of well-defined acidity, soft chalk minerality and excellent persistence. The fragrant appeal of pinot noir has ultimately triumphed, fully subsuming the oak flavours and aromas that dominated its early life and the firm, fine tannin grip that marked its middle age.

DUMÉNIL

(Dew-mehn-neel)

—

38 RUE DE PUITS 51500 SACY
www.champagne-dumenil.com

PROPRIÉTAIRE · D · DEPUIS 1874

CHAMPAGNE
Duménil
— PREMIER CRU —

The elegant fruits of the gentle slopes of the premier crus of the northern Montagne de Reims call for a particularly sensitive touch, in tending both the vines and the wines. Emile-Paul Duménil established his eponymous estate in Chigny-les-Roses in 1874, and today winemaking is handled by the gentle touch of his great-granddaughter, Fréderique Poret-Duménil. From a long line of vignerons in nearby Sacy, her husband Hugues manages the family vineyards with attentive care. Sourcing exclusively from the premier crus of Chigny-les-Roses, Rilly-la-Montagne, Ludes and Sacy, the family moved operations to escape the congestion of the narrow streets of Chigny during harvest, finding a new home in Sacy, where they are also the only saffron producer in Champagne. Their cuvées capture the eloquent mood of refined terroirs.

Privileged to old vineyards, Hugues manages his vines with gentle sensitivity. Soils are ploughed and grasses cultivated in the mid-rows to encourage roots to plunge deep into the chalk. Manual labour is favoured, and a lightweight tractor and horses are employed in the oldest vineyards to minimise soil compaction, improving soil aeration, drainage and root growth. Prunings are mulched and applied as organic fertiliser, and moderate yields are upheld to achieve concentration and aromatic depth.

Adopting a similarly attentive approach in the winery, Fréderique uses only the cuvée (the first and best juice) from her Coquard press. Débourbage (cold settling) takes place over 24 hours before juices are seeded to initiate alcoholic and malolactic fermentations in temperature-controlled stainless steel vats to preserve delicate aromas. Cuvées are long aged, with non-vintage blends enjoying a minimum of three years in the cellars, special cuvées five years and vintages eight to ten. Non-vintage cuvées are built on generous proportions of a deep solera of more than 20 vintages of reserves.

The year of disgorgement is indicated in the last four digits of the lot number, so GR092018 is 2018.

Duménil Grande Réserve Premier Cru Brut NV $$

91 points • 50% 2014 BASE VINTAGE • DISGORGED APRIL 2018 • TASTED IN AUSTRALIA

33% Chigny-les-Roses chardonnay, 33% Ludes pinot, 33% Rilly-la-Montagne meunier; average vine age 30 years; 50% reserves from an ongoing solera of more than 20 vintages; aged 3 years on lees; 8g/L dosage; cork

Capturing the acid tension and restraint of the northern Montagne de Reims premier crus, this is a cuvée that unites the crunchy apple and grapefruit of primary fruit with the savoury charcuterie and roast chestnut notes of a generous 50% inclusion of a deep solera. Balancing such depth with the elegant fruits of these villages is a precarious tightrope act, especially in the understated season of 2014, and Fréderique and Hugues have handled this confidently. It concludes with fine chalk minerality and balanced, honeyed dosage.

Duménil Rosé Vieilles Vignes Premier Cru NV $$

86 points • 50% 2014 BASE VINTAGE • DISGORGED APRIL 2018 • TASTED IN AUSTRALIA

Same base as Grande Réserve; 33% Chigny-les-Roses chardonnay, 33% Ludes pinot, 33% Rilly-la-Montagne meunier; average vine age 30 years; 7% meunier red wine from vines planted in Chigny-les-Roses in 1956 and aged in oak; 50% reserves from an ongoing solera of more than 20 vintages; aged 3 years on lees; 8g/L dosage; cork

A delicate inclusion of 7% old-vine Chigny-les-Roses meunier red wine infuses a pale salmon hue, red apple notes and gentle tannins, which serve to amplify the savoury, chestnut core of the deep solera. This is all too much for the subdued fruit of the 2014 vintage, making for a style of firm tannin bite and woody, savoury character, lacking in fruit lift, fragrance and persistence.

Duménil Millésimé Premier Cru 2007 $$

93 points • DISGORGED APRIL 2018 • TASTED IN AUSTRALIA

60% chardonnay, 20% Ludes pinot, 20% Chigny-les-Roses meunier; aged 10 years on lees; 5g/L dosage; cork

There is an elegant beauty to the 2007 season on the northern slopes of the Montagne de Reims, and while chardonnay is rare as the lead varietal in these parts, Duménil plays it eloquently to capture this mood. Seven years on lees has drawn out pronounced complexity of buttered toast and roast almonds, which unites seamlessly with the preserved lemon and pear flavours of chardonnay. The lowest dosage of the range is well gauged for this style, highlighting the lingering lemon juice acidity of these cool slopes. Classy, confident and well crafted.

Duménil Les Pêcherines Prestige Vieilles Vignes Premier Cru NV $$

93 points • 2012 BASE VINTAGE • DISGORGED APRIL 2018 • TASTED IN AUSTRALIA

80% chardonnay, 20% pinot, from the family's oldest single vineyard, 'Les Pêcherines', planted in 1969 in Chigny-les-Roses; 20% reserves; aged 5 years on lees; 8g/L dosage; cork

Previously named Cuvée Prestige Vieilles Vignes and now renamed in recognition of the vineyard, Les Pêcherines, because peaches were once grown here. Vines of more than 50 years of age infuse character and power unusual for Chigny-les-Roses, infused with outstanding depth and complexity that spans white peach, fig, even hinting at tropical notes of mango. Chardonnay is Duménil's unexpected strong suit, and here it reaches its finest expression, holding line and length of outstanding confidence. Five years on lees has built layers of nougat, vanilla and honey that mesh seamlessly with gentle acidity and a soft finish that concludes just a little too sweet.

Duménil Amour de Cuvée Blanc de Noirs NV $$

89 points • 2012 base vintage • Disgorged April 2018 • Tasted in Australia

50% Ludes pinot, 50% Chigny-les-Roses meunier; reserves from three previous vintages of 2011, 2010 and 2009; aged 5 years on lees; 8g/L dosage; cork

Chigny and Ludes unite in a savoury and understated blanc de noirs of bright, medium straw hue and red apple skin and pear character, with subtle red berry persistence. Fine tannin grip and phenolic bite make for a grainy mouthfeel and a dry, firm finish. It nonetheless upholds good persistence, elegant acid line and well-integrated dosage.

Duménil Special Club Premier Cru 2012 $$$

94 points • Disgorged April 2018 • Tasted in Australia

First release; 40% Chigny-les-Roses chardonnay, 60% Ludes pinot; aged 5 years on lees; 7g/L dosage; cork

The Duménil family joined the Club Trésors de Champagne in 2012, and their Special Club is an outstanding first attempt by any measure! A pretty pale-straw hue celebrates this elegant season on the cool north-facing slopes of the Montagne de Reims. Chardonnay and pinot noir unite to compelling effect, in a refreshing and primary style true to both place and season. Crunchy apple and lemon are granted depth by the succulent notes of white peach, underscored by fine chalk minerality. The elegant acid line of 2012 is the focus here, holding the finish very long, perfectly harmonised with integrated dosage. A wine of restraint rather than showy glamour, true to the integrity of its vineyards, and all the better for it.

Sacy, harvest 2017

DUPERREY

(Dew-peh-reh)

17 RUE DES CRÉNEAUX 51100 REIMS
www.champagneduperrey.com

CHAMPAGNE
DUPERREY

Duperrey is the brand of Australia's Woolworths supermarket group, made by the house of G.H. Martel in Reims from its huge resource of 200 hectares of estate vines and 700 hectares of growers. Named after the French explorer who mapped the southern Australian coastline, it's a creamy style sourced from premier cru and unclassified villages. The brand comprises just two cuvées, a non-vintage and a vintage blend, and there was once also a non-vintage rosé. These are inexpensive cuvées which Woolworths reports to be one of its top ten bestsellers.

DUPERREY PREMIER CRU BRUT NV $

85 points • 2014 BASE VINTAGE • DISGORGED 12 JULY 2018 • TASTED IN AUSTRALIA

48% chardonnay, 23% pinot, 29% meunier; crus include Verzy, Chouilly and Chamery; no oak; 10g/L dosage; DIAM

One of the cheapest champagnes on the shelves in Australia, this buyer's-own brand of the Woolworths supermarket group is a case in point that you get what you pay for. It contrasts the lemon-zest bite of chardonnay with the biscuity complexity of lees age, dusty and lacking in fruit expression, concluding with a firm, bitter, coarse phenolic finish that reflects too much tailles in the blend. Even a full 10g/L dosage does little to remedy its challenging finish.

DUPERREY VINTAGE BRUT 2012 $

84 points • DISGORGED 12 JULY 2018 • TASTED IN AUSTRALIA

41% Côte des Bar chardonnay, 12% Montagne de Reims pinot, 47% Vallée de la Marne meunier; no oak; 10g/L dosage; DIAM

To make a vintage cuvée at this price in Champagne, too many corners must be cut, voiding any hope of integrity, balance or drinkability. Composed almost exclusively of Aube chardonnay and Vallée de la Marne meunier, this is a cuvée in which the tinned-pea notes of underripe fruit collide with the tension of immature acidity, the bitterness of harsh phenolics and an earthy overlay that swamps any semblance of fruit purity.

DUVAL-LEROY

(Dew-val-Lair-wah)

5/10

69 AVENUE DE BAMMENTAL 51130 VERTUS
www.duval-leroy.com

CHAMPAGNE

DEPUIS 1859

DUVAL-LEROY

The scale of Duval-Leroy's modern winery is a physical statement of the rapid progress at this family-owned company. Celebrating its 160th birthday in 2019, it now ranks in the 15 largest champagne houses, thanks to its dynamic, visionary leader, Carol Duval-Leroy, who has courageously grown the estate since 1991, now confidently supported by her three sons, Julien, Charles and Louis. Chardonnay takes the lead in these graceful and elegant wines, reflecting the bright fruit purity of the village of Vertus.

The imposing Duval-Leroy building looks more at home in Silicon Valley than a small village in Champagne. The entire façade is covered by 250 square metres of solar panels, sufficient for the electrical needs of the barrel room, tasting room and reception area. It makes a bold, immediate statement that Duval-Leroy has sunk a serious investment into its modernisation and growth. And that's just the beginning.

Step inside the largest facility in Vertus and you're greeted by lines of gleaming new tanks, all temperature controlled to between 16°C and 20°C to preserve delicacy during fermentation. Five gentle eight-tonne pneumatic presses are cleverly positioned above 30 settling tanks, delivering the must by gravity. Dug deep underground, this facility operates on multiple levels. Operations were modernised in 2001, 2007 and 2008, when extensions were made to integrate the entire production under one roof to improve efficiency and quality. A new barrel room was also added for fermentation of grand cru parcels.

Estate holdings are led by 60% chardonnay. The house controls 200 hectares in the Côte des Blancs (including an impressive 150 hectares in Vertus, and holdings in every grand cru), Montagne de Reims and Côte de Sézanne, providing a generous one-third of all fruit required to produce around 4 million bottles annually. Its key villages after Vertus are Chouilly and Le Mesnil-sur-Oger for chardonnay, and Cumières, Mareuil-sur-Aÿ, Avenay-Val-d'Or, Bouzy, Ambonnay, Verzy and Verzenay for pinot.

Duval-Leroy manages a sustainability regime that's more than just a solar panel façade. A 10-page document on its website details a diverse list of initiatives. Herbicide use has more than halved in the past decade, and all estate vineyards are cultivated organically or biodynamically – quite a feat for a house of this size. Fruit purchased from a number of organically certified growers finds its way into two organic cuvées. The house claims to be the first to market an organic champagne and first to obtain High Environmental Value certification.

The house is serviced by five press centres, the biggest of these in Vertus. A stock of 16 million bottles represents four years of sales, with non-vintage cuvées stored mostly in Vertus. Vintage cuvées reside in chalk cellars 30 kilometres away in Châlons-

en-Champagne. The broad bottle of its Femme de Champagne prestige cuvée dictates riddling by hand.

The house style celebrates the accessible fruit and elegant structure of Vertus. 'I want to make champagne that everybody will enjoy, not just connoisseurs,' says Sandrine Logette-Jardin, who has been with the house since 1991 and chef de cave since 2005. 'I love minerality that is integrated in vinosity.'

Only the best wines from each harvest are held as reserves, from a large majority of premier and grand crus. Reserves are held in large tanks of 500hL at 12°C. 'I have trialled different conditions for reserve wines and found the larger volume and lower temperature keeps freshness,' Sandrine explains. 'If I want to increase the aged character in reserves, I keep them in smaller tanks at ambient temperature.'

Malolactic fermentation is completed in all parcels, at least for now. 'I am ready to adapt the level of natural acidity by blocking malolactic in the future in the non-vintage cuvées if I need to,' she admits. 'With climate change, the acidity can vary, and it is important not to forget that champagne is a fresh wine!'

Duval-Leroy has made the bold and surprising decision to market its vintage cuvées as non-vintage in all but the very finest vintages. 'We have a problem in Champagne, a big problem,' Sandrine declares. 'Because of the climate evolution, we have the ability to make more and more vintage cuvées, but we don't have the ability to sell all of them.'

Hence, Blanc de Blancs Grand Cru Brut NV is currently 100% 2006, with the next release to be 100% 2007, though unfortunately without any indication of the vintage on the label. Blanc de Blancs Grand Cru Brut 2008 will then be released as a vintage.

This also explains the 2017 release of Duval-Leroy's flagship Femme de Champagne Brut Grand Cru NV, sourced entirely from 2004. 'Now everyone releases a prestige cuvée in every vintage, but we want to recognise only the very finest vintages,' Sandrine reveals. Femme de Champagne 2002 and 2008 will be released as vintage cuvées, while 2004, 2006 and 2007 will be labelled non-vintage, with no indication of their vintage composition (although, confusingly, there was a release of 2004 as a vintage cuvée in half bottles in 2015). I suggested an edition number to distinguish each release, and Sandrine promised to propose this to her marketing team. The intention is to always have a vintage and a non-vintage Femme in the market at the same time

Duval-Leroy maintains 300 oak barrels for fermentation of select plots. Since 1995, Femme de Champagne has been vinified and matured in used oak barrels, in proportions varying from 8% to 25%, depending upon the vintage.

Second-use Sauternes barrels were obtained from Château d'Yquem in the past. However, these have been phased out since 2006 in response to inconsistent honeyed characters of oxidation that interfered with the purity of chardonnay in sporadic barrels. 'It's more pleasant to use young oak barrels and see the characteristics of each wine,' Sandrine observes. Since 2006, her single-vineyard Clos des Bouveries has been fermented in 10% new oak.

The disgorgement date can be easily ascertained from the first four digits of the lot code on each bottle. The first digit is the year of disgorgement, and the next three digits are the Julian day number of that year. For instance, L8011AG18 is the 11th day of 2018.

Duval-Leroy's strength lies in its chardonnay-focused cuvées, achieving a lofty pinnacle in the towering magnificence of Femme de Champagne, in both vintage and non-vintage guise. Its 1996 re-release is spellbinding.

DUVAL-LEROY BRUT RÉSERVE NV $$

89 points • 2014 BASE VINTAGE • DISGORGED JANUARY 2018 • TASTED IN CHAMPAGNE

10% chardonnay from Sézanne, Côte des Blancs and Épernay, 60% pinot from Côte des Bar and a little from Montagne de Reims, 30% meunier from the right bank of the Vallée de la Marne (Fleury-la-Rivière, Venteuil and Châtillon-sur-Marne); 40% reserves from 2013 and 2012; 8g/L dosage; around 1.4 million bottles, currently the majority of production of the house

Conceived 30 years ago when the company was ramping up its sourcing from all over Champagne, this is a cuvée led by pinot noir. The house seeks a rich style of pinot, but not too structured or powerful, hence favouring Côte des Bar, and just a little from Ambonnay and Bouzy. With a medium straw hue, its fruity presence is announced in characters of red apple and pear, culminating in a finish of firm, fine phenolic grip and some biscuity, dry-extract complexity. At odds with the chardonnay theme of the house, this cuvée has never hit the high notes.

Duval-Leroy Extra-Brut Prestige Premier Cru NV $$

92 points • 2014 base vintage • Tasted in Champagne

New cuvée since 2017; 65% chardonnay from Vertus, Chouilly and Le Mesnil-sur-Oger, 35% pinot from Cumières, Mareuil-sur-Aÿ, Avenay-Val-d'Or, Bouzy, Ambonnay, Verzy and Verzenay; 50% reserves from 2013, 2012 and 2011; 2% of reserves vinified in oak barrels; 4g/L dosage; 100–200,000 bottles

A new release as Duval-Leroy begins to transition from Brut Premier Cru to Extra-Brut Prestige Premier Cru. While the *cépage* and crus remain unchanged, the shift is a noble one, and not insubstantial, not so much in evolving from brut to extra brut, but in stepping up from 15% to a generous 50% of reserve wines. 'The concept was to create an extra brut, but I refused to do that if I couldn't start by changing the blend,' Sandrine explains. 'Dosage is not the reason; it is a complementary solution to marry a blend and integrate the acidity.' For her, this cuvée is an opportunity to value reserve wines to add complexity and richness. It is her hope to produce this cuvée every year or every second year, and in spite of such strong representation of reserves, uniformity is not the goal. 'I want to target the character of the base year, rather than consistency from one year to the next,' she explains.

It is no small ambition for any sizeable champagne house to reinvent its second-largest cuvée, and Duval-Leroy's dynamic and fresh new apéritif represents an exciting new twist for the company. Projecting a beautiful pale straw hue that Sandrine describes eloquently as 'silver green', this is a very pure and precise blend that captures the dynamic mood of the house in vibrant freshness of lemon, grapefruit and crunchy beurre bosc pear. Devoid of the distraction of dosage, it celebrates the minerality and salinity of a veritable who's who of many of Champagne's top grand and premier cru villages. Chardonnay leads confidently on the front, gracefully supported by the red fruit flickers of pinot on the finish.

Duval-Leroy Fleur de Champagne Brut Premier Cru NV $$

91 points • 2013 base vintage • Disgorged November 2017 • Tasted in Champagne

70% chardonnay, 30% pinot; 15% reserves; 8g/L dosage; the second cuvée of the house, currently in a period of transition as the volume is lowered to make more Extra-Brut; currently 600–800,000 bottles

Fleur de Champagne is the historic cuvée of Duval-Leroy, purposely an elegant and fine summer apéritif style. It meets the brief in a medium straw hue, with chardonnay singing in notes of lemon and lime, while pinot noir lends its red apple presence, culminating in an elegant finish of vibrant acidity and well-integrated dosage.

Duval-Leroy Blanc de Blancs Grand Cru Brut NV $$$

90 points • 100% 2006 vintage • Tasted in Champagne

Chardonnay exclusively from the six grand cru villages; 4% vinified in oak barrels; 100% 2006, but labelled NV, as the house struggles to sell vintage cuvées, so only the very finest seasons like 2008 will be marketed as vintages; 3g/L dosage

Sandrine Logette-Jardin likes 2006, a vintage of high maturity and low acidity, for its balance and 'perspective on the future', anticipating more vintages of richness and ripeness as the climate continues to evolve. 'I remember the chardonnay from Le Mesnil-sur-Oger in 2006,' she recalls. 'Normally the aromas are of lemon and lime, but here they were mandarins and oranges.' For such a warm season, its bright, medium-straw hue is refreshing. True to the harvest, this is a generous blanc de blancs of ripe pear and fruit mince spice, with a creamy, supple mouthfeel and a biscuity, dry-extract finish of phenolic grip, amplified by subtle coffee bean and mocha notes derived from a little touch of barrel fermentation. For such proportions, it concludes vibrant and long.

DUVAL-LEROY ROSÉ PRESTIGE PREMIER CRU NV $$$

91 points • 2012 BASE VINTAGE • DISGORGED 17 JULY 2017 • TASTED IN CHAMPAGNE

Pinot from Vertus, Ambonnay and Bouzy, macerated on skins for 20 hours; blended with typically 20-35% (depending on the season) grand cru chardonnay post-fermentation for freshness and elegance; 9g/L dosage

Duval-Leroy's rosé has never enjoyed the freshness and endurance of its chardonnay-led cuvées, and more than four years on lees has only amplified its developed personality. With a medium salmon-copper hue, there is a contrast here between the juicy red strawberry and raspberry fruits and rose hip fragrance of macerated pinot and savoury complexity of tomato and charcuterie. Maturity has heightened its complexity and creamy structure, which offset fine tannin grip on the finish.

DUVAL-LEROY PETIT MESLIER EXTRA BRUT 2007 $$$$

90 points • TASTED IN AUSTRALIA

Barrel fermented; 3717 bottles; 7g/L dosage

Petit meslier is making a comeback in Champagne, garnering interest for its ability to hold acidity even in increasingly hot vintages. Duval-Leroy have conjured a beautifully fresh and energetic meslier that transcends its variety and its season. It's at once tense and intense, with baked apple concentration, crab apple bite and layers of ginger spice, even exotic notes of star anise. The toasty, biscuity and creamy complexity of a decade on lees contrasts with meslier's bitter phenolics and tart grapefruit notes, culminating in a finish of lingering, zesty lime and tense, firm acidity.

DUVAL-LEROY CLOS DE BOUVERIES CHARDONNAY PREMIER CRU EXTRA BRUT 2006 $$$$

88 points • TASTED IN CHAMPAGNE

100% chardonnay from 50-year-old vines in a single clos of 3.5 hectares in the heart of Vertus, with chalk 60 cm below the surface, belonging to the company for more than a century; made in every vintage; completion of fermentation, malolactic fermentation and maturation in oak barrels, 10% new for the first time; 2g/L dosage; 15,888 bottles, less than half the production volume of 2005

Sandrine Logette-Jardin describes Clos de Bouveries chardonnay as mineral, smoky and flinty, very similar to that of Le Mesnil-sur-Oger. Unfortunately, its nuances are lost in this powerful cuvée that brims full of the coffee and dark chocolate of oak barrel maturation. This is a Vertus of significant impact and proportions, colliding the rich, ripe power of 2006 with the full texture and flavour overlay of new oak for the first time. It upholds the deep fruit intensity of mirabelle plums that defined its release two years ago, now evolving into golden fruit cake complexity. It's designed to age, and was released altogether too young, though time has done little to soften the bitter phenolics of the season, heightened by oak. The concept of releasing a single-variety, single-vineyard wine in every single vintage in a climate as fickle as that of Champagne is more than a little disconcerting and, like the 2005 before it, this vintage is sadly not worthy.

DUVAL-LEROY CLOS DES BOUVERIES BRUT 2003

89 points • Disgorged 2013 • Tasted in Champagne

As for the Clos de Bouveries Chardonnay Premier Cru 2006; completion of fermentation, malolactic fermentation and maturation in oak barrels from 2001, 1999 and 1998; just 5 tonnes per hectare, half the usual yield, due to losses to frost; 3g/L dosage

Flaunting a full golden yellow hue, the flamboyance and exuberance of 2003 is on full parade amidst the grand spectacle of toasty, creamy oak. The result is a broad-shouldered champagne of hearty main-course proportions, true to its warm, low-yielding season, though lacking in finesse.

DUVAL-LEROY CUMIÈRES PINOT NOIR PREMIER CRU BRUT 2005 $$$$

87 points • Tasted in Champagne

Single vineyard; organic; 100% fermented and matured in oak barrels; 4.5g/L dosage; 5648 bottles

Joining Clos des Bouveries in Duval-Leroy's growing portfolio of single-clos releases, this is a powerful cuvée of full straw hue that encapsulates the impact of Cumières pinot noir. Now devoid of the primary fruits of its release two years ago, it has been trumped by heightened, spicy oak flavour that leaves the finish biscuity, firm and dry, signalling that it has now reached the end of its life. It is very much a child of its season, and the pronounced dusty, dry-extract, dank peanut notes and coarse phenolic grip that define the vintage completely overwhelm the bouquet, palate and structure, heightened by full barrel fermentation.

DUVAL-LEROY BOUZY GRAND CRU EXTRA BRUT 2007 $$$$

90 points • Tasted in Champagne

Single vineyard; 100% fermented and matured in oak barrels; 2g/L dosage; 3960 bottles

Duval-Leroy is joining the ranks of houses releasing more single-clos cuvées, inspired by the terroir focus initiated largely by the growers of Champagne. It's no easy task to achieve balance and appeal in single-vineyard champagne, particularly in vintages with their own inherent challenges. But the presence and generosity of the great pinot noir grand cru of Bouzy makes this a pretty solid attempt at this pursuit. All the generosity of the village, the variety, the vintage and full barrel fermentation are compacted into a medium to full straw-yellow thing rumbling with the power of Bouzy in red and black fruits layered with fruit mince spice. Oak heightens its spicy personality, hints of charcuterie and structure, lending some grip to the finish, though the fruit in the strong 2007 season has the confidence to sustain it, concluding with good length and tense acidity.

DUVAL-LEROY FEMME DE CHAMPAGNE NV $$$$

97 points • 100% 2004 VINTAGE • TASTED IN CHAMPAGNE

80% Côte des Blancs chardonnay, 20% Ambonnay pinot; only selected plots from the middle of the grand cru slopes; one plot per village: Chouilly Montaigu, Avize La Chapelle, Oger Terre Noël, Le Mesnil-sur-Oger Chétillons; 15% vinified in old oak barrels of three, five and six vintages of use; 100% 2004 but labelled NV, as the house struggles to sell vintage cuvées, so only the exceptional seasons like 2002 and 2008 will be marketed as vintages, with 2006 and 2007 coming next as non-vintages; 5g/L dosage

Femme is built on a core of four incredible Côte des Blancs grand cru sites, though it is Ambonnay pinot that Sandrine Logette-Jardin surprisingly upholds as defining its longevity in this release (pinot for Femme usually hails from Bouzy, and sometimes a little from Aÿ). She describes 2004 as a classic harvest with good balance of freshness and 'just correct richness, no more and no less'.

As spectacular as ever two years on from its release, radiating an amazingly bright, brilliant medium-straw hue at a full 15 years of age, this is a remarkable Femme that encapsulates the glory and energy of 2004. It articulates the understated power of some of the greatest sites in the Côte des Blancs grand crus, the tension and endurance of 2004 and the spicy complexity of long lees age and a touch of barrel maturity. The result presents tremendous line and length, a wine that walks the tightrope between tension and character with great confidence. Mineral expression is profound, mouth-filling, deeply salty and chalk mineral, given full voice thanks to low dosage, articulating the resonant glory of the Côte des Blancs. It has a grand future before it yet.

DUVAL-LEROY FEMME DE CHAMPAGNE 1996 $$$$$

99 points • DISGORGED MARCH 2017 • TASTED IN CHAMPAGNE AND AUSTRALIA

76% Côte des Blancs chardonnay, 24% Aÿ and Bouzy pinot; same chardonnay plots as per NV above; 8% barrel fermented; aged on cork rather than crown seal, though today Femme is aged on crown seal; 4.5g/L dosage; a significant quantity held back for re-release

The youthful endurance of grand cru Côte des Blancs chardonnay in this cuvée has long captivated me, but never has it reached the heights that it has attained in 1996, and with a larger dose than usual of grand cru pinot noir, too. Even on the occasion of its 22nd birthday, and no less than two decades on lees, it projects a glowing straw hue and even – astonishingly – a green tint. The sheer, bombastic energy and towering concentration of 1996 are on grand display, yet with a harmony, focus, creaminess, even an elegance and sheer allure so many failed to capture in this lauded yet controversial season. Flattering notes of struck flint, gunsmoke and fennel lend a layer of reductive intrigue I've not seen in other bottles. Primary lemon, apple, pear and grapefruit are still here, layered with the toast and nougat of middle age and hints of pipe smoke and green olives that declare its two decades in the cellar. Tense acid line and fine, frothing chalk minerality unite on a finish of profound focus and endurance, holding every promise of yet another decade of life. A triumph. One bottle opened by the house was corked.

Duval-Leroy maintains 300 oak barrels for fermentation of select plots.

EGLY-OURIET

(Eglee-Ou-ree-yair)

10/10

15 RUE DE TRÉPAIL 51150 AMBONNAY

EGLY-OURIET
Propriétaire - Récoltant

Some in Champagne can achieve grandeur of dizzying proportions, and the most talented can summon delicacy of light-footed grace, but no village marries the two as effortlessly as Ambonnay, and no practitioner as masterfully as Francis Egly. His fabled domain enjoys a cult status shared by no other grower on the Montagne de Reims. This tiny, pristine operation deserves its acclaim, capturing the profound complexity, intensity and grandeur of the Montagne's finest terroirs, without sacrificing the precision that underlies the most revered champagnes. These are ravishingly vinous sparkling wines, consistently among the most exactingly balanced of Champagne's power set, handcrafted by a creative, thoughtful artisan who painstakingly tends his vines naturally to full maturity. To uphold the calibre of his non-vintage cuvées even in the wake of the harrowing 2011 and tricky 2010 seasons calls for wizardry I have witnessed from no other grower or house. On this basis, Egly-Ouriet remains the finest grower in Champagne right now, and my only 10/10 grower. This name just might be the hardest to pronounce in Champagne, but it's one you must remember and seek out at every possible opportunity.

Egly-Ouriet now owns 40 parcels spanning 13 hectares of vineyards planted to 70% pinot noir and 30% chardonnay, encompassing a glorious 10 hectares of grand crus, primarily in Ambonnay, 1.4 hectares in Verzenay, a few rows in Bouzy, and a two-hectare plot of very old meunier vines in Vrigny that produce a single-vineyard premier cru. Francis Egly has recently acquired vines in the premier cru of Bisseuil and in Trigny near Vrigny, both of which will soon become their own cuvées. Francis Egly, fourth-generation head of the estate, has bottled the entire harvest since he took over in 1982, growing from just six hectares then to sales of 100,000 bottles today. Previously, his father, Michel, bottled a small proportion since the 1970s, and his grandfather, Charles, bottled tiny quantities for family and friends since the 1950s.

'Champagne is like Burgundy,' Egly upholds. 'You go one kilometre and it is different. Ambonnay is completely different to Bouzy, where the soils are deeper. Ambonnay is a very "solaire"

village, south-orientated, which is very important for maturity. The soil is very poor, generally only 20–30 centimetres deep, so you can smell the minerality of the chalk.' Egly works intuitively to preserve the detail of his grapes and their terroirs.

His approach in the vineyards is as natural as possible, without aspiring to organic or biodynamic certification. 'It is too complicated to practise specific regimes,' he maintains. An eco-friendly approach has seen a radical reduction in the use of fertilisers and the complete elimination of herbicides and insecticides. The soil is manured and ploughed for aeration, and old vines and green harvests reduce crop levels by up to 50% for red wine for rosé and Coteaux Champenois. Otherwise, his yields are at the full level of 10 tonnes per hectare.

From vines averaging more than 45 years of age, Egly harvests at full maturity, typically at 11 or 12 degrees of potential alcohol, extremely ripe for Champagne, and never chaptalises. 'We are

always the last to harvest in Ambonnay,' he reveals. His goal is to harvest grapes as ripe as possible, and he cites the best vintages as those of high maturity, naming under-maturity as Champagne's biggest problem. 'A lot of houses say the acidity is very important, but for us this is wrong because we always have very good acidity in Champagne.' His aspiration is 'elegance and strength, but never heaviness'. He says champagne is like a bird; 'it has to stay aromatic and light'.

Champagne's warming vintages do not concern him. 'For now, the weather in Champagne is for the better,' he suggests. 'Twenty or thirty years ago, we sometimes had very difficult years in which it was very hard to achieve good ripeness, but now this is easier. The sun is very important for the grapes, but the difference in temperature between day and night is also very important for building complexity. And even if the temperature is warmer, we still have very cold nights in summer. So it is very good!'

'A problem in Champagne now is that a lot of champagnes are very similar, but we are aiming for something that represents its style distinctively,' he declares. 'It is very important for us to maintain consistency in quality and to be the best that we can. Our clients are not ordinary people, they are very passionate about wine and they know about the diversity of champagne. In Champagne you have to make a good wine first. We can't only make champagne because it is champagne, but we must make wine which has its own specificities and is well recognised all over the world.'

The distinction of Egly-Ouriet is founded in its terroir. 'Ambonnay is very chalky,' Francis emphasises. 'In Champagne we have chalk everywhere, but it depends on the depth of the soil. In Bouzy and Trépail the chalk is deeper under the surface, so the wines are heavier and more winey. Ambonnay is different. The majority of the vines are on the slope where the soil is very chalky and the topsoil is only 30 centimetres deep, so the vines are able to draw the minerality out of the chalk.' This is the key to the freshness, vitality and endurance of his ripe style.

In order to preserve this freshness and detail, grapes are pressed slowly and ferments are run for two to three months at a cool 15°C. All grand crus are fermented entirely in barriques, with some premier cru parcels in enamelled and stainless steel tanks, using only natural yeasts. Egly maintains more than 200 barrels, in which the majority of his production is fermented (apart from 20% of Brut Tradition), not only for structure and longevity, but to facilitate vinification of all 40 parcels separately to draw out more character of the terroir. Used barrels are purchased from his friend Dominique Laurent in Nuits-Saint-Georges.

Malolactic fermentation is allowed or barred (by chilling) depending on the vintage, and completely blocked in the warm 2018 season. Very low dosages are used – typically just 1–3g/L. 'I prefer to use a little sugar rather than following the fashion of no dosage,' he says. Long ageing on lees in barrel for 8–10 months and in bottle for at least 3–4 years furnishes considerable longevity.

A 2006 cellar expansion brought all winemaking operations together in the same building, with pressing, vinification and storage on three successive levels, temperature controlled at every stage. Wines are aged in barrel until May following harvest, held at 12°C to preserve freshness. In 2008, Egly replaced his old horizontal press with two new vertical presses, which he says have improved quality.

Such is the duration of lees age that annual sales of 100,000 bottles are facilitated by an incredible cellar stock of 700,000. Production has now reached 150,000, with sales anticipated to match in a few years' time. Cellar stocks will rise to 1 million bottles accordingly.

Francis is now assisted by his daughter Clémence in the office and his son Charles in the vineyards. 'With my parents and children, we are now six in the domain, so it is necessary to expand a bit, and we have a new objective to fulfil with new cuvées,' he explains.

Egly purchased a vineyard in Bisseuil in 2012, but has only had access to the fruit since 2016. 'Les Vignes de Bisseuil' will be released

To Francis Egly, the key to Ambonnay is its chalk.

in 2021 as a blend of 70% chardonnay, 15% pinot and 15% meunier. He also purchased a tiny plot of just 0.17 hectares of chardonnay planted in 1902 in Verzy. The *vins clairs* already look exciting, true to their distinctive terroirs, with the clear signature of Egly. 'It is very important for me to uphold the distinctiveness of each of the different terroirs, and also the style of Egly-Ouriet,' he emphasises.

The back labels are among Champagne's most informative, declaring disgorgement dates, terroirs and number of months on lees. Wines are bottled in July following harvest, so it's easy to determine the base vintage. Important details appear on every bottle, alongside the philosophy of the house: 'This champagne is the expression of a "family" style that comes first and foremost from perfectly tended vineyards. The quality of grapes, the precision of blending and long *élevage* in the cellar allows us to offer you non-filtered champagnes in the purest champagne style.' A breath of fresh air in a region saturated with marketing froth.

I first had the privilege of meeting Francis Egly in 2015 and of visiting his hallowed estate in 2019. He is a man of generous warmth, careful precision, and quietly spoken confidence, just like his champagnes.

EGLY-OURIET LES VIGNES DE VRIGNY PREMIER CRU BRUT NV $$$

95 points • 2014 BASE VINTAGE WITH 30% 2013 AND 20% 2012 RESERVES • TASTED IN CHAMPAGNE
95 points • 2013 BASE VINTAGE WITH 30% 2012 AND 20% 2010 RESERVES • DISGORGED JULY 2017
• TASTED IN AUSTRALIA

100% meunier from 2 hectares of 40-year-old vines on a south-facing slope in premier cru Vrigny; aged 36 months on lees; 4g/L dosage

'Vrigny is sandy, without a lot of chalk or great minerality, but it's perfect for making a fruity and easy-to-drink meunier,' Francis says. 'We need to wait at least three years for the yeast and ferment character to subside.'

He crafts one of Champagne's most flattering single-vineyard meuniers, faithfully translating every detail of the succulent depth of this grape's enticing full golden-yellow hue, overflowing in fleshy black cherry, red plum and white nectarine fruit. It resonates with varietal mixed spice and the biscuity complexity and crème brûlée of long lees age and deep reserves. Tangy, vibrant acidity lingers long through a finish at once salty and mineral, and at the same time creamy and luscious. Deliciously rich, ripe and alluring, this is meunier that radiates with the full grandeur of Egly.

EGLY-OURIET BRUT TRADITION GRAND CRU NV $$$$

96 points • 2013 BASE VINTAGE WITH 50% RESERVES FROM 2012, 2011 AND 2010 • AGED 5 YEARS
ON LEES • 4G/L DOSAGE • TASTED IN CHAMPAGNE
96 points • 2012 50% BASE VINTAGE WITH 30% 2011 AND 20% 2010 RESERVES • AGED 4 YEARS
ON LEES • DISGORGED JULY 2017 • 2G/L DOSAGE • TASTED IN AUSTRALIA

30% chardonnay, 70% pinot; 80% Ambonnay and the remainder Verzenay and a little Bouzy; at least 50% wild fermented and aged in oak casks

From the very first cuvée, Egly-Ouriet is distinguished for its ability to preserve exacting precision and outstanding chalk mineral focus in the midst of magnificent generosity. This is a vinous wine of calm authority, carrying the full grandeur and complexity of carefully tended, old-vine pinot noir on some of Champagne's most revered grand crus. Reverberating with the deep spice of pinot noir, this is a cuvée of magnificent complexity that unites deep reserves with long lees age to achieve silky texture and grand complexity of magnificent red and black cherries, succulent peach, fig, fruit mince spice and red plums. It culminates in a finish of seamless harmony, uniting fine chalk mineral texture with long-lingering, silky yet vibrant acidity and heightened salt minerality. At once luscious and creamy, with vanilla custard notes, yet eminently fresh, bright, and oh so long. In line, length and mineral definition this is a cuvée of profound definition and jubilant enticement. Two brilliant Brut Traditions from outstanding seasons.

Egly-Ouriet Brut Rosé Grand Cru NV $$$$

96 points • 2013 base vintage • 3g/L dosage • Tasted in Champagne
97 points • 2012 base vintage • Disgorged July 2018 • Tasted in Champagne
94 points • 2011 base vintage with 20% 2010 and 20% 2009 reserves • 2g/L dosage
• Disgorged May 2017 • Tasted in Australia

30% chardonnay, 70% pinot including 5% Ambonnay red wine; aged 58 months on lees

Francis Egly's Rosé is a similar composition to his Brut Tradition, with a very small addition of just 4–5% red wine, 'since it is very concentrated'. Red wine is sourced from plots close to those for his Ambonnay Rouge, a little lower in quality here. 'Our aim is to make the best wine possible and then blend a little red wine into it,' he explains. 'I am looking for a wine with a lot of tension, unlike a saignée style.'

Rumbling power with delicate finesse, this is a delightful rosé of pretty pale salmon hue that bears witness to Francis Egly's talent in drawing out the succulent, luscious, creamy structure of ripe fruit fermented in barrel and transposing it gracefully on the lively freshness and chalk minerality of Ambonnay. The 2012 and 2013 represent spectacular renditions, bursting with the exuberance and beguiling transparency of Ambonnay pinot noir. Sensational perfume of rose hip, fig and mixed spice sings with the pinpoint purity of the village, to a thundering undercurrent of grand complexity of dark fruit cake and spice, yet at every instant light, refreshing and breathtakingly energetic. Francis Egly's genius is on grand display here in achieving acidity so lively and so focused, and yet ripe, full and enticing. Chalk minerality underscores every magnificent moment. The 2011 base transcends its season, now a medium copper hue, though beginning to fade from the glory of its 2017 release.

Egly-Ouriet Grand Cru V.P Vieillissement Prolongé Extra Brut NV $$$$

96 points • 2009 base vintage • Disgorged May 2017 • Tasted in Australia

30% chardonnay, 70% pinot from Ambonnay, Bouzy and Verzenay; 33% 2008, 33% 2007 reserves; aged 80 months on lees; vinified and aged in oak casks; 2g/L dosage

In an age when single-vineyard, single-varietal, single-vintage champagnes are all the rage, it remains that blends triumph most often, even in an estate as tiny as this. Egly's 'prolonged ageing' blend unites three vintages in equal proportions. Power meets effortless calm as three of Champagne's finest pinot noir crus unite with breathtaking expression. The depth and complexity on display here are a grand testament to the collision of the deep 2009 season, the grandeur of Ambonnay and the exacting precision of Egly. It ripples with mirabelle plums, peaches and all the fanfare of a Parisian boulangerie. For all its complexity, it concludes with sensational tension and focus on an exacting finish of precise minerality that bores to the core of grand cru chalk. A brilliant V.P, albeit without the dazzling minerality or towering magnificence of the 2008 before it.

Francis Egly remains Champagne's finest grower.

Egly-Ouriet Blanc de Noirs Grand Cru Vieille Vigne NV

98 points • 2012 base vintage with 50% 2011 reserves • Aged 72 months on lees • Tasted in Champagne

97 points • 2011 base vintage with 50% 2010 reserves • Aged 66 months on lees • Disgorged December 2017 • Tasted in Australia

99 points • 2010 base vintage with 50% 2009 reserves • Aged 70 months on lees • Disgorged May 2017 • Tasted in Australia

100% pinot, from a single lieu-dit, 'Les Crayères', planted in 1946 in shallow 30cm-deep soils in a warm, south-facing amphitheatre high up the Ambonnay slope; fermented and matured in barriques; 3g/L dosage

Francis Egly describes the grapes of Les Crayères as 'very small and very aromatic', producing a champagne 'for gastronomy, with presence and structure', quoting with pride that others have dubbed it 'Burgundy with bubbles'.

This warm amphitheatre high up the Ambonnay slope epitomises the golden sunlight, glowing warmth and magnificent mineral expression of Egly-Ouriet and gives birth to his finest cuvée of all. In sheer length, line and juxtaposition between exacting chalk mineral focus and grandeur of other-worldly depths, this is one of the greatest sparkling pinots on the planet. An anthem to pinot noir, the depth and complexity on parade here are of grand cru Burgundian proportions, welling up from a deep core of black cherries, black plums and figs, erupting with hedonistic layers of violets, plum liqueur, fruit mince spice, dark chocolate and vanilla nougat. The 2011/2010 blend transcends its season, 2012/2011 is at least the equal of the great 2009/2008, and 2010/2009 trumps them all. In sheer volume, depth and persistence, this cuvée pushes champagne into another world. Yet, crucially and mesmerisingly, it is never for a moment heavy or blowsy, pulled exactingly into tight line by gorgeous, bright, dynamic yet perfectly ripe and generous acidity. It exudes a red cherry purity at once deep and yet light and airy, the essence of pinot noir, of Ambonnay, and of Egly-Ouriet. With barely a foot of topsoil before the chalk, the mineral character of this hallowed site speaks articulately in softly salty tones that will stir the depths of your soul.

Egly-Ouriet Brut Grand Cru Millésime 2009 $$$$

97 points • Tasted in Champagne

30% chardonnay, 70% pinot noir; vines 40 years of age; fully fermented and aged in barrels; no malolactic fermentation; 6g/L dosage

'With big temperature extremes and very good maturity, 2009 was a very good vintage,' recalls Francis Egly. 'We had a lot of wind from the north, which was very good for freshness.' He selects the vines to reserve for the vintage cuvée before the harvest, and sorts the grapes as they come in to be pressed, looking for clean and ripe fruit of high quality and good maturity. He considers this a cuvée for food. The long-enduring stamina of 2008 prompted him to release 2009 first.

The full exuberance of Ambonnay is on grand display here in full orchestral scoring of fruit mince spice and golden fruit cake, reverberating with thundering waves of crème brûlée and honey. Its concentration embodies the full crescendo of pinot noir with epic line and length, underscored by all the spicy complexity of barrel fermentation. Creamy, succulent and oh so luscious, it controls its flamboyant concentration to exacting effect, rejoicing in Francis Egly's mastery in upholding freshness, vitality and poise. In the wake of its exuberance, to uphold pitch-perfect high notes of structural finesse is a breathtaking triumph. Intricately and exactingly structured with outstanding, bright malic acidity, it's awash with a cascade of mouth-filling chalk minerality that bears testimony to carefully tended old vines on shallow soils. Another exhilaratingly thrilling Millésime.

EGLY-OURIET BRUT GRAND CRU MILLÉSIME 2007 $$$$

96 points • Disgorged May 2017 • Tasted in Australia

30% chardonnay, 70% pinot, harvested very late from 40-year-old vines in Ambonnay; fermented and aged completely in oak barrels; no malolactic fermentation; aged 106 months on lees; 4g/L dosage

The tension of Egly-Ouriet in contrast to the grand depth of long lees age makes for a magnificent cuvée of deep pinot noir cherry fruit, tangy morello cherry acidity and long-lingering acid drive. This is a powerful statement of pinot noir, wrapped in layers of golden fruit cake and fruit mince spice that linger very long. Exacting chalk mineral freshness meets malic acidity of vitality and energy. Another brilliant Egly. One bottle was corked and another exhibited some oxidation in notes of burnt orange and a touch of volatile acidity.

EGLY-OURIET COTEAUX CHAMPENOIS AMBAONNAY ROUGE CUVÉE DES GRANDS CÔTES 2015 $$$$

97 points • Tasted in Australia

Single parcel of four plots of mid-slope Ambonnay old vines in an amphitheatre; low yields of just 35hL/hectare; vinified and aged for 18-22 months entirely in oak barrels; miniscule production of 200 cases

'It is very difficult to make red wine in Champagne,' admits Francis Egly, who tries to produce his Coteaux Champenois every year. 'We have tried with different parts of Ambonnay, and if it's too chalky and mineral it doesn't work. There is only one area that works, this little amphitheatre on the mid-slope, where the soil is 80 centimetres before the chalk, much deeper than the 30 centimetres across most of the village.' He harvests shortly after he picks for his champagnes, and typically around 14 degrees of alcohol potential.

From a plot of very old pinot noir vines in a sun-catching amphitheatre on the mid-slope of Ambonnay, Francis Egly produces the finest Coteaux Champenois in all of Champagne. His 2015 goes further, one of the greatest pinot noirs on earth outside of the fabled grand crus of Burgundy itself, and the first Coteaux Champenois that I have ever seen achieve true grand cru heights, by lofty Burgundian standards. Its perfume is enticing and alluring, beckoning with exacting red cherry fruit of the most gorgeous purity, swept with sublime fragrance of pure violets. Brimming with white pepper, beetroot, sarsaparilla and exotic spice, yet it is not its grand complexity that elevates it to hitherto unknown heights, but its core of enthralling red cherry, hovering motionless, haunting and spellbinding, like a silent mist over a sea of fine chalk minerality. A tannin web of silky-fine grace juxtaposes a high-cocoa dark chocolate grip, infusing a confidence that will sustain it for three decades and beyond.

Ambonnay, winter 2013.

EMMANUEL BROCHET

(Eman-yoo-el Bro-sheh)

7 IMPASSE BROCHET 51500 VILLERS-AUX-NŒUDS

Champagne

EMMANUEL
BROCHET

PREMIER CRU

In the turning wheel of Champagne succession, it is virtually unheard of for a young grower-producer to be the first in his family to tend vines. All the more daring in the little-known premier cru village of Villers-aux-Nœuds, in which no one has made champagne for generations. Emmanuel Brochet defines a bold new frontier, bringing an old terroir to life with an intuition derived not from local knowledge, family history or personal experience, but from the sheer courage to respond to each plot, each season and each ferment individually. Most remarkable of all is the beautiful fruit character and pronounced terroir expression he has drawn from this place in a very short time. I know of no one in Champagne today who has achieved so much from so little so quickly as Emmanuel Brochet.

In the plains between the slopes of the Montagne de Reims and the sprawling southern suburbs of Reims, Villers-aux-Nœuds was once the proud custodian of 250 hectares of vines. The quaint little village is now home to just 27 hectares, planted on its best south-east slopes, spanning a wide diversity of soils, with chalk just 30 centimetres below the surface.

Emmanuel Brochet's family has owned vines here for generations, leasing them to others to tend until Emmanuel commenced in 1997. His mother's 2.5 hectare single vineyard 'Le Mont Benoit' is one of the better sites in the village, with a thin layer of 40 centimetres of topsoil directly over chalk, and just 25 centimetres at the top of the slope. The vineyard is visible from the motorway, under the power lines, adjacent to the toll station near Champfleury. Planted to 37% meunier, 30% chardonnay and 23% pinot noir dating from 1962, half the block was replanted after the devastating frosts of 1986. Emmanuel manages the site for his mother, paying her a rent of 0.6 hectares of fruit, leaving 1.9 hectares for his modest production of 10,000 bottles.

Without the constraints of family and village history, Brochet is blessed with the freedom to forge a brave path with a spontaneity rarely possible in this staid region. 'As the first winemaker of the family, I am lucky I do not have my family telling me what to do!' he grins. 'I do things because I want to, not because I have to.' This affords full licence to pursue his elegantly simple philosophy: 'A wine is good because the grapes are good. If there is good balance in the soils and in the vine, there is good balance in the wine. Every year is different, and we work it according to the season, not because we did it that way last year,' he says, admitting he's never written down anything he's done each vintage. 'I practise biodynamics, but this is not the most important thing, no more important than the soil, the vines or my state of mind.'

To achieve a good balance of acidity and sugar, Brochet harvests his fruit ripe; many of his neighbours have finished picking before he even starts. In respect for the soil, he commenced biodynamic certification in 2008 and completely abandoned use of chemicals in 2009, though he has no intention of mentioning biodynamics

on his labels once certification is granted. 'It is important that my wines have no residues of pesticides, but many other elements are equally important,' he explains. 'If I put biodynamic certification on my labels, then I should also include my press, the house, the grapes, the soil, the place and my state of mind!'

Brochet has found the period of transition to organic certification difficult, selling all his reserve wines prior to 2010 to a négociant, as they were not organic. An annual production of 10,000 bottles is little over half of what 1.9 hectares would normally produce in Champagne, even with some *vins clairs* sold to négociants for cash flow. Biodynamics has reduced Brochet's yields to a tiny 35hL/hectare. He does not perform a green harvest and upholds that balanced fruit relies upon yields that are neither too large nor too small. 'Perhaps it's not that we produce too little yield, but that conventional viticulture produces too much?' he pointedly suggests. The equilibrium he has achieved in his vines produces a balance of sugar and acidity sufficient that he has no need to chaptalise, unusual in Champagne, and virtually unheard of in a lesser premier cru village.

MINIMALIST WINEMAKING

With no winery to inherit, Brochet sold his grapes until 2002 to finance the purchase of his equipment. He found a traditional 1960s two-tonne Coquard press in 2006, half the size of a traditional champagne press, and restored it 'like an old car'. He admits he prefers driving a tractor to driving a horse. 'I am a boy and I love machines!' says this off-road rally driver. Grapes are pressed on the day they are harvested and settled overnight before fermentation with wild yeasts entirely in barrels, in which the wine remains for 11 months.

The soil and the vines are Brochet's first priority, and he says that with good fruit he has little to do in the winery. 'My winemaking

is very simple: an oxidative vinification and ageing on lees, which consume the oxygen, creating a balance between oxidation and reduction.' Adamant champagne should not have a woody taste, he buys old barrels as well as new, and keeps wines in barrel on their lees for an extended period of 11 months to reduce pick-up of oak flavours. Brochet likens winemaking in barrels to biodynamics: 'It's easier than in tanks, and the wines are more natural.' There is no bâtonnage, no filtration and no cold stabilisation.

Brochet is continually experimenting and refining his style. 'I tried putting my reserve wines in barrel, but without lees they became tired and woody, so I've since kept reserve wines in tank.' Generally he blocks malolactic fermentation in his vintage wines, but in 2012 he allowed it to proceed. 'With our warming weather, some people are saying that we should stop malo so as to retain acidity, but if you don't have a lot of acidity it's very hard to stop malo,' he explains. 'I would have to use a lot of preservative, and I don't want to do that.'

Brochet uses very small levels of preservative, and an extra brut dosage of around 4g/L in his cuvées, and trialled a zero-dosage wine from the same blend as his Le Mont Benoit NV, but found the acidity too pronounced at low temperatures. 'Sugar is a mediator, and a little is a technical support if you drink champagne too cold!' he says. The blend of this cuvée changes each year. 'The *cépage* is not important,' he upholds, 'and we can achieve great consistency each year even with different proportions of each variety. The wines taste of the vineyard and the soil, and that's the important thing. The soil is more important than the varieties.'

He maintains the flexibility to release wines 'when they are good to drink, not because I need the money', a rare opportunity in any young business. His wines are consequently aged long, NVs generally 2–3 years and vintages 5–8 years. He has also broken with Champagne tradition in releasing vintage and even non-vintage blends non-sequentially, releasing 2009 before 2007 and 2008. He tastes vintages blind with his friends and releases those that are ready. Back labels are informative, specifying vintages, varieties and vinification details.

Brochet's wines showcase the unique mineral expression of his vineyard in a savoury chalk mouthfeel, a little coarser-grained in texture than that of the Côte des Blancs. I ask if this is unique to the village, or particular to the accessible chalk in his vineyard, and he says he has no idea. 'There is just one producer who makes wine in this village and it is me!' he exclaims. 'Everyone else sells their grapes to the cooperatives and négociants. Old winegrowers always said they could make very good wines in this village. Two generations ago they kept the grapes separate and made very good wines.'

To Brochet, state of mind is an important ingredient of terroir. 'There is no stress here during harvest,' he says, having employed his two best friends to assist. 'It's very important to enjoy your work and I like working in the vineyard on the tractor. When I was young I played with toys and now I like to have fun playing with bigger toys in the vineyard and the winery!' A refreshing mindset for one who has achieved so much so quickly.

EMMANUEL BROCHET LES HAUTS MEUNIERS EXTRA BRUT 2011 $$$$

91 points • 2014 base vintage • Tasted in Australia

100% meunier from the old vines at the top of the vineyard in Villers-aux-Nœuds; 20% 2013 reserves; 8000 bottles

This is Brochet's favourite cuvée, which he variously describes as 'extraterrestrial' and the 'soul music' of his range. Boasting a full straw hue, it's quite dark for its youth, reflective of its ripe, full and characterful style. Meunier is on grand display here, in all its spicy fig, ginger and cherry kernel character, laced with the coffee and high-cocoa dark chocolate persona of fermentation and maturation in oak barrels. The salty minerality of Villers-aux-Nœuds defines a finish of vibrant, firm acidity and good persistence.

EMMANUEL BROCHET LES HAUTS MEUNIERS EXTRA BRUT 2009 $$$$$

90 points • Tasted in Australia

As above

With a ravishing medium-gold hue, all the exuberant quince, berry fruits, golden fruit cake, fruit mince spice and Christmas fanfare of meunier meets the smoked bacon, charcuterie and milk chocolate of barrel fermentation. It's fleshy, creamy and spicy, embodying the full panoply of meunier's extroverted personality in this ripe and powerful season. For its generous benevolence, it upholds admirable poise and definition for meunier hailing from an immediate vintage in a lesser terroir at a full decade of age. One bottle showed some oxidative aldehyde notes, impacting its precision on the finish, suggesting premature development.

Emmanuel Brochet (opposite) is the only grower in generations to make champagnes in his village of Villers-aux-Nœuds.

ERIC RODEZ

(E-ri Roh-dez)

(7/10)

Rue de Isse 51150 Ambonnay
www.champagne-rodez.fr

RODEZ
CHAMPAGNE
AMBONNAY
AUTEUR DE CHAMPAGNE
R

Organic viticulture has become something of a catch cry in the modern wine world, but never have I seen a more profound statement of its impact than in Eric Rodez's magnificently positioned vineyard of 6.5 hectares on the glorious mid-slopes of Ambonnay. Standing on the edge of his rows of vines, he showed me tiny, sparse bunches. In the very next row, not more than a metre away, his neighbour's vines were loaded with full-sized bunches. The fanatical approach of this eighth-generation winegrower permeates every detail of his work, which embraces vinification in barriques, light dosages and a colossal resource of reserve wines spanning 20 years. The aspiration is to let the salty minerality and generous expression of one of Champagne's greatest grand crus sing through every cuvée. And sing they do.

When I first met Eric Rodez, who moonlights as mayor of Ambonnay, he immediately admitted his English is very limited and, my French being far worse, he proposed, *Nous pourrons parler la langue des bulles!* – 'We can speak in the language of the bubbles!'

As I soon discovered, where his bubbles are concerned, a particularly fine language it is.

Rodez's extensive portfolio has now grown to 13 cuvées, which he thinks of as 13 'melodies'. He likens them to a concert, where every tune evokes a different emotion. 'There is not enough emotion in champagne today!' he exclaims. 'I will not be the Coca-Cola of champagne – I will make emotional wine!' He thinks of his 35 parcels as 35 notes of music, each expressing five emotions, in their grape variety, vintage, vineyard location, method of fermentation, and malolactic fermentation ('forte') or not ('allegro').

The Rodez family have grown grapes in Ambonnay since 1757, and have made their own champagnes since the time of Eric's grandparents, but things changed when Eric began in 1984. 'That was not a good vintage,' he recalls, and it prompted him to do things differently in the vineyard, initiating a methodology that he prefers to call 'integrated' rather than 'ecological'. He upholds that it is 'very important to respect the conditions for the production of the grapes, not for you or for the pickers but for the wine and for the future.' Eric's son Mickael now manages the vineyards.

He borrows practices of organics and biodynamics, without seeking certification under either. 'Every year it is a new logic,' Eric explains. 'I do not have only one vision or one consistent process. My philosophy is to be free. Real life is not about following a recipe.' Use of chemicals is limited, grasses are cultivated in the mid-rows and yields are restricted to a tiny 30–40% of the permitted levels. 'To achieve music in the wine you need music in the grapes to begin with, and to achieve this you cannot have too high a yield,' he maintains. He is working hard to reduce the use of copper sulphate as a fungicide, just six kilograms per hectare in 2014, and ultimately aiming for four kilograms per hectare.

'To my colleagues, I am a little crazy!' he exclaims. 'But I am very happy. When you want to see the soil in the glass, you need to get the vine roots to go into the chalk,' he says. In his vineyards, the chalk is just 40 centimetres below the surface, but this is still deeper than in many parts of the Côte des Blancs, and it took 10 years from when he commenced biodynamics in 1989 before the roots tapped deep into the minerality of the chalk.

His philosophy now translates accurately into his profoundly salty mineral champagnes. He showed me a stunning barrel sample of 2010 pinot noir that displayed none of the botrytis problems that dogged this wet vintage. 'Thanks to low vegetation in the canopy, we had good ventilation and no botrytis in the vineyard,' he explains.

Expression of terroir is everything to Rodez, and he cheerfully admits that he doesn't aspire to make consistent wine each year. 'Every year is different and I will adapt my processes in the vineyards and in the cellar to suit. It is very important to me to make a wine of terroir, where you can taste the emotion.'

Exclusively in the heart of Ambonnay's mid-slope, his vineyards are planted to 60% pinot noir and 40% chardonnay, with an average vine age exceeding 30 years. As we left his vineyard and passed Krug's Clos d'Ambonnay on the lower slopes, he commented, 'There is more complexity in the mid-slopes and more minerality lower on the slopes.' I asked which was better and he paused for a long time, smiled knowingly and responded, 'Both are very important for blending!'

There are few small growers who understand blending more intricately than Rodez. His annual production of 45,000 bottles and 13 cuvées includes six non-vintage blends, benefiting from a deep stock of reserve wines, currently extending as far back as 20 years. Disgorgement dates are clearly marked on every back label.

His 35 plots of two varieties are vinified separately to produce 60 different wines, 80% of which are fermented and matured for six months in small Burgundian barrels, mostly aged between three and 20 years. Three vintages in Burgundy and one at Krug taught him how to use barrels 'for sensuality, not oak flavour'; Rodez maintains that new barrels are not good for the equilibrium and personality of champagne. He is currently increasing old barrel vinification, finding that it offers greater persistence and complexity.

Ferments occur naturally, and any that don't spontaneously kick off he will seed one week after débourbage (cold settling following pressing) with five yeast strains that he isolated from the domain.

Reserve stocks presently comprise barrels of eight vintages, representing 52 different wines. He recently showed me very fresh 2012 and 2013 reserves, energised by malic acidity.

He tactically utilises the generosity of Ambonnay and the complexity of barrel fermentation, then enlivens his cuvées with low dosage and selective use of malolactic fermentation, according to the parcel and the season. He neither seeds malolactic fermentation nor blocks it, warming the cellar to 16–17°C in the summer after harvest, to allow each barrel and tank the opportunity to proceed or not. Grape juice rather than sugar is used to sweeten liqueurs, and his wines contain no more than 5g/L dosage, allowing the character and minerality of these distinguished vineyards to sing with clarity and harmony.

Rodez recently constructed a magnificent new cuverie, cellar and tasting room at his home in the village, including an atmospheric upstairs barrel room.

When I visited Rodez during and after the 2014 harvest, I was taken aback by the exceptional expression of salt minerality in his *vins clairs*. 'When you want emotion in your glass, you cannot create this in the cellar, you must have it in your grapes before the vinification,' he emphasises. 'The vinification is only make-up. I am very lucky, Ambonnay is one very nice terroir. A Stradivarius, very well known and respected.' Yet, for all they represent, the wines of Eric Rodez are largely undiscovered, and offer incredible value for money.

Eric Rodez and his magnificent new cuverie, cellar and tasting room.

ERIC RODEZ CUVÉE DES CRAYÈRES AMBONNAY GRAND CRU NV $$

88 points • 2013 BASE VINTAGE • TASTED IN CHAMPAGNE

40% chardonnay, 60% pinot; 100% Ambonnay from at least 11 vineyards; average vine age 34 years; 28% 2013, 29% 2012, 20% 2011, 12% 2010, 11% 2009; 75% vinified in small oak barrels; 65-70% reserves; 65% malolactic fermentation; 4.5g/L dosage

Eric Rodez's very first cuvée traditionally captures the personality of Ambonnay, in depth, complexity and structure, but this release is sadly foiled by premature development that I've not seen in this estate before, nor anywhere else in his current line-up. It's a forward style of tangy acidity and some developed volatile notes, culminating in a finish of chalky salinity. Sadly lacking in the freshness, vibrancy and integrity that is integral to the rest of Rodez's range.

ERIC RODEZ BLANC DE BLANCS AMBONNAY NV $$

92 points • 2013 BASE VINTAGE • TASTED IN CHAMPAGNE

100% Ambonnay chardonnay from five vineyards; average vine age 39 years; 28% 2013, 21% 2012, 20% 2011, 15% 2010, 9% 2009, 7% 2008; 95% vinified in barrels; 10% malolactic fermentation; 3.5g/L dosage

Eric Rodez describes his blanc de blancs as more 'masculine' and his blanc de noirs as more 'feminine'. Strength here is derived from tremendous depth of more than 70% reserves, bolstered eloquently by the richness and creamy texture of fermentation almost entirely in oak barrels. The expression of blanc de blancs in Ambonnay serves to provide breadth of stone fruits, apple and pear. For such a recipe, it upholds great liveliness and lemon tang, energised by crunchy malic acidity and the freshening influence of prominent chalk mineral texture that glitters on a long and complex tail.

ERIC RODEZ ROSÉ AMBONNAY NV $$

92 points • 2012 BASE VINTAGE • TASTED IN CHAMPAGNE

45% pinot noir macerated for 4 days, 30% pinot noir white wine, 25% chardonnay; 100% Ambonnay from at least seven vineyards; average vine age 39 years; 50-55% reserves; 80% vinified in oak barrels; 4.5g/L dosage

'I will not assemble a red wine and a white wine as I do not want the tannin of red wine,' declares Rodez. 'For harmony, I will assemble pink wine of pinot noir macerated on its skins with white wine,' thus merging the maceration and blending techniques of rosé production. His pinot noir suits rosé very well, making, as he puts it, the red berries more explosive. It's a complex style of pretty pale-salmon hue, uniting vibrant red fruits, focused malic acidity and the subtle charcuterie notes and soft texture of barrel fermentation. The fine chalk minerality of Ambonnay brings persistence, freshness and texture that hold the finish with focus and vibrancy amidst its savoury complexity.

ERIC RODEZ BLANC DE NOIRS AMBONNAY NV $$

94 points • 2012 BASE VINTAGE • DISGORGED JUNE 2017 • TASTED IN CHAMPAGNE

100% Ambonnay pinot from 11 vineyards; average vine age 39 years; 24% 2012, 29% 2011, 14% 2010, 11% 2009, 13% 2008, 9% 2007; 90% vinified in barrels; 10% malolactic fermentation; 4g/L dosage

Eric Rodez crafts one of the best-value blanc de noirs anywhere in Champagne. The enticing purity of Ambonnay pinot noir on show is something to behold, encapsulating the personality of the village in gorgeous intensity of satsuma plum and black cherry fruit, layers of fruit mince spice and even sarsaparilla. The power and poise of great terroirs are exemplified in a style that resonates with lively yet ripe and well-integrated acidity, beautifully honed by the frothing salt minerality of ancient chalk. With a full, bright straw hue, it's at once generous and succulent and at the same time refined and poised, lingering with terrific line and length. Benchmark Rodez and standout blanc de noirs.

ERIC RODEZ DOSAGE ZÉRO AMBONNAY NV $$$

94 points • 2010 BASE VINTAGE • TASTED IN CHAMPAGNE

30% chardonnay, 70% pinot noir; 100% Ambonnay from 10 vineyards; average vine age 37 years; 100% vinified in small oak barrels; 60-70% reserves of six vintages; 10-20% malolactic fermentation; zero dosage

Rodez admits that it's very difficult to create a good equilibrium in zero-dosage champagne every year, yet he consistently manages to craft one of Champagne's richer zero-dosage offerings, and one of its most delicately balanced. While others tend to create bone-dry champagne from taut, young fruit vinified in stainless steel and softened with malolactic, Rodez turns the entire concept on its head and ingeniously blends a tremendous depth of old wines vinified and aged in barrel from his wonderfully opulent Ambonnay fruit, kissing it with just the lightest touch of malolactic. Already a magnificent eight years of age on release, the purity he achieves is game-changing, utilising the lively energy and vibrant lemon fruit and citrus zest freshness of Ambonnay, tactically deploying the honey, brioche and almond-nougat complexity of barrel vinification and a deep stock of reserves to create internal harmony without any need for dosage. It's a captivating fanfare of yellow and red fruit succulence, culminating in a very long finish, drawn out by the inimitable salty mineral signature of Ambonnay. For the record, you'd never guess it had no dosage. And I don't think I've ever said that before.

ERIC RODEZ CUVÉE DES GRANDS VINTAGES AMBONNAY GRAND CRU BRUT NV $$$

96 points • 2009 BASE VINTAGE • TASTED IN CHAMPAGNE

30% chardonnay, 70% pinot; 100% Ambonnay from at least 12 vineyards; average vine age 41 years; 26% 2009, 28% 2008, 14% 2006, 11% 2005, 10% 2004, 11% 2002; no malolactic fermentation; 100% vinified in barrels; 3g/L dosage; before champagne it is a wine of Champagne

An assemblage of the fruits of the first pressings of the best parcels across many years, this is a cuvée built on a mind-blowing roll-call of vintages, not only in that its youngest season is already nine years of age on release, but that it plunders many of the great harvests of two decades, in proportions that must be unparalleled in Champagne, except perhaps in Krug itself, at three times the price. Throbbing with a full straw hue, this is a wonderfully exotic release that basks in succulent peach juice, layered with honey and butter cake, heaped with dried fruits and mixed spice. Its deep, layered complexity matches the recipe, countering the grand intensity of Ambonnay pinot noir with the finesse of chardonnay and the tension of malic acidity, bringing definition and poise to its generous exuberance, thanks to balanced acidity and fine chalk minerality that proclaims distinguished terroirs tapped by great old vines. It all culminates in a grand crescendo of pristine line and length. The harmony on show in this melody is a masterpiece of Rodez's talent as a composer.

Eric Rodez Les Fournettes Ambonnay Pinot Noir 2009 $$$$

96 points • Tasted in Champagne

100% Ambonnay pinot noir; single-vineyard Les Fournettes; south-east facing with 65cm of soil before the chalk; average vine age 18 years; 100% vinified in oak barrels; no malolactic fermentation; 2g/L dosage

An exciting newcomer to Rodez's splendid hall of single-site cuvées, this release is the ultimate paradox, amplified four-fold by pinot noir from a strong grand cru in a powerful season fermented in barrels, yet toned masterfully and euphorically by malic acidity and low dosage. Rippling with the depth and magnitude of this looming season, this is a cuvée of captivating complexity and full straw hue that spans all manner of citrus and stone fruits, plum liqueur, spice, honey, even nuances of liquorice. Its dark fruit depth is something to behold, yet never heavy or tired, well supported by balanced acidity and most of all by the prominent chalk of this great site. An outstanding juxtaposition of the power and poise of Ambonnay, this is a gloriously main-course-ready cuvée.

Eric Rodez Les Beurys & Les Secs Ambonnay Pinot Noir 2008 $$$$

96 points • Tasted in Champagne

100% Ambonnay pinot noir, 95% Les Beurys, 5% Les Secs; east and south-east exposures; 30–35cm of soil before chalk; average vine age 38 years; just one press load of 4000kg; 100% vinified in oak barrels; no malolactic fermentation; 2g/L dosage

The energising play of 2008 in the powerful style of Ambonnay pinot noir serves to create a blanc de noirs of ravishing splendour. A generous medium to full straw hue and spectacular depth of black fruits and spice are honed exactingly by focused acidity and the rippling, dancing presence of prominent Ambonnay chalk minerality. It is understated and coiled by Rodez standards, projecting fantastic energy and brilliant line and length that promise long-enduring potential, although it's delightfully enticing even in its youthful state a few months prior to release. Benchmark.

Eric Rodez Empreinte de Terroir Pinot Noir Brut 2006 $$$$

93 points • Tasted in Champagne

100% Ambonnay pinot noir from six vineyards; average vine age 42 years; 100% vinified in oak barrels; no malolactic fermentation; to be renamed Empreinte Noir from 2007 onwards; 2.5g/L dosage

Power and complexity attain new heights in this full straw-gold cuvée, as a rich season in Ambonnay is amplified by full barrel fermentation and more than a decade on lees. Dried fruits, orange and lemon zest and prominent spice of all kinds flow rich, luscious and honeyed, just beginning to dry out on the finish, suggesting that it is now at the close of its life. Nonetheless, it upholds great persistence, charged by malic acidity and refreshing, fine chalk minerality.

Eric Rodez Empreinte de Terroir Pinot Noir 2005 $$$$

90 points • Tasted in Champagne

100% Ambonnay pinot noir from five vineyards; average vine age 38 years; 100% vinified in oak barrels; no malolactic fermentation; 2.5g/L dosage

The ripe and firmly structured 2005 season has not well upheld the test of time. Powerful citrus and stone fruits are layered with the roast nuts, honey and fruit mince spice of maturity, with the firm grip of 2005 bringing structure to its generosity. Burnt orange and honey define a style beginning to tire, showing some oxidative dryness on the close.

FLEURY

(Floo-ree)

6/10

43 GRANDE RUE 10250 COURTERON
www.champagne-fleury.fr

CHAMPAGNE
FLEURY
En biodynamie depuis 1989

Jean-Pierre Fleury pioneered biodynamic viticulture in Champagne, tending his vines organically since 1970 and biodynamically since 1989. His family have been growers in the village of Couteron in the south of the Côte des Bar since 1895, and his grandfather was selling his own champagnes as early as the 1930s. Since 2004, the estate has been under the keen eye of Jean-Pierre's son, Jean-Sébastien, a trail-blazer who brings a sense of flair and daring no less courageous than his father's, constantly trialling new and at times brave techniques in the vineyard and winery. His wines encapsulate the character and expression of Côte des Bar fruit with carefully balanced oak, limited dosage and malolactic fermentation tweaked to draw out the personality of each cuvée. These value-for-money champagnes rightfully rank among the most respected in the Aube.

PIONEERING BIODYNAMICS

Jean-Pierre Fleury was regarded by some as a 'crazy hippie' when he started composting and tilling in 1970. 'When my father first talked about biodynamics, it was like something from a different planet!' Jean-Sébastien recalls.

Jean-Pierre's first trial in 1976 was a catastrophe, producing no grapes at all, due to excessive silicon sprays supposed to control mildew. It was not until 1989 that he trialled biodynamics again, and the whole estate was certified in 1992.

Within three years, two other growers in the village followed. Fleury now sources from 15 hectares of its own vines across 10 different parcels and eight hectares from these two neighbours, all biodynamically certified. Characteristic of the area, the estate is planted to a vast majority of pinot noir and a little chardonnay, pinot blanc and pinot gris.

'Our philosophy is to have healthy grapes,' emphasises Jean-Sébastien. Celebrating 30 years of biodynamics in 2019, they have found biodynamics delivers more consistent crops. 'In seasons when others have low yields, we have higher volumes, and when they have high volumes, ours are medium.' Aiming for lower yields is not Fleury's philosophy.

'We try to take what the vines can bring,' Jean-Sébastien explains, adding that every vineyard brings something different each year, and he needs to be very careful to manage each parcel individually to maintain balance. In 30 years of biodynamics, Fleury was able to reach the yield set for the appellation in every year but three (2003, 2007 and 2012).

A biodynamic approach in Champagne's wild climate can be a nail-biting affair, and it's not getting any easier. The year 2012 was 'a good year for us to learn some new things, and we hope we won't have another year like it!' Jean-Sébastien bemoans. Winter brought frosts of -15°C for two weeks straight, followed by two spring frosts, rain disrupting flowering, and outbreaks of mildew, followed by two singeing summer days of 38°C and 41°C. 'The worst conditions for a good harvest,' he says.

Fleury continues to learn more from its biodynamic approach and the dividends it pays in Champagne's warming climate. Recent comparisons between organic, biodynamic and traditional viticulture in the Côte des Bar have found Fleury to achieve 1g more acidity at harvest in regular years, and 2.5g more in hot years. 'Acidity is very important to us,' Jean-Sébastien emphasises. 'Before we embarked on biodynamics, our malolactic fermentation was inconsistent, but high acidities now make it more consistent.' Malolactic fermentation is employed strategically, according to the acidity of each parcel.

Fleury has discovered that the roots of its vines have plunged deeper into the chalk following biodynamic conversion. With topsoil depths of between 40 centimetres and 1.5 metres, such deep roots are important for tapping into the mineral expression of each site. Prior to full conversion, comparisons were made between biodynamic and traditional viticulture and Jean-Sébastien recalls many tasters enquiring as to the percentage of chardonnay in blanc de noirs, such was the mineral expression of biodynamic parcels.

Fleury's inquisitive approach remains strong. 'We are always experimenting!' Jean-Sébastien announces, with wide eyes. Fleury is part of a group of biodynamic producers trialling alternatives to spraying copper sulphate as a fungicide, including essential oils and lower doses of new copper sprays. Others are trialling preparations based on local plant concoctions, harvesting on particular days of the biodynamic calendar, even playing different music to the vines. Fleury's own trials are somewhat less far-fetched, employing a horse to cultivate the soil to determine whether or not there is a reduction in soil compaction, replanting using a massal selection of a variety of clones from biodynamic producers, and testing different grafting techniques.

BIODYNAMIC WINEMAKING

In the winery, Fleury has sought ways to introduce the principles of biodynamics in vinification. Its small, gravity-fed winery is intelligently constructed to follow the slope of the hill, with the press house at the top, cuverie directly underneath, and barrels suspended on high frames on the lowest level. Jean-Sébastien's aim is to use no pumps, but admits that this is complicated. Two vertical presses were installed in 1990 and an automatic Coquard press in 2004. 'The pressing makes 50% of the quality,' claims Jean-Sébastien, who loves the delicacy of the new press for reducing colour pick-up and oxidation.

Reducing oxidation is a key priority for the house, which hasn't added sulphur as a preservative since 2008. 'In 2011 we made a half press with sulphur and half without and found that adding sulphur removed purity and expression of flavour,' Jean-Sébastien explains. 'We only adjust sulphur levels at disgorgement, because this is crucial for the wine to travel. I hope, touch wood, that we will not have a bad experience!' So far, so good. His no-sulphur Sonate No 9 cuvée showed pristine freshness in Australia nine months after disgorgement.

Fleury vinifies all parcels separately and, since 1997, 10% of production has been fermented and aged in oak barrels, mostly destined for vintage and reserve wines. To downplay oak flavour, barrels are purchased after three or four uses and maintained for 10–15 years. Reserve wines are stored in an impressive line of 6000-litre foudres. Jean-Sébastien is keen to trial different fermentation vessels, and hopes to buy egg fermenters and concrete tanks this year to assess their effect.

Jean-Pierre Fleury retired recently, leaving the estate in the capable hands of Jean-Sébastien, who takes charge of winemaking, his brother Benoît in the vineyards and sister Morgane, who oversees exports and marketing. Their imperative is to uphold the style of Fleury's existing cuvées, while actively pursuing the introduction of new labels, including a 100% oak-fermented pinot blanc, a low-sulphur, zero-dosage pinot noir and a distinctive extra brut pinot noir. The estate has doubled production to a total of 200,000 bottles in recent years, and is working to increase its export markets.

While disgorgement dates are printed on every bottle, they're not always easy to read. Labelling dates are printed much more clearly. Labelling generally occurs one to six months after disgorgement.

'Biodynamics explains how we can make our wines unique, but ultimately it's about the wine,' Jean-Sébastien emphasises. 'We'd like to be considered not only because our wines are organic or biodynamic, but because we have good grapes and make good wines.'

The champagnes of Fleury certainly live up to this aspiration and are worth discovering for their noble philosophy and, more importantly, for the character they bring at an affordable price.

Jean-Sébastien Fleury

FLEURY BdN BLANC DE NOIRS BRUT NV $$

94 points • 2013 BASE VINTAGE • DISGORGED MAY 2018 • TASTED IN AUSTRALIA
92 points • DISGORGED MAY 2017 • TASTED IN AUSTRALIA

100% pinot; 43% 2012 reserves; vinified in enamelled tanks; 26% reserve wines vinified in oak tuns and aged in 60hL oak foudres; vines 20-25 years of age; full malolactic fermentation; 5.5g/L dosage; cork

Fleury's is a thrilling blanc de noirs that consistently captures the tension between the generous succulence and the poised energy of pinot noir. This year it's crunchier and fresher than ever, and yet every bit as juicy and expressive. Pretty red cherry, raspberry and strawberry fruits are energised by a refreshing backbone of tangy lemon and morello cherry acidity and fine, soft, Aube chalk mineral texture. It glides effortlessly through fields of crunchy strawberries and orchards of tangy white cherries on a long, even and refreshing finish nuanced with pink pepper and hints of fruit mince spice. Dosage is lower than ever, and it's all the better for it. Drink it young and vibrant, as older disgorgements are beginning to dry out on the finish. Don't discount the Aube – this cuvée again walks all over many Marne blanc de noirs this year.

FLEURY RS ROSÉ DE SAIGNÉE BRUT NV $$$

94 points • DISGORGED JANUARY 2017 • TASTED IN AUSTRALIA

100% pinot; 20-year-old vines; fermented in enamelled tanks; full malolactic fermentation; 5.3g/L dosage; cork

Fleury's Rosé de Saignée is a wonderful tribute to the personality of Côte des Bar pinot noir, with its detail and character heightened through skin contact. Enticing layers of morello cherries, wild strawberries and even blackberries and tomatoes are structured with tangy acidity and well-handled, fine-grained tannins. Lees age has brought creamy structure that unites its elements seamlessly. Particularly sensitive in clear glass, I have encountered some bottles exhibiting the cabbagey hydrogen sulphide grubbiness of lightstruck degradation. As always, keep it in the dark.

FLEURY CÉPAGES BLANCS EXTRA BRUT 2009 $$

94 points • DISGORGED DECEMBER 2017 • TASTED IN AUSTRALIA

94% chardonnay, 6% pinot blanc; vines 20 years of age; 66% vinified in oak barrels and 34% in enamelled tanks; full malolactic; 2.7g/L dosage; cork

Fleury captures a tension, focus and purity in its chardonnay that belies nine years of age, the warm 2009 season and majority fermentation in barrels. It upholds a brightness to its medium straw hue and a core of crunchy golden delicious apple, grapefruit and lemon. The subtle spice and cohesive texture of barrel fermentation unite with the brioche of lees age, energising and propelling its yellow fruits, which ever remain the hero. It concludes long and strong, with unashamed acidity and structure making for a cuvée that is not for the uninitiated, though promising great things over the next decade and beyond. Wait at least another five years. Patience.

FLEURY BOLÉRO EXTRA BRUT 2006 $$$

93 points • DISGORGED APRIL 2018 • TASTED IN AUSTRALIA

100% pinot; 50% fermented in oak barrels and 50% in enamelled tanks; tiraged under cork; vines 25 years of age; full malolactic; 2.6g/L dosage; cork

The full exuberance of Aube pinot noir is on parade here, with the tension and energy to uphold its poise and stature. A full straw hue with a blush tint proclaims both grand fruit depth and partial fermentation in oak barrels. Its fruit presence is all-conquering, exploding with black cherries, satsuma plums, even prunes. Oak sets a backdrop of roast nuts and high-cocoa dark chocolate, which jostles for supremacy a little with the fruit. The latter wins out in the end, lingering rich and long amidst a well-focused and lingering line of tangy acidity and fine Côte des Bar minerality.

FRANCK BONVILLE

(Fronk Bon-vee)

(6/10)

9 RUE PASTEUR 51190 AVIZE
www.champagne-franck-bonville.com

CHAMPAGNE

FRANCK BONVILLE

GRAND CRU

À AVIZE

As demand for the greatest Côtes des Blancs grand crus continues to spiral, the privilege of substantial, well-placed holdings cannot be overstated. Gilles and Ingrid Bonville and their son Olivier are in command of 20 glorious hectares of prime grand cru turf, largely in Avize, with old vines on the slope of Oger and a little in Le Mesnil-sur-Oger and Cramant. Tended and vinified with precision, their polished blanc de blancs contrast the tension and brilliance of Avize with the generosity and exoticism of Oger.

The Bonville family has been growing grapes on the Côte des Blancs for more than a century, and bottling their own champagnes since 1947. Their old 1936 press still stands in pride of place on display in their house in Avize, purchased by Olivier's grandfather, Alfred Bonville, in 1937, complete with press, oak casks and five levels of glorious nineteenth-century chalk cellars.

Olivier Bonville is the third generation of his family to make champagnes in Avize, tending his 77 plots sustainably since 2011, with High Environmental Value certification granted in 2016. Herbicides and pesticides have been eliminated, half of the vineyards are now ploughed and one-quarter are planted with grasses in the mid-rows.

To preserve aromatic freshness, slow fermentation takes place in climate-controlled, stainless steel vats, with the exception of the family's flagship from old vines in Oger, fermented in oak barrels sourced from Meursault. Some reserves are also barrel fermented for roundness to counter the tension of Avize.

Chardonnay is the theme of these tense, powerful champagnes, with red grapes only for rosé sourced from the great estate of Paul Déthune in Ambonnay. A modest production of 140-150,000 bottles leaves some excess to sell to top houses like Deutz.

The portfolio has grown to 10 cuvées, with the addition of three distinctive monocru cuvées since the 2012 vintage. All details are printed on back labels.

Avize, summer 2018

FRANCK BONVILLE GRAND CRU BLANC DE BLANCS BRUT NV $$

91 points • 2016 BASE VINTAGE • DISGORGED JULY 2018 • TASTED IN CHAMPAGNE

100% chardonnay; 70% Avize and 30% Oger; 30% 2015 reserves and a little 2009 from barrels; 9.17g/L dosage

A beautiful expression of the tension and precision of Avize, bolstered with the generosity and exoticism of Oger. Apple, grapefruit, lemon and fragrant pink lady apple lead out, with lees age and a touch of barrel-fermented reserves contributing notes of nougat and vanilla that soften and build the finish. A cuvée of body and presence, marked with slightly firm phenolic texture on the finish. Dosage is adjusted each year to maintain consistency of the style, usually 6–7g/L, making 9.17g/L quite high, rounding out its phenolic grip.

FRANCK BONVILLE GRAND CRU ROSÉ NV $$$

93 points • 2015 BASE VINTAGE • DISGORGED JUNE 2018 • TASTED IN CHAMPAGNE

90% Avize chardonnay, 10% Ambonnay pinot red wine made by Paul Déthune; 25% 2014 reserves; 6.67g/L dosage

Ambonnay shares a similar chalky terroir to Avize, hence the choice of red wine for this cuvée. The two harmonise evenly and seamlessly in a pretty medium-salmon hue. The aspiration here is a light style and it meets the brief in a wonderful array of red cherries, wild strawberries, mixed spice and lifted hints of rose petal. Acidity and dosage meld seamlessly on a long finish that glides very long and harmonious with the signature, fine chalk minerality of Avize and the, gentle, fine tannin grip of Ambonnay. A rosé of elegance and salt mineral precision.

Franck Bonville Prestige Blanc de Blancs Grand Cru Brut NV $$$

94 points • 2014 base vintage • Disgorged July 2018 • Tasted in Champagne

100% Avize chardonnay; 50% 2013 reserves; aged 3.5 years on lees; 6.67g/L dosage; 25–30,000 bottles

The second wine of the house after Grand Cru Blanc de Blancs Brut is conceived in the cuverie after fermentation, from tanks that show the greatest maturity. It's a cuvée of exuberant complexity that rejoices in the multi-layered panoply of flavours and textures that build with lees age. Beautiful notes of vanilla nougat, brioche and subtle spice abound, while upholding the lemon, apple and grapefruit purity of Avize chardonnay. It concludes with beautifully creamy texture that melds eloquently with the fine salt minerality of the village. A cuvée of polish and precision, representing a delightfully enticing expression of this great cru.

Franck Bonville Grand Cru Extra Brut Blanc de Blancs Vintage 2012 $$

93 points • Disgorged July 2018 • Tasted in Champagne

100% Avize chardonnay; aged 5 years on lees; 2.5g/L dosage

A powerful and exotic Avize, built with layers of apple and pear, even star fruit exoticism, fragranced with chamomile and linden blossom. A hint of green olive is not out of place in the Côte des Blancs, if unexpected in such a youthful cuvée. Concentration and ripeness contrast the racy acidity and pronounced chalk mineral signature of this fabled village, making for a characterful and bold Avize of great length and room-filling presence.

Franck Bonville Grand Cru Brut Blanc de Blancs Vintage 2012 $$

91 points • Disgorged January 2017 and April 2018 • Tasted in Champagne and Australia

As above, with 6.67g/L dosage; cork

A profound statement of the impact of more dosage and greater duration of time on cork, this cuvée is a stark contrast with the Extra Brut edition. The effect is an amplification of its power and development to surprising levels for a young expression of a lively vintage in Avize. Boasting a full straw-yellow hue, this is a cuvée that unites the brioche, buttered toast and even dark honey and mixed spice of four years lees age with the apple, pear, lemon drops and grapefruit of Avize. The salty minerality of the village unites with gentle phenolic grip and creamy lees texture on a finish of good persistence. A vintage to drink right away. One bottle opened by the house was corked.

Franck Bonville Grand Cru Blanc de Blancs Pur Oger 2012 $$$

93 points • Disgorged April 2018 • Tasted in Champagne

100% chardonnay from two plots in Oger, Les Noyerots and Les Rumigny; co-pressed; tank fermented; aged 5.5 years on lees under cork; hand disgorged; 2g/L dosage; 2500 bottles

All the flamboyant power of Oger is on grand parade here, embracing a universe of cumquat, grapefruit, succulent white peach and even fig and fruit mince spice, bolstered by all the complexity and texture of long age on cork, swimming with vanilla custard, butter and nougat. Its texture is at once creamy and buttery, yet with a subtle phenolic bite of cork tannin that amplifies the grainy minerality of Oger, making for some bitterness on the finish. Its generosity holds it true, concluding very long and complex.

FRANCK BONVILLE GRAND CRU BLANC DE BLANCS PUR AVIZE 2012 $$$

93 points • TASTED IN CHAMPAGNE

100% chardonnay from three plots, Les Avats, Les Maladries and l'Argentière, very close to the village on the best chalk in the heart of the terroir; co-pressed; aged on lees under cork; 2g/L dosage

A powerful Avize in ripeness, stature and structure, bursting with baked apple, orange and lemon fruit and the layered complexity of lees age in biscuit, custard and spice. Aged on lees under cork, the phenolic bitterness and fine tannin grip of cork tannins jostles a little with the pronounced chalk minerality of Avize.

FRANCK BONVILLE GRAND CRU BLANC DE BLANCS PUR MESNIL 2012 $$$

94 points • TASTED IN CHAMPAGNE

100% chardonnay from three plots, in a triangle, one above, one to the left and one to the right of the village; co-pressed; aged on lees under cork; 2g/L dosage

The confidence and energy of Le Mesnil makes for the most complete and the most exciting of Bonville's inaugural monocru cuvées, a wine of tension and poise that contrast with the complexity of lees age under cork. Lemon and apple fruit of precision and focus are underlined by vanilla and brioche. Fine salty minerality lingers very long, accented by the fine phenolic tannin grip and creamy texture of cork age, culminating in a finish of great line, length and freshness.

FRANCK BONVILLE CUVÉE LES BELLES VOYES GRAND CRU BLANC DE BLANCS 2012 $$$$

92 points • DISGORGED MAY 2018 • TASTED IN CHAMPAGNE

100% Oger chardonnay from a single vineyard of vines over 60 years of age, always ranking among the top three sites of the house for maturity; vinified in oak barrels; aged on lees under cork; hand riddled; 2.5g/L dosage

Full in colour and in amplitude, this is cuvée at the far extreme of Côte des Blancs concentration, exploding with the full, voluptuous, exotic presence of Oger and the creamy texture and biscuity complexity of barrel fermentation. It's intensely spicy, full bodied and firm in structure, uniting dry tannin grip with the stony minerality of Oger.

FRANCK BONVILLE 1976

96 points • TASTED IN CHAMPAGNE

100% chardonnay

A grand old bottle from deep in Bonville's chalk cellar under Avize, this is a cuvée in fabulous condition, proclaiming the vast longevity of one of the world's most enduring sparkling grand crus. The passage of time has evolved its hue to full copper, while piling on layers of green olive, cedar, glacé fruit and the inviting aromas of old hearth. Intensely umami, it's sustained by a frame of inimitable Avize chalk minerality. Its ability to sustain fruit intensity for more than four decades is truly astonishing, upholding sensational persistence of honey and apricot.

GARDET

(Gar-day)

---

13 Rue Georges Legros 51500 Chigny-les-Roses
www.champagne-gardet.com

CHAMPAGNE
GARDET

Depuis 1895

The house of Gardet was established in Épernay in 1895 by Charles Gardet, sold to Mercier in 1920 and refounded by Charles' nephew Georges Gardet in Chigny-les-Roses in 1930. Owned by the Prieur family since 2009, the house tends just five hectares of its own, mostly in Chigny and neighbouring Ludes, supplemented substantially by some 95 hectares of grower vines, largely in the Montagne de Reims, Vallée de la Marne, Côte des Blancs and the Aube. With production and cellars in Chigny, the house style is built on pinot noir from the Montagne de Reims, aged long on lees. Gardet itself comprises just 400,000 bottles of a total production of around 1 million, the remainder declassified to second labels and buyer's-own brands. Most cuvées are fermented in stainless steel vats, with a deep reserve for Brut Réserve aged in large oak foudres, and some dosage liqueurs in oak barrels. Malolactic fermentation is encouraged, except in Prestige Charles Gardet. The first two digits of the lot code laser-etched on the bottle are the base vintage, and the last three digits are the week and year of disgorgement. For instance, 09S1277K denotes the 2009 base vintage, disgorged in the 27th week of 2017.

GARDET BRUT TRADITION NV $$

87 points • 2014 BASE VINTAGE • DISGORGED FEBRUARY 2018 • TASTED IN AUSTRALIA
89 points • 2013 BASE VINTAGE • DISGORGED OCTOBER 2017 • TASTED IN AUSTRALIA

10% chardonnay, 45% pinot, 45% meunier; Montagne de Reims, Vallée de la Marne, Côte des Blancs, Côte des Bar; 40% reserves back to 2008; aged 24–36 months on lees; fermented and matured in stainless steel tanks; malolactic fermentation encouraged; 8g/L dosage; cork; the majority of production of the house

A fresh, lively and precocious cuvée in a soft, rounded, early-drinking guise that celebrates the generosity and spicy red apple and berry fruits of pinot and meunier and the biscuity, nutty complexity of three years lees age. It's marked by earthy, mushroomy notes of imperfect fruit, concluding short, a little skinny, and dried out by dusty tannins and phenolic bite.

Chigny-les-Roses, harvest 2014

GARDET BRUT RÉSERVE NV $$

88 points • 2009 BASE VINTAGE • DISGORGED DECEMBER 2016 AND JULY 2017 • TASTED IN AUSTRALIA

33% chardonnay, 33% pinot, 33% meunier from Montagne de Reims (Trépail, Vaudemange, Ludes), Vallée de la Marne (Hautvillers, Mareuil-sur-Aÿ, Avenay-Val-d'Or) and Côte des Blancs (Cuis); 25% reserve solera aged in 40hL 50-year-old and 25hL 100-year-old foudres, dating from the early 1990s and 75% renewed every year, comprising 18.75% 2008, 4.69% 2007, 1.17% 2006, etc; aged 6–7 years on lees; 6g/L dosage; cork

Gardet's Brut Réserve is a very different proposition to its Brut Tradition, a much older blend and built on very deep reserves. Very much in its secondary spectrum, this is a cuvée characterised by bubblegum, boiled sweets, gingernut biscuits and red cordial. Spicy, toasty, biscuity and faintly earthy notes expresses its age in secondary complexity that looks a little tired and lacking in freshness and energy. Long lees age has built a creamy bead, which contrasts with bitter phenolic bite on the finish.

GARDET BRUT PREMIER CRU BLANC DE NOIRS NV $$

87 points • 100% 2015 • Disgorged September 2018 • Tasted in Australia
90 points • 100% 2014 • Disgorged October 2017 • Tasted in Australia

60% pinot, 40% meunier; 100% from Hautvillers, a blend of different parcels from the bottom of the village to the top, from a single, longstanding grower; no reserves, but not declared as a vintage, as the house doesn't want to focus on it as a vintage wine; fermented and matured 6-8 months in stainless steel tanks; full malolactic fermentation; aged 2.5 years on lees, not 4-5 years as declared on the back label; 8g/L dosage; cork

Released earlier than in the past to enhance freshness, this is a single vintage, single cru and even single grower, though the front label sadly misses the opportunity to declare any of these. It's a fruity and rich style, with a core of red fruits reminiscent of candied cranberries and red apples, layered with spice and the biscuity complexity of age. It showcases the succulent generosity of pinot noir and meunier, well balanced by gentle acidity and soft minerality. The ripe 2015 harvest imposes an overlay of dustiness, quashing fruit purity and lending a graininess to a short finish. The 2014 vintage, by comparison, is a generous, friendly and immediately appealing style.

GARDET EXTRA BRUT MILLÉSIME 2012 $$

90 points • Disgorged July 2017 and September 2018 • Tasted in Australia

30% chardonnay (mostly from Avize), 70% pinot (mostly from Ludes, Ville-Dommange, Mareuil-sur-Aÿ and Hautvillers); aged 5 years on lees; fermented and matured in stainless steel tanks; full malolactic fermentation; aged 4-5 years on lees; 4g/L dosage; cork

Purposely a younger blend to contrast the age of Charles Gardet, the bright purity of 2012 is presented in a style of lemon juice and crunchy red apples, accented with the toasted meringue complexity of four years lees age. The palate is built around a core of spicy red cherry, strawberry and red apple of pinot noir, faithfully reflecting the northern Montagne de Reims and Vallée de la Marne. It's well supported by bright, fresh, northern acidity, marked by a touch of phenolic bite on the close. A style of sweet, ripe fruit focus and gentle salt minerality.

GARDET PRESTIGE CHARLES GARDET MILLÉSIMÉ 2005 $$$

84 points • Disgorged November 2018 • Tasted in Australia

70% chardonnay from Trépail and Cuis, 30% pinot from Aÿ; fermented and aged in stainless steel tanks; no malolactic fermentation; aged 12.5 years on lees; 8g/L dosage; cork

The challenge of uneven ripeness in 2005 inflicted green capsicum, tinned pea and nasturtium characters, particularly pronounced in this cuvée. Such is their dominance that little other fruit definition is apparent. Firm malic acidity and the coarse, grainy phenolics of 2005 make for a rustic structure.

GARDET PRESTIGE CHARLES GARDET BRUT MILLÉSIME 2004 $$$

89 points • DISGORGED DECEMBER 2017 • TASTED IN AUSTRALIA

70% chardonnay from the Côte des Blancs, 30% pinot from the Montagne de Reims; fermented and aged in stainless steel tanks; no malolactic fermentation; aged 12.5 years on lees; 9g/L dosage; DIAM

A powerful and spicy style of oxidative development apparent in notes of blood orange, toasted marshmallow, brioche and honey. It shows good length and fine, salty chalk mineral structure, though looks tired on the finish.

GARDET PRESTIGE CHARLES GARDET ROSÉ DE SAIGNÉE MILLÉSIMÉ 2011 $$$

86 points • DISGORGED SEPTEMBER 2018 • TASTED IN AUSTRALIA

50% pinot, 50% meunier from Chigny-les-Roses and Taissy; partial maceration (saignée), fermented and matured in stainless steel tanks; malolactic fermentation encouraged; aged 6.5 years on lees; 8g/L dosage; DIAM

A full crimson hue announces a rosé of powerful red-fruit presence, filled with pomegranate, cranberry and red apple skins. It's marked by a smoky, savoury dominance reminiscent of smoked paprika, campari and orange bitters, perhaps a consequence of impure and underripe fruit or stalk influence in the saignée in this challenging season? This quashes fruit vibrancy and renders the finish firm, phenolic and grainy.

GARDET PRESTIGE CHARLES GARDET ROSÉ DE SAIGNÉE MILLÉSIME BRUT 2008 $$$

89 points • DISGORGED SEPTEMBER 2017 • TASTED IN AUSTRALIA

50% pinot, 50% meunier; 100% Chigny-les-Roses; 9g/L dosage; DIAM

A characterful Rose de Saignée energised by the vibrant 2008 season in characters of rose hip, pomegranate, strawberries, pink pepper and red apple. It's sadly let down by savoury notes of charcuterie and earth, which diminish purity on the finish.

GARDET 120 ANNIVERSARY LIMITED EDITION NV $$$$

86 points • 2011 BASE VINTAGE • TASTED IN AUSTRALIA

Approximately 70% chardonnay, 30% pinot; 15% reserves from 11 vintages in magnums: 1943, 1947, 1959, 1988, 1995, 1996, 1997, 1998, 2000, 2001 and 2002, some disgorged and the younger magnums undisgorged; 2g/L dosage; cork; 12,000 bottles

In celebration of the 120th anniversary of Gardet in 2015, a special cuvée was conceived, not in an attempt to make the best wine from the best vintages, but rather to reflect the work of the house through different times. The precise blend is unknown, since the exact blend of the older wines is uncertain and may contain a little meunier. The choice of the challenging 2011 harvest for such a cuvée is confounding. The green astringency of the season makes for a herbal and sappy style of hard underripeness, transposed against the mature-tobacco complexity of deep reserves. Why subject such old reserves to such a poor harvest?

GASTON CHIQUET

(Gas-toh Shi-khe)

5/10

912 Avenue du Général Leclerc 51530 Dizy
www.gastonchiquet.com

CHAMPAGNE Gaston Chiquet
PROPRIÉTAIRE-RÉCOLTANT

'The point is to make "vin de terroir",' emphasises the young, eighth-generation Dizy grower Nicolas Chiquet. 'We are lucky to have some very nice vineyard locations, so our goal is to preserve the character of the fruit.' His assessment of the family's 23 hectares is politely modest. These are well-established vineyards on the privileged mid-slopes of Dizy, Hautvillers, Aÿ (including an impressive five hectares of chardonnay), Mareuil-sur-Aÿ, as well as in the Vallée de l'Ardre, close to Reims. With careful attention to sustainable viticulture, meticulous fruit handling and sensitive vinification, Nicolas and his brother Antoine's 'vin de terroir' ambition is brought to life in champagnes of fruit purity and fine, chalky minerality that represent impressive value for money.

The Chiquets have tended vines since 1746 and were among Champagne's first growers to make their own wines in 1919. The property in Dizy was purchased by the brothers' grandfather, Gaston, in 1935, with a deep and extensive cellar, more than sufficient for a production of just 150,000 bottles, even in the high-yielding 2018 harvest. This is more than conservative, from a vineyard resource that could produce 230,000 bottles even in an average season.

In villages famed for pinot noir, Gaston Chiquet is unusual in its 50% holdings of chardonnay and 30% of meunier. 'We speak well of the quality of meunier, even though it does not have the finesse to age like chardonnay or pinot noir. It provides roundness in the mouth for our non-vintage wines,' Nicolas Chiquet explains.

Sustainable viticulture is practised, with minimal use of chemicals, elimination of herbicides, hormones for sexual confusion in place of insecticides, and up to half of the vineyards ploughed and planted to grasses in the mid-rows. The estate was certified as High Environmental Value in 2015.

'Terroir is the most important thing and we have to be very humble in our approach,' suggests Chiquet, who continuously adapts his vinification in response to the season. 'We want to work more on our vineyards than our wine, making "vin de terroir" rather than adding oxygen through vinification in oak.' He compares it to cooking.

'When you have good produce you have very little to do and it is perfect! This is why we have very natural winemaking processes. We do not want to change our fruit. We are very careful to adapt our vinification to keep the freshness in the juice, as we have a lot of power in our fruit.'

Vinification begins with one of the most sophisticated presses in Champagne, extracting the purest juice, though the old press is still sometimes used. 'The new press has had little influence, but how it's controlled is the key,' Chiquet says. Each of 35 different parcels is vinified separately in small, temperature-controlled stainless steel tanks, not oak barrels. 'Our terroirs can tend towards oxidation, so we phased out barrels since the 1940s,'

Chiquet explains. To further protect against oxidation, wines are only held in tank for three or four months, with bottle ageing preferred. Malolactic fermentation is carried out on all parcels, and low dosages of typically 8g/L are used.

To preserve fruit character and reduce oxidation, DIAM closures have been used on every cuvée since 2009. 'The crown caps we use in the cellars are the best closures, but we can't sell our wines with them,' he says. 'DIAMs are very reliable, with a consistent level of oxygen ingress and no cork taint.' Every bottle is labelled with its disgorgement date. 'This is very important to us. We have educated our customers and they know not to open a bottle soon after it has been disgorged.' An informative website provides detailed data sheets on every cuvée.

In 2014, Antoine's daughter, Marion, was employed as chef de cave. 'She's well travelled and it's excellent to have the involvement of the wider family,' says Nicolas.

In recognition of the growth of oenotourism, in 2018 the family opened a new tasting room on the main street in Dizy, open for visits six days a week, even without an appointment. A refreshing initiative in a region whose doors are all too often closed to visitors.

Along with their cousins around the corner at Jacquesson, the Chiquets make the finest champagnes of Dizy. True 'vin de terroir'.

The house of Gaston Chiquet in Dizy

GASTON CHIQUET TRADITION PREMIER CRU BRUT NV $$

91 points • 2013 BASE VINTAGE • DISGORGED JULY 2018 • TASTED IN CHAMPAGNE

35% chardonnay, 25% pinot noir, 40% meunier; 10% reserves dating from 2009; 8g/L dosage

The same blend since the brothers' grandfather created the brand, hence the name. The lively 2013 season has made for an accurate Tradition, in which the red fruits and citrus crunch of Dizy take the lead in a clean and fruity style of balanced integrity. Age has built gentle texture and gingernut biscuit, honey and spice complexity. Well-integrated dosage melds with vibrant acidity on an even finish.

GASTON CHIQUET ROSÉ PREMIER CRU BRUT NV $$

92 points • 2014 BASE VINTAGE • DISGORGED MARCH 2018 • TASTED IN CHAMPAGNE

35% chardonnay, 25% pinot noir, 40% meunier; Brut Tradition with red wine in place of reserves; red wine of pinot noir and meunier, 7% from 2009 and 7% from 2013; 9g/L dosage

The clean, fruity integrity of Gaston Chiquet's Tradition makes a cracking base for rosé. With a pretty medium salmon-copper hue, this is a release that captures the body, presence, character and complexity of Dizy. Crunchy red apple and succulent strawberry fruit is backed by subtle layers of mixed spice. Finely structured salt minerality melds evenly with fine tannins, culminating in a finish in which ripe yet bright acidity finds harmonious balance with understated dosage. The result is friendly, refreshing and delightful.

Gaston Chiquet Blanc de Blancs D'Aÿ Grand Cru Brut 2014 $$

93 points • Disgorged June 2018 • Tasted in Champagne

100% Aÿ chardonnay from lieux-dits Vauzelles and Haut Crohauts; aged 3 years on lees; 8g/L dosage

Gaston Chiquet was among the first to plant chardonnay in Aÿ in 1935, and today claims five hectares of chardonnay and the only blanc de blancs in the village, a blend made by Nicolas' father and grandfather since 1955. It's always been a vintage wine, though traditionally labelled non-vintage, since the aspiration was always to showcase the character of chardonnay in Aÿ, highlighting the terroir rather than the year. It's great to see it now celebrating its vintage distinctiveness for the first time. To make 30,000 bottles, sufficient chardonnay is harvested to make double this capacity, with only the best parcels making the cut. Holding more acidity and freshness than pinot and meunier, chardonnay is planted on sunny, south-west exposed slopes in Aÿ. The body, breadth and succulence of the village unites with the tension of chardonnay and the salty minerality of its terroir, layered with mixed spice, fig and the ginger-biscuit notes of bottle age, lingering with excellent acid line and mixed spice complexity.

Gaston Chiquet Or Premier Cru Brut 2008 $$$

95 points • Disgorged March 2018 • Tasted in Champagne

40% chardonnay from Dizy, 60% pinot noir from Mareuil-sur-Aÿ; 8g/L dosage

Gaston Chiquet sets aside parcels for vintage wines based on their power and ability to age for 10 years without sensitivity to oxygen – criteria very easy to fulfil in the spectacularly enduring 2018 season! They have succeeded resoundingly in capturing a beautiful purity integral to 2008, defining a wine of pretty, medium-straw hue that unites youthful jubilance and the creamy softening complexity of a decade of age. It is the epitome of effortless, with a poise and silkiness of alluring balance that marries the understated red cherries of Mareuil with the lemon citrus of Dizy and the subtle gingernut biscuits and fruit mince spice of age. Its minerality is heightened, salty, fine and energetic, fusing confidently with excellent 2008 acidity that carries the finish with enduring harmony. This is a very classy cuvée that ranks among the greatest hits of Gaston Chiquet, irresistible now, yet with the perseverance to take at least another decade in its confident stride.

Gaston Chiquet Spécial Club Brut 2011 $$$

91 points • Disgorged September 2017 • Tasted in Champagne

70% chardonnay from Aÿ and Dizy, 30% pinot noir from Dizy; aged 5.5 years on lees; 8g/L dosage

The house selects the more elegant parcels for its Spécial Club, providing an enticing contrast to the richness of its other cuvées. The aspiration here is delicacy, long ageing and slow oxidation. Chardonnay is deployed for its citrus and mineral notes, and pinot for its body and persistence. The wines that come forward are naturally more acidic and less fruity, hence the impression of dosage is diminished and it looks much lower than 8g/L. Apple, beurre bosc pear and grapefruit unite in a structured style of medium straw hue and salivating, salty minerality. Fennel notes are reflective of the uneven ripeness of the difficult 2011 season, contributing a little bitterness to its structure and dustiness to the finish. It concludes with good acid tension and persistence, holding the potential to continue to age.

GATINOIS

(Ga-tin-wah)

---

7 RUE MARCEL MAILLY 51160 AŸ
www.champagne-gatinois.com

CHAMPAGNE
GATINOIS
AŸ GRAND CRU

In the elegant reception room of Gatinois in the back streets of Aÿ, alongside a magnificent wine press still standing where it was constructed five generations ago, the Gatinois family tree is proudly displayed, tracing their history in the village back to 1696. Young Louis Cheval-Gatinois is the 12th successive generation to farm seven hectares of the family vineyards, enviably positioned on the majestic slopes of Aÿ. His family has made champagne here since probably the mid-1800s, which must place Gatinois among Champagne's oldest grower-producers. Gatinois' generously coloured champagnes are among the finest in this revered village, resonating with the history of the house and the thundering power of its grand cru slopes, at every moment retaining exceptional definition and freshness.

In the convoluted history of Champagne succession and inheritance, the vineyards of the ancient village of Aÿ have been divided into ever-smaller plots, creating what Louis Cheval-Gatinois describes as 'a mosaic on the hillside'.

Gatinois has been privileged to retain seven hectares that have scarcely changed since the inception of the house, divided into 27 parcels of exclusively south-facing vines. Old vines provide depth and structure, blended with young vines for freshness and vivacity. A wide spread of sites across the full breadth of the village creates complexity 'Some respond better in particular seasons, so we can pick what we want in each vintage,' explains Cheval-Gatinois, who knows his vineyards so well that he can recognise each plot purely on the appearance of the grapes when they arrive at the press house.

Pinot noir comprises some 90% of plantings, with a little less than one hectare of chardonnay to add freshness and endurance to pinot's fleshy structure and aromatic intensity. Fruit is green harvested if appropriate to give low harvests of 65hL/hectare, yielding an annual production of just 50,000 bottles. Less than 10% of the harvest is sold to a few top houses, including Bollinger. Low yields enable Gatinois to pick at high maturity, bringing colour and intensity to its champagnes.

The house employs its own team of pickers, who are instructed to be very selective and, importantly, are paid by the hour and not by the kilogram. Every bad grape is sorted from each basket that is brought to the press.

'The quality of the grapes is the thing that makes our champagnes,' Cheval-Gatinois declares. 'The secret to the colour and style of our champagnes is what we put in our press. My father taught me to be proud of what is in the press before we close it, to be able to pick any grape and have the very best quality.'

Vinification is meticulously hands-on, shared between just three workers in the vineyards and cellars. The house still maintains its manual press. 'People are surprised to see me working with a traditional vertical press, but this is important to ensure that we do not lose any quality,' he explains. 'We have a very humble vinification as we do not want to have too much impact on the taste.' Vinification takes place entirely in small stainless steel tanks, parcel by parcel to preserve detail and purity of grape aromas. 'I produce wines more in an oxidative than a reductive style as I like generous champagnes, but with the freshness imparted by the acidity of Aÿ.' The only barrels in the house are for red wines, and these are very old, so as to produce gentle oxidation without imparting wood characters.

GATINOIS AŸ GRAND CRU BRUT RÉSERVE NV $$

94 points • TASTED IN CHAMPAGNE

20% Aÿ chardonnay, 80% Aÿ pinot noir; aged 3 years on lees; 7g/L dosage

Made in the same manner and from similar parcels as his entry Brut Tradition, and aged on lees for another year, this is purposely a more generous style that Cheval-Gatinois describes as more textural, more velvety and a more comfortable winter cuvée. A full-straw colour unashamedly blush in hue hints at its exuberance, trumpeting the magnificence of Aÿ in gloriously accurate red cherry and strawberry fruit that glides long into a tail defined by the cool, refreshing acidity and fine chalk minerality that is Aÿ. It's a pure expression of Gatinois' mosaic of great sites on this legendary hillside. Brilliant and enthralling, it epitomises the contrast between fruit depth and structural tension that only Aÿ can achieve.

Aÿ, winter 2013

GEOFFROY

(Zhof-wah)

6/10

4 RUE JEANSON 51160 AŸ
www.champagne-geoffroy.com

CHAMPAGNE
GEOFFROY
PROPRIÉTAIRE · RÉCOLTANT · ÉLABORATEUR

'I am a winegrower,' says young, fifth-generation vigneron Jean-Baptiste Geoffroy. 'I need to be in the vineyard, this is my passion.' There is a well-considered sensibility about Geoffroy, and every detail of his work in the vineyard and winery follows a stringent regime, while maintaining practical common sense. With 11 glorious hectares in Cumières, and one in each of the nearby villages of Damery, Hautvillers and two in Fleury-la-Rivière, he is well placed to capture the fruit purity, poise and deep mineral fingerprint of some of the finer premier crus of the Vallée de la Marne. The sustaining presence of malic acidity makes his champagnes particularly long-lived.

The finest grower in Cumières is no longer in Cumières. With winemaking facilities and cellars shared between his grandmother's house, his father's house and a neighbour, when the opportunity came to consolidate in 2008, Jean-Baptiste Geoffroy moved the whole operation 20 minutes (by tractor) down the road to a proud and spacious facility in Aÿ.

'Nothing has changed in the vineyards,' asserts Jean-Baptiste. 'I want to create a champagne of terroir, to achieve the best expression of the soil in the grapes.' To this end, his highest goal in the winery is to maintain freshness in every cuvée. This proved to be a challenge, working from three sites in Cumières, necessitating regular pumping and moving of bottles.

Now he can guarantee that his grapes are on the press less than an hour after they are harvested, in a facility ingeniously designed to do away with pumping altogether. Taking advantage of the hill behind, the harvest is delivered to the press on the third level of the building, and the juice flows by gravity to settling tanks immediately below the press on the second level,

then to fermentation on the first level, and finally to two levels of deep maturation cellars below. In 2012 he purchased a further 500 square metres of storage space in the village, not to increase production, but to relocate bottles to provide space to move his barrels deeper into the cellar, where the temperature is more stable.

Every step of production is geared towards maintaining freshness and vineyard character, which Geoffroy achieves with admirable consistency, even with low use of sulphur dioxide as a preservative. Grapes are sorted in the vineyard and again in the winery when necessary. A traditional press is employed, which he admits is difficult to operate by hand, but worth every effort for quality. Each of 45 different parcels is pressed and vinified separately, and the tailles of each pressing separated and vinified independently.

Ferments rely on wild yeast, but are inoculated if they don't start naturally. To further preserve freshness, malolactic fermentation is avoided (but will occasionally start spontaneously). Fermentation

is conducted variously in the best vessels to facilitate controlled oxidation, generally small enamelled vats for non-vintage wines, and small barrels and large foudres for vintage wines and the best pinot noir parcels, and Geoffroy has shown a preference for 350-litre barrels and recently for 600L demi-muids. Previously using only older barrels from Burgundy and the Loire, he now prefers new barrels and purchased four new foudres in 2015. 'I like to work with barrels with only the memory of my wine,' he explains. 'In the past, when I bought used barrels, I tried to block malolactic, but there was lactic bacteria in the oak, and once you have it, it is hard to block.' He ferments directly in his new oak barrels and is pleased with the results. His wines today exhibit less of the wild ferment and oak flavours and tannins that have at times conflicted with the elegance of his fruit in the past – though his new oak ferments are yet to come through in his cuvées.

Only concentrated grape juice is used for dosage, because he says he couldn't find a good balance using sugar. 'This emphasises the taste of the grapes and the character of the soil,' he says.

Geoffroy generally uses extra brut dosages of less than 5g/L. As he puts it, 'A champagne must always be very fine, elegant and fresh. If you have good ripeness and good practice in the winery you don't need dosage.'

Ripeness is achieved through painstaking attention to every detail in the vineyard. Geoffroy's annual production of 120,000 bottles is sourced exclusively from his own vines, apart from 5% permitted under récoltant-manipulant registration. Pinot rules in this part of the world, and his holdings comprise 42% pinot noir, 34% meunier and 24% chardonnay.

EARTH-FRIENDLY APPROACH

His eco-friendly approach is close to organic, but falls purposely short of the constraints of certification. 'I like to say I am biological, without being biodynamic,' he says. To best express the soil in the grapes, vineyards are ploughed to discourage surface roots and drive the vines deeper into the subsoils. To the same end, several species of natural grasses are cultivated in the mid-rows to provide surface competition. He is currently intro-ducing a horse to plough one vineyard in an attempt to reduce

tractor compaction. Organic fertilisers encourage soil health, and herbicides are avoided. Sulphur and copper sulphate sprays are used where possible, but here he sometimes deviates from a strict organic regime, calling on other chemicals as required.

Geoffroy knows each of his 45 plots intimately, and treats each separately, regarding them variously as grand cru, premier cru or unclassified. The blanket classification of Cumières as premier cru makes no sense to him. 'On the poor soil and sand at the top of the hill near the forest, it is inferior to Damery, which is unclassified,' he clarifies. 'The early-ripening middle slope of the south-facing amphitheatre of Cumières north of the city is of grand cru quality, and to the west it is premier cru.' He points out each on a satellite photo, and his designations correspond precisely with green patches that betray the most vigorous vines. There is a natural regulation of vigour in Geoffroy's vines, with old vines and mid-row grasses limiting yields, ensuring earlier ripeness.

COTEAUX CHAMPENOIS RED WINES

This approach allows him to produce one of the most celebrated Coteaux Champenois still red wines, a passion he inherited from his father and grandfather. 'I make a red wine from the best grapes of my terroir, from the oldest vines and the lowest yields,' he says.

After experimenting extensively with red wine production in Beaujolais and Burgundy, Geoffroy produces red wine only in warmer vintages from Cumières pinot noir (meunier for the first time in 2008), releasing it as both a non-vintage and a vintage cuvée. The wines undergo malolactic fermentation and mature in 600-litre demi-muids for at least 12 months. These are long-ageing wines, with the potential to live for decades, and are only released when he deems them ready. Production is small and sporadic. 'It's good to make Coteaux Champenois when you don't need to!' he says. 'You can't make it to demand or in every vintage.' He made none in the challenging 2017 vintage, and then 100hL in the gloriously warm 2018. 'Normally I would alternate between pinot and meunier for Coteaux Champenois in the right years,' he explains, 'but in great years like 2015 I make both.'

In 2012, Geoffroy simplified the name of the estate from 'René Geoffroy' to 'Geoffroy' and introduced a new label, depicting the gate of the house in Aÿ to represent his new identity. 'It is not my philosophy to put my first name on the label, as I hope to one day pass the estate on to my children. There is no point changing the name with every generation,' he suggests.

Vintages, varieties, dosage and date of disgorgement are displayed on the back of every label, a laudable commitment for a small grower who disgorges every 2–3 months and tweaks the dosage for each disgorgement. He now uses DIAM closures on his red wines, 'as I had too many problems with cork taint'. In 2008 he bottled a trial of 800 bottles under cork and DIAM, but is yet to open them to assess their progress.

With undeviating attention to well-situated vineyards, an enviable production facility larger than his needs – and no intention to grow production – Cumières' finest grower is as fine as ever.

Jean-Baptiste Geoffroy in his cuverie at his home (opposite) in Aÿ.

GEOFFROY EXPRESSION BRUT PREMIER CRU NV $$

92 points • 2014 BASE VINTAGE • DISGORGED SEPTEMBER 2018 • TASTED IN CHAMPAGNE

29% chardonnay, 36% pinot, 35% meunier; 47% reserves of the previous blend; aged 3.5 years on lees; 6g/L dosage; 60,000 bottles, of which 15,000 are Pureté

Geoffroy describes Expression as his base wine, equal to the production of his eight other cuvées and three Coteaux Champenois put together. His aspiration here is easy-drinking freshness, 'to appeal to everyone'. It rises to the brief in a beautifully spicy expression of the voluptuous black grapes of Cumières, brimming with blackberries, raspberries and mixed spice. Ginger-cake complexity of lees age has built a creamy structure, while upholding the grapefruit-pith bite of very subtle, fine phenolic grip, textured salt minerality and vibrant, lingering acidity. Malic tension is well gauged to counter the luscious mood of Cumières, confirming a cuvée of fruit integrity and poise.

GEOFFROY PURETÉ BRUT NATURE PREMIER CRU NV $$

91 points • 2013 BASE VINTAGE • DISGORGED OCTOBER 2018 • TASTED IN CHAMPAGNE

28% chardonnay, 32% pinot, 40% meunier; 34% 2012 reserves; aged 4.5 years on lees; zero dosage

Pureté is Expression with another year on lees and no dosage. The luscious, golden fruits of the solar premier cru of Cumières make for a rich Nature of grilled pineapple and white peach fruit with golden delicious apple crunch. Full malic acidity and no added sugar made for a tense and steely champagne in the past, but Geoffroy has expertly massaged it into a more friendly style, enabling him to grow production from 5000 to 15,000 bottles. It maintains great tension on a long and crunchy finish, thanks to the fine, bitter bite of crab apple, in unison with focused malic acidity and pronounced salt minerality.

Geoffroy Meunier Millésime 2013 $$$$

90 points • **Disgorged April 2018** • **Tasted in Champagne**

New cuvée of 100% meunier from 100% lieu-dit Les Tiersaudes in Cumières planted to 'selection massale' in 1972, with no herbicides from the beginning; fully fermented and aged in older barriques until March; aged 4 years on lees; zero dosage

Geoffrory describes 2013 as a vintage of good ripening, giving birth to a cuvée of full yellow-gold hue that marries the exuberance of Cumières with the creamy structure and spicy personality of older barrel fermentation. A touch of reduction adds complexity unusual in barrel-fermented meunier, but which Jean-Baptiste attributes to the vintage. No malolactic keeps the acidity vibrant and poised. Figs, golden fruit cake and roasted almonds unite in a style that finishes dry and astringent and would appreciate a little dosage to soften it.

Geoffroy Blanc de Rose Rosé de Saignée Premier Cru Extra Brut NV $$$

92 points • **100% 2012** • **Disgorged March 2018** • **Tasted in Champagne**

50% chardonnay and 50% pinot noir, co-macerated; could label this as a vintage now, as it is aged long enough; Geoffroy keeps 300 bottles from each vintage to re-release as a vintage later as it is ageing well; no malolactic fermentation; aged 5 years on lees; 4g/L dosage

Full crimson-red hue. A characterful and delightful rosé that ricochets with pink pepper, pomegranate, pink lady apple and white cherry fruit, with a subtle violet lift, supported by a confident structure that unites the zip of malic acidity with the salt minerality of the village and the fine tannins of maceration. It holds a fresh, peppery finish of understated persistence. A unique and intriguing style.

Geoffroy Les Houtrants Complantés Brut Nature Premier Cru NV $$$$$

91 points • **2011 base vintage** • **Disgorged November 2017** • **Tasted in Champagne**

A blend of Geoffroy's four best plots in Cumières, planted to pinot noir, meunier, chardonnay, arbane and petit meslier in 2004; first harvest 2008; 75% reserves of 2010, 2009 and 2008 from magnum; wild fermented in enamelled vats; aged under cork; aged 5.5 years on lees; zero dosage; 1002 bottles

'My aim is to express the character of the soil, not the grapes,' says Geoffroy, of his decision to co-plant his four best plots in Cumières to five varieties. From the outset, he has ploughed these vineyards by horse, and commenced a biodynamic approach in 2018. Each year, 1200 magnums are bottled as reserves under three atmospheres of pressure (sufficient for disgorgement, which he performs by hand, after hand-riddling).

The result is as characterful and complex as its recipe, brimming with stone fruits, berry fruits, apples and even tropical fruits of all kinds, reflecting both its fruit salad of varietal diversity and the golden sunshine of the Vallée de la Marne's ripest cru. A generous majority of reserve wines lays down deep-set spice and luscious pâtisserie and wild honey complexity. The salty minerality of Cumières speaks articulately on a dry finish, with a firm grip amplified by zero dosage. It would appreciate some dosage to tone its structure. One bottle was corked.

GEOFFROY EMPREINTE MILLÉSIME BRUT PREMIER CRU 2012 $$

93 points • DISGORGED MARCH 2018 • TASTED IN CHAMPAGNE

25% chardonnay, 75% pinot noir from a selection of very early-ripening plots above Cumières on clay and chalk soils with fragments of flint; average vine age 30 years; 80% vinified in large oak vats and oak barrels; no malolactic fermentation; aged 5 years on lees; 5g/L dosage

Geoffroy's goal with Empreinte is to express the personality of Cumières pinot noir, which he describes as 'rich on the front, yet elegant and detailed on the end'. Always pinot-dominant, from 2014, this cuvée will be 100% pinot. It meets its aspiration confidently in 2012 in a wonderfully characterful style of medium to full straw hue. The luscious, juicy white peach and ripe pear flamboyance of Cumières is embellished by the creamy texture and spicy, toasty and even milk-chocolate complexity of barrel and oak vat fermentation. The personality of 2012 is captured in both depth and focus, well poised thanks to carefully deployed malic acidity and fine salt minerality. An outstanding Empreinte of impressive length and line, precisely articulating its brief.

GEOFFROY VOLUPTÉ BRUT PREMIER CRU MILLÉSIME 2011 $$$

89 points • DISGORGED OCTOBER 2018 • TASTED IN CHAMPAGNE

Volupté is always focused on Cumières chardonnay, 100% since 2010; mostly two of Geoffroy's three chardonnay plots in the village – La Montagne, south-east facing, just above the road to Hautvillers, with 50cm of topsoil before the chalk, giving very small yields and hence fruitiness to the blend, the other Le Tourne Midi, just 0.8 hectares on the Damery side of Cumières, steeply west-facing, planted in 1989 on just a few inches of soil above the chalk, bringing minerality; launched before the 2010, which will be labelled as blanc de blancs (Geoffroy forgot for the 2011); aged 6.5 years on lees; 3g/L dosage

Geoffroy says he can always find a few barrels to make Empreinte and Volupté, even in a difficult vintage like 2011, in which he said the attack of rot was more of a problem for the black grapes than chardonnay. The rot took off quickly, so he had to harvest very early. The result has upheld apple and pear fruit, accented with notes of fig and spice. The dry grip and coffee bean character of unhealthy, underripe fruit inherent to the harrowing 2011 season unfortunately makes for a firm and strict style of dry, astringent grip and short finish.

GEOFFROY VOLUPTÉ BRUT PREMIER CRU MILLÉSIME 2004 $$$

94 points • DISGORGED 2008 • TASTED IN CHAMPAGNE

100% chardonnay; partial oak fermentation; 8g/L dosage

A magnificent Volupté that exemplifies the endurance of Cumières chardonnay, electrified by the glorious tension of malic acidity in this bright and brilliant season. The generosity of the village shines in gorgeous white peach and white nectarine lusciousness, layered with spice that propagates very long on the finish. It sustains impressive poise and freshness, entwining fine salt minerality with seamless, silky texture.

Geoffroy Rosé de Saignée Brut Premier Cru 2014 $$$$

91 points • Disgorged September 2018 • Tasted in Champagne

Saignée of 100% skin-contact pinot noir, sourced from clay and silt soils with some marl; average vine age 25 years; no malolactic fermentation; aged 3.5 years on lees; 7g/L dosage

Renowned for his long-lived Cumières rouge Coteaux Champenois, Geoffroy's Rosé de Saignée predictably also improves with time. Now released with sufficient age for the vintage to be declared, it's come a long way from the stark, young non-vintage releases of the past. Flaunting a medium bright crimson-pink hue, this is a saignée that sings with the exuberant, precocious fruit of Cumières pinot noir in all of its youthful glory, basking in fresh plum, raspberry lolly, watermelon and fresh strawberry vibrancy. It holds its integrity and stature, thanks to a backbone of fine tannin structure, salt minerality and well-integrated malic acid freshness. A versatile food wine; Geoffroy recommends it with spicy Chinese food because it works well with soy.

Geoffroy Terre Extra-Brut Premier Cru Millésime 2006 $$$$

92 points • Disgorged October 2018 • Tasted in Champagne

30% chardonnay, 70% pinot; vinified in oak barrels and foudres; no malolactic fermentation; aged 11.5 years on lees; 3g/L dosage; 2000 bottles

Terre is the new name for Geoffroy's black label Millésime, only made in his best vintages. The selection is made at blending, from the best barrels of his oldest plots, always vinified in oak, generally barrels and sometimes foudres. It's a different blend and different quantity according to the harvest, sometimes as little as 2000 bottles.

With a rich colour of medium straw tinted with gold, this is a luscious style that revels in the ripeness of 2006 on the generous, sun-drenched slopes of Cumières. Layers of grilled pineapple, golden delicious apple and fig are amplified by the creamy texture and vanilla flavours of oak fermentation, making for a style of silky, soft structure. Definition and poise are upheld by salt minerality and well-entwined, gentle malic acidity. It holds with very good line and length.

Geoffroy Terre Millésime Extra Brut Premier Cru 2004

91 points • Disgorged January 2018 • Tasted in Champagne

71% chardonnay, 29% pinot; 100% vinified in oak barrels; aged 13 years on lees; 4g/L dosage

Upholding a bright, medium straw-yellow hue even paler than the 2006, the tension and restraint of 2004 in concert with a majority share of chardonnay blesses the generosity of Cumières with poise and confidence. Salt minerality and malic acidity mark out a long and focused finish. Prominent oak lends layers of nuts and toast, which sit apart from the fruit even after an impressive 13 years on lees, and will appreciate more time on cork to integrate.

Geoffroy Terre Millésime Extra Brut Premier Cru 2002

94 points • Disgorged January 2014 • Tasted in Champagne

35% chardonnay, 65% pinot, 5% meunier; aged 11 years on lees; 4g/L dosage

This is the fourth time that this magnificent vintage for Geoffroy has graced this Guide, since my first tasting way back in 2011. It's evolving slowly and confidently as it basks in the glory of yet another few years on lees, shedding the fresh lemon of its youth and arriving in a happy place of full yellow straw hue. A champagne of expansive presence and focused elegance, this is a wonderful take on the flamboyant expression of 2002 in Cumières. It's at once rich and exuberant in its layers of fig and grilled pineapple, and at the same time projecting all the focus and energy of its early years, tapping deep into chalk minerality, energised by well-defined malic acidity. Hints of coffee bean and mocha provide complexity to a finish of creamy silkiness, seamless line and fantastic persistence. Impressive.

GEOFFROY TERRE MILLÉSIME EXTRA BRUT PREMIER CRU 2000

90 points • DISGORGED JANUARY 2014 • TASTED IN CHAMPAGNE

70% chardonnay, 30% pinot; aged 13 years on lees; 4g/L dosage, 5565 bottles

When I first tasted this cuvée for the inaugural edition of this Guide way back in 2010, after seven years on lees, I described it as 'wild and decadent'. A retaste in 2015 suggested that its strict malic acidity needed longer still to soften – and soften it now has, relaxing into a full yellow gold hue. The glowing, golden personality of 2000 shines through in rich layers of grilled pineapple, luscious white peach, locut and fig, layered with spice and nougat. It is now beginning to build tertiary notes of green olive. Salty minerality and balanced acidity provide poise to the finish. It's beginning to tire and dry out now, but holds itself impressively for such a generous season.

GEOFFROY COTEAUX CHAMPENOIS CUMIÈRES ROUGE PINOT NOIR 2015 $$$

91 points • TASTED IN CHAMPAGNE

Bottled November 2018 and tasted in January 2019; DIAM

Geoffroy is one of Champagne's best-known names for Coteaux Champenois, thanks to well-situated plots of sun-drenched Cumières pinot and meunier. His tendency is to alternate the two varieties in the right years, but great seasons like 2015 afforded the opportunity to produce both. This is a spicy and structured style of impressive line and length, scaffolded with a fine and rigid oak chassis. It looks particularly firm and coiled in this recently bottled guise. Geoffroy's Coteaux Champenois always needs time to blossom, and this vintage is packed with particularly enduring potential. Patience.

GEOFFROY COTEAUX CHAMPENOIS CUMIÈRES ROUGE PINOT MEUNIER 2015 $$$

87 points • TASTED IN CHAMPAGNE

Bottled November 2018 and tasted in January 2019; DIAM

Firm, dry oak takes a strong lead here. A touch of brettanomyces spoilage accentuates savoury overtones, making for a firm and coarse style with a dry and astringent finish.

GEOFFROY COTEAUX CHAMPENOIS CUMIÈRES ROUGE PINOT NOIR 2012 $$$

90 points • TASTED IN CHAMPAGNE

Just one new barrel of 350 litres, in which it was fermented and aged for 2.5 years until January 2015, followed by ageing in a stainless steel tank for 3 years prior to bottling in January 2018; DIAM

A spicy and structured Coteaux Champenois of dark berry fruit character, toasty oak support and firm, fine tannins. Very long élevage has well toned the impact of 100% new French oak, drawing out impressive black-fruits depth and integrity. It will age very long and will appreciate at least another decade to soften and integrate.

GOSSET

(Goh-say)

(7/10)

3 RUE DE MALAKOFF 51200 ÉPERNAY
www.champagne-gosset.com

Established in 1584, centuries before the bubble was ever put into champagne, Gosset rightfully claims to be the oldest wine house in the region. Far from a staid, traditional establishment, Gosset is on the move, having relocated its production to the impressive Épernay cuverie and cellars of Château Malakoff, purchased from Laurent Perrier just in time for vintage 2009. In the midst of change, the house maintains an unwavering consistency, thanks largely to one man, the late Jean-Pierre Mareigner, its talented chef de cave of 33 years. Under his legacy, the house style of no malolactic fermentation, clean-cut structure and enduring longevity remains as fine as ever, with the exception of its Brut Excellence NV entry wine, which seems a strange misfit, in both philosophy and quality.

Previously operating from five different locations, Gosset is now basking in the opportunity to grow into the huge cuverie of Château Malakoff, with a capacity of 2.6 million litres, far exceeding the requirement for an annual production of 1.1 million bottles. There is a long-term hope to gradually increase to 1.2–1.4 million, but this will take a long time for a style as long-aged as Gosset.

The substantial premises, constructed in 1860 on two hectares of parkland next door to Pol Roger, came fully equipped with vinification facilities and disgorgement and labelling lines. Its 1.5 kilometres of deep cellars have a capacity for 2.5 million bottles, and house part of Gosset's stock of more than 4 million. The rest remain in Gosset's historic headquarters in Aÿ, where riddling and disgorgement are still conducted.

Gosset's roots in Mareigner's birth town of Aÿ remain strong in spite of the move and the company's tiny vineyard holdings.

With just one hectare to its name, Gosset purchases 99% of its fruit from 200 growers in 60 different villages, exclusively premier and grand crus in the Marne department.

The consistency of supply is a credit to Mareigner's long-term relationships with growers, some of whom have supplied Gosset for three generations. He knew them all so well that when they phoned him they announced themselves by first name only. As evidence of its faith in these relationships, Gosset does not operate press houses in the villages, instead entrusting its growers to crush on its behalf.

Every village and grower is kept separate during vinification, which is performed in stainless steel tanks, the temperature regulated to maintain ferments below 18°C. 'Our goal is to keep what nature has given us,' explained Mareigner. 'No centrifuge, no filtering until immediately before bottling, and no malolactic fermentation.'

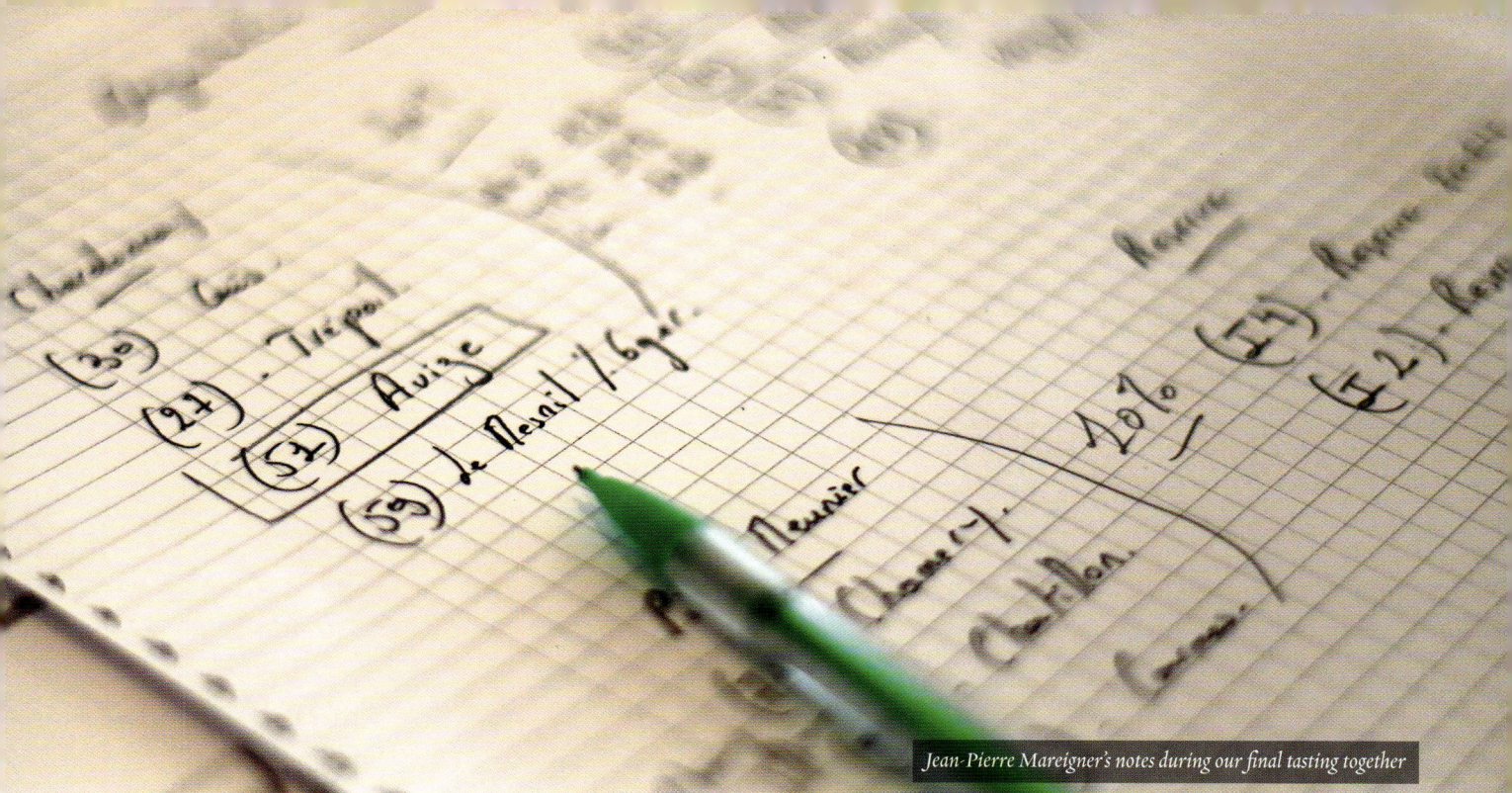

A little oxidation early in production builds resilience. No sulphur dioxide preservative is added at bottling, though a little remains in the wine from earlier in production.

Jean-Pierre Mareigner passed away in May 2016, leaving the house in the hands of his team, capably led by Odilon de Varine, his offsider for just over a decade. The house remains in good stead, as Mareigner had been training de Varine and his team in anticipation of his intended retirement in January 2017.

Mareigner's legacy lives on. 'He always said, "I am the first consumer of Gosset, so I want to make the wine that I want to drink every day,"' de Varine reflects. 'And now *I* am the first consumer!'

Upholding malic acidity is fundamental for de Varine. 'Right from the beginning, the grapes have tartaric and malic acidity; they do not have lactic acidity. For me, it is easier to create the right balance with tartaric and malic than with tartaric and lactic. But it takes time on lees for the malic acidity to find its balance, and if you don't take the time, the acidity is tighter. *C'est pas fondue!* It's not melted!'

The impressive freshness and remarkable ageing potential of malic acidity thus calls for long cellaring prior to release, and the great vintages of Gosset will live exceedingly long. The house has recently been tasting Mareigner's very first blends of Grande Réserves from the 1980s, and reports that they are still magnificent. 'Without malolactic fermentation, the plateau of a wine's peak development is longer,' observes de Varine.

'Time on lees is important for the balance in our wines, more important than the vintage,' de Varine proposes. 'The vintage is a consequence, nature makes all the difference, but age is a purpose, an ID. As a winemaker, I am lazy, so I prefer to have something I can do!' he grins.

Like Pol Roger next door, Gosset's deep cellars maintain a temperature below 11°C, drawing out the second ferment over six months to produce a very fine bead. A low dosage of 8g/L or less is used across the Grande range, and no more than 5g/L across the prestige Celebris trio, which accounts for a tiny 2% of the production of the house. Dosage is changed for each cuvée and even each disgorgement, determined by blind-tasting trials to create the right balance.

The beautifully poised Grande Réserve is on the rise, now representing more than 40% of production, pushing Brut Excellence down to just 40% (a tiny representation for an entry wine in the grand scale of champagne house production). The aim is to increase Grande Réserve and diminish Brut Excellence to just 20% in the coming years. This is just as well, because this cuvée is something of an ironic aberration in the excellence of the house, made using partial malolactic fermentation and a full dosage of 11g/L, and the house no longer shows me samples. There's quite a disparity between this bottle and the rest of the portfolio, which is referred to by the house as the 'antique' range. It is here that Mareigner's great talent was showcased, evidenced perhaps most demonstrably in his exceptional ability to achieve texture, finesse and harmony without malolactic fermentation.

I greatly admire de Varine's precision in his winemaking and his frank, open and humble approach, traits he shares with his predecessor. He is very well considered and precise about the details that define and distinguish Gosset, upholding Mareigner's legacy and his masterful skill in crafting clean-cut and enduring cuvées that make this distinguished old house what it is today.

GOSSET GRANDE RÉSERVE BRUT NV $$

95 points • 2013 BASE VINTAGE • DISGORGED JUNE 2018 • TASTED IN CHAMPAGNE AND AUSTRALIA

45% chardonnay, 45% pinot, 10% meunier; predominantly Aÿ, Bouzy, Ambonnay, Le Mesnil-sur-Oger, Villers-Marmery; aged 4 years on lees; 7g/L and 8g/L dosage in successive disgorgement; cork

Grande Réserve is the key focus of Gosset, progressively growing in volume to overtake Brut Excellence, and the first priority for fruit allocation before vintage cuvées. It represents a blend of 50 villages, all vinified separately, with reserves built both from single years and from the full blend of the previous year, in what Mareigner likened to 'a partial solera system'. In Champagne, 2013 was a great season, which de Varine suggests might have been a little forgotten after such a strong year in 2012. This cuvée has been aged nine months longer than in the past, which he suggests is very important.

The tension and energy of Grande Réserve are on full display in the great 2013 base vintage, filled with crunchy, exact red gala apple, lemon and even a hint of fennel. Power meets tension in a celebration of impressive fruit sources, showcasing their pedigree in depth and tension, blessed with all the toasted brioche and spice of long bottle age, illuminated by bright malic vitality and Gosset's signature of prominent, gently rolling, fine chalk mineral finesse. A very fine mousse wraps around a spine of magnificent, ripe yet confident malic acidity. Chalk minerality is heightened to profound levels, lingering very long with frothing salt mineral texture. Every detail lingers with generous length and accurate line. This is a Grande Réserve of greater precision, harmony and persistence than ever before – the finest I have seen this cuvée.

GOSSET GRAND BLANC DE BLANCS BRUT NV $$$

94 points • 2013 BASE VINTAGE • DISGORGED APRIL 2018 • TASTED IN CHAMPAGNE AND AUSTRALIA

100% chardonnay; predominantly from longstanding growers in Avize, Le Mesnil-sur-Oger, Chouilly, Cramant, Villers-Marmery, Trépail and Ambonnay; new clear bottle sold in a gift box with a clear message in three places: 'This gift box protects the wine against damage from UV light. We therefore recommend removing it just before serving'; 6g/L dosage; cork

The Gosset house style of refined minerality and thrilling malic acidity has shone in its blanc de blancs since its inaugural 2011 base release, and never more brilliantly than it does in this 2013 base of bright, pale straw hue. Youthful purity and focus rise with grand cru fruit presence and impressive concentration of pinpoint lemon and generous white peach, pear and golden delicious apple. This pristine fruit melds seamlessly with the brioche, almond nougat, shortbread, fresh vanilla and spice of lees age, and reductive nuances of struck flint. Ripe yet full and energetic malic acidity brings drive and focus to a finish of impressive length and tension, energising frothing salt minerality of heightened presence. It holds excellent harmony and poise on the finish, with fruit, minerality, dosage and malic acidity intricately entwined and uplifting. A thrilling blanc de blancs with the confidence to hold its poise for many years to come.

GOSSET GRAND ROSÉ BRUT NV $$$

95 points • 2013 BASE VINTAGE • DISGORGED MAY 2018 • TASTED IN CHAMPAGNE AND AUSTRALIA

Roughly 50% chardonnay, 50% pinot as always; predominantly Avize, Chouilly, Villers-Marmery, Bouzy, Ambonnay and Verzenay; 8% pinot noir red wine; 8g/L dosage; cork

The aspiration of Gosset Rosé is freshness, delicacy and elegance, without too much structure. 'Jean-Pierre always said, "We don't want to have red flavoured wine in our Rosé, just more red fruit aromas,' de Varine recalls. 'The idea is rosé on the nose but white on the palate.' Red wine is blended from the base vintage and the preceding year from three suppliers in Cumières, Ambonnay and Bouzy.

A confident chardonnay lead, low proportion of red wine and signature cut of malic acidity fulfil the brief for this delicate and graceful style. A pretty pale-salmon hue heralds a beautifully eloquent rosé that articulates the restrained mood of Gosset and the delicacy of a touch of pinot noir red wine. Pretty red cherry and strawberry fruit is fragranced with rose petal perfume, building to complex nuances of tamarillo with time in the glass. Tension and structure are defined equally by the salty chalk minerality of the great crus of the Côte des Blancs and Montagne de Reims, and the drive of excellent, ripe malic acidity. It glides very long and harmonious.

GOSSET GRAND BLANC DE MEUNIER EXTRA-BRUT NV $$$$

93 points • 2007 BASE VINTAGE • DISGORGED SEPTEMBER 2017 • TASTED IN CHAMPAGNE

New cuvée of 100% meunier from Dizy, Pierry, Moussy, Chavot, Cumières and Hautvillers; vinified on chardonnay lees; aged 9 years on lees; 5000 bottles

A one-off release of a new cuvée. 'One shot! For fun!' declares de Varine. 'And to share! Sharing is very important for me. Meunier is a good friend of ours and we wanted to show that meunier can age if it comes from great terroirs.' Sourced from almost all of the villages surrounding Épernay – 'meunier terroirs'. Having worked extensively with lees in Burgundy, de Varine fermented meunier on chardonnay lees to add minerality.

The soft and rounded personality of meunier is on grand display here, snapped into sharp focus by the poise of malic acidity. This is a cuvée that cleverly and confidently achieves the precarious balance of upholding the personality of meunier with the complexity of considerable age, achieving this with the inimitable tension and precision of the house. With a full straw hue, the spicy dark berries, dark fruit cake and fruit mince spice of meunier meet the roast nuts and buttered toast of a decade of age.

GOSSET GRAND BLANC DE NOIRS EXTRA-BRUT NV $$$$

94 points • 2007 BASE VINTAGE • TASTED IN CHAMPAGNE

New cuvée of 100% pinot from Verzy first, then Aÿ, Ambonnay, Tauxières, Louvois, Chigny-les-Roses, Pierry and Cumières; less than 5% reserves; vinified on chardonnay lees; aged 9 years on lees; 5g/L dosage

There is tremendous richness and exuberance of pinot noir personality here, fleshy, spicy and generously black-fruited, with gorgeous satsuma plum and black cherry definition. All of the complexity of a decade of age is on grand parade in toasty character and a medium to full straw hue. Like the meunier, it proudly declares its Gosset DNA, confidently flying the house flag of definition and focus. It concludes with fantastic balance and integrity, holding wonderfully rounded, succulent presence with outstanding line and poise.

GOSSET GRAND MILLÉSIME BRUT 2006 $$$

92 points • Disgorged September 2017 • Tasted in Champagne and Australia

44% chardonnay predominantly from Avize, Cramant, Le Mesnil-sur-Oger, Vertus and Trépail, 56% pinot predominantly from Aÿ, Avenay-Val-d'Or, Louvois, Ambonnay and Chigny-les-Roses; aged 10.5 years on lees; 6g/L dosage; cork

De Varine describes his first vintage at Gosset as a 'good friend' vintage, 'a nice guy, round, easy to vinify and easy to drink. It was round and ripe but with vitality, not fat or spineless.' True to this season of heightened amplitude, this was a cuvée of exotic complexity and cuddly roundedness when I first met it on release three years ago, sadly without the energy and stamina to sustain it. Its hue of full straw with gold tints has deepened further, and its full panoply of toffee, honey, golden fruit cake, glacé peach, fig, mirabelle plums, ginger, vanilla and nutmeg remain. Some bottles cling to shades of their former integrity, maintaining presence and flesh, with gentle salt minerality drawing out a long aftertaste, while others teeter on the brink of burnt-orange oxidation which truncates the finish. A rich vintage that lacks vitality and tension at 12 years of age, now in the dim twilight of its glory days.

GOSSET CELEBRIS VINTAGE EXTRA BRUT 2007 $$$$

96 points • Disgorged August 2017 • Tasted in Australia

57% chardonnay predominantly from Vertus, Avize, Le Mesnil-sur-Oger, Verzy and Trépail, 43% pinot predominantly from Cumières, Avenay-Val-d'Or, Aÿ, Bouzy and Ambonnay; aged 9.5 years on lees; 3g/L dosage; cork

Celebris is intricately crafted for heightened elegance with amplified stamina, downplaying fruit concentration while zapping it with a charge of malic acidity that jolts everything into a state of frenzy, slaying innocent, youthful white flowers, white cherries and golden delicious apples with an ice shard of acidity that screams out for years to soften. Fresh coconut, almond nougat and creamy texture declare the magic of long lees age, trailing long into a grand finish of pronounced, mouth-filling salt minerality that bores to the core of Champagne's greatest grand crus.

GOSSET CELEBRIS ROSÉ EXTRA BRUT 2007 $$$$$

95 points • Disgorged February 2016 • Tasted in Australia

59% chardonnay predominantly from Avize, Chouilly, Cramant and Vertus, 41% pinot predominantly from Aÿ, Bouzy and Ambonnay; 7% pinot noir red wine; aged 8 years on lees; 5g/L dosage; cork

The most subtle rosés are the most enchanting, and Mareigner has conjured the epitome of elegance by seeking a small selection of what he calls the most 'shy' villages in the very fresh vintage of 2007. This cuvée has mapped out quite a trajectory in the six years since its first release after five years on lees (now eight years, and longer on cork, too). Its hue has evolved to a copper shade of salmon and its mood has awoken to a more contemplative and savoury style that upholds the spicy berry fruits and blood orange of its youth with freshly baked bread and roast almonds of secondary development, beginning to build the pipe smoke of tertiary maturity. As in its youth, it takes time to unravel to depth of black cherries, strawberry hull and mixed spice. Its intricate framework of chewy structure and tannin presence is so fine it's impossible to tell where tannins finish and pronounced grand cru salt minerality begins. Malic acidity sits as comfortably and confidently in the midst of this as ever, drawing its finish out very long.

HATT ET SÖNER

(At e Soh-neh)

---

10 Avenue des Comtes de Champagne 51130 Bergères-lès-Vertus
www.hatt-soner.com

CHAMPAGNE
HATT *et* SÖNER

When the Ruscon family established their small estate in the village of Bergères-lès-Vertus at the southern end of the Côte des Blancs in 2011, they were to become the first Swedish family to own a champagne house. Their recipe is daring to say the least. Sourcing from 40 parcels entirely in the premier and grand crus of the Côte des Blancs is certainly admirable, but to vinify these tense, young blanc de blancs exclusively as vintage cuvées with low or no dosage and without malolactic fermentation makes for assertive wines. The house is privileged to 13 hectares of estate vines exclusively in the southern Côte des Blancs strip of Bergères-lès-Vertus, Vertus, Le Mesnil-sur-Oger and Oger. Cuvées produced prior to 2012 were made by the coopérative in Vertus. Since then, the house has vinified only its own grapes, but upholds négociant status for flexibility if it chooses to buy in future. A new cuverie permits small-batch vinification, mostly in temperature-controlled stainless steel cuves partitioned into eight sections. A single parcel of Bergères-lès-Vertus for Le Grand-Père Omnes is half fermented in barrels previously used for three seasons to ferment white Bordeaux. Some malolactic fermentation proceeds, since it is tricky to block in used barrels. The business represents a progressive take-over of fourth-generation Bergères-lès-Vertus grower François Vallois, who retains half ownership and remains in control of production. The launch of the brand in 2012 certainly stirred some controversy in Sweden, not least because François Vallois' cuvées were rebadged with evocative metal label plates at much inflated prices, soliciting comparisons with Armand de Brignac from the Swedish press.

HATT ET SÖNER GRANDE CUVÉE PREMIER CRU BLANC DE BLANCS BRUT 2012 $$$

91 points • TASTED IN AUSTRALIA

100% chardonnay from 10 parcels in Oger, Les Mesnil-sur-Oger, Vertus and Bergères-lès-Vertus; no malolactic fermentation; 5g/L dosage

Generous, exotic and spicy, this is a cuvée that captures the exuberance of Vertus and Bergères-lès-Vertus. Impressive ripeness makes for approachability even with no malolactic fermentation and low dosage in young blanc de blancs. It leads out rich and full and pulls into a focused tail of malic acidity and prominent, fine chalk minerality. A cuvée that contrasts generous presence with focused structure and well-defined minerality.

Hatt et Söner Grande Cuvée Premier Cru Blanc de Blancs Brut Nature 2010 $$$

90 points • Tasted in Australia

100% chardonnay from 50-year-old vines in the single lieu-dit Les Martin in the centre of the slope in the middle of Bergères-lès-Vertus; fermented in stainless steel tanks; no malolactic fermentation; zero dosage; 4300 bottles

With a pale straw hue, this is a focused and tense style that exemplifies the mineral definition and tension of Bergères. Notes of nutmeg and spice hint at the beginnings of secondary complexity, which lingers long. In the absence of dosage, malic acidity serves to heighten the mid-slope chalk minerality of the village.

Hatt et Söner Vieille Vigne 2008 $$$$

91 points • Tasted in Australia

100% chardonnay from a single plot planted in 1954 on a warm site at the top of the slope in the middle of Bergères-lès-Vertus; vinified in stainless steel tanks; no malolactic fermentation; 6g/L dosage

A cuvée from François Vallois, prior to the establishment of Hatt et Söner, this is a spicy and exotic style that expresses a warm site in a cool vintage with complex notes of kerosene, reminiscent of the secondary phase of maturity of ripe phenolics. It's a complex cuvée that contrasts its exoticism with the malic acid tension of the house and the chalk mineral structure of the southern Côte des Blancs.

Bergères-lès-Vertus, summer 2011

Henri Abelé

(On-ree Ab-leh)

---

50 Rue de Sillery 51100 Reims
www.henriabele.com

1757
Henri Abelé
· MAISON FONDÉE EN 1757 ·
· A REIMS · FRANCE ·
CHAMPAGNE

Founded in 1757, Henri Abelé is the fifth oldest house in Champagne, and played a famous role in the history of riddling and disgorgement. In 1834, the house was joined by Antoine Müller, former chef de cave at Veuve Clicquot, where he developed the process of remuage with the Widow. When Henri Abelé himself took over in 1903, he fine-tuned the riddling rack and was the first to freeze the bottle neck in disgorgement. The house was bought by the Spanish giant Freixenet Group in 1985, which joined forces with Henkell in mid-2018 to become the biggest sparkling group in the world, though Henri Abelé has admirably shunned the trend to grow, capping production at a modest 500,000 bottles. The merger unites the house with Henkell-owned Alfred Gratien (page 88), and Nicolas Jaeger now oversees production for both brands. With limited vineyard resources under its ownership, sourcing is primarily from growers spanning the Marne, Sézanne, Vitry and Aube. To celebrate its 250th anniversary in 2007, a new cuverie and vat room were constructed and a large supply of small vinification vats procured. The aspiration of the house is for a fresher style, and to this end the presence of chardonnay has been increased as the leading varietal in all cuvées except the flagship blanc de noirs, Le Sourire de Reims Rosé. The house style this year is sadly variously plagued by imperfect fruit, phenolic bitterness and oxidation. Under Jaeger's capable watch, I hope that Henri Abelé might now enjoy a similar trajectory to that of the recent rise of Alfred Gratien.

Henri Abelé Brut NV $$

86 points • 2016 base vintage • Disgorged February 2019 • Tasted in Australia

40% chardonnay, 35% pinot, 25% meunier; Grande Montagne de Reims, Côte des Blancs, Massif de Saint-Thierry, Sézannais; 30% reserves from 2011, 2009, 2008 and 2007; no oak; aged 2 years on lees; 9g/L dosage; DIAM

A young and crunchy chardonnay-led style of grapefruit and golden delicious apple fruit, backed by the spicy complexity of deep reserves. It's a firm cuvée of hard acidity, bitter phenolic bite and coarse phenolic graininess, which even candied dosage is helpless to counter. The base vintage is four years younger than it was two years ago, though the reserves are still listed as hailing from the same vintages, which appears to be an anomaly.

Henri Abelé Blanc de Blancs NV $$$

88 points • TASTED IN AUSTRALIA

100% chardonnay, sourced mainly from the Côte des Blancs; DIAM

The apple, pear and lemon fruit of largely Côte des Blancs chardonnay is underlined by fine salt minerality, supported by an integrated interplay between bright acidity and harmonious dosage. It's marked by the mushroomy charcuterie imperfection of unhealthy fruit that foils an otherwise delicate and pretty style.

Henri Abelé Brut Rosé NV $$

87 points • 2016 BASE VINTAGE • DISGORGED FEBRUARY 2019 • TASTED IN AUSTRALIA

40% chardonnay, 40% pinot, 20% meunier; Grande Montagne de Reims, Côte des Blancs, Massif de Saint-Thierry, Sézannais; 30% reserves from 2011, 2009, 2008 and 2007; no oak; aged 2 years on lees; 9g/L dosage; DIAM

A savoury and secondary rosé of medium salmon-copper hue and flavours of tomato, tamarillo, white pepper and a note of sage. Bright, tangy acidity and balanced dosage are interrupted by coarse, firm tannin bite. It concludes short and abrupt. Like the Brut, the base vintage has progressed four seasons in two years, but the stated reserves have not changed.

Henri Abelé Brut Millésimé 2009 $$$

85 points • DISGORGED FEBRUARY 2019 • TASTED IN AUSTRALIA

70% chardonnay, 30% pinot; Grande Montagne de Reims, Côte des Blancs; no oak; aged 9 years on lees; 8g/L dosage; DIAM

A fully developed take on this ripe season, this cuvée exhibits some oxidative degradation in its deep hue of full straw yellow and notes of burnt-orange oxidation that render the finish dry and contracted. No back-up bottle was supplied.

Henri Abelé Brut Millésimé 2006 $$$

89 points • TASTED IN AUSTRALIA

70% chardonnay, 30% pinot; Grande Montagne de Reims, Côte des Blancs; 8g/L dosage; DIAM

Two years ago I wrote that this ripe and forward vintage was 'just edging past the peak of its trajectory, so tuck in quick smart'. Predictably, it's now a full straw-yellow hue and has shed its primary fruit, quite developed in its profile, with its secondary layers of honey, burnt toffee, roast almonds, dried apricots and fruit mince spice tending towards burnt-orange oxidation, beginning to fragment and dry out on the finish.

Henri Abelé Le Sourire de Reims Rosé 2006 $$$$

92 points • Disgorged March 2019 • Tasted in Australia

100% Les Riceys pinot; macerated on skins for 36–48 hours; aged 12 years on lees; no oak; first launched from the 2003 vintage to commemorate the 800th anniversary of the Reims Cathedral in 2011; 7g/L dosage; DIAM

Les Riceys is Champagne's largest cru and the most famous in the Aube, sought after by virtually every house with a keen interest in rosé. This saignée of 100% pinot noir pronounces a powerful and characterful expression of this village. It has now grown to a full crimson-copper hue, upholding its full flamboyant exuberance on the bouquet, leaping from the glass in powerful characters of pomegranate, guava, wild strawberries, musk, blood orange and burnt orange zest – even savoury, stalk-derived nuances of tamarillo, Campari and pipe smoke. The bouquet is quite an affair, and the palate leads off with similar gusto, though its freshness is now fading. Skin tannins lend bitter grip to the finish, more prominent now than in its youth, as its juicy and extroverted fruit begins to lose momentum on the finish.

The cathedral Notre-Dame de Reims dates from 1211.

HENRI GIRAUD

(On-ree Zhi-row)

---

71 BOULEVARD CHARLES DE GAULLE 51160 AŸ
www.champagne-giraud.com

The Giraud-Hémart family has diligently tended vines on the south-facing slopes of Aÿ since 1625, making this the oldest champagne house still owned by its founding family. It was not until the current head of house, twelfth-generation Claude Giraud, that champagnes were made under the family name. An annual production of about 250,000 bottles is sourced from the family's 10 hectares, spread across 35 small plots, supplemented with fruit purchased largely from family and friends, all of which is pressed by Giraud. Planted to 70% pinot noir and 30% chardonnay, the magnificence of Aÿ is captured, thanks to vines of a minimum 30 years of age, planted on thin topsoils and deep chalk, tended according to organic principles and harvested at full ripeness. Musts are cold settled at 10°C prior to fermentation, to enhance clarity and aroma, and all cuvées go through full malolactic fermentation. Stainless steel tanks have recently been completely rejected and all cuvées are now vinified in terracotta, sandstone eggs or 228-litre barrels from the Argonne forest south-east of Aÿ, an oak industry which Claude has been instrumental in reviving since 1989. He says his generous and silky Fût de Chêne and Code Noir cuvées are fresher and more lively as a result, though across the range, fruit purity and definition have gravely suffered in the wake of both increasing use of oak and decreasing sulphur dioxide preservative, which is greatly disappointing. Disgorgement dates are laser etched on bottles.

HENRI GIRAUD ESPRIT NATURE NV $$

90 points • 50% 2016 BASE VINTAGE • TASTED IN AUSTRALIA

20% chardonnay, 80% pinot; 50% reserves matured in small Argonne oak casks; alcoholic and malolactic fermentations in sandstone egg fermenters; 6-7g/L dosage; cork

Giraud's line-up kicks off with a characterful cuvée that celebrates a rich, fruitful expression of Aÿ pinot noir with the depth and complexity of 50% reserves matured in small oak barrels. A progression towards increased oak fermentation and low sulphur has deepened its colour and heightened savoury, charcuterie character, while muting the juicy strawberries and raspberries of Aÿ pinot noir that once defined the style. Characteristic notes of sage and saltbush are upheld, underscored by salty chalk minerality and softly integrated acidity.

Dawn frost in Aÿ, winter 2019

HENRI GIRAUD DAME-JANE ROSÉ NV $$$

87 points • 2014 BASE VINTAGE • TASTED IN AUSTRALIA

30% chardonnay, 70% pinot; 6% Aÿ rouge from 1952 plantings; alcoholic and malolactic fermentations in sandstone egg fermenters and Argonne oak barrels; maturation in terracotta; 6–7g/L dosage; cork

I have long admired the accord that this cuvée struck in the past between the succulent fruit expression and tense focus of Aÿ pinot noir, boldly and accurately embracing the impeccable cut of bright acidity and the frothing salt minerality of Aÿ old vines. Its mandate is upheld, though its freshness, purity, detail, grace, finesse and flesh have sadly now been lost in the wake of oak structure and low sulphur. It has unfortunately collapsed into a brittle shell of firm tannin grip and callow development, merely a skeleton of its former glory.

HENRI GIRAUD GRAND CRU FÛT DE CHÊNE MV13 BRUT NV $$$$$

94 points • 2013 BASE VINTAGE • DISGORGED 20 MARCH 2018 • TASTED IN AUSTRALIA

20% chardonnay, 80% pinot; 30% perpetual reserve, dating back to 1990; alcoholic and malolactic fermentations in Argonne oak barrels; 6–7g/L dosage; cork

The voluptuous curves of pinot noir are amplified three-fold, in the stature of Aÿ, the luscious warmth of ripe fruit, and the voluminous mood of small-barrel fermentation, flinging Fût de Chêne to the deep end of champagne concentration. This extreme style sits more confidently than ever in the vibrant 2013 season, infusing poise and focus to its classic bombastic power of juicy white peach and pineapple, bolstered by all the toasty, dark chocolate and coffee exuberance of barrel fermentation. It's backed with all manner of complexity of ginger and roast nuts, declared in a full straw hue and grand fruit persistence. The vibrant acid line of this impressive season tones this maelstrom with focus and confidence, heightening the fine, salty minerality of Aÿ in a compelling accord that lingers long and seamless with silky, slippery generosity. Its fruit presence and structure hold its poise more confidently than ever, and the result is characterful, succulent, enticing and ready for main-course fare of whole turkey proportions. A low-sulphur regime unfortunately necessitates drinking right away, as there is no staying power to resist oxidation in the cellar or after the bottle is opened.

HENRIOT

(On-ree-oh)

7/10

81 RUE COQUEBERT 51100 REIMS
www.champagne-henriot.com

Champagne
HENRIOT
MAISON FONDÉE EN 1808

To Henriot chef de cave Laurent Fresnet, blending is more than just uniting varieties, crus and vintages. 'I say I do a human blending because each area is a group of people,' he says. 'We are close to our wine growers and they care about the quality they give us. We are a small house and we don't have a second wine, so I have a lot of tastings with them to improve our relationships. If I have bad grapes I cannot make good blends.' His are meticulously assembled and long-aged cuvées, seamlessly crafted with balance and order in a classic approach, built on a core of Côte des Blancs chardonnay.

In 2008 Henriot celebrated its 200th year of independent family ownership, one of the last remaining houses to be run continuously by the founding family from the outset. Joseph Henriot passed away suddenly in 2015 and his son Thomas left the group in the same year. Joseph's nephew and eighth-generation member of the family, Gilles de Larouzière, is now president of the group.

The Henriot family is privileged to a considerable wine empire and has been masterful in elevating the quality across its estates, including Bouchard Père & Fils in Burgundy, William Fèvre in Chablis, Villa Ponciago in Beaujolais, Lejay Cassis and Beaux Frères in Oregon.

Family ownership has afforded the privilege of building a long-ageing house style that might otherwise be infeasible for a house producing 1.4–1.5 million bottles annually. This is achieved through a strong reliance on chardonnay and virtually no meunier.

Long ageing on lees is reflected in a whopping 5–6 years of stock held continuously in the company's extensive cellars under Reims, as well as reserve wines back to 1990.

Thirty-three hectares of estate vineyards are located mainly in the great crus of the Côtes des Blancs, with smaller holdings in Avenay-Val-d'Or, Verzy and Verzenay. The focus of the house is on premier and grand cru villages, which comprise at least two-thirds of non-vintage blends and 100% of vintage cuvées. Vines averaging 25–30 years of age are tended respectfully, with grasses cultivated in mid-rows, and herbicides and fertilisers avoided. The family sources from a further 100 hectares of vineyards under long-term contracts.

Every parcel is kept separate and fermented in small stainless steel vats (there are no oak barrels here), which can lead some cuvées to tend towards a reductive savouriness, not unusual for chardonnay-led blends. 'We work reductively with our wines

Trépail, winter 2013

and this is why they age so confidently,' explains Fresnet, who recommends drinking them from large glasses. Full malolactic fermentation provides soft structures, while dosages have been progressively lowered to now between 5g/L and 8g/L.

With exacting attention to the finest details, Fresnet has quietly dedicated himself to refining Henriot's style since he began with the house in 2005, while upholding a deep respect for the long history of the house. 'I have a collection in my cellar of 10 years of Brut Souverain and 10 years of Blanc de Blancs, and every year before I blend the new vintage, I taste the full vertical to remember what we did in the past, and how it has evolved,' he reveals.

Non-vintage cuvées are privileged to a small quantity of a deep perpetual reserve of grand cru chardonnay dubbed 'Cuve 38'. In 1990, Joseph Henriot set aside a special vat of grand cru Côte des Blancs chardonnay. An addition has been made in each of the best vintages since, largely from Chouilly and Avize, with lesser contributions from Le Mesnil-sur-Oger and Cramant, in something of a solera system. The proportion of each vintage addition may be as little as 1% of the blend, or as much as 18%, according to taste. The blend has grown to fill a 467hL tank, held at 14°C to retain freshness. A little is drawn every year as reserve for the three non-vintage cuvées and replaced with the current vintage.

In 2015, Henriot unveiled Cuve 38 as a release of just 1000 magnums, secretly held in production for an incredible 25 years. I was privileged to be the first outside the house to see a sneak preview of this unprecedented new concept. This was not the first time I've witnessed the other-worldly freshness that can be sustained by annually refreshing a grand old solera in a big tank, but nothing prepared me for the unbridled joy of youth radiating from this cuvée. I was stunned that a blend whose youngest component was seven years old at the time, and the oldest no less than 24 years, could trap such a bright straw hue, breathtaking lemon blossom and lemon zest fragrance and vibrant focus. A remarkable reserve that impeccably complements the elegance of Henriot's non-vintage style.

Henriot has released its Blanc de Blancs NV under DIAM since 2007 and its Rosé NV since 2017, with Brut Souverain cued to join in 2020, when Fresnet completes his trials to determine the right level of permeability. This can't come too soon, as I've encountered cork taint in more than one Henriot cuvée under natural cork this year. I hope he extends DIAM across his glorious set of vintage cuvées.

The last four digits of the lot code clearly printed on back labels are the month and year of disgorgement. For instance, 1017 is October 2017.

Verzenay, harvest 2014

HENRIOT BRUT SOUVERAIN NV $$

92 points • 2013 BASE VINTAGE • DISGORGED OCTOBER AND NOVEMBER 2017 • TASTED IN CHAMPAGNE AND AUSTRALIA

50% chardonnay, largely from the Côte des Blancs, particularly Le Mesnil-sur-Oger, Oger, Avize, Cramant and Chouilly; 50% pinot, mostly from the Montagne de Reims, particularly Aÿ, Verzy, Verzenay, Beaumont, Sillery and Mailly-Champagne; 65% premier and grand crus; 30% reserves, including Cuve 38 (see previous page); aged 3.5 years on lees; 7–8g/L dosage; cork; 70% of production, hence around 1 million bottles

Fresnet describes 2013 as a great year of high acidity and fruitiness, which he has captured beautifully in his entry blend. It lands pre-charged with impressive bottle-age complexity of toast, brioche, roasted almonds, gingernut biscuits and dried peach, with a flicker of grilled-bread reductive complexity, while holding admirable, lemon fresh vibrancy, energy and elegance thanks to its strong Côte des Blancs chardonnay lead. Upholding a medium straw hue, this is a beautifully balanced and refined blend energised by the prominent, salty chalk minerality of the great Côte des Blancs grand crus. Apple, pink grapefruit, lemon and pear fruit melds seamlessly with fine-grained structure and perfectly gauged dosage on a long and even finish. A bargain apéritif.

HENRIOT BRUT ROSÉ NV $$$

93 points • 2013 BASE VINTAGE • DISGORGED SEPTEMBER 2016 • CORK • TASTED IN AUSTRALIA
93 points • 2014 BASE VINTAGE • DISGORGED DECEMBER 2017 • DIAM • TASTED IN CHAMPAGNE

40% chardonnay from the Côte des Blancs, particularly Avize, Chouilly, Vertus and Épernay; 50% pinot, mostly from the Montagne de Reims, particularly Mareuil-sur-Aÿ, Verzy, Verzenay, Avenay-Val-d'Or and Trépail; 10% meunier; 10% of very light and aromatic red wine made in house with pre-ferment maceration and regular plunging to extract flavour and colour; 70% premier and grand crus; 35% reserves, including Cuve 38 (see previous page); aged 4.5 years on lees; 8g/L dosage; 7–8% of production, hence 100–120,000 bottles

Fresnet's ambitions with rosé are fruitiness and creamy texture, not colour, so he blends in dark glasses. It's always an impressive colour considering, and surprisingly pale for 10% red wine, reflecting the delicacy of his reds. The result is a rosé of pretty pale to medium-salmon hue that occupies a place midway between the extremes of elegance and depth on the grand rosé spectrum, alive with rose hip, strawberry and morello cherry poise, contrasting with savoury notes of tomato and cracked pink pepper, even a note of sarsaparilla. The succulent fruit presence of pinot noir defines a juicy mid-palate, while gently handled pinot noir red wine offers a fine-grained structure of well-gauged tannin presence, melding harmoniously with fine, salty chalk mineral texture and bright acidity on a long finish of even line and well-integrated dosage. Celebrating the calibre of largely grand cru sourcing, this is a compellingly complex and alluringly precise, bright and fruity rosé of creamy bead, elegant appeal and savoury complexity. One bottle of the 2013 base was corked. Thank goodness the 2014 base is under DIAM.

Henriot Blanc de Blancs NV $$$

93 points • 2012 BASE VINTAGE • DISGORGED NOVEMBER 2017 • TASTED IN AUSTRALIA
94 points • 2013 BASE VINTAGE • DISGORGED MARCH 2017 • TASTED IN CHAMPAGNE

100% chardonnay; predominantly Le Mesnil-sur-Oger, Chouilly and Avize for longevity and salty minerality, with Vertus and Trépail for white peach and nectarine fruit, and Sézanne, Montgueux and sometimes Vitry for an exotic touch; 70% premier and grand crus; 40% reserves including Cuve 38; aged 3–4.5 years on lees; 7g/L dosage; DIAM

Two additional years on lees since I saw it last has amplified the toasty complexity and bitter almond notes of the 2012 base, while upholding hints of reductive complexity, all the while transforming the fresh lemon and white peach of youth into preserved lemon and dried peach. Line, length and fine chalk mineral texture remain transfixed and delightful. The 2013 base is even more thrilling, leading out with grilled toast and gun-smoke reduction, providing an elegantly complex air to a cuvée of great precision and character. It's at once precise in its lemon and sugared mandarin freshness, generous in white peach succulence and complex in the almond nougat and creamy texture of age. A blanc de blancs of completeness and class.

Henriot Rosé Millésime 2008 $$$$

95 points • TASTED IN CHAMPAGNE

45% chardonnay from the Côte des Blancs, particularly Avize and Vertus, 55% pinot mostly from the Montagne de Reims, particularly Mareuil-sur-Aÿ, Verzy, Verzenay, Avenay and Trépail; less than 8% red wine; 100% premier cru and grand cru; 6g/L dosage

The focus for Fresnet in crafting vintage rosé is to emphasise both the style and the year, while respecting the blend. Never has he captured the potential of the season more emphatically than he did in the enduring 2008 vintage. Four years ago I announced this as a rare 2008 to drink now, such was its gorgeous drinkability on release, but such is the sheer stamina of the sensational 2008 season that it is still singing with full voice after more than a decade. Its hue has now evolved to a medium salmon copper, while magnificent, tangy morello cherries and strawberries hold confident amidst rising complexity of roast almonds. Testimony to this great season, the acidity of the year upholds magnificent vibrancy, with line and length of exacting precision. Exalting now more than ever in the wonderful texture of long lees age, it has relaxed from youthful verve into creamy maturity. Silky texture harmonises the magical touch of bottle age with soft chalk-infused minerality, and beautifully poised tannin support, drawn out by the fine acid line of the inimitable 2008 vintage, lingering undeviating for minutes.

HENRIOT MILLÉSIME 2008 $$$$

96 points • DISGORGED FEBRUARY 2018 • TASTED IN CHAMPAGNE AND AUSTRALIA

50% chardonnay, 50% pinot; 10 premier crus and grand crus; aged 9 years on lees; 6g/L dosage; cork

Fresnet describes 2008 as 'the most gifted vintage of the 2000s, complex, generous, fresh, elegant yet expressive – the DNA of Henriot'. A fitting vintage to celebrate the 200th birthday of the house. The juxtaposition he's captured here is captivating, a pronounced contrast between the exciting tension and vivacity of 2008 acidity and the depth of creamy texture and complexity instilled by a decade on lees. It ripples with toasted brioche, almond nougat, Parisienne baguette and gingernut biscuits, carrying captivating complexity of subtle spice, even white pepper. Upholding a medium straw hue even at such age, it concludes with magnificent drive and focus, its line and length on another order and its energy and drive promising decades of potential. Acidity as bright as stark pure daylight illuminates the chalk minerality of tremendous crus to mouth-embracing heights. One of the greats from the most exceptional vintage in decades, it stands as a grand testimony to Fresnet's precise attention to detail and seamless craft. One bottle showed low-level cork taint which stripped its fragrance and contracted its finish.

HENRIOT CUVÉE HEMERA BRUT 2005 $$$$$

93 points • DISGORGED JULY 2018 • TASTED IN AUSTRALIA
94 points • DISGORGED 2017 • TASTED IN CHAMPAGNE

50% chardonnay from Chouilly, Avize and Le Mesnil-sur-Oger, 50% pinot from Mailly-Champagne, Verzy and Verzenay; 5g/L dosage; cork

'When I first arrived at Henriot in 2005, my first mission was to evolve Enchanteleurs, the prestige cuvée of the house, to be closer to the range,' Fresnet recalls. 'It was more about oxidative autumn flowers and mushrooms, but we needed to bring some spring and summer to the style! Hence, I created Hemera, which means "light of day", in a similar blend, but with grapes of different maturity. The old oxidative style is not my focus, but I instead aspire to uphold fresh flavours of chardonnay and pinot, to keep acidity and freshness.' He admits 2005 was a very complicated year, in which not every house produced vintage cuvées. 'We did it because our suppliers for this cuvée are only in grand crus, so we could select very beautiful fruit, which was simply too good for us not to produce our prestige cuvée!'

Draped in a full yet bright straw robe with a gold tint, this is a powerful and structured cuvée, rigidly scaffolded by the dry phenolic grip of the warm 2005 season, contributing grainy mouthfeel and notes of bitter hazelnuts, coffee bean, high-cocoa dark chocolate and dust. The wisdom of maturity is articulated in all the character of toasted corn on the cob, butter, gingernut biscuits, vanilla bean, crème brûlée and dark fruit cake, lending a silky, buttery, creamy smoothness that goes some way towards dissipating its phenolic dryness. Ripe fruit of grilled pineapple, golden delicious apple, layers of fruit mince spice and even prune falls away quickly on the finish, leaving callow, bitter phenolic grip amidst long-lingering fine salt minerality. It has been blessed by age, but this is not a vintage to mature longer.

J. LASSALLE

(J. Lah-sahl)

7/10

21 RUE CHÂTAIGNIER 51500 CHIGNY-LES-ROSES
www.champagne-jlassalle.com

CHAMPAGNE
J. LASSALLE

— PROPRIÉTAIRE DE VIGNOBLES —

It takes great sensitivity to create wines that communicate the subtleties not only of the place that has given them birth, but also the very personalities of those who have brought them to life. When I first tasted the enchanting champagnes of J. Lassalle, I knew nothing of the estate or the family behind them and was immediately captivated by their dainty restraint and feminine beauty, arousing my curiosity to discover how such delicate sophistication could be achieved. It all made sense when I met the three generations of delightful women who, for almost 40 years, have nurtured this immaculate estate in the charming village of Chigny-les-Roses.

Ever since Jules Lassalle passed away in 1982, his wife, Olga, daughter Chantal and granddaughter Angéline Templier have worked closely together to treble the size of their family estate to 16 hectares and an annual production of 120,000 bottles. Angéline oversees winemaking, ably assisted by her mother. Olga, now 96, still helps with management and administration. 'We don't need any men to help!' she grins.

The meticulous attention to detail of these women shines in every stage of production. The winery at their home in the village is pristine, bathed in white light, one of the cleanest little facilities I've visited anywhere. 'We do everything as my grandfather did, but because we are girls we have a feminine touch, and you can feel it in the wines,' says Angéline.

The Lassalles have been making champagnes exclusively from their premier cru vineyards since 1942. Their aspiration is to express the clay soil terroir of the northern slopes of the Montagne de Reims, and in particular of their home in Chigny-les-Roses, with all vineyards tightly located within six kilometres of the house.

The domain now spans 60 different parcels, two-thirds of which are located in Chigny-les-Roses. No insecticides or herbicides are used, and every plot is ploughed. 'Finally, the revolution is doing what was done 80 years ago, but we have small plots, so it is hard work!' exclaims Angéline.

'I would love to be like Vilmart with 10 or 12 parcels, but with plots in each of the different parts of Chigny, we have an opportunity to share the terroir of the village. The more plots we have, the better we can express the Chigny terror. We are growers and we are observing our vineyards more and more closely, with an aspiration to more accurately express our terroirs. We are making an evolution, not a revolution.'

Meunier is king here, comprising 50% of plantings, which

Angéline describes as 'the expression of Chigny', well suited to its northerly exposure and humid, limestone-rich soils. Chardonnay (25%) takes a confident, if surprising, lead in Lassalle's most sublime cuvées, and pinot noir makes up the remaining 25% of the estate. The family is privileged to own a significant proportion of old parcels, upholding an average vine age of 40 years, none less than 30, and some up to 50. 'My grandfather started planting vineyards in 1942 and they make great wines, so I am very proud to say that we keep the old vines and don't replant them!' Angéline exclaims. Any fruit of insufficient quality is sold to large houses.

Old vines make for low yields, and Angéline harvests a miniscule 30–50hL per hectare in an average year – half the usual champagne yield. 'Sometimes I need to green harvest, but these volumes are mostly a result of the old vines,' she clarifies.

Blends comprise all three champagne varieties in proportions varied according to the season, bolstered with reserve wines from the preceding vintage. Preserving freshness at every stage is a high priority. Grapes are pressed on the first floor in a new press installed in 2013, and the juice flows by gravity directly to settling tanks below to avoid oxidation, where it undergoes cold settling for 24 hours.

The philosophy in the winery is to maintain the tradition of Angéline's grandfather, while growing progressively. 'I don't want to follow trends, I just want to be respectful of the traditional style of the product we make,' she says. 'The wine we make today is a tribute to my grandfather, and our work in the vineyards looks like the work he did 30 years ago.' Much of the historical equipment of the estate is still in use, including enamelled tanks, and all cuvées are still riddled by hand. New technology, including a modern press, was installed, 'to be more precise'.

Long ageing is inherent to the house style, and when rosé demand outstripped supply, the cuvée was put on allocation rather than earlier release. 'The only thing we have to sell the house is our quality, and it is very important for us to respect this, so we told our clients to wait,' Angéline explains. In the harrowing 2017 season she made only her Preference cuvée.

Angéline Templier

Non-vintage cuvées are claimed to be aged at least four years, vintage cuvées nine and Special Club blanc at least ten, though typically less in my tastings. Nonetheless, this necessitates a large cellar stock of 400,000–450,000 bottles. The estate also holds back unusually large reserves, and currently holds as much reserve as new wine in storage. 'We're always full and running out of room!' says Angéline.

To facilitate growth, the building next door was bought in 2007 and the winery expanded to a capacity of almost 100,000 litres. New cellars were dug under the building, and temperature-controlled stainless steel tanks installed to allow separate vinification, although 60 small plots do not permit the opportunity to keep every parcel separate. 'I prefer stainless steel to express the terroir and not interfere with the style of the wine,' explains Angéline, who is also playing with demi-muids, foudres and barrels, but emphasises that these are purely experimental. She will, however, make a special magnum release of both white and rosé cuvées wild fermented in demi-muids from Châteauneuf-du-Pape.

Every cuvée undergoes full malolactic fermentation, even in the warm 2018 season. 'I like the roundness of malolactic for our style, and they don't seem to lose freshness, even with long ageing,' she suggests. The acidity of the northern Montagne de Reims is certainly charged with great endurance. Cuvées are blended after malolactic and stored in 50-year-old ceramic tanks for four months prior to bottling in April.

Angéline uses dosages of consistently around 7–8g/L. 'We are getting lighter in dosage, which is the natural trend, but we never go as low as extra brut,' she explains. 'We make expressive, round wines with malolactic fermentation, rather than being all about minerality and salinity, so we are more traditional and don't want 1–2g/L of dosage. I'm not having fun when I have a whole glass at 2–3g/L!'

In late 2013, the Lassalles were presented with their biggest growth opportunity yet: an invitation to buy the neighbouring estate of a cousin in the village, providing much-needed production and cellar space and, most of all, 4.5 glorious hectares of vineyards in Chigny-les-Roses, Ludes and Rilly-la-Montagne, all conveniently neighbouring existing Lassalle plots.

When I visited during vintage 2014, the first of the new fruit was arriving and I was privileged to the first tour of the new premises. The Lassalles are excited about the opportunity to expand production from 100,000 to 150,000 bottles, but are cautious about maintaining quality, so are slowly evolving production progressively over four years. Half of production is currently sold to the United States, where Lassalle was one of the very first growers to market its cuvées in 1975.

Refined new labels were introduced in 2015, with elegant white space reflecting the graceful appeal of the house and courtyard. The lot code laser-etched on every cuvée is the disgorgement date.

Don't miss these impeccably crafted cuvées of generous fruit presence, purity, and the most intricately judged balance.

J. Lassalle Preference Premier Cru NV $$

93 points • **2015 base vintage** • **Disgorged late 2018** • **Tasted in Champagne**

20% chardonnay, 20% pinot, 60% meunier; 2014 reserves; mostly Chigny-les-Roses with some parcels of Puisieulx and Montbré at the bottom of the slope; aged 2.5 years on lees; 8g/L dosage; 87,000 bottles

Angéline Templier's aspiration for her entry cuvée is to capture the freshness of Chigny-les-Roses, by emphasising the aromas of meunier, structured with chardonnay and pinot noir. She describes it as 'purposely affordable and designed to make people happy, not for sommeliers!' – though she is delighted that a three-Michelin star restaurant in California has offered it by the glass for 10 years. Dosage has been lowered from 9g/L to 8g/L in response to global warming.

In the hands of the most sensitive practitioners, the elegant crus of the northern Montagne de Reims take the warmer seasons in their stride, and Lassalle's delicate entry cuvée exemplifies this emphatically in the warm 2015 harvest. Preference meets its brief of capturing the personality of Chigny-les-Roses meunier in crunchy red apples and wild strawberry fruits, accented with spice and hints of golden fruit cake. It unites flesh with elegant tension and persistence. A touch of dry-extract grip from the warm 2015 harvest is well restrained and does not topple the flow of the finish. As intricately crafted and graceful as ever, this is a wonderful expression of berry fruit freshness in the elegant tension of the house and the northern Montagne.

J. Lassalle Rosé Premier Cru Brut NV $$

94 points • 2016 base vintage • Disgorged late 2018 • Tasted in Champagne

Majority pinot noir with some meunier and chardonnay; 2015 reserves; 3% red wine from Chigny-les-Roses vines planted in 1942; aged 18 months on lees; 8g/L dosage

'Delicate and light, our rosé is an expression of the three generations of the feminine style of the house,' says Angéline Templier. 'An exercise of balance rather than set percentages, there are no rules for the blend, except that it is a majority of pinot noir, with a little meunier and chardonnay, because I love the *cépage* of these varieties.' Red wine is added the day before bottling, made from the estate's oldest plot in Chigny, planted in 1942. Typically only 2–4% red wine is used, and as little as 2% due to the dark extraction of red wine in recent vintages, 'because we don't want something too full-bodied'. With one year less on lees, it is always a year younger than Preference. Like Preference, dosage has been lowered from 9g/L to 8g/L.

The epitome of the dainty refinement and clean precision that I adore of this cuvée, this is a delightfully elegant rosé with a gorgeous, pale salmon hue and a fairy touch of rose petal perfume. Lighter than air freshness is graced with pretty, subtle notes of red cherries and strawberries, invigorated by bright acidity and magnificently fine, salt chalk minerality that bears the stamp of the north-facing slopes of the northern Montagne. For all its refinement, it lacks nothing in presence or personality, with a mid-palate that coasts with the body of pinot noir of intricate, effortless harmony. Graceful and confident, it beautifully embodies its aspiration of articulating the delicate feminine touch of the house. One of the benchmarks of elegant champagne rosé, this is a breathtakingly subtle and primary apéritif that deserves to be showcased with as little culinary distraction as possible.

J. Lassalle Blanc de Blancs Premier Cru Brut 2009 $$$

94 points • Disgorged late 2018 • Tasted in Champagne

Single-site Chigny-les-Roses chardonnay; aged 8.5 years on lees; 7g/L dosage; 5000 bottles

Jules Lassalle was ahead of his time in showcasing the terroirs of his vineyards, and Angéline Templier's aspiration for her blanc de blancs is to continue his legacy. Previously sourced from a single parcel in Villers-Allerand and now from a single site in Chigny-les-Roses. The slope in the village is gentle, never more than 11%, so the family's steepest slope was chosen, with 50-year-old vines on chalky soils. With a south-east exposition, it's a particularly sunny site. 'We like to express this roundness of Chigny terroir, with minerality and floral fragrance, not abrasive or strict,' Angéline explains. 'It's so expressive, I have the sensation that we are making a wine rather than a champagne.' This is particularly pronounced in 2009, a season she describes as 'a solar vintage, very hot in temperature and very complicated for chardonnay, but we wanted to present this experience'.

It takes both talent and a sensitive touch to extract a cuvée of refreshing balance from a sunny site in a vintage as warm as 2009. Lassalle's Blanc de Blancs meets its aspiration of expressive body and character confidently, yet preserves the restraining elegance that characterises Chigny-les-Roses. Leading out strong with pineapple, succulent white peach and fig, it glides gracefully into a long finish of refreshingly balanced acidity and deep salt minerality. Age has blessed it with brioche and wild honey notes, which carry a very long finish.

Sacy, harvest 2017

J. LASSALLE CUVÉE ANGÉLINE PREMIER CRU BRUT 2011 $$$$

86 points • DISGORGED JANUARY 2019 • TASTED IN CHAMPAGNE

40% chardonnay, 60% pinot from two vineyards planted on the slope of Chigny-les-Roses in the early 1970s; aged 7 years on lees; 7g/L dosage; 7000 bottles

'We have not had a vintage like 2011 any time in 200 years!' exclaims Angéline Templier. 'It was a complicated vintage as the phenolic maturity came before the alcoholic maturity, particularly in pinot and meunier. Our decision was to wait to harvest, and this proved to be a good decision.'

The flagship of the house, created from the same parcels since 1973, epitomising the elegance of northern Montagne pinot noir and the exacting precision of Lassalle. Locking into two parcels denies the insurance of blending in the tougher seasons, making this a cuvée that sways vividly with the wild swings of Champagne's climate. It sadly suffered dramatically in the wake of 2011. This is a vintage of herbal, sappy, green, even woody, smoky notes and astringent phenolic grip, leaving the finish awkward and firm. It shows fleshy stone fruits, crunchy grapefruit and the grainy texture and astringency of underripe pear, presenting particularly stark and lean, just a week after disgorgement.

J. LASSALLE SPECIAL CLUB PREMIER CRU BRUT ROSÉ 2012 $$$$

96 points • DISGORGED LATE 2018 • TASTED IN CHAMPAGNE

Inaugural release; 60% chardonnay, 40% pinot; aged 7 years on lees; 4% red wine; 8g/L dosage; just 500 bottles

Lassalle has released its first Special Club Rosé with the same philosophy and the same blend that Special Club blanc has maintained since its first vintage in 1979. 'I like the approach of showcasing the terroir of the village,' is Angéline Templier's ambition. 'I wanted to uphold the tradition of my grandfather, but also to adapt to the new tradition with our red wine of Chigny-les-Roses, crossing the past and the future.'

Lassalle has always made delightful rosé, so its inaugural Special Club Rosé has arrived with great anticipation. The result meets the expectation with resounding success. A wonderfully characterful wine of gorgeous pale salmon hue (very impressive for such a tiny proportion of red wine), it wells up with refreshing lift of red cherry and wild strawberry fruit, flowing seamlessly into the gingernut biscuits and brioche of seven years of age. It articulately embodies the terroir of Chigny in deep salt minerality that dances and glides through a super-fine tannin structure of confident, effortless, incredible persistence.

J. Vignier

(J. Vii-niay)

427 Rue de la Libération 51530 Cramant
www.champagnevignier.fr

Nathalie Vignier is the tenth generation of her family to grow grapes in Champagne, and the sixth in her village of Cramant. In team with her family friend Sebastian Nickel, their substantial estate spans 16.5 hectares, planted exclusively to chardonnay in Cramant, Oiry and Chouilly and the Coteaux du Sézannais, providing for an annual production of around 140,000 bottles (though the four cuvées I tasted each declare a production of only 3500 bottles). Vines date from as far back as 1950 and are tended today without herbicides or insecticides. These are generous champagnes, built around ripe fruit, vinified in stainless steel vats with full malolactic fermentation and aged long on lees, with little need for dosage, and all are bottled at an extra-brut level of 5g/L. Disgorgement dates, base vintages, cépage, dosage and even the number of bottles produced have been declared on back labels since 2018.

J. Vignier Ora Alba Brut Grand Cru NV $$

87 points • Disgorged September 2016 • Tasted in Australia

100% chardonnay from Cramant, Chouilly and Oiry; aged 6 years on lees; 3500 bottles; 5g/L dosage

Vignier turns the reserve concept on its head in her entry cuvée, using younger rather than older vintages in small proportions. With its oldest vintage dominant, this is an unusual recipe, though it makes good sense for a rich and ripe house style in these days of ever-warmer vintages – though the logistics of holding such large parcels for three years prior to blending must be a nightmare. The vintages are undeclared here, but I suspect it's based on 2009, which would make it 65% 2009, 25% 2010 and 10% 2011. A bright, medium straw hue heralds a generous and rich expression of the northern Côte des Blancs. This is a ripe and powerful style, true to the mood of the house and the exuberance of 2009, brimming with honey, spice and gingernut biscuits, even exotic tropical fruit nuances, concluding with the phenolic grip of dry extract.

Cramant, harvest 2014

J. Vignier Silexus Sezannensis Brut NV $$

88 points • 100% 2011 • Disgorged September 2016 • Tasted in Australia

100% chardonnay from parcels of Le Chatet on chalky subsoil in the heart of Sézannais; 100% 2011, though not declared; aged 5 years on lees; 5g/L dosage; 3500 bottles

A bright, medium straw hue announces a blanc de blancs that showcases the dry, grainy structure of the Sézanne, heightened by the challenging 2011 season, with a note of grapefruit-pith bitterness. Almond meal notes of lees age are more prominent than the subtle fruit character of neutral apple and pear. Five years on lees provides a textural creaminess, though helpless to resolve its bitter grip.

J. Vignier Les Longues Verges Brut Grand Cru NV $$$

89 points • Disgorged September 2016 • Tasted in Australia

100% chardonnay from a single plot, Les Longues Verges, of slow-ripening and low-yielding vines on chalk, crossing the boundary between Cramant and Chouilly; aged 4 years on lees; 5g/L dosage; 3500 bottles

A rich take on Cramant and Chouilly, layered with ginger, spice and butter cake. It's full and broad, with oxidative development creating a dry and slightly grainy finish.

J. Vignier Deux Terres Brut 2008 $$

92 points • Disgorged September 2016 • Tasted in Australia

100% chardonnay from two plots, one in Cramant for vivacity, and one in Barbonne-Fayel south of Sézanne for roundness and breadth; aged 8 years on lees; 5g/L dosage; formerly named 'Cuvée 2008'; 3500 bottles

The ripe exuberance of J. Vignier is neatly juxtaposed by the tension of the 2008 harvest. There is a compelling generosity here that contrasts ripe white peach fruit with a panoply of layers of aged complexity: golden fruit cake, fruit mince spice, wild honey and brioche. Eight years on lees has built buttery, creamy structure, well countered on the finish with a touch of bitter grapefruit bite.

J.L. VERGNON

(J.L. Vair-ngoh)

7/10

1 GRANDE RUE 51190 LE MESNIL-SUR-OGER
www.champagne-jl-vergnon.com

J.L. Vergnon

*D*aring' is the only word to describe the little estate of J.L. Vergnon in Le Mesnil-sur-Oger. In a village renowned for chardonnay of greater longevity than any other in Champagne, no other estate besides the long-aged Salon itself dares avoid malolactic fermentation. And Vergnon goes further. Dosages are very low, never more than 5g/L, and often just 3g/L. Its top cuvée, appropriately named 'Confidence', is vinified entirely in oak, a whopping 50% of which is brand new. With such an ambitious recipe, the proof of the skill of this house is a well-crafted range of long-lived blanc de blancs that capture the vibrant, clean expression of the finest grand crus of the Côte des Blancs and, most of all, Le Mesnil-sur-Oger.

And herein lies the secret of J.L. Vergnon. With nothing but chardonnay harvested ripe from just 5.5 hectares of vines averaging more than 30 years of age, enviably situated primarily in Le Mesnil-sur-Oger, Oger and Avize, there is no need for malolactic fermentation, chaptalisation, dosage, or any other trick to soften or mask such riveting fruit.

The aim at harvest is to achieve maximum maturity so as to produce balanced wines of vinosity and finesse. To this end, an average vine age of more than 30 years is upheld and cover crops are used to naturally regulate yields. There is a focus on sustainable viticulture with High Environmental Value certification, completely shunning herbicides for the past 15 years, and avoiding pesticides where possible.

Didier Vergnon and his son Clement are the fourth and fifth generations to manage the estate, which has existed in Le Mesnil since 1950, though has only produced its own cuvées since 1985.

With supply limiting current production to 50,000 bottles, they surrendered their grower-producer status in late 2012 to function as a négociant and purchase fruit from the 2013 harvest, with the plan to increase the volume of their Conversation cuvée.

'I buy grapes in the vineyard, like they do in Burgundy, though this is not done much in Champagne,' explained Christophe Constant, J.L. Vergnon's talented chef de cave since 2000. 'I don't want to buy must, only grapes, so we can press everything ourselves, with one exception. We have found an old vineyard in Le Mesnil managed by someone who works like me and makes wine without malolactic fermentation, and we would like to one day buy vins clairs from him.'

In October 2017, Christophe Constant announced his retirement after 17 years at Vergnon. He invited the young and capable Julian Goût to apply for his position. A wise choice, Goût shares Constant's fanatical attention to detail and arrived in 2018

with a wealth of experience, having worked at the coopérative in Les Mesnil, and with Anselme Selosse, Taittinger and most recently at Henri Giraud (where he was happy to move on, 'because I didn't like the style – too much barrel and too much sugar').

He is much more at home with the style of Vergnon. 'Our goal is to pick late with lots of maturity and aromas, no malolactic fermentation and low dosage,' he sums up. 'With no malolactic and low dosage you cannot make wines that lack purity as there is no artifice.'

Goût oversees not only the winemaking but also the vineyards, and had just come in from six hours of ploughing when I first met him. Managing the estate is no simple task, not that 5.5 hectares is a large holding, but they are spread over 30 parcels, one in Avize, three in Oger, one in Vertus, one in Villeneuve and the remaining 25 or so in Le Mesnil-sur-Oger, including four in the legendary Les Chétillons.

Goût vinifies in stainless steel tanks or oak, according to the cuvée, and all reserve wines have been fermented in oak since 2010. One or two new barrels are purchased each year and are used unseasoned to ferment cuvées from the outset – courageous, but his rich fruit tends to handle it. Disgorgement is by hand, and disgorgement dates are printed on every back label and cork. The first two digits are the month and the second two are the year.

These are engaging wines of characterful endurance and riveting structure that are not to be judged hurriedly. It takes some time to get to know these cuvées, and the longer I sip and swirl, the more I admire their harmony.

Blending of different plots creates distinct personalities in five cuvées, whose evocative names neatly sum up the character of the house in both French and English: 'Conversation', 'Éloquence', 'Résonance', 'Rosémotion' and, most of all, 'Confidence'.

Le Mesnil-sur-Oger, summer 2011

J.L. Vergnon Murmure Brut Nature Premier Cru Blanc de Blancs NV $$

90 points • 2015 BASE VINTAGE • DISGORGED APRIL 2018 • TASTED IN CHAMPAGNE AND AUSTRALIA

100% chardonnay, 50% from one vineyard in Vertus, vinified and aged in oak barrels on lees; 50% from one vineyard in Villeneuve, vinified in stainless steel; no reserves, but only aged 2 years on lees, so not labelled as a vintage; zero dosage; 7000 bottles; cork

Vergnon's ripe style colliding with the warm 2015 season in the generous red clay soils of Vertus and Villeneuve, amplified by half oak vinification, conspire to make for a powerfully concentrated and densely structured blanc de blancs. The tension of lemon, grapefruit and apple is heightened by the cut of malic acidity and zero dosage, contrasting an exotic mood true to these crus, evoking in honeydew melon, mandarin, orange and nashi pear. Salty minerality is underscored by the drying phenolic bite of 2015, sufficient to completely strangle any mortal cuvée, yet here the stature of looming fruit presence and powerful chalk/malic interplay rise to meet it, uniting in a finish of confident endurance. This is a piercing style of stark purity and virile youthfulness that will improve in time and looks set to live for decades.

J.L. Vergnon Conversation Brut Grand Cru Blanc de Blancs NV $$

95 points • 2013 BASE VINTAGE • DISGORGED 7 FEBRUARY 2018 • TASTED IN AUSTRALIA
94 points • 2014 BASE VINTAGE • TASTED IN CHAMPAGNE

100% chardonnay from Le Mesnil-sur-Oger, Avize and Oger; 20% reserves; aged 3 years on lees; 80% 2013 base vinified in stainless steel; 20% reserves vinified and aged for 3 months in oak barrels; 5g/L dosage; 30,000 bottles; cork

This Conversation is as engaging as ever, leading out with the articulate lemon, apple and pear that classically define the ripe Le Mesnil style of Vergnon. A touch of barrel fermentation and more than three years on lees have built a medium straw hue, delightfully creamy texture and glorious layers of brioche, almond nougat, gingernut biscuits, crème brûlée, even a note of spicy white fruit cake. Perfectly ripe malic acidity is seamlessly integrated, amplifying the frothing salt chalk minerality of Le Mesnil to wonderful effect. This is the quintessential apéritif with the potential to age long, a captivating and enticing cuvée of sensational coherence, brilliant definition, great line and enduring length. It takes considerable talent to harmoniously unite malic acidity, oak fermentation and low dosage in a village as tense as Le Mesnil, and to achieve such a compelling result in the lead cuvée of the house is grand testimony to the calibre of this fabled estate. All the more profound that Vergnon makes as much Conversation as every other cuvée put together.

J.L. Vergnon Eloquence Grand Cru Blanc de Blancs Extra Brut NV $$

93 points • 2014 BASE VINTAGE • DISGORGED 17 MAY 2018 • TASTED IN CHAMPAGNE AND AUSTRALIA

100% chardonnay from Le Mesnil-sur-Oger, Avize and Oger; 80% 2014 base vinified in stainless steel; 20% reserves vinified and aged 3 months in oak barrels; aged 3 years on lees; Conversation with 2g/L dosage; 15,000 bottles; cork

Back in the days when Conversation held 7g/L dosage, there was a subtle distinction in the 3g/L dosage of Eloquence. Conversation has since progressively dropped to 5g/L, and Eloquence to 2g/L, narrowing the gap, yet still as profoundly and astonishingly distinct as ever! I love them both, Conversation with a whisker more generosity, and Eloquence for its dazzling display of fine chalk minerality and strict malic drive. Such detail of distinction is testimony both to the fanatical attention to detail of Christophe and Julian and to the articulate expression of the finest nuances in their cuvées. With lower dosage, Eloquence is more coiled and closed on the bouquet and palate, building a core of apple, pear and preserved lemon fruit with generous layers of spicy, toasty, biscuity complexity from three years of lees contact. The generous mid-palate of ripe Le Mesnil fruit pulls into a honed finish of sparkling, crystalline minerality and well-composed malic acidity, making for an enlivening apéritif.

J.L. VERGNON ROSÉMOTION GRAND CRU EXTRA BRUT NV $$

95 points • 2013 BASE VINTAGE • DISGORGED 12 APRIL 2018 • TASTED IN AUSTRALIA
94 points • 2014 BASE VINTAGE • TASTED IN CHAMPAGNE

90% chardonnay from Le Mesnil-sur-Oger, Avize and Oger, Eloquence with 10% pinot noir red wine from Mailly Grand Cru; 20% reserves; aged 3 years on lees; 3g/L dosage; 2000 bottles; cork

Blended according to taste rather than colour, the aspiration for Rosémotion is rosé with the specificity of chardonnay. Mailly-Champagne red wine blesses Eloquence chardonnay with a pale salmon-copper hue and nuances of red apple, tangy morello cherries, red berries and a savoury edge of fresh tomato, tamarillo and a touch of pink pepper. Texture and structure are the game here, and the inimitable, fine, salty chalk mineral presence of Le Mesnil is all-encompassing, heightened by the bright malic acidity of the energetic 2013 harvest and invisibly low dosage. It carries with great persistence and savoury refinement. A masterfully crafted, beautifully elegant and consummately engaging apéritif rosé.

J.L. VERGNON OG GRAND CRU BLANC DE BLANCS BRUT NATURE 2011 $$

87 points • DISGORGED NOVEMBER 2017 • TASTED IN CHAMPAGNE AND AUSTRALIA

100% chardonnay from the single plot, Le Chemin de Flavigny, of old vines low on the slope on the border of Oger and Le Mesnil-sur-Oger; vinified in stainless steel; aged 5 years on lees; zero dosage; 3121 bottles; cork

Julian Goût describes 2011 as 'the worst vintage', and recalls Christophe's assessment: 'In 2010, everyone picked too late, and so they all picked too early in 2011, and hence there is a problem with vegetal taste and lack of maturity.' The underripe-fruit notes of green capsicum and green bean, marked by the dusty, dry, green coffee bean notes of this challenging harvest, make for a dry, firm and callow style of astringent, grainy structure, without the safety net of malolactic or dosage.

J.L. VERGNON EXPRESSION GRAND CRU BLANC DE BLANCS EXTRA BRUT 2010 $$

92 points • DISGORGED 12 APRIL 2018 • TASTED IN AUSTRALIA

100% chardonnay from Le Mesnil-sur-Oger, Avize and Oger; vinified in stainless steel; aged 6 years on lees; 2011 vintage to be renamed Expression de Terroirs (though no change in recipe or terroirs); 3g/L dosage; 2500 bottles; cork

The harmonious accord between ripe fruit presence, toasty development, prominent chalk minerality and malic tension that define Vergnon works to compelling effect, even in the tricky 2010 season. Lemon, granny smith apple and beurre bosc pear fruit are marked by a little underripe note of green bean, which heightens the tension between malic acidity and phenolic bite on the finish. Nonetheless, the interplay between the creamy silkiness of six years lees age and the fine salt minerality of Le Mesnil is well-composed and persistent.

J.L. Vergnon Resonance Blanc de Blancs Grand Cru Extra Brut 2009 $$$$

93 points • Disgorged 7 February 2017 and May 2017 • Tasted in Champagne and Australia

100% chardonnay from two plots, Les Chétillons and Les Mussettes in Le Mesnil-sur-Oger; vinified and aged in stainless steel; aged 7 years on lees; 2010 vintage to be renamed MSNL (though no change in recipe or terroirs); 3g/L dosage; 3222 bottles; cork

Goût describes this cuvée as typical of these two sites, delivering great concentration with lots of chalk minerality. In the wake of the eternal endurance of the scintillating 2008 season, the generosity of 2009 follows with great confidence and absolutely no lack of tension or potential. With a brilliant pale straw hue, grapefruit, ripe granny smith apple and lemon zest are backed by the toasty, biscuity, ginger-accented spice of a decade of age. The generosity of fruit picked ripe in the powerful 2009 season makes for depth and richness of mandarin and orange fruit, honey and almond, even a touch of molasses, all kept in strict line thanks to the double act of malic acidity and the heightened, salty chalk mineral texture of these two great terroirs. The grip of phenolic structure of late harvest in this warm vintage makes for a firm finish, and it will benefit from a lot longer in the cellar yet, promising to go down among the most enduring 2009s of all.

J.L. Vergnon Confidence Blanc de Blancs Grand Cru Brut Nature 2010 $$$

94 points • Disgorged 19 December 2017 • Tasted in Champagne and Australia

100% chardonnay from the single plot Les Hautes Mottes in Le Mesnil-sur-Oger; 100% vinified and aged in 300-litre oak barrels; aged 6 years on lees; 2011 vintage be renamed Hautes Mottes, as a coopérative trademarked Confidence (though no change in recipe or terroir); zero dosage; cork

The big terroir of Les Hautes Mottes sits at the bottom of the village of Le Mesnil, where the soil infuses great richness in its fruits. The powerful structure and amplified ripeness of Vergnon rise confidently to the challenge posed by new oak. The result presents a full, bright straw hue amidst a swirling maelstrom of lemon meringue, white chocolate, brazil nuts, bran, toffee, even a hint of pine nettles. A shard of lemon and grapefruit erupts triumphantly, charged by high-tensile malic acidity and the omnipresent, larger-than-life, all-singing, all-dancing salt minerality of Le Mesnil. A cuvée of exacting execution, delivering all the confidence that its name anticipates, exemplifying the unlikely truth that balance and harmony can be found even in larger-than-life proportions, provided every element rises equally to the challenge.

J.L. Vergnon Confidence Blanc de Blancs Grand Cru Brut Nature 2009 $$$

94 points • Tasted in Champagne

As above

It takes confidence indeed to half vinify in a forest of new oak, and this tense and structured fruit of Le Mesnil is infused with no shortage of vanillin oak flavour and tannin. Even in the two years since I tasted it last, it has upheld its grand power of grapefruit, fennel and lemon, with the heightened tension of malic acid and zero dosage, pulled in firmly on a finish accented with wood spice. Yet for all of its stark, contrasting tension, this is a cuvée that immaculately and astonishingly finds a harmony and balance with ripe white peach and apple confidence, propagating very long and true amidst the frothing salt chalk minerality that defines Le Mesnil. The exuberance of 2009 knows no bounds, yet the definition and control brought by malic acidity is all-encompassing. The result stands in stark contrast to this voluptuous and immediate vintage, and this is set to go down as one of the most enduring cuvées of the season. Hold off until at least 2025, and preferably longer.

JACQUART

(Zhah-khah)

(5/10)

34 BOULEVARD LUNDY 51100 REIMS
www.champagne-jacquart.com

CHAMPAGNE
JACQUART

Jacquart is the brand of the Alliance Champagne Group, a cooperative representing one of Champagne's largest sources of grapes. The group is owned by 1800 growers, holding over 2200 hectares (and counting), vinifying 900 separate parcels spanning more than 150 crus across the Côte des Blancs, Vallée de la Marne, Montagne de Reims and Côte des Bar. Jacquart has grown dramatically since it was founded just over 50 years ago, selecting 300 parcels from 300 hectares of its vineyard pool to create 2.6 million bottles of pleasant chardonnay-led blends. Freshness, purity and elegance are the mandates of the house, upheld by 38-year-old chef de cave Florian Eznack, who left Veuve Clicquot to join the house in 2011. Its chardonnay-focused style calls for long ageing, and non-vintage cuvées are matured a minimum of four years, blanc de blancs at least six years and Cuvée Alpha seven or more.

In 2010, Jacquart ranked as the fifth largest house in Champagne, boasting a production of 5.8 million bottles. 'But Jacquart got lost in promotions and supermarket listings and so lost its image,' Eznack admits. With 18 different cuvées in the portfolio, the house was ready for a refocus. 'With 2200 hectares you could do anything you want to please the market, but we don't want to do this,' she says.

When Eznack came on board, production was slashed by more than half, aspiring 'to be recognised as a premium brand, though not a luxury brand – we are not trying to compete with LVMH or Pernod Ricard.' She is comfortable with the current production level to maintain consistency in Brut Mosaïque and to introduce the prestige Alpha cuvées. 'I could produce a little more volume if I wanted to, but to do much more would compromise quality,' she explains.

The complexity of this scenario is compounded because Eznack finds herself in a unique position in Champagne overseeing three winemakers, each responsible for their own distinct brand and their own production facility. The group makes Devaux in Bar-sur-Seine, Collet in Oger and Pannier in Château-Thierry. Each produces just 400–500,000 bottles, making the much larger volume of Jacquart the prime priority of the group.

Eznack's exclusive priority rests on Jacquart, and she says she gets to choose all the parcels she wants. She's the youngest in the team, yet enjoys strong relationships with each of her winemakers. 'Having three wineries is a weakness and the logistics can be hard to manage,' she reveals. 'But it is rare in Champagne to have the opportunity to create a brand together in addition to each of their own brands.'

Vinification of the cuvée (no tailles is used) for each of the group's 900 separate parcels takes place in small vats, no larger than 400 hectolitres. Of these, just 300 are preselected for blending for Jacquart and the remainder are sold to other houses.

The freshness, straightforward appeal and power of chardonnay are the aspirations, sourced predominantly from the Côte des Blancs (particularly Vertus) and the Montagne de Reims, fleshed out with the fruitiness of meunier from the very far west of the Vallée de la Marne and the premier crus around Épernay, and the finesse of pinot noir, half from the northern slopes of the

Montagne de Reims and half from the eastern parts of the Aube.

This mandate of freshness and appeal does not call for a heavy reliance on reserve wines, which are used selectively to fill out the flesh of the blends for consistency and longevity. 'We are looking for refined texture, elegant bead and graceful and immediately accessible wines, with sufficient richness to enjoy,' Eznack sums up. Her current cuvées meet the brief with pleasant appeal.

In June 2019, Eznack announced that she was moving on after eight years with Jacquart. At the time of writing, her successor is yet to be announced.

JACQUART BRUT MOSAÏQUE NV $$

90 points • 2013 BASE VINTAGE • DISGORGED SECOND QUARTER OF 2018 • TASTED IN AUSTRALIA

35–40% chardonnay for freshness and delicate aromas, 35–40% pinot for structure, 25–30% meunier for fruit; a blend of 60 villages with a focus on the grand crus of the Côte des Blancs and Montagne de Reims; 20% reserves; no oak; 9g/L dosage; 1.1–1.2 million bottles; cork

'The essence of Jacquart is to be a mosaic,' says Florian Eznack. A fresh and refreshing style of medium straw hue and red apple, raspberry, lemon and candied citrus is true to her aspiration, accurately reflecting more elegant pinot and meunier parcels to highlight the structure and elegance of chardonnay. It concludes with accurate acid line and elegant persistence in a fresh and lively apéritif style. The dosage has always shown a little in this cuvée, and while its level hasn't changed on paper, it looks more candied on the finish in the 2013 base than it did in 2012. Its phenolics are better controlled than ever, which means it would shine with less sugar in a great base year like this.

JACQUART ROSÉ MOSAÏQUE NV $$$

89 points • 2012 BASE VINTAGE • DISGORGED SECOND QUARTER OF 2017 • TASTED IN AUSTRALIA

34% chardonnay, 45% pinot, 21% meunier; 28% reserve wines; 18% pinot noir red wine selected from Neuville, Les Riceys, Vertus, Cumières and Aÿ; a blend of 63 crus; aged 3 years on lees; 9g/L dosage; more than 300,000 bottles; cork

Jacquart builds its rosé on the same base as its white Mosaïque, with a mandate of impact and attack, achieved with a solid dose of pinot noir red wine, contributing body, fine tannin grip and a medium salmon colour, now tending towards copper. The same base I tasted two years prior has benefited from an additional year on lees, upholding primary strawberry and raspberry fruit over a savoury core of roast nuts and tomatoes. This bottle has shed the gamey, charcuterie suggestions of the past, though retains a firm grip to its tannins, which 9g/L dosage helps to soften.

JACQUART BLANC DE BLANCS 2012 $$$$

94 points • DISGORGED THIRD QUARTER OF 2017 • TASTED IN AUSTRALIA

100% chardonnay from Avize, Le Mesnil-sur-Oger, Vertus, Villers-Marmery, Aÿ and Hautvillers; aged 5 years on lees; no oak; 8g/L dosage; cork

'Freshness, minerality, chalk, creaminess, ampleness and richness' are the diverse aspirations for Jacquart's Blanc de Blancs, and 2012 meets this ambitious brief more confidently than any before it. This was the first great season since Florian Eznack joined the house, and this cuvée resoundingly proclaims her elegant yet confident touch. Sourcing is adjusted according to the season, always from the Montagne de Reims or the Côte des Blancs; in 2012 a union of grand and premier crus from both, seamlessly uniting the generosity of Aÿ, Hautvillers, Villers-Marmery and Vertus with the tension and focus of Avize and Le Mesnil-sur-Oger. Bright lemon and succulent white peach fruit are generously underscored by the almond nougat and cream of five years of lees age, uniting seamless and poised on a finish of great line and length. The mineral signature of Avize and Le Mesnil are pronounced, deeply chalky and finely mineral, charging the finish with great freshness and finesse. A little jump from 6g/L to 8g/L dosage is not out of place in this vibrant season. All hail the new Jacquart!

Jacquesson vinifies exclusively in oak foudres.

Jacquesson's attention in the vineyard allows its cuvées to capture the expression of the soil, exemplified in its quartet of single-vineyard, single-varietal, single-vintage wines produced in minuscule volumes (never more than 10% of production in total), from four special little plots in Aÿ, Dizy and Avize. 'Terroir is the most unfair part of the wine business – you either have the right place or you don't!' Jean-Hervé says. 'It is very important to talk about terroir in champagne.' And talk terroir these cuvées do, articulating chalk mineral textures of disarming clarity. J

HANDS-OFF WINEMAKING

Jacquesson's scrupulous practices in the vineyard are mirrored in its hands-off approach in the winery. All fruit is pressed using its own presses, three in Dizy and one in Avize. 'Pressing is very important in Champagne because we have this stupid idea of making white wine from red grapes!' he exclaims. 'We must hand-pick and press close to the vineyard or we'll end up with jam.'

Gentle vertical presses are used, 'because they offer better visibility of the fruit, better self-filtration due to the higher surface

area, and they provide the opportunity for *retrousse'* (separation and redistribution of the press cake between pressings). The very first juice is removed 'because it has washed the outside of the grapes'. Dry ice is used to reduce oxidation. No chaptalisation has been performed since 2007. 'You only need to chaptalise when there is a problem,' Jean-Hervé points out.

The Chiquets prefer what they describe as an oxidative rather than reductive style of winemaking. Each parcel is vinified separately in large 45hL oak foudres to allow the wine to breathe, after which it is left on lees and stirred until a relatively late bottling in June or July up until 2014. Since that time, *élevage* has been extended to a full year, with wines racked into tanks just before harvest and bottled after harvest.

Occasional *bâtonnage* (lees stirring) produces creaminess and body, and has stabilising and antioxidant effects, and so no sulphur dioxide is generally required between pressing and disgorgement, though on this Jean-Hervé is refreshingly unpragmatic: 'If a barrel needs sulphur, we give it, but only very rarely do they need it.'

'Malolactic fermentation is the eternal debate in Champagne,' Jean-Hervé suggests. 'We favour malolactic fermentation as we don't want to use heavy sulphur dioxide additions or filtration.' Traditionally, Jacquesson has run malolactic fermentation to completion, but more recently has discouraged it in less than 20% of ferments by using cooling. 'Strictly blocking malolactic can be too intrusive, but sometimes we try to discourage it, in order to achieve balance.' There is also no cold settling, filtering or fining, 'to maintain the aromatic potential of the fruit'. Cold stabilisation occurs naturally in barrels.

To build complexity, reserves for the 700 series wines are the previous blends, kept separate in foudres, demi-muids and enamelled tanks. No single parcels are kept as reserves, which makes allocation of parcels a simple choice between the 700 series, the four single vineyards or discarding them to sell. 'Our blending is very easy because we sort of blend everything except the single vineyards,' Jean-Hervé explains. A trial blend is created using the single vineyards, and if the blend needs them, no single vineyard cuvées are made. 'It is not often that we produce the four single vineyards, as we need them to uphold the integrity of the 700 series, and all the more so since it has to age confidently as a Dégorgement Tardif.'

All Jacquesson cuvées have been extra brut (less than 6g/L dosage) since 2000, although only recently declared on labels. Dosages have become progressively lower, but this trend has never been a conscious decision. 'Some of our wines have no dosage, not because we wanted to make zero-dosage wine, but because they were better wines this way,' says Jean-Hervé. All current cuvées have no more than 2.5g/L dosage.

Since 2008, Jacquesson's single-vineyard cuvées and Dégorgement Tardif have been aged on lees under cork. The house reports that it has found this to increase the freshness and liveliness of its long-aged cuvées. Tasting these for the first time this year, I am a little troubled by the subtle phenolic grip that this lends, particularly in Dégorgement Tardif and Champ Cain.

Jacquesson's website is one of the coolest and most informative in Champagne, and back labels are among the most forthcoming of any champagne house, shamelessly declaring the crus for the first time, alongside disgorgement date, dosage, base vintage, blend and even precise production quantities. 'Declaring the number of bottles not only shows how small we are, but also that each cuvée is uniquely identified.'

There are no secrets here, just great champagnes, and better than ever. As Jean-Hervé puts it, 'At Jacquesson, it is very simple, we just want to make good wine from good places.'

JACQUESSON CUVÉE 742 EXTRA BRUT NV $$

94 points • 2014 BASE VINTAGE • DISGORGED JUNE 2018 • TASTED IN CHAMPAGNE

41% Avize and Oiry, 59% Aÿ, Dizy and Hautvillers; 1.5g/L dosage; 222,408 bottles, 10,000 magnums, 300 jéroboams

Jean-Hervé Chiquet describes 2014 as a difficult vintage with some tense acidity, so he had too make a selection. Chardonnay was very good and the finished result was better than he was expecting from a challenging harvest. There is no question that the house is better positioned than ever to deal with the vagaries of Champagne's seasons. The characterful distinction of the Jacquesson style is ever more defined as the house more tightly hones its sourcing, viticulture and vinification. The fruit hails from more noble sources than in the past, gripping grand terroirs with greater confidence of structure and tension, upholding taut focus of lemon and grapefruit amidst characterful expression of red apple fruit, tangy grapefruit and crunchy crab-apple bite. It's riper, too, in a full straw hue, with flickers of exoticism reflected in persimmon, tangelo and pomegranate, yet at every moment vibrant, citrus-driven and honed. Skilfully managed barrel work spins beautifully woven texture without oxidation or oak character, building a fine, creamy mouthfeel that amplifies salty minerality. A well-crafted and characterful wine of great persistence and tension.

JACQUESSON CUVÉE 741 EXTRA BRUT NV $$

93 points • 2013 BASE VINTAGE • DISGORGED MAY 2018 • TASTED IN CHAMPAGNE

Aÿ, Dizy, Hautvillers, Avize and Oiry; 212,788 bottles, 8086 magnums, 302 jéroboams; 2.5g/L dosage

In the Grande Vallée de la Marne and Côte des Blancs, 2013 was a superb vintage, and Jean-Hervé Chiquet reports the pinot noir from Aÿ and Dizy and the chardonnay from Avize as particularly successful. He has encapsulated all the body and personality of Jacquesson in this great season, creating an even and harmonious accord between the red apple and grapefruit intensity of ripe fruit and the deeply spicy layers of barrel fermentation character. Bright acidity lends crunch and bite amidst the subtle grip of phenolic texture, uniting in a confident finish of great length, tension and character. At once energetic and crunchy, and at the same time contemplative and multifaceted, it coasts on a fine line of focused acidity and salty minerality. This release exemplifies the acute sense of detail and inimitable personality of the house more accurately than ever.

JACQUESSON CUVÉE 737 DÉGORGEMENT TARDIF EXTRA BRUT NV $$$$

93 points • 2009 BASE VINTAGE • DISGORGED NOVEMBER 2017 • TASTED IN CHAMPAGNE

43% chardonnay, 30% meunier, 27% pinot noir; 30% reserves; aged 7.5 years on lees under cork for the first time; original release 250,000 bottles and Dégorgement Tardif just 14,640 bottles and 660 magnums; 1.5g/L dosage

Holding prime position among the best Cuvée 700 series releases of the past decade, 737 ranks second only to the sensational 2008 base of 736. It unwound magnificently across its release cycle five years ago, shedding its crystalline brittleness for silky finesse. A glorious 7.5 years on lees has deepened its mood to a full straw hue and heightened its rich complexity with layers of butterscotch, fruit mince spice and gingernut biscuits, while projecting the crunchy apple confidence and grapefruit tension of its youth. It holds its integrity with outstanding line and length, and will continue to age confidently for the next few years. The first 700 series release aged on lees under cork, Jean-Hervé Chiquet is impressed with the freshness and liveliness that this brings, though I am a little troubled by the phenolic bite it lends to the finish.

JACQUESSON AŸ VAUZELLE TERME RÉCOLTE 2008 $$$$$

97 points • DISGORGED APRIL 2018 • TASTED IN CHAMPAGNE

100% pinot noir; tiny plot of just 0.3 hectare, due-south-facing on the mid-slope of Aÿ, not far from the Dizy border; planted by Jean-Hervé Chiquet in 1980 on calcareous soil 60-70 cm over Campanian chalk; vinified and matured in oak casks on lees; zero dosage; 2652 bottles and 198 magnums

Jean-Hervé Chiquet is modest about the terroir that he has always known to be his most exceptional. 'It is just a tiny vineyard, and can we be proud of that? We just take a great terroir and wait for a great vintage!' he grins. That vintage came in 2008, giving birth to an enchanting Vauzelle Terme, and the greatest since the mesmerising 2002. It's an entrancing paradox: so light, fresh and floral that it will lift you clean off the ground, yet reverberating with monumental depth that infuses its full straw hue with a blush tint and its palate with all the red fruits of Aÿ, even candied raspberries and jelly powder. Encapsulating the full heights of fruit purity, poise and tension of its fabled cru, its mineral depth is cavernous and immensely chalk-infused. This is a rousing celebration of Aÿ pinot noir, a cuvée of coiled tension that epitomises the sheer endurance of 2008. With undeviating length and unwavering line, it's a champagne so complete it defies resistance. Few will ever experience what magnificence will unfold when it one day reaches its glorious maturity. That day will not come until at least 2038.

Jacquesson Dizy Corne Bautray Extra Brut Récolte 2008 $$$$$

97 points • Disgorged April 2018 • Tasted in Champagne

100% chardonnay; south-west-facing single-vineyard Dizy of 1 hectare on the boundary with Aÿ, planted in 1960 on millstone-grit gravel over clayey marl and Campanian chalk; vinified and aged in oak casks on lees; zero dosage; 5488 bottles and 304 magnums

This is one of the most profound chardonnays of the Vallée de la Marne, and the most surprising of all. To this day, Jean-Hervé Chiquet has no idea why his father planted chardonnay in Dizy in 1960, nor even from where he obtained it, as there was no chardonnay in the village at the time. No one believed good chardonnay could be grown here, and it was discovered only by the Chiquets when a 1995 *vin clair* stood out. Even today, Jean-Hervé still describes it as 'chardonnay from the wrong place that should not be this good!' And he still has no idea why.

The profound mineral impression of this wine is inexplicable, from a site with chalk no less than 2.5 metres under the surface (very much deeper than in neighbouring Aÿ or any of the great crus of the Côte des Blancs), in a village unrecognised for chardonnay of structure. Over half a century, these old vines have tapped so deep into the terroir that the voice of the soil speaks above the tones of the fruit and the expression of the barrels. Its violent, deep, frothing, salty minerality is a revelation, infusing the palate with immense texture, drawn out with incredible persistence by the high-tensile acid cut of 2008. Lifted, primary lemon tang leaps from the glass with freshness impossible for a decade of age, a shard of purity that remains transfixed with profound line and length. For all of its tension and crunch, the ripeness of the house delivers wonderful presence of almost ripe white nectarine, white peach and layers of spice. Nine years on lees has united every detail in seamless texture, playing out an intense background track to its mineral solo. At least the equal of the soaring 2002, 2008 represents the greatest Corne Bautray yet, a stunning blanc de blancs with an effortless 20-year future before it. It singly takes Dizy to all new (dizzying) heights.

Jacquesson Avize Champ Cain Extra Brut Récolte 2008 $$$$$

96 points • Disgorged April 2018 • Tasted in Champagne

100% chardonnay; due-south-facing single vineyard of 1.3 hectares at the bottom of the slope of Avize, planted in 1962 on surface chalk; vinified and matured in oak casks on lees; 2.5g/L dosage; 8296 bottles and 402 bottles

The terroir of Avize is so all-consuming that you can literally smell the violent tidal wave of heaving salt minerality coming, surging with the full force of heightened 2008 acidity. This cuvée is a salty sea breeze, a steamy whiff of bath salts heralding an intricately crystalline salt structure. The frothing, energetic interplay between chalk minerality and high-tensile acid line is captivating, amplified by subtle barrel texture and long lees age that gently massage the cut of Avize. Nine years on lees has laid down great complexity of roast nuts and spice, without for a moment interrupting its pristine acid drive and exceptional persistence. Its tightly clenched core is a little unsettled by the phenolic grip, subtle toastiness and dusty notes of cork oak, the first vintage to be matured under cork.

Avize, summer 2018

JEEPER

(Zhee-pehr)

---

3 RUE DE SAVIGNY 51170 FAVEROLLES-ET-COËMY
www.champagne-jeeper.com

CHAMPAGNE JEEPER

SINCE 1949

L'ASSEMBLAGE DE L'EXCELLENCE

Taking its name from the jeep in which Armand Goutorbe made his way around the vineyards when he returned from World War II, Jeeper was established in 1949 and became a supermarket brand of the Pressoirs de France group in 2009. The group went into insolvency in early 2013, and the house was rescued by the Reybier group and relaunched in 2015. From its home in Faverolles-et-Coëmy, 15 kilometres to the west of Reims, Jeeper sources from 40 hectares of estate vineyards in the Vallée de la Marne and Côte de Sézanne, substantially supplemented by a declared 160 hectares of growers, though it must be more than this to facilitate an annual production of 2.5 million bottles. Originally created in Damery with a focus on pinot and meunier, today chardonnay takes the lead in every cuvée. Since 2010, chardonnay has increasingly been aged (not fermented) in 1000 barrels of 228-litre capacity and 200 demi-muids of 600 litres, sourced after two to three vintages fermenting chardonnay in Meursault in Burgundy. Jeeper boasts Champagne's third largest stash of barrels after Bollinger and Krug, increasing at 10–15% annually, and time in barrel has extended from 3–6 months to now two years. The aspiration of Jeeper is elegance, but this is sadly foiled by the oxidative development of long barrel age. Sales are mostly in France, and the house is working to build exports. Back labels declare labelling dates, and disgorgement dates are laser etched on bottles, with the year followed by the day of the year (for instance, 18-211 denotes the 211th day of 2018).

JEEPER BRUT GRAND ASSEMBLAGE NV $$$

87 points • 2012 BASE VINTAGE • DISGORGED 18 JULY 2018 • TASTED IN AUSTRALIA

60% chardonnay, 25% pinot noir, 15% meunier; 2010 reserves; 37 villages; 20% of chardonnay aged in oak barrels for 2 years; 7g/L dosage; cork

With a medium straw hue, this is a complex style, led by the biscuity, bready notes and roasted hazelnut character of long lees age, amplified by a portion of barrel age. Dosage adds a honeyed overtone, which is not sufficient to counter the bitter phenolic bite of a firm finish.

JEEPER BRUT GRANDE RÉSERVE NV $$$

85 points • 2012 BASE VINTAGE • DISGORGED 15 JANUARY 2018 • TASTED IN AUSTRALIA

100% chardonnay; 11 villages, mostly from the Côte des Blancs, Marne Valley, Vitry and Sézanne; 2010 reserves; 40% aged in oak barrels for 2 years; 7g/L dosage; cork

With a bold yellow label, this is a blanc de blancs (though only declared on the back label). It's a developed and forward style, with burnt-orange oxidation notes giving the impression it is older than it is. Two years in barrel is too long for 40% of the blend. It consequently lacks vibrancy, definition and carry, though acid/sugar balance is harmonious.

JEEPER BRUT GRAND ROSÉ NV $$$

86 points • 2012 BASE VINTAGE • DISGORGED 27 JUNE 2018 • TASTED IN AUSTRALIA

88% chardonnay (Vitry, Sézanne, Ville-Dommange, Cumières, Oger, Avize, Le Mesnil-sur-Oger, Vertus, Cramant, Verzy and Savigny), 12% Ambonnay pinot red wine; 2010 reserves; 40% chardonnay aged in oak barrels for 2 years; 6g/L dosage; cork

True to the chardonnay-led style of the house, this is a blanc de blancs coloured with Ambonnay pinot noir. It's a savoury and developed style of medium copper-salmon hue, amplified with the richness, toastiness, roast hazelnut bite and charcuterie complexity of 40% of its chardonnay aged in oak barrels for two years. The subtle red berries of Ambonnay are lost in this firm and developed style of phenolic bite.

JEEPER EXTRA BRUT NATURELLE NV $$$

84 points • 2011 AND 2012 BASE VINTAGE • DISGORGED 17 JULY 2018 • TASTED IN AUSTRALIA

60% chardonnay, 40% pinot noir; Cumières, Damery and Verneuil; 2% chardonnay aged in oak barrels for 2 years; organic; zero dosage; cork

The developed style and firm bite of Jeeper have nowhere to hide without the protection of dosage, and this is a dry and astringent style of soapy character and quashed fruit definition. I suspect there is a higher proportion of oak-aged chardonnay than the declared 2%.

JEEPER BRUT PREMIER CRU NV $$$$

90 points • 2012 BASE VINTAGE • DISGORGED 25 MAY 2018 • TASTED IN AUSTRALIA

80% chardonnay, 18% pinot noir, 2% meunier; Ville-Dommange, Sacy, Écueil, Jouy-lès-Reims and Vertus; 27% chardonnay aged in oak barrels for 2 years; 2010 reserves; 6g/L dosage; cork

With a medium, bright straw hue, Jeeper's Premier Cru boasts the best colour of its range. It also carries the most accurate balance and fruit definition, without the oxidation and oak that dog the other cuvées. Gentle stone fruits and citrus are harmoniously wrapped in the nougat and candied almond complexity of long lees age, concluding with soft and gentle balance of acidity and dosage.

JEEPER BRUT GRAND CRU NV $$$$$

89 points • DISGORGED 16 APRIL 2019 • TASTED IN LONDON

98% chardonnay, 2% pinot noir; vinified in barrels; 6g/L dosage; cork

A powerful chardonnay bolstered by the spicy complexity and oxidative development of oak maturation, this is a style of blood orange, bruised apple and pear fruit, underscored by fruit mince spice. It's fleshy and full, though oxidation makes for a dry and contracted finish, lacking in fruit definition and freshness.

JÉRÔME PRÉVOST

(Zheh-rowm Preh-voh)

(7/10)

2 RUE DE LA PETITE MONTAGNE 51390 GUEUX
www.champagnelacloserie.fr

CHAMPAGNE
La Closerie

Across every style and region of the wine world, the very greatest makers share an intuitive approach that transcends any prescriptive grapegrowing or winemaking regime. Besides Anselme Selosse (of Jacques Selosse) himself, no one in Champagne personifies this more dramatically than Jérôme Prévost. When others follow regimes of traditional viticulture, organics or biodynamics, Prévost adopts a natural approach, keeping his senses attuned to the vines and responding gently. In a region that strives to mould every vintage into a house style, Prévost makes only a vintage wine and sees it as his role to support the vines to maximise the expression of the season, though sadly releases it too early to label it as a vintage. He harvests not on sugar or acidity, but on the sensation of the skins of the grapes in his mouth. He can't tell you if his wines go through malolactic fermentation ('I don't do analysis — the wines do what they want'). And he doesn't add dosage, not because this is his philosophy, but because the wine doesn't need it. 'Wine is not about philosophy,' he declares. This is winemaking by emotion, a world away from the formal, clinical approach of Champagne. With a big smile and a genuine, warm and unflustered approach, Prévost makes wines much like himself. Fleshy, vinous and brimming with exotic spice, these are some of the finest expressions of pure, single-vineyard, single-vintage meunier in all of Champagne.

In 1987, at the age of 21, Prévost inherited the 2.2 hectare Les Béguines vineyard planted in the 1960s by his grandmother in Gueux on the Petite Montagne. There is only one vineyard and one variety and, until a foray into rosé since 2007, there was only one wine, too.

Prévost made his first wine in 1998, with the help of his friend, Anselme Selosse. It was a sign of the regard in which Anselme held the young Jérôme that he lent him space in his winery in Avize to make his first four vintages. There is a clear synergy of philosophy between the two.

Prévost treasures the 55-million-year-old soils of his village in Champagne's youngest geological area, and proudly showed me a sample, teeming with fossils of ancient sea life like some geology museum artefact — the secret, he says, to the minerality of his wine. Here, the chalk is deep, starting 80 centimetres below the surface, and he has spent 12 years working the soil to encourage deeper roots to build minerality in his wines. This is very much a lesser terroir of Champagne. 'I cannot understand how Jérôme Prévost can make wines as good as he does where he is,' Jacquesson's Jean-Hervé Chiquet told me. 'He is very talented.'

And he pays close attention to his vineyard. 'The soil used to be very hard, but now it is very easy to work. I plough the mid-rows and avoid herbicides. It's all about building up the micro-organism population in the soil, and that takes time,' Prévost says.

He has completely shunned insecticides since 1994, herbicides since 1996 and minimises use of copper sulphate as a fungicide.

Like his mentor Selosse, he is emphatic that this is not biodynamics. 'Biodynamics is like a religion and I don't agree with that,' he explains. 'It's too much like a recipe, but every plot of land is different. You have to work with emotion and sensation and learn from nature, not from a book. You have to go out in the vines and feel the sun and the wind, with all of your senses attuned, to taste with your eyes and your ears.'

Interspersed with meunier planted in 1964, Prévost's Les Béguines vineyard contains 2% each of pinot gris, chardonnay and pinot noir planted in 2000. Grapes are harvested at a high level of maturity, achieved with tiny yields of 45hL/hectare, less than half Champagne's average. His role is to support his vines to draw out the expression of the year. 'I do not know which years are good years because for me every year is different,' he says. 'I have two girls, educated in the same way, but each is different and I love them both with the same love. My wines are the same. In the vineyard, every year is very different and this is what I enjoy about it.'

'I do not understand the philosophy of making champagne taste the same every year. It is not my role to determine the style of the wine. The wine is the wine and it has its own way. In the winery, I do not want my stamp to show. I have to work very softly. To make a white wine I do nothing in the cellar — I work hard in the vineyard, press and put it in barrels,' he says.

Fermentation relies exclusively on natural yeasts from the vines — 'lazy vinification', in his words. 'Different yeasts give different aromas, so you have to use natural yeast to make complex wines,' he explains. Since different yeasts have different tolerances to sulphur, he uses only very low levels of sulphur, so as not to inhibit weaker strains. Fermentation takes place entirely in barrels, three-quarters in Burgundy barrels, and variously in larger barrels of up to 600 litre capacity, including a few acacia barriques for the first time in 2012, and wines remain in barrel for 10 months, so as to breathe and not develop reductive characters. There is only one wine (the rosé is made from the same base as the white and named 'Fac-simile', because 'in Latin it means to do the same thing — and for me it is all about the vineyard, not the cellar'), so the blend is made up of every barrel. Prévost prizes the complexity achieved by blending many small ferments of parcels from one vineyard. Every wine receives the same dosage of a minute 2.5g/L, and rosé 2—3g/L. 'I don't think about that, they all get the same!' he says.

It's a shame Prévost's wines are released so young, as it takes years for them to blossom. My scores are uniformly higher years later than they are on release. Bottles are not vintage dated, but the year of harvest is coded in the fine print of the front label, beginning 'LC'.

Prévost was excited to make red wine for rosé from meunier for the first time in 2007. A tiny production of just 3300 bottles is worked by hand, even using a bucket to 'pump' over twice a day. 'It's a marvellous thing!' he exclaims. 'Working directly with the grapes to make red wine is like a gift for me. In Champagne traditionally we never put the skin in the wine, but I don't understand this because all the good things about the grape are just under the skin!' Harvesting at full ripeness is the key, because maturity of the skin is more important to him than sugar and acid levels. This is achieved by sourcing red wine from an old part of the vineyard affected by a virus which produces very small and very few berries, reducing yields and intensifying the fruit. He now adds 13% (previously 10%) to the white of the vintage to produce a rosé of slightly different colour each year.

In 2016 he experimented with adding 2% of still red wine prior to fermentation, 'because I am obsessed with the skins of the red grapes; I feel I can add something from the skin to the wine by fermenting together.' He reports that this has improved the mouthfeel without changing the aromas.

In 2017, Prévost finally upgraded from his tiny cellar in his World War I armaments store in the outhouses of his charming 1924 cottage, and built a wooden winery on the edge of Les Béguines, next to his mother's house. 'It is much easier for me to work here, with a level floor!' he exclaimed when he showed me through. 'The winery opens to the vineyard so the yeast can transfer in.'

Les Béguines is low in altitude and frost prone, and the challenge of relying exclusively on a single site in Champagne's temperamental climate came to bite in 2017, when the temperature plummeted to -9°C and Prévost lost 80% of his crop. For the first time, he purchased fruit and consequently changed his status from récoltant to négociant. 'I fear this problem will repeat in the future,' he told me, 'so I buy grapes from just 0.1 hectares on another part of Les Béguines, and I work this site just like it is my own.' He also purchases from Les Champs, within a stone's throw of Les Béguines. 'The problem is not to buy grapes, but to buy good grapes,' he revealed.

Prévost makes just 13,000 bottles every year in his little space. 'It is very small, but enough for my two hands,' he says. Such is his tiny scale that he refers to his friend Pierre Larmandier's small estate of Larmandier-Bernier as 'a factory'.

Prévost's elegant new website is evidence that his talents extend beyond the vineyard and the winery and into eloquent poetry and stunning photography.

The scarcity of Prévost's wines makes them hard to find, but the hunt is richly rewarded. Don't look for a bottle with his name on it. The name of the vineyard is prominent and his name is lost in the fine print. This is just as he would have it.

I know I ought to name this chapter and its cuvées La Closerie, but unlike every other house in six editions of this Guide, it just would not seem right to do so. The man is the story, every bit as much as Selosse, Egly and Agrapart.

55-million-year-old fossils from Les Béguines

Jérôme Prévost La Closerie les Béguines LC15 NV $$$$

93 points • 100% 2015 • Tasted in Champagne

94% meunier, 2% pinot gris, 2% chardonnay, 2% pinot noir; wild fermented and aged 10 months in barrels; 2.5g/L dosage

For Prévost, 2015 was an easy harvest of perfect grapes and low yields, though without the acidity of 2016, 'a vintage that is easy to drink early'. His is a wonderfully accurate articulation of the true character of meunier. Boasting a full straw hue, this is a complex and fleshy vintage of dried peach and mixed spice flavour, balanced by gentle acidity and softly poised minerality. It lingers long, with enticing succulence and cuddly approachability, a vintage to drink now.

Jérôme Prévost La Closerie Fac-simile LC15 NV $$$$$

93 points • 100% 2015 • Tasted in Champagne

As above, with 10% red wine added at bottling in July

The soft, fleshy, immediate 2015 season is well suited to Prévost's rosé, the fine tannins of his red wine elevating its gentle chalk mineral structure sensitively yet confidently. With a pretty medium salmon hue, he's created a characterful and approachable Fac-simile of elegant rose-hip red fragrance over a core of lingering spicy berries, apples and crab apples, underscored by gentle toasty barrel complexity on a precise and elongated finish.

JÉRÔME PRÉVOST LA CLOSERIE FAC-SIMILE LC14 NV $$$$$

93 points • 100% 2014 • TASTED IN CHAMPAGNE

Same as for Fac-simile LC15 NV

Prévost describes 2014 as a 'crazy harvest' – fighting, among other things, the *Drosophila suzukii* fly and its menacing tendency to turn the grapes to vinegar. To his credit, I saw no volatile acidity (vinegar) in this bottle, which he had opened a few days earlier. A generous and fleshy Fac-simile, it captures the evocative layers of meunier in succulent red cherries, fresh strawberries and mixed spice. The fine tannins of red wine unite in harmony with gentle minerality and soft acidity on a long finish.

JÉRÔME PRÉVOST LA CLOSERIE LES BÉGUINES CLIMAX EXTRA BRUT 2012 $$$$$

94 points • DISGORGED OCTOBER 2016 • TASTED IN CHAMPAGNE AND AUSTRALIA

As above; aged 2 years in barrel, 2 years on lees and 2 years on cork; 2.5g/L dosage; 600 bottles

I love Prévost's 2012, my favourite in his cellar since 2008. He loved the vintage, too, and kept a small parcel of just 600 bottles in barrel for two years – though he now admits that while he likes the wine, 'this length of time in barrel is not my way' and, feeling it needed longer, he held it on cork for two years post-disgorgement. The vintage is not indicated on the bottle, and in fact it's labelled LC15, because those were the labels he happened to have at the time. Not to worry, it's what is inside that counts, and this is a great example of Prévost in top form. It's an especially powerful, pronounced and characterful cuvée, even by Prévost standards, revelling in a full straw hue tinted with gold, and brimming with the pineapple of ripe meunier, played to a full orchestral backing track of spice, buttered nuts, fig and butterscotch, even fruit mince spice. It concludes long, dry and taut, with lingering spice and juicy flesh well countering the fine, dry tannin grip of long barrel age. A great expression of an outstanding season, holding confidently with finely poised acid drive. Give it plenty more time still to unravel.

Jérôme Prévost recently built a new wooden winery on the edge of his Les Béguines vineyard.

JmSÉLÈQUE

(J.M. Se-lek)

9 ALLÉE DE LA VIEILLE FERME 51530 PIERRY
www.jmseleque.fr

JmSÉLÈQUE
CHAMPAGNE

'The first thing is that I am trying to make wine before making champagne,' says the young Jean-Marc Sélèque, who has transformed his vineyards and created a brand-new winery since returning to his family estate in 2008. 'I like empty bottles!' he says. 'Purity and drinkability are very important to me, and these come with balance between minerality and richness in the wine — these are my style!' He achieves this not by following regimes, but instead, 'Winemaking is about following the wines with sensibility and not following a recipe.' His cuvées capture the fruit freshness, spicy complexity and stony minerality of his home in the premier cru of Pierry, just south of Épernay.

Jean-Marc's father, Richard, first started making his own champagnes in Pierry in the 1970s, and since that time has amassed a diverse holding of 45 parcels of an impressive average vine age of more than 40 years, spanning nine hectares across seven villages: Pierry, Moussy and Épernay in the Coteaux Sud d'Epernay; Dizy, Mardeuil and Boursault in the Vallée de la Marne, and Vertus in the Côte des Blancs.

Meunier comprises the majority of plantings in Pierry, but the geographical spread of their vineyards makes for a 50% representation of chardonnay, 40% meunier and 10% pinot noir. These they blend into 75–80,000 bottles of a diverse portfolio of 12 cuvées, including two Coteaux Champenois and a ratafia.

'When I took over, I made quite a few changes, mostly in the vineyards,' Jean-Marc explains. 'In order to make wine before champagne, I started working on the soils to significantly lower the yields.'

Sustainable viticulture is the focus, with grasses planted in the mid-rows and ploughing to promote root growth and microbial life in the soil. One hectare is ploughed by horse, and there is a

desire to increase this to half the estate. 'I would love to see a total ban on herbicides in Champagne,' Jean-Marc reveals.

His work in the vineyards has increased ripeness, though high ripeness is not the goal — 'but not underripe like most growers in Champagne!' Ripeness has enabled him to completely avoid chaptalisation and to lower dosage levels across his cuvées to extra brut or zero dosage.

'To achieve our style of purity, balance, minerality and drinkability, we need perfect quality of grapes and a natural winemaking approach, with no fining, no filtration, and long ageing,' he explains. 'You lose flesh if you filter, and you need flesh if you want to make wines with low dosage.' He bottles in July and August, to provide time for the wines to settle naturally. 'I see people bottling in January or February, but they need to filter, as the wines are too cloudy.'

In 2015, Jean-Marc constructed a 'very practical' new winery in Pierry to facilitate transfer by gravity and space to mature his cuvées in a wide variety of vessels, including vats, oak barrels of different volumes and origins, concrete ovoid vats and sandstone

amphorae. Around 60% of parcels are fermented in tanks, mostly for his entry cuvées, with barrels devoted to his top wines.

Low sulphur dioxide preservative is a priority for Jean-Marc, which he is able to achieve, thanks to the gentle handling that is possible in his new facility. 'For years I was sulphuring the wines too much and they were not expressive, not ageing, and sometimes oxidised right away. Winemaking is about following the wines with sensibility and not following a recipe.' He adds a little sulphur at the press and again in the New Year, but no more until bottling, with the final addition at disgorgement, 'but just a little'. Jetting is employed to avoid oxygen pick-up at disgorgement.

A low-sulphur regime makes it difficult to block malolactic fermentation. 'Malolactic depends on the vintage,' he explains. 'We used to block malolactic in barrels, but for the past two years I've been thinking about it differently. We have such low sulphur that sometimes malolactic happens. And if it happens, it happens. I check the wine every month, but I try not to control it. The wine has life, and you block part of its expression if you control it with sulphur.'

Jean-Marc changed the name of the estate to JM Sélèque in 2013 to distinguish it from his Sélèque cousins in the village. He prints disgorgement dates on back labels.

Pierry, winter 2013

JmSÉLÈQUE Solessence 7 Villages NV $$

91 points • 2016 base vintage • Tasted in Australia
88 points • 2015 base vintage • Disgorged November 2017 • Tasted in Australia

50% chardonnay, 10% pinot noir, 40% meunier from all 7 crus of the estate; 50% perpetual reserve dating from 2000; largely tank fermented; 3g/L dosage; cork

Jean-Marc's aspirations for drinkability and ripeness are fulfilled right from his first cuvée. The 2016 base blend is packed with expression, character and fullness, in a style of rich breadth of baked apple, mixed spice and even fruit cake. The ripeness of the fruit is the hero here, and it has no need for much dosage, thanks to soft acidity carrying a finish of body and length. The 2015 base is marked by the dry, phenolic graininess of this warm season.

JmSÉLÈQUE Solessence Nature 7 Villages NV $$

93 points • 2012 base vintage • Disgorged April 2017 • Tasted in Australia

50% chardonnay, 10% pinot noir, 40% meunier from all 7 crus of the estate; 50% perpetual reserve dating from 2000; largely tank fermented; no dosage; cork

Solessence Nature is Solessence Extra Brut without dosage, aged three to four more years on lees. The methods in his old winery required more protection from sulphur here, but it does not seem to be any the less for it, upholding impressive depth of berry fruits, apple and fig. Its ripe, spicy fruit richness contrasts the tension of the great 2012 season and all the character of long lees age in biscuity, brioche and vanilla-custard notes. It has no need for dosage, with a harmonious and complex finish lingering long. Excellent acid drive and chalk minerality unite with the texture of deep maturity to produce a style of harmony, character, persistence and presence.

JmSÉLÈQUE Solessence Rosé 7 Villages NV $$

88 points • 2015 base vintage • Disgorged January 2018 • Tasted in Australia

45% chardonnay, 15% pinot noir, 40% meunier from all 7 crus of the estate; 40% perpetual reserve dating from 2000; maceration of meunier and red wine of pinot noir; 4g/L dosage; cork

Sélèque's ripe style makes for strong phenolic impact in the rich 2015 season. His rosé boasts a medium, bright salmon hue, in a dry and firm style of crab-apple grip. Low dosage amplifies its salty minerality, concluding firm and tense.

JmSÉLÈQUE Quintette Chardonnay 5 Terroirs NV $$

92 points • 2014 base vintage • Disgorged February 2018 • Tasted in Australia

Five parcels: 1950 vines in Vertus La Justice near Le Mesnil-sur-Oger, the chalky Chouilly side of Épernay, the chalky mid-slope of Pierry, a ripe site in Dizy on the road to Champillon, and an early-ripening site just after Épernay in Mardeuil; half fermented in barrels and half in tanks; 20% reserve solera in a 2000-litre barrel, dating from 2012; partial malolactic fermentation; aged 3 years on lees; 2g/L dosage

A chardonnay that well juxtaposes the richness of Sélèque's ripe fruit style with the vivacity of youth and the tension of the high malic acidity of the 2014 harvest. This accord makes for a characterful style that unites tangy lemon and crunchy apple fruit with a touch of grapefruit bitterness on the end. It holds with impressive length and style.

JOSÉ MICHEL & FILS

(Zho-say Mee-shell e Fees)

5/10

14 RUE PRÉLOT 51530 MOUSSY
www.champagne-jose-michel.com

Dubbed 'king of meunier' for his remarkable cellar of grand old vintages, José Michel has been making champagne since 1955 in the little village of Moussy, just south of Épernay. Sourced from 10 hectares mostly in his village and six nearby villages of the Coteaux Sud d'Épernay and Vallée de la Marne, the estate today relies on chardonnay as much as it does meunier (45% of each), with just 10% pinot noir. José was the first in his family to plant chardonnay in 1958, making him the fourth generation of his family to grow grapes in the village since 1847; his grandfather, Paul Michel, was bottling since 1912. Vines of average age 30 years (and some up to 70 years) are farmed sustainably, with High Environmental Value certification. Grasses are cultivated in the mid-rows to moderate yields. Vinification and malolactic fermentation take place variously in temperature-controlled tanks, large old demi-muids and foudres. His generous wines are well crafted, testimony to the skill that comes with more than six decades of experience, showcasing the heights which meunier can attain in Moussy, and its seamless marriage with chardonnay.

JOSÉ MICHEL & FILS PINOT MEUNIER BRUT NV $$

91 points • 2013 BASE VINTAGE • TASTED IN AUSTRALIA

100% meunier; 2012 reserves; 10g/L dosage

A spicy, exuberant and exotic meunier of medium straw hue and a generous air of wild honey and incense. The palate is an accurate representation of this luscious variety, with ripe, golden pineapple and mango meeting baked apple and the biscuity complexity of age. Honeyed dosage is well integrated with balanced acidity on the finish.

José Michel & Fils Blanc de Blancs Brut 2008 $$

90 points • Disgorged January 2017 • Tasted in Australia

100% chardonnay; alcoholic and malolactic fermentation in temperature-controlled, stainless-steel tanks; aged 8 years on lees; 9g/L dosage

A generous blanc de blancs for the energetic 2008 vintage, layered with caramel and roast nuts, true to José's more oxidative winemaking style, though in no way oxidised or tired. This makes for an immediately approachable style ready to drink right away, gently supported by soft chalk minerality and rounded, integrated acidity on a long finish.

José Michel & Fils Grand Vintage Brut 2008 $$

92 points • Disgorged January 2017 • Tasted in Australia

55% chardonnay, 45% meunier; aged 8 years on lees; 9g/L dosage

A beautifully crafted cuvée of definition that transcends its terroirs, showcasing José's talent with meunier and its synergy with chardonnay. The strawberry, red apple and red cherry fruits of meunier are layered with spice, seamlessly meshing with the confident poise of chardonnay. A lingering, creamy structure marries soft, fine phenolic presence with salty chalk minerality and crunchy acidity.

José Michel & Fils Spécial Club 2010 $$$

93 points • Disgorged 2017 • Tasted in Australia

50% chardonnay, 50% meunier; from the oldest plots, some dating to 1927; aged 6 years on lees; meunier fermented in stainless-steel tanks and chardonnay in barrels; full malolactic fermentation; 7g/L dosage

José Michel exemplifies the heights which Moussy can attain, and his Spécial Club shows just how seamlessly meunier and chardonnay can marry together. The bright, juicy red cherries and strawberries of meunier carry a backdrop of mixed spice and an elegant lift of rose hip, while chardonnay heightens it gentle salty chalk mineral undertone and lemon and orange rind bite. The phenolic bitterness of the season has been well managed, and the finish carries very long, with the brioche and buttered croissant complexity of lees age bringing seamlessness and silky texture.

José Michel & Fils Cuvée du Père Houdart NV $$$

91 points • 2011 base vintage • Disgorged July 2016 • Tasted in Australia

20% chardonnay, 40% pinot noir, 40% meunier; 60% of equal parts 1971, 1975, 1976, 1982 and 1984, from bottles opened and checked in 2012; fermented in stainless-steel tanks and old barrels; 4g/L; 3200 bottles

Grand testimony to José Michel's remarkable cellar of old vintages, the sheer weight of ancient reserves in this cuvée must be unparalleled not only in Champagne, but anywhere in the beverage world outside the most ancient fortified blends. Boasting an insane average age of more than 29 years, it exudes the full, expansive complexity that would be expected from such ridiculous maturity and rarity. And yet it, of course, tastes nothing like a 29-year-old cuvée. It's at once deeply mature and intriguing in its complexity, and yet it springs from the glass with the life and confidence of its young base. Pipe smoke, old hearth and bruised apple are all here, uniting with layers of mixed spice, ginger, candied orange and dark fruit cake. Its old components show the dryness of age in bottles, with the challenging 2011 season bringing dry phenolic grip and bright yet integrated acidity. An idiosyncratic style as unusual as its inimitable recipe.

KRUG

(Khroo-k)

10/10

5 RUE COQUEBERT 51100 REIMS
www.krug.com

To those of us gazing in from the outside in wide-eyed wonder, Krug is to Champagne as Domaine de la Romanée-Conti is to Burgundy and Pétrus is to Bordeaux. It possesses a grandeur, an other-worldliness, an amplitude that is as lofty as its mesospheric price. Krug's grand hierarchy of prestige begins at a higher price than any other in Champagne, and its single-vineyard wines rank among the most expensive in the world. I have been visiting the hallowed halls of Krug for 19 years, and assessing its wines spanning four decades on countless occasions. Cuvée for cuvée, my ratings declare a house in a league all of its own. Krug is the king of champagnes, singly the greatest sparkling estate on the planet today. And it has something mystical, too.

I've always wondered if the magic of Krug is real. If one worked here for long enough, would the sparkle evaporate, the cellar turn into just a dank, dark hole, the barrels become just dirty old kegs, the cracks in the walls reveal these old buildings for what they are, and the day-to-day reality expose the hyperbole of one of the most clever of all French marketing spiels?

I'm not the only one who has wondered. Julie Cavil, one of four in a talented young winemaking team headed by Eric Lebel, made a flippant passing comment when I first met her in 2010.

'When I joined here, I went behind the scenes because I suspected that not everything was done as it is said to be. But I found that it is,' she said. The sparkle in her eye and that glimmer of don't-pinch-me-in-case-I-wake-up wonder told me this was no rehearsed marketing line. The magic, it seems, is real.

And it has to be, hasn't it? Some can fake wines of mediocre standards – but no one, anywhere, ever, can fake wines at this level. The wines of Krug are among the most revered in the world.

'I've been talking about Krug for over 20 years, but in 2011, I really discovered what it is about!' exclaims sixth-generation director, Olivier Krug. The revelation was the discovery of a book buried in the company archives for more than 160 years, the personal notebook of Olivier's great-great-great-grandfather, written to document the philosophy of Krug just five years after he founded the house in 1843. In it he expounded the principles of creating a champagne of great richness and yet great elegance, of selecting only the finest elements from the greatest terroirs, rejecting mediocre fruit and, revolutionary at the time, making both a non-vintage and a vintage cuvée. It sent shivers down the spine of Eric Lebel to read the philosophy that articulated everything that he had for so long aspired to achieve. To this day, a resolute commitment to these same ideals has secured Krug's position as the most luxurious, most exclusive and most decadent of all champagnes. And, most extraordinary of all, it's only getting better.

PERFECTIONISM BEFORE TRADITION

From the outset, Krug has courageously pursued perfectionism ahead of traditionalism.

'Joseph was not a non-conformist, he was a very serious German guy, but he was ready to go beyond the rules to create something different,' Olivier reflects. 'He left the stability of the largest house in Champagne in 1842, with a vision to create a champagne that didn't exist.'

That same daring spirit flows in Olivier's blood, relentlessly pursuing the very finest grapes, regardless of variety, vineyard classification or village reputation, and fanatical vinification, regardless of cost.

Meunier is prized, even in these wines of untiring longevity. Classification tastings are conducted blind, with no regard for a vineyard's cru. Krug purposely does not constrain itself to grand cru, nor even to premier cru, and its reach has extended as far even as the village of Les Riceys at the most southerly extreme of the Côte des Bar, on the border of Burgundy.

In a region not traditionally associated with longevity, its winegrowers were amazed when Krug invited them to taste their reserve wines at two, three, five and even 15 years of age. 'They were astounded that their wines could be kept all that time, and were extremely moved and very emotional,' Julie recalls.

Krug owns just 21 hectares, less than 35% of the vineyards required to meet annual sales of an undisclosed figure somewhere in the vicinity of 650,000 bottles. Olivier says that Krug is not selling any more bottles today than it was 15 years ago, though production has increased by an undisclosed amount to facilitate a slow future growth in sales. My estimation is that Krug is currently producing between 900,000 and 1 million bottles annually.

Estate vineyards are supplemented with fruit from 73 hectares owned by 100 loyal growers, some of whom have supplied the house since its foundation. More than 90 percent of Krug's contracts are signed according to individual plots. 'Ten years ago, people laughed at us, as most growers will not commit to a plot,' Olivier reveals. Flexibility is upheld to maintain quality in difficult vintages.

'One grower called us in 2010 and said, "I have a different plot for you because yours was done by rot",' he says. Few champagne houses can claim such loyalty. Olivier personally visits the vineyards every day during harvest.

I was privileged to tag along for a day during vintage 2014 and witness the calibre of their sites and the pristine condition of their fruit. Olivier personally visits many of the plots and tastes the grapes, as he has done for more than 30 years. He enjoys deep relationships with his growers and is warm and friendly with the workers in the press houses, showing them photos on his phone when he visits. 'My best moments are sharing with the growers!' he beams. 'I grew up with this idea that Champagne was about the growers and the maisons, but Champagne has moved on, and today I feel closer to many of the growers than I do to the houses.'

Eric Lebel knows the names of the dogs and cats of his 100 growers. He drives 4500 kilometres to walk every vineyard prior to harvest – 'because you make wine in the vineyard, not in the cellar', declares Olivier.

Krug pays a premium for higher-quality grapes, and pays its picking teams mostly by the hour rather than the usual rate by the kilogram, an important distinction in ensuring stringent selection in the vineyards. Pickers are instructed to drop anything with rot and burnt or weak berries. I was surprised by just how much fruit was dropped in the mid-rows of Clos d'Ambonnay.

Krug is working with its growers on an internal sustainability program to achieve Viticulture Durable en Champagne certification in biodiversity and carbon and water footprints. Olivier admits it is very difficult to encourage growers into a program of sustainability, with its inherent risks. 'Certification costs money and takes a lot of paperwork, so we are building a program to manage this for our growers,' he says.

'This is a collaboration, and it is our objective to show our growers the road and help them achieve this,' adds Julie. 'We do the administrative stuff and help them with the audit, so they can concentrate on their field.' One-fifth of growers are certified to date, with the hope of having the majority on board within four or five years. The company has been herbicide-free for three years.

OBSESSED WITH DETAIL

Krug's long-ageing style begins with fruit harvested with more acidity and less sugar, so pHs are usually lower than the rest of the region. When I visited mid-harvest in 2017, Krug finished harvesting Clos du Mesnil on the same day everyone else in the village started. This is a polar-opposite approach to the riper style of houses like Louis Roederer, whose chef de cave Jean-Baptiste Lécaillon told me unprompted later that very same day, 'I told Olivier I think he picked Clos du Mesnil a little too early!'

'In 2010 we started in Clos du Mesnil two days before the official regulated start of harvest,' Olivier recalls. 'Everyone in the village said we were mad, but they were all watching for when we started because they know we are obsessed with detail!'

The secret at Krug lies in the detail. 'Joseph set some rules for absolute detail for everything,' Olivier says. 'And we focus even more intently on the details today.' Grapes are selected plot by plot and pressed individually by their growers. 'Even if a grower chooses grapes from the same part of the village, we ask him to press as many parcels as he can.'

Olivier's late father, Henri Krug, told him, 'If you have a chance to vinify a wine on its own, you will express more of its personality. The more individuality you get, the more precise you can be with your selection.'

'It is as if I have a friend who paints the most beautiful panorama covering a wall, so lifelike and so detailed that it is as if the wall is not there,' says Olivier. 'And he paints the sky using 200 different shades of blue. Pale for the horizon, grey-blue for the east and deep blue for the west. But if he mixed all 200 shades of blue together and used the same proportions to paint the sky, it would have nothing of the same detail. So it is with blending

champagne. We make 250 separate vinifications of parcels that could all be blended into just three vats.'

To facilitate this, 36 stainless steel double vats of small capacity were installed in 2007, increasing the small-batch storage capacity of the winery. In keeping each plot separate, reserve wines can be kept fresher. 'Some plots have more potential to age than others, and if they were all vinified together, the blend would lose the freshness of the freshest parcels,' he explains.

Last year one of Krug's largest growers in Avize came to taste his six reserve wines back to 1998. 'He knows which plots are in each sample and we don't,' Oliver recounts. 'He went white when he tasted them. Out of 20 plots that he has supplied us over 13 years – more than 250 wines in all – five of those six reserves were from the same plot. None of us had any idea, because what we do is by taste, not by recipe. Such is our attention to detail in the tasting room.'

Krug's winemaking team admits to an obsession with numbers. Krug works with 200–250 very small parcels of fruit every vintage, all of which are tasted after vintage and again the following year. 'We know all of the musicians through pre-listening before we assemble the orchestra!' waxes Olivier, adding that Krug is the conductor. Any not up to Krug's exacting standards go somewhere else in the Louis Vuitton–Moët Hennessy (LVMH) group. Olivier and his uncle Rémi join the winemaking team for the tastings, which comprise 15 wines each day. Olivier personally attends about half the tastings, between an increasingly busy travel schedule.

'The reserve tanks are the heart of Krug,' says Olivier. Since 1990, Krug has more than doubled its reserves, without increasing production. In 2006 alone it added 36 new double vats to house its growing reserve collection, which has grown from 60 to 150 different wines in 15 years. Reserves are kept fresh in 150 small tanks, deep in the cellar at a stable 11–12°C. At any time, all of these 'treasures' are under consideration for Grande Cuvée, and all are tasted annually. The final blend comprises more than 100 parcels, spanning eight to 10 vintages, reflecting a different recipe every year. 'Our job every year is to recreate the most generous character of champagne,' says Olivier. A particular 1995 reserve wine from Bouzy has been tasted every year for 16 years and is yet to be allocated to the blend. There are still two 2001 reserve wines in Krug's cellar. As always, taste before reputation. 'Even in a crap vintage, there are still great wines,' grins Olivier.

At any given time there are 5 million bottles in the cellar, 10 times the annual production, a massive ratio, testimony to this long-ageing style.

MAGNIFICENT LONGEVITY

Krug attributes its longevity to the primary fermentation of all its wines in more than 4000 small, 205-litre oak barrels. When I arrived in September 2015, I was confronted by a sea of barrels in preparation for vintage packed tightly into Krug's large courtyard. And Krug has more barrels on site at its Clos du Mesnil and Clos d'Ambonnay vineyards. It uses these not for oak flavour or aroma,

but to build richness, complexity, balance and a 'high fidelity' not possible in stainless steel.

This is achieved by using only old casks, of average age 20 years, currently dating back to 1964. They are decommissioned after about 50 years, when they become too difficult to repair. Seguin Moreau barrels were used exclusively in the past, but Taransaud have been introduced recently. 'It took six years of tasting trials to establish the best coopers for Krug,' Julie tells me. Such is the attention to detail here. All barrels are purchased new and are seasoned for a few years by fermenting the second and third press before it is sold for distillation. A waste of a new barrel, but that's Krug!

Olivier is adamant that Krug is not special just because it is fermented in oak. 'When we started, every champagne was fermented in oak, and it still was 50 years ago!' he points out. When I asked to take his photo in front of the barrels, he politely proposed a different backdrop, eager to downplay the focus on oak.

To uphold freshness, Krug's wines spend just a short time in cask and are transferred to tanks following fermentation. When I visited in early January 2019, half of the 2018 harvest had already been racked to tanks. Contact with oxygen during fermentation furnishes Krug with a resilience when it contacts oxygen as it ages, infusing its wines with rock-solid consistency. I have not seen the degradation of freshness in Krug bottles that plagues many other champagnes as they travel around the world. These are wines capable of ageing magnificently for decades.

When a bottle in Krug's museum cellar popped as its cage was replaced a few years ago, the board and winemakers were immediately assembled to taste the wine blind. Vigorous debate ensued as to whether it was from the 1950s or the 1960s, but it was decided it was too fresh for the 1960s. It turned out to be 1915 – all the more remarkable because the Côte des Blancs was under occupation during World War I and the wine was made exclusively from pinot noir, without the structural longevity of chardonnay.

Olivier doesn't like talking about malolactic fermentation, but lab analysis reveals the presence of malic acid as a key agent in Krug's longevity. 'Eric Lebel says he doesn't care about malolactic, but of course he cares,' reveals Olivier. 'Nothing is done to start it and nothing is done to stop it.' Sometimes it even takes off in reserve vats three or four years after harvest. In 2013, just two or three of Krug's 240 fermentations went through malolactic fermentation. Even some parcels of the searingly high-acid 1996 vintage retained full malic acidity.

Although Grande Cuvée is released when it is ready to drink, after a long ageing process, Olivier has been intrigued by the number of collectors who age it further. 'Visitors now talk about Grande Cuvées from the '40s, '50s, '60s and '70s,' he reports. 'Many of our customers now put it down for five years or more.' He enjoys hosting dinners around the world for Krug lovers to bring their oldest Grande Cuvée.

The age of Krug's cuvées is revealed, first thanks to an ingenious ID code printed above the barcode of every bottle, the first three digits of which indicate the trimester (first digit) and year (second

Krug's Clos du Mesnil is surrounded by the village of Le Mesnil-sur-Oger.

and third digits) in which it was disgorged. Using this code, Krug.com and the Krug app reveal the season and year in which the bottle was shipped, the number of years over which it has aged, the blend and the vintage story for vintage wines. For non-vintage blends, it reveals the number of wines and each of the vintages. Eric has recently been elaborating wonderful insights into the crus and the seasons, making Krug.com an increasingly powerful and invaluable resource. There is even a Twitter robot that will reply with the details when you tweet #KrugID with the code.

Secondly, in 2016 Krug began printing the edition number on the front label of every Grande Cuvée, though this has been discontinued on half-bottles, because the house doesn't want to encourage people to age these. Edition 166 is based on the 2010 harvest, the 166th release in its history. This edition number comes with another exciting promise from Krug, the release of older editions of Grande Cuvée in the future.

Such disclosure ushers in a brand-new era for Krug, initiated by Maggie Henriquez, Krug's dynamic CEO since 2009. 'I was resisting the concept of disclosing the disgorgement date,' admits Olivier. 'But the world has changed. People want to know. I have changed. And we are keen to be more transparent now.' Bravo, Maggie.

RELENTLESS PURSUIT OF QUALITY

Krug's quest for quality in spite of the cost knows no limits. Krug Clos du Mesnil 1999 was to be released in 2010, but the final tasting pre-labelling was a disappointment. 'It did not have extravagant purity, it was shy and boring, you don't want to sit next to this wine!' Olivier explains.

So the decision was made to cancel its release, in spite of an offer from China to purchase the entire production of more than 10,000 bottles at full price. Olivier opened a bottle for me, 'to show that there is no compromise at Krug'. It was tense, introverted, deeply mineral and magnificent, though not as coherent as the 1998 or 2000. A secure 96 points. 'We will destroy the bottles and blend it away,' he declared.

'The first thing you learn here is patience,' admits Julie. 'There is a different time here. The clock in the courtyard is a symbol of the house. Time is very important in this place.'

Long ageing prior to release makes it impossible for Krug to follow trends, even if it wanted to. It takes 25 years to make a bottle of Grande Cuvée, since reserve wines are built up over more than 10 years, and seven or eight years of stock is perpetually ageing on lees.

Ownership of Krug rests with LVMH, which has remained sufficiently detached to leave most of the decisions in the hands of the family. Since he joined the company in 1989, Olivier has built the Japanese market into the most important for Krug. 'Everyone in Champagne was laughing when we went to Japan,' he said. 'And that's the reason they are still not there today!'

Olivier is travelling to more countries than ever today. Such is the demand for Krug that the company put Grande Cuvée on allocation worldwide since mid-2017, for the first time in Olivier's 30 years at Krug. 'We are paying today for some bad decisions in 2009 and 2010, when we produced less Grande Cuvée,' he says.

Krug's respect for a timeless tradition of rigorous selection, genius winemaking and masterful blending secures its inimitable position at the pinnacle of sparkling wine in the world today.

Krug Grande Cuvée 166ème Édition Brut NV $$$$$

97 points • 2010 BASE VINTAGE • DISGORGED WINTER 2016–2017 • TASTED IN CHAMPAGNE AND AUSTRALIA

39% chardonnay, 45% pinot noir, 16% meunier; ID 117012; 42% reserves; 140 wines from 13 vintages back to 1996; aged 6 years on lees; cork

Krug leads off where most other champagne houses end, and its entry wine is every bit a prestige cuvée. Krug is adamant that it has no hierarchy in its cuvées, but price and style dictate that Grande Cuvée is always the starting point. Interestingly, the house pours in reverse order, tasting Grande Cuvée last. 'My father said, "Red carpet for every Krug!"' explains Olivier. 'There is no special treatment here, and every grape at Krug is given the same respect.'

Krug's winemaking team describes Grande Cuvée as its most exciting and most challenging wine to produce each year. It is a blend of the three champagne varieties, but there is no formula or recipe except to maintain, not so much the consistency of the style (as the house has claimed in the past), but the best that can be produced each year, a philosophy reinforced first by the ID code on the back label and now the edition number on the front. Krug Grande Cuvée and Rosé are built on a high proportion (30–50%) and wide spectrum (6–12 vintages) of reserve wines, kept in tank for five, 10 and even 20 years. Krug's unique reserve philosophy is a key to its blends. 'I don't like the expression "base wine",' declares Olivier, 'as this assumes it is most important. A non-vintage is where you try to erase the influence of the base vintage, but for me it is not about erasing this or about being consistent, but about bringing the elements that the youngest vintage does not offer.' After blending, Grande Cuvée spends at least a further six years on lees in bottle to build its characteristic golden amplitude. An additional year of ageing (formerly five years) was added thanks to slow sales during the financial crisis of 2008 and 2009. It is aged a further year after disgorgement (formerly six months). Grande Cuvée accounts for 90% of the production of the house, which would equate to sales close to 600,000 bottles, and production perhaps more than 800,000.

Grande Cuvée smells and tastes like no other wine, a monumental paradox of tense freshness, profound maturity and inimitable complexity. Its current 166ème Édition bears a full straw hue, embracing the full, marvellous expanse of the universe of Krug complexity. It opens with a fanfare into a maelstrom of molten wax, incense, truffles, pipe smoke, glacé apricot, preserved lemon, crème brûlée, even notes of mocha and charcuterie. Decadently rich, extravagantly complex and thunderingly expansive, Grande Cuvée is a vinous champagne of multifaceted personality, yet ever-heightened tension. Its structure is more dynamic and defined than ever, uniting the electric tension of no small retention of malic acidity with deep wells of scintillating, swirling, salty minerality, lacing everything together with the creamy, silky seamlessness of barrel fermentation and long lees age. It soars with spiralling expansion, then touches down gracefully, with unerring focus and breathtaking persistence. Every bit as enchanting and ethereal as its legendary reputation promises, this is a champagne to drink slowly from large glasses, to witness an entire universe of captivating theatrics unfold as it warms. Édition 166ème is a grand achievement as always, and more than ever in the challenging 2010 season, described by Eric Lebel as 'tumultuous'. Chardonnay from the Côte des Blancs consequently lacked its habitual freshness, and he responded with both the vivacity of the year's meunier, and the structure of relatively young reserve wines, most notably from 2000. Oger was included for its generous roundness, and 2006 wines from Verzy and Bouzy for harmony.

Le Mesnil-sur-Oger, winter 2019

KRUG GRANDE CUVÉE BRUT NV $$$$$

97 points • 163ème Édition • 2007 base • Disgorged winter 2015–2016 • Tasted in Champagne

32% chardonnay, 37% pinot noir, 31% meunier, foremost from Villers-Marmery, Trépail, Mareuil and Ambonnay; ID 116003; 27% reserves; 183 wines from 12 vintages back to 1990; aged 7 years on lees; cork

98 points • 160ème Édition • 2004 base vintage • Disgorged spring 2014 • Tasted in Champagne

33% chardonnay, 44% pinot noir, 23% meunier; ID 214031; 35% reserves, most notably 1990 Avize and Oger, and 1995 Avize; 121 wines from 12 vintages back to 1990; aged 9 years on lees; cork

97 points • 158ème Édition • 2002 base • Disgorged winter 2007–2008 • Tasted in Champagne

36% chardonnay, 44% pinot noir, 20% meunier; ID 108002; 42% reserves, predominantly from the 1990s; 76 wines from 10 vintages back to 1988; aged 5 years on lees; cork

Older disgorgements of Grande Cuvée served at the house and around the world demonstrate the enduring consistency of this cuvée and its profound propensity to retain vitality. The house showcased the 2004 base (160ème Édition) to coincide with the launch of its vintage wine from the same season, a staggering celebration of the radiant white light and profound minerality of this enduring season. Édition 163ème (2007 base) holds incredible freshness, while the original disgorgement of Édition 158ème embodies the smouldering depth of maturity of reserves back to 1988. The precision of recent releases is unprecedented, and just how many decades they might hold in the cellar, only time will tell.

KRUG ROSÉ 22ÈME ÉDITION BRUT NV $$$$$

97 points • 2010 base vintage • Disgorged Fourth quarter of 2016 • Tasted in Australia

17% chardonnay, 51% pinot noir, 32% meunier; 22 wines back to 2005; 9% pinot noir red wine from a single plot in Aÿ; ID 416041; 47% reserves; aged 6 years on lees; cork

Like Grande Cuvée, Krug Rosé is a multi-vintage blend, but the association strictly ends here. This is a much smaller volume, representing less than 10% of the production of the house, assembled from the ground up. Pinot noir is treated to a short fermentation on skins and then blended with pinot noir, meunier and chardonnay fermented in small oak casks as white wine, before ageing for a minimum of now six years in bottle. Rosé is a relative newcomer at Krug, first released in the 1980s. Such was the visionary daring of Olivier's late father Henri Krug, and his brother Rémi, that when their father opposed the creation of a pink wine, they secretly produced a trial rosé. On pouring it blind for their father in 1976, he exclaimed, 'It is finished for us because someone in Champagne has copied Krug!'

Ethereal restraint and a delicate air seem a paradox in the grand decadence of Krug, but such is the detailed intricacy of this pretty medium salmon-copper cuvée that it dances with light-footed grace on a stage of euphoric complexity. There is no detail of the panoply of Krug expansiveness that is missing from this captivating spectacle. It has basked in the passage of time, slowly guided into a savoury spectrum, rejoicing in roast hazelnuts, molten wax, incense, dark fruit cake, pipe smoke and all manner of spice. Two-and-a-half years post-disgorgement, its primary fruit has been assimilated on the bouquet, while the palate upholds reflections of tangy white cherries, spicy berries and strawberry hull of exceptional length. The dynamic drive of malic acidity and the omnipresent, consummate definition of emphatic, fine chalk minerality are all-encompassing. A cool end to the tumultuous 2010 season proved to be a challenge, yielding what Eric Lebel described as 'unctuous chardonnays, beautifully fresh meuniers and pinots of fruit and finesse', producing a soft and generous blend in need of youthful tension from young reserves, representing a considerable 47% of the blend. Regrettably, the only bottle I had the opportunity to taste did not present quite the same freshness of the blends of the past.

KRUG VINTAGE BRUT 2004 $$$$$

98 points • DISGORGED SECOND QUARTER OF 2014 AND THIRD QUARTER OF 2016 • TASTED IN CHAMPAGNE AND AUSTRALIA

39% chardonnay, 37% pinot noir, 24% meunier; aged more than 11 years on lees; IDs 214041 and 316034; cork

Krug's vintage comprises just 4–5% of production, making a statement to reflect the story of the year, rather than a creative expression. Olivier Krug says, '2004 is all about the elegance', while Eric Lebel highlights its generosity, describing it as a year of radiant sunshine. He was blessed by nature's elation, affording him a breadth of choice of more characterful yet mature grapes than any previous harvest, making wines highly expressive, bright and elegant. He achieved balance by uniting the vivacity and tension of meunier with shining chardonnay and the backbone of pinot. This is one of the rare vintages of Krug to have more chardonnay than pinot. Letting down his guard during my most recent tasting, he revealed, 'a generous year, but 2002 is my darling!'

The astonishing freshness, staggering purity, pitch-perfect precision and sheer vitality of the energetic and enduring 2004 season find a new lease on life at 15 years of age in Krug's capable hands, making for a Krug Vintage of thrilling flair, charged with enormous potential. With a bright, full straw hue, the 'luminous freshness' description of the house is apt. The sustaining presence of malic acidity is all the more prominent in the modern Krug style, and here lays out a tense backbone of exacting structure. The result is slow-motion evolution, upholding a core of fresh-picked lemon tang, crunchy apple, quince and white pepper that sits upon an expansive stage of majestic Krug complexity, in rumbling depth of molten wax, wild honey, truffles and incense. The 2004 season captures Champagne's stark, white, salt minerality in profound detail, frothing and churning with mouth-embracing presence of heightened proportions. In extraordinary persistence, profound line and sheer, enduring longevity, this is a Krug that hovers, unchanging, for minutes, confidently set for a lifetime spanning many decades. At 15 years of age, it screams out for at least as many years again before it attains its full potential. That is when the true magic will begin.

KRUG VINTAGE BRUT 1998 $$$$$

100 points • DISGORGED WINTER 2012 • TASTED IN AUSTRALIA EN MAGNUM

46% chardonnay, 35% pinot noir, 19% meunier; chardonnay sourced mostly from the Côte des Blancs and Trépail, pinot almost all from the southern Montagne de Reims, meunier mainly from Leuvrigny's less sunny, left side of the Marne; ID112005; aged 14 years on lees; cork

A dramatic year made for a controversial Krug vintage. The hottest August since 1991 saw 40°C heat burning some vines and destroying 15 percent of the crop. Chardonnay held its freshness better than pinot, so this wine became the second in the history of the house to comprise predominantly chardonnay (the other was 1981). 'Krug is all about pinot noir, but this wine is much more about chardonnay,' Olivier explained. His father Henri declared, 'This is not Krug!' But the brief for Krug vintage, as Olivier puts it, is that 'every vintage has to taste as different as possible from the previous one, otherwise there is no interest. We do not try to force the vintage into the house style.'

I have always adored Krug Vintage 1998, transcending its season to rank among the greats of the 1990s, but it had been five years since our last meeting, and nothing was to prepare me for the intoxicating brilliance of this magnum. Billowing in clouds of pipe smoke and truffle, its ageless freshness vitalises an air of lemon blossom that rings in clear peals like church bells. The velocity of its fruit has shed nothing of its youthful agility, even at a full 20 years of grand maturity, darting from pure lemon sunshine into a remarkable finish that glides with glacé peach. An icy shard of malic acid sustains its great vitality and exceptional freshness, yet at every moment integrated, effortless and soaring. It swirls into a river of minerality that flows deep and swift across the palate, frothing with whitewash of mouth-filling, salty minerality that lingers and splashes long and strong. A majestic Krug that delivers incredible power with impossible finesse, it ranks alongside Clos d'Ambonnay, Clos du Mesnil and Clos Saint-Hilaire as the finest I have ever seen this vintage. This magnum was shared on the occasion of James Halliday's 80th birthday. It was voted the champagne of the night and declared by Australian sparkling winemaking legend Ian McKenzie as the greatest champagne he had ever tasted.

The clock in the courtyard at Krug is a symbol of the house.

KRUG VINTAGE BRUT 1995 $$$$$

98 points • DISGORGED WINTER 2008–2009 • TASTED IN AUSTRALIA EN MAGNUM

35% chardonnay, 48% pinot noir, 17% meunier; ID109095; a blend of 18 crus; aged 13 years on lees

The endless summer of 1995 made way for cool autumn nights that infused tremendous freshness and endurance, giving birth to the most underrated season of the decade. While 1996 made the headlines, with the benefit of long hindsight, many now favour the more affable 1995. After almost a quarter-century in the deep, this is a radiant, glowing and generous take on the season, holding incredible integrity and allure in magnum. The energising, vibrant freshness of malic acidity in tandem with the deep chalk minerality of the finest crus infuses timeless potential, enlivening a finish that floats motionless with incredible endurance.

KRUG VINTAGE BRUT 1988 $$$$$

100 points • DISGORGED SPRING 2015 • TASTED IN AUSTRALIA

32% chardonnay, 50% pinot noir, 18% meunier; aged 26 years on lees; ID 215027

Olivier Krug knows 1988 intimately, having worked the full harvest at Krug, visiting all the growers and vineyards with the chef de cave. 'There was a debate about 1988 in the early 1990s, because it was so shy compared with 1989, which was so clearly a vintage year,' he recalls 'In that era, ripeness and body were valued more highly than the character of the year. And so 1979, 1981 and 1988 were not considered strong vintage years at the time.' How opinions change! '1988 is perhaps the best vintage in 40 years for some houses,' he says today. Hindsight has confirmed 1988 as one of the most spectacular and enduring harvests of the decade, charged with the longevity of the slow maturation of a mild summer, described by Eric Lebel as timid initially, with beauty drawn out by time's precious influence. It was first released a year after the 1989, and will be re-released as Krug Collection when it is ultimately deemed sufficiently mature.

Krug 1988 epitomises the focused tension of this long-enduring vintage, charged with life and huge potential yet. It sets forth with spellbinding purity and succulent precision of mango and peach, opulently supported by layers of truffle, fig and wonderfully spicy pipe smoke. Long age has caressed it into silky softness and wild honey succulence that strike a triumphant harmony with its energetic tension. An ethereal old Krug of spellbinding integrity, line and length. This bottle was beautifully fresh and pristine, and Olivier typically finds more buttery roundness in average bottles.

KRUG CLOS DU MESNIL BRUT BLANC DE BLANCS 2004 $$$$$

99 points • DISGORGED AUTUMN 2016 AND JANUARY 2017 • TASTED IN CHAMPAGNE AND AUSTRALIA

ID 416040; aged 11 years on lees; undeclared production less than 19,000 bottles

Clos du Mesnil is the most famous vineyard in all of Champagne, and one of the world's finest chardonnay sites outside the hallowed grand crus of Burgundy. An inscription in the vineyard states that vines were planted and the wall built in 1698. Olivier discovered recently that Krug has bought grapes from Clos du Mesnil since 1864. The 1.84 hectare clos is divided into five or six plots and 19 separate vinifications. On pure chalk in the heart of the finest and most age-worthy of Champagne's chardonnay villages, this east-facing slope achieves less ripeness than some of Le Mesnil-sur-Oger's due-south-facing slopes, all the more suited to Krug's long-ageing style.

'My father purchased the plot in 1971 to secure a supply of chardonnay,' Olivier explains. 'They didn't expect this plot to produce amazing wines, but when they tasted all the still wines that year, they realised this little clos behind the big rusty gate in the middle of the village did not taste the same as the other wines from Le Mesnil. It was used in the blend at the time, but the same story repeated until the outstanding 1979 harvest, when my father suggested they should make a single wine. My grandfather said, "Never! You will ruin the philosophy of Krug! This is only one grape and one year and one little garden!" But my father made a test and they fell in love with it.'

There's something remarkable about Clos du Mesnil that is infused in its fruits from the outset. The powerful, intoxicating aroma of the cask hall at the vineyard mid-vintage is enthralling. A taste of the 2014 vintage from barrel mid-ferment, just eight days old, revealed the most concentrated and structured champagne of the season. Its DNA is infused in the vineyard, and it holds in the bottle for time eternal.

The exacting precision of 2004 unites with the commanding presence of Le Mesnil in a sensational statement of sheer, coiled power. Depth and focus of grapefruit, white peach and apple reach almost grand cru Burgundian proportions, struck with a lightning bolt of malic acidity that illuminates a focus of astonishing tension. All the fanfare of Clos du Mesnil is on full display in molten wax, almond nougat, vanilla and truffles. The inimitable chalk minerality of these hallowed soils is all-conquering, delving to thundering depths with a bath salts presence of proportions unequalled by any other champagne, elevating the palate with freshness as light as air. It rises with an ethereal flourish on the finish, expanding in line and length, spiralling upwards in slow motion to larger-than-life proportions. Clos du Mesnil is again one of the most dramatic, phenomenal, stupendous sparkling releases of the year. The 2004 vintage possesses an inherent generosity and calm that make it more approachable on release than the 2002, making this the vintage to drink over the coming decades until the 2002 finally, one day, comes into its glorious own.

KRUG CLOS DU MESNIL BRUT BLANC DE BLANCS 2002 $$$$$

100 points • DISGORGED AUTUMN 2015 • TASTED IN AUSTRALIA

As for the Blanc de Blancs 2004; aged 12 years on lees; ID 415068; 14,000 bottles

The only 100-point new release in the previous edition of this Guide singly and emphatically declared its superiority on every level: concentration of fruit, monumental acid structure, disarming chalk minerality and mesmerising persistence. It immediately transported me back to my first encounter with Etienne Sauzet Le Montrachet 2006 from barrel in the little domaine in Puligny-Montrachet in 2007. Such was its sheer force of haunting persistence, building and spiralling with no end, that it was only after I had farewelled its maker Gérard Boudot and was well down the road that its true greatness revealed itself and I increased my score to 100 perfect points.

My two encounters with Krug Clos du Mesnil 2002 were nothing like that. From the first molecule of hedonistic aroma and time-arresting sip, this cuvée instantly and unequivocally projected itself so far beyond anything else I had tasted that awarding it 100 points was no wishful triumph, but simply a necessary formality. And yet Clos du Mesnil was everything like Etienne Sauzet, instantly evoking Le Montrachet itself, for no other vineyard infuses chardonnay with such explosive concentration and force with a shining white sabre of razor precision. Its youthfulness at 16 years of age is disarming, a blinding flash of white sunshine, of lemon freshness and white pepper, layered with molten wax, even glimpses of green olives. Grand malic acidity of dizzying proportions is swept up in an immense, all-consuming tidal wave of frothing, sea salt minerality, crashing with such force that any mortal wine would collapse breathless in its wake. Yet herein lies the triumph of 2002, the vintage more than any other that reverberates with looming structure, yet meets it commandingly with awe-inspiring fruit presence. This sets it with a life expectancy of a century, no less. Do not dare approach this eternal soul for at least another 20 years and, if you can possibly muster the stamina, much, much longer. For all this, the one irrefutable trait that sets Krug Clos du Mesnil 2002 apart among the most profound wines of our era is a line and length so undeviating and enduring that it hovers, unwavering, for minutes, teasing and beckoning, as if taunting any who might have missed the point in that first spellbinding moment. None will miss it now.

An inscription in Clos du Mesnil reveals that vines were planted and the wall was built in 1698.

L. BÉNARD-PITOIS

(L. Bear-nah-Pee-twah)

5/10

23 RUE DUVAL 51160 MAREUIL-SUR-AŸ
www.champagne-benard-pitois.com
www.champagne-laurentbenard.com

CHAMPAGNE

L. Bénard - Pitois

PROPRIÉTAIRE-RÉCOLTANT

Vignobles Premier Cru et Grand Cru

In Champagne's finest villages, the carving knife of succession can be sharp in slicing down the estate of each generation, but the Bénard-Pitois family has been blessed with something of the opposite. Laurent Bénard's paternal grandfather was privileged to holdings in Le Mesnil-sur-Oger and Oger, his mother in Avenay-val-d'Or and neighbouring Mutigny since 1850, and his wife in Bergères-lès-Vertus. The estate now draws from all five villages from its home in Mareuil-sur-Aÿ, one of the Vallée de la Marne's finest premier crus, and source of half its fruit. These are refreshingly affordable, terroir-driven wines, built around majestic pinot noir (two-thirds of the estate), from vines of average age exceeding 25 years.

Bénard's grandfather made his own champagne in Mareuil-sur-Aÿ in small quantities from 1950, his father increased annual production to 20,000 bottles, and since 1991, Bénard has grown it to 70,000.

This is a conservative production for a 12-hectare estate. Meunier has very little place in these cuvées 'because I don't like it', Bénard admits candidly.

His philosophy is to make wines that express their terroirs. To this end, he upholds a natural approach in his vines, cultivating grasses in the mid-rows of every vineyard. Two hectares just behind the house in Mareuil-sur-Aÿ have been tended organically and ploughed with a horse since 2009, with certification approved in 2012. Organic fruit has already shown greater floral aromatics and complexity, as well as 20–30% lower yields, to less than 60hL/hectare – under two-thirds of Champagne's average.

Yields in 2012 were even lower, after outbreaks of mildew and oïdium. 'It is easy to plough to control the weeds, but mildew is our biggest problem,' he reveals. There is a hope to convert all estate vineyards to organics, though Bénard acknowledges that this will be quite a challenge across 40 far-flung plots (his four plots in Oger together only comprise 0.3 hectares). He has used some biodynamic preparations and practices for the past two years, though not to the extent that he aspires, as he finds these labour-intensive.

Bénard released his first organic champagne from Mareuil-sur-Aÿ in 2014 under the label 'Laurent Bénard'. As a grower, he is not permitted to market certified organic wines under the same brand as his traditional wines.

'Organics is currently on standby for L. Bénard-Pitois,' he reveals. 'We have stopped using chemicals altogether, but we are not certified, and we will wait for the next generation to decide which way we should go.'

Practice is more important than certification, and his organic philosophy carries over into vinification, with wild ferments, minimal use of sulphur as a preservative, and an attempt to make sulphur-free wine in recent years.

Mareuil-sur-Aÿ, winter 2013

'We prefer to use just enough sulphur at the beginning of vinification and a tiny addition at disgorgement,' Bénard explains. As a result of these low levels of preservative, tanks and barrels which develop too much acetic acid (vinegar) are discarded.

Sadly, his Laurent Bénard cuvées have always been devoid of the fruit purity, integrity, finesse and clarity of terroir expression of his L. Bénard-Pitois range, suffering at the hands of both too little sulphur dioxide and too much oak.

All cuvées go through full malolactic fermentation, as it's very difficult to block with a low-sulphur regime. This creates something of a dilemma for Bénard, concerned by declining acidity in the wake of global warming. Warm summers are building good sugar concentrations and he has very little need to chaptalise, if at all. Reconstituted grape must rather than sugar is used for dosage. To balance lowering acid levels, Bénard has lowered dosage from 15g/L to less than 9g/L over two decades.

Each parcel is vinified separately in small enamelled tanks, or oak barrels for chardonnay and reserve wines. To minimise oak influence, barrels are purchased after three vintages in Burgundy. 'But the problem is that you're not sure of the quality of cleanliness,' he points out. He therefore sometimes buys new barrels and seasons them for two years before fermenting his cuvées. 'We are using less barrels than we were in the past,' he explains. 'Warming climate and earlier harvests mean the must is more powerful, so the problem is now keeping the acidity, freshness and tension, and for me, putting it in barrels adds to much body.' Growth of production over the past two decades has put pressure on space, and bottles are now aged in a rented cellar.

Disgorgement dates are now printed on back labels, and also coded on the cork. The letter is the month, and the numbers are the year, so I18 is September 2018.

L. Bénard-Pitois Carte Blanche Premier Cru Brut NV $$

90 points • 2016 base vintage • Disgorged 20 November 2018 • Tasted in Champagne

20% chardonnay, 75% pinot noir, 5% meunier from Avenay-Val-d'Or, Mutigny, Bergères-lès-Vertus, with a little Mareuil-sur-Aÿ meunier; 2015 reserves; 8.5g/L dosage

Comprising half the production of the estate, Bénard-Pitois' entry wine is a rousing celebration of the pinot noir of the premier crus of the southern Montagne de Reims. A pale straw hue with a blush tint heralds a vibrant and pretty style of spicy red apple fruit and firm lemon juice acidity. It's a simple and clean starting point, though lacking in polish and seamlessness of structure, marked by a little phenolic grip of the warm 2015 season. Tasted just a couple of months after disgorgement, it will appreciate cork age to soften from its stark newly disgorged guise.

L. Bénard-Pitois Brut Réserve Premier Cru NV $$

91 points • 2015 base vintage • Disgorged 20 November 2018 • Tasted in Champagne

40% chardonnay, 60% pinot noir; Le Mesnil and Mareuil-sur-Aÿ; 2014 reserves

Few champagne producers offer the chance to trade up from their entry NV for such a tiny outlay. It's an altogether different proposition, too, not only boasting both a larger representation of chardonnay and an extra year in the cellar, but it's also the only label of the house, besides the vintage cuvées, privileged to fruit from Le Mesnil-sur-Oger. Celebrating its pinot noir lead, the hue is pale straw tinted with blush. Crunchy red apple fruit is toned by the toasty complexity of lees age, with the grip of dry extract of the warm 2015 season making for firmness and herbal notes on the finish.

L. Bénard-Pitois Brut Nature Premier Cru NV $$

92 points • 2012 base vintage • Tasted in Champagne

40% chardonnay, 60% pinot noir; Brut Réserve kept longer on lees; zero dosage

Brut Nature exemplifies the ability of Bénard-Pitois Brut Réserve to both age confidently and stand up without added dosage. Age has blessed it with a medium straw hue, complexity and integration, uniting golden delicious apple and grapefruit with vanilla and lemon meringue. It revels in the great 2012 season, with purity that highlights pronounced chalk minerality. Its grainy texture and acid tension are heightened by zero dosage, making for a little firm bite on the end.

L. Bénard-Pitois Rosé Premier Cru NV $$

89 points • 2015 base vintage • Disgorged 30 November 2018 • Tasted in Champagne

35% chardonnay, 50% pinot noir, Brut Réserve with 15% meunier red wine from 41-year-old vines in Mutigny; 8g/L dosage; 3000–4000 bottles

The pristine freshness, purity and chalk mineral expression of Brut Réserve typically makes for the perfect base for a beautifully elegant rosé, but here the warm 2015 base vintage challenges the delicacy of the style. Pretty medium salmon-pink hue is unimpeded, but the clash of sunny-season phenolic grip with the tannins of red wine makes for a herbal astringency and sappy, chewy-tannin texture. Dried mango and tomato leaf notes are underscored by salt minerality on a long finish.

L. Bénard-Pitois Rosé LB Brut Premier Cru NV $$

93 points • 2014 BASE VINTAGE • DISGORGED 30 NOVEMBER 2018 • TASTED IN CHAMPAGNE

88% chardonnay from Mareuil-sur-Aÿ and Bergères-lès-Vertus; 12% pinot red wine from Mutigny; 30% vinified in barrels; 8g/L dosage; 2000 bottles

It takes keen eyes to spot the difference between Bénard-Pitois's two non-vintage rosés, but look for the little 'LB' in the border of the front label. There is no mistaking the distinction in the glass. The goal in this tiny-production cuvée is to contrast the vibrancy and mineral texture of chardonnay (a strong 88% of the blend) with the red berry fruits of pinot noir red wine (12%) and the spicy complexity of barrel age. Sporting a medium salmon hue, it meets the brief with flamboyance and confidence, harmonising the succulent white peach fruit of Mareuil-sur-Aÿ chardonnay with the apple crunch and citrus of Bergères-lès-Vertus, and the subtle strawberry hull of Mutigny pinot noir red wine. Partial barrel fermentation has been well played to build creamy structure without impacting its elegant fruit profile. It finishes long, creamy and harmonious, with gentle tannin grip.

L. Bénard-Pitois Blanc de Blancs Millésime Premier Cru 2008 $$

94 points • TASTED IN CHAMPAGNE

100% chardonnay; 30% Mareuil-sur-Aÿ from 55-year-old vines on 0.5 hectares with only 50 cm of soil before the chalk, 30% Le Mesnil-sur-Oger and Oger (blended since four plots in Oger comprise just 0.3ha), 30% Bergères-lès-Vertus; 4g/L dosage

The four disparate crus of Mareuil-sur-Aÿ, Le Mesnil-sur-Oger, Oger and Bergères-lès-Vertus are united here not by design but by family circumstance, yet the recipe makes very good sense and works to compelling effect in the enduring 2008 season. The result is a wonderfully approachable take on this high-acid vintage, which unites the fleshy generosity of Mareuil with the freshness of Bergères-lès-Vertus and the structure of Le Mesnil and Oger, wonderfully polished by the silky texture and all the vanilla custard and butter croissant complexity of a decade of age. It holds fine salt minerality and excellent persistence.

L. Bénard-Pitois Blanc de Blancs Millésime Premier Cru 2009 $$

92 points • DISGORGED SEPTEMBER 2018 • TASTED IN CHAMPAGNE

As above

Exuding all the generosity of its warm season, this vintage was astutely released before the 2008, as many smart houses have done in Champagne. The golden delicious apple richness of Mareuil in this generous vintage is freshened by the elegance of Bergères-lès-Vertus and deepened with the inimitable chalk mineral structure of Le Mesnil. This makes for a style of medium to full straw hue, emphasising fruit presence and textured salt structure, embellished with the vanilla-cream effect of lees age. It lingers with good persistence, and just a little warm vintage phenolic grip on the close.

L. Bénard-Pitois Brut Millésime Premier Cru 2012 $$$

92 points • DISGORGED NOVEMBER 2018 • TASTED IN CHAMPAGNE

50% chardonnay, half from Le Mesnil-sur-Oger and half from Mareuil-sur-Aÿ, 50% pinot noir from Mareuil-sur-Aÿ; 10% barrel fermented; 5g/L dosage; 3000 bottles

I was privileged to be the first to taste this new vintage, boasting a higher proportion of chardonnay than usual after significant losses in pinot noir after outbreaks of mildew and oïdium. Chardonnay declares its lead in a crisp and fruit-focused 2012 of medium straw hue, with crunchy apple, pear and spicy grapefruit, accented with the star-fruit exotic complexity of a sunny year. The salt minerality of Le Mesnil melds with subtle phenolic grip to make for a dry and structured finish. Good acid line and tension suggest confident medium-term potential.

L. Bénard-Pitois Brut Millésime Premier Cru 2008 $$$

93 points • Tasted in Champagne

20% chardonnay, 80% pinot noir; 30% fermented in barrels

Laurent Bénard is open in expressing concern surrounding Champagne's challenging seasons, citing 2008 as the refreshing counter-example, delivering the right level of sun and rainfall to produce balanced vines that drew mineral expression from their terroirs. The impressive acid line, heightened energy and strict tension of the season contrast the structure, grip and toasty roast-almond characters of barrel fermentation. It screams out for plenty more time yet for oak and fruit to integrate. Patience promises to be rewarded.

Laurent Bénard La Clé des Sept Arpents Extra Brut NV $$

87 points • 100% 2014 base vintage • Disgorged 25 October 2018 • Tasted in Champagne

17% chardonnay, 17% pinot noir, 60% meunier, from the organic vineyard immediately behind the house in Mareuil-sur-Aÿ; meunier tank fermented; pinot and chardonnay barrel fermented; full malolactic fermentation; low sulphur dioxide preservative; 2g/L dosage

With a medium straw hue, this is a complex and savoury cuvée that collides the peanut and gingernut biscuit character of oak fermentation with crunchy, almost ripe pear fruit. It's a dry and firm style that finishes with crunchy tension of firm acidity and slightly sappy phenolic grip.

Laurent Bénard Vibratis Extra Brut 2013 $$

88 points • Disgorged 18 July 2018 • Tasted in Champagne

20% chardonnay, 40% pinot noir, 40% meunier, from the organic vineyard immediately behind the house in Mareuil-sur-Aÿ; meunier tank fermented; pinot and chardonnay barrel fermented; no added sulphur; 2g/L dosage; previously 'Vibrato' but another producer trademarked it

A dry, tense and firm style of medium straw hue, led by the peanut flavours of oak, which dominate a dry and crunchy profile of almost ripe beurre bosc pear. The grip of oak tannins unites with phenolic firmness on a dry and short finish.

Laurent Bénard Vendange Blanc de Noirs Extra Brut 2011 $$

89 points • Disgorged 25 October 2018 • Tasted in Champagne

50% barrel-fermented pinot noir, 50% tank-fermented meunier; 2g/L dosage

Laurent Bénard describes 2011 as a vintage that achieved sugar ripeness, but not flavour of phenolic ripeness. The toasty, spicy impact of oak barrels is heightened by the dry, phenolic grip of fruit harvested before flavour ripeness or phenolic maturity could develop. The result is spicy and crunchy, concluding with the dry, bitter grip of crab apple. Barrel fermentation brings some creamy persistence to this tussle.

LAHERTE FRÈRES

(La-airt Frair)

3 RUE DES JARDINS 51530 CHAVOT-COURCOURT
www.champagne-laherte.com

CHAMPAGNE

DEPUIS 1889

Laherte Frères
à CHAVOT

The young Aurélien Laherte describes himself as a farmer, not a winemaker. 'More than anything, my father and I are trying to respect the soil, expressing the style of the clay and limestone,' he says. This is the soil of the historic little village of Chavot-Courcourt, on the border of the Côte des Blancs and the Vallée de la Marne. 'The clay gives us chardonnay that is fruitier than the Côte des Blancs, and the limestone meunier that is finer than the Vallée de la Marne,' he explains. For a production of less than 120,000 bottles, Laherte Frères boasts a very large portfolio of 12 cuvées that preserve the detail of its terroirs in wines of taut, linear persistence, and at times assertive structure.

With a history of grape-growing in the village spanning seven generations, the extended Laherte family accounts for almost one-third of Chavot's population of 350. The 11 hectares from which the estate sources across 80 parcels in 10 nearby villages have been passed down through the generations, and all are still owned and tended by members of the immediate family. French law dictates registration of the domaine as a négociant-manipulant, but for all practical purposes it should be considered a grower-producer, with the exception of its entry Brut Ultradition NV, for which supply is supplemented with two hectares of purchased fruit.

A complex array of vineyard parcels span the Coteaux Sud d'Épernay (close to seven hectares in Chavot, and a little in Brugny, Moussy, Épernay, Vaudancourt and Mancy, with chardonnay, pinot noir and meunier), Côte des Blancs (small holdings of chardonnay in Vertus and Voipreux) and Vallée de la Marne (less than half a hectare of meunier in each of Le Breuil and Boursault).

With almost two-thirds of the estate in Chavot, Aurélien explains that 'we would like our wines to express that they are not from the Côte des Blancs or the Montagne de Reims, but to be expressive of our village'. In tasting young *vins clairs*, the distinctive saltiness, glassy chalk minerality and north-facing freshness of Chavot are unique compared with his parcels from other villages. The oldest vines have been cultivated here by different generations of the family for more than 70 years. Since 2011, Aurélien has also purchased biodynamic pinot noir from a friend in Chamery on the Petite Montagne de Reims, since 'we are very poor in pinot noir in our own vineyards'.

Aurelien decided to 'work in the natural way' when he arrived to work with his father in 2005. He has adopted an ecological approach, with half the vineyard holdings managed

biodynamically, and the rest essentially organically, 'to facilitate the natural expression of the vine and increase its aromatic potential'. He reports seeing increased mineral character in biodynamic plots as vines push deeper into the chalk, encouraged by ploughing by horse in spring and autumn to break up the surface. Natural pesticides and herbicides are used, and yields are limited.

'When we started with biodynamics in 2005, we found the fruit was cleaner and more consistent during vinification,' he says. 'The wines were fruity, held good acidities, and the bottles maintained their freshness for longer after they were opened.'

A vintage wine is made every year, even in the challenging 2010 season. 'If you work diligently, you don't need to be afraid of the quality of the vintage,' he suggests. 'In Champagne, many people just add more sugar or leave a wine on lees for longer if it's not right, but for us we simply make the wine.'

Villages, crus and varieties are separated, and matched to the age and style of one of now 350 barrels as the musts leave one of two traditional presses. 'We have lots of complexity in the vineyard, so we try to obtain the same complexity in the winery using different fermentation vessels,' explains Aurélien. He considers the matching of parcels to the right vessels to be his most important task in the winery. 'The work we are doing in the vineyards has increased the potential of our fruit, so we have increased the quantity of oak in the last five years.' More than 80% of parcels are fermented and aged in oak, as has been the tradition here for more than 25 years. Barrels vary from four to 40 years of age, and include six large foudres between three and 100 years of

Aurélien Laherte

age from Alsace for reserve wines. Five small barrels are purchased each year from Domaine de la Romanée-Conti, where they have aged Le Montrachet, no less. Since 2011, pinot noir and meunier have been selectively vinified in barrels used for red Burgundy in the hope of increasing red fruit character and tannins.

In 2012, a cellar with capacity for 600,000 bottles was built, and Aurélien challenged his father that it was too big. 'A cellar is never too big!' came the response. A current stock of 250,000 bottles facilitates an average age of three years. 'It is the work of my generation to increase the ageing of our cuvées, and if I could extend it to four years by the end of my life, that would be an important step,' declares Aurélien, who aspires to add a month or two of age every year. An increase in production of 10,000 bottles in 2014 equated to an increase of four months of ageing in the cellar.

Some lees stirring is performed to build richness. Malolactic fermentation is blocked in most cuvées, but may proceed spontaneously or by design for particular years and varieties. 'Every year, the personality of the vintage is different, so partial malolactic gives the opportunity for me to respond to the style of the season,' Aurélien explains. In Laherte's structured and savoury terroirs, malic acidity makes for a tricky balance in young cuvées with increasing use of small-format oak, all too often resulting in assertive and drying structures. Laherte has trialled some barrels without sulphur, but is not yet convinced. 'Good acidity and low pH mean we don't need to use much sulphur, but without any we lose something of the soil and the precision of the fruit,' he says.

A unique 'Le Clos' vineyard of just 0.3 hectares in Chavot has been co-planted to seven varieties to preserve the heritage of the estate. 'We found the lost varieties of our ancestors in our old plots, and we have embarked on a project to recreate champagne with the same taste as 250 years ago,' Aurélien explained as he showed me through the prized site at the top of the village. Chardonnay, meunier, pinot noir, fromenteau, petit meslier, pinot blanc and arbane are harvested and pressed together, wild-yeast fermented in barrel without malolactic fermentation, blended with a reserve solera of every vintage since 2005 and bottled as 'Les 7'.

Attention to every detail is the key at Laherte, right down to the cork. Every wine has been sealed with DIAM for more than eight years. 'I don't want to lose all our work to the cork!' Aurélien exclaims. 'Our goal is to preserve freshness, fruit and minerality in our wines, and our tests indicate that DIAM is most effective, providing protection against changes in temperature and humidity as our wines travel around the world.'

Aurélien has worked hard to slowly evolve the estate since he began working alongside his father, uncle and grandparents in 2005, and his spirit of experimentation and evolution continues. They have rationalised their large portfolio a little to now nine cuvées each year, all but two of which are made in tiny volumes of just a few thousand bottles. Each boasts a refreshingly informative back label, detailing villages, assemblage, vinification, dosage and disgorgement date.

Église Saint-Martin de Chavot dates from 1108.

LAHERTE FRÈRES EXTRA-BRUT ULTRADITION NV $$

89 points • DISGORGED APRIL 2018 • TASTED IN AUSTRALIA

30% chardonnay, 10% pinot noir, 60% meunier; from 8 villages of the Coteaux sud d'Épernay and Vallée de la Marne on limestone and chalky soils; vinified in foudres, tanks and oak barrels; partial malolactic fermentation; 40% reserves aged in barrels; 4.5g/L dosage; DIAM

Cleverly named Ultradition, Aurélien explains, 'because our work in the vines and the winery now is not traditional. We are trying to do something different.' It is in this cuvée that he feels they have made their greatest progress in the vines and the barrels and foudres over the past decade, and still have the most potential to improve. 'People ask which is my favourite wine, and this is it, because there is so much we can do with the blend!' he discloses. This is certainly a complex expression of an entry cuvée, a characterful and representative take on the Coteaux sud d'Épernay, with plenty of complexity led by meunier in crunchy strawberry hull, red apple, crab apple and grapefruit. Barrel and foudre fermentation works in concert with lees age to build biscuity complexity and some creaminess to its grainy structure. It captures the glassy, chalk mineral texture of the village, with some grip and phenolic bitterness. Tense malic acidity marks out a long and energetic finish.

LAHERTE FRÈRES BLANC DE BLANCS BRUT NATURE NV $$

89 points • 2015 BASE VINTAGE • DISGORGED JANUARY 2018 • TASTED IN AUSTRALIA

100% chardonnay from the family's most mineral soils in Chavot and Épernay; 50% reserves from 2014 and 2013; 100% wild fermented in barrique, foudre and truncated cone vat; aged 2 years on lees; hand disgorged; 60% malolactic fermentation; zero dosage

Sourced from the sites Aurélien considers best represent the personality of the estate, the aspiration here is to draw out the salinity of young chardonnay through vinification in barrels and lees contact. It lives up to his hopes, singing with the salty chalk expression of the Coteaux sud d'Épernay. Crunchy grapefruit and golden delicious apple fruit is marked by the charcuterie character of wild ferment in cask. It's at once full and mouth-filling, with the creamy, buttery texture of two years lees age, and at the same time high-tensile, its youthful acidity exacerbated by blocking 40% of malolactic fermentation and zero dosage. It concludes with good length and energy.

Laherte Frères Les Empreintes NV $$

89 points • 2011 base vintage • Disgorged March 2017 • Tasted in Australia

50% chardonnay from Les Chemins d'Épernay in Chavot, planted in 1957 on clay and chalk, 50% pinot noir from Les Rouges Maisons in Chavot, planted in 1980 on deep soil, rich in clay, flint and schist; fermented in old Burgundian barrels; 4g/L dosage

A selection of Laherte's best barrels from his two finest terroirs in Chavot, this is a very spicy and intense cuvée that bores deep into the salt mineral texture of the earth. It unites the charcuterie, savoury and biscuity notes of oak and the cut and tension of taut malic acidity, heightened by low dosage. Coarseness, phenolic grip and impurity reflect the harrowing 2011 season. Aurélien is rightfully disappointed that this challenging vintage disrupts the purity of mineral expression.

Laherte Frères Les Vignes d'Autrefois Extra Brut 2013 $$$

93 points • 2013 base vintage • Disgorged January 2017 • Tasted in Australia

100% meunier from vines planted between 1947 and 1953 in two chalky plots in Chavot and Mancy; one 4 tonne press load; no malolactic fermentation; aged in old Burgundy barrels; aged 30 months on lees; 3g/L dosage

Laherte produces Les Vignes d'Autrefois every year regardless of the vintage, a daring philosophy for a small estate, whose meunier invariably swings dramatically according to the mood of the seasons – a blessing in a wonderful year like 2013! It was a late harvest, yet one that Aurélien admires for freshness and delicacy. Layers of meunier complexity of blood orange, mandarin and mixed spice are underlined by tension of lemon and grapefruit. Excellent poise and great length are energised by the pronounced, glassy salt chalk minerality that defines the Coteaux sud d'Épernay. An impressive meunier.

Laherte Frères Les Longues Voyes Blanc de Noirs 2013 $$$

87 points • Disgorged January 2017 • Tasted in Australia

100% pinot noir from 1 hectare of 35-year-old biodynamic vines planted in clay and flint over limestone, purchased from a friend in Chamery on the Petite Montagne de Reims; one 4 tonne press load; wild fermented and matured for 18 months in barrels; aged more than 2 years on lees; 4g/L dosage; 3000 bottles

The pronounced charcuterie complexity, bacon fat and creamy texture of barrel fermentation and maturation create austerity in the presence of youthful, tense malic acidity and low dosage. Underscored by salty minerality, this is a rustic style that holds its poise with good persistence.

Laherte Frères Les Beaudiers Rosé de Saignée NV $$$

85 points • Disgorged March 2016 • Tasted in Australia

100% meunier, interplanted with a few other varieties, planted in 1953, 1958 and 1965 in Les Beaudiers on the lower slopes of Chavot on hard limestone with clay; macerated 20 hours on skins (compared with 14-16 hours typically) before bleeding and wild fermentation and at least 6 months maturation in old oak barrels; no malolactic fermentation; aged 4 years on lees; 3g/L dosage

A rosé de saignée of medium crimson hue with a copper hint. Pink pepper and pomegranate character are sadly foiled by composty notes and dominant volatile acidity that leave the finish heavy, austere and awkward, the unfortunate victim of oxidative degradation in barrel.

LAHERTE FRÈRES LES 7 SOLERA 05-15 NV $$$$

88 points • 2015 base vintage • Disgorged January 2018 • Tasted in Australia

Single-vineyard Chavot field blend; formerly labelled Les Clos; 18% chardonnay, 18% meunier, 17% pinot blanc, 15% petit meslier, 14% pinot noir, 10% fromenteau, 8% arbane; planted on chalky clay soils in 2003; blended at the press; 40% perpetual reserve blend of 2005 through 2014; co-fermented with wild yeast in Burgundy barrels of at least 10 years of age; matured in barrel for 6 months with regular lees stirring; no malolactic fermentation; 4g/L dosage

As idiosyncratic and characterful as its complex recipe predicts, the tension of taut acidity and the salty minerality of Chavot underscore the vast complexity of multidimensional fruit salad anticipated by the full monty of every variety in Champagne. The dry, phenolic grip of 2015 does not harmonise well with the perpetual reserve, making for a rustic and savoury release of dusty earthiness. The grip of oak tannin and phenolic bitterness conspire to create a firm finish. Age has lent an element of creaminess to a finish carried by the salt minerality of Chavot. It's great to see an NV cuvée sensibly named with a declaration of its vintages.

LAHERTE FRÈRES LES 7 SOLERA 05-13 NV $$$$

89 points • 2013 base vintage • Disgorged January 2016 • Tasted in Australia

As above; 40% perpetual reserve blend of 2005 through 2012

The bright 2013 base marries with the deep complexity of Laherte's solera more seamlessly than the 2015. Barrel fermentation lends gentle charcuterie complexity, providing a softening influence to subtle phenolic bitterness.

Église Saint-Martin de Chavot

LALLIER

(Lah-liay)

(6/10)

4 Place de la Libération 51160 Aÿ
www.champagne-lallier.fr

DEPUIS 1906

CHAMPAGNE
LALLIER

À Aÿ-FRANCE

Navigating a trajectory of rising quality in the wake of mushrooming growth is a monumental undertaking for any establishment, and the rise and rise of the young house of Lallier over the past 15 years stands as an exemplar of just what can be achieved. Established only in 1996, the family's history in Aÿ spans five generations, having overseen Deutz from 1906 until Louis Roederer took ownership in 1996. Chef de cave since 2000, fourth-generation Champagne winemaker Francis Tribaut purchased Lallier when René-James Lallier retired in 2004. At the time, production totalled only 50,000 bottles. In just one decade, it mushroomed to a cool 400,000 bottles, where it is capped today. Its clean, well-balanced and fruit-focused champagnes have stepped up another level again this year.

Such rapid growth necessitates space, and in 2012 production was moved from Aÿ to a new, state-of-the-art facility in Oger with a capacity for 1 million bottles.

The heart of the company, its 18th-century vaulted cellars and the core of its sourcing, remain in Aÿ, whose pinot noir is the basis of every cuvée except Blanc de Blancs. The estate has doubled its holdings in recent years, and is now privileged to 15 hectares of largely grand crus centring around Aÿ, providing for 40 percent of its production, the remainder sourced from across the Montagne de Reims and Côte des Blancs. No meunier is used.

Tribaut personally oversees management of his vineyards and selection of fruit, working closely with his growers. Vineyards are tended sustainably and no pesticides are used.

His philosophy of vinification is 'less is more'. Fermentation takes place in temperature-controlled stainless steel tanks using only natural yeast, which he cultured in 2007 from his best plot in Aÿ. The number of fermentation vats has been increased to 50, of all different sizes, to keep parcels separate. Partial malolactic fermentation maintains freshness in all cuvées.

Reserves are used only in small quantities of less than 20 percent; 'it doesn't take much for a lot to happen!' Tribaut says. Small dosages are based on a liqueur of his Blanc de Blancs and Ouvrage cuvées.

Lallier's entry non-vintage blend has been cleverly re-engineered to reflect the character of its base vintage, with the year proudly displayed in the name of the cuvée. Back labels now disclose disgorgement dates, dosage, blends and crus, with further detail expounded via his informative website.

Tribut is to be lauded for the dramatic leap in precision and finesse of every cuvée that has emerged from his Oger facility.

LALLIER R.013 BRUT NV $$

91 points • DISGORGED MARCH 2017 • TASTED IN AUSTRALIA

44% chardonnay, 56% pinot noir; 85% Grand Cru (Avize, Cramant, Oger, Aÿ, Verzenay, Bouzy and Ambonnay); 17% reserves from 2010, 2008 and 2002; partial malolactic fermentation; 7g/L dosage

Tribaut describes his 'Serie R' as the result of a 'deep reflection upon one year's harvest', and more than 80% is sourced from 2013. Grand crus comprise the majority of the blend, and will grow to 100% in future releases. A lovely freshness of golden delicious apple with a creamy structure and notes of vanilla bean and subtle exotic notes of star fruit. Succulent and nicely balanced, it has its own personality, true to 2013 and distinct to 2012, more succulent and exotic in 2013.

LALLIER BLANC DE BLANCS BRUT GRAND CRU NV $$

94 points • DISGORGED MARCH 2017 • TASTED IN AUSTRALIA

100% chardonnay; 60% Aÿ, 40% Avize, Cramant and Oger; 12% reserves; aged 4 years on lees; 9g/L dosage

Always a highlight of Lallier's portfolio, this is a cuvée that balances the expressive depth and intensity of Aÿ with the freshness of the Côte des Blancs, and never has it looked more exact than it does from Lallier's new facility, basking in the glory of the great 2012 harvest. Blessed with another year of lees since I reviewed it in my last edition, it has perfectly preserved all of its succulent white peach generosity of Aÿ and citrus cut of the Côte des Blancs. Time has overlaid lemon meringue and marzipan complexity, at every moment underlined by the definition and grip of the pronounced, fine chalk minerality of its profound crus. An enticing blanc de blancs, with dosage well integrated on a finish of exacting line and seamless persistence.

LALLIER GRAND ROSÉ BRUT GRAND CRU NV $$

95 points • 2013 BASE VINTAGE • DISGORGED MARCH 2017 • TASTED IN AUSTRALIA

20% chardonnay, 80% pinot noir; sourced mostly from Aÿ, Bouzy and Avize; 8% reserves; 8g/L dosage

Tribaut's elegant touch with the pinot of the legendary crus of Aÿ and Bouzy, freshened with the zing of Avize, makes for a delightfully captivating rosé. He dubs his unique method 'millefeuille' (only in France!), blending pinot and chardonnay by layering the crushed grapes in the vat for warm maceration, just for a few hours to extract fruitiness and a pale colour, before bleeding and chilling for alcoholic fermentation. Landing in a new classy wide bottle, never has this distinctive method looked more triumphant than it does in 2013. It's a beautifully fragrant, fine and characterful articulation of Aÿ and Bouzy, rising stature and presence of red cherry and strawberry fruit, beautifully laced with the brioche and vanillin of bottle age. Wonderfully fine chalk mineral structure and excellent length are elevated by the distinguished energy of Avize.

LALLIER MILLÉSIME GRAND CRU BRUT 2008 $$$

95 points • DISGORGED FEBRUARY 2016 • TASTED IN AUSTRALIA

45% chardonnay, 55% pinot noir; Côte des Blancs chardonnay; Aÿ pinot noir; aged 7 years on lees; 7g/L dosage

I love the way this cuvée has blossomed with a few years on cork since its disgorgement. Boasting a medium straw-yellow hue, it has exuded its rich, voluptuous curves from the outset, now more generous than ever in its layers of spicy golden delicious apples, brioche and vanilla custard. The purity and energetic acid drive of 2008 elevate its fine chalk mineral presence. A rare 2008 that's ready to drink right away.

LANSON

(Lohn-soh)

(6/10)

66 RUE DE COURLANCY 51100 REIMS
www.lanson.com

*Exciting new developments are unfolding to usher in a brand-new era at an historic estate that has always struck me as quite
extraordinary. For the ninth-largest Champagne house, with a 4 million bottle annual production (the majority of which is Black
Label Brut NV, frequently discounted to one of the lowest prices of any champagne on the shelves), Lanson is a house that has maintained
remarkable consistency. All the more astonishing considering that it was purchased by Moët in 1991 and cunningly on-sold less than six
months later, retaining just two of its 208 hectares of magnificent vineyards. It should take 15 years for a house of this magnitude to recover
from such a blow, but I have admired Black Label consistently over the past two decades, and in recent tastings of vintage wines spanning
30 years, that ominous dip that everyone anticipated simply never came. How is this possible?*

One man. Jean-Paul Gandon commenced here in 1972, making
his tenure of more than 40 years extraordinary, even in a region
as historic as Champagne. More than this, he spent his first
15 years overseeing the sourcing of the grapes and must in the
vineyards, a role which he retained when he was promoted to
chef de cave in 1986.

His new owners astutely left him free rein to source, make
and blend the wines as he saw best. He was a talented winemaker,
certainly, but more than this, he was connected, and his relationships
with the growers spanning 500 hectares of Lanson sourcing across
Champagne infused this house with a startling resilience in the
midst of its tumultuous corporate ride of recent decades.

In 2013, Hervé Dantan joined Lanson as assistant chef de
cave in anticipation of Jean-Paul Gandon's retirement in 2015.
With a progressive intuition for innovation and experimentation

in the vineyards and the winery, Dantan had dedicated 22 years
to transforming Mailly Grand Cru into one of Champagne's top
coopératives. 'In Lanson, I found the same family spirit that I
enjoyed at Mailly, in a bigger place!' he exclaimed.

He immediately ushered in an exciting new era at Lanson.
'Many things have changed, while respecting the traditions of
Lanson,' he told me recently. 'We need to uphold a consistent
style, keeping the soul of Lanson, while improving the quality.'

Dantan's first priorities were to facilitate small-parcel
vinification and to increase texture in the wines. To this end,
€17 million was invested into the winery in 55 new small tanks of
50–100hL capacity, a new reserve wine cellar and 23 new foudres
installed just in time for the 2014 vintage.

'Without malolactic fermentation, we need to add creamy
texture, and we hope that the use of oak and micro-oxygenation

can help with this,' he says. 'We want to keep the style fresh and crisp, while adding creamy complexity.' His foudres are thus for complexity and not for wood character, by ageing (not fermenting) chardonnay and pinot noir. 'I don't envisage making a special oak-matured cuvée, but expect that a very small contribution of just 5–6% will add complexity and depth to our blends.'

Following primary fermentation, the wine is cooled to 8°C and sulphur dioxide preservative is added to block malolactic fermentation. This creates a distinctive house style of excitingly high-strung, age-worthy champagne, true to Gandon's aspiration of 'maintaining freshness, power and fruit character'. In 2015, Dantan put 10% of Black Label components through malolactic, which he considers important, not to change the style, but for maintaining consistency in Black Label and Rose Label in certain vintages.

'We are not dogmatic about malolactic,' he explains. 'The idea is not to be full malolactic or no malolactic, but to be flexible according to the balance of the harvest. In a warm season we might avoid malolactic altogether.' He expects to land at around 20-25% malolactic on average, with Vintage and Noble cuvées remaining with no malolactic. 'The idea with the non-vintages is to give more depth and complexity, while upholding the traditional Lanson style.'

Long ageing is facilitated thanks to a considerable stock of 20 million bottles, resting in 7 kilometres of galleries under Reims at a stable 10°C. The non-vintage receives complexity from a minimum of three years ageing on lees and a generous 20–30% reserves, power and structure from a 50% dose of pinot noir from the Montagne de Reims and Côte des Bar, minerality from chardonnay on the southern slopes of the Montagne de Reims, and a balancing touch of just 15% Vallée de la Marne meunier.

Lanson uses meunier only in its entry non-vintage cuvées.

Over the past decade, Lanson has added 16 hectares to its estate vineyards, which now comprise 57 hectares, including 16 hectares of biodynamic vines in Verneuil in the Vallée de la Marne. Sustainability is a high priority for Dantan, who received a wake-up call in 2017.

'The 2017 vintage was the most complicated harvest I have ever faced,' he recalled. 'I was worse than stressed, I was disoriented. This vintage demonstrated to me that we need to change things in the vineyards in Champagne. And I saw that the growers who managed to have the best level of quality were all those that were certified Viticulture Durable en Champagne (VDC).'

Concerned that Champagne will increasingly face vintages of such challenge, Dantan was prompted to invest in VDC. 'We are working very hard with our growers and have created a collective structure to make it easier and less expensive for them to become certified.' He will pay growers a little more for their fruit under VDC, and hopes to have a majority certified in the coming years. 'This is important for our relationships, for the quality of vine growing, and for the future,' he emphasises.

Dantan maintains Gandon's legacy of grand cru fruit sources for Lanson's Gold Label Vintage, which is generally a 50/50 blend of pinot noir and chardonnay, aged a minimum of five years on lees prior to release, and usually considerably longer – remarkable for one of the lowest-priced vintage wines on the shelves.

Lanson has long maintained a deep reserve stock, and Dantan has filled his new reserve cellar with an incredibly diverse palette of blending options. The collection currently includes every vintage from 2017 back to 1998, besides the dog years of 2001,

2010 and 2011. Three different years of Black Label are kept as reserves, 'as a link between the harvest and the reserves'. A reserve solera is maintained for complexity and freshness. And from vintage 2013, Dantan has introduced oak casks to store reserve wines. Only pinot and chardonnay from grand and premier crus are held in reserve.

Lanson is a house whose wines age effortlessly, building slowly and purposefully in bottle, and I have recently been stunned by the stamina of late-disgorged 1979, 1983, 1988, 1990 and regular-disgorged 1996 and 1998.

To commemorate its 250th anniversary in 2010, Lanson launched a series of 'Extra Age' cuvées. The concept was unusual but inspired, a trilogy of three non-vintage cuvées, each from three mature vintages chosen to complement each other. These were not simply late-disgorged versions of its non-vintage cuvées, but purpose-assembled to age gracefully.

Lanson is impressive in printing disgorgement dates on the back of every cuvée. Sadly, the wonderfully informative detail on every cuvée appears to have disappeared from its website.

Lanson seals its Organic, Père et Fils and all half-bottles with DIAM closures and continues to experiment with other cuvées. 'I am convinced that when you do a blind tasting of a classic cork and a DIAM, it is impossible to perceive the difference for Lanson wines,' Dantan reveals. 'We can only recognise a natural cork when it has a corky taste.' I look forward to a move to DIAM across his range, as I have experienced some cork taint in Lanson again this year.

Lanson recently released Dantan's first blend, and it is the best Black Label I've tasted. He is modest: 'It was the beginning, I was but a child at Lanson. Now I am a teenager.' There are great things to come in the reinvention of this grand historic estate.

CLOS LANSON

In 2016, Lanson launched Clos Lanson from its unique single hectare alongside the winery in Reims. When Philippe Baijot purchased Lanson in 2006, he began conversion of the site to organic viticulture and resolved to create the first vintage from one of the last remaining vineyards in the city of Reims. 'It was here in the 18th century, and was on the edge of town at the beginning of the 19th,' reveals Dantan. Surrounded by development today, the environment of the city influences its microclimate, pushing temperatures 2–2.5°C warmer than the Montagne. The Clos is subsequently harvested as early as Avize and Oger.

It was planted to 100% chardonnay in 1962 and 1986 in 15 metres of topsoil above pure, white, friable, well-draining chalk. According to Dantan, it's the warmth and the chalk that make it possible for this site to produce a vintage every year.

The vineyard is divided into two plots, which ripen between three and seven days apart, and are hence harvested separately. The entire harvest of 8000 bottles (and as few as 5000) is fermented and matured in oak barrels of three to four vintages of age. True to Lanson, malolactic is fully blocked.

Clos Lanson is a generously expressive cuvée that captures the elegance of the Lanson style with ripe intensity and the chalky, saline signature of its unique site.

It is a tricky calling to create a single-varietal, single-vintage wine from a single plot in every year, yet a vertical tasting of every vintage from 2006 to 2015 revealed a surprising consistency and impressive integrity. Oak impact is astonishingly subtle and colours are surprisingly pale, with fruit and oak presence diminished thanks to the absence of malolactic fermentation.

Lanson is the primary brand of the Lanson-BCC group, champagne's third largest after LVMH and Vranken-Pommery Monopole.

LANSON BLACK LABEL BRUT NV $

92 points • 2013 BASE VINTAGE • DISGORGED OCTOBER 2017 AND JANUARY 2018 • TASTED IN CHAMPAGNE AND AUSTRALIA

35% chardonnay, 50% pinot noir, 15% meunier; 100 different villages including 50 grand and premier crus; 30% reserves from 10 vintages from 1995 to 2012; no use of oak; a little inclusion of malolactic for the first time; aged more than 3.5 years on lees; 8g/L dosage; cork

Black Label remains the confident barometer of Lanson, and Dantan's first blend is a class act, a resounding statement of his talent in preserving the style and integrity of the house while meticulously polishing the edges. For all it represents, this is a very important cuvée in the grand scheme of champagne, upholding its throne as one of the best and most consistent of the readily available bargain set. It contrasts the crunch of lemon zest, red apple and pear with the toasty, spicy, honeyed complexity of maturity. The purity and freshness of pinot noir are more exact than ever, layering pretty notes of red cherries, raspberries and a wisp of musk. This release has enjoyed more than 3.5 years on lees – impressive, even by Lanson standards. With seamless integration of malic acidity and chalk minerality, it steps the style up to a new level of harmony, precision and persistence, making this the best Black Label yet. Bravo, Dantan.

Pinot noir ready for pressing in harvest 2014.

LANSON ROSE LABEL BRUT ROSÉ NV $$

92 points • **2013 BASE VINTAGE** • **DISGORGED JUNE 2017 AND FEBRUARY 2018** • **TASTED IN CHAMPAGNE AND AUSTRALIA**

32% chardonnay, 53% pinot noir, 15% meunier; 100 different villages; 6.5% red wine in equal thirds from Les Riceys pinot, Bouzy pinot and Cumières meunier; 30% reserves of Rose Label base 2010, 2011 and 2012; no oak; aged more than 3.5 years on lees; 8.5g/L dosage; cork

Lanson first produced rosé in the 1950s and the style is increasingly important for the house, now representing an impressive 18% of its production, close to double the region's average. The base wine is not the same as Black Label, and while the *cépage* is not far from it, the recipe of crus is simpler, with more grand and premier cru sourcing in the Rose Label, and more reserves. Mareuil-sur-Aÿ, Cumières and Côte des Bar are important for fruitiness, balanced with the freshness of chardonnay from Montgueux, Vitry and Trépail. Blended with just a small proportion of red wine, it's intentionally a refreshing, fruity, apéritif style, purposely not too heavy or structured. Dantan is seeking wines that express delicate prettiness. He includes 30% reserves of the previous three year's Rose Label blend, as 'a vaccination against the evolution of colour', because the colour, freshness and fruitiness remain very stable in these reserves.

There is a pretty elegance and an understated delicacy to this gorgeous rosé that its blatant strawberry mousse-coloured livery belies. Don't be put off by this or its teeny price, because this is a finely crafted rosé of purity and subtlety, and never has it looked prettier. Pinot noir and chardonnay are blended from the most elegant premier and grand crus with a judicious dose of red wine of pretty aromatics and soft tannins to create a medium salmon hue and layers of vibrant, gentle strawberry hull, raspberry, red apple and tangelo fruit. It's been aged longer than ever (more than 3.5 years here) and yet it's fresher and more fruit pure than before. The refreshing drive of malic acidity is well poised, yet in no way aggressive, directing a long and tangy finish of fine chalk minerality. Rose Label confidently upholds its position among the true bargains of rosé champagne.

Lanson Père et Fils Brut NV $$

92 points • 2012 BASE VINTAGE • DISGORGED 2016 • DIAM • TASTED IN AUSTRALIA
89 points • 2011 BASE VINTAGE • DISGORGED FEBRUARY 2015 • CORK • TASTED IN AUSTRALIA

35% chardonnay, 50% pinot noir, 15% meunier; 100 different villages; no oak; Black Label aged 4 years on lees with a slightly lower dosage of 7g/L

I have always admired the way Black Label blossoms with cellar age post-disgorgement, and Père et Fils is a celebration of its endurance. It upholds bright, crunchy lemon zest and red apple fruit amidst the rising toast, biscuits, roast nuts and spice of maturity. The 2012 base presents a freshness that belies its age, even paler in hue and more elegant in style than the 2013 base Black Label, radiating with bright, focused lemon and tangelo, sustained by scintillating malic acidity. The harrowing 2011 season marks its release with subtle underripe, grassy notes and hints of coffee-bean dryness and phenolic bitterness. Nonetheless, it's a pretty good result for the season and the price. One bottle of 2011 base showed low-level cork taint, thankfully a thing of the past, with subsequent releases under DIAM.

Lanson Vin Biologique Green Label Organic Brut NV $$

90 points • 2013 BASE VINTAGE • DISGORGED SEPTEMBER 2016 AND OCTOBER 2017 • TASTED IN CHAMPAGNE AND AUSTRALIA

20% chardonnay, 50% pinot, 30% meunier from Verneuil; no oak; no malolactic fermentation; 6-8g/L dosage; DIAM

In the heart of the Vallée de la Marne, Dantan describes Verneuil as a village that always yields very fruity characters with floral notes and a touch of honey. Spanning 30 different plots, Lanson's 16-hectare organic vineyard was originally acquired from the great estate of Le Brun de Neuville.

The tense cut and tang of malic acidity presents a compelling juxtaposition to the plush red berry presence, red apple crunch, rounded generosity and spicy complexity of Verneuil pinot noir and meunier. Edginess is accentuated by low dosage, making for a distinctive and tense style of crab-apple bitterness that contrasts the crowd-friendly appeal of Lanson's other non-vintage cuvées. With a pale straw and a blush tint, it's bright, crunchy, firm and primary, showcasing fragrant red fruits amidst tangy citrus that lingers long on the finish. I tasted this blend on four separate occasions, and it progressively improved post-disgorgement, becoming spicier and more honeyed. It will age confidently and deserves at least a few more years to integrate and mellow.

Lanson Extra Age Brut NV $$$$

95 points • 2006 BASE VINTAGE • DISGORGED NOVEMBER 2017 • TASTED IN CHAMPAGNE AND AUSTRALIA

40% chardonnay from Avize, Cramant, Oiry, Oger and Le Mesnil-sur-Oger (the same base as Extra Age Blanc de Blancs), 60% pinot noir from Verzenay and Bouzy; reserves from 2005 and 2004; no malolactic fermentation; aged more than 10 years on lees; 8g/L dosage

Lanson's Extra Age blends are only produced in 'the most interesting vintages' from 'a higher level of grapes', not always grand cru, though they are here. The leader of its senior citizen trio is a majestic blend that bores deep into the chalk bedrock of seven of Champagne's most distinguished and profound crus. Its medium straw-yellow hue proclaims its freshness even after more than a decade in the deep. The focus of Côte des Blancs chardonnay harmoniously melds with the red fruits of pinot noir, underscored by prominent salt chalk minerality amplified by the freshness of malic acidity. A seamlessly composed blend that unites fresh fruit definition with the deep complexity and texture of long lees age.

Pinot noir harvest 2014 at Lanson

LANSON EXTRA AGE BRUT BLANC DE BLANCS NV $$$$

94 points • 2006 BASE VINTAGE • DISGORGED NOVEMBER 2016 • TASTED IN CHAMPAGNE

100% chardonnay from Avize, Cramant, Oiry, Oger and Le Mesnil-sur-Oger; 2005 and 2004 reserves; no malolactic fermentation; aged more than 9 years on lees

A beautifully precise blanc de blancs of alluring grace and precise definition. For a wine of this age, purity is proclaimed in a medium straw-yellow glow that resonates with grand cru fruit presence of fleshy white peach and zesty lemon. Almost a decade on lees has unravelled a creamy texture and characters of brioche, almond nougat and vanilla cream. Malic drive and pronounced chalk minerality unite effortlessly on a long finish.

LANSON EXTRA AGE BRUT ROSÉ NV $$$$

90 points • 2009 BASE VINTAGE • DISGORGED MARCH 2018 • TASTED IN CHAMPAGNE

30% chardonnay from Avize, Cramant, Le Mesnil, Trépail, 70% pinot noir from Verzenay, Bouzy, Aÿ and Mareuil-sur-Aÿ; 6% Bouzy red wine; 2008 and 2007 reserves; no malolactic fermentation

This is a young release by Extra Age standards, and it looked precocious and stark three months post-disgorgement. A rosé of personality and energy, it leaps from the glass with flamboyant pink pepper and Campari. It's a savoury and dry style of medium copper-salmon hue, with the tension of malic acidity amplifying the grip of fine tannin structure. It concludes focused and taut, desperately in need of time to unravel.

LANSON GOLD LABEL BRUT VINTAGE 2008 $$

96 points • DISGORGED FEBRUARY AND OCTOBER 2016 • TASTED IN CHAMPAGNE AND AUSTRALIA

47% chardonnay from Avize, Cramant, Le Mesnil-sur-Oger, Oger and Trépail; 53% pinot noir from Aÿ, Bouzy and Verzenay; no oak; no malolactic fermentation; 7g/L dosage; cork

Lanson Gold Label is only made in the golden years, and with no 2006 or 2007, Hervé Dantan was nervous about releasing the 2008 in 2017. It was desperately too young then, as it is now, the electric zap of 2008 malic acidity all-conquering. True to the season and the no-malolactic and low-dosage mandate of the house, this is a tightly coiled cuvée of elegant refinement, a vector of astounding energy. I love the endurance of malic acidity in charging Lanson Vintage with tremendous potential in the cellar, and I cannot recall when this was more pronounced than in 2008, with the stamina to age confidently for three or four decades. Just one decade into its odyssey, it's still a pale straw hue, a magnificent contrast of the tension, energy and lemon freshness of 2008 malic acidity, massaged with the glorious layers of age, slowly beginning to build nougat, crème brûlée, vanilla, brioche, ginger and spice. There is ripeness here of mirabelle plums, juicy peaches and pears, yet this is not for the uninitiated, having lost nothing of its drive, energy and chalk mineral cut. For goodness sake, do not over chill it, for risk of being impaled by an ice shard of malic acidity! In line and length, it's an absolute triumph that will go down among the most sublime Gold Labels of the modern era. After spouting many superlatives in my last edition, my esteem of this cuvée and its endless potential have not diminished one bit over four recent tastings. I bought many cases and will take my own advice and hold off until at least 2030.

LANSON NOBLE CUVÉE BRUT BLANC DE BLANCS 2002 $$$$

94 points • DISGORGED NOVEMBER 2016 • TASTED IN CHAMPAGNE

100% chardonnay from Avize, Cramant, Le Mesnil-sur-Oger, Oger and Chouilly; aged more than 13 years on lees

Noble Cuvée is only made in the classic years, blended from the best wines of the house. Dantan is looking for 'those that express vibrancy, saltiness, delicacy, finesse and ageability, not rich or showy', so as to uphold stamina for at least 15 years until release. He describes 2002 as 'a fantastic year', and it certainly shows off in this captivating and entrancing release. Veiled in a medium, bright straw-yellow hue, the primary definition of pear, lemon, white peach and fennel are accented with the generosity of glacé pear and fig, evolving into wonderful toasty complexity that evokes nuances of vanilla and brioche over a core of silky, buttery smoothness. Subtle wisps of grilled-toast reduction glide high on a palate of great harmony, lingering with fine, salty minerality on a finish charged with the drive of malic energy.

LANSON NOBLE CUVÉE BRUT 2002

95 points • DISGORGED JUNE 2016 • TASTED IN CHAMPAGNE

70% chardonnay, 30% pinot noir from Verzenay; no malolactic fermentation; aged 13 years on lees

A resounding and compelling case for the marriage of chardonnay and pinot noir, with the definition of the great crus of the Côte des Blancs holding hands intimately with the elegant yet generous presence of Verzenay pinot noir. Maintaining a medium yellow hue, it is unravelling with all of the captivating theatrics of 17 years of age, boasting brioche and almond complexity amidst creamy texture. A very long finish is sustained by the eloquent draw of malic acidity.

Lanson Noble Cuvée Brut Rosé NV $$$$

93 points • 100% 2002 • Disgorged October 2017 • Tasted in Champagne

100% Noble Brut 2002 with 6% Bouzy rouge; Dantan doesn't know why it isn't labelled as a vintage (it will be in future); no malolactic fermentation

A dribble of just 6% Bouzy rouge completely changes the game for Noble Brut, and I would never guess it was the same wine (the ultimate options game twist!). It adds a medium copper hue and layers of toasty maturity and savoury complexity of roast tomato, dried herbs and dried apple It concludes long and complex, yet well focused and taut, thanks to the tension between finely poised tannin structure, bright malic acidity and fine, salty chalk minerality.

Lanson Noble Cuvée Brut 1988 $$$$$

98 points • Disgorged early 2000 • Tasted in Champagne

On more than one occasion many years ago, when I was but a poor associate judge in high-profile wine shows, my contribution to the grand spectacle of indulgent bottles that paraded the table at judges' dinners was a magnum of Lanson 1988. I was proud and relieved that the eternal stamina of the house in the longest-lived vintage of the decade stood up confidently alongside even grand old magnums of Dom Pérignon. I had a flashback to those moments when Dantan poured this remarkable old Lanson, from a bottle in epic condition, and my stab at guessing its vintage was more than lucky. After more than 30 years, it remains a profound, inimitable and instantly recognisable 1988 that masterfully wields the gleaming malic sabre of the season. It has finally relaxed into its happy place of generous complexity of luscious stone fruits, juicy plums, layers of dried fruit, ginger, fruit mince spice, golden fruit cake, even marmalade. The slow parade to grand old age is beginning in evocative suggestions of green olive and sweet pipe smoke. Sustained by the long-life battery pack of malic acidity, the great vintages of Lanson evolve in freeze-frame slow motion, and finally this one has attained that perfect moment in its maturity when the three universes of primary, secondary and tertiary development coalesce in wonderful harmony.

Lanson Clos Lanson 2006 $$$$$

94 points • Disgorged December 2014 • Tasted in Champagne

100% chardonnay; 1-hectare single vineyard in Reims; warm site on friable chalk; fermented and aged in oak barrels of 3-4 vintages of age; no malolactic fermentation; 3g/L dosage; ~8000 bottles; inaugural release; full detail in the introduction on page 348

There is a wonderfully seamless contrast here, between the understated generosity of this warm site, the ripe intensity of the early 2006 season, and the enduring malic precision of the Lanson style. True to its lavishness, it has progressed faster than Lanson's other vintage cuvées, attaining a point in its sweeping arc of evolution of full, bright-yellow hue and deep, reverberating complexity of rich layers of vanilla and the prominent, smoky character of barrel fermentation. Layers of luscious, primary white peach, pineapple and pear hold long and strong, uplifted by gentle malic acceleration and the salty, elegantly chalky texture that defines this unique Clos. A wine of great persistence and characterful singularity.

LARMANDIER-BERNIER

(Lah-mohn-diay-Bear-niay)

7/10

19 Avenue du Général de Gaulle 51130 Vertus
www.larmandier.fr

CHAMPAGNE
LARMANDIER-BERNIER

'To create a wine that deeply expresses its terroir' is Pierre Larmandier's aim, stated on the back of every one of the 150,000 bottles that leave his little cellar in Vertus each year. But to this fastidious grower, terroir in itself is not enough. 'Terroir is to wine what the score is to music,' he suggests. 'What's the point if the grape variety, the vine plant (the instrument) and the winegrower (the performer) are not up to standard?' Some growers are known for their focus on the vines, others for their attention in the winery, but few find a symphonic harmony in every detail like Pierre Larmandier.

Since he came back to the family estate in 1988, Larmandier has grown holdings from 10 hectares to now a substantial 18 glorious hectares, blessed with impressive terroirs that represent one of the most expansive holdings of any grower on the Côte des Blancs. Spread across a total of 65 plots, his vineyards span the premier cru village of Vertus – including substantial holdings on the mid-slopes close to Le Mesnil-sur-Oger, supplemented with an impressive 2.5 hectares in the grand cru of Cramant, nearly 1 hectare in each of Avize and Chouilly, 0.2 in Oger, and 0.5 in the little villages of Bergères-lès-Vertus, Voipreux and Villeneuve-Renneville-Chevigny surrounding Vertus. In 2018 they added new plots of chardonnay in Avize and in Bisseuil, between Tour-sur-Marne and Mareuil-sur-Aÿ. Chardonnay is king here, covering more than 90% of his holdings, and Larmandier tends just two hectares of pinot noir in Vertus for rosé and red wine.

'Chardonnay is very adaptable, and if you cultivate it carefully it will take its expression from the soil,' he explains, likening the diversity of his various plots to that of Puligny-Montrachet and Chablis.

'It would be a shame if we didn't bring our vineyards to your glass!' Larmandier says. And bring them he has, through one of the most sensible and diligent regimes anywhere in Champagne.

ORGANO-REALIST
Practising biodynamically since 1999 and certified since 2004, Larmandier describes himself as an 'organo-realist'. Every time I visit, he whisks me off in his four-wheel drive to one of his key plots in Vertus. One year, he'd heard rumours of an oïdium breakout around the village and wanted to get onto it right away. As we approached one of his plots, we passed other growers out treating for oïdium. 'That man', he said, pointing out one, 'is the worst in the village for always treating.' We found a little oïdium in Larmandier's plot, 'but it is not so bad so we will not treat yet. We're not too concerned about a little disease in the vineyards. Some people say grass is a disease, too!'

Larmandier cultivates grasses in the mid-rows during winter and ploughs until close to harvest. He considers an absence of

Pierre Larmandier takes a sample from a foudre.

herbicides to be the key. 'Organic or not is less important than abandoning herbicides,' he upholds. 'Everyone says they control weeds by ploughing, but I see them spraying with herbicide!' With neighbouring vines in such close proximity, it's impossible to conduct a biodynamic regime without some influence from those who do not farm naturally. Larmandier is matter-of-fact: 'We try to do the best we can, but it is not ideal. We still manage to be different to the others, even though we are among them.'

Biodynamics is difficult to manage across so many plots, particularly the smaller ones, some just 200 square metres, spanning 15 kilometres north to south. 'We spend more time on the road than in the field with the tractor!' he says. And he calls his cousins in each village to check how much it has rained. 'We need to time our copper applications very carefully to combat disease.'

Since beginning conversion to biodynamic viticulture in 2000, Larmandier has noted a drop in yields, regulated by grasses in the mid-rows. He currently produces just 60–70hL/hectare. 'In the village, you are considered a bad grower if you do not produce 100hL/hectare,' he reveals. 'People produce too much in the Côte des Blancs, and the big houses just buy everything. They say I'm crazy to produce less than 100hL.'

He says 2012 was one of the toughest seasons he can recall in 25 years of managing his vines, yielding just two-thirds of his usual small harvest. Incessant rain made it difficult for him to get into the vineyards to cultivate the soil. 'We do our best with biodynamics, but when it's crazy, it's crazy!' he exclaims.

Larmandier likes old vines and tries to keep them as long as he can; some are as old as 80 years. 'My ideal is to never replace them, which is all very well, but then you don't have any grapes!' he says. In order to create more competition and push the roots deeper, he is slowly replanting at 10,000 vines per hectare, more than the regional average of 7500. 'This is contrary to the way of thinking in Champagne, but if I want to improve concentration without increasing my harvest, I think this is the way,' he explains.

'You can only extract so much minerality per square foot before

it is diluted, but with more vines you can extract more.' While others focus on grapes per square metre of leaves to produce more aromatic wines, for Larmandier the key is the more Burgundian focus on grapes per square metre of soil.

'The soil is the most important thing,' he emphasises. 'With deep roots in good soils, 80% of the work is done.' Here, on the lower slopes below the village of Vertus, the chalk lies 80 centimetres below the surface. He considers his average vine age of 35 years to be very important. 'The roots have a better depth and are better able to extract the minerality from the chalk. We are very lucky to have the place we do, and we work very hard in the vineyard to make the most of it,' he says.

Along with an expression of minerality, his priorities are roundness and linearity achieved by harvesting grapes at optimal ripeness of around eleven degrees of potential, compared with most in Champagne who aim for around nine. 'It is important for us to work the soil to achieve a lower pH in the wine, allowing us to wait longer to harvest, to achieve ripeness without lacking freshness.'

Even in the record heatwave of 2003 he was able to achieve liveliness in his wines. 'Attention to the soil is increasingly important in these warmer vintages, so as to achieve phenolic maturity and not just sugar ripeness.' Larmandier harvests on taste rather than sugar levels.

NON-INTERVENTIONIST WINEMAKING

His sensitive and non-interventionist approach informs all he does. 'My philosophy used to be that terroir was everything and the hand of man was nothing, that our work in the vineyard was all that mattered,' Larmandier clarifies. 'But now we understand that the work we do and the choices we make in the winery are important, too.' Larmandier did not study oenology and says it's impossible to simplify winemaking to a recipe. 'If you work in the vineyards, your mind is not only on acid and alcohol numbers but on expression,' he says. 'Every year I have an oenology student come to work with me and they want to measure everything but I say, "First, you must taste!"'

To draw out the character of each site, wild yeast is used for primary and malolactic fermentations, with every parcel kept separate, and every ferment relying exclusively on its own natural yeasts. There is no filtration, 'because every time you filter or fine you lose a part of what you have worked hard to achieve in the vineyard'. Very low levels of preservative (sulphur dioxide), and ever lower extra-brut dosages of never more than 4g/L are used. 'After all the care lavished on our wines, we are not going to add anything which might go against them!' Larmandier exclaims. 'And a warmer climate means we can have a lower dosage.' Low sulphurs dictate that every wine is free to proceed through malolactic fermentation, and reserve wines are kept in tank under temperature control to maintain freshness.

Each year since 2004, a proportion of his non-vintage Latitude and Longitude cuvées has been held as a perpetual reserve for the next year's blend.

Larmandier doesn't like the 'austerity' of stainless steel fermentation, and has increased the proportion of oak vinification from 40% to 80%, for controlled oxidation and complexity. Wines are matured in oak until the end of July. He is very careful with barrel hygiene, having had 10% of his wines turn volatile when he first started with barrels, and now cleans them carefully and sulphurs three times in the lead-up to harvest. He appreciates the expression achieved in oak, and has experimented with egg fermenters for rosé for some years (though finds the result too rounded and intense, so balances this with an equal proportion fermented in tank) and an amphora for rosé. 'Perhaps it can give us a little bit more complexity for the blend?' he suggests. He confesses he likes to follow fashions 'a little bit', but won't go too far as he doesn't like oxidation.

'In Champagne we are blenders, and different fermentation vessels give us more components for the blends. With more concentration in our fruit, stainless steel is too closed and there's more risk of reduction,' he explains. He maintains a delicate balance to keep his wines fresh, admitting that he's afraid of oxidation.

When I first visited in 2011, he was putting the finishing touches on a new 'chai' to provide space for more wooden casks and vats and longer ageing. He still uses the first barrels he purchased in 1988, and has bought new barrels every year since 1999, 'because a used barrel has a personality of the wine, but we only want to express the personality of our vineyards'.

He doesn't want new oak characters to interfere, so new barrels comprise just 3% of his larger non-vintage blends for their first two years. Even tastings of his young vins clairs from second-use barrels display very subtle oak influence. He has purchased large foudres of the more subtle Austrian oak since 2001, and three more arrived in 2013.

Extra space also provides an opportunity to hold stock in bottle for longer, and his cellar now houses 700,000 bottles (up from 500,000 a couple of years ago), sufficient for an average of more than four years on lees across his cuvées (3.5 years previously), having increased his non-vintages from two years to three.

Larmandier's non-vintage philosophy is to let every vintage express its character. 'We are not blessed with making our non-vintage wines taste the same every year,' he says. Bottling codes are easy to decode, with the last four digits denoting the month and year of disgorgement. The other digits in the code are the base year. A refreshingly informative website presents the full detail of every cuvée.

The Larmandier and Bernier families have been winegrowers on the Côte des Blancs for eight generations since 1765. Today, Pierre's wife Sophie remains as actively involved in the business as ever, and their son Arthur has joined them since harvest 2017.

Larmandier-Bernier exemplifies the levels of purity and mineral focus that can be drawn out of primarily premier cru terroirs with sufficient care and attention. These exceedingly fine wines rightfully rank high among the greatest of Champagne's grower-producers.

Pierre Larmandier disgorging by hand.

LARMANDIER-BERNIER LATITUDE BLANC DE BLANCS EXTRA BRUT NV $$

90 points • 2015 BASE VINTAGE • TASTED IN CHAMPAGNE

Exclusively from plots sharing the same latitude in southern Vertus, a generous terroir yielding fully ripe grapes; wild fermented and matured until July in oak casks and vats; 40% perpetual reserve of previous Latitudes since 2004; aged at least 2 years on lees in bottle; 4g/L dosage

The generous southern slopes of Vertus yield a less mineral, easy to drink blanc de blancs. It projects the classic exoticism of the village in apple, pear and grapefruit. This is a cuvée that sings in the more classic, brighter vintages, but wanes in warmer vintages. The phenolic firmness of the ripe 2015 harvest makes for an austere style of dry-extract grip, making this release the least I have seen this cuvée since it was first named Latitude. Nonetheless, it concludes with admirable persistence.

LARMANDIER-BERNIER LONGITUDE PREMIER CRU EXTRA BRUT NV $$

92 points • 2014 BASE VINTAGE • TASTED IN CHAMPAGNE

From villages sharing roughly the same longitude: Vertus, Oger, Avize and Cramant; wild fermented and matured until July in oak casks and vats; 40% perpetual reserve of previous Longitudes since 2004; aged at least 2 years on lees in bottle; 3g/L dosage

A captivating take on the hallowed strip of the Côte des Blancs, this is a cuvée that heroes the engaging, finely poised chalk mineral texture of magnificent crus. The tension in the 2014 base makes for a crunchy style that contrasts the exotic flamboyance of Vertus, confidently bolstered with the concentration and structure of Oger, Avize and Cramant. The toasted brioche and caramel of barrel fermentation and lees age linger on the finish, empowered by nicely balanced acid drive.

LARMANDIER-BERNIER ROSÉ DE SAIGNÉE PREMIER CRU EXTRA BRUT NV $$$

92 points • TASTED IN CHAMPAGNE

Vertus single vineyard, co-planted to 85% pinot noir and 15% pinot gris; old vines harvested ripe at low yields; grapes are selected on a sorting table, partially destemmed and cold macerated for 2-3 days for colour without tannin before wild fermentation in tanks or concrete eggs; aged 2 years on lees; 3g/L dosage

This rosé is a paradox of the highest order, a salute to the genius of its maker and the depth of old-vine sources. How a 100% Côte des Blancs rosé from an elegant east-facing Vertus site can land midway between a graceful champagne rosé and an expressive red cherry pinot noir is truly astounding. Pierre Larmandier set out to make 'a rosé, not a white champagne with colour', marrying the power of pinot noir with the elegance of the village and, goodness, has he done it! 'We are different,' he says. 'We don't make pinot with just red fruit,' referring to 15% (by vine count) of pinot gris, co-planted among his pinot noir in 2003. 'Pinot gris brings more complexity and more florals than fruit,' he reveals.

This is an exuberant and exotic rosé of medium salmon-copper hue, brimming over with the red berry compote of pinot noir and the honey and frangipane florals of pinot gris bringing allusions of Alsace. It's alive with all the jubilant personality of Vertus in ginger, tamarillo and pawpaw, framed in fine, well-structured tannins. An increasing inclusion of gris makes for a rosé more characterful and complex than ever, if a little more precocious.

LARMANDIER-BERNIER TERRE DE VERTUS PREMIER CRU 2013 $$$

93 points • TASTED IN CHAMPAGNE

Single-vineyard Les Barillers, on delicate, saline terroir in the mid-slope of Vertus; wild fermented in small oak barrels and foudres; aged at least 5 years on lees; zero dosage

The intense mineral texture and layers of mouth-filling chalk of the northern slopes of Vertus learn much from the neighbouring grand cru of Le Mesnil-sur-Oger, and Larmandier is astute in separating these from the more rounded character of southern Vertus. Terre de Vertus is all about preserving this salt mineral fingerprint, which it does with laudable prowess, swimming with salivating salt minerality. It encapsulates the signature of the village, with its classic flamboyance on full parade in a panoply of spice and tropical fruit of persimmon and even pawpaw of lifted proportions, set against a silky, creamy, buttery palate, thanks in part to fruit ripeness and in part to barrel and foudre fermentation and maturation. A finish of beautiful persistence is accented with finely textured structure. Larmandier describes 2013 as being 'in the spirit of 2004, strict, and not very complex when it is young – but maybe this will come?'

LARMANDIER-BERNIER TERRE DE VERTUS PREMIER CRU 2012 $$$

94 points • TASTED IN CHAMPAGNE

As above

To Larmandier, '2012 is not a classical Terre de Vertus, very rich and not so sharp.' It presents a wonderful harmony between the creamy texture of barrel fermentation, the stone fruit generosity of the sunny 2012 season in exotic Vertus and the salt minerality of the north of the village. Nuances of freshly ground nutmeg are the lingering memories of barrels. A beautifully complete cuvée of character and allure, this is a rich expression of Terre de Vertus and ready to drink right away.

LARMANDIER-BERNIER LES CHEMINS D'AVIZE GRAND CRU 2012 $$$$

93 points • DISGORGED MARCH 2018 • TASTED IN CHAMPAGNE

Two vineyards, Chemin de Plivot and Chemin de Flavigny, of 50-year-old vines planted on chalky sites with thin top soils in the heart of Avize; wild fermented in one 2000-litre oak foudre, which Larmandier suggests was a bit young, plus some small barrels; aged 5 years on lees; disgorged a little earlier than usual to allow time for oak integration; 2g/L dosage

Tasted on the eve of its release, the presence of oak is more prominent than this cuvée has seen before, and Pierre admits that the foudre was a bit young and its impact is a little too much. His wines come into their oak with time in bottle, so this is a cuvée to afford plenty of patience. The generosity of white peach and the cut of grapefruit in Avize define a very long finish, supported by the creamy texture and vanilla custard notes of barrel fermentation. It finishes long and full, dazzling with the ever-present glitter of deeply textured, inimitable Avize salt minerality.

LARMANDIER-BERNIER VIEILLE VIGNE DU LEVANT GRAND CRU 2009 $$$$

93 points • TASTED IN CHAMPAGNE

Single-vineyard Bourron du Levant, south-east-facing on a particularly rich and powerful slope of Cramant, with vines 56–80+ years of age; wild fermented in casks and vats; aged 7–8 years on lees; 2g/L dosage

To Larmandier, Cramant is a different world that deserves to be showcased solo. Like all of his vintage cuvées, the vintage is now displayed on the front label, though purposely in small print at the bottom, 'because the place is more important than the vintage'. He says that in this special part of Cramant, his carefully cultivated old vines are less sensitive to seasonal fluctuations, and he could make a vintage every year. There's inherent power here, indicative of a particularly intense pocket of one of the Côte des Blancs' strongest villages, tamed with the classic finesse of Larmandier's sensitive touch. The succulent yellow fruits of Cramant, toasty, spicy influence of barrel fermentation and the frothing seaspray of chalk-embedded vineyards make for a style of character, presence and structure. It's firm and drying, with the subtle tannin and phenolic grip of the warm 2009 season in harmony with chalk minerality on a very long finish. Previously named Vieille Vigne de Cramant, but changed because of confusion between Cramant and crémant, now I suppose it will be confusion between Cramant and Levant!

LARMANDIER-BERNIER VIEILLE VIGNE DU LEVANT GRAND CRU 2008 $$$$

96 points • TASTED IN CHAMPAGNE

As above

The warmest sites of Cramant come into their own in the most classic and enduring seasons, and the signature acidity of 2008 presents a stark juxtaposition to the phenolic drive of 2009. The enticing yellow fruit presence of this intense slope of Cramant is oozing with white peach, contrasting the crunchy lemon and grapefruit of 2008. Barrel fermentation layers complexity of brioche and nougat, lending creaminess to its structure, without ever losing sight of the focused energy that defines this scintillating season. Boring to the core of its terroir, salt minerality heaves and churns on an incredible finish. This is a vintage that insists upon patience. As Larmandier puts it, '2009, you drink it, and 2008 you think about it'.

LARMANDIER-BERNIER SPECIAL CLUB VERTUS 1994

93 points • TASTED IN CHAMPAGNE

Disgorged on release, perhaps around the year 2000

The exotic immediacy of Vertus can give the impression of a lack of stamina, but Larmandier's great old vintages prove the endurance of the village, even in weaker seasons. Exuding a full yellow gold hue, cumquat and grapefruit play out the exoticism and crunch of Vertus, layered with marmalade and mixed spice, even hints of madeira. A glacé apricot note reflects some botrytis in the harvest. Acidity and salt minerality meld seamlessly on a finish of good persistence and outstanding integrity for a lesser season at a full quarter-century of age.

LARMANDIER-BERNIER VERTUS ROUGE PREMIER CRU COTEAUX CHAMPENOIS 2012
$$$$

90 points • TASTED IN CHAMPAGNE

100% old-vine Vertus pinot noir; partially destemmed with 20% stalks remaining and macerated for 12 days; wild fermented; aged 2 years in barrels; a little more than 2000 bottles

The Larmandier family has a long and deep tradition of still red wine, producing one of the great Coteaux Champenois, naturally more tense and mineral-focused in Vertus than the deeper style of the warmer slopes of the Montagne de Reims. It's now only made in exceptional years, and the excellent, very ripe, small grapes of 2012 beckoned a red wine instead of a rosé. I first tasted this cuvée in all of its rose petal and red cherry fragrance in 2015. It's now shed its youthful freshness, evolving to a secondary place of game and spice, now a little dried out by a touch of brettanomyces, but it holds its confidence, definition and persistence, sustained by finely structured tannins.

LARMANDIER-BERNIER VERTUS ROUGE PREMIER CRU COTEAUX CHAMPENOIS

94 points • TASTED IN CHAMPAGNE

The grand endurance of Coteaux Champenois is exemplified in the grand old vintages in Larmandiers' cellar, and this is not the first time I've been wowed by the impeccable condition of a mythical old bottle that finds its way to the surface. Hailing from his father's era, with no indication of its age; Larmandier suspects 1976 or earlier, and it may have been a blend of more than one vintage. A glorious bottle, in equally stunning condition to the last old Coteaux Champenois he poured for me in 2015, it still upholds primary fruit of black cherry, blackberry and plum, layered with spice, with a long finish sustained eternally by a backbone of super-fine tannins.

LAURENTI

(Lohr-ren-tee)

(6/10)

RUE DE LA CONTRESCARPE 10340 LES RICEYS
www.champagnelaurenti.fr

*L*es Riceys is the biggest cru in Champagne and the best in the Côte des Bar, increasingly sought after by the great houses for pinot noir. The Laurenti family is privileged to a tremendous estate of 45 hectares of mostly pinot noir and some chardonnay exclusively in the village. Founded in 1923 by Joseph Laurenti, the vineyards and winemaking are today managed by third-generation brothers Dominique, Joseph and Bruno Laurenti. A production of 300,000 bottles of just four cuvées celebrates the full expanse and majesty of the village in at times hedonistic proportions.

LAURENTI GRANDE CUVÉE BRUT NV $$

93 points • 2015 BASE VINTAGE • 20% CHARDONNAY, 80% PINOT NOIR • TASTED IN AUSTRALIA
92 points • 2014 BASE VINTAGE • 30% CHARDONNAY, 70% PINOT NOIR • TASTED IN AUSTRALIA

Reserves from the previous vintage; no oak; aged 3 years on lees; 12g/L dosage; cork

From its very first cuvée, Laurenti rejoices in the full breadth and glory of the best cru of the Côte des Bar. Pinot noir commands a confident and exuberant lead in a medium straw hue in the 2015 base, layered with succulent plums and black cherries of impressive fresh definition and presence. It's wrapped consummately in the spicy and characterful personality of the village in mixed spice and ginger, seamlessly married to the shortbread complexity of lees age. For all of its proportions, its full dosage is not overbearing, concluding with soft, rounded Les Riceys acidity and excellent line and length. The 2014 base presents a deeply spicy and characterful style, layered with fig, plum, pineapple and poached pear, accented with spice and the crunch of grapefruit on the finish. Dosage is well married to fine phenolic grip and lively acid drive, making for an exact and characterful take on Les Riceys.

Laurenti Grande Cuvée Rosée NV $$

91 points • 2015 base vintage • Tasted in Australia
92 points • 2014 base vintage • Tasted in Australia

30% chardonnay, 70% pinot noir; Les Riceys; reserves from the previous year; 2–3% pinot noir red wine from old vines more than 55 years of age, aged 3–4 years in the cellar; no oak; aged 3 years on lees; 12g/L dosage; cork

Les Riceys is one of Champagne's key sources of red wine for rosé, and it is testimony to the village that just 2–3% here represents one of the smallest proportions in all of the region, yet still infuses a beautiful pale to medium salmon hue. The spicy exuberance of pinot noir is the theme, flamboyantly celebrating the full succulence and presence of the region in the ripe 2015 season. Red berry fruits take on a savoury and spicy edge, even notes of balsamic and sun-dried tomato. For such proportions and juicy generosity, its full dosage feels a little heavy-handed, and it doesn't quite have the acid poise to hold it on the finish. Nonetheless, excellent line and length. The 2014 vintage has birthed a generous yet determined rosé in a succulent style that shows better balance, layered with plum, red cherries, fig, mixed spice and pear. It carries with excellent body and presence, with fine phenolics, focused acidity and elegant dosage working in seamless accord.

Laurenti Grande Cuvée Tradition NV $$$

94 points • 2010 base vintage • 70% chardonnay, 30% pinot noir • Tasted in Australia
92 points • 2009 base vintage • 50% chardonnay, 50% pinot noir • Tasted in Australia

Reserves from the previous year; 2–3% of reserves aged in oak barrels for 3 years; aged 3 years on lees; 12g/L dosage; cork

The label presents no hint of the considerable depth of maturity wrapped into the folds of this hedonistic cuvée, yet there is no mistaking this in the wine, which looks, smells, tastes and feels even older than it is. The colour is a deep, full gold, proclaiming the trifecta of age, ripeness and oak, and the bouquet and palate follow, a richly exuberant blend of hedonistic proportions. You name it, this cuvée has it: pineapple, fig and marmalade exoticism, layered with incredible character of vanilla custard, spice, burnt toffee, nougat and a full assortment of dried fruit and mixed nuts. For all of its flamboyance, it propagates with outstanding persistence and focus. A daring recipe which has been magnificently executed in the 2010 base vintage, a main-course cuvée of the most generous proportions. Two identical bottles of the 2009 base showed the fragility of the style in a warm season, riding the edge of collapsing into oxidation, but holding on for dear life for now, upholding integrity of succulent fruit persistence, helped in no small part by a full dose of sweetness. It explodes with grilled pineapple, baked fig, burnt orange, muscadelles, golden fruit cake, glacé apricots, crème brûlée that's been slightly over-fired, vanilla, even hints of cedar, warm hearth and antique sofa. For complexity and maturity at an affordable price, this cuvée over-delivers. Selosse for the masses.

Laurenti Grande Cuvée Blanche NV $$$

91 points • 2014 base vintage • Tasted in Australia

100% chardonnay; Les Riceys; 2013 reserves; no oak; 12g/L dosage

Laurenti has long built its personality on the exuberance of Les Riceys pinot noir, making the new arrival of blanc de blancs a foray in a very different direction for this impressive outfit, yet confidently upholding the shape and not inconsiderable size of the house. Generosity remains the theme, in succulent layers of peach, pineapple, golden delicious apple and the idiosyncratic mixed spice that is evidently more regional than varietal here. Chardonnay inherently brings with it a more confident cut of acid drive, all the more apparent here in 2014 by comparison with the warmer base vintages of 2015 and 2009 currently frequenting the Laurenti stable. In this context, its full dosage gives something of a sweet and sour impression and looks a little candied. A long finish confirms impressive fruit integrity and generosity.

LAURENT-PERRIER

(Lohr-rohn-Peh-riay)

5/10

51150 TOURS-SUR-MARNE
www.laurent-perrier.com

CHAMPAGNE

Laurent-Perrier

MAISON FONDÉE
1812

Laurent-Perrier is on a steep growth curve. Substantial expansion in recent years has seen the house climb to number five in Champagne by volume. A new cuverie, constructed in time for the 2009 harvest, added capacity for another 150 vins clairs and now handles production for the group, including de Castellane, Delamotte and Salon, now Champagne's fourth largest group. With an annual production of 7 million bottles (almost two-thirds of which are La Cuvée Brut), Laurent-Perrier is unusual in having found a reasonably comfortable equilibrium in that precarious balance between volume and finely tuned quality. Its famous rosé, beautiful vintage cuvée and distinguished Grand Siècle present a flattering demeanour of precision, delicacy, elegance and tension.

Laurent-Perrier's success is less by virtue of its domain vineyard holdings, which supply just 11% of its total needs of 150 hectares, than of the skill and vision of its people. The talented Alain Terrier was its longstanding chef de cave from 1975 to 2005, and was succeeded by Michel Fauconnet, his offsider for more than 20 years.

The secret to Laurent-Perrier's wines today is buried deep within the history of a house that celebrated its 200th birthday in 2012. The late Bernard de Nonancourt, founding president of the Laurent-Perrier Group, was a visionary who spent half of the last century transforming and expanding the company. His innovations changed the face of modern champagne. Under his leadership, the house boldly launched its non-vintage prestige cuvée, Grand Siècle, in 1957, a rosé well ahead of its time in 1968 (then considered a joke by the Champenois, now the best-selling champagne rosé in the world). Perhaps most influential of all, inspired by brewers of beer, Laurent-Perrier was the first house in Champagne to use stainless steel tanks in the 1960s.

De Nonancourt's vision was one of freshness, finesse and elegance based on chardonnay, which to this day maintains the majority stake in every cuvée (representing double Champagne's average) except rosé. No meunier is used, apart from now just 10% in La Cuvée Brut. This creates a house style of precision and tension, unusual among houses of this scale.

To celebrate its bicentenary in 2012, the house commissioned a major addition and renovation to its cuverie. In the same location as Champagne's first stainless steel tanks, the Grand Siècle winery is an atmospheric display of stainless steel reserve tanks custom-built with graceful curves, no seams, and narrow spouts to reduce oxidation.

Across the Laurent-Perrier group, sourcing spans 1550 hectares of vines, about 10% of which is from its own vineyards and 90% from more than 1200 growers and coopératives, providing for an annual production of 11.8 million bottles.

Laurent-Perrier has a declared commitment to sustainability in reducing the use of herbicides, ploughing, cultivating grasses in mid-rows and using only non-invasive chemicals in estate

vineyards, as well as in reducing the environmental impact of its winery, which is almost self-sufficient in its use of water. Former vineyard manager Christelle Rinville went even further, refusing to fly in aeroplanes and encouraging workers to use bicycles.

The house uses only the first pressing and no tailles, even in La Cuvée. Its tight, chardonnay-driven style is softened through malolactic fermentation in all cuvées, and long lees ageing of close to four years or more at 11°C in 10 kilometres of cellars under the house in Tours-sur-Marne. These are enduring wines of clean sophistication that transcend the scale of this operation.

Laurent-Perrier's long ageing is regrettably difficult to ascertain, as the house does not disclose disgorgement dates or base vintages, although it is possible to decode disgorgement dates from cork codes. The two digits represent the year (inverted) and the first letter (A–D) is the quarter – so, for instance, B81KB was disgorged in the second quarter of 2018.

I have requested an audience with Fauconnet countless times when visiting Champagne, and I am sorry to have never had the opportunity to meet him. In May 2019, the house announced the appointment of Dominique Demarville as Fauconnet's successor, effective from the beginning of 2020. The talented Demarville has spent the past quarter of a century transforming first Mumm and then Veuve Clicquot. Exciting things are indeed in store for Laurent-Perrier.

LAURENT-PERRIER LA CUVÉE BRUT NV $$

89 points • DISGORGED SECOND QUARTER OF 2018 • TASTED IN AUSTRALIA
89 points • 2012 BASE VINTAGE • DISGORGED FOURTH QUARTER OF 2016 • TASTED IN CHAMPAGNE

55% chardonnay, 35% pinot noir, 10% meunier from more than 100 crus; 20-30% reserves; 9g/L dosage; cork; around 5 million bottles

La Cuvée replaced L-P Brut two years ago, and its transformation went far deeper than just the label. Chardonnay was increased from 45% to 50% and now 55%, meunier correspondingly diminished from 15–20% to just 10%, and the inclusion of premier and grand crus was increased. The house disclosed that it took 15 years of preparation to get its supplies in line for this upgrade. At 62% of Laurent-Perrier's production, this cuvée alone accounts for around 5 million bottles annually, which makes its high proportion of chardonnay and long ageing all the more impressive. It's a happy party apéritif quaffer of pale straw hue that contrasts crunchy red apple, grapefruit and beurre bosc pear fruit and elderflower fragrance with fresh green notes reminiscent of fennel. Lees age brings impressive depth of spicy ginger cake complexity to the party. Bright acidity finds harmony with integrated yet slightly candied dosage that attempts to cover a subtle bite of almond-skin bitterness on the finish.

LAURENT-PERRIER ULTRA BRUT NV $$

92 points • 2009 BASE VINTAGE • DISGORGED FOURTH QUARTER OF 2017 • TASTED IN CHAMPAGNE
55% chardonnay, 45% pinot noir from 15 crus; reserves only from 2006; the 12th release since 1976

Laurent-Perrier has a very long history with zero dosage, having first launched its 'Grand Vins Sans Sucre' in the 1800s, relaunched by Bernard de Nonancourt in 1981 from the 1976 vintage, the warmest in Champagne in 45 years. The story goes that Alain Terrier, his chef de cave at the time, was resolved to make zero dosage, egged on by his friends in Burgundy who jeered, 'It's easy in Champagne – you make mistakes, you just add sugar!' When he took his new cuvée to the CIVC to ask how it should be labelled, they had no category, so proposed 'Extra Brut sans Dosage'.

Today, Ultra Brut is champagne's best-selling brut nature, in a well-balanced and high-strung apéritif style. With a pale, bright straw hue, this is a very pure and precise Ultra Brut that transcends both its age and the depth and power of its two composite vintages of 2009 and 2006. Pure apple, pear and lemon fruit are the primary focus here, with very little nuance of maturity. It is fine and mineral, with salt chalk definition and highly coiled poise. Anything it lacks in complexity and length it confidently makes up for in purity, freshness and mineral definition. A well-assembled zero dosage for champagne die-hards to drink with oysters.

LAURENT-PERRIER CUVÉE ROSÉ BRUT NV $$$

93 points • 2012 BASE VINTAGE • DISGORGED FOURTH QUARTER OF 2017 • TASTED IN CHAMPAGNE
94 points • DISGORGED SECOND QUARTER OF 2018 • TASTED IN AUSTRALIA

100% pinot noir from 10 crus, mostly in the Montagne de Reims; reserves only from the previous year; aged 5 years on lees; 8g/L dosage; cork

Laurent-Perrier picks fruit specifically for its famous rosé, sorts it in its press houses in Oger and Tour-sur-Marne, and destems it prior to maceration at 15°C for 48–72 hours, depending on fruit ripeness, until the colour is fixed and the aroma resembles freshly picked raspberries. So crucial is this timing, legend has it that the first chef de cave, Edouard Leclerc, slept by the tank to stop it just in time! Today, Michel Fauconnet tastes it every half hour when it gets close, and posts one of his team in the other village to do the same. The moment it's ready, they drain off the free-run juice, and only include a little pressing.

This wine has achieved that elusive ideal of volume and finesse; the world's best-selling rosé champagne epitomises the ultra-restraint of rosé's finest expressions. All the more remarkable for the challenging saignée method. Its latest incarnation is a medium to full, vibrant crimson hue, singing with the personality of pinot noir in white raspberries, crunchy wild strawberries, redcurrants, pomegranates and tangy morello cherries. Ripe pinot noir is the resounding theme here, in all of its fruity, spicy and tangy glory, uniting finely managed tannin structure with salty chalk mineral texture and well-integrated 'boiled sweets' dosage. Five years in the deep has built texture without interrupting its primary vibrancy. Older disgorgements begin to take on balsamic notes. An unashamed saignée style to drink young, with the structural scaffolding and confidence to partner effortlessly with protein. Jamón would be perfect!

LAURENT-PERRIER HARMONY DEMI-SEC NV $$

87 points • DISGORGED FIRST QUARTER OF 2017 • TASTED IN CHAMPAGNE

45% chardonnay, 40% pinot noir, 15% meunier from 55 crus; 10–20% reserves; aged 3 years on lees; 40g/L dosage

Like every Laurent-Perrier cuvée, Harmony is a unique blend, not simply a sweetened-up rendition of a dry cuvée. Lemon zest and lemon meringue contrast the toasty, biscuity complexity of maturity. Some dry-extract grip makes for a harsh and short finish with subtle nuances of mushrooms, which even a solid 40g/L dosage proves helpless to counter.

LAURENT-PERRIER MILLÉSIMÉ BRUT 2007 $$$

94 points • DISGORGED FIRST QUARTER OF 2018 • TASTED IN CHAMPAGNE

50% chardonnay from Chouilly, Cramant, Oger and Le Mesnil-sur-Oger; 50% pinot noir from Verzy, Verzenay, Mailly, Louvois and Bouzy

Laurent-Perrier's vintage aspiration is elegance and freshness that contrast the structure of pinot noir and the elegance of chardonnay. De Nonancourt's vision was never for his company to be a 'vintage house', and hence supplies for Brut NV were given first priority, which is why only the best seasons are released as vintage cuvées.

The 2007 has always been an approachable vintage for Laurent-Perrier, and it had already attained a wonderful apogée in its development on release two years ago. It retains its bright, medium straw hue and its nashi pear vibrancy and golden delicious apple generosity today, having shed its lemon zest freshness. At 12 years of age, the complexity of buttered toast and vanilla cream are on the rise, as is its creamy texture, which completely envelops any suggestion of phenolic grip that once marked the finish. It remains a beautifully approachable and seamless cuvée of lingering, calm, silky persistence.

LAURENT-PERRIER GRAND SIÈCLE NV $$$$

96 points • 2004 BASE VINTAGE • DISGORGED SECOND QUARTER OF 2017 • TASTED IN CHAMPAGNE AND AUSTRALIA

55% chardonnay from Avize, Cramant and Le Mesnil-sur-Oger, 45% pinot noir from Ambonnay, Bouzy and Mailly-Champagne; 2002 and 1999 reserves; aged more than 12 years on lees; 7g/L dosage; cork

When De Nonancourt conceived a prestige cuvée in 1955, there were only three prestige champagnes, and all were vintage cuvées. His grandfather had instilled in him that champagne was not about vintage – that the great years possessed structure, finesse and elegance, but not always all three, hence the need to blend. His vision was therefore to produce a prestige cuvée in his style, a multi-vintage able to maintain consistent quality. This he achieved by blending only grand cru fruit from the best crus in the finest years. Fifty-five years on, his recipe remains. It's a blend of select plots, comprising 60% of the youngest vintage of more pinot noir than chardonnay, with two older vintages contributing more chardonnay than pinot. The glorious age of the blend places it among the oldest champagnes on the shelves. Sadly, the consumer is oblivious to all this, as the bottle gives no clue to either its disgorgement date or its splendid maturity. Even the Laurent-Perrier website declares only 7–8 years of maturity, when the truth is close to double. Despite a huge internal debate, the house refuses to budge on this. Such archaic secrecy makes managing collections a challenge, which is a shame, as Grand Siècle ages magnificently, long beyond its release.

A full, bright straw hue with gold tints, this is a cuvée that boldly declares its maturity in both colour and character, brimming with luscious layers of crème brûlée, toasted meringue, tarte tatin, ginger, honey, blood orange and fig. A seamless and harmonious blend, it leads with the elegant finesse and youthful endurance of 2004 and continues with the depth and definition of 2002, bolstered by the richness of 1999. Ageing slowly and confidently, more than 12 years on lees has built a silky, creamy mouthfeel that contrasts layered, salty chalk minerality and subtle, well-gauged phenolic bite. It holds excellent length and line, nudging at tertiary complexity of toffee. Idiosyncratic and distinctive, at once lusciously decadent and at the same time elegantly strict, this is signature Laurent-Perrier and characteristic La Grande Siècle. Distinguished, refined and immediately alluring, this is a release to drink in the next few years.

LAURENT-PERRIER ALEXANDRA GRANDE CUVÉE ROSÉ 2004 $$$$$

92 points • DISGORGED FIRST QUARTER OF 2017 • TASTED IN CHAMPAGNE

20% chardonnay from Avize, Cramant and Le Mesnil-sur-Oger, 80% pinot noir from Ambonnay, Bouzy and Verzenay; macerated together in a saignée of free-run juice with no pressings; aged 10 years on lees; 7.5g/L dosage; the seventh vintage since 1987

Laurent-Perrier includes a little chardonnay in its flagship rosé to inject extra stamina in this long-aged style. This vintage has now been in the market for six years, evolving with a wonderful flourish in its early years, now fading into the twilight of its life. Its hue has deepened to a medium copper, and the bright red fruits of its youth have progressed to an evocative realm of savoury, secondary, toasty, spicy complexity reminiscent of fruit cake, dried apple and dried peach. It holds its fruit integrity through a long finish, carried by a silky, buttery mouthfeel, soft chalk mineral texture and gentle tannin structure.

Le Brun de Neuville

(Ler Bru deh Neh-vil)

5/10

ROUTE DE CHANTEMERLE 51260 BETHON
https://lebrundeneuville.fr

CHAMPAGNE
Le Brun de Neuville

DEPUIS 1963

The largest coopérative in the Sézanne, Le Brun de Neuville unites 170 growers and 150 hectares of vines spanning the Sézannais villages of Bethon, Villenauxe-la-Grande, Chantemerle, Barbonne-Fayel, La Celle-sous-Chantemerle, Montgenost and Fontaine-Denis. The majority of the crop is sold to négociants, and the group produces just 500,000 bottles of 12 cuvées. Chardonnay is the hero of Sézanne's shallow soils over granulated calcite, and comprises 88% of sourcing, supplemented with 11% pinot and just 1% meunier. Vinification is sensibly intuitive according to the parcel and the season, with the majority of fermentation in temperature-controlled stainless steel tanks and the balance in oak barrels. The adaptability of the house is impressive between seasons, even in the same cuvée, with blends tweaked and malolactic fermentation encouraged or blocked in whole or in part. Barrel-fermented components are used judiciously across its Authentique range, which are tiraged under cork. Cuvées are long aged in cellars 15 metres underground. Le Brun de Neuville presents an accurate, complex, characterful and well-assembled take on the Sézanne, articulating its salty chalk minerality in chardonnay-led cuvées blessed by long lees age.

Le Brun de Neuville Blanc de Blancs Brut NV $$

90 points • 2012 BASE VINTAGE • PARTIAL MALOLACTIC • AGED 4 YEARS ON LEES
• DISGORGED JULY 2017 • 8G/L DOSAGE • TASTED IN AUSTRALIA
90 points • 2010 BASE VINTAGE • FULL MALOLACTIC • AGED 5 YEARS ON LEES
• DISGORGED APRIL 2016 • 9.8G/L DOSAGE • TASTED IN AUSTRALIA

100% Sézanne chardonnay; 33% reserves; fermentation in stainless steel tanks; cork; 128,886 bottles

A crunchy blanc de blancs of tangy grapefruit, tense lemon and golden delicious apple. Long lees age has built a deep, spicy core reminiscent of dates, dark wild honey, fruit mince spice and gingernut biscuit complexity. The rustic, salty minerality of the Sézanne and a note of bitter phenolic bite are well softened by the creamy texture of maturity. The 2012 base holds good persistence on the finish, while the 2010 finishes a little short with a touch of candied dosage. Nonetheless, a well-made and expressive take on Sézanne chardonnay.

Le Brun de Neuville Authentique Par Champagne Brut Assemblage NV $$

92 points • 2012 base vintage • 65% chardonnay, 35% pinot • Disgorged September 2017 • 6g/L dosage • 5006 bottles • Tasted in Australia

93 points • 2010 base vintage • 70% chardonnay, 30% pinot • 6.5g/L dosage • 6102 bottles • Disgorged November 2016 • Tasted in Australia

Sézanne; 30% reserves; fermentation 92% in stainless steel tanks and 8% in oak barrels (chardonnay); full malolactic fermentation; aged 5 years on lees under cork

Le Brun presents a complex, characterful and well-crafted take on the Sézanne. Authentique unites the salty, grainy minerality of chardonnay with the juicy stone fruits of pinot noir and the deep shortbread complexity of lees age, enhanced by a vanilla note from a touch of oak. Crunchy golden delicious apple, fennel and kiwi fruit lend an exotic crunch to this 2012 base. A blend of impressive character and complexity, evenly uniting tension and concentration, concluding long and distinctive. The 2010 base upholds even more freshness of lemon tension and spicy red berry fruits.

Le Brun de Neuville Authentique Par Champagne Brut Blanc de Blancs NV $$

93 points • 2013 base vintage • Disgorged February 2018 • Tasted in Australia

100% chardonnay; Sézanne; 30% reserves (including 4% reserve wine solera aged in oak); fermentation 92% in stainless steel tanks and 8% in oak barrels; partial malolactic fermentation; aged 4 years on lees under cork; 6g/L dosage; 6950 bottles

A rich celebration of the blessings of lees age, building a wonderfully creamy style of vanilla custard, freshly baked croissants, butterscotch and almond nougat. It counters this secondary maturity with the granny smith apple crunch and lemon tang of chardonnay, even a touch of star fruit exoticism, enlivened by the energy of partial malic acidity. Its Sézanne credentials are declared articulately in a prominent backdrop of salty minerality and grainy chalk texture. Every detail lingers long on a finish of great line and character. Quintessential Sézanne.

Le Brun de Neuville Tendre Rosé Brut NV $$

89 points • 2013 base vintage • 66% chardonnay, 16% pinot noir; 18% pinot noir red wine • No malolactic fermentation • Disgorged April 2017 • 9g/L dosage • 26,208 bottles • Tasted in Australia

89 points • 2012 base vintage • 57% chardonnay, 28% pinot noir, 15% pinot noir red wine • Partial malolactic fermentation • Disgorged August 2016 • 10.8g/L dosage • 19,975 bottles • Tasted in Australia

Sézanne; fermented in stainless steel tanks; aged 3 years on lees under cork

A rosé of medium to full crimson hue and precocious fruit intensity, led by a pronounced note of orange bitters and fresh mandarin, backed by candied raspberry and ripe wild strawberry fruit. Fine tannins unite with phenolic bitterness and grainy Sézanne salt minerality to lend a firm bite to the finish, countered both by the creaminess of lees age and the boiled-sweets note of plenty of dosage. The result is characterful and inimitable, if a little rustic and awkward. The 2013 base is fresher, more fruity and less savoury than the 2012, which contrasts tomato savouriness with redcurrant and blackberry fruitiness, backed by tannins ready to take on protein fare.

Le Brun de Neuville Lady de N Cuvée Clovis Brut NV $$$

93 points • 2007 base vintage • Disgorged October 2017 • Tasted in Australia

20% chardonnay, 80% pinot noir; Sézanne; fermented in stainless steel tanks; full malolactic fermentation; 8% reserves; aged 9 years on lees; 8g/L dosage; 25,631 bottles

With a full yellow-gold hue much deeper than last year's disgorgement, this is a complex cuvée, layered with all of the pâtisserie character and creamy texture of long lees age and a touch of smoky allure of tertiary development. It upholds the lemon juice, orange zest and juicy nectarine notes of primary fruit and the subtle vanilla of a touch of new oak fermentation, finishing long, spicy and inviting. One bottle was afflicted by oxidative development in a touch of burnt-orange bite, burnt toffee, pipe smoke complexity and dry, contracted finish.

Le Brun de Neuville Lady de N Cuvée Blanc de Blanc Brut NV

94 points • Believed to be 2008 base vintage • Disgorged August 2016 • Tasted in Australia

100% chardonnay; Sézanne; fermented in stainless steel tanks; full malolactic fermentation; 5% aged in oak barrels; 10% reserves; aged 7 years on lees; 9g/L dosage; 37,787 bottles

A beautiful bouquet of fresh almonds, apple blossom and freshly baked baguette heralds a wonderfully crafted Sézanne blanc de blancs, and the best from Le Brun de Neuville in recent years. A dash of barrel age adds toasty spice in a manner reminiscent of Taittinger Comtes de Champagne, no less. It carries bright lemon freshness amidst all the creamy blessing of seven years on lees, concluding very long with great integrity, enticing appeal, and a touch of honeyed dosage.

Le Brun de Neuville Grand Vintage Brut 2008 $$$

89 points • Disgorged 2018 • Tasted in Australia

96% chardonnay, 4% pinot noir; Sézanne; fermented in stainless steel tanks; full malolactic fermentation; aged 9 years on lees under cork; 8g/L dosage; cork

The 2008 season infuses its distinctive energy and freshness, making for a style of structural cut and zest, which tussles with the firmly structured tannins and phenolic grip of long age under cork. This is unfortunate, as its core of citrus and apple fruit is otherwise pure, long and enduring. It may ultimately integrate in time, but another decade is a long time to wait.

LE BRUN SERVENAY

(Ler Bru Sair-veh-nay)

6/10

14 PLACE LÉON BOURGEOIS 51190 AVIZE
www.champagnelebrun.com

When the late Patrick Le Brun's parents were married in 1955, they brought together the house of Le Brun in Avize and the estate of Servenay in Mancy in the Coteaux Sud d'Épernay. His estate remains a seamless, if somewhat unusual, union of the two families, maintaining the Le Brun cellars directly next door to Erick de Sousa in Avize, and the Servenay press house and cuverie, six kilometres over the hill in Mancy, rebuilt in 2013. Le Brun's almost six hectares of enviably positioned chardonnay in Cramant, Oger and (especially) Avize provide 80% of the estate's needs, supplemented by about 1.5 hectares of pinot noir and meunier from Mancy and its surrounding villages. These are distinctive champagnes in their remarkable freshness, pristine purity and staggering longevity, particularly expressive of the salty chalk mineral signature of Avize, heightened through the blocking of malolactic fermentation across all cuvées.

It wasn't many generations ago that malolactic fermentation became commonplace in Champagne, before which every wine of the region was blessed with the sustaining endurance, if at times disarming austerity, of malic acidity.

Those houses and growers who have conscientiously retained malic acidity while upholding carefully balanced ripeness are due high admiration.

Patrick Le Brun struggled to convince his father to block malolactic fermentation, maintaining that malic acidity is crucial for preserving the freshness and smoothness in his grapes' aromas. It also charges his cuvées with tremendous sustaining power. I have tasted Patrick's cuvées back to the 1970s on more than one occasion with him, and it is breathtakingly apparent that these champagnes mature at but half the pace that one might expect. Even pre-1982 cuvées with full malolactic fermentation still look backward in their evolution.

Built on majestic grand cru chardonnay and finished with low dosages of typically 5–7g/L, with most cuvées also available as extra brut of typically 3.5g/L dosage, these would be challenging champagnes were it not for Le Brun's meticulous attention to picking at perfect ripeness, his exacting precision in vinification, and his patience in long ageing in the cellar. Freshness is preserved through vinification in tank, with just a small amount of red wine in barrel for rosé.

'Our purpose is to translate in the glass the elegance and minerality of the terroir of our vineyards,' declares Le Brun, the fifth generation of the Servenay family, and the fourth on the Le Brun side to tend grapes in these sites. His vines are old by Champagne standards, some older than 80 years, with roots that plunge 10–12 metres into the chalk. 'We plough and plant grass in the mid-rows to encourage competition and force the roots deeper,' he explains. Yields of 60–80hL/hectare (60–80% of

Champagne's average) are important for achieving full ripeness.

Le Brun Servenay represents outstanding value for money, and the consistency of every cuvée is preserved under DIAM closure.

Patrick Le Brun was tragically killed in an accident while repairing his tractor after harvest in September 2017. His son Gauthier immediately stepped in to manage his family's estate.

Patrick leaves a tremendous legacy in his vineyards and wines. 'Because we aim to reach perfection, our wines openly display the elegance, minerality and freshness that make them unique,' he once said. 'They stem from both our terroir and the winegrower spirit.' His spirit lives on in champagnes that fulfil his aspiration with exacting clarity.

LE BRUN SERVENAY ODALIE BRUT NV $$

93 points • 2015 BASE VINTAGE • DISGORGED DECEMBER 2017 • TASTED IN CHAMPAGNE
94 points • 2014 BASE VINTAGE • TASTED IN CHAMPAGNE

50% Avize chardonnay, 25% Mancy pinot, 25% Mancy meunier; reserves from the previous three harvests; DIAM

Previously named Brut Réserve, Le Brun Servenay's lead cuvée contrasts tightly coiled restraint with exacting fruit presence and ripeness. Lemon, grapefruit and nashi pear purity are well backed by the body and depth of the 2015 harvest, with just a touch of earthy complexity on the finish, which will appreciate time to wrap into its folds. The 2014 base is charged with a bolt of malic acidity that illuminates scintillating Avize minerality. The ripeness of the fruit is exactingly played for the tension of the style, making for the quintessential apéritif of great line and length.

LE BRUN SERVENAY GRAND CRU MÉLODIE EN C BRUT NV $$

94 points • 2015 BASE VINTAGE • TASTED IN CHAMPAGNE

100% chardonnay from Avize, Cramant and Oger; 2014, 2013 and 2012 reserves; 7g/L dosage; DIAM

The pristine delights of Le Brun Servenay are proclaimed for all to relish, even in its refreshing entry apéritif. Previously named Seléction, three exquisite grand cru villages unite in a lively, exacting apéritif of dazzling purity. Chardonnay is the game for Le Brun Servenay and it radiates from the glass in a pale, bright-straw brilliance. The purity of the house sings in high notes of lemon and apple, magnificently expressive of the salty chalk mineral purity of Avize, massaged with the presence of Cramant and Oger. Malic acidity keeps it pitch perfect, pure and energetic, making for an exceptionally affordable and accurate expression of the Côte des Blancs.

The cellars of Le Brun Servenay under Avize.

Le Brun Servenay Juste Rosé Brut NV $$

94 points • 2015 BASE VINTAGE • TASTED IN CHAMPAGNE

90% chardonnay, Mélodie en C with 10% 2009 pinot and meunier red wine from Mancy, half aged in barrel; 2014, 2013 and 2012 reserves; 7g/L dosage; DIAM

Rosé was the first cuvée I ever tasted from Le Brun Servenay, and its achingly pristine elegance singly inspired me to visit the house, now a regular stop on all of my Champagne sojourns. For a house led by such sensational chardonnay, it's perhaps a surprise that rosé remains one of its star attractions. With a pretty, bright pale-salmon hue, it's a beautifully pure and elegant almost blanc de blancs rosé of delicate rose hip, strawberry hull, white cherry and pink grapefruit poise. The deep, fine chalk minerality of Avize sets its palate alight with dazzling structure, illuminated by a brilliant flash of malic acidity. It holds its fanfare long, pure and ultra-refreshing. It takes real craftsmanship to create such a graceful rosé without malolactic fermentation.

Le Brun Servenay Exhilarante Vieilles Vignes Extra Brut 2008 $$$

92 points • TASTED IN CHAMPAGNE

80% chardonnay from Avize, Cramant and Oger; 10% pinot noir for structure, 10% meunier for fruitiness; Le Brun's oldest vines, 60–80 years old on soil 15 cm above chalk; aged at least 9 years on lees; 4g/L dosage; DIAM

The suggestion of full malic acidity in chardonnay from the austere village of Avize in the electric 2008 season, vinified in stainless steel, with extra-brut dosage, should be enough to instil terror in even the most seasoned champagne fanatic. In mere mortal hands, its piercing tension would be disarming. And yet, testimony to the fruit depth and ripeness of Le Brun's old vines, his strategically placed tweaks of pinot noir and meunier, and not least to his mastery in both the vines and the cellars, this is a cuvée infused with a presence and generosity that epitomise seamless balance, immense presence and great confidence. Tense, yes, but with the breadth and length to balance its lofty heights, underscored by a foundation of precise Avize chalk minerality, and just the beginnings of almond, marzipan and vanilla complexity. When I first previewed it two years ago, it lacked a little in freshness. Sadly now, at its moment of release, this has developed into a heaviness that threatens to unsettle its purity on the finish

Le Brun Servenay Grand Cru Vieilles Vignes Extra Brut 2006 $$$

92 points • DISGORGED EARLY 2017 • TASTED IN CHAMPAGNE

Blanc de blancs from Avize for elegance, Oger for minerality and Cramant for body and freshness; from vines 80–100 years old; aged 10 years on lees; 4.5g/L dosage; DIAM

I tasted this vintage with Patrick first in 2015, again in 2017 and finally with Gauthier in 2018, who noted that it is only now beginning to lose freshness as they move on to release the 2008. The presence and weight of 2006 has brought great generosity to this old-vine fruit, now finally evolving into its secondary phase. Le Brun-Servenay's malic freshness and exceptionally mineral grand crus unite to energise even the otherwise rounded and early-drinking 2006 season with a definition and stamina that lift it above most from this vintage. The talent of old vines to tap into the deep, salty chalk mineral structure of Avize, Oger and Cramant is proclaimed resoundingly in a magnificently structured palate of focused malic acidity and bright, enduring chalk minerality. Age has ushered in toasty, honeyed complexity that piles on layers of orange, fig and golden syrup intensity. It coasts long and effortlessly through a finish that froths and foams with pristine bubbles of chalk minerality.

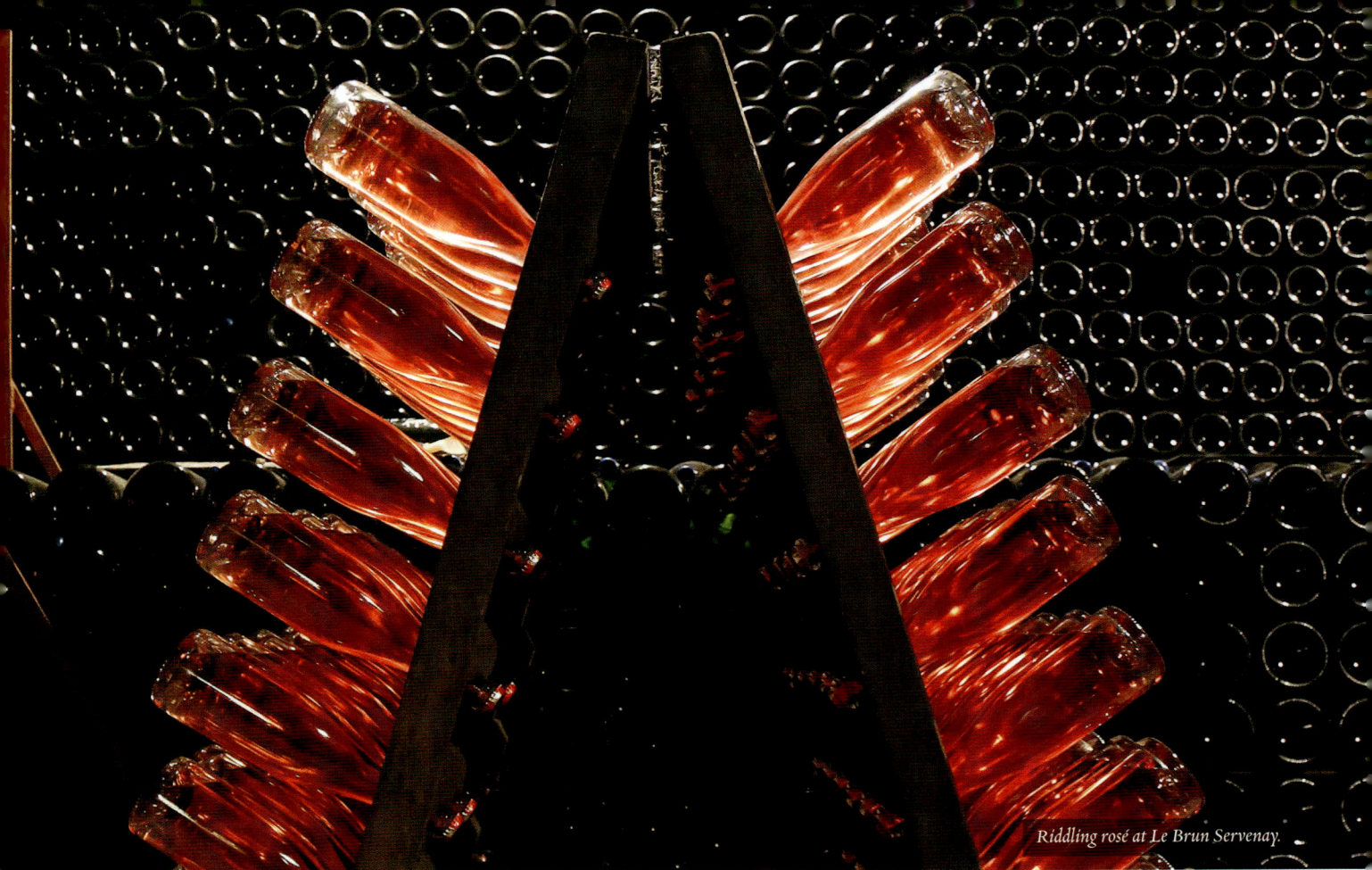

Riddling rosé at Le Brun Servenay.

Le Brun Servenay X.B. Blanc de Blancs Grand Cru Extra Brut 2.5 NV $$$

91 points • 2011 BASE VINTAGE • TASTED IN CHAMPAGNE

100% Avize chardonnay; 2010, 2009 and 2008 reserves; DIAM

Patrick Le Brun teamed up with former Les Crayères sommelier Philippe Jamesse to create his X.B. (Extra Brut) cuvées. Low dosage heightens the tension and coiled potential of electric malic acidity and pronounced chalk minerality in this persistent and lemon and apple flavoured blanc de blancs. I have greatly admired their dexterity in creating harmony in previous releases, but the dismal 2011 vintage was always going to challenge such an ambitious recipe. A touch of bruised apple development on the finish suggests a style to drink soon.

Le Brun Servenay X.B. Rosé Ultime Réserve Privée Extra Brut 3.2 NV $$$

89 points • TASTED IN CHAMPAGNE

90% chardonnay, predominantly from Cramant and Avize, aged 1 year in tank; 10% red wine of 80% pinot noir and 20% meunier from Mancy, aged 1 year in barrel; no malolactic fermentation; 3.2g/L dosage; DIAM

A pale, bright salmon hue has always been merely window dressing in this cuvée, where the game has always been the definition of grand cru chalk minerality and the focused malic acidity of chardonnay. There are, however, subtle nuances of pure strawberry hull and pink grapefruit visible in this release. Notes of reduction make for hints of egg on the nose, but the palate holds its purity and poise.

Le Mesnil

(Ler Meh-neel)

(6/10)

19–32 Rue Charpentier Laurain 51190 Le Mesnil-sur-Oger
www.champagnelemesnil.com

CHAMPAGNE
Le MESNIL

Le Mesnil rivals only Mailly Grand Cru as Champagne's greatest coopérative, and in value for money it has no competition. This large establishment has more than 600 member growers who tend a good 310 hectares, spanning some of the best sites in the most age-worthy grand cru of the Côte des Blancs. It presses grapes for many of the big names of Champagne, and bottles just 8% of production under its own label. Vinification is performed in stainless steel at a controlled temperature of 18°C to preserve the fresh expression of the village. The house is clever in progressively lowering dosage, and in selectively blocking malolactic, in full or in part, according to the season. Its finest cuvées proclaim the racy tension and commanding presence of Le Mesnil-sur-Oger, at enticing prices.

Le Mesnil Sublime Blanc de Blancs Grand Cru 2012 $$$

93 points • Disgorged mid 2018 • Tasted in Australia

100% chardonnay from the grand crus of the Côte des Blancs; 89% malolactic fermentation, oak used; aged 5 years on lees; 8g/L dosage; DIAM

An enticing juxtaposition of concentration and tension, an accurate articulation of the great 2012 season on the Côte des Blancs, capturing the power of its grand crus from mature vines in layers of apple, pear and grapefruit, backed by the brioche, almond nougat and subtle gingernut biscuits of five years lees age. Retention of 11% malic acidity lends impressive energy to the finish, enhancing the natural structure of its commanding crus. It concludes with impressive length, well-integrated dosage and magnificent fine, salty chalk minerality, the inimitable fingerprint of grand cru chalk. 2012 is the most sublime I have yet seen this cuvée.

Le Mesnil-sur-Oger, summer 2018

LE MESNIL PRESTIGE GRAND CRU MILLÉSIME 2006 $$$

94 points • DISGORGED 2017 • TASTED IN AUSTRALIA

100% chardonnay from the coopérative's best south-facing parcels in Le Mesnil-sur-Oger; average vine age 38 years; no malolactic fermentation; aged 10 years on lees; 8g/L dosage; DIAM

Le Mesnil has made impressive work of upholding tension and poise from south-facing plots in the warm and rich 2006 season, and it has retained great energy and life, even after a decade on lees. Full retention of malic acidity has proven to be an astute gamble in this season, and its acid tension has found a comfortable balance with primary white peach and lemon purity, and waves of brioche, crème brûlée, almond nougat and ginger cake of long age. Tension and concentration define a long finish underscored by great presence of fine-ground, salty chalk minerality. Definitive Le Mesnil, a credit to the astute attention to detail of this great coopérative, and a triumph for 2006.

LECLERC BRIANT

(Leh-clair Bree-on)

6/10

67 RUE CHAUDE RUELLE 51200 ÉPERNAY
www.leclercbriant.fr

CHAMPAGNE

LECLERC
BRIANT

Depuis 1872 à Épernay

It takes great tenacity to embark upon a biodynamic or organic path in the erratic climate of Champagne today. All the more so in the 1950s, when such practices were unheard of in the region. It was then that Bertrand Leclerc first introduced organic principles in his vineyards. His experiments in the following decade made him one of the pioneers of biodynamics in Champagne, alongside Fleury in Couteron (page 251). His son, Pascal Leclerc-Briant, set about obtaining the first certifications after he took over in 1978, expanding his biodynamic practices across the estate over three decades. By 2002, the entire estate of 30 hectares was in conversion, representing the biggest organic and biodynamic producer in Champagne at the time. Today, Leclerc Briant claims to be the only négociant in Champagne whose entire grape supply is organic.

The Leclerc family has grown grapes in Champagne since 1664, and Pascal was the fifth generation since 1872 to produce his own champagnes. A charismatic visionary, he was also a leader in the movement to single-vineyard champagnes when he released his Collection les Authentiques series in 1994.

Pascal passed away suddenly and tragically during the harvest of 2010, and his 30 hectares of biodynamic vineyards were subsequently sold, mostly to Lanson and Louis Roederer (for which it established the core of its glorious Cumières biodynamic estate). Leclerc Briant was saved from oblivion in 2012 when it was acquired by American power couple, ex-capital investment fund managing director Mark Nunelly and Harvard professor Denise Dupré. Owners of the phenomenal new Royal Champagne Hotel and a number of properties in Burgundy, the couple was not only equipped with the financial resources to resurrect this historic estate, they also had the nous to make two strategic appointments.

After 20 years' experience at Moët & Chandon, Frédéric Zeimett was appointed general manager. Biodynamic and organic specialist Hervé Jestin was brought on as chef de cave, following two decades of experience at Duval-Leroy. He was the perfect choice, already knowing Leclerc Briant intimately, having worked alongside Pascal since 1999.

At the time of its acquisition, the only vineyard remaining was the tiny 0.6 hectare plot behind the house in Épernay, so Zeimett and Jestin set about acquiring vineyards, extending holdings to 14 hectares today, all certified organic or biodynamic. These are located mostly in the grand and premier cru villages of Mailly-Champagne, Le Mesnil-sur-Oger, Hautvillers, Cumières, Mareuil-sur-Aÿ, Bisseuil, Rilly-la-Montagne, Villers-Allerand and Trépail, as well as some pinot noir the Aube. Supply is supplemented from 15 hectares of growers, all certified organic or biodynamic.

Leclerc Briant still occupies the premises in Épernay into which it moved in 1955 from its home in Cumières since 1872, and its new owners invested considerably in the extensive refurbishment

Hautvillers, summer 2018

of its winery, cellars and offices, recently opening a new reception house on the Avenue de Champagne.

Jestin variously made the wines at Château d'Avize and at a joint facility with Benoît Marguet in Ambonnay, prior to commissioning of Leclerc Briant's new facility in Épernay in time for harvest 2015.

In tune with its natural approach in the vines, the house describes its vinification as 'soft and natural'. All fermentations are spontaneous, in a combination of stainless steel tanks, terracotta eggs and oak barrels. Malolactic fermentation occurs naturally, and cuvées are unfined and unfiltered, clarified only by settling. After at least nine months ageing prior to bottling, its wines are aged in the company's cool cellars extending over one kilometre. 35 metres deep under Épernay. All cuvées are blessed with low dosages of no more than 4g/L.

Back labels disclose impressive detail of *cépage*, crus, base vintage, dosage and date of disgorgement, and an informative website presents all the detail on the story of the house, alongside data sheets for each cuvée.

Sales today are a conservative 140,000 bottles, with the assumed capacity to grow to almost double over the coming years, in line with the company's vineyard resources.

The house has recently been responsible for making champagne in a 24-carat gold barrel and ageing bottles 60 metres under the ocean, but we can forgive them for such expensive marketing stunts because, in spite of all the odds, its core range of wines is remarkably good.

Cuvées from the new facility are yet to emerge, and the current range spans the full transition from Pascal's vintage cuvées to Jestin's earliest blends. Expertly crafted, these are cuvées that capture the expression of sensitively grown and handled fruit. Upholding consistency and purity with organic and biodynamic rigour is an impressive feat by any standards, and quite remarkable in the context of the rollercoaster ride that Leclerc Briant has experienced over the past decade. Now that it has settled into its new facilities, I very much look forward to everything that is in store in this brand-new day for this pioneering house.

Leclerc Briant Brut Réserve NV $$

94 points • 2013 base vintage • Disgorged May 2016 • Tasted in Australia

20% chardonnay, 40% pinot noir, 40% meunier from Hautvillers, Avenay-Val-d'Or, Épernay, Verneuil, Cramant and Montgueux; aged 2 years on lees; 4g/L dosage; 90–100,000 bottles

There's no greater testimony to the rosy future of Leclerc Briant than the entry cuvée of the house from the first harvest after its resurrection was set in place. All things considered, the result is not just impressive, it's downright astonishing. A showcase for the depth and presence of pinot noir and meunier, it presents pristine red cherry and strawberry fruit with fresh lemon accents. Lees age has built lovely creamy texture and gingernut biscuit, toast and honey complexity that lingers with great focus and persistence. A classy cuvée that accurately presents fruit grown and handled with sensitivity and care.

Leclerc Briant Rosé Brut NV $$

92 points • 2013 base vintage • Disgorged May 2016 • Tasted in Australia

95% chardonnay from Chouilly, Montgueux and Essoyes; 5% pinot noir red wine from Les Riceys; 3g/L dosage

A pretty and elegant almost blanc de blancs with a pale salmon tint, this is a cuvée more about chardonnay than pinot. It unites three disparate crus, harmonising the tension of Montgueux with the luscious generosity of Chouilly and the spicy depth of Essoyes in the Aube. The result carries depth and presence, with Montgueux and Essoyes contributing oyster shell aromas and a pronounced salty, slightly grainy mineral finish. Low dosage is attractively balanced and well integrated with its finely structured texture.

Leclerc Briant Millésime Brut 2007 $$$$

90 points • Disgorged December 2015 • Tasted in Australia

70% pinot noir, 30% meunier from Hautvillers, Cumières and Verneuil; 2g/L dosage

Hailing from the core of Pascal Leclerc Briant's glorious biodynamic estate, this is a vintage that is now showing the effects of time. Its full straw-yellow hue is deep for 2007, reflective of pinot noir and meunier in generous crus. A bouquet of fresh cocoa powder announces a black cherry and black plum palate with deep coffee notes layered with biscuity complexity. Low dosage lets salty chalk minerality speak articulately on a long finish. It holds good acid line, without quite the precision and freshness of Jestin's wines, just beginning to dry out on the finish.

Leclerc Briant La Croisette Blanc de Blancs Parcelle à Épernay Brut NV $$$$

92 points • 2013 base vintage • Disgorged July 2016 • Tasted in Australia

100% chardonnay; single plot of 0.6 hectares behind the house in Épernay; vinified and aged in oak for 9 months; zero dosage; 2000 bottles

Farmed organically since it was planted by Bertrand Leclerc in 1966, the tiny 0.6-hectare plot of La Croisette behind the house in Épernay is the last standing remnant of its historic vineyards. The 2013 base upholds precise apple and grapefruit of freshness and focus, in the midst of all of the buttery creaminess, toasty complexity and subtle charcuterie of oak fermentation and maturation. Well-managed and impeccably ripe fruit stands confidently without dosage. It is structured around beautifully fine and pronounced chalk minerality, amplified by careful oak management.

Leclerc Briant Blanc de Meuniers Premier Cru Brut Zéro NV $$$$

94 points • 2013 base vintage • Disgorged September 2016 • Tasted in Australia

100% meunier from a single plot of 1 hectare in Chamery; vinified and aged in oak for 9 months in oak barrels; zero dosage; first release

A new cuvée that confidently heralds the start of an exciting new era for the house, this is a meunier of great fruit integrity that showcases a lesser cru magnificently. A medium straw hue is bright for oak-matured meunier. Notes of cocoa and dark chocolate underline excellent expression of strawberry hull and white cherry fruit with very good structure of fine salt mineral and bright acid line, amplified by zero dosage. Oak is beautifully gauged to build creamy texture without interfering with refined fruit expression, culminating in a finish of length and line, possessing refreshing precision and tension for meunier.

LOMBARD

(Lom-bar)

---

1 RUE DES CÔTELLES BP118 51024 ÉPERNAY
www.champagne-lombard.com

CHAMPAGNE
LOMBARD

Thierry Lombard is the third generation of his family to run the medium-sized Épernay house of Lombard. An annual production of about 750,000 bottles of 15 cuvées is produced from 5.5 hectares of family vines, largely in premier crus of the Montagne de Reims and Épernay, supplemented substantially from long-term growers managing 100 hectares, mostly in 21 premier crus and 11 grand crus. The house harvested the first organic fruit from its own vineyards in 2015, and hopes to obtain certification.

When I visited Lombard's premises in Épernay for the first time in 2015, I was impressed by the number of shiny little temperature-controlled stainless steel tanks of 500–2500 litres, facilitating parcel by parcel vinification, producing a house style of freshness and vitality. Malolactic fermentation is usually allowed to proceed to completion, but is blocked in low-acid harvests.

In recent years, the house has followed the trends towards single-cru and single-vineyard cuvées, as well as moving its style towards lower dosages, increasingly blocking malolactic, shorter ageing and decreasing levels of reserves. These are all in keeping with its fresh aspirations, but the pendulum has unfortunately swung too far. This lends a feeling that the wines have been made to rigid mandates rather than to sensitivity, intuition or taste.

Progressively lower dosages of now 4g/L or less represent a refreshingly low level of sweetness, but the acidity can look bracingly firm in these young blends that largely rely on little or no reserves. The house keeps a stock of 3 million bottles in its cellars, though its cuvées are often released with shorter times on lees than the house declares. Its youthful style appreciates further bottle age to show its full potential.

Thomas Lombard returned to the estate to work alongside his father Thierry in 2017. Together they have released a series of single-cru and single-vineyard cuvées to showcase their grand cru sites, selectively fermented in oak barrels. 'Our philosophy and values are oriented towards the world of fine wines and terroir, and we strive to express all the diversity and complexity of our terroirs,' says Thomas.

DIAM closures have been introduced in some cuvées to protect and preserve freshness. Informative back labels declare *cépage*, dosage and disgorgement dates, with further detail expounded via detailed tech sheets on the website.

Verzenay, winter 2013

LOMBARD EXTRA BRUT PREMIER CRU NV $$

89 points • DISGORGED 15 MARCH 2017 • TASTED IN AUSTRALIA

40% chardonnay from Grauves and Vertus, 40% pinot noir from Sermiers and Ville-Dommange; 40% meunier from Coulommes-la-Montagne; 20% reserves; fermented in stainless steel tanks; aged 36 months on lees; 4g/L dosage

A tense and lively style, with the apple and spice of pinot noir from the sandy soils of the western Montagne de Reims freshened by the citrus of Côte des Blancs chardonnay, completed by a long, fresh finish of fine minerality. Tense acidity is heightened by low dosage. A clean and lively style, if a little simple.

LOMBARD BRUT NATURE GRAND CRU BLANC DE BLANCS NV $$

88 points • DISGORGED 24 MARCH 2016 • TASTED IN AUSTRALIA

100% chardonnay; 50% Le Mesnil-sur-Oger (without malolactic fermentation), 25% Chouilly, 15% Avize, 10% Cramant; no reserves; aged 6 months on lees in 600-litre barrels and 4–5 years in bottle; no dosage; DIAM

Le Mesnil-sur-Oger with full malic acidity delivers tension and minerality, rounded with the presence of Chouilly and Cramant, freshened by Avize. A tense cuvée lacking in reserves, in which abrasive malic acidity clashes with the spice of six months in barrel, a discord that is accentuated by an absence of dosage. It concludes hard and astringent.

LOMBARD BRUT NATURE GRAND CRU NV $$

89 points • DISGORGED 4 MAY 2017 • TASTED IN AUSTRALIA

50% chardonnay from Le Mesnil-sur-Oger (without malolactic fermentation), Chouilly, Avize and Cramant, 50% pinot noir from Ambonnay and Verzenay; 20% reserves; aged 4–5 years on lees; no dosage; DIAM

A young and tense style of crunchy strawberry hull and lemon with a firm finish accentuated by zero dosage. It presents good fruit freshness, but its soaring acidity would appreciate the calming effect of a touch of dosage.

LOMBARD EXTRA BRUT PREMIER CRU BLANC DE NOIRS NV $$

88 points • DISGORGED 18 JULY 2016 • TASTED IN AUSTRALIA

100% pinot from Rilly-la-Montagne, Chigny-les-Roses and Ludes; no reserves; aged 3-4 years under cork; 4g/L dosage

The premier crus of the northern Montagne de Reims produce an elegant pinot noir, expressed here in a simple style of neutral apple and citrus fruit, in a fresh guise of bright acidity and balanced dosage. It's balanced, yet finishes short, simple and lacking character. Labelled as a non-vintage, but it contains no reserves, which could help to bolster depth and complexity.

LOMBARD BRUT NATURE LE MESNIL SUR OGER GRAND CRU NV $$$

91 points • DISGORGED 2 MARCH 2017 • TASTED IN AUSTRALIA

From vineyards half on the hillside and half in the heart of the terroir, with south and south-east exposure; no malolactic fermentation; fermented in stainless steel vats; no reserves; aged 4–5 years on lees; zero dosage

The searing malic acidity of young Le Mesnil-sur-Oger fruit makes for a daring style in the absence of the softening influence of reserves and dosage. It's a predictably tense style of firm and slightly abrasive acidity. The creaminess of lees age brings texture to the finish, although some dosage, reserves and longer lees age would help. Give it time in the cellar.

LOMBARD BRUT NATURE VERZENAY GRAND CRU NV $$$

92 points • 2014 BASE VINTAGE • DISGORGED 20 JUNE 2017 • TASTED IN AUSTRALIA

20% chardonnay, 80% pinot noir; Verzenay Grand Cru; no reserves; fermented in stainless steel vats; aged 2 years on lees; zero dosage; cork

A medium straw hue with a faint blush tint announces an accurate take on the tension of Verzenay pinot. Crunchy red apple and beurre bosc pear fruit is accented by notes of spicy red cherries and wild strawberries, which in time grow to nuances of black cherries and fruit mince spice. It holds impressive persistence, underlined by frothing salt minerality and focused acid line. This is a tense, young cuvée that could have been very impressive with sufficient time on lees and a little dosage to balance its high-tensile finish. Give it at least a decade in the cellar.

LOMBARD BRUT NATURE AVIZE GRAND CRU LIEU-DIT «CHEMIN DE FLAVIGNY» NV $$$$

88 points • 2015 BASE VINTAGE • DISGORGED 12 NOVEMBER 2018 • TASTED IN AUSTRALIA

100% Avize chardonnay, from the south-east-facing plot Chemin de Flavigny; no reserves; no malolactic fermentation; 75% aged in oak barrel with bâtonnage for 6 months; aged less than 3 years on lees in bottle; no dosage; cork

Avize is one of Champagne's most tense and structured crus, which explains why its most famous growers make full use of malolactic and age to calm its tension. Not labelled as a vintage, this cuvée is 100% 2015, making it a very young expression of this plot. Without any of the calming agents of malolactic, reserves or dosage, the result is searingly stark. A bright, pale straw hue, this is a crunchy, tense and young blanc de blancs in which the hard cut of acidity begs for flesh and softness. The bitter phenolic grip of 2015 only heightens the austerity of the finish. Nonetheless, it's clean, fresh and lively, with understated apple and crunchy pear fruit, and a distinctive note of fresh vanilla, thanks to six months in barrels. It concludes short and oh so tense. It might age well, but it will take some decades to find out.

LOMBARD BRUT NATURE VERZENAY GRAND CRU LIEU-DIT «LES CORETTES» NV $$$$

86 points • 2015 BASE VINTAGE • DISGORGED 24 JULY 2018 • TASTED IN AUSTRALIA

100% Verzenay pinot noir, from the north-west-facing plot Les Corettes; no reserves; no malolactic fermentation; 75% aged in oak barrel for 6 months with bâtonnage; aged 2 years on lees in bottle; zero dosage; cork

A savoury, structured and tense blanc de noirs of medium yellow hue with a blush tint, this is a wine that boldly contrasts the bitter phenolic bite of the warm 2015 season with the high-tensile austerity of firm malic acidity. Without the calming assistance of malolactic, dosage, reserves or long age, the result is callow and hard. Subtle, muted red apple fruit is underscored by the almond meal notes of just two years bottle age. There's classy fruit here, but it needs support to get across the line. There's a feeling the wine has been made to a rigid mandate rather than to intuition or taste.

LOMBARD BRUT NATURE GRAND CRU MILLÉSIMÉ 2008 $$$$

89 points • DISGORGED 4 JULY 2017 • TASTED IN AUSTRALIA

80% chardonnay from Le Mesnil-sur-Oger and Avize, 20% pinot noir from Ambonnay; fermented and aged 2 years in steel vats; bottled in 2011; aged 6 years on lees in bottle; zero dosage; cork

Two years is a long time in tank before bottling, and the result is a developed take on the energetic 2008 season. Pear and bruised apple fruit is accented by notes of spicy grapefruit and fig, underscored by the roast hazelnuts and crème brûlée of more than a decade of age. The high-tensile acidity of the season persists amidst fine chalk minerality, concluding with a touch of bitter grip on a dry finish. It would have appreciated some dosage to calm its firm conclusion. One bottle showed premature oxidation, with a premature yellow hue with a gold tint, with oxidative notes of honey and burnt orange.

LOUIS ROEDERER

(Loo-ii Roh-dehr-air)

9/10

21 BOULEVARD LUNDY 51053 REIMS
www.champagne-roederer.com

MAISON FONDÉE EN 1776

LOUIS ROEDERER
CHAMPAGNE

Louis Roederer is unlike any other champagne house of its magnitude. The largest independent, family-owned and managed champagne maker of all is privileged to a monumental 240 hectares of superbly located vineyards, supplying a grand 70% of its needs for an annual production of a little over 3 million bottles. With 410 blocks and 450 tanks and casks at his disposal, chef de cave Jean-Baptiste Lécaillon describes his role as 'à la carte winemaking'. He hates the word 'blend'. 'We don't blend, we combine,' he says. 'I love art, and like a great painter we add colour rather than blending.' There are few in Champagne today with an intellect as sharp, an attention to detail as acute and a nerve as strong as Lécaillon. This year he celebrates his 20th year of extraordinary initiatives in Roederer's vineyards unparalleled in the region, and a revolution in the winery to match. His are spectacular cuvées, carefully tended and nurtured to full ripeness in magnificent sites, energised with malic acidity and textured judiciously with oak fermentation. Never have they looked more characterful or more pure, effortlessly juxtaposing jubilant precision, deep complexity, long-lingering endurance and the smiling, self-assured, gracious confidence of their creator.

There was once a time when Louis Roederer was purely a négociant house, but over the years it has strategically acquired vineyards to amass one of the largest proportions of estate vines among the big champagne houses. These are well situated across some 16 villages, spanning the Montagne de Reims, Vallée de la Marne and Côte des Blancs, including a glorious 126 hectares of grand crus, 88 of premier crus and just 26 hectares unclassified.

All of Louis Roederer's vintage wines are assembled exclusively from estate properties, and even its entry Brut Premier NV now boasts 55% estate fruit, and rising.

'People call us "maison vigneron",' says Lécaillon. 'I do not say that Roederer is a champagne house for the vintage wines. We are three growers, one in Montagne de Reims, one in Vallée de la Marne and one in Côte des Blancs.'

Roederer is continuing to expand its estate and has averaged an additional two hectares every year for the past decade, all on chalk soils. 'Chalk is the style of Roederer,' Lécaillon declares. 'It produces more focused wines, while clay produces more round and soft styles.'

The vast majority of estate vines are on chalk, with a strong focus on the chalk-rich Côte des Blancs, home to 80 hectares of Roederer vines. The company owns no vineyards beyond Cumières in the Vallée de la Marne due to their higher clay content. Some 45 parcels spanning 50 hectares are devoted to Cristal, all on chalk.

'We have wonderful terroirs and our goal is to express each of them,' Lécaillon says. 'We have a new era in Champagne today, coming back to the terroir; forgetting about all the know-how in the cellar, forgetting about the salt and the pepper, but getting back to the raw ingredients.'

Lécaillon commenced at Louis Roederer in 1989, and after '10 years of learning' was appointed chef de cave in 1999, at the age of 33. Not only did this make hime the youngest chef de cave in Champagne, he also requested of owner Jean-Claude Rouzaud that he be granted responsibility for managing the vineyards as well, making him the first chef de cave to take on this role. 'The story of wine is about contact with terroir,' he says. 'Staying in touch with the soils and the vines.'

For an operation of this scale, his attention to detail in the vineyards is unprecedented. Old vines are used to limit yields (Cristal vineyards average a huge 43 years of age and some date from 1930), as is green harvesting, in what Lécaillon dubs 'haute couture viticulture'. Over the past 17 years, he has customised the pruning, budding, trellising, ploughing and harvesting of each vineyard to suit the cuvée to which it is destined. 'Each vineyard is crafted to make the wine,' he suggests. 'Our job is to balance nature intelligently.'

A team of 800 pickers sorts fruit in the vineyard, and it is sorted again before it is pressed. 'The only way I can get quality is by paying pickers by the hour, not by the kilogram,' he emphasises. This is rare in Champagne.

BIODYNAMICS ON A GRAND SCALE

When Lécaillon was appointed in 1999, he was charged with taking Cristal to the next level. Visiting Burgundy, he observed that the top estates were predominantly biodynamic, even if they didn't declare it.

Of Roederer's 240 hectares of vineyards, 134 hectares are now certified organic, representing close to one-fifth of Champagne's organic surface, and the entire estate was farmed organically in the immensely challenging 2017 season. Most remarkably, the house now tends 100 hectares of vineyards biodynamically (though only 10 hectares are certified biodynamic), including more than half of those that contribute to Cristal, with a goal of reaching 100% by 2020. An incredible 25 hectares are ploughed by horse. Biodynamics on such a scale is unheard of in Champagne, and Roederer's operation is the biggest in the region by an order of magnitude, and one of the biggest in France.

Critics have written this off simply as 'a strategy for their environmental image'. Does it make any real difference in Roederer's wines?

'I am not a biodynamicist,' Lécaillon reveals. 'But I think biodynamics is the best school. Organics simply says "No to chemicals" — but biodynamics says "Yes to life"! I am not a believer in biodynamics as such, but I believe what I see. I have been doing trials of biodynamic and organic wines for 18 years, and there is always more texture and depth in the biodynamic

wines. It stretches the wine into more dimensions. And you see your vines changing, and your wines changing, and your world changing, and you cannot go back! My team is much more passionate, much more daring to take risks rather than resorting to convention and safety. And you sleep better because you are not using strong chemicals on your vineyards or on your people!'

He has set aside plots for experimentation in each of the three regions of Champagne, and fruit from biodynamic vines is compared with traditional viticulture from the same village. In tasting *vins clairs* with him, I am continually amazed at just how much more chalk minerality, texture and seamless integration is evident in *vins clairs* from biodynamic sources.

In the village of Cumières, where Roederer has a strong presence, the tiny, fanatical biodynamic grower Vincent Laval mentioned to me that he prefers Roederer's attention to viticulture to that of small growers using industrial methods. High endorsement.

'When the soil looks better, the vines look better, the fruit looks better, and we get more ripeness, more acidity and more iodine salinity to the minerality,' explains Lécaillon, for whom ripeness is 'the game'. His aim is to pick ripe and 'make wine first, champagne second'. He believes that 'dry extract, ripeness and fruitiness are the key, and a great champagne needs phenolics from oak or from fruit', and goes so far as to suggest that ripe skin phenolics are more important than acidity for ageing potential, though he does qualify this by emphasising that acidity and phenolics must be in balance.

Lécaillon goes into the vineyards every day in the lead-up to harvest, 'to feel the development'. He picks fruit on taste and acid ripeness, not on sugar levels. 'Malic acid indicates the physiological ripeness of the vine,' he explains. 'I want to pick when the phenolics are ripe, and this is linked to the acid.' He consequently picks later than most. 'Krug typically picks Clos du Mesnil 15 days before I start picking chardonnay!' he reveals.

He attributes greater precision in biodynamic fruit to decreased vigour in the vines, and greater mineral expression to deeper roots. 'We cannot explain this with measurements, but this is the way with biodynamics — we can only see it by tasting.'

Roederer began experimenting with biodynamics in 2003, after a false start in 2000. Nineteen years on, Lécaillon says it will take 40 years to draw any solid conclusions. But he has discovered that a different approach is necessary in each region, easier on well-draining chalk in the Côte des Blancs and Montagne de Reims, and harder on clay in the Vallée de la Marne.

'There are some years in which biodynamics is much better and some years in which it is not so effective,' Lécaillon explains. 'It performs well in vintages in which the vines struggle under particularly wet or dry conditions.' In the wet 2011 and 2014 seasons, he harvested his best fruit in biodynamic vineyards. He suspects this may be a result of thicker skins providing greater resilience in biodynamic fruit.

The old and the new at Louis Roederer.

While he is convinced of the philosophy of biodynamics, certification is not the goal, and he upholds that it will never be advertised on the label or in the marketing. 'The wine is not good because it is biodynamic, it is good because of everything else. We see it as just one means of achieving terroir expression,' he says. 'We are constantly learning.'

This learning curve was particularly steep in 2012, and Roederer reported losses equivalent to 10 hectares of fruit, and greatest under biodynamics. 'It involves so much risk,' Lécaillon explains. 'Biodynamics removes all the safety of chemicals, and if it's not done properly you can really get caught quickly.' He accepts the loss of 2012 and suggests that the experience was helpful for his team to really get on top of biodynamics.

At the end of vintage 2014, I shadowed Lécaillon for a day in his vineyards and was stunned by a stark difference between healthy biodynamic vines and struggling organic plots on neighbouring sites. I took 7500 words of notes and learnt more about viticulture in Champagne that day than ever before. 'In order to survive we must decrease the chemicals that we use,' he told me. 'By removing the comfort of chemicals, my team has to work like vignerons, to really understand the terroir, not like robots. It really is a culture of coming back to the terroir.'

It was climate change that motivated Lécaillon's conversion to biodynamics, and his aspiration is to change the balance of pH, acidity, sugar and ripeness back to what it was in the 1950s and 1960s – 'the golden age of champagne!' To him, biodynamics and organics are not goals in themselves, but rather tools to work towards the balance the region achieved before it relied on herbicides and other chemicals.

À LA CARTE WINEMAKING

Lécaillon's aim is to emphasise terroir and downplay house style and varietal character, which he achieves by pushing for ripeness, encouraging a little oxidation at harvest, and blocking malolactic fermentation.

At every stage in the process, he upholds a refreshingly intuitive agility. 'Recipes can be good at one period in time, but we need to challenge our recipe every year, because the fruit changes every year,' he emphasises. 'My work in the vineyards is more important than my job in the cellar.'

Roederer's focus on its vineyards opens up opportunities for greater refinement in the winery. Regulated yields allow harvesting at full ripeness, rendering chaptalisation unnecessary, unless the season is very difficult – an impressive mandate, and

I believe unprecedented at this scale in Champagne. In recent years, wild yeast ferments have been introduced to increase integration and balance. The ripest bunches in biodynamic plots are harvested early, fermented wild, and used to seed other ferments. A record 40 percent of the harvest was fermented wild in 2018. Lécaillon builds texture and silkiness in his wines through long, slow ferments of two to three weeks, compared with the usual seven days.

Malolactic fermentation is generally avoided, except in some higher-acid parcels destined for the non-vintage Brut Premier, generally just 20–30% of the blend. 'The only way to avoid malo is to produce fruit in the vineyard that doesn't require it — ripe fruit with soft malic acid,' notes Lécaillon, who prefers to obtain the right acid balance in the vineyard than the winery.

'Malolactic fermentation was first conducted in Champagne in 1965,' he points out. 'It can be useful in a difficult year, but it must be a safety tool, not a systematic procedure, and this is especially true with global warming.' The house completely blocked malolactic fermentation on all estate and contract fruit in 2016, 2015, 2012, 2009, 2006, 2003, 2002 and 1999.

'Malolactic and oak are not the house style,' he reveals. 'Terroir is the house style, and malolactic and oak are just there according to what the grapes need.'

Basket presses run 24/7 throughout vintage, as it takes three hours to press the first cuvée. Unusually, the solids are retained, producing a cloudy juice. 'We feel this expresses terroir better and gives greater protection against oxidation,' Lécaillon explains.

A new cuverie was built in 2007 to enable every block to be vinified separately in a custom-made tank or large oak vat,

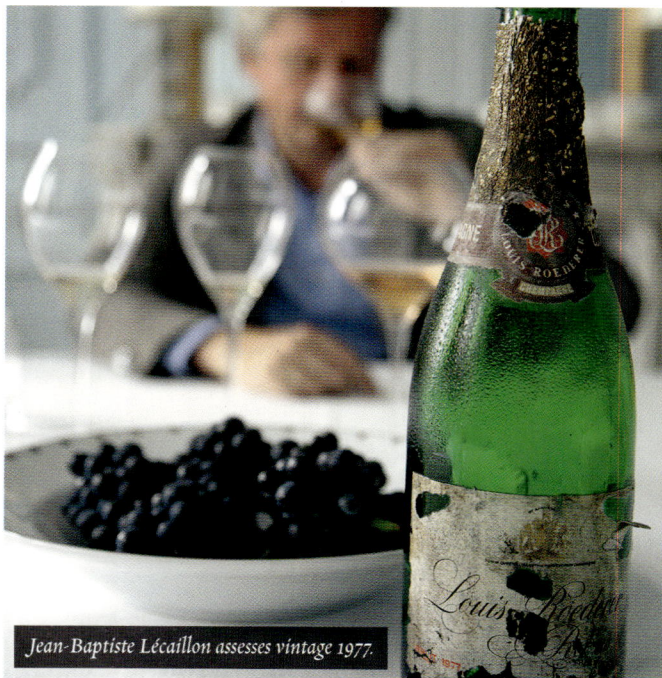

according to the power of the fruit tasted in the vineyard. 'Each tank and vat is a vineyard with a roof!' Lécaillon suggests. 'My workers must think of each parcel in the winery as a site, not as a lot.' Oak fermentation was reintroduced in 1999, and today about 20% of the vintage is fermented in oak, and aged on lees with bâtonnage for texture, phenolics and roundness.

Lécaillon does not consider phenolics to be a dirty word in Champagne. 'Oak phenolics and the right fruit phenolics draw out salinity on the sides of the tongue and bring out another dimension to the flavour. We hate oxidation — it is a betrayal of terroir,' adds Lécaillon. 'Lees contact and bâtonnage protect from oxidation.'

This creates a reductive style, which has at times produced savoury overtones that distract from fruit purity in Roederer's vintage wines, though this has been better controlled in recent years. 'I make wines reductively because I want them to age.' Vins clairs fermented in oak show richer texture, without taking on oak flavour. Reserve wines are aged in 150 large old oak foudres (15–50 years of age), and *liqueur d'expédition* is kept in casks for as long as a decade. Four vintages of *liqueur d'expédition* are kept in vat at all times to allow the dosage for each blend to be tweaked. Dosages of typically 8–11g/L sometimes appeared a little high in the past. Today, 7–9g/L sits more comfortably with the natural ripeness of Roederer's fruit.

Non-vintage wines are aged on lees in bottle for three years, vintage wines for four years, and Cristal for six or seven (with the enduring 2008 Cristal boasting a record nine years, launched after the 2009, the first ever non-sequential release). This requires a large stock of 18 million bottles squirrelled away in Roederer's cellars, with 3 million leaving every year.

Roederer's attention to detail in its vineyards and winery shine even in its non-vintage Brut Premier. In 2007, Lécaillon constructed a gleaming, state-of-the-art, all-new facility devoted exclusively to this cuvée (and a dedicated rosé facility in the same year). This facilitated its own dedicated team, earlier classification of fruit, fewer bottlings (just five each year of an identical blend) and less pumping, all of which he credits for the rise in Brut Premier. This is a masterfully assembled cuvée, previously representing 80% of the production of the house, but today just 65–75%. 'I very much have a vintage philosophy,' says Lécaillon, who likely makes a higher proportion of vintage cuvées than any other major house.

Lécaillon describes champagne as a 'permanent innovation'. Such is his attention to tuning the finest details that he sells 5–10% of his crop that is not up to standard every year. He also tweaks the pressure to suit every cuvée, bottling riper vintages at five atmospheres, sometimes as low as four, and more classic, lean seasons at six. 'Lower pressure creates finer bubbles, creamier texture and greater integration,' he reveals.

A low level of sulphur is added at disgorgement, hence jetting is employed to reduce oxidation.

He emphasises that age in bottle on cork is crucial for his

cuvées, and after three years he prefers the effect of natural cork to DIAM. His batch testing of corks is the most rigorous I have seen anywhere. Of every batch of 100,000 corks, 460 are agitated in water for 45 minutes and the water then tasted. This is repeated for 200 batches every year, and sometimes a batch is tested twice. If a single tainted cork is found, the entire batch is rejected. His team rejects one batch in three. 'If you are strict, you get the best corks,' Lécaillon reveals. However, even such rigour is not foolproof, and of the 41 bottles of Louis Roederer that I tasted for this year's reviews, two were cork tainted. I applaud his move to Mytik DIAM for Brut Premier in some markets.

In a fantastic development in disclosure, Louis Roederer has followed Krug's lead, and its website and app reveal the base vintage, year of bottling and year of disgorgement from the labelling code or QR code of any cuvée. Detailed tech sheets are featured for every cuvée. May more houses do likewise!

In 2019, Jean-Baptiste Lécaillon nominated his successor, Johann Merle, his colleague for 18 years and vineyard director for 10, with whom he will now work for 10 years before retiring. 'He knows the vineyards perfectly, even better than me,' he says. 'He does biodynamic farming every day.'

The Louis Roederer revolution continues.

LOUIS ROEDERER BRUT PREMIER NV $$

94 points • 2015 BASE VINTAGE • TASTED IN AUSTRALIA
94 points • 2014 BASE VINTAGE • DISGORGED 2018 • TASTED IN AUSTRALIA
95 points • 2013 BASE VINTAGE • TASTED IN CHAMPAGNE AND AUSTRALIA

40% chardonnay, 42% pinot noir, 18% meunier, from 55% estate vineyards; a little more pinot noir in 2015, 'as it was a warm year and the pinot was beautiful'; 16% fermented and matured in oak casks with weekly bâtonnage; 30% malolactic fermentation; 10% reserves from five vintages, fermented in tanks and matured in large oak casks for up to 8 years; 5-5.25 atmospheres of pressure; 9g/L dosage; cork; previously 80% of production, now just 65-75%, hence 2-2.2 million bottles

Jean-Baptiste Lécaillon's aspirations for Brut Premier are 'light and fresh and yet rich and powerful, walking the line between apéritif and gastronomic'. He does not aspire to blanket consistency, but rather wants it to declare its base vintage. The rise and evolution of this cuvée over the past 15 years, and particularly since the construction of its dedicated facility in 2007 (see introduction above) has showed no sign of slowing today, as he continues his fanatical regime of experimenting, tweaking and refining every detail. Until the 2009 base, Brut Premier reserves came from a solera, in his view, lacking focus and 'showing too much character of having been made in the cellar'. The solera was dropped, bringing greater precision, more accurate mineral articulation and greater emphasis on ripe fruit. Dosage was sensibly lowered from 10–11g/L to now 8.5–9g/L. Pressure was dropped from the usual 6 atmospheres to 5–5.2, for finer bubbles, creamier texture and greater integration. His latest initiatives have focused around differentiating the style from other non-vintage cuvées by increasing the oak-fermented component from 5% to 16%, as it was in the 1960s, and by increasing the time between disgorgement and release.

I've long adored Brut Premier, a masterful presentation of impeccably ripe fruit of intricate balance and abundant appeal: a grand pinnacle and dependable bargain in the non-vintage champagne stakes. Its latest three incarnations are the fulfilment of the fanatical focus that Lécaillon and his team have poured into this cuvée. The 2015 base is a magnificent Brut Premier, a wine of great tension and focus for this warm season. It leaps forth in freshness of red apple crunch, lemon and grapefruit, accented with a hint of fennel, encapsulating the wonderful juxtaposition of ripe fruit body, acid tension and beautifully textured mouthfeel that inscribes the signature of Brut Premier. There's even a suggestion of white chocolate from oak-aged reserves. It concludes with terrific line and length, uniting fine chalk mineral structure with the expansive mouthfeel of oak fermentation and the harmonious texture of lees age.

By contrast, the 2014 base is fantastically tense and cut, a streamlined supercar of intricate precision, more about white-knuckle corners and screaming acceleration than it is about raw horsepower. For its aerodynamic curves, it boasts impressive engineering of fruit presence and body under the bonnet. Crunchy red apple and zippy lemon take a confident lead, supported by the subtle almond nougat of three years of lees age. It concludes with fine, salty minerality, laser line and persistence that follows a dead straight road all the way to the horizon. The 2013 base might just be the fairest of them all, growing into seamless complexity of brioche, baguette, honey and spice, while ever upholding vibrant brightness, thanks to the impeccable malic acidity of this lively season.

LOUIS ROEDERER BRUT VINTAGE 2012 $$$

94 points • DISGORGED 2018 • TASTED IN AUSTRALIA

20-30% Chouilly chardonnay; 70-80% Verzy pinot noir; 33% fermented in large oak casks; 9g/L dosage; cork

Louis Roederer Brut Vintage is a precise and calculated juxtaposition of just two vineyards, with a core of cool pinot noir from a north- and east-facing site on the Verzenay border of Verzy acquired by the house in 1841, contrasting chardonnay from a ripe, south-facing slope in Chouilly near Cramant. Jean-Baptiste Lécaillon uses this chardonnay to 'bring a smile and sunshine to an austere pinot noir'. He believes the best blend is created by uniting opposites. 'Blending is about playing with contrasts to stretch your palate,' he explains. 'If all the tanks taste the same, you cannot create a great blend. Diversity is the key.' He likes to ferment pinot from Verzy and Verzenay in oak, 'as it adds an extra sweetness, dimension and comfort to super-racy pinot noir!', and suggests this is what champagne was like 50 years ago – 'strong pinot noir from a cool climate, with classic oak fermentation'.

He describes his 2012 as a very gastronomic wine, from a complicated yet 'dream' vintage. 'A pinot year and we like those years! It delivered succulent, textured, round, creamy, precise pinot – and the most beautiful chardonnay I have met in my career, concentrated and deep!' Though he claims no credit for this. 'It is not me who is important in making the taste of the vintage wines, it is the farmer and the vineyard team. My role is only to eliminate the parcels that I don't want, but it is the terroir that speaks, and I cannot change this.'

Lécaillon is a master of juxtaposing not only the contrast of tense, north-east-facing pinot noir with generous, south-facing chardonnay, but also the complexity of oak fermentation with the cut of malic acidity, and the amplitude of ripe fruit with the subtlety of chalk minerality. He achieves this marriage with masterful seamlessness in 2012 in a cuvée that embodies the mood of the modern face of Roederer: jubilant precision, deep complexity and long-lingering endurance. The red apple crunch of cool pinot meets the golden delicious apple and pear richness of ripe, spicy chardonnay, layered with the biscuity, toasty brioche complexity of vat fermentation and lees age. Flinty reductive expression of struck match is heightened by a subtle smokiness that Lécaillon associates with the iron soil of Verzenay. It's rich and powerful, and at once creamy and crunchy, with malic acidity and salt minerality uniting in concert to draw out a very long and focused finish of great potential and endurance. It's only going to get even better over the next eight years, too. One bottle showed subtle cork taint.

LOUIS ROEDERER BRUT VINTAGE 2008 $$$

96 points • DISGORGED 2014 • TASTED IN CHAMPAGNE

As above; 32% Chouilly chardonnay, 68% Verzy pinot noir

The planets aligned as the vivacious 2008 season collided with the full impact of Lécaillon's innovation in the vines and the wines. The fallout unequivocally confirms the greatest Roederer vintage in modern history, embodying the dynamic freshness of Verzy pinot, countered by the richness of Chouilly chardonnay. The ethereal perfume that runs through the palate is enthralling, lending a fragrant rose petal air to spectacular pinot noir expression, purity and drive of fresh lemon, white cherry, red apple and grapefruit. A magnificent confluence of electric energy and resonating depth, as the racy, streamlined tension of 2008 malic acidity traces out a high-tensile cage that will support many decades of evolution. All manner of barrel- and bottle-derived personality infuses flesh, body and nuances of fig, nutmeg, even mocha, underlined emphatically by epic minerality, drawn out by roots thrust deep into chalk. Fairly light delicacy, breathtaking primary definition and impeccably ripe fullness make for a captivating display right away, but the full pyrotechnics display is yet to come. Such is its freeze-frame endurance that it has not evolved one millimetre since I first tasted it on its much-heralded release four years ago.

LOUIS ROEDERER BRUT VINTAGE 1990

94 points • ORIGINAL DISGORGEMENT 1995/1996 • TASTED IN CHAMPAGNE

No malolactic fermentation; no oak

Jean-Baptiste Lécaillon describes 1990 as a super-fruity vintage of superb pinot noir. At a full three decades of age, it's draped in a full copper-gold hue, reverberating with an expensive universe of fresh apricot, orange rind, pipe smoke, honey, mixed spice, truffles, mocha and green olives. It holds with excellent length and integrity, sustained by enduring malic acid drive, with just a little oxidation evident in this bottle.

LOUIS ROEDERER BRUT VINTAGE 1988

97 points • ORIGINAL DISGORGEMENT 1994 • TASTED IN CHAMPAGNE

Jean-Baptiste Lécaillon showcased this bottle in a flight of four decades of '8' vintages for my little visiting group on the release of Cristal 2008. 'The 2008 reminds me of 1988 and 1996,' he shared. '1989 was my first year at Louis Roederer and we tasted the 1988s and they were so acidic I almost quit!' But for him, acidity is not the key to longevity – '1988 and 2008 are concentrated; this is why they can age forever. The key to ageing is not the acidity, it's the concentration. Acidity is just salt and pepper on concentration!' His is one of the greatest 1988s I have tasted. At a full three decades of maturity, it has put on a full gold hue and grand concentration of grilled pineapple, mixed spice and roast fig. It is presence, concentration, persistence and tension that jettison it to another level, thanks to breathtaking acidity.

LOUIS ROEDERER BLANC DE BLANCS 2011 $$$$

93 points • TASTED IN CHAMPAGNE AND AUSTRALIA

Four parcels in Avize; 20% fermented in 9000-litre casks of 10-15 years of age; no malolactic fermentation; 4 atmospheres of pressure

Since 2009, Jean-Baptiste Lécaillon resolved to focus exclusively on four parcels in Avize for blanc de blancs: one on the border of Cramant, one on the border of Oger and two in the middle of Avize, all on the mid-slope. 'Such high-chalk soils give low pH and high acidity, so we push the ripeness to balance the tension and salinity with fruity roundness.' He picks very ripe, at 11.5 degrees potential, typically a week after everyone else. 'Only Anselme Selosse is still picking when we are!' he observes. Malolactic is always completely blocked as it creates too much butteriness, while retaining malic acid enhances salinity and chalk integration. A low pressure of four atmospheres gives 'finer bubbles, a creamier mousse and a more sexy touch!' He described 2011 as a 'very, very challenging season', with botrytis wiping out pinot noir, making chardonnay the champion of the season.

Lécaillon's mandate of ripeness strategically dodges the full impact of underripeness and rot in the harrowing 2011 season. The result projects a ripe, medium straw-green hue, exuding ripe pear and apple fruit with grapefruit tension and a focused line of malic acid energy. Subtle notes of fennel and green pea are true to this challenging season. Outstanding, inimitable Avize salt minerality lingers on and deep and long, making for a finish of well-integrated tension. A little dry grip on the finish is true to the season, though this is an impressive result for the year, finishing with energy, persistence and drive. It will age long, too.

Chouilly, winter 2013

LOUIS ROEDERER BLANC DE BLANCS 2010 $$$$

94 points • DISGORGED 2017 • TASTED IN AUSTRALIA

5% of Roederer's estate fruit is devoted to this cuvée; 20% vinified in oak casks; 9g/L dosage; cork

Ripe for drinking on release two years ago, this release has taken another year on lees confidently in its stride, downplaying its youthful struck-flint and gunsmoke reductive complexity and amplifying its baritone notes. Succulent, ripe white peach generosity has evolved to dried peach richness and just the right contrast of grapefruit bitterness, beautifully enveloped in the roast almond, vanilla nougat and mixed spice allure and creamy texture of both partial oak fermentation and six years on lees. The sustaining endurance of malic acidity is a wonder indeed, and for a cuvée so rounded and approachable in its youth, I am astounded at its confidence and undeviating line two years on, and astonished that I like it even more now than I did then. It's not going to get any better than this, so drink it now. But then again, that's what I thought two years ago.

LOUIS ROEDERER BLANC DE BLANCS 1998

96 points • TASTED IN CHAMPAGNE

Equal thirds of Avize, Le Mesnil-sur-Oger and Cramant; original disgorgement; no malolactic fermentation; 4 atmospheres of pressure; cork

'I am not a fan of the 1998 vintage,' confesses Jean-Baptiste Lécaillon, 'too open, too sexy, not classic enough… except blanc de blancs.' If the test of time is the ulitmate proof of any wine's credentials, he made the resoundingly correct decision to release this cuvée. At a full two decades of age, it upholds a bright, full yellow hue, even straw in the best bottles. All the majesty of the ripe 1998 year builds enticing succulence of white peach and grilled pineapple, bathed in preserved lemon, contrasting delightful struck-flint and grilled-toast reduction true to chardonnay and to Roederer. It lingers long with dried peach and mixed spice, while subtle green olive and warm hearth complexity tell of the beginnings of tertiary development. Opulent and delightful, it has now achieved its wonderful peak.

LOUIS ROEDERER ROSÉ 2013 $$$

96 points • DISGORGED 2018 • TASTED IN CHAMPAGNE AND AUSTRALIA

30% Chouilly chardonnay, 70% Cumières pinot noir; 33% fermented in oak casks; 22% malolactic fermentation; 5 atmospheres of pressure; 8g/L dosage; cork

'The art of blending is when different elements make something that is seamless that doesn't exist alone,' says Jean-Baptiste Lécaillon. 'This is the precision of blending, and this is the only idea of blending – the start, middle and end in one piece of fuselage!' His Rosé exemplifies this philosophy more emphatically than any other blend. It's built on Cumières pinot that unifies the ripeness of south exposure with the elegance of chalk. Yields of just half of the usual Champagne level makes for high phenolic ripeness and sweet, fruity tannins. Lécaillon amplifies ripeness through increasing exposure by sending 100 workers into the vineyard to remove leaves after flowering. Such ripe, fruity pinot lacks freshness, which he injects with a little chardonnay from a north-facing vineyard in Chouilly, 'very underripe, for minerality and freshness!' He thus balances ripe pinot with tense chardonnay, in the opposite manner to his Brut Vintage blend of tense pinot with ripe chardonnay.

The two are married in a brilliantly inspired and more than slightly courageous 'infusion' method developed uniquely by the house, first for Cristal Rosé in 1974. Pinot bunches are chilled, destemmed on the sorting table and sealed uncrushed in cold tanks for 7–10 days. They burst their skins, releasing flavours and aromatics but not tannins, to achieve his goal of softness without tannin structure. The juice is run off without pressing, and chardonnay juice is blended at this point, prior to fermentation, typically between 20% and 40%. 'We call this "infusion" like a Japanese tea,' explains Lécaillon, 'and we do the tea ceremony during harvest to decide how much chardonnay to add.' The risk in this method lies in fixing the blend prior to fermentation. 'The process is very uneven, since we can miss the colour, because some vintages have more colour than others,' he discloses. 'The colour is whatever the vintage delivers; some are almost white and some are darker. The key is that it tastes like rosé.' The 2013 vintage was a cool, classic, long-ripening season, so he put 22% through malolactic fermentation, the maximum for this cuvée.

The courageous premonition to blend chardonnay and pinot noir pre-fermentation is daring in itself, but to do so for rosé, one needs to be a either psychic, crazy or uber-talented. If there was ever evidence that Jean-Baptiste Lécaillon is unequivocally and emphatically the last of these, his 2013 is surely it. To unite such pure, glorious fragrance of rose petals and red cherries, gorgeous tang of pristine red cherries and strawberry hull, purity of crunchy redcurrants, tension of malic acidity, texture of chalk minerality, complexity of oak fermentation, and to do so with silky, undeviating harmony and graceful allure is nothing short of sheer genius. The silky integration that he has achieved through co-fermentation is mesmerising, and matched by no other rosé, saignée, blend or otherwise. It delivers the radiant generosity of Cumières in a pretty pale-salmon hue and flavours of yuzu, pink grapefruit, wild strawberry and cracked pepper, gracefully underscored by the fine chalk minerality of Chouilly. A one-third portion of oak fermentation brings no suggestion of oakiness, but works harmoniously to enhance creamy integration. This is an astonishingly delicious rosé, not only one of the most distinguished to emerge from this lauded estate, but one of the finest you'll find anywhere outside the rarefied air of uber-prestige this year. An expertly crafted masterpiece of breathtaking beauty.

LOUIS ROEDERER ROSÉ 2012 $$$

95 points • DISGORGED 2018 • TASTED IN AUSTRALIA

As above; 37% chardonnay, 63% pinot noir; 24% vinified in oak casks; aged 5 years on lees; 9g/L dosage

Lécaillon says north-facing Chouilly chardonnay is the New World equivalent of adding acid and life. This beautifully medium salmon-tinted rosé unites the body and flesh of Cumières pinot noir with the tension of Chouilly chardonnay. Five years on lees has built grand depth and texture, contrasting full, creamy confidence with the brilliance of chalk minerality and the enlivening tension of bright malic acidity. Glorious roast almond complexity is on the rise, yet at every moment holding wonderful harmony with crunchy red apple and tangy pink grapefruit. Lécaillon is a master of rosé – and 2012 is set to go down among his long line of greats.

Louis Roederer Rosé 1996

96 points • Tasted in Champagne

On the occasion of the launch of his spectacular Rosé 2008 in 2013, Jean-Baptiste Lécaillon lined up each of his best vintages since 1988. The star of the show was unequivocally the 1996, and my review at the time declared, 'few rosés are capable of sustaining their integrity post-disgorgement as effortlessly as Louis Roederer, and no vintage is charged with enduring stamina quite like 1996.' That was a full decade after disgorgement, and today, another five years on, it has ventured to an intriguing and enchanting place of medium copper hue and magnificent toasty complexity of roast chestnuts, hazelnuts, butterscotch, burnt butter and spice. The high-wire tension of its youth has now relaxed into a beautiful space of calm poise and seamless integration, while sustaining gorgeous peach fruit integrity, delightful malic acid balance and unrelenting persistence.

Louis Roederer et Philippe Starck Brut Nature 2009 $$$$

95 points • Tasted in Australia
95 points • Tasted in Champagne en magnum

Cumières field blend of roughly 34% chardonnay, 41% pinot noir, 25% meunier; co-planted, co-picked and co-pressed; 25% vinified in oak casks; aged on lees prior to bottling for 8–9 months; no malolactic fermentation; low pressure of 4.5 atmospheres to heighten creaminess; zero dosage; about 5% of Roederer's estate fruit is devoted to this cuvée

Roederer's first new cuvée since 1974 was conceived in the estate's remarkable 10-hectare biodynamic vineyard planted on dark clay in Cumières. All three varieties are picked together on the same day when pinot is ripe, which usually means meunier is a little overripe and chardonnay a little underripe. 'We do this to kill the variety and let the terroir shine,' Lécaillon told me as we stood in the heart of the vineyard. 'We want to capture the soil and not the variety. The terroir had to be the key. This was the secret to making this wine. I didn't set out to make a zero-dosage wine; I just found that the terroir didn't need it. The paradox of this cuvée is that the marketing is about Philippe Starck, but the cuvée is all about the terroir.' After the inaugural 2006 release heralded a remarkably well-balanced wine thanks to its warm and ripe season, Lécaillon has tactically waited until the sunny 2009 vintage to repeat the same act. The 2012 vintage will yield both a blanc and, for the first time, a rosé, made by the Roederer 'infusion' method. The distinctive label of this cuvée is polarising yet purposeful. 'I did not want to surf on the grower fashion, and hence the label – it is clearly not a grower wine!' Lécaillon outlines.

Here is evidence that the masterful harmony achieved with malic acidity without dosage in the first release was no fluke, and kudos to Lécaillon for pulling off the same tactical act again. On its release two years ago, I wrote that this unique and crafted cuvée would benefit from at least five years to fully come together. It's progressing down that path precisely as predicted and I love it even more today than I did then. Rich and powerful from the outset, its bouquet and palate ripple in waves of golden delicious apple, grapefruit, ripe white peach, even pineapple, fig and fruit mince spice, over a bed of roast nut complexity. Lovely umami notes and oyster shell salinity are wonderfully present, if surprising for Cumières' dark clay soils. It delivers body and richness of white Burgundian proportions, yet pulls magnificently into a focused and crunchy tail of tremendous persistence and presence, and yet exacting tension and line. Brilliantly executed, definitively Roederer and characteristically Cumières. I don't mind the uncharacteristic informality of its love-or-hate label, but I wish it declared its Cumières origins and the remarkable story of the most incredible biodynamic vineyard in all of Champagne. That's what this cuvée is really all about.

Cumières, summer 2011

LOUIS ROEDERER CRISTAL 2009 $$$$$

96 points • TASTED IN CHAMPAGNE AND AUSTRALIA

40% chardonnay, 60% pinot noir; aged 6 years on lees; sourced from a pool of 45 parcels over some 50 hectares of vines averaging 42 years of age on the most chalky mid-slopes, yielding 50% less than the appellation; 60% biodynamic vineyards, with a goal of 100% by 2020; 16% fermented in 60hL casks with bâtonnage for power, vinosity and a touch of spice and vanilla complexity; no malolactic fermentation; 8.5g/L dosage; typically 150,000–300,000 bottles

The secret of Cristal is that it's built to age, and its reductive style screams out for time to truly blossom. For its price and reputation, Cristal has until recently been a relatively early release in the world of prestige cuvées, though Lécaillon points out that 30 years ago it enjoyed only three years on lees, when he joined the company 20 years ago it only had four, and now it has six or seven. Notwithstanding, Cristal was the first 2009 prestige cuvée to hit the streets. He describes 2009 as a 'tutti-fruity year', yet holding its freshness, luminous and bright. He gave it the lowest dosage of any Cristal at the time.

This cuvée has revelled in the blessing of another two years since its release, confidently upholding its poise, refinement and pale, bright-straw hue. The gunflint reductive complexity of the house leads out, ushering in youthful definition of lemon and apple fruit. It changes up a gear on the finish, with pinot noir's red berries rising in depth and presence, gaining velocity and energy from the cut of malic acidity and the pronounced fine chalk mineral fingerprint of Cristal. It is still but a babe, primary, reticent and shy even for this generous vintage. As ever with Cristal, all it asks for is time.

LOUIS ROEDERER CRISTAL 2008 $$$$$

99 points • TASTED IN CHAMPAGNE AND AUSTRALIA (ON SIX OCCASIONS)

40% chardonnay, 60% pinot noir; Verzenay, Verzy and Beaumont-sur-Vesle, Dizy, Aÿ, Mareuil-sur-Aÿ, Cramant, Avize and Le Mesnil-sur-Oger; from a pool of 50 hectares of vines of 25–70 years of age (average 47 years), on the most chalky mid-slopes, yielding 50% less than the appellation; 35 parcels from a pool of 45 dedicated to Cristal (10 declassified in 2008); 40% biodynamic then (100% for the first time in 2012); 22% fermented in 60hL oak casks; 16% malolactic fermentation; aged 9 years on lees; 8g/L dosage, the lowest ever for Cristal; cork

'2008 was a legendary vintage, very close to 1996,' Lécaillon recalls. 'But we were disappointed with 1996; it was not as exceptional as we had hoped. So we made this wine thinking of 1996, and did four things differently that we didn't do very well then. 2008 was a cool year and I knew I had to add sunshine which was not in the vineyards, so I brought it in the cellar in malolactic, oak and time on lees. I always considered that we picked 1996 a week too early. So when 2008 arrived with a similar pattern, I became obsessed, so I waited, to make sure I picked ripe. Second, 1996 had only 3% oak fermentation, and we bumped it up to 22% in 2008 for more sweetness, and to round its firm acidity. There was no malolactic fermentation in 1996, so I went for 16% in 2008, not much, but sufficient to soften the acidity a bit and give the feeling of an oiliness to the mid-palate. Finally, when we came to disgorge at seven years, like we always do with Cristal, it was not ready, so for the first time ever we released non-sequentially and launched 2009 first. This gave 2008 nine years on lees before disgorgement, much more than we did in 1996, which really helped to soften the texture.' This made 2008 the first Cristal to be released at 10 years of age.

Cristal 2008 is the ultimate and absolute embodiment of Jean-Baptiste Lécaillon's fanatical work in the winery and, most of all, in the vineyards – a magnificent, towering monument to the lofty chalk aspiration that defines Cristal. Many have declared 2008 to be the greatest Cristal of the modern era, not least Lécaillon himself. It achieves this ambition not by a fanfare of pyrotechnics, but by the precision and focus that define the greatest Champagne vintage of recent decades. The struck-flint and gunpowder complexity of the reductive Roederer style lends a subtle complexity to the start. This is quickly swept up in a beautifully focused flow of chardonnay's lemon freshness and pinot noir's red berry and apple fruit. On first release, the most delicate strawberry hull, more recently graduating to wonderful depth of black cherry. A decade of age lends the subtle beginnings of almond nougat and understated mixed spice. The chalk mineral mandate of Cristal is exemplified in all-consuming presence like no vintage before it, as the planets aligned when the exacting purity and energy of 2008 met the ever more focused regime of Jean-Baptiste and his team, benefiting from all the learnings of 1996 and every season since. The result is a brilliant flash of signature 2008 malic acidity, stark as high-noon daylight, illuminating in dazzling radiance the crystalline chalk minerality of old vines deeply rooted in the greatest terroirs. It churns and froths with sea salt minerality, a beach-fresh, aquamarine landscape that at once confronts you with its vivid, stark brilliance and simultaneously calms you with its peaceful, ordered beauty. In line and length it is other-worldly, hovering motionless literally for minutes, at once lighter than air, yet thunderingly expansive, soaring to the epitome Cristal heights. A true masterpiece by every definition, quintessential Cristal and unreservedly the greatest I have tasted. It will not attain its full potential until at least 2038, and its mesmerising spectacle will continue for at least half a century.

Cramant, harvest 2014

LOUIS ROEDERER CRISTAL 2002 $$$$$

98 points • ORIGINAL DISGORGEMENT 2010 • TASTED IN CHAMPAGNE EN MAGNUM AND AUSTRALIA

40% chardonnay, 60% pinot noir; the first of the Cristal Collection Privée program, re-releasing the original disgorgement after 8 years on lees and 8 years on cork; 20% fermented in oak casks; no malolactic fermentation; just a few thousand bottles; only select vintages (the next will be 2008)

'Before 2008 was born, 2002 was king of the first decade of the millennium, but now 2008 will make it the queen,' Jean-Baptiste Lécaillon proposes; '2002 is richer, more powerful and more Burgundy, while 2008 is more classic.' Of 45 parcels in the Cristal pool, he generally eliminates 15 and sometimes 20 in each blend. 'But in 2002, for the first time, I couldn't do it,' he reveals. 'Whatever blend I tried, the estate was stronger than me. So it's all 45 parcels.' Equal time on lees and on cork is his ideal. 'I love this idea of half and half, a half life on lees (the Champagne way) and a half life without lees, to build wine expression, lose some yeastiness and come back to the fruit. I am not making Vegemite! There are two kinds of winemakers in Champagne: the yeast makers and the winemakers. I am a winemaker!'

An ethereal Cristal that encapsulates the magnificent 2002 season in a glorious, glowing straw-yellow hue, tinted with gold. Building incrementally in magnitude, body and power, this grand vintage is unravelling with incredible generosity, beginning to evolve from its primary fruits of white peach and pineapple, into a vast universe orbiting with roast nuts, melted butter, mixed spice, ginger, dried peach, baked fig, pâtisserie, toasted meringue, vanilla, even hints of incense. Its succulent, silky generosity contrasts the deep salt minerality and poise of legendary terroirs A true expression of 2002, rich, full, voluptuous and eminently ready to drink now. In magnum it is emphatically more youthful, elegant and refined, luminous in its bright straw hue, and intensely reductive, with struck-match notes. One bottle was tragically corked.

LOUIS ROEDERER CRISTAL VINOTHÈQUE 1995 $$$$$

98 points • TASTED IN CHAMPAGNE

43% chardonnay, 57% pinot noir; 7% vinified in oak casks; 10% malolactic fermentation; aged 8 years *sur latte*, 8 years *sur pointe* and 7 years on cork; 8g/L dosage; 600 bottles

Just 600 bottles of the stunning 1995 vintage were held back for Roederer's first ever Vinothèque re-release of Cristal. This late-disgorged, lower-dosage rendition is testimony to the magical transformation of Cristal with bottle age. Few will have the chance to partake, but we can all be inspired to have the stamina to leave the great vintages of Cristal in our cellars for 20 years, the age at which Lécaillon finds an ideal balance of youth and evolution. After more than two decades, this classic and benchmark season has attained a magical place of ravishingly silky refinement, perfectly seamless, yet still breathtakingly backward, lively and refined. Its youthful clarity and focus are disarming, holding a hue brighter even than the 2002 today, and wafting with classic Roederer struck-flint and grilled-toast reduction. Stunning poise and harmony define a finish of outstanding persistence, with an ever-present undercurrent of fine salty chalk acidity that ripples with grand complexity and drive.

LOUIS ROEDERER CRISTAL 1993

96 points • DISGORGED 2008 • TASTED IN CHAMPAGNE

58% chardonnay, 42% pinot noir; 7g/L dosage

In line for Cristal's first Vinothèque release, 1993 didn't ultimately make the cut. It was a difficult and wet season in which pinot suffered, hence an unusually high proportion of chardonnay for Cristal. Extended time on lees has proven to be a blessing, piling on layers of richness that Lécaillon observes weren't there in this less intense season. It's in a fabulous place at 25 years of age, holding a medium yellow-gold hue and sustaining a wonderful core of glacé fig and candied almonds, rolling into a tertiary realm of toffee, pipe smoke and green olives. It concludes with seductive silkiness, graceful completeness and calm confidence.

LOUIS ROEDERER CRISTAL ROSÉ 2009 $$$$$

97 points • TASTED IN AUSTRALIA

45% chardonnay from one parcel in Avize and one in Le Mesnil-sur-Oger, 55% pinot from two parcels in Aÿ, all biodynamic since 2007; 12% vinified in oak casks; no malolactic fermentation; Roederer 'infusion' method of maceration and blending (see Rosé Vintage 2013 and Cristal Rosé 2008); aged 6 years on lees; 8g/L dosage; cork

A gorgeous rosé that captures the elegance of the modern Louis Roederer, even in the powerful and structured 2009 season. With a dazzling, bright pale-salmon hue, pretty red cherry and strawberry hull fruit is underlined by savoury notes of tomato and the roast hazelnuts of secondary development of this fast-maturing vintage. An impressive core of exact pinot noir generosity of succulence and allure is seamlessly integrated with the lemon tension of chardonnay, thanks to the magnificent polish of Roederer's daring co-fermentation technique. Upholding 100% malic acidity has cunningly sustained energy and tension, amplifying fine salt mineral structure, integrating neatly with the super-fine grip and bite of warm season phenolic structure. It coasts with exceptional line and length.

LOUIS ROEDERER CRISTAL ROSÉ 2008 $$$$$

100 points • TASTED IN AUSTRALIA

44% chardonnay from one parcel in Avize and one in Le Mesnil-sur-Oger, 56% pinot from two parcels in Aÿ, all biodynamic since 2007; 17% vinified in oak casks; 16% malolactic fermentation; Roederer 'infusion' method of maceration and blending (see Rosé Vintage 2013); aged 6 years on lees; 8g/L dosage; cork; just 5% of Cristal production

In Cristal Rosé, Jean-Baptiste Lécaillon aspires to capture the essence of Cristal (chalk, freshness and precision) with an extra-deep fruit concentration that links the sweetness of Burgundy with the delicacy of champagne. The house has made vintage rosé since 1832, but it was only in 1974 that it conceived its unique and daring 'infusion' method of maceration and blending prior to fermentation (see Rosé Vintage 2013). 'I love doing it!' Lécaillon waxes. 'I get my whole team in our special rosé cellar and we spend two hours on the blend. It is the end of harvest and we are in the swing of the mood of the season, so our intuitive decision reflects the mood of the harvest, unlike doing the blend in December, January or February, when we are away from the pure spirit of the harvest.'

The 2007 release heralded a brand-new day for Cristal Rosé, the first to emerge from Roederer's new facility dedicated to rosé, and the first year in which all four vineyards were farmed biodynamically. The planets aligned when 2008 delivered the perfect season into Roederer's 'organic revolution', as Lécaillon dubs it; '2008 has such finesse,' he suggests. 'There are many, many pixels in high definition. This is the magic of 2008!' Yet he points out that its release was overshadowed by Cristal 2008.

In any pursuit, it is only the most daring and courageous who succeed at the very highest level, only the trailblazers who risk everything and take the biggest gambles who define new horizons. Lécaillon's 'infusion' technique has everything to lose and everything to win, and never has he won like he did in 2008. The desperate, beguiling purity of the superlative 2008 season attains a breathtaking pinnacle in Cristal Rosé. The sheer purity and elegance of exact white cherry fruit, cherry kernel and pristine rose petals is ravishing, perfectly and seamlessly interwoven with the almond nougat and vanilla of a decade of age. Subtle wisps of the gunflint reductive complexity of Roederer quickly evaporate into a desperately gorgeous cuvée of pretty pale-salmon hue, blending its elements with such wizardry that it is impossible to distinguish where one concludes and the next begins. The seamless integration, silky harmony and creamy texture of Jean-Baptiste's daring co-fermentation has reached hitherto unattained heights in this beguiling season. For all there is to adore about Cristal Rosé 2008, it is the magnitude and harmony of its breathtaking salt mineral texture that elevate it above all before it, locked in an interplay with malic acidity of lightning brilliance and shuddering tension that would shatter any mere mortal cuvée. And yet here they are somehow, shockingly, impossibly – harmonious, calm, perfection. The only question that this cuvée begs is whether to drink it now or in 50 years. And like all the very greatest wines of all, there is of course no wrong answer, and there will never be a wrong time to revel in the delights of the most monumental release of the year. This is, singly and unequivocally, the greatest champagne that has landed since the thundering Clos du Mesnil 2002. And it just might be the greatest rosé I have ever tasted.

LOUIS ROEDERER CRISTAL ROSÉ 2002 $$$$$

97 points • TASTED IN CHAMPAGNE EN MAGNUM
96 points • TASTED IN CHAMPAGNE

As above; 45% chardonnay from one parcel in Avize and one in Le Mesnil-sur-Oger, 55% pinot from two parcels in Aÿ

Cristal Rosé presents the ultimate juxtaposition between the breathtaking freshness of Champagne's two most enduring chardonnay grand crus and the glorious concentration of ripe fruit from its most historic pinot cru. Consummate definition, exacting poise and undeterred persistence are reinforced by the tension of scintillating crystal mineral structure, propelling subtle red apple fruit and the most understated elements of secondary development, more in texture than in flavour. Magnificently mineral and eminently refined, time has built creamy structure without diminishing any of its remarkable energy. A brilliant Cristal Rosé, with many more glorious years stretching before it yet.

LOUIS ROEDERER CHARMONT MAREUIL-SUR-AŸ COTEAUX CHAMPENOIS BY LOUIS ROEDERER 2016

95 points • TASTED IN CHAMPAGNE

100% pinot noir; single-parcel Charmont of 0.4 hectares, mid-slope, south-facing in a well-sheltered location on chalky soils, on the Aÿ side of Mareuil-sur-Aÿ, just under Bollinger's La Côte aux Enfants and Selosse's La Côte Faron; biodynamically farmed and organically certified; yielding just 35hL/hectare; fermented in stainless steel barrels, stood on their ends with open tops; 25% whole bunches; hand *pigéage*; one-third each of new barrels 1 and 2 years old; wild fermented; natural malolactic fermentation; less than 1500 bottles

Ever the innovator, Jean-Baptiste Lécaillon has been secretly working on both Coteaux Champenois red and white wines since 2002. 'Coteaux Champenois is innovation backwards,' he suggests. 'Before 1850, there was more still wine than sparkling wine produced in Champagne. Whenever they had lunches here in the 1950s, they had a glass of champagne and a glass of Coteaux Champenois blanc and a glass of Coteaux Champenois rouge. Maybe in years to come we won't make sparkling wine anymore? And that would not be a problem. In 20 years time we might be making super white wines or red wines in Champagne!'

In creating his Coteaux Champenois, Lécaillon searched for the best terroir in Cumières, Aÿ, Bouzy and Ambonnay, and found a little plot in Mareuil-sur-Aÿ was the best. 'The idea is to express the full terroir,' he says. White Coteaux Champenois has proven to be more of a challenge for him. 'I have done many bottlings and I was never happy, as it was never as good as my champagne,' he reveals. 'And so I asked, "What is the point if it is not at least as good as champagne?" So I changed my focus. Your normal feeling would be to oak-ferment it, but you cannot ferment it like you can in Burgundy; it is much more amazing in stainless steel barrels and in white clay and limestone jars! We must invent a Coteaux Champenois blanc that is unique, more Chablis in style than Burgundy.'

I was privileged to be the first to taste Lécaillon's secret project, just a few days after visiting Francis Egly, who Lécaillon and I both uphold as creating Champagne's most sublime Coteaux Champenois, and Veuve Clicquot, second only to Egly, though not commercialised (yet). Louis Roederer instantly joins the holy trinity of rouge with its ethereal inaugural release. An impressive purple-red hue heralds a bouquet of fantastic violet fragrance, gliding into a palate of delightful purity and finesse of black cherry and black plum fruit. Whole-bunch has been impeccably gauged, lifting its spicy complexity and lending a subtle smokiness, while sensitively toned oak plays a gentle support role. The structure is refined and crafted, with super-fine tannins meshing harmoniously with well-gauged acidity, providing a platform for the fine chalk minerality of Mareuil-sur-Aÿ to be the rightful hero. Like all great Coteaux Champenois, it will be very long lived. Keep it for a decade and watch the magic unravel.

MAILLY GRAND CRU

(My-ii Groh Khrew)

5/10

28 RUE DE LA LIBÉRATION 51500 MAILLY-CHAMPAGNE
www.champagne-mailly.com

CHAMPAGNE

MAILLY

GRAND CRU

Of Champagne's 137 coopératives, only 42 market their own cuvées, and Le Mesnil rivals Mailly Grand Cru as the fairest of them all. Mailly's 80 owners supply fruit for 500,000 bottles each year, from some 480 parcels on 75 hectares, exclusively in one village, representing more than one-quarter of the glorious Mailly-Champagne grand cru on the northern slopes of the Montagne de Reims. Mailly is unusual in dedicating 90% of its fruit to its own label, selling just 10–15% to négociants and none back to its own growers. With no contracts, the house upholds the flexibility not to sell in some years. Mailly's range of nine cuvées showcases the deep colour, rich complexity and up-front fruit character of this celebrated cru, and its finest prestige cuvées capture the elegant mineral precision of the northern Montagne.

In the erratic climate of Champagne, the inability to blend with other villages makes a single-cru estate particularly challenging.

Wine critic Michel Bettane upholds Mailly-Champagne and Aÿ as the two villages in the region with sufficiently varying exposition and soils to confidently produce a monocru. Half of Mailly's slopes are north-facing, and the remainder have easterly, westerly and even southerly aspects, since the hill slopes gently back up below the village. Soils likewise vary dramatically from the top of the village to the bottom, in some places with chalk very close to the surface, and in other areas two metres below.

Mailly has taken strategic advantage of this diversity, and Hervé Dantan, its talented and longstanding chef de cave from 1991 to 2013, set up the coopérative with some 150 tanks, an incredible number for its size, to facilitate individual vinification of small parcels. Every tank displays a map of the village to indicate the plots. In 2012, a new area of the winery was dug to provide space for more small tanks, providing for a blending palette of

some 70-80 vins clairs each vintage, plus more than 10 vintages of reserves, stored in small stainless steel and enamelled tanks and oak foudres. A solera system for reserves has been in operation for more than 20 years. The house sources two-year-old barrels from Burgundy.

Malolactic fermentation is completed on most parcels, according to the plots and the vintage. In the warm 2018 season, malolactic was blocked on 40% of parcels. Jetting is performed at disgorgement to reduce oxidation. Dosages have been lowered from 9g/L to 7–8g/L in response to warmer growing seasons. Mailly suffered from substantial losses to frost in the past, and the warmer conditions of recent decades have blessed it with much more consistent yields.

After years of strong investment in the winery, the coopérative is now increasing its efforts in the vineyards. It describes its approach as 'Burgundian', with so many plots in the same village, all within one kilometre and all pressed at the coopérative. Its

vineyards are managed by 25 families, with whom it works closely. It has divided the village into 35 areas and has established a test plot in each, which it has analysed since 1998. The results have enabled it to better support its growers, setting the start of harvest for each part of the village, and decreasing use of chemicals in the vineyards by 75% over 15 years. The coopérative is working closely with its growers to further reduce herbicides and insecticides, and pays the cost for them to be certified *Sustainable Viticulture en Champagne*, with 75% already on board, and a target of 100% in the next few years. It is also working with 15 growers to trial organic techniques. In 2018 it was the second in France to be verified sustainable as a collective structure.

Mailly's north-facing slopes on chalk subsoils draw out the mineral freshness of pinot noir, which comprises 75% of plantings, with chardonnay making up the remainder. The coopérative is proud to uphold an average vine age of 25 years, though has been asking its growers to plant more chardonnay. The old growers in the village say that their pinot noir has the elegance and minerality of chardonnay, and their chardonnay has the weight of pinot noir.

The coopérative's glass building stands proudly in the village, above seven levels of cellars, permitting gravity flow without pumping. A kilometre of chalk crayères, dug by hand 20 metres below the surface by the founders of the coopérative every winter from 1929 to 1965, is home to 2 million bottles, representing an impressive four years of stock.

Mailly Grand Cru now boasts informative back labels, detailing the plots, oak vinification and base years.

Hervé Dantan accepted a position at Lanson in 2013 and was replaced at Mailly by Sébastien Moncuit, from a family of growers in the Côte des Blancs, with a decade of experience at Château Malakoff and three years consulting for growers, including Pascal Agrapart, Francis Egly and Anselme Selosse.

MAILLY GRAND CRU BRUT RÉSERVE NV $$

92 points • 2015 BASE VINTAGE • TASTED IN CHAMPAGNE

25% chardonnay, 75% pinot noir; 34% reserves from 10 years as always; 5-8% of 2015 vinified in oak barrels; reserves mostly from stainless steel and a little from enamelled tanks and barrels; 7.5g/L dosage

Mailly's entry cuvée aims to be an apéritif style of minerality and precision, but most of all approachable from the roundness and freshness of pinot noir, which assumes a three-quarters lead in the blend, in line with the sourcing of the coopérative. It's on great form, taking the warm 2015 season in its stride. With a medium straw hue, it presents a particularly vibrant and tangy take on pinot noir, true to its northern Montagne location, thanks to lively acidity that brings focus and accuracy to bright, tangy strawberries, crunchy red apple freshness and gentle spicy complexity. Projecting the character of the village in fine chalk minerality, it concludes with excellent integrity and balance of bright acidity and well-integrated dosage.

MAILLY GRAND CRU BLANC DE PINOT NOIR BRUT NV $$

91 points • 2015 BASE VINTAGE • DISGORGED 22 MAY 2018 • TASTED IN CHAMPAGNE

100% pinot noir; 24.2% reserves; 26.6% vinified in oak; lieux-dits Les Côtes, Les Champs de 8 Jours, Sous la ville Monument, Les Feugeres; 8g/L dosage

The house upholds Blanc de Pinot Noir as its flagship, sourced from just four plots, named on the back label. It's a particularly deep hue of medium orange copper, presenting a spicy and complex take on northern Montagne blanc de noirs, exuding succulent apricots, peaches and fruit mince spice. One quarter oak vinification brings creaminess and layers of vanilla custard and honey cake. Fine chalk minerality and honeyed dosage meld seamlessly on the finish, making for a complex style, albeit lacking a little in freshness.

MAILLY GRAND CRU ROSÉ DE MAILLY BRUT NV $$

93 points • 2014 BASE VINTAGE • DISGORGED SEPTEMBER 2018 • TASTED IN CHAMPAGNE

6% chardonnay, 94% pinot noir; 90% of pinot skin macerated for 15-18 hours and racked every 2 hours; 4.5% pinot noir white wine; two key lieux-dits close to the village, Sous la Ville Monument and Les Roses; 7.6g/L dosage

Flaunting a full crimson hue, this is a confident and flamboyant saignée rosé of wonderful fruit definition and freshness, masterfully side-stepping the tannin grip that almost invariably accompanies this method of production, particularly with this level of colour. It presents beautiful notes of pomegranate, raspberries and even musk. A classy rosé de saignée that captures the elegance of Mailly, holding primary fruit of integrity and poise, with fine minerality, good acid line and eloquent persistence.

MAILLY GRAND CRU DÉLICE NV $$

90 points • 2014 BASE VINTAGE • TASTED IN CHAMPAGNE

25% chardonnay, 75% pinot noir; Brut Réserve aged 1 year longer, with 35g/L dosage

With a medium yellow hue, this is demi-sec of clean, fruity appeal and boiled-sweets candied character, with a firm, structural grip and simple finish. It's well made, but there's no escaping the fact that this base was designed for low dosage as Brut Réserve.

MAILLY GRAND CRU EXTRA BRUT MILLÉSIMÉ 2011 $$

87 points • DISGORGED 14 FEBRUARY 2018 • TASTED IN CHAMPAGNE

25% chardonnay, 75% pinot noir; principal lieux-dits Les Côtes, Le bas des Chalois, Sous la Ville Regards, Les Coutures; 7.7% vinified in oak; 2.6g/L dosage

Mailly creates a specific blend for its vintage cuvée, built around riper plots. It's consequently a deeply coloured and richly fashioned cuvée of full yellow-gold hue, presenting ripe fruits of apricots and peaches, showing some burnt-orange oxidation that accentuates the dry coarseness of the challenging 2011 harvest, only amplified by low dosage. This results in a short, firm and dry finish.

MAILLY GRAND CRU L'INTEMPORELLE BRUT 2011 $$$$

89 points • TASTED IN CHAMPAGNE

40% chardonnay, 60% pinot noir; less than 5 atmospheres of pressure; 6-7g/L dosage; 25,000 bottles

L'Intemporelle aspires to finesse, elegance and precision, and hence the blend is built around lieux-dits on pure chalk soils with north-facing orientations, especially for pinot noir. With a full yellow-gold hue, it's a contrast between the ripeness of loquat fruit and the green notes of dried mango and smoke marked by the challenging lack of ripeness of 2011. Its acid line carries long, and the structure is creamy, successfully side-stepping the coarseness inherent to so many in this season, though there is a little bitter grip to a close that lacks fruit generosity. A good attempt for such a tough season.

MAILLY GRAND CRU L'INTEMPORELLE ROSÉ 2010 $$$$

93 points • TASTED IN CHAMPAGNE

40% chardonnay, 60% pinot noir; L'Intemporelle with 2.5-3% pinot noir red wine from vines more than 40 years old; 8g/L dosage; 4900 bottles

It is a profound lesson in the intricacies of champagne blending to see the tremendous impact that less than 3% of red wine can make in transforming a cuvée. The colour has shifted to a medium orange copper hue, making for a characterful rosé, brimming with mandarin and loquat flavours, with an elegant palate of strawberry hull tang. The fine-boned tension of the northern Montagne de Reims defines a tangy style of elegant focus, accented with spicy berry compote complexity. It concludes with great fruit persistence, fine chalk minerality and excellent acid line. An impressive result for a not so easy season.

MAILLY GRAND CRU LES ÉCHANSONS 2008 $$$$$

95 points • DISGORGED MARCH 2018 • TASTED IN CHAMPAGNE

25% chardonnay, 75% pinot noir; aged 9 years on lees; 6g/L dosage; 6029 bottles

Sourced predominantly from the oldest vines of the village, boasting an impressive 80–90 years of age, Les Échansons is intentionally a contrast to the elegance of L'Intemporelle – and a powerful village, large majority of pinot noir, old-vine concentration and a decade of bottle age make for a compelling foursome, conspiring in a full yellow-straw hue with a blush tint. The poise and youthfulness of the stunning 2008 season is the perfect foil, and it rejoices in all the glory of Mailly pinot noir, rumbling with grilled pineapple, layers of mixed spice, golden fruit cake, vanilla and candied almonds. It is at once succulent and luscious and at the same time bright, with tense acid line and finely textured salt minerality, concluding with triumphant line and length.

EXCEPTION BLANCHE BLANC DE BLANCS 2007 $$$$

96 points • TASTED IN CHAMPAGNE

100% chardonnay; 50% Mailly, 50% Avize; aged 10 years on lees; 10,000 bottles

Mailly's 'Exception' to its rigorous monocru status is the injection of Avize into its Mailly chardonnay. The result is one of the greatest cuvées to emerge from this laudable estate in the modern era, a tribute to grand terroirs, fastidious blending and magnificent bottle age. Mailly chardonnay does not stand confidently flying solo, so Hervé Dantan exchanged grapes with a grower in Avize. Aged for 10 years, the idea was to create something unique to the great blanc de blancs of the Côte des Blancs. An anomaly for the coopérative, this cuvée cannot be named Mailly Grand Cru as it is not sourced exclusively from the village, and hence was registered as its own brand in 1999. This is a masterfully crafted blend, and 2007 stands tall among the greatest to date. Its body, complexity and full yellow hue encapsulate the signature of Mailly, seamlessly integrated with the energy, tension and deep chalk mineral structure of Avize to compelling effect. A full decade on lees has built wonderfully creamy, silky texture and layers of nougat and brioche. The finish is long, linear and beautifully salt mineral, with an enticing interplay between youthful vibrancy and the slow-rising complexity of bottle age. It concludes confident, refined, creamy and ever so long.

MAILLY GRAND CRU MAGNUM COLLECTION MILLÉSIMÉ 1998 $$$$$

93 points • DISGORGED 2017 • TASTED IN CHAMPAGNE EN MAGNUM

25% chardonnay, 75% pinot noir; 2g/L dosage; 1808 magnums

Two decades in Mailly's cool, deep cellar has built a full yellow-gold hue to this magnificently complex and multi-faceted 1998, swimming with tarte tatin, roast peach, vanilla pod, dried nectarine and fruit mince spice. A little bitterness on the finish offers bite and tension, beginning to dry out now as it edges past its peak of maturity. Nonetheless, it holds with persistence, acid line and fine chalk mineral structure.

MARC HÉBRART

(Mark E-brah)

7/10

18 Rue du Pont 51160 Mareuil-sur-Aÿ

Champagne
MARC HEBRART

Behind the village of Mareuil-sur-Aÿ, directly under the vineyards, a sheer chalk cliff stands as a dramatic and stark testimony to the profound terroir that forms the bedrock of what is the greatest premier cru of all. Experiencing the masterfully crafted creations of the most famous grower in the village is an equally profound encounter with the confronting minerality of Mareuil-sur-Aÿ. 'My greatest aspiration is to let the soils speak,' declares Jean-Paul Hébrart, for whom harmony is more important than intensity. Each of his cuvées contrasts elegant fruit expression with the mineral signature of great terroirs, tapped by the deep roots of old vines.

Jean-Paul's father Marc Hébrart has been making his own champagnes in Mareuil-sur-Aÿ since 1964, and Jean-Paul joined him from the age of nineteen in 1983, taking over in 1997.

The estate is privileged to 15 hectares of vines of average age 28 years, spread across 75 plots of 70% pinot noir, proudly positioned in Aÿ, Dizy, Hautvillers, Avenay-Val-d'Or, Bisseuil, Mutigny, Louvois and most of all Mareuil-sur-Aÿ, including many gently south-facing plots around and above Clos des Goisses. These are cunningly married with 25% chardonnay from Avize, Chouilly and Oiry. No meunier is used.

Sustainable *lutte raisonnée* (reasoned viticulture) is the mandate, and synthetic treatments are avoided as much as possible.

Jean-Paul recently completed a new facility on the bank of the river in Mareuil to increase his production and storage space, where all parcels are vinified separately, mostly cool fermented in temperature-controlled stainless steel tanks. Some natural fermentation in small barrels was introduced in 2004, and foudres were introduced for some reserves in 2018. *Moût concentré rectifié* (MCR) from grape must is used for dosage rather than cane sugar, since it is more neutral and less oxidative. No sulphur is added at disgorgement, and his attentive winemaking doesn't call for it – every cuvée I've tasted upholds freshness and purity.

His cuvées enjoy a minimum of two years on lees, and more often three to four years, though he aspires to increase this by another year within the next four years.

Jean-Paul is married to Isabelle Diebolt of Diebolt-Vallois, though the businesses function autonomously. His annual production has grown to around 125,000 bottles.

MARC HÉBRART SÉLECTION BRUT PREMIER CRU NV $$

94 points • 2013 BASE • 40% 2012 RESERVES • DISGORGED JULY 2018 • TASTED IN AUSTRALIA
93 points • 2012 BASE • 15% 2010 RESERVES • DISGORGED APRIL 2017 • TASTED IN AUSTRALIA

30% chardonnay from Oiry and Chouilly, 70% pinot noir from Mareuil-sur-Aÿ vines of 45–55 years of age; fermented in stainless steel tanks; full malolactic fermentation; aged 4-4.5 years on lees; 7-7.5g/L dosage; cork

A magnificent entry cuvée that articulates the inimitable talent of Mareuil-sur-Aÿ to magnificently juxtapose the elegance and the presence of pinot noir. For its age, pinot noir predominance and generous reserves, it upholds impressive freshness of Mareuil old-vine lift in precocious red cherry and red berry fruits and waves of anise and fruit mince spice. It concludes with an enticing and seamless fanfare of vibrant morello cherry acidity and well-harmonised dosage. It's at once succulent and juicy and at the same time lively and fresh, with the pronounced salty chalk minerality of Mareuil tapped as only old vines can do. All hail the great 2013/2012 duo!

MARC HÉBRART BLANC DE BLANCS BRUT PREMIER CRU NV $$

92 points • 70% 2015 BASE VINTAGE • 20% 2014, 10% 2013 RESERVES • 88% MAREUIL-SUR-AŸ, 12% OIRY AND CHOUILLY • DISGORGED JULY 2018 • TASTED IN AUSTRALIA
92 points • 65% 2014 BASE VINTAGE • 29% 2013, 6% 2012 RESERVES • 85% MAREUIL-SUR-AŸ, 15% OIRY AND CHOUILLY • DISGORGED APRIL 2017 • TASTED IN AUSTRALIA

100% chardonnay; fermented in stainless steel vats; full malolactic fermentation; aged 38 months on lees; 7g/L dosage; cork

On the gently south-facing slopes of Mareuil above Clos des Goisses, chardonnay takes on a fleshy generosity, especially in a warm season like 2015. Jean-Paul Hébrart presents a masterfully crafted take on this, in a blanc de blancs of bright, pale straw hue that heralds its elegant freshness. A core of mirabelle plum and white peach is accented with the zest of grapefruit and lemon sherbet in an approachable and succulent style of generous spice complexity and ripe fruit persistence. The salt minerality of Mareuil upholds freshness on the finish, amplified strategically by a well-placed touch of the structure of Chouilly/Oiry. The 2014 base is a fleshy style hinting at exotic, ripe pineapple, ready to drink now.

MARC HÉBRART BRUT ROSÉ PREMIER CRU NV $$

94 points • 55% 2015 CHARDONNAY, 39% 2014 AND 2013 PINOT, 6.5% 2014 PINOT RED WINE • AGED 2.5 YEARS ON LEES • DISGORGED JULY 2018 • TASTED IN AUSTRALIA
94 points • 50% 2014 CHARDONNAY, 43.5% 2013 AND 2012 PINOT, 6.5% PINOT RED WINE • AGED 2 YEARS ON LEES • DISGORGED JULY 2017 • TASTED IN AUSTRALIA

100% Mareuil-sur-Aÿ; cool fermented in temperature-controlled stainless steel tanks; red wine vinified in oak; full malolactic fermentation; 6.5-7g/L dosage; cork

Graced with Hébrart's delicate touch, this magnificent cuvée embodies everything that makes Mareuil such a gorgeous terroir for refined rosé. An elegant dash of just 6.5% Mareuil pinot noir red wine creates a pretty, bright pale-salmon hue and delightful perfume of strawberry, red cherry, pink pepper and rose petal, uniting fragrant restraint with red fruit presence and outstanding poise and persistence. It contrasts primary, precocious freshness with the gorgeous, succulent fruit generosity that defines Mareuil — no small task, especially in the warm 2015 season. Its fragrant perfume lingers from start to finish, holding very long, flattering and characterful, sustained by beautifully poised acidity and the prominent, fine, signature chalk minerality of the village.

Marc Hébrart Mes Favorites Vieilles Vignes NV $$

96 points • 2014 BASE VINTAGE • DISGORGED 24 APRIL 2018 • TASTED IN AUSTRALIA

25% chardonnay, 75% pinot noir; Jean-Paul's favourite parcels of Mareuil-sur-Aÿ from vines older than 50 years; 2013 and 2012 reserves; fermented in temperature-controlled stainless steel tanks; full malolactic fermentation; aged 3 years on lees; cork

Behind the village of Mareuil, directly under the vineyards, a sheer chalk cliff stands as a dramatic and stark testimony to the profound terroir that forms the bedrock of what is the greatest premier cru of all. To drink Jean-Paul Hébrart's new cuvée is an equally profound experience of the confronting minerality of Mareuil-sur-Aÿ. The ability of the deep roots of old vines to extract the chalk signature of the terroir of great sites is remarkable indeed, and Hébrart bores to the very core of the chalk of Mareuil. Old vines infuse sensational concentration, too, rippling and rumbling with layers of generous white peach, fig and layers of spice. Chalk brings dynamic freshness to this succulent generosity, holding pronounced persistence and impeccable line. It's little wonder that these plots, Hébrart's most representative of his village, are the closest to his heart. Mes Favorites, indeed. Mine too.

Marc Hébrart Special Club 2014 $$$

95 points • DISGORGED 25 APRIL 2018 • TASTED IN AUSTRALIA

45% chardonnay, 55% pinot; 35% Mareuil-sur-Aÿ pinot from 3 parcels, 20% Aÿ pinot from 4 parcels; 25% Mareuil-sur-Aÿ chardonnay from 3 plots, 20% Oiry and Chouilly chardonnay; 45+ year old vines; fermented in temperature-controlled stainless steel tanks; full malolactic fermentation; aged 4 years on lees; 6.5g/L dosage; cork

Hébrart's skill as a blender in concert with his deep resource of old vines in legendary terroirs makes for a fantastic and harmonious cuvée of profound terroir expression and fruit purity that utterly transcends its tricky season. The articulate expression of fine, chalky minerality defines a super-fine finish of profound persistence and line. Pinot noir takes a glorious lead in notes of liquorice and morello cherries, underlined by the youthful lemon freshness of chardonnay. Four years on lees has brought a seductive almond nougat subtlety. A fantastic 2014.

Marc Hébrart Special Club 2012 $$$

94 points • DISGORGED JULY 2016 • TASTED IN AUSTRALIA

45% chardonnay, 55% pinot; 35% Mareuil-sur-Aÿ pinot from 3 parcels, 20% Aÿ pinot from 4 parcels; 25% Mareuil-sur-Aÿ chardonnay from 3 plots, 20% Oiry and Chouilly chardonnay; 45+ year old vines; fermented in temperature-controlled stainless steel tanks; full malolactic fermentation; aged 4 years on lees; 6g/L dosage

Jean-Paul Hébrart lists 2012 alongside 2008 and 1998 as his greatest vintages. He is privileged to grand sites atop Clos des Goisses, and the presence and depth of character tapped from his old vines is articulated emphatically in his Special Club. Pinot noir takes the lead in glossy red cherry and crunchy red apple fruit, building to black cherries and even blackberries in time, confidently supported by the juicy white peach and ripe pineapple of chardonnay from generous terroirs. It's spicy and characterful, hinting at candied orange rind, building into a generous and fleshy finish of buttery, silky succulence, beautifully toned by the salty minerality of pure chalk. In depth and character it captures the fragments on the edges of Clos des Goisses.

MARC HÉBRART RIVE GAUCHE RIVE DROITE EXTRA BRUT 2010 $$$$

95 points • **DISGORGED 2016** • **TASTED IN AUSTRALIA**

50% Oiry, Chouilly and Avize, 50% Aÿ pinot noir; fully fermented and aged in old 205-litre oak barrels; aged 4 years on lees; 5g/L dosage; cork

Fermented and matured entirely in small, old barrels makes this an anomaly in the Hébrart style, yet upholding the DNA of the house and its grand cru terroirs. It has hardly moved in the two years since I last tasted this disgorgement. This is a spicy and characterful cuvée of pale-straw hue that accurately accomplishes its aspiration of expressing the two sides of the river, by confidently uniting the red berry fruit and fig depth of Aÿ pinot noir, the white peach definition of ripe northern Côte des Blancs chardonnay, and the spicy, toasty, coffee bean complexity of well-handled old barrel fermentation. Oak is sensitively handled, making more of a contribution in creamy, seamless texture than in flavour or colour. The result has body, power and flesh, tempered by fine phenolic grip, well-integrated acidity and invisible dosage on a long finish.

MARC HÉBRART COTEAUX CHAMPENOIS BLANC NV $$$

92 points • **BOTTLED 3 MAY 2018** • **TASTED IN AUSTRALIA**

100% chardonnay; vinified and aged for 18 months in barrel; no malolactic fermentation; cork; 1169 bottles

A beautiful and pure Coteaux Champenois blanc that seamlessly unites pristine white peach and lemon fruit with the vanilla of high-class French oak. Full malic acidity is rare in Coteaux and makes for a tense acid line, yet is held confidently, thanks to impeccably ripe and poised fruit concentration rising on the palate to meet its towering heights of acidity. It's commanding, classy and will be profoundly long-lived.

Mareuil-sur-Aÿ, summer 2011

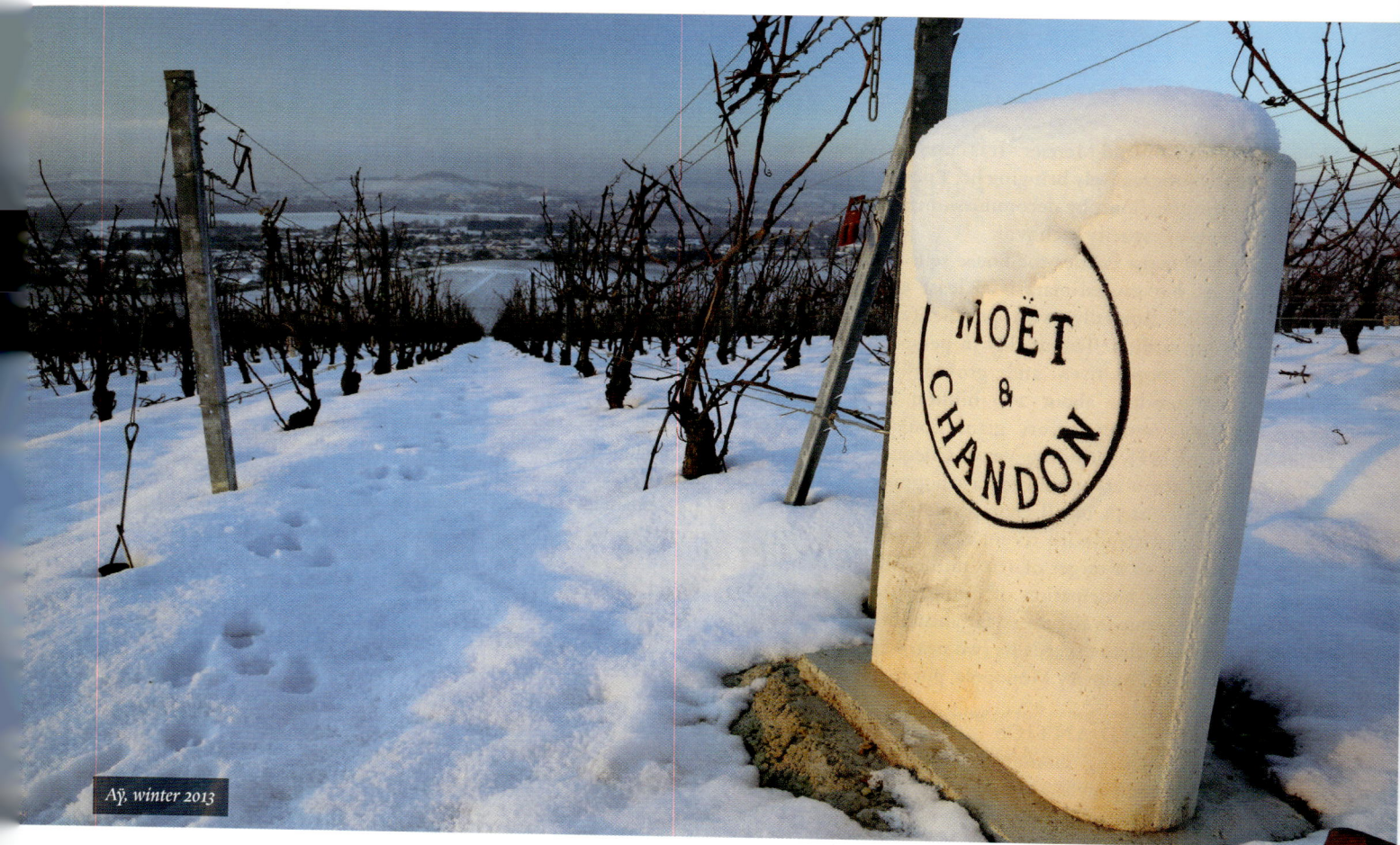

Aÿ, winter 2013

weather. Grower wines are very good, and I have friends among many of them, but by nature the quality of champagne is uneven. The more grapes you can access, the more you can be consistent.'

It's a principle that appears to have worked for Moët in recent years. At more than 20 million bottles every year, its Brut Impérial is the biggest blend in Champagne, and currently as fresh as I've seen it. 'This is a wine that is always evolving, because the climate, the technology, the market, the consumers and the world have changed,' Gouez explains.

Of course, quality does not automatically come with quantity, and his team has embraced innovation and worked hard to refine the style. 'We have worked on the preparation of our ferments to provide the right level of oxygenation so they don't get too stressed,' Gouez says. 'This reduces the reductive flavours, allowing room for expression of the precision and cleanliness of the fruit.' Lower dosage has also been a refreshing trend in recent years, and more refined than ever in his current cuvées. 'Lower dosage allows us to be more precise at every stage, in everything we do,' he points out. 'In the past, we were known for higher dosage, but today Brut Impérial is no more than 9g/L and sometimes as low as 7g/L, one of the lowest among the *grandes marques*. When I started at Moët 20 years ago, it was 14g/L and now we have halved, without losing fruitiness or appeal.' This comes in response to both riper fruit and a changing consumer palate, seeking elegance and purity. 'We will continue to evolve,' he says. 'It's perpetual, and we need to continually revisit our style and our values.'

The Moët ambition is a fruit-driven style of freshness, brightness and purity. He prizes the ripeness and phenolic maturity of warmer vintages over acid definition, not a philosophy I subscribe to, but nonetheless a valid house style. 'Eighteen years ago, when I started here, phenolic bitterness was "no way!", but now I think that this is the next thing for us,' he reveals. He considers it something of a quest to build structure with bitterness and not just acidity. 'Since we are looking for fruitiness and roundness, we tend to harvest our grapes at a higher level of ripeness, so sometimes the acidity might be lower. We are looking for structure through phenolic bitterness rather than acidity.

'We want our champagnes to taste of the grapes they're made of,' he says, pointing out that 90% of winemaking is simply getting the grapes and the pressing right. He tries not to do too much in the winery. To this end, the winemaking is purposely reductive, vigorously minimising oxidation and religiously avoiding oak. 'The size and diversity of our vineyard sources is the key to consistency,' he says.

Richard Geoffroy, who oversaw Moët's production until his retirement in 2019, named tightening up consistency and improving viticulture as the two key focus areas for the future of the house. Complexity is built through fermentation using yeasts produced in its own lab. All Moët & Chandon cuvées are blends of the three champagne varieties, and all undergo malolactic fermentation.

Moët has introduced DIAM closures and three other brands of 'technological' micro-agglomerate corks across its full range in 2019, after first beginning with its vintage cuvées from the 2004 vintage, so as to send the message that this is a quality initiative. 'These technological corks are more consistent not only in avoiding cork taint, but in other characteristics also,' he observes. All corks are batch tested 200 at a time, and rejected if more than 2.5% defects or 1% critical defects are detected. Gouez maintains that it's impossible to ask for zero defects for fear of rejecting everything (though Louis Roederer successfully maintains zero tolerance). He is currently trialling Amorim's new NDtech sparkling cork on a sample of a few thousand bottles, which he will assess for cork taint and oxidation every six months over three years before making a decision.

Moët has long published disgorgement dates on the back labels of its vintage cuvées, and in a groundbreaking new initiative, the biggest blend in Champagne will now declare its disgorgement date. Every bottle of Brut Impérial now boasts the numerical date laser etched into the neck of the bottle. For instance, 31072017 denotes 31 July 2017. You'll just need to peel back the neck foil to see it.

These are rounded, commercial champagnes, but recent efforts have certainly refined the style in spite of the monumental scale of production. The phenolic maturity of the Moët house style is not my favourite in Champagne, but the more I get to know Gouez and Geoffroy and their philosophies, and the more I see behind the curtain of this incredible operation, the more profound respect I have for their attention to detail while producing tens of millions of bottles. The philosophy, the technology and the execution are, quite simply, unprecedented on this scale anywhere on earth.

'Whatever we do at Moët, we like to do it big and bold, to share Moët with the world!' Gouez rejoices. That they do.

MOËT & CHANDON BRUT IMPÉRIAL NV $$

88 points • TASTED IN AUSTRALIA
88 points • 2014 BASE VINTAGE • DISGORGED JULY 2017 • TASTED IN CHAMPAGNE

20-30% chardonnay, 30-40% pinot, 30-40% meunier; first blend of the year 50-55% reserves, third blend 30-35%, mostly from the previous year; a blend of more than 100 different wines; aged 24 months on lees; 7-9g/L dosage; cork

At well over 20 million bottles, and rising steeply, this one wine accounts for more than 7% of Champagne's production. To put this in perspective, the vines that supply this label alone would cover an area close to 2000 rugby fields! The blend represents the proportions of the three varieties across the appellation, with pinot noir sourced roughly half from the Marne and half from the Aube. 'Brut Impérial represents the grape supply from the region,' Gouez explains. 'The goal is to use as many wines as possible in the blend. The more you blend, the more harmony you can create – this is the basis of the consistency of Brut Impérial.' The oceanic scale of this blend of everything from everywhere makes a single blend impossible, dictating three quite different blends every year. Gouez and his team blend from December until June. The aim is to use young and fruity reserves of two vintages to build consistency by contributing any elements missing from the latest harvest. On average, the proportion of reserve wines in this blend is much higher than in the past (another reason for Moët's recent huge investment in storage capacity), particularly in the challenging vintages of recent years, as much as 55% in the first blend of the year, though fruitiness remains the goal, not maturity. There is thus no recipe, with a different dosage from 7g/L to no more than 9g/L, and a different liqueur for every batch and every disgorgement. 'I call this tailor-made winemaking,' says Gouez. 'We have to adapt and be flexible. How can a house of this size be flexible? For me, craftsmanship is not about being small, but about having an ambition to focus on every detail.'

The mind-boggling scale and complexity of composition of Brut Impérial makes its improvement in recent years all the more admirable, and it's as lively and fresh as ever. Red apple, lemon and grapefruit zest are underlined by the biscuity, spicy complexity of a couple of years of lees age. The dusty hazelnut and coffee bite of phenolic bitterness that defines the style lends some firmness and astringency, melding with tangy, fresh, lemon-accented acidity and ever lower, nicely balanced dosage. A good Brut Impérial and an impressive result for this scale of production.

MOËT & CHANDON ROSÉ IMPÉRIAL NV $$

87 points • TASTED IN AUSTRALIA
89 points • 2014 BASE VINTAGE • DISGORGED 9 JANUARY 2017 • TASTED IN CHAMPAGNE

10-20% chardonnay, 40-50% pinot, 30-40% meunier; 20% red wine, half pinot, half meunier; 7-9g/L dosage; DIAM

Moët has a very long history with champagne rosé, evidenced by a letter of order from Napoléon Bonaparte dated 1801. Today, rosé represents a phenomenal 20% of total sales, which Gouez has grown from just 3% when he commenced in 1998, prompting the 2014 opening of a new facility in the Aube to double red wine production capacity. Prior to this time, red wine was largely meunier from the Marne; now it's half pinot from the Aube. Rosé Impérial is intentionally in the same style as Brut Impérial, though crafted from a unique blend. To create intensity of colour and lightness on the palate, Moët is unique in Champagne in employing a Beaujolais technique of heating and macerating meunier at 70°C for a couple of hours to extract colour and flavour without tannins. In a groundbreaking initiative, the press has now been completely replaced with a horizontal centrifuge to produce a more rounded style of intense colour and aroma without phenolic grip. Short macerations produce red wines of lighter colour, which explains a large dose of 20–25% red wine, though recent improvements in both the maturity of the grapes in warm seasons like 2018, and advances in methods of extraction, bring it as low as 12% in future releases.

A full salmon crimson hue heralds a generous and bold rosé, led by the red apple, strawberry, gentle macerated red berry fruits and pink pepper accents of pinot noir, with a subtle sense of savoury tomato, concluding with a bitter grapefruit-pith feel. Drying tannin texture, phenolic grip and firmness make for a grainy and structured finish. Low dosage heightens the tang of fine acidity, upholding bright strawberry fruit line. One bottle was atypical, particularly dusty and dry, with an astringent palate stripped of fruit presence, concluding callow and truncated.

MOËT & CHANDON GRAND VINTAGE EXTRA BRUT 2012 $$$

91 points • DISGORGED FEBRUARY 2018 • TASTED IN CHAMPAGNE

41% chardonnay, 33% pinot noir, 26% meunier; aged 5 years on lees; 5g/L dosage; DIAM

Vintage production is just 1% of the house, making this cuvée significantly less than 300,000 bottles. Gouez replaced 'Moët & Chandon Vintage' with 'Vintage by Moët & Chandon', and labels of bold vintage declaration since the release of the 2002, to focus more on the style of the season than the house. He is looking for four things in a vintage: sufficient maturity of at least 9.5 degrees potential, no rot, ageing potential from either acidity or phenolic structure, and finally character – something special, not simply the stamp of the season. 'The idea is not to follow a recipe, but to listen to the wines and create a vintage with uniqueness and charisma,' he says. The blend and the selection of parcels change to reflect the character of the season, looking for those that are most interesting and original. 'We start from scratch. I choose the grapes from anywhere I want, and I don't care if it's meunier or if it isn't grand cru.' The maturation has also evolved, with Grand Vintage previously released after five years on lees and now after seven, allowing the dosage to be lowered to just 5g/L since. Disgorgement date, dosage and blend are clearly displayed on the back label – impressive detail for a house of this magnitude.

'The challenge of blending the low-yielding and uneven 2012 vintage was to keep the balance between sugar and acidity,' explains Gouez, who describes the vintage as a synthesis of the high sugar of 2009 (up to 10.5 potential alcohol), and high acidity of 2008 (consistently above 7.2g/L). With clean fruit and no rot, he used a higher than usual proportion of meunier in his vintage blend. 'It is challenging to make good meunier, and when we have it, I like to use it!' This vintage saw a shorter time on lees of just five years (2008 and 2009 were both seven years) because no 2010 or 2011 were released – the first time since the 1960s that the house hasn't released two consecutive vintages.

This is a cuvée that captures and harmoniously unites the ripeness and the vibrancy of the great 2012 season, rising to the challenge of the vintage in moving 'seamlessly from the initial generosity to a seamless flow of final tension'. Grapefruit and apple are accented with a coffee bean complexity that lends a biscuity dryness and grapefruit-pith bitterness to the finish. The tangy, bright acidity of the season bursts through, defining a vibrant finish of accurate acid line and good persistence, promising potential for the coming decade.

MOËT & CHANDON GRAND VINTAGE EXTRA BRUT 2009 $$$

90 points • DISGORGED JANUARY AND OCTOBER 2017 • TASTED IN AUSTRALIA

36% chardonnay, 50% pinot noir, 14% meunier; the highest proportion of pinot since 1996; aged 7 years on lees; 5g/L dosage; labelled Extra Brut for the first time, even though it has been extra brut since 2002; DIAM

Benoît Gouez favours 2009 to 2008, which always surprised me, but in tasting this cuvée, I understand for the first time. Holding a particularly vibrant, medium straw hue for this generous vintage at a decade of age, this is a crunchy 2009 of nashi and beurre bosc pears and fennel, underscored by the tang of grapefruit and lime. The reductive style of the house lends an attractive note of grilled bread to the biscuity, toasty, roast almond notes of seven years on lees. Its low dosage integrates neatly with vibrant acid, marked by the dusty, dry, bitter phenolic grip of a hot and dry summer, so much so that it's evident even on the bouquet, in notes of green coffee bean and mocha. It holds impressive acid line on the finish for this warm vintage, maintaining fruit presence and persistence, promising to hold its own for the short term. Its low dosage lends gentle, honeyed notes, more than adequate for the fruit sweetness of this season.

MOËT & CHANDON GRAND VINTAGE ROSÉ EXTRA BRUT 2012 $$$

88 points • DISGORGED FEBRUARY 2018 • TASTED IN CHAMPAGNE AND AUSTRALIA

35% chardonnay, 42% pinot, 23% meunier; 13% pinot noir red wine; aged 5-7 years on lees; 5g/L dosage; DIAM

Moët harvests red wine for its vintage rosé from its best estate pinot plots of low-yielding old vines in Mareuil-sur-Aÿ, Bouzy and most of all Aÿ, green harvested to reduce yields when necessary. Twice the necessary vineyard area is prepared, to permit choice of the grapes with the best phenolic maturity to provide structure. Red wine is macerated for 5–7 days to draw out ripe, soft character, without hard tannins. The proportion of red wine has halved in just eight years, from 27% in 2004 to 20% in 2008, 19% in 2009 and ultimately just 13% here. In 2018 it might even be less than 9%. By contrast to the thermal vinification and centrifuge used for the non-vintage rosé, this is traditional red wine vinification for depth of flavour, presence and endurance-building structure.

A full crimson hue heralds a savoury rosé true to the reductive house style. Tamarillo savouriness contrasts red apple, red berry, beurre bosc pear and subtle strawberry fruit, which carry the bright lemon tang of the vibrant 2012 season. A dry finish accents the dry grip of tannin structure and phenolic bitterness, making for a callow and short close.

MOËT & CHANDON GRAND VINTAGE ROSÉ EXTRA BRUT 2009 $$$

88 points • DISGORGED FEBRUARY 2017 • TASTED IN AUSTRALIA

30% chardonnay, 59% pinot noir, 11% meunier; 19% pinot noir red wine; labelled Extra Brut for the first time, even though it has been extra brut since 2002; 5g/L dosage; DIAM

Boasting a powerful 19% of pinot noir red wine, there is no subtlety to the medium crimson-copper hue of this bold rosé. It's a savoury style of tomato, olive and even artichoke character, with the dry phenolic grip of the season heightened by firm, fine pinot noir tannins. Pinot noir takes a confident lead in the flavour spectrum, too, with gentle red berry fruits and spice loitering in the background, lingering with good length. Age has brought pronounced toasty complexity, true to the rapid evolution of this sunny season, heightened by the coffee and mocha notes of the Moët style. Acidity and dosage find harmonious balance on the finish.

MOËT & CHANDON GRAND VINTAGE COLLECTION 2002 $$$$

92 points • DISGORGED JANUARY 2017 • TASTED IN CHAMPAGNE

51% chardonnay, 26% pinot noir, 23% meunier; aged 14 years on lees; 5g/L dosage

Benoît Gouez believes '15 years of age is a sweet spot for Moët', and hence he's holding back substantial volumes for his Collection release (and even more than Veuve Clicquot's significant Cave Privée program). 'I love 2002,' he says. 'It is perfect.'

I first tasted Grand Vintage 2002 on release in 2011 after seven years on lees, and it is testimony to the endurance of this vintage that after twice as long in the cellar, my notes today are almost identical, and my score unchanged. A glowing medium yellow hue, youthful lemon and preserved lemon are still here, amidst grapefruit, peach and fennel that contrast the ripeness and tension of this great season. Lees age has built seamlessness, while a bitter grapefruit-zest bite on the finish upholds definition, if a little firmness.

MOËT & CHANDON MCIII BRUT 001.14 $$$$$

95 points • 2003 BASE VINTAGE • DISGORGED JULY 2014 • TASTED IN CHAMPAGNE EN MAGNUM

37.5% 2003 (50% chardonnay and 50% pinot noir); 37.5% three vintages, 2002, 2000 and 1999, vinified in stainless steel tanks and aged for 5-7 months in 50hL oak foudres; 25% three vintages of Moët Grand Vintage Collection disgorged from the cellar, 1999, 1998 and 1993; '001.14' on the front label denotes the first batch, disgorged in 2014; 5g/L dosage; just a few thousand bottles in the first release; 1000 magnums produced

Moët's prestige cuvée was in creation for 15 years, first trialled in 2000, a blend of wines spanning 10 years, aged in three different 'universes', then matured on lees for a further 10 years. The focus is on 'ripe, rich, solid vintage years' (hence a choice of 2003 for the first release, with 2006 coming next; Gouez showed me an embargoed pre-release and it's another step up), and base wines of 'richness, intensity and weight'. He says he doesn't understand the idea that acidity is a key in the ageing of champagne. 'The warmer vintages age well, as the wines are based more on phenolic structure than on acidity. We need the warm-vintage phenolic bitterness of pinot noir to sustain this blend.'

When I first tasted MCIII in 2015, I wrote that I had every suspicion it would only get better with another five years post-disgorgement. That day has come, and the definition and energy it has upheld in magnum is nothing short of stunning. For one of the most complex recipes in all of champagne, spanning all dimensions of production, maturation and age, its complexity is predictably multidimensional, yet wonderfully vibrant. Now a full yellow-gold hue, the crunch of citrus zest is evenly harmonised with the ripe succulence and complexity of stone fruits, the exotics of glacé pineapple and spice, and the brioche, mocha and ginger cake of long age. The structure upholds the dry phenolic grip of the ripe 2003 vintage, yet fine-grained and tense, polished by the creamy effect of deep maturity. Excellent acid line drives a finish of outstanding persistence.

Moët's Montaigu Lodge, Chouilly

Moutard Père et Fils

(Moo-tahr Pear e Feess)

6 Rue des Ponts BP1 10110 Buxeuil

www.champagne-moutard.fr

CHAMPAGNE

M

MOUTARD

PÈRE & FILS

The Moutard-Diligent family have been vignerons in the little village of Buxeuil just outside Troyes in the Côte des Bar since 1642, and have made their own champagne since 1927. The domaine encompasses 23 hectares of vines, planted largely to pinot noir (14 hectares) and chardonnay (6 hectares), with one hectare each of the rare arbane and petit meslier, and half a hectare each of pinot blanc and meunier. Estate holdings provide for 40% of an annual production of 750,000 bottles, over a diverse portfolio spanning 19 cuvées, supplemented with sourcing from a further 60 hectares of vineyards. Vineyards are ploughed, and only natural fertlisers are employed. Cold settling is used to settle the coarse lees prior to fermentation and ageing, mostly in small and large Burgundian barrels. Use of sulphites as perservatives is minimised. The family also produces Rosé des Riceys, Chablis and Burgundy. Its champagnes are largely inexpensive and rustic in character. Disgorgement dates are printed discretely on back labels.

Moutard Père et Fils Grande Cuvée Brut NV $

85 points • 2015 base vintage • **Tasted in Australia**

100% Côte des Bar pinot noir, predominantly Buxeuil, Polisy and Polisot; no oak; 25% reserves; aged 3 years on lees; full malolactic fermentation; 10g/L dosage; DIAM

A blanc de noirs, though not labelled as such, and it needn't be, because this is a pale and neutral style. Astringent and firm, with coarse palate texture and a truncated finish, it lacks character, harmony, appeal and grace.

Moutard Père et Fils Rosé Prestige Brut NV $

83 points • 2014 base vintage • **Tasted in Australia**

30% Buxeuil chardonnay, 55% Buxeuil pinot noir, 15% Buxeuil rouge; no oak; 60% reserves; aged 4–5 years on lees; full malolactic fermentation; 10g/L dosage; cork

As heavily regulated as Champagne is, there are no criteria or accountability surrounding the designation of 'prestige'. This is an astringent style of volatile acidity, vinegar and balsamic character that render the finish austere, countered by a generous dollop of candied dosage, which serves to lend a sweet and sour sensation. Prestige?

Moutard Père et Fils Cépage Arbane 2012 $$$$

89 points • **Tasted in Australia**

100% Buxeuil arbane, planted in 1966; vinified in oak barrels; 7g/L dosage; 1500 bottles

While small by comparison with its plantings of pinot and chardonnay, Moutard's arbane, petit meslier and pinot blanc vineyards are both substantial and mature by modern Champagne standards, making these traditional varieties a key focus for the family. Its arbane brings varietal spice and exoticism in custard apple, honeydew, dried fig and honey. It's a creamy and soft style of barrel-fermentation texture that well tones the grapefruit-pith bite of the variety. Barrel fermentation lends notes of charcuterie.

Verzy, summer 2018

Mouzon-Leroux

(Moo-zoh Leh-roh)

16 Rue Basse des Carrières 51380 Verzy

www.champagne-mouzon-leroux.com

Champagne
MOUZON LEROUX
& FILS

B iodynamic practices are labour intensive to uphold in the vagaries of Champagne's climate at the best of times, all the more so spread across 50 separate plots spanning 7.5 hectares of vineyards. The Mouzon family has been growing vines since 1776 and bottling its own champagnes since 1930, sourced mostly from the revered grand cru of Verzy on the north-eastern edge of the Montagne de Reims. Vines have been farmed organically since 1997 and biodynamically since 2008, with certification achieved in 2011. The youngest vines are tended with a horse to minimise soil compaction, and plants and flowers are encouraged in the mid-rows. Today, Pascale, Philippe and Sébastien Mouzon achieve the impressive feat of vinifying all 50 plots separately. Their natural approach continues in the winery, where every cuvée is wild fermented before ageing for around six months on lees in vats or barrels, with no fining or filtration, disgorged with low dosage. One of the lowest levels of sulphur dioxide in champagne (and one cuvée with none at all) dictates completion of malolactic fermentation. Mouzon-Leroux has in the past been an exemplar of the fine signature of Verzy. However, the natural pendulum has swung too far, and its latest releases have regrettably begun to lose touch with their terroirs and their fruit purity, as the artefact of barrel fermentation begins to dominate, and the repercussions of a low-sulphur regime impact freshness and integrity. Back labels are particularly informative in declaring the villages, blend, base vintage, disgorgement date and dosage.

Mouzon-Leroux L'Atavique Tradition Verzy Grand Cru NV $$

89 points • 2013 base vintage • Disgorged January 2017 • Tasted in Australia

35% chardonnay, 65% pinot noir; 100% Verzy; 20% 2012 and 2011 reserves; wild fermented, 75% in stainless steel vats, 25% in barrels and demi-muids; full malolactic fermentation; aged 30–40 months on lees; low sulphur; 3g/L dosage; 31,193 bottles

A crunchy young blend of exact red apple fruit that sings with the elegance of north-east-facing pinot noir in Verzy. Barrel fermentation heightens its dryness and lends a little oak tannin grip, which exaggerates its phenolic firmness. It finishes youthful, crunchy and firm. With low sulphur, it loses a little in the perfume and lift that blessed the 2012 base.

Mouzon-Leroux L'Ascendant Verzy Grand Cru Solera NV $$$

89 points • 2013 base vintage • Disgorged January 2017 • Tasted in Australia

40% chardonnay, 60% pinot noir; 100% Verzy; 50% reserve solera of l'Atavique base 2012, 2011 and 2010; fully wild fermented and aged 6 months in barrels and demi-muids; full malolactic fermentation; low sulphur; aged around 3 years on lees; 3g/L dosage; 5900 bottles

The savoury complexity and subtle charcuterie notes of barrel fermentation in concert with a low-sulphur regime make for a dry and savoury style. It's creamy and firm, with a sherry-like volatility and bruised apple oxidative dryness to the finish, heightened by a generous proportion of reserve solera. A firm and oxidised style.

Verzenay, winter 2013

MUMM

(Moom)

29 RUE DU CHAMPS DE MARS 51199 REIMS
www.mumm.com

An annual production of 8.5 million bottles ranks Mumm number four by volume in Champagne after Moët, Clicquot and Feuillatte. Despite a turbulent history of acquisitions over the past century, Mumm has retained almost 218 hectares of vines, mostly planted to pinot noir, meeting 25% of its needs. The house has come a long way since my first visit during the snowfalls of Christmas 2001, recovering from its dark days of the 1980s and 1990s under ownership by Seagram, then then largest alcoholic beverage producer in the world, due in part to the appointment of the 31-year-old Dominique Demarville as chef de cave in 1998 and his 35-year-old successor, Didier Mariotti, in 2006. Mumm now enjoys a higher percentage of chardonnay in its 'Cordon Rouge' house blend, as well as more reserve wine, longer maturation times and lower dosages. And there is more at hand.

'The end of the Seagram era in the 1990s marked the beginning of the decline of Mumm, due to a strong quest for financial profitability, without taking into account the quality of the wines,' Mariotti reveals. 'The quality of Cordon Rouge was so bad, because of insufficient and mismanagement of reserve wines, reduced ageing in the cellar to the legal minimum, and several inconsistent blends in the same year.'

In 1995, Mumm launched a 12-year plan to resurrect Cordon Rouge, encompassing harvesting, pressing and vinification, with a focus on building reserve wines since the late 1990s, but it was not until Pernod Ricard purchased the company in 2005 that sufficient funds were injected to fully realise this vision.

A gleaming new winery was constructed in Reims in 2008 and extended in 2010 to house row after row of sparkling new stainless steel tanks, new disgorgement and bottling lines, and space for greater stocks of reserve wines. 'With a new winery and smaller vats we are able to home in on the terroir more accurately by producing smaller parcels for the blends,' Mariotti explains. New press centres were constructed in Mailly-Champagne and Verzy in 2010 to address concerns with fruit waiting for up to 10 hours to be pressed. Grapes can now be moved just a few kilometres between press houses to avoid these delays.

Cordon Rouge is moving from 20% to an impressive 30–35% reserve wines, spanning six vintages, which Mariotti upholds as crucial for maintaining the consistency of the blend. It spends a minimum two and a half years on lees in the cellar. Mariotti has worked to lower the dosage from 10g/L to 8g/L. 'I am very proud of this dosage, one of the lowest of any of the houses,' he claims. Every other Mumm cuvée is just 6g/L.

Mumm completes its blending schedule earlier than most houses. When I visited in early January 2019, I tasted a sample of the 2018 blend, ready to be blended the following week.

Most other houses were only beginning to taste their *vins clairs* at the time.

The magnitude of Mumm's new winery is sufficient that all 5–8 million bottles of Cordon Rouge are now the same blend each year, a remarkable feat of logistical engineering. An identical blend is made once a week for 15–20 weeks. An extra 30% is produced, and kept in tank as the reserve for the following year.

Enthusiastic about raising quality, Didier Mariotti brings acute attention to detail to every part of the process, from vineyard to market. He spends 70% of his time during harvest visiting growers, building relationships, seeing the quality of the fruit and gaining insight into the vintage. Mumm's 218 hectares of estate vineyards are enviably located, including 39 hectares in Ambonnay, 26 in Avenay-Val-d'Or, 23 in Mailly, 21 in each of Verzenay and Verzy, 20 in Cramant, 14 in each of Bouzy and Aÿ, 13 in Vaudemange, 10 in Avize and three in Dizy.

Mariotti is equally attentive to the other end of the process, tasting every wine from each warehouse in most export markets every six months, and checking the disgorgement date of cuvées in every restaurant he visits. He binned a couple of pallets of Rosé NV from the warehouse in Australia some years ago and reserved some de Cramant 2006 for internal use only because they were too old.

'It is important to be sure that the quality is maintained at every step,' he emphasises. 'You can work hard on the blend, ageing and disgorgement, but if you don't focus on the supply chain you can destroy everything.' Mumm now prints bottling and disgorgement dates on the back labels of its RSRV range, as Mariotti believes it is always best to disclose the disgorgement date.

In a region where change comes slowly, Mariotti is eager to embrace innovation, even appointing a new winemaker dedicated to this purpose, with a focus on testing stoppers, lightstruck damage, matching champagne glasses to particular cuvées, as well as driving all manner of experiments in the winery.

'If you are not trialling, you are not moving,' he declares. 'Global warming, the markets and other things are changing, so we need to be asking questions about winemaking all the time.' This philosophy has inspired small trials of bâtonnage, malolactic fermentation, barrel ageing of liqueurs, even barrels of different coopers and varying levels of toast. All Mumm cuvées traditionally undergo full malolactic fermentation, though parcels with no malolactic are trialled each vintage. 'We need to be prepared for global warming,' Mariotti reveals, 'but so far our only response has been to harvest earlier.' RSRV Blanc de Blancs now includes components in which malolactic fermentation has been blocked, as much as 30% in the very mature 2018 vintage.

Mariotti has a vision to bring more structure and complexity to non-vintage cuvées, by increasing ageing on lees, facilitated by maintaining 25 million bottles maturing at any time, and through greater proportions of reserve wines. 'With five years of wines in reserve I'm able to think about which reserves I use for each blend,' he explains. Barrel ageing with bâtonnage may in future be the third step, though he admits that 'in some of our experimentation with barrels, the results have been very, very bad! But it's good for the kids to play!'

Mumm has gradually increased its use of DIAM closures to 60% of production, including all of its RSRV range, and some Grand Cordon and Vintage cuvées. Mariotti is convinced of DIAM's superiority. 'If we can guarantee no more cork problems, I don't know why we are waiting!' he exclaims.

'It takes a long time to turn things around in Champagne!' he adds. This is especially true in a house the size of Mumm. Its non-vintage cuvées are on a slow ascent, with hope for further gains in years to come.

Mumm's evolution continues. In 2016, the house launched new bottles, classy new labels and a change of branding from G.H. Mumm to Maison Mumm, though the G.H. Mumm branding still lingers on all cuvées besides its RSRV range and Cuvée Lalou.

Mumm has evolved its branding to introduce its RSRV range, sporting bold, modern labels. Confusingly, RSRV means 'reserve', but not in the traditional sense of reserves for non-vintage blends (there are three vintage wines in the range), but rather to pay tribute to the tradition of the house to keep some wine aside to hand deliver to friends. Its de Cramant cuvée is now RSRV Blanc de Blancs, Blanc de Noirs de Verzenay is now RSRV Blanc de Noirs (both vintage cuvées), Brut Selection is RSRV 4.5, and a non-vintage RSRV Rosé has been introduced. Cuvée Lalou is also currently transitioning to join the RSRV range.

After all its quality initiatives of recent decades, I can't help but wonder if the house today isn't investing more energy in its branding, marketing and discounting to build market share than it is in improving Cordon Rouge. Pernod Ricard's most recent annual report devotes a page to Usain Bolt's association with Mumm, and mentions the new Cordon Rouge red sash bottle, but says nothing of the wines. In 2018, it launched Grand Cordon Stellar, a champagne bottle designed for drinking in space. But does this vital and substantial brand still have its feet on the ground?

Shortly after harvest 2018, Didier Mariotti sent me a note to announce, 'It's with a lot of sadness that I wanted to inform you that I have left Mumm... This is not a voluntary departure... Today Mumm has decided that I had to leave the house.' He did not elaborate, but rumour has it there was disagreement with the company surrounding his aspiration to raise quality through increased lees age. Eleven months on, he has not yet been replaced.

Of course, it would never be long before a chef de cave as capable as Mariotti was snapped up, and in July 2019 it was announced that he would replace Dominique Demarville as chef de cave of Veuve Clicquot. It is a noble path indeed from Mumm to Clicquot!

Mumm Grand Cordon Brut NV $$

87 points • 2014 base vintage • Tasted in Champagne

At least 45% pinot noir, mostly from the Montagne de Reims and Côte des Bar; roughly 30% chardonnay, mostly from the Côte de Blancs, Montagne de Reims and Sézannais; roughly 25% meunier, mostly from the Grande Vallée de la Marne and Vallée de l'Ardre; 0-5% tailles; 30-35% reserves spanning six vintages, including 30% of the previous year's blend kept as reserve; 8g/L dosage; 5-8 million bottles

In the past, Cordon Rouge has represented more than 85% of Mumm's production, but the house recently suggested that it is only 60%, which would seem unlikely. This places it somewhere between five and eight million bottles annually. Wherever it falls, Cordon Rouge is a massive blend of between 300 and 450 tanks from more than 100 villages.

The aspiration for Cordon Rouge is a fruity and round style. It was in its heyday in the 2008 and 2009 base vintages around five years ago, and has since dipped slightly, excusable in the tough 2010 and 2011 seasons, rallying a little in 2012, but I expected more in 2014, after everything that has been poured into its production over the past decade. This is a cuvée that contrasts the rounded, toasty caramel effect of full dosage with the firm, dry grip of phenolic structure. It presents red apple fruit and bready autolytic complexity, finishing firm and sweet. Its coarse phenolics prompted me to enquire as to the inclusion of tailles in the blend, and the response was just zero to five percent, to balance its fruity roundedness.

Mumm Le Rosé Brut NV $$

87 points • Tasted in Champagne

15% chardonnay, 60% pinot noir, 25% meunier; 15% pinot and meunier red wine from 4-7 crus; 6g/L dosage

Mumm Le Rosé is based on 60% of its Grand Cordon blend, around which different crus are added to create balance according to the season. The blend of red wine is adapted each year to maintain consistent colour and typically comprises a blend of between four and seven wines from the Aube, Montagne de Reims and meunier from the Vallée de L'Ardre.

Mumm sets out to add an accent of fresh red fruits to its Grand Cordon blend, with a generous dose of 15% red wine infusing a medium salmon crimson hue. It's an elegant celebration of red berry fruits, strawberry hull, red apple and watermelon, though the phenolic grip of its base conspires with the tannin structure of its red wines in a firm structure of coarse grip, concluding short and hard.

Mumm Brut Millésimé 2012 $$$

90 points • Tasted in Champagne and Australia

28% chardonnay from Oger, Avize and Cramant, 72% pinot from Mailly-Champagne, Bouzy, Ambonnay and Verzenay; aged 6 years on lees; full malolactic fermentation; new bottle to celebrate its 60th vintage; 6g/L dosage; DIAM

Mumm only produces its vintage cuvée in the best years, and hence did not release 2011. It describes 2012 as an elegant season, with good potential to age. With a medium straw hue, this is a cuvée of bitter crab apple, grapefruit and pear skin, in an astringent and coarse style of bitter phenolic grip. Six years on lees has coaxed out buttery, brioche notes which serve to tone its firm edges. It holds good persistence, nicely integrated dosage and bright, vibrant lemon-focused acidity, energised by pronounced salt minerality. It concludes dry and structured and will benefit from age to soften.

MUMM RSRV BLANC DE BLANCS BRUT GRAND CRU 2013 $$$$

93 points • DISGORGED MARCH 2018 • TASTED IN CHAMPAGNE

100% Cramant chardonnay; 4.5 atmospheres of pressure; 90% malolactic fermentation; aged 4 years on lees; 6g/L dosage

RSRV Blanc de Blancs replaces de Cramant. In philosophy, pedigree and fruit resources, this cuvée is an altogether different tier in the world of Mumm, and it has long been their only cuvée that I buy. It's great to now see Mariotti's initiative in introducing other RSRVs of similar calibre and philosophy. De Cramant was always one variety (chardonnay), one village (Cramant) and one vintage, though never labelled as a vintage (which made managing collections tricky – it always needed more age). It's now aged four years on lees (de Cramant was always 2.5–3 years) and it's great to see it now sporting its vintage, and a front label proclaiming '100% chardonnay du Village de Cramant', though ironic and confusing that it took RSRV (reserve) labelling for it to finally declare its vintage – and of course the implication that it has no reserves! As a relatively young release, it's bottled at 4.5 atmospheres of pressure rather than the usual 6, to soften the impression of acidity. To maintain consistency, Mumm plays with selection of plots, yeasts, fermentation temperature (some plots are fermented at 12°C rather than 18°C, to enhance exotic fruit aromas), addition of lees, blocking of malolactic fermentation and even micro-oxygenation in some tanks to build developed maturity of butter and vanilla character. Bâtonnage is utilised to enhance creaminess.

The hero here is the chalk minerality of Cramant – fine, lingering and churning with frothy waves of sea salt. It's a deeply textured and complex style that delivers all the mouthfeel and character that its plethora of winemaking and blending techniques promise. These serve to downplay zestiness and aromatics, instead building a leesy style that hints at lactic goats cheese, enhancing its almond meal complexity and emphasising its minerality. Heightened, dry, salty texture melds seamlessly with tangy grapefruit acidity on a long and linear finish.

MUMM RSRV CUVÉE 4.5 BRUT NV $$$

94 points • 2010 BASE VINTAGE • DISGORGED SEPTEMBER 2016 • TASTED IN CHAMPAGNE

30-40% chardonnay from Cramant and Avize, 60-70% pinot nir from Bouzy, Aÿ and Verzenay; 20% reserves from 2009 and 2006; 5% aged in oak barrels for creaminess and texture; aged 4 years on lees; 6g/L dosage

An impressive brand-new blend for Mumm, oddly named 4.5, the four in reference to the number of years on lees and the five to the number of crus. The recipe is built on that of Mumm's Brut Selection Grand Cru (a cuvée that I have never seen), uniting five grand crus in which the house is privileged to historic parcels of estate vineyards.

A splendid testimony to five of the finest grand crus of all, this is a characterful blend that taps deep into the structure of great historic vineyards. Already boasting a full straw hue, it melds the crunch of grapefruit zest, red apple and beurre bosc pear with hints of wild strawberry and spice. Rounded fruit body is supported by fine structure, well-integrated acidity and creamy texture enhanced with a subtle touch of barrel maturation. Salty minerality rises and froths with prominent structure, marking out a long finish of excellent line and integrity.

Mumm RSRV Blanc de Noirs Brut Grand Cru 2009 $$$$

88 points • Disgorged November 2017 • Tasted in Champagne

100% Verzenay pinot noir; Village de Verzenay; aged 7.5 years on lees; full malolactic fermentation; disgorgement dates on back labels of all RSRV cuvées

RSRV Blanc de Noirs replaced Blanc de Noirs de Verzenay, and now declares its vintage, and a front label proclaiming '100% Pinot Noir du Village de Verzenay'. My favourite village of the northern Montagne de Reims has been a historic stronghold of the house, privileged to great vineyard resources and ownership of the Moulin de Verzenay itself, the most famous icon perched proudly and distinctively among the vines. I have consequently always held high expectations for this cuvée, which it has sadly always failed to meet. A full straw hue with a yellow tint, this is a dry and tense style of muted fruit expression, notes of crab apple and beurre bosc pear. Bready, yeasty characters dominate, more pronounced than its fruit, making for a dry style that lacks brightness, presence and persistence.

Mumm RSRV Rosé Foujita Brut NV $$$$

90 points • 2012 base vintage • Disgorged July 2016 • Tasted in Champagne

30% chardonnay from Cramant and Avize, 70% pinot noir from Bouzy, Aÿ and Verzenay; a similar base to RSRV 4.5, with 15% red wine from Ambonnay; 20% reserves from 2010, 2009 and 2006; dosage liqueur aged in oak barrels; 6g/L dosage

Named in tribute to René Lalou's godson, Japanese painter Léonard Foujita, who built and decorated the Foujita chapel in the grounds of the house, Mumm's new rosé is a bold style of full crimson hue. It boasts deep complexity of well-mannered redcurrant, cumquat, quince and tamarillo. Gentle presence is interrupted by firmly structured, jarring tannins and phenolic grip, making for a dry finish of coarse structure. The deep salt minerality of distinguished crus and the lingering, tangy acid line of the great 2012 harvest are sadly overpowered by domineering tannins.

Mumm Cuvée Lalou Vintage 2006 $$$$$

91 points • Disgorged September 2017 • Tasted in Champagne

50% chardonnay, 50% pinot noir; Bouzy, Ambonnay, Verzy, Verzenay, Cramant, Avize, Aÿ; dosage liqueur aged in new oak barrels; 6g/L dosage

Lalou was the prestige wine of the house from 1969 to 1985, but the bottle cast and recipe were lost in the wild ride of ownership changes, and revived by Demarville in 1998. It's always an equal blend of chardonnay and pinot, but only at the point of blending is the decision made of which 12 potential parcels of estate grand cru vineyards will win the golden ticket (as few as two, if the vintage is deemed worthy at all). The 2006 is a blend of just seven villages. A liqueur of Cramant and Bouzy is aged 9–10 months in new oak barrels, including some acacia barrels, to lend vanilla notes and build sufficiently to meet the power of the wine.

Lalou is unashamedly fashioned as a strong wine, and consequently shows at its best in the most elegant and energetic seasons. The warm and generous 2006 harvest has produced a rich and luscious Lalou of full straw-yellow hue. It's already advanced to a place of prominent secondary character, brimming with roast chestnuts, bitter almond, rich dried apricot, tart grapefruit and dry crab apple. True to the proportions and structural grip of its powerful season, it concludes with the bite of phenolic bitterness, its long finish a little dried out on the close.

NICOLAS FEUILLATTE

(Ni-khoh-lah Fer-yat)

CD 40A PLUMECOQ 51530 CHOUILLY
www.feuillatte.com

CHAMPAGNE

Nicolas Feuillatte

EPERNAY - NEW YORK - AILLEURS

'Centre Vinicole–Champagne Nicolas Feuillatte' is Champagne's oldest and largest coopérative, and Nicolas Feuillatte is its key brand. The gargantuan operation comprises a collective of 82 coopératives, with more than 5000 growers (and rising) tending more than 2100 hectares of vines covering 7% of Champagne's surface, spanning more than 300 villages, though only 182 crus form the selection pool for Nicolas Feuillatte. Production facilities span a full 12 hectares of high-tech buildings, with a capacity of 33.5 million litres — so large that they act as a second production and storage site for Moët & Chandon. Extensions were added in 2007 and 2012 to facilitate growing production. Fermentation occurs entirely in temperature-controlled stainless steel vats, and state-of-the-art robotic printing and dressing lines can process 9000 bottles per hour. Once focused on producing champagnes for its growers and other houses, today the key priority has shifted to 60–70% of production for Nicolas Feuillatte. In 2017 it produced 19 million bottles and sold 10.3 million, making the brand Champagne's third largest and the best selling in France. At any time, 90 million bottles of Nicolas Feuillatte are ageing here, with a capacity of 100 million. It's a primary, fruity style, with dosage now evenly balanced most of the time.

Most coopératives in Champagne were based in the Vallée de la Marne and the Aube when Nicolas Feuillatte was established in 1972, and to this day these areas remain the focus of the sourcing of the house. This explains its reliance on a high proportion of meunier (45%), and lesser amounts of pinot noir (35%) and chardonnay (25%). This is slowly changing (from 50% meunier a few years ago), as the region moves away from meunier towards chardonnay. In 2007 chardonnay overtook meunier as the most planted variety in the Marne.

Palmes d'Or is the prestige brand of the house.

NICOLAS FEUILLATTE RÉSERVE EXCLUSIVE BRUT NV $$

87 points • TASTED IN AUSTRALIA

20% chardonnay, 40% pinot noir, 40% meunier; aged 3-4 years on lees; cork

A clean and fresh style that presents vibrant fruit of lemon and lime tang and red apple crunch, backed with the biscuity complexity and subtle toastiness of lees age. The firm grip of raw acidity and subtle phenolic bitterness create bite and tension, which jostle with boiled-sweets dosage typical of this cuvée to produce a sweet and sour effect on the finish.

NICOLAS FEUILLATTE RÉSERVE EXCLUSIVE ROSÉ NV $$

89 points • Tasted in Australia

10% chardonnay, 45% pinot noir, 45% meunier; 16% red wine; aged 2–3 years on lees; cork

There's no mistaking that this is rosé, with a generous 16% red wine furnishing a full, vibrant crimson hue. The Nicolas Feuillatte team have performed an admirable job in tannin and phenolic management for such proportions, creating a firm, fine apple skin-like grip of seamless and even graceful appeal. It meets its mandate of being as fruity as possible, in fresh raspberry, spicy strawberry and red apple flavours of sweet fruit appeal, with a subtle tamarillo and pink pepper nuance contributing savoury complexity. Sweet dosage is well deployed to keep things approachable.

NICOLAS FEUILLATTE PALMES D'OR BRUT VINTAGE 2006 $$$$

89 points • Tasted in Australia

50% chardonnay from Chouilly, Cramant, Oger, Le Mesnil-sur-Oger, Avize and Montgueux (7%); 50% pinot noir from Bouzy, Verzy, Verzenay, Aÿ and Ambonnay; cork

Now a couple of years into its release, its reductive opening of struck flint and grilled bread has evolved to funky, composty hydrogen sulphide notes that quickly dissipate on the bouquet, yet dig in firm on the finish. Behind this, the fast-developing personality of the 2006 vintage is displayed in a toasty, shortbread, secondary style of spice, now evolving to an assertive walnut bitterness. The integrity it displayed on the finish two years ago has been left in the cellar, and its phenolic bitterness has now overwhelmed the vibrant acidity and fine chalk minerality of some of Champagne's most revered grand crus. A vintage that has sadly passed its prime.

Chouilly and Avize, harvest 2014

NICOLAS MAILLART

(Ni-khoh-lah My-yah)

6/10

5 RUE DE VILLERS AUX NOEUDS 51500 ÉCUEIL
www.champagne-maillart.fr

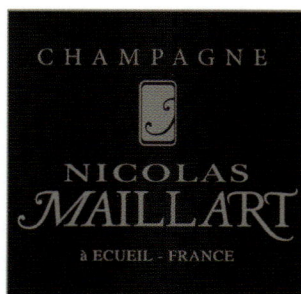

The blessing of holdings and contracts purposefully assembled over generations to strategically build an ideal blend is an opportunity afforded only to the most privileged in Champagne. The vagaries of succession and inheritance more often dictate a haphazard collection of disparate and diverse crus. Uniting such an estate seamlessly and coherently calls for special talent indeed, and in this the young Nicolas Maillart is particularly gifted. In his home premier cru of Écueil on the Petite Montagne de Reims, he inherited three hectares from his father, but more significantly from his mother, eight hectares eight kilometres away in the premier cru of Villers-Allerand, and four in the glorious grand cru of Bouzy, 25 kilometres on the other side of the Montagne. His adaptable intuition as a winemaker makes him a master of uniting 55 plots spanning these three distinct terroirs with the creaminess of fine-tuned barrel fermentation and the gentle tension of ripe malic acidity.

Returning to his family estate in 2003, Nicolas Maillart is the ninth generation of his family to grow grapes in Écueil and its surrounding villages since 1753, and perhaps much longer, having found a document in the abbey in neighbouring Chamery referring to an ancestor growing grapes in 1533. His grandfather made wine a century ago, and his father sold still wine in barrel in Reims.

Maillart crafts an annual production of 130,000 bottles from well-established vineyards planted mostly on the mid-slopes of his three villages. Pinot noir is the hero of the Montagne de Reims, making up the lion's share of 75% of his plantings, supplemented with chardonnay mostly in Écueil, a little meunier largely in Villers-Allerand and a tiny amount of petit meslier, which he considers interesting for acidity in increasingly warmer seasons.

While he produces single-vineyard cuvées of 100% meunier from Villers-Allerand, 100% chardonnay from Écueil and 100%

pinots from both Bouzy and Écueil, his non-vintage cuvées represent blends of pinot and chardonnay from across all three villages, and his core vintage cuvée is a blend of Bouzy and Écueil.

He deploys pinot noir from the sandy soils of Écueil to build bright aromatics and crispness, Villers-Allerand on clay soils for structure and endurance in his reserve wines, and the mighty, south-facing slopes of Bouzy for power.

Maillart's most important village of Villers-Allerand neighbours Rilly-la-Montagne, and although it boasts almost the same area of vineyards, this is a cru that keeps a lower profile, with no growers in the village bottling their own cuvées, for reasons Nicolas and his parents cannot ascertain. He finds pinot from the village to be monotone, lacking in aromatics, but meunier stands alone more confidently, thanks to its fruitiness. He bottles meunier from a single site of a substantial 1.8 hectares. 'Meunier

has a bad reputation because it's been traditionally planted in lesser sites where chardonnay and pinot noir can't ripen,' he suggests, 'but planted in the best sites it can be a great wine.'

The ownership of Maillart's vineyards is shared with his cousins by means of a family company, of which he is a shareholder. On paper, this classes him as a négociant-manipulant, since he purchases grapes. 'But I am like a grower,' he says, 'because I take care of all of the vines.'

He farms using organic methods as well as biodynamic soil fertility sprays, upholding ploughing as important. While he is certified High Environmental Value and Sustainable, he does not aspire to full organic certification. 'If it were just me, I would be organic, but I don't want to expose my other shareholders in the family to the risk,' he clarifies, adding that he is considering pursuing organics in some of his vineyards.

His sustainable approach extends beyond the vines, recycling water in the winery and installing 130 square metres of solar panels in 2009 to provide 90% of his electricity.

Maillart's aspiration is to capture the essence of his grapes and where they come from. 'For me as a grower, I want to create something unique, an expression of my terroir,' he explains. 'I am really focused on harvesting at the right time, maybe a little later than others. This gives a fruitiness and creaminess without sacrificing freshness.'

Texture is enhanced through wild fermentation and maturation for six months in Burgundy barrels, which he has progressively increased to 50% of his harvest (the balance in temperature-controlled stainless steel vats). Parcels are allocated to tanks or barrels according to the source of the grapes. 'I am looking for gentle oxidation rather than oakiness from my barrels,' he says. 'The barrels open the wine and make it more approachable.' He also selectively matures reserve wines in barrels to increase complexity.

Malolactic fermentation is not encouraged, so it generally does not progress in most ferments, though a low sulphur dioxide regime means that many of his reserves naturally go through malolactic.

Maillart is a master in creating texture that unites fine-tuned barrel fermentation creaminess and silkiness with the gentle tension of ripe malic acidity — no easy balance, and yet one that he has nailed in every one of his cuvées this year. His barrels bring texture and seamlessness without any oakiness. His is an intuitive winemaking approach, significantly adapting blends, vinification and finely tweaked dosage (never more than 6g/L) according to every harvest. Such dexterity makes for wines that reflect his acute attention to detail. 'I experiment every harvest and change the details,' he explains. 'Every detail is important and I try to really respect each terroir.'

He experimented with zero sulphur in some ferments in the 2018 harvest, and the *vins clairs* he showed me in January 2019 were holding admirable freshness. He's not yet certain whether these will be released as a new cuvée, but for him such experimentation is 'more about understanding my wines better and making tweaks to the details in how they are made'.

To this end, he is also trialling tiraging under cork rather than crown seals, but it will be some years yet before he draws any conclusions. Maillart's cuvées are generally aged 3.5 years on lees, and he holds a considerable stock of 500,000 bottles in order to facilitate annual sales of 130,000.

His talents extend beyond grape growing and winemaking, and he recently designed elegant new labels to adorn his new releases. Informative back labels declare the blend, crus, vinification, disgorgement date and base vintage. His website presents detailed technical sheets on every cuvée.

Nicolas Maillart exemplifies the harmonious marriage that can be achieved between diverse terroirs in Champagne, with a concerted attention to every detail in the vineyards and production. 'I try to make wine for pleasure — wines that are easy to drink,' he sums up.

NICOLAS MAILLART PLATINE PREMIER CRU NV $$

92 points • 2014 BASE VINTAGE • 16% CHARDONNAY, 78% PINOT NOIR, 6% MEUNIER • 35% RESERVES • 40% WILD FERMENTED AND AGED 6 MONTHS IN YOUNG BARRELS • DISGORGED APRIL 2018 • 6G/L DOSAGE • TASTED IN CHAMPAGNE

92 points • 2011 BASE VINTAGE • 45% CHARDONNAY, 55% PINOT • 25% RESERVES FROM 2007-2010 • 29% WILD FERMENTED AND AGED 6 MONTHS IN YOUNG BARRELS • DISGORGED JULY 2017 • 1G/L DOSAGE • 13,452 BOTTLES • TASTED IN AUSTRALIA

Villers-Allerand, Écueil and Bouzy; no malolactic fermentation

Nicolas Maillart refers to Platine as his 'classical non-vintage' in which he is seeking 'balance between freshness, fruitiness and aromatics, not too sweet but easy drinking, not too complicated or sharp'. The harmony of his craft is exemplified from his very first cuvée, a beautiful pinot-led style of full straw hue that captures red cherry, strawberry and red apple fruits of freshness and elegance, accented with the citrus of chardonnay, and gently massaged by the subtle brioche character of lees age. Laced with subtle spice, barrel work is very sensitively managed, a credit to his skill. It finishes long and graceful with salty minerality and nicely integrated, ripe malic acidity keeping even tension. A master blender, he upheld the integrity of his entry cuvée even in the harrowing 2011 harvest, and with less reserves than usual, by tactically side-stepping meunier.

Bouzy, harvest 2014

NICOLAS MAILLART ROSÉ GRAND CRU NV $$

94 points • 2014 BASE VINTAGE • DISGORGED APRIL 2018 • TASTED IN CHAMPAGNE

35% chardonnay, 65% pinot noir; 100% Bouzy; saignée of pinot noir on skins for 52 hours, plus 7% pinot noir red wine; 25% reserves; 50% fermented and aged 6 months in young barrels; no malolactic fermentation; 6g/L dosage; 15,077 bottles

Nicolas Maillart designs his rosé to be 'delicate and gentle as an apéritif', not 'too tannic or winey'. He devotes a plot in Bouzy to red wine and blends this with a maceration saignée and other plots in the village as required, including chardonnay. 'We have chalk under just a couple of feet of soil in Bouzy, and the chardonnay vines really capture the minerality,' he reveals. His focus is to harvest at the right time for this cuvée, perhaps a little later than others, to provide 'fruitiness and creaminess without sacrificing freshness'.

A spectacular contrast of the presence and tension of Bouzy, this is a rose built around crunchy red fruits, white cherries, pomegranates and raspberries, even a hint of redcurrant. It meets its brief of elegant freshness with aplomb. Fine tannins meet pronounced salt minerality from Bouzy chardonnay, and malic acidity upholds brightness while never asserting itself. A wine of excellent texture, at once creamy and crunchy, projecting with outstanding line, enduring length and effortless seamlessness.

NICOLAS MAILLART EXTRA BRUT PREMIER CRU NV $$

92 points • 2013 BASE VINTAGE • DISGORGED MAY 2018 • TASTED IN CHAMPAGNE

50% chardonnay, 50% pinot noir; Villers-Allerand, Bouzy and Écueil; 60% fermented and aged 6 months in young barrels; no malolactic fermentation; 3g/L dosage

'I am looking for maturation in all of my parcels, and those I choose for Extra Brut have good maturity and freshness without the need to add sugar for balance,' explains Nicolas Maillart. He thus chooses a different selection of parcels each vintage, which means the volume changes each year, and in years like 2017 when he doesn't have the maturity in the fruit, he doesn't make it at all.

With a focus on riper fruit in this blend, the style is exotic and characterful, even tropical in its exuberant fruitiness. There are notes of passionfruit, star fruit and grapefruit, yet in no way blowsy, held taut thanks to beautifully gauged and refreshing malic acidity that guides the finish very long and straight. In the Maillart style, barrels bring texture and seamlessness without in any way appearing oaky. A purposely composed Extra Brut, and a good one.

NICOLAS MAILLART MONT MARTIN PREMIER CRU 2015 $$

90 points • DISGORGED DECEMBER 2018 • TASTED IN CHAMPAGNE

100% Villers-Allerand meunier; single vineyard of 1.8ha planted 1972; 100% vinified and aged 6 months in oak barrels; no malolactic fermentation; zero dosage; 3750 bottles

Classic meunier, exploding with crunchy redcurrants, raspberries, strawberries and spice. The warm 2015 season contributes some ripe tannin grip, which lends coarseness to the finish. Tasted just a month after disgorgement, it showed some dusty, dry astringency in its stark, young state, and will benefit from time to soften and harmonise.

NICOLAS MAILLART PREMIER CRU 2012 $$$

94 points • DISGORGED SEPTEMBER 2017 • TASTED IN CHAMPAGNE

45% chardonnay, mostly from Écueil, 55% pinot noir, mostly from Bouzy; 60% wild fermented and aged 6 months in barrels; no malolactic fermentation; 4g/L dosage; 15,912 bottles

Admirably, Nicolas Maillart only makes his vintage cuvée in top seasons, and 2012 followed 2002 and 2008, with 2015 yet to come and potentially 2018. For him, 2012 was a season that contrasts great maturity with great freshness. He has composed an even and harmonious assemblage of the gentle strawberry and red cherry fruit of pinot noir, the apple and grapefruit of chardonnay, and the gentle brioche and subtle vanilla-custard complexity of barrel fermentation and lees age. In signature Maillart style, it's at once creamy and crunchy, thanks to carefully fine-tuned barrel fermentation in the presence of ripe malic acidity. Subtle spice lingers very long in this beautifully enticing style.

NICOLAS MAILLART CHAILLOTS GILLIS ECUEIL PREMIER CRU 2012 $$$

93 points • DISGORGED JULY 2018 • TASTED IN CHAMPAGNE

100% Écueil chardonnay; two parcels, Les Chaillots and Les Gillis, planted 1963 on mid-slope clay soils; fully wild fermented and aged 6 months in young barrels; no malolactic fermentation; zero dosage here, but can be 1-3g/L in other vintages; 3648 bottles

A complex and characterful cuvée that welds the power of ripe and exuberant chardonnay with the flavours and textures of barrel fermentation. The combination makes for a succulent, creamy and soft style, layered with white peach, custard apple, crème brûlée, baked fig, even toffee. It carries very long and finishes with even harmony, the gentle tension of ripe malic acidity melding seamlessly with enticing fruit, and no need for dosage whatsoever (an extremely rare achievement).

Écueil, summer 2014

NICOLAS MAILLART FRANC DE PIED ECUEIL PREMIER CRU 2012 $$$$

93 points • DISGORGED MAY 2017 AND MARCH 2018 • TASTED IN CHAMPAGNE AND AUSTRALIA

100% Écueil pinot noir; one of Nicolas' most prized sites, a single plot of ungrafted vines planted by his father in 1973; wild fermented and aged 6 months in young oak barrels with bâtonnage; no malolactic fermentation; zero dosage; 3651 bottles

Evidence of the heights to which the premier cru of Écueil is capable of attaining, Maillart's aspiration for fruit ripeness makes for a blanc de noirs of expression, character and power more often found in a grand cru than an elegant, north-facing premier cru. A medium to full straw-yellow hue with a blush tint, this is a blanc de noirs of wonderful fruit presence of red and black cherries, figs, even mulberries and blackberries. Wild fermentation in young oak barrels has drawn out spicy complexity, while blocking malolactic has upheld freshness and brightness without undue tension. A long finish unravels magnificently with layers of black fruits and spice, entwined seamlessly with fine tannin structure, subtle minerality and seamless malic acidity. Testimony to its generosity and ripeness, it has absolutely no need for dosage. Achieving such balance without sugar or malolactic fermentation is no simple task, and this cuvée exemplifies the skill and spirit of Nicolas Maillart.

NICOLAS MAILLART JOLIVETTES BOUZY GRAND CRU 2015 $$$$

95 points • DISGORGED DECEMBER 2018 • TASTED IN CHAMPAGNE

100% Bouzy pinot noir; from a single site of just 0.6 hectares, planted in 1987 on the mid-slope in the heart of the village; fully fermented and aged 8 months in oak barrels; no malolactic fermentation; 1g/L dosage

Nicolas Maillart has created some of the finest expressions I have tasted of his villages of Écueil and Villers-Allerand, yet it is in Bouzy that he crafted his greatest achievement. The heart of this legendary grand cru has been well defined in all of its characterful presence by the focused style of Maillart, with freshness, crunch and tension. This is no easy feat in a season of generous ripeness in the most powerful cru in all of Champagne. More red berries than black, it's laced with mixed spice that lingers with excellent persistence. Chalk minerality infuses texture and freshness, while ripe malic acidity drives a refreshing and elongated finish. A dosage of 1g/L is indicative of an acute attention to detail — most would simply revert to zero, but even 1g/L makes a difference. A terrific take on one of Champagne's greatest crus.

PALMER & CO

(Pal-mair e Co)

5/10

67 RUE JACQUART 51100 REIMS
www.champagne-palmer.fr

CHAMPAGNE

Palmer & Co

Reims-based coopérative Palmer & Co is on an impressive growth curve, now boasting 320 member growers spread across some 40 villages and 415 hectares of vineyards, almost half of which are classified as grand or premier crus. Production under the brand has recently expanded to close to 800,000 bottles, though this still represents less than 20% of the capacity of its vineyards. Half of its annual pressing is locked into long-term contracts with houses, and 500,000 bottles are sold back to its growers, leaving the equivalent of about 850,000 bottles of supply flexible for it to manage vintage by vintage. The standard of the current releases suggests that the coopérative is diligent in reserving the finest for Palmer & Co. These are eloquently refined cuvées that capture the bright, radiant purity of chardonnay.

Palmer & Co is privileged to source from 220 hectares in the Montagne de Reims, in an arc that runs from Rilly-la-Montagne to Ambonnay, rising to a grand crescendo in the north-east corner of Mailly-Champagne, Verzenay, Villers-Marmery and Trépail, where it sources more than any other house.

'We love the chardonnay from these regions and it is very important in our signature, bringing fitness and elegance to the style of Palmer,' says managing director and oenologist, Rémi Vervier.

Chardonnay comprises a high 50% of sourcing, and it is the generous concentration and bright structure of these villages that define the house style (supplemented with a little chardonnay from Barbonne in the Sézanne), bolstered with 40% pinot noir and 10% meunier, sourced mostly from the villages of the northern Montagne de Reims (and a little from Les Riceys in the Aube).

'The villages of the eastern Montagne de Reims produce chardonnay of less richness and more citrus definition than the Côte des Blancs,' explains Vervier. 'Trépail is more mineral in style, and Villers-Marmery more fruity and more elegant.'

This produces *vins clairs* that he describes as 'very strong and sharp', which require long ageing for balance. 'Time is a crucial ingredient in the winemaking process for us,' he emphasises. 'We are lucky to have the opportunity to take the time to mature our wines.' Cuvées are aged for a minimum of three years, and more often four or five. 'Brut Réserve is not ready when we taste it at two or three years, lacking finesse and elegance,' he reveals.

The house keeps three deep soleras to bring further balance and complexity to its racy chardonnay-led style. Solera components are vinified in old oak barrels (by contrast to fermentation in stainless steel tanks for the base blends of the house). A 25–30-year-old solera of Trépail chardonnay is used as the *liqueur d'expédition* (dosage) across all cuvées. A younger solera of pinot noir dating back 10 years forms a reserve for its Blanc

Trépail, summer 2014

de Noirs, while the oldest solera of the house is of pinot noir red wine for Rosé Réserve. 'It's at least 38 years old, but we don't have records prior to that!' Vervier discloses. It might just rank as the oldest solera in the region.

He is unusual in Champagne as a managing director who is also a member of the winemaking team. 'This is very important, as the spirit and philosophy of Palmer is that everything is dedicated to and focused on the wine,' he says.

Sustainability is a key emphasis for the company, which is currently working with its growers to assist them on the path towards sustainability, with 70% on board to date. The house credits this for its success even in the high-rot year of 2017, and with active vigilance in the vineyards and stringent sorting in the winery, it reports ultimately rejecting only one tank to be sent off for distillation.

Palmer's relationship with its growers is attracting others who wish to work with the same philosophy, and the house is progressively expanding its grower base by 5–10 hectares annually.

Its sustainable focus extends to its facilities, and in mid-2018 it opened a substantial new €11 million facility on the outskirts of Reims in Bezannes, with capacity to store more than 2.1 million litres of reserve wines. Certified High Environmental Quality, its sustainability encompasses gravity flow, water recycling and energy efficiency in controlling lighting, temperature and humidity.

Palmer was established from the outset with a different mandate to other coopératives. Created in 1947, its seven founding growers were already producing their own champagnes, with their own press centres in their own grand cru villages, so the coopérative was founded not to create common facilities, but to create a special blend. 'This is the total opposite of the goal of other coopératives, whose goal is generally to create facilities together,' Vervier suggests. 'For the first 20 years, if you wanted to enter the Palmer club, the condition was that you had to have your own press centre.'

PALMER & CO BRUT RÉSERVE NV $$

91 points • 2013 BASE VINTAGE • 50% CHARDONNAY, 40% PINOT NOIR, 10% MEUNIER • DISGORGED JUNE 2018 • TASTED IN AUSTRALIA
89 points • 2011 BASE VINTAGE • 55% CHARDONNAY, 30% PINOT NOIR, 15% MEUNIER • DISGORGED AUGUST 2017 • TASTED IN AUSTRALIA

Montagne de Reims, Côte de Sézanne, Vallée de la Marne, Aube; more than half the chardonnay is from Villers-Marmery and Trépail (hence 30% of the blend); 30-35% reserves, mostly from the year prior and two years prior; aged 4 years on lees; 8-9g/L dosage; cork

The bright, radiant purity of Palmer's chardonnay focus, in the eloquent refinement of the modern guise of this house, makes for a magnificent starting point in the confident and lively 2013 season. Pale, bright straw hue. A core of impressive definition and concentration of grapefruit, golden delicious apple and beurre bosc pear takes a confident lead, well supported by the toasted brioche, vanilla bean and almond nougat of four years lees age. It concludes with well-integrated dosage, good acid line and gentle phenolic bitterness. The 2011 base suffers a little from the underripeness of the season, with some green vegetal and coffee bean notes, concluding with coarse phenolic grip.

PALMER & CO BLANC DE BLANCS NV $$$

92 points • 2013 BASE VINTAGE • 80% TRÉPAIL AND VILLERS-MARMERY, 20% BARBONNE • DISGORGED JULY 2018 • 7.5G/L DOSAGE • TASTED IN AUSTRALIA

93 points • 100% 2012 • 85% TRÉPAIL AND VILLERS-MARMERY, 15% BARBONNE • DISGORGED JUNE 2017 • 7G/L DOSAGE • TASTED IN AUSTRALIA

100% chardonnay; aged 4 years on lees; cork

Palmer's Blanc de Blancs is a vintage cuvée but labelled non-vintage, 'because we want to achieve a consistent style every year', claims Rémi Vervier. This is attempted by adjusting the blend each vintage (with as much as 40% Barbonne), the dosage for each disgorgement, and by avoiding tricky seasons like 2011. This is all very well in theory, but of course every season is intrinsically unique, and to downplay this is to diminish something of its integrity. Aged four years on lees, its maturity should be something to celebrate and promote, not to disguise.

The chardonnay terroirs of the eastern Montagne de Reims possess an inherent juxtaposition between yellow-fruits approachability and eloquent restraint, and this is the theme of Palmer, captured here with character and tension. The bright and lively 2013 season furnishes a style of grapefruit tang, beurre bosc pear crunch and a note of crab apple bite. Four years on lees brings a creaminess to its crunchy structure, and flattering layers of vanilla custard and ginger. It culminates in a finish of salty minerality, well-integrated dosage and impressively harmonious line and length. The 2012 is a delightful Palmer that articulates the lily fragrance of Montagne de Reims chardonnay with the fine mineral oyster shell texture of Trépail that contrasts the exotic ripe pineapple and star fruit notes of Barbonne. A benchmark Palmer that eloquently showcases the aspiration of the house in capturing finesse and presence.

PALMER & CO BLANC DE NOIRS NV $$

91 points • 2013 BASE VINTAGE • DISGORGED APRIL 2018 • TASTED IN AUSTRALIA

91 points • 2012 BASE VINTAGE • DISGORGED JUNE 2017 • TASTED IN AUSTRALIA

50% pinot noir from Mailly-Champagne, Verzy, Verzenay, Rilly-la-Montagne, Ludes and Les Riceys, 50% meunier from Rilly-la-Montagne and Ludes; 30-40% reserve solera of pinot, more than half from Mailly-Champagne and Verzenay, dating back 10 years, fermented in old oak barrels and aged in tank; 6.5g/L dosage; cork

'The aim is Blanc de Noirs with finesse,' announces Rémi Vervier. 'We know we will always achieve body and fruitiness, so we select vats that are very, very fresh, to uphold the elegant style of Palmer.' Palmer's DNA is chardonnay, but its historic home on the northern slopes of the Montagne de Reims is the territory of pinot noir and meunier. An even blend of the two, this cuvée expresses the understated mood of this part of the world in a savoury style of strawberry hull, gingernut biscuit and red apple. It lacks aromatic lift, though the lively, bright morello cherry acidity of 2013 ensures a finish of poise and definition. The 2012 base delves to a deeper place of black cherry and black plum fruit, yet upholds the restrained freshness, definition and focus of Verzenay and Mailly, marked a little by a bitter phenolic bite on the finish.

Aÿ chardonnay, harvest 2014

PALMER & CO ROSÉ RÉSERVE NV $$$

91 points • 2014 BASE VINTAGE • DISGORGED JULY 2018 • TASTED IN AUSTRALIA
92 points • 2013 BASE VINTAGE • DISGORGED AUGUST 2017 • TASTED IN AUSTRALIA

45% chardonnay, 45% pinot noir, 10% meunier; Montagne de Reims, Côte de Sézanne, Vallée de la Marne, Aube; Brut Réserve plus 8% red wine solera dating from at least 38 years ago; aged 4 years on lees; 8g/L dosage; cork

'Every year we make red wine from pinot noir of Les Riceys, because we love the fruity pinot of this village!' exclaims Rémi Vervier. Fruit is picked at high maturity, sorted on a sorting table, gently handled with plunging in small vats and no pumping, and macerated for one week post-ferment, so as to extract maximum fruit and minimum tannin. It's aged in old oak barrels for eight months before it's used to refresh 20–25% of the red wine solera of more than 38 years of age. 'The idea of the solera is to achieve two different ranges of aromas, fresh red and black fruits from the young wines, and at the same time spicy notes like cinnamon and vanilla – aromas from the past,' he explains.

Palmer's old solera of pinot noir elevates the savoury complexity of its Brut Réserve, adding a spicy and charcuterie edge to blackberry and red apple fruit. True to the understated 2014 season, it's a restrained style of fine tannin structure, creamy bead, well-integrated dosage and bright acid vibrancy, boasting a pretty medium salmon hue. The 2013 base is supple and rounded, well balanced by finely handled tannin grip and the bright acidity of the northern Montagne de Reims, a characterful rosé that reflects a unique and complex recipe.

PALMER & CO VINTAGE 2012 $$$

94 points • DISGORGED NOVEMBER 2017 • TASTED IN AUSTRALIA

52% chardonnay from Trépail and Villers-Marmery, 48% pinot from Mailly, Verzy and Verzenay; 7g/L dosage; cork

The chardonnay of the eastern slopes of the Montagne de Reims in concert with the pinot noir of the north-eastern grand crus unite to compelling effect in the impressive 2012 season. Confident fruit concentration of grapefruit, golden delicious apple and strawberry hull is tensioned with the vibrant acidity of these cool slopes. More than four years on lees has made for a creamy texture and layers of vanilla bean, brioche and freshly churned butter. It concludes with fine, salty minerality and excellent line and length. A well-crafted cuvée that eloquently and consummately articulates the distinctiveness of its terroirs.

PALMER & CO VINTAGE 2009 $$$

94 points • DISGORGED JULY 2017 • TASTED IN AUSTRALIA

50% chardonnay from Trépail, 50% pinot noir from Mailly and Verzenay; 8g/L dosage

Palmer's mandate for its vintage cuvée is an expression of the Montagne and of the season. 'We are looking for freshness and body, structure and fitness, trying to join the two worlds of Trépail and Mailly,' Rémi Verviers enunciates. While 2009 was a warm vintage, 'thanks to the north-facing slopes of Mailly and Verzenay, we have been able to uphold a high level of acidity'.

The freshness of lemon drops and preserved lemon express the refreshing restraint of the northern slopes of the Montagne de Reims, triumphantly trouncing the heaviness of the season. The result is beautifully mineral, chalky, salty and fine, with wonderful focus of refined acidity and delightful line and length. Chardonnay assumes a strong and confident lead, articulating the elegant restraint of the house effortlessly, upholding excellent crunch, line and length with a linearity and focus unusual for the Montagne and remarkable for a season as warm as 2009.

PALMER & CO AMAZONE DE PALMER NV $$$$

94 points • 2006 BASE VINTAGE • DISGORGED NOVEMBER 2017 • TASTED IN AUSTRALIA

52% chardonnay from Trépail and Villers-Marmery, 48% pinot noir from Mailly, Verzy and Verzenay; roughly 30% 2006 with reserves equally from 2002, 2004 and 2005; aged 10 years on lees; 7.5g/L dosage; cork; 10,000 bottles

Amazone is a blend of reserve wine from four vintages. 'The idea is to show three things: the potential of the reserve wines, the selection of the terroir, and the blessing of time in the cellar,' explains Rémi Vervier. 'Every year when we taste each vat, if we find any that are particularly strong and powerful yet closed, we will keep them aside, and every five or six years we will create an Amazone blend.' It's always built around Mailly, Verzenay and Trépail, and aways roughly equal parts chardonnay and pinot. A portion of the total production of 10,000 bottles is to be disgorged and released each year for five years. It's disappointing that the vintages are not declared on the label, particularly for a cuvée of such age, created with a philosophy that it will naturally change as its vintages roll.

It's triumphant fanfare of the reverberating complexity and body of a deep set of reserve wines, with luscious richness amplified by the succulent generosity and subtle exoticism of the ripe 2006 harvest. The result is a deeply complex and exuberantly confident main-course style that unashamedly ripples with the blessing of a decade on lees in golden fruit cake, crème brûlée, vanilla, persimmon, honey, gingernut biscuits and fruit mince tarts. In the midst of such flamboyance, it holds its cool with consummate poise, thanks to the vibrant acid line and fine, glassy chalk minerality of the greatest crus of the north-eastern and eastern slopes of the Montagne de Reims. It concludes succulently enticing and effortlessly persistent. Classy.

PASCAL DOQUET

(Pas-khal Doh-khay)

(6/10)

44 Chemin du Moulin de la Censé Bizet 51130 Vertus
www.champagne-doquet.com

CHAMPAGNE

*T*he annual release letter Pascal Doquet sends to his customers from his cellar on the edge of Vertus reads more like that of a tiny boutique in Burgundy than a champagne producer. In it he recounts the stories of recent vintages, the tribulations of a rigorous organic regime in far-flung vineyards and the intricacies of 10 different cuvées, in their limited availability. Every detail of the philosophy and practice of this tiny estate translates into wines of effortless form and beguiling beauty, making this a mailing list to which every lover of blanc de blancs ought to subscribe.

Third-generation winemaker Pascal Doquet has been making champagne under his parents' label of Doquet Jeanmaire since 1982, and has led the estate since 1995. It was not until 2004 that he gained independent control and began marketing the brand under his own name, following acquisition of shares held by his sisters. This opened up the opportunity for Doquet to embark upon a daring organic regime to more accurately draw out the terroirs of each plot.

While he abandoned the use of herbicides as early as 2001, it was not until 2004 that he fully tuned in to sustainable viticulture, resolutely pursuing practices in harmony with nature and the planet, as he puts it. Full organic certification was granted in 2007. 'Respect of the soil is important,' he explains as he proudly shows photos of the health of his vines compared with neighbouring plots.

Today, Pascal is an increasingly vocal leader and exemplar for organics in the region, president of Champagne's organic body,

Association des Champagnes Biologiques, and elected as a board member of the Syndicat Général des Vignerons in 2018. 'It was significant for them to have an organic grower in this position!' he exclaims.

His is an intuitive approach, constantly experimenting and adapting his techniques and treatments to suit the site and the season. All plots are ploughed and herbicides have been completely eliminated since 2001, with spontaneous flora maintained in the mid-rows for a rich and complex biodiversity.

Doquet prepares his own organic composts and applies hardwood bark, grape marc and shredded prunings to encourage biological activity. He is exploring new alternatives to copper and sulphur sprays for protection against disease.

He admits that a meticulous organic approach is a constant challenge in Champagne's climate, and particularly tricky to manage in vineyards separated by 75 kilometres. His 8.66-hectare estate is solidly rooted in the Côte des Blancs, with 3.5 hectares

in Vertus, Bergères-lès-Vertus and Le Mont Aimé just south of Bergères, and a magnificent 1.7 hectares in Le Mesnil-sur-Oger. A further 3.5 hectares are located in he communes of Bassuet and Bassu in the region of Perthois in the Vitry to the east. Vines boast an impressive maturity of up to 77 years, with a weighted average of 37 years, very high for Champagne. Chardonnay rules across the estate, with just 5% pinot noir, and no meunier. Vintage cuvées are sourced exclusively from mid-slopes in the heart of his finest terroirs.

Doquet's goal is to harvest at full maturity of above 10.5 degrees potential, to avoid chaptalisation. 'Chaptalisation should be the exception in Champagne,' is his radical suggestion. Vine age and organics regulate his yield down to around 65hL/hectare, just two-thirds of the permitted appellation volume. This provides an annual production of 70,000 bottles, exclusively from estate vines.

Pascal Doquet makes wine by the philosophy of letting the vines and the wine tell him what to do, while forever experimenting and striving to improve. There are no strict rules and he varies his techniques in the cellar from year to year. Some wines go through malolactic fermentation, others do not. About one-third are fermented in oak, largely his vintage cuvées, and two-thirds in enamelled steel vats, which he says are less prone to developing reductive characters than stainless steel. He has also increased barrel fermentation in recent years, with several cuvées now progressing towards 100%. 'I am using some 600-litre puncheons with thick staves now, and I prefer this size for lower porosity and less oxidation,' he explains. He has recently introduced limestone

fermenters to hold freshness. The natural yeasts of each vineyard are used for fermentation, and wines spend 4–5 months on lees in vats, and 11 months in barrels with bâtonnage. Doquet has always used a low dosage, and it is now lower than ever. Every cuvée is extra brut, no higher than 5g/L, and usually around 3.5g/L. Concentrated grape must is used instead of sugar because it tastes closer to the natural sweetness of the grapes.

A massive stock of 350,000–450,000 bottles is held in large cellars cut into chalk to permit long ageing of typically 4–5 years, crucial for blanc de blancs that hold their youthful vigour with pristine clarity. Vintages are released only when they're ready. DIAM closures have been used for exports since 2007. Doquet likes the closure, but admits that it's not so popular in France. Back labels are informative, declaring disgorgement date, dosage, base vintage and percentages of reserves. 'It is important to me to have all the detail on the label, to explain that my champagne is a terroir wine,' he explains.

Pascal was joined in 2018 by his oldest son Noel and his partner Amandine. 'He is projecting some new energy into the estate, and we have decided to start a new activity as a négociant,' Pascal reveals. The two began sourcing organically certified grapes in 2018, including from a cousin in Vertus, and are currently constructing a new facility in Vertus to accommodate increased production.

The intuitive and sensitive approach of Pascal Doquet creates beautifully expressive and deeply terroir-driven wines. All but three non-vintage blends showcase individual villages, of which Le Mesnil-sur-Oger and Vertus are his jewels.

Le Mesnil-sur-Oger, winter 2019

Pascal Doquet Horizon Blanc de Blancs NV $$

90 points • 2015 base vintage • Disgorged 12 December 2017 • Tasted in Champagne

100% chardonnay; Vertus, Le Mont Aimé and Bassuet; 42% perpetual reserve since 2012; vinified in enamelled tanks; 5g/L dosage

Horizon now includes sourcing from Vertus and Le Mont Aimé to supplement the chalk and grey clay soils of Bassuet, 60 kilometres to the east on chalk soils in the Côte de Perthois in the Vitry. It's a young and edgy style of tight acid drive, contrasting tense citrus fruit with crunchy apple. Youthful and lively, it's acid driven and expressive, with assertive acidity which will benefit from time to mellow.

Pascal Doquet Anthocyanes Premier Cru Rosé NV $$

89 points • 2012 base vintage • Disgorged 13 December 2017 • Tasted in Champagne

66% chardonnay from Vertus, Bergères-lès-Vertus, Le Mesnil-sur-Oger and Mont Aimé, 34% pinot noir from Vertus and Bergères-lès-Vertus; co-fermented in a blended maceration; 20% 2012, 46% 2011, 34% 2010; 4.5g/L dosage

Pascal Doquet describes his rosé as 'not rosé de saignée, and not a blend, but a blended maceration rosé'. Entirely from Côte des Blancs fruit, he prefers rosé with chardonnay for its energy: 'A century ago, Vertus and Bergères-lès-Vertus were planted to 80% pinot, but close to Le Mesnil-sur-Oger the chardonnay was fetching a similar price to Le Mesnil, so the village has been replanted to 92% chardonnay today. But the clay in the soil in Vertus gives a higher potential for colour in the black grapes, making the village similar to Bouzy, Ambonnay and Aÿ, and very different to Le Mesnil.' He planted pinot noir in Vertus in 2006, which is now the most important component of this cuvée.

Doquet's rosé is unusual in both composition and method, not least in that its youngest vintage represents its smallest component. Vibrant Vertus pinot noir is structured with the dry apple-skin notes of the 2011 harvest. It leads out with vibrant wild strawberry and red cherry liqueur notes and contrasts these with a firm, dry finish of phenolic structure and firm grip.

Pascal Doquet Arpège Premier Cru Blanc de Blancs Brut Nature NV $$

94 points • 2014 base vintage • Disgorged 18 September 2018 • Tasted in Champagne

100% chardonnay; Vertus, Villeneuve and Mont Aimé; 27% 2014, 49% 2013, 24% 2012; zero dosage

The finest I have ever seen this cuvée, Arpège is an impressively assembled expression of the freshness of the southern Côte des Blancs captured with all of the precision and detail of Pascal Doquet. Bright in hue and restrained in style, it unites crunchy apples and pears with unadulterated tension, pristine purity, lingering persistence and profound, heightened, salty chalk minerality.

Pascal Doquet Arpège Premier Cru Blanc de Blancs Extra Brut NV

94 points • 2014 base vintage • Disgorged 18 September 2018 • Tasted in Champagne

As above, with 3.5g/L dosage

A profound expression of the effect of even a small addition of dosage, this is Arpège with enticing notes of honey and biscuit, and slightly softer salt mineral grip and acid tension on the finish. I love it equally in both guises.

PASCAL DOQUET DIAPASON GRAND CRU LE MESNIL SUR OGER NV $$

95 points • 2009 BASE VINTAGE • DISGORGED JANUARY 2018 • TASTED IN CHAMPAGNE

Le Mesnil-sur-Oger; 61% 2009, 39% 2008; 45% vinified in barrels; 3.5g/L dosage

Pascal Doquet's finest cuvées hail from his 1.7 magnificent hectares of superb plots in Le Mesnil-sur-Oger, a glorious expression of all the concentration and theatrics of what is arguably Champagne's most confident grand cru. Traditionally utilising just a small component of reserves, here he has tactically enlivened the glowing generosity of 2009 with the heightened acid cut of 2008, accurately capturing the assertive endurance of the village in this tensely poised blanc de blancs. It's judiciously toned by the toasty, spicy complexity and softening influence of barrel age, which has been strategically increased from 25–30% to 45% of the blend. The result is a cuvée of textured mouthfeel, characterful personality and mineral drive, in which the inimitable voice of Le Mesnil-sur-Oger's salt minerality echoes very long.

PASCAL DOQUET LE MONT AIMÉ PREMIER CRU COEUR DE TERROIR 2006 $$$

92 points • DISGORGED JULY 2017 • TASTED IN CHAMPAGNE

Mont Aimé; 64% vinified in tanks and 36% in barrels (it will be 100% in barrels from 2008); 3.5g/L dosage

In the extreme south of the Côte des Blancs in the commune of Coligny, Le Mont Aimé unites varied soils of sand and stone from an ancient river bed. Without the pure chalk of the crus to its north, its minerality is softer. Mont Aimé is an elegant terroir, maturing 8–9 days later than Vertus, and its restrained tension serves it well in the generous 2006 harvest. Apple and pear fruits unite with the spicy complexity of barrel fermentation, in a gentle style, accented with very fine dry extract, true to the warm 2006 harvest. It concludes with balance and harmonious persistence.

PASCAL DOQUET VERTUS PREMIER CRU COEUR DE TERROIR 2006 $$$

94 points • DISGORGED JULY 2017 • TASTED IN CHAMPAGNE

Vertus; 40% vinified in barrels with malolactic fermentation; 3.5g/L dosage

Vertus is the biggest and one of the most diverse villages in the Marne, and Doquet is astute in presenting his northern vineyards separately to those of the south. This cuvée rejoices in the strength, longevity and mineral structure of terroirs that clearly have more in common with nearby Le Mesnil-sur-Oger than they do with southern Vertus. This is particularly pertinent in the warm 2006 season, enlivening red apple and white peach fruit generosity with grapefruit crunch, underscored by the roast nut and mixed spice complexity of barrel fermentation. The salt minerality of Vertus lingers long, effortless and seamless.

PASCAL DOQUET LE MESNIL SUR OGER GRAND CRU COEUR DE TERROIR 2006 $$$$

93 points • DISGORGED DECEMBER 2017 • TASTED IN CHAMPAGNE

100% vinified in barrels for the first time; full malolactic fermentation; 3.5g/L dosage

Assembled in tiny volumes from four different lieux-dits — the thundering Chétillons, Champ d'Alouette, Finciart and Coullemets du Midi — this is a powerful take on Le Mesnil-sur-Oger. The richness of the ripe 2006 season in concert with full barrel fermentation builds deep layers of honey, spice and toast. Doquet progressed from 30% oak vinification in 2002 to 50% in 2004, which served to eloquently frame the thrilling poise of Le Mesnil-sur-Oger. A jump to 100% in 2006 is stark, not only in creamy texture and vanilla custard flavour, but also in hazelnut bitterness on the finish. The crystalline minerality and fruit purity of the village are left lurking somewhere between the trees.

PAUL BARA

(Pawl Bah-rah)

(7/10)

4 RUE YVONNET 51150 BOUZY
www.champagnepaulbara.com

CHAMPAGNE

Paul Bara

BOUZY
DEPUIS 1833

Paul Bara knew Bouzy history so well he wrote the book on it. Celebrating its 185th anniversary recently, the family estate has long been one of the top names in the village, boasting 11 magnificent hectares of low-yielding grand cru vineyards on 32 parcels in Bouzy, and one in neighbouring Ambonnay. Boasting 9.5 hectares of pinot noir and 1.5 hectares of chardonnay, an annual production of 100,000 bottles embodies the characterful grandeur of Bouzy pinot noir, energised by impeccable malic acidity.

The Bara estate boasts impressive vine age averaging 35–40 years, keeping yields in check and ripeness in balance. Vines are managed sustainably, with herbicides and insecticides avoided and cover crops planted in the mid-rows.

The exuberance of ripe fruit is well toned, with freshness and vibrancy preserved by fermenting in small enamelled and stainless steel tanks, with the single exception of a new cuvée fermented fully in barrels, in honour of the family's first ancestor in Bouzy, who made his living as a cooper.

Low dosages of 8g/L or less are used in all cuvées, and malolactic fermentation has been completely blocked since 1996. Malic acidity appreciates long periods to soften, hence NV cuvées rely on generous proportions of reserve wines and bottle ageing of almost three years; vintage wines at least five years.

Some 500,000 bottles reside in a climate-controlled warehouse behind the winery and 11 metres below the village in cellars dug by Paul Bara after World War II. The winery was renovated and extended in time for the 2015 harvest.

The fifth generation of his family to grow grapes in Bouzy, Paul was the first to sell champagne in the 1950s. His daughter Chantale began working with him in 1980 and took the lead in 1986. She retired in 2018, following the death of her father in 2015. Their legacy lives on in the hands of her sister, Evelyne Dauvergne, who took over management in 2018.

Paul Bara Bouzy Extra Brut NV $$

92 points • 2012 base vintage • Tasted in Champagne

20% chardonnay, 80% pinot noir; Bouzy; vines averaging 30 years of age; 3g/L dosage

The freshness and energy of malic acidity, crunchy red apple fruits of Bouzy pinot noir and subtle biscuity complexity of long age unite in a style of spicy complexity and harmonious balance. A little crab-apple grip provides definition to the finish, in harmony with salt minerality and fine-spun malic acidity.

Paul Bara Bouzy Réserve Brut NV $$

93 points • 2012 base vintage • Tasted in Champagne

As above, with 7g/L dosage

In these days of ever lower dosage, here's evidence that a little more sweetness can sometimes be a blessing, especially in the presence of malic acidity, even in a village as exuberant as Bouzy. A stark contrast to the Extra Brut, a little more dosage lends more lift to its red fruit core, and a more honeyed feel to its structure, lengthening the finish.

Paul Bara Bouzy Grand Rosé Brut NV $$

94 points • 2013 base vintage • Tasted in Champagne

20% chardonnay, 80% pinot noir; Bouzy; 12% Bouzy rouge vinified in stainless steel; 7g/L dosage

A beautiful rosé that shines with the bright intensity of Bouzy pinot noir and the crystalline definition of salt minerality zapped with tangy malic acidity. A dose of 12% Bouzy rouge lends but a hint of pink to its delicate, pretty, bright straw hue. It's a wonderful expression of the character of Bouzy translated with detail and finesse, filled with strawberry and cranberry fruits and fragranced with rose petals of lifted, lively character. Fine tannin structure melds with salt minerality to provide grip and structure in unison with tangy and persistent malic acidity. It's thrillingly primary and enticingly moreish, with just subtle allusions of ginger-cake spice beginning to appear on a long finish.

Paul Bara Bouzy Grand Millésime Brut 2012 $$

93 points • Tasted in Champagne

10% chardonnay, 90% pinot noir; 8g/L dosage

Such has been the popularity and demand for Bara's Millésime that sales have overtaken supply and lees age has been shortened, to the point where it coincides with the base vintage of the current Réserve Brut. 'We might need to hold back and be out of stock in the future, so as to have longer ageing,' Evelyne Dauvergne suggests.

This is a fleshy, luscious, textured and spicy cuvée that revels in the exuberance of Bouzy in layers of fig, white peach, mixed spice and honey. It holds its poise thanks to evenly integrated malic acidity and the salt minerality of chalk bedrock, defining a long, calm, full and enticing finish. Well-balanced phenolic grip provides just the right level of bite to hold its succulent roundness in check.

PAUL BARA SPECIAL CLUB 2009 $$$

94 points • TASTED IN CHAMPAGNE

30% chardonnay, 70% pinot noir

Drawing vibrant energy, mineral-laden texture and impeccable control from vast, expansive fruit of old-vine Bouzy magnitude calls for quite some wizardry. Paul Bara uses a strong dose of chardonnay to counter pinot noir's exuberance, for now at least (it will become blanc de noirs from 2017). This is a powerful Special Club that colliers the luscious exuberance of Bouzy with the ripe depth of 2009. The poise and harmony of Paul Bara keep this tenuous union in check, with chardonnay assisted in no small part by fine chalk minerality and well-balanced malic acidity to bring definition and vibrancy to a long finish. Lingering with enduring red apple, gingernut biscuit and spice, this is a grand celebration of the full depth of Bouzy pinot noir in all of its wonderful splendour

PAUL BARA SPECIAL CLUB ROSÉ 2013 $$$$

95 points • TASTED IN CHAMPAGNE

30% chardonnay, 70% pinot noir; Bouzy; 5% Bouzy rouge 2013

Taming Bouzy's extravagant fervour is an art of the highest order, and this wine is a case study in graceful strength. A monumental contrast of intensity and elegance, at once delicate and bright and at the same time deep, concentrated and complex, this is a cuvée that epitomises the grandeur of Bouzy, transposed by the fresh and lively definition of this celebrated grower. Just 5% Bouzy rouge is all it takes to stain its pretty pale-salmon hue. It's soaked in wild strawberry, raspberry and red cherry fruit, even hints of berry compote and layers of spice and cherry kernel. Fine salt minerality and ripe, well-integrated malic acidity make for a beautifully fine structure and very long finish. A feisty enchantress.

PAUL BARA COMTESSE MARIE DE FRANCE 2006 $$$$

95 points • TASTED IN CHAMPAGNE

100% pinot noir; stainless-steel fermented; 8g/L dosage

Unashamedly blanc de noirs, celebrating vast, expansive fruit presence of old-vine Bouzy magnitude, this is purposely a more voluminous style to Bara's Special Clubs. It ripples with the full grandeur of brooding layers of grilled pineapple, figs, juicy stone fruits, almond nougat, honey, crème brûlée and golden fruit cake. Quite some wizardry is called for to draw impeccable control and refinement from such extravagant fervour, and Bara masters this with poised, well-integrated malic acidity, the creamy texture of long lees age and the soft, chalk-laden minerality of its legendary sites. Ready to drink now, this is a larger than life representation of Champagne's most exuberant village, bathed in velvety warmth, all the while upholding sure-footed balance and graceful strength.

PAUL BARA ANNONCIADE 2005 $$$$

95 points • TASTED IN CHAMPAGNE

30% chardonnay, 70% pinot noir; fermented in old oak barrels and one new

Fully fermented in oak barrels, Bara's new cuvée is a salute to cooper Auguste François Bara, the family's first ancestor in Bouzy. The inaugural 2004 release was 100% pinot noir, and the powerful 2005 season has been astutely tempered with a dose of chardonnay. Ricocheting with grand intensity and complexity, the booming black plum, black cherry, fig and grilled pineapple of Bouzy pinot noir rise to meet the coffee bean and dark chocolate of oak fermentation, brought together by the brioche and gingernut biscuit complexity of long age. It's spicy and full-bodied, with length and breadth on another plane, yet it holds its poise in spite of such proportions thanks to the blessing of well-balanced malic acidity and all-pervading, fine chalk minerality.

PAUL DÉTHUNE

(Pawl Deh-tune)

6/10

2 RUE DU MOULIN 51150 AMBONNAY
www.champagne-dethune.com

CHAMPAGNE

PAUL DÉTHUNE
Propriétaire-Récoltant
GRAND CRU
À AMBONNAY

The Déthune family has tended its vines on the privileged slopes of Ambonnay since 1610, and produced their own wines since 1890. Today, Pierre Déthune and wife Sophie sensitively manage seven hectares of 70% pinot noir and 30% chardonnay entirely within the village. Ten cuvées draw complexity and diversity from 34 different Ambonnay parcels vinified separately, some in large oak foudres and small oak 'pièces' from the forests of Champagne. 'We want to show that the same grapes from the same village can produce seven different styles by varying the blends, the ageing and the use of oak,' Sophie explains. Their 50,000 bottles confidently express the luscious power and characterful poise of Ambonnay and quickly sell out every year.

The Déthunes proudly uphold an average vine age of 34–36 years and effectively tend their vineyards organically, having employed organic composts and avoided insecticides and herbicides for more than 20 years, though they have purposely shunned organic certification over concerns surrounding copper sulphate fungicide.

'Pierre's grandfather was organic without knowing it, and 100 years later we still have copper in the vineyard from his treatments. This is not good for the vines,' Sophie explains. 'Champagne's difficult climate calls for liberal use of fungicides, particularly in wet vintages like 2012, but we do not want to use massive amounts of copper sulphate.'

Pierre is instead trialling essential oils in the vineyards. 'I need every grape I can harvest, so I cannot take risks that might jeopardise any of our crop,' he reveals. The Déthunes report that their yields have halved since they commenced working sustainably, now harvesting 11 tonnes per hectare, quite a contrast to the 28 tonnes of one of their neighbours. 'Other growers laugh at us for not having many grapes, but we laugh at them for not having deep colour in their skins!' he says.

Pierre's father, Paul, introduced mechanisation in 1960. 'They had an easier job – and we are going backwards!' he exclaims, detailing the time and attention required to control grasses planted in the mid-rows since 2001. 'We intend to leave the vineyards for the next generation, so it is important for us to preserve the environment.'

Fifty-four square metres of solar panels on the roof of the 17th century buildings provide one-fifth of the winery's electricity, and rainwater services a similar proportion of water requirements.

The Déthunes are careful not to harvest too late, to hold freshness and check the exuberance of Ambonnay pinot noir. Sophie works with the picking teams to inspect the fruit and ensure a stringent selection.

They aim to complete harvest of all 34 parcels within eight days. All are vinified separately, those destined for Brut NV in

stainless steel, and reserves and other cuvées in large 3200-litre vats and small 205-litre barrels of up to 20 years of age. Vats work harmoniously with the Déthunes' fruit, though small oak barrels have at times tended to assert themselves, but are finding a more harmonious balance recently. They buy a few new 205-litre champagne oak barrels each year. 'We have 50 in all, and that's all we have room for!' says Sophie.

Non-vintage blends are built on generous inclusions of deep reserves from oak casks, including a solera of more than 40 different vintages, made and aged in oak vats, created by Pierre's father, to which every vintage since has contributed. It must rank among the oldest of its kind in the region. I have noted some charcuterie-like savouriness creeping in to the current blends from this ever maturing solera.

Having invested significantly in vineyards (purchasing four hectares and taking 20 years to pay it off), the focus since 1990 has been on investment in the winery, particularly in the purchase of new barrels and five new temperature-controlled vats. Space constraints have necessitated storage of their longest-aged cuvées off-site. They purchased the house next door and dug an impressive new cellar, to double their storage capacity to 200,000 bottles (much more than current requirements of 50,000 bottles), increase reserve wine stocks, and introduce a few new foudres.

This will permit a small increase in production, enabling them to keep the 15% of their fruit that they previously sold to Veuve Clicquot for La Grande Dame. Blends, bottling and disgorgement dates are printed on the back of every bottle.

Pierre and Sophie Déthune

Paul Déthune Extra Brut NV $$

93 points • 2014 base vintage • Disgorged May 2017 • Tasted in Champagne

30% chardonnay, 70% pinot; 50% reserves from oak cask, including a solera of more than 40 vintages; 5g/L dosage

Déthune's core cuvée comes in Extra Brut, Brut Nature and Demi-Sec, a wonderfully deep and complex celebration of Ambonnay pinot noir in all of its alluring red cherry, red apple and mixed spice character. The spicy, savoury complexity of an ever more mature reserve solera lends a note of charcuterie for the first time and sits comfortably behind the brightness of its red fruits, underlined by well-focused acidity. Fine tannins are well married with the fine chalk minerality of Ambonnay on a very long finish.

Paul Déthune Brut Rosé NV $$

92 points • 2014 base vintage • Disgorged November 2017 • Tasted in Champagne

20% chardonnay, 80% pinot noir; 50% reserves; Extra Brut with 10% pinot noir red wine; 3000 bottles

Déthune blends rosé from its Extra Brut NV rather than macerating pinot noir, to retain higher acidity and freshness in its rich Ambonnay fruit. The effect is a bright medium-crimson hue and a spicy style that resonates with the expansive and characterful mood of Ambonnay pinot noir. Red cherry, raspberry and strawberry fruit carry hints of charcuterie complexity from its deep reserves, and wood spice notes from barrels, culminating in a supple and enticing finish. Its clear bottle is no more, now well protected in green bottles for the first time.

The Champagne Guide

Paul Déthune Blanc de Noirs Brut NV $$$

93 points • 100% 2014 • Disgorged May 2017 • Tasted in Champagne

100% pinot noir from Les Crayères in Ambonnay, with excellent exposition and accessible chalk; 100% 2014, though not stated; entirely vinified in 205-litre oak barrels and 3000-litre oak casks; 4000–5000 bottles; next year Les Crayères will be declared as a vintage blanc de noirs, and a new Blanc de Noirs NV of around 9000 bottles will be announced

The rounded generosity of this well-exposed site in Ambonnay infuses a full straw hue and fills a palate rippling with pineapple and mirabelle plums. Oak vinification and maturation coaxes out vanilla, roasted almonds and the complexity of charcuterie. Fine chalk minerality meshes seamlessly on a long and fleshy finish.

Paul Déthune Millésime 2008 $$$$

93 points • Disgorged January 2017 • Tasted in Champagne

60% chardonnay, 40% pinot noir; 100% vinified and aged in 3400-litre oak casks; 3000 bottles

Paul Déthune's vintage cuvée is selectively released from only the top seasons, and in tiny volumes. The next will be 2012, and not released until 2022. The 2008 is a powerful release for such a tense vintage, a bold blend that will stand up confidently alongside main-course fare. It presents a seamless unity between the red berry fruit of pinot noir and the grilled pineapple and succulent peach of chardonnay, with not inconsiderable presence of spice, toast and texture from oak barrel vinification. It will benefit from more time for the grip and flavour of oak to integrate, and it confidently holds the magnificent line and length to go the distance.

Ambonnay, summer 2016

PERRIER-JOUËT

(Per-riay Zhoo-et)

---

28 AVENUE DE CHAMPAGNE 51201 ÉPERNAY
www.perrier-jouet.com

CHAMPAGNE
PERRIER-JOUËT

The past 20 years have been turbulent for Perrier-Jouët, changing hands three times before it was taken over by current owners, Pernod Ricard, in 2005. In the midst of this rollercoaster, the house has been fortunate to retain most of its vineyards, with 65 hectares now providing for one-quarter of its annual production of 3.5 million bottles, up 2.5 million in just a decade, now ranking as Champagne's tenth-largest house. From its founding just over 200 years ago, the vision of the house has focused on the floral elegance of chardonnay, and today more than half of the estate's holdings lie in the Côte des Blancs, particularly in the grand crus of Cramant (27 ha), Avize (9 ha) and, to a lesser extent, Chouilly. The jewel of the house is the glorious Cramant, where it is privileged to the very finest sites in the village, acquired by the house since the 1870s. For chef de cave Hervé Deschamps, 'Perrier-Jouët is about the elegance, freshness, fruitiness and roundness of chardonnay, with power and biscuity complexity.' His is a house style of soft, rounded, creamy generosity.

For Deschamps, the origin of the fruit is of utmost importance, and he sources from no less than 70 villages across Champagne. 'It's all about which village and which location and which age of vines,' he says. 'The best chardonnay comes from the Côte des Blancs, Trépail, Villers-Marmery, the Sézanne and the Vitry, and for Perrier-Jouët, it's all about the Côte des Blancs,' he says, listing Cramant, then Avize, then Chouilly as the greatest villages, adding that Villers-Marmery is also an important source. He uses pinot noir for perfume rather than strength, favouring Mailly-Champagne (the most important source of pinot for the house, with nine hectares under its ownership), Verzy, Verzenay, Aÿ, Avenay-Val-d'Or and Les Riceys, and meunier from Dizy, Damery, Venteuil and Vincelles. Maintaining acidity and avoiding high ripeness is his priority in the vineyards, which he admits is a challenge in the wake of global warming.

A total of 300 tanks allows the flexibility to keep not only each village separate, but the early, middle and late picks also. 'For me, a blend is not about percentages of products, it is about a list of tanks. And to me, every tank has its own personality.' Everything is vinified in stainless steel, with full malolactic fermentation.

Since my very first meeting with Hervé I have been drawn to his warm smile, humility and candour. 'When I joined Perrier-Jouët 32 years ago, I knew about winegrowing, as my grandfather grew grapes, but I'd never blended a wine before!' he revealed. He learnt his art over a decade under his predecessor, André Bavaret.

Deschamps' openness is rare and refreshing in the big-brand champagne world, and as he methodically presents each of the cuvées of the house, no topic is off limits, even production volumes of each cuvée.

Together with Mumm, its sister house within Pernod Ricard (Champagne's fifth-largest group), Perrier-Jouët aspires to double volume in 10 years, and is already increasing production in response to growing demand, particularly from Japan, China and Australia. The biggest challenge lies in sourcing fruit, Deschamps admits. Without space to extend its historic premises, the house has rented cellars off-site.

Of Perrier-Jouët's current production of around 3.5 million bottles, roughly 2 million are Grand Brut and a massive 1 million are Belle Epoque, making this label a much larger proportion than the vintage cuvée of most houses, though it is labelled, marketed and priced very much at prestige level. At such a production level, it takes a truly great vintage like 2008 for it to really shine.

Symbolic of its focus on chardonnay's floral elegance, the Belle Epoque flagships are presented in a distinctive, enamelled bottle of Art Nouveau Japanese anemones. The luscious branding of the house is likewise a tribute to the Art Nouveau era.

Every bottle of Perrier-Jouët is now reliably sealed with DIAM, except those destined for the US.

Deschamps has been with Perrier-Jouët since 1983 and chef de cave since 1993. In September 2018, he announced his successor in Séverine Frerson, who joined the house after 16 years at Piper-Heidsieck. She will work alongside him until his retirement, which has not yet been announced. 'Our goal is to maintain the Perrier-Jouët style with Séverine as the new cellarmaster,' Deschamps stated.

PERRIER-JOUËT GRAND BRUT NV $$

91 points • 2015 BASE VINTAGE • TASTED IN CHAMPAGNE

20% chardonnay, mostly from the Côte des Blancs, Trépail, Villers-Marmery and Vitry; 40% pinot noir, mostly from the Montagne de Reims and Aube; 40% meunier, mostly from the Vallée de la Marne; a blend of 200 tanks from 50-70 villages; 9g/L dosage; roughly 2 million bottles

Hervé Deschamps' ambition for Grand Brut is to bring more of an impression of chardonnay than its small inclusion suggests, to tease out floral aromas, citrus, fresh, juicy fruits and biscuit. 'Pinot noir and meunier work together to build mineral saltiness in the chardonnay style of the house,' he suggests.

This is the best I've tasted Grand Brut, a clean, lively and fresh blend that presents red apple and lemon amidst well-structured, finely mineral salt texture. Mandarin citrus notes reflect the warm 2015 season. Bottle age has built subtle gingernut biscuit notes and a creamy structure. Kudos to Deschamps for dispelling the dusty dryness and phenolic grip of the past.

PERRIER-JOUËT BLANC DE BLANCS BRUT NV $$$

88 points • 2015 BASE VINTAGE • TASTED IN CHAMPAGNE

Côte des Blancs, Montagne de Reims, Hautvillers, Chavot and Vitry; 8g/L dosage

Perrier Jouët's brand-new Blanc de Blancs NV aspires to present the chardonnay style of the house — 'but with charm, more than just citrus and acidity,' Deschamps explains. 'We are aiming for gentleness and smoothness, not sharp acidity or assertive saltiness.'

For a house with such a deep history with chardonnay, enviable resources in the northern Côte des Blancs, a stunning track record with Belle Epoque Blanc de Blancs and recent advances in Grand Brut, its inaugural foray into Blanc de Blancs NV comes with enormous anticipation. In the pretty, clear 'Blason de France' bottle of the house, it certainly looks the goods in its pale straw hue. Apple, pear and grapefruit all arrive on cue, but then it collapses into the dry-extract grip and firm structure of the warm 2015 season, disrupted by notes of tobacco and coffee bean, leaving the finish firm and coarse. Such a disappointment after promising so much.

PERRIER-JOUËT BLASON ROSÉ NV $$$

89 points • 2015 BASE VINTAGE • TASTED IN CHAMPAGNE

25% chardonnay, 50% pinot noir, 25% meunier; 15% red wine from Bouzy, Ambonnay, Aÿ, Cumières, Vertus and Les Riceys; 15% reserves; 8g/L

The aspiration for Blason Rosé is an elegant colour and red fruit aromas, more about red berries than the floral focus of the white cuvées. This is created with red wine of fruity aromas, strong colour and soft tannin. Perrier-Jouët has been making rosé since 1959 and is currently increasing its production, though only makes it in vintages in which the red wine is of sufficient quality. Blason Rosé is built on a similar base to Grand Brut, with a difference. 'I need more chardonnay and more power of pinot here, to balance the red wine,' Hervé Deschamps explains.

The warm 2015 season was well suited to red wines in Champagne, and a strong inclusion of 15% establishes a medium salmon hue. In newly disgorged guise, this is a fresh Blason Rosé of lively strawberry notes and cracked pink pepper accents. The phenolic grip of fine tannin structure of 2015 collides with salivating salt minerality to create a firm, coarse mouthfeel. The fruit drops away quickly, leaving its phenolic bitterness exposed unadorned in the stark light of day, making for a callow and assertive finish.

PERRIER-JOUËT BELLE EPOQUE 2012 $$$$

92 points • TASTED IN CHAMPAGNE

50% chardonnay from Cramant, Avize, Le Mesnil-sur-Oger, Chouilly and Oger; 45% pinot noir, mainly from the northern Montagne de Reims, Mailly-Champagne, Verzy and Verzenay; 5% meunier from estate vines in Dizy; aged 5–6 years on lees; 8g/L dosage; DIAM; roughly 1 million bottles

For Hervé Deschamps, 2012 was a good year for Perrier-Jouët chardonnay, producing a good balance between acidity and ripeness. He uses a dash of meunier 'to create harmony by bridging chardonnay and pinot, like the dash between Perrier and Jouët'.

Cramant and Mailly-Champagne are the pillars of Belle Epoque, uniting in a fresh and lively style in 2012. Chardonnay assumes a confident, citrus-driven lead, with elegant northern Montagne pinot noir providing gentle support. This is a Belle Epoque of grip and definition, with bitter grapefruit notes and crunchy apple fruit jostling with fine salt minerality. It holds freshness on the finish, though bitter grip truncates its persistence.

PERRIER-JOUËT BELLE EPOQUE 2011 $$$$

89 points • TASTED IN AUSTRALIA

50% chardonnay from Cramant and Avize, 45% pinot noir from the Montagne de Reims, 5% meunier from estate vines in Dizy; aged 6 years on lees; 9g/L dosage; DIAM

Vegetal and composty with chlorophyll notes that reflect underripeness, this is a cuvée that finishes with firm, dusty phenolic grip that betrays the imperfect fruit of a dismal vintage marked by underripeness, dilution and widespread rot. Its dosage looks candied. Very few houses declared a vintage. Why did Perrier-Jouët release a prestige cuvée? Perhaps because the house was founded in 1811?

PERRIER-JOUËT BELLE EPOQUE 2008 $$$$

96 points • TASTED IN AUSTRALIA

50% chardonnay from Cramant and Avize; 45% pinot noir from the Montagne de Reims; 5% meunier from estate vines in Dizy; 9g/L dosage; DIAM

The generous, sunny, buttery mood of Perrier-Jouët is well countered by the tension and definition of the great 2008 season, creating the most compelling Belle Epoque I can recall. Since its release two years ago, it has subsumed its heightened lemon purity as the creamy generosity of ripe Cramant chardonnay expands. The prominent strawberry fruit of the Montagne de Reims remains, bolstered by the toasty, candied notes of dosage. The acidity of 2008 triumphs, defining greater focus, line and energy than ever, illuminating the elevated chalk minerality of Cramant and Avize, while never deviating from the silky succulence and creamy approachability that scream Perrier-Jouët.

PERRIER-JOUËT BELLE EPOQUE ROSÉ 2010 $$$$$

90 points • TASTED IN CHAMPAGNE

45% chardonnay, 50% pinot noir, 5% Dizy meunier; 11% red wine from Vertus and Aÿ; 8g/L dosage

With rain during harvest, Perrier-Jouët elected not to release Belle Epoque or Belle Epoque Blanc de Blancs in 2010, but decided to proceed with Belle Epoque Rosé, on the strength of its red wines. This label is purposely a more elegant style than Blason Rosé, blended with red wines that aspire to dark colour and elegant structure.

A savoury vintage for Belle Epoque Rosé, this is a cuvée of medium salmon-copper hue and flavours of tomato and redcurrant. The structure is pronounced and firm, with dry-extract grip and fine tannins quashing salty minerality. It lingers long on the finish, though lacks fruit brightness and lift, a victim of its imperfect season.

PERRIER-JOUËT BELLE EPOQUE BLANC DE BLANCS 2006 $$$$$

94 points • TASTED IN CHAMPAGNE

Two legendary mid-slope lieux-dits of south-south-east exposure in Cramant, Bouron Leroi and Bouron du Midi; vinified separately; aged more than 10 years on lees; 8g/L dosage; DIAM; never more than 30,000 bottles

Perrier-Jouët has been building its clutch of Cramant vineyards since 1870, before the village was ever officially classified. It was celebrated grower Pierre Larmandier who once told me that the house owns the finest terroir in the village. No doubt these two plots were foremost in his mind. The third release of this cuvée is a contrast to the glittering triumph of the 2002 and 2004. The gentle, rounded, creamy succulence of the 2006 harvest defines a Perrier-Jouët flagship of deep complexity and soft, calm mood. It's buttery and secondary, with long bottle age piling on layers of vanilla and brioche. The structure is led more by the subtle phenolic bitterness of the season and the salt minerality of Cramant than by the soft acidity of 2006. It concludes with the same grand dimensions with which it led out, carrying a line of expansive volume and spicy complexity from start to very long finish, yet at every moment tamed by impeccable salt minerality, the definitive Cramant. It's ready to drink right away. Alongside Perrier-Jouët's 2 million bottles of Grand Brut NV and 1 million of Belle Epoque, its 30,000 bottle production of this cuvée is minuscule. One bottle was rejected by Deschamps as inconsistent..

PHILIPPE FOURRIER

(Fi-lip Faw-riay)

39 RUE DE BAR SUR AUBE 10200 BAROVILLE
www.champagne-fourrier.com

MAISON FONDÉE EN 1847

CHAMPAGNE
PHILIPPE FOURRIER
BAROVILLE

The Fourriers have been growing grapes in the village of Baroville in the Côte des Bar for five generations since 1847, and were the first growers to produce their own champagne in the village in the early 1900s. Today, the family estate comprises nearly 18 hectares in the village, planted predominantly to pinot noir (70%). Unusually for this part of Champagne, the balance is made up almost entirely of chardonnay (29%), with meunier comprising a tiny 1%. Sustainability is the mandate of not only the vineyards, where vines are ploughed manually and mulch is used to protect the soil, but also the winery, which is equipped with substantial rainwater recovery and solar systems. Disgorgement dates are now printed prominently on both back labels and corks of all Fourrier cuvées. These are characterful wines, confidently holding full levels of dosage, brimming with the personality of Côte des Bar pinot noir, at times lacking a little in polish, but with the propensity to shine in a great season.

PHILIPPE FOURRIER BLANC DE NOIRS NV $$

91 points • DISGORGED JUNE 2018 • TASTED IN AUSTRALIA

100% Côte des Bar pinot noir; aged 3 years on lees; 11g/L dosage; cork

This is Côte des Bar pinot noir in all of its glory, and one certainly feels closer to Burgundy than to the Marne in the presence of this cuvée. It's as black fruited as ever this year, brimming with crunchy blackberries and even blackcurrants. It's juicy and fresh, yet at the same time tangy and tense, holding a full dosage with balance and poise. A magnificent expression of Côte des Bar pinot noir of integrity, allure and purity.

PHILIPPE FOURRIER CUVÉE PRESTIGE NV $$

90 points • DISGORGED JUNE 2018 • TASTED IN AUSTRALIA

100% Côte des Bar chardonnay; aged 4 years on lees; 10g/L dosage; DIAM

This estate bottles the essence of the Aube, and this is chardonnay of character and structure. True to this part of the world, it does not have the finesse, chalk mineral texture or polish of the Côte des Blancs, but what it lacks in structure it delivers in fruit. Grapefruit and strawberry-hull fruit character is evidence of chardonnay's ability to take on red fruit nuances in terroirs more commonly planted to pinot noir. A fleshy stone-fruit core counters tangy acidity, finishing primary, fruity and long.

PHILIPPE FOURRIER PINOT BLANC NV $$$

88 points • DISGORGED JUNE 2018 • TASTED IN AUSTRALIA

100% Côte des Bar pinot blanc; aged 2.5 years on lees; 11g/L dosage; cork

Brimming with the exuberant personality of pinot blanc, this is a cuvée of star fruit, dry straw, crab apple and white pepper. Creamy texture contrasts the fine phenolic grip of the variety, well massaged by a full 11g/L dosage. What it lacks in refinement it makes up for in character. A good example of the variety.

Les Riceys, winter 2012

PHILIPPE GLAVIER

(Fi-lip Glah-viay)

6/10

82 RUE NESTOR GAUNEL 51530 CRAMANT
www.champagne-philippe-glavier.com

CHAMPAGNE
PHILIPPE
GLAVIER
À CRAMANT

Twelfth-generation grower in the village of Monthelon, Véronique Glavier swore she would never marry a grower, until she met third-generation grower Philippe Glavier on a skiing trip in 1993. By 1995, they had created their own little house from scratch, and have since achieved a great deal in a quarter of a century in building their holdings, facilities and brand. Devoted exclusively to grand cru chardonnay, they have grown their estate to 4.5 hectares in Le Mesnil-sur-Oger, Oger, Avize and Cramant. While production is based in the facilities of her family in Cramant, the majority of their vineyards are in Le Mesnil-sur-Oger and Oger. Spanning a substantial spread of 49 distinct plots, a mandate of vinifying terroir by terroir is no simple exercise, necessitating a small 2000-kilogram pneumatic press, many small temperature-controlled vats, oak barrels and a 2000-litre foudre. All nine cuvées in their portfolio go through full malolactic fermentation, and receive dosages of less than 5g/L. Informative back labels declare full details of crus, dosage, base vintage and bottling and disgorgement dates. Minimal lees ageing is explained on the basis of a desire to accentuate terroir and chalk mineral expression, but chardonnay as serious and expressive as this would benefit from longer on lees.

PHILIPPE GLAVIER LA GRÂCE D'ALPHAËL BLANC DE BLANCS GRAND CRU NV $$

92 points • 2015 BASE VINTAGE • DISGORGED 12 OCTOBER 2017 • TASTED IN AUSTRALIA

100% chardonnay; 38% Avize, 33% Le Mesnil-sur-Oger, 19% Oger, 10% Cramant; 30% 2014 and 2013 reserves; 4.5g/L dosage; cork

Philippe Glavier captures his aspiration in a bottle from the very first cuvée: youthful vibrancy and purity that articulate the mineral personality and seriously strict structure of the grand crus of the Côte des Blancs. A full straw hue, this is a savoury cuvée of apple skin and spicy pear character, cut with a line of vibrant grapefruit acidity. Purposely aged for the minimum duration on lees, it hasn't had sufficient time to build integration and silkiness, which leaves a firmness and bite to the finish. Phenolic grip melds confidently with heightened, fine, salty chalk mineral personality that define its core components of Avize and Le Mesnil-sur-Oger. It concludes with impressive persistence and confidence; a cuvée brimming with character and terroir detail, if not polish.

Philippe Glavier La Grâce d'Alphaël Blanc de Blancs Grand Cru Zero NV $$

90 points • 2015 base vintage • Disgorged 12 October 2017 • Tasted in Australia

As above, with zero dosage

There is a beautiful white floral fragrance to La Grâce d'Alphaël, unusually and surprisingly even more pronounced in the Zero version than the Brut Nature rendition. On the palate, by contrast, the absence of the calming influence of dosage heightens the tension and austerity of this young and raw style, emphasising the impact of bitter phenolics. Strictly for die-hard champagne masochists.

Philippe Glavier Génésis Blanc de Blancs Grand Cru NV $$$

94 points • 2014 base vintage • Disgorged 12 October 2017 • Tasted in Australia

100% chardonnay; 40% Le Mesnil-sur-Oger, 24% Oger, 20% Avize, 16% Cramant; 30% 2013 reserves; 4.5g/L dosage; cork

Richer parcels and a year longer on lees than Grâce d'Alphaël build a very serious and captivating representation of the four neighbouring grand crus that define the core of the Côte des Blancs. Spicy apple, crunchy nashi pear, tangy lemon curd and grapefruit contrast the subtle toasted biscuit and honey character of two-and-a-half years on lees. The chalk minerality of Le Mesnil takes the lead in a super-fine and salty structure, beautifully toned by the silky creaminess of lees age. It holds with grand cru persistence and impressive line on a long finish..

Cramant, harvest 2014

PHILIPPONNAT

(Fi-li-poh-nah)

8/10

13 Rue du Pont 51160 Mareuil-sur-Aÿ
www.philipponnat.com

PHILIPPONNAT

CHAMPAGNE

If the finest vineyard sites are the most important asset of any Champagne house, the little house of Philipponnat is particularly privileged. Its 21 hectares of mostly pinot noir span Mareuil-sur-Aÿ, and its neighbours Aÿ, Mutigny and Avenay-Val-d'Or, but its most prized is the splendid, sun-drenched Clos des Goisses, one of the most powerful and distinctive sites in all of Champagne. The house is masterful in toning the exuberance of ripe pinot noir with judiciously deployed malic acidity, energising the scintillating chalk minerality of the greatest premier cru in all of Champagne. This year, this dynamic estate has ascended to unprecedented heights across its extensive portfolio, soaring from a position in the top 60 champagne houses to a proud and lofty rank in the top 20.

POWERFUL VINEYARDS

The walled Clos des Goisses of 5.5 hectares lies directly to the east of Mareuil-sur-Aÿ at the very heart of Champagne, the juncture at which the Côte des Blancs, the Vallée de la Marne and the Montagne de Reims intersect. With a perfect south-facing aspect, a dramatic slope of 30–45 degrees towards the Marne ('Gois' means 'very steep' in the local dialect), catching the sun in its full perpendicular strength, and shielded from the westerly winds, this is one of the warmest microclimates in Champagne, boasting temperatures to equal those of Burgundy. The subsoil is pure chalk, following the gradient of the hill under a thin layer of poor topsoil, so roots quickly strike chalk, pervading the wines with minerality. Mareuil-sur-Aÿ is a mere premier cru, and Clos des Goisses is perhaps the most striking case of all for a much more detailed classification of Champagne vineyards.

Philipponnat's house style is particularly intense, relying primarily on the power of Montagne de Reims pinot noir from south-facing estate vineyards. Additional supplies are sourced from a further 45 hectares of vines, particularly from the Côte des Blancs and Vallée de la Marne, and excess is purchased each vintage to permit lesser parcels to be declassified.

Yields are restricted and optimal physiological maturity is sought through slightly delayed harvests. 'We aim to harvest late and mature, and we buy from the end of the harvest rather than the beginning,' explains Charles Philipponnat, president of the house. 'We start picking at the time Billecart stops. There is a risk involved, but we gain from this strategy.' Clos des Goisses is 1–1.5°C warmer than other nearby vineyards, and is harvested at 12–13 degrees potential, the maximum permitted in the appellation.

The opulence of Philipponnat's ripeness can be disarming, and in warm seasons, its looming proportions in the midst of oak fermentation can be disconcerting.

Are increasingly warmer vintages a concern for a house built on such powerful vineyards?

'It is true that on average grapes are riper, but so far it has been a good thing for Champagne that the harvests have been warmer than in the past,' Charles Philipponnat declares. 'We now have only one bad harvest in a decade, but in the past it was many. Clos des Goisses is a good case study for warming seasons, because it is too warm by Champagne standards, but it hasn't been a problem.

'I believe the soil, the slope and the regime are more important than the temperature,' he reveals. 'Pure chalk and thin topsoils are perfect for upholding freshness through minerality. You can also influence the microclimate by the way you cultivate the vineyards. There is no reason why we have to lose the precision of the minerality even when we maintain high ripeness. Our wines today have grown in warmer conditions than 20 years ago and we have gained precision, so what is the problem?'

For Philipponnat, underripeness is the biggest concern. 'If you want the ideal fruit, you want to pick at the peak of phenolic maturity, not before, when there is greenness and vegetal character in the wine. If one thing worries me it's that I don't want to pick too early.

'The biggest problem, if there is one, is that instead of ripening in the cooler weeks of mid- and late-September, the grapes will be ripening towards the beginning of September and the end of August, and so we lose some finesse, even if we pick at the same degree of ripeness.'

He is sceptical of initiatives by the INAO and the Comité Champagne to experiment with hybrid varietals of lower ripeness and longer maturation periods. 'I am not sure these are true to the Champagne tradition,' he observes. 'Personally, I think we should maintain the best of what we have.'

He has worked very hard to this end, ever since Philipponnat owners Lanson-BCC invited him to return from Moët to manage the family business in 2000. He has focused on improving viticulture through natural fertilisation and abolishing pesticides and herbicides, which have enhanced grape ripeness, allowing for lower dosage, and every cuvée above the entry non-vintages is extra brut.

'One of the main things we have done over the years has been to eliminate meunier,' Philipponnat discloses. 'Our style is a pinot noir style, especially the riper style from the southern side of the Montagne de Reims.' Meunier thus appears only in his non-vintage blends, and never more than five percent. From the 2014 base it will be just a few percent residual. 'We have almost no meunier in our vineyards and in our contracts, as we let go of our meunier contracts in favour of pinot.'

By planting more pinot, Philipponnat has shifted Clos des Goisses from 60% to 70% of the variety. 'The old habit was always to plant chardonnay on the chalk soils, so it was a majority of chardonnay until 1964,' he points out. 'In the future, I'd rather buy a beautiful vineyard in the Côte des Blancs and focus on pinot noir in Mareuil-sur-Aÿ.'

Currently resourcing a little under one-third of its needs from its own 21 hectares of vineyards, Philipponnat owner Lanson-BCC has announced a strategic decision for the house to increase its vineyards, particularly in chardonnay from the Côte des Blancs and pinot noir from the Montagne de Reims. 'The only reason for buying vineyards is to control the quality, because it is not financially rewarding,' Philipponnat admits.

REFRESHING WINEMAKING

Fruit of ripeness as high as Philipponnat's calls for winemaking processes that preserve freshness in every detail. This begins with vinification close to the vineyards in Mareuil-sur-Aÿ. Charles Philipponnat's first initiative when he joined the house in 2000 was to construct a new winery in Mareuil-sur-Aÿ and discontinue processing in Reims. He has also focused on longer oak ageing, cleaner blends from vats and barrels, and introducing new smart, minimalist, modern front labels and detailed back labels across the range. He remains personally actively involved in the tastings and blendings of the house.

'Our objective is twofold,' he outlines. 'To preserve and enhance the fruit, while preserving the freshness and the crisp impression of pleasant acidity and minerality.'

This is achieved through use of only the first pressings, cool fermentation in temperature-controlled stainless steel, blocking of malolactic fermentation in the most powerful parcels according to the vintage, use of a minimum of 30% chardonnay, and moderate dosage.

The strongest parcels of pinot noir and chardonnay (about 20% in all, representing 40–60% of vintage cuvées) are fermented in barrels, which are relatively young – though not new, and no older than six years of age – for complexity, development and antioxidative properties. 'We are keen to avoid oxidation,' Philipponnat emphasises. Walking into the barrel hall, the aroma of young oak is intoxicating, like nowhere else in Champagne. Such is the strength of Philipponnat's bold fruit that oak flavour does not tend to dominate, though its structure risks disrupting the already heightened phenolics of ripe fruit in increasingly warm seasons.

The barrel hall is climate controlled to block malolactic fermentation in every barrel, which Philipponnat emphasises as most important for preserving freshness and for avoiding buttery aromas. All reserve wines are matured for six months in small- and large-format oak. Reserve wines for Royale Réserve are kept in a solera system of fractional blending in foudres for six months, then in small barrels, re-blended every year to incorporate mature wines without losing freshness. Non-vintage cuvées receive 20–30% reserve wines and are aged 3–4 years in bottle. The house doubles the minimum ageing times across its cuvées, necessitating a stock of 2.5 million bottles in its 1.5 kilometres of 17th-century cellars. It

Clos des Goisses, summer 2015

Clos des Goisses is produced every vintage, but not always released. The house believes that it represents the first single-vineyard bottling in Champagne, and it is testimony to the site that since 1936 all but seven vintages have been released.

THE NEW PHILIPPONNAT

Philipponnat sells 500,000 bottles annually, all of which boast some of the most informative back labels of any house, declaring the date of disgorgement (since 1997), the blend, barrel maturation, dosage and even the number of bottles of vintage cuvées. The house claims to be the first in Champagne to also indicate the base year of its blends. An excellent website adds informative tech sheets on every cuvée.

The house has instituted a re-release program featuring an older vintage of every vintage cuvée and two vintages of its top-tier cuvées. 'The market is changing, and people no longer have space to store their wines,' observes international marketing and sales director Antoine de Boysson.

Philipponnat has introduced three single-vineyard cuvées of pinot noir since the 2006 harvest: Le Léon in Aÿ, Mareuil-sur-Aÿ and Les Cintres at the heart of Clos de Goisses. In tiny volumes of roughly just 2000–3000 bottles each, and only in the best harvests, Charles Philipponnat emphasises that only part of the best plots are taken, so as not to compromise or impoverish the Clos des Goisses blend. 'The idea of these single plots is not to turn Philipponnat into a single-plot house, but to showcase the best of what the south Montagne de Reims can craft from a single variety. It was very easy to do! So much harder to make a good blend.'

Its 2008 single-vineyard series represents some of the finest cuvées Philipponnat has ever created. Their release marks the ascent of the house to an all new level this year, with my reviews reading like a roll-call of 'best ever's thanks to a stunning set of vintage cuvées and, most laudable of all, a non-vintage tier that now ranks high among the very best in Champagne. Philipponnat has consequently leapt from a position in the top 60 champagne houses to a proud and lofty rank in the top 20. For this reason, it has done what no other house has achieved this year and ascended two tiers in my Hall of Honour, from 6/10 to a coveted 8/10.

Such ascension has not happened overnight, and two decades after Charles Philipponnat commenced his regime of refinement, I asked him what has changed today.

'We are doing exactly the same as before, but we are doing it better,' he responded. 'Our objective is precision of fruit with character and freshness, and everything must converge into the completion of this objective. This is the sum of many details that are very important.'

The ebullient and insightful Charles Philipponnat is a man of beaming generosity and exacting focus, a master of crafting wines that share his own virtues. Everything he has accomplished at Philipponnat is not only an exemplar of the rise of modern Champagne, it is a shining light for what can be achieved in powerful sites in Champagne's ever warmer climate.

maintains some 250 barrels, purchased after two or three vintages in Burgundy, and upheld for about 10 seasons at Philipponnat.

All 17 Clos de Goisses parcels are vinified separately, half in tank and half in barrel, as has been tradition since 1935. Comprising about 70% pinot and 30% chardonnay, its vines are aged 8–45 years, with an average of 30 years.

While 5.5 hectares has the capacity to produce some 55,000 bottles, on average just 17,000 bottles are made annually – sometimes as few as 5000 or as many as 20,000 – with the remainder declassified into other Philipponnat cuvées.

Philipponnat Royale Réserve Brut NV $$

95 points • 2013 BASE VINTAGE • DISGORGED OCTOBER 2017 • TASTED IN CHAMPAGNE

30% chardonnay, 65% pinot noir, 5% meunier; two-thirds premier and grand cru; 30% reserves from a solera aged in oak barrels; partial malolactic fermentation; aged 3 years on lees; 8g/L dosage

I have long loved Royale Réserve, revelling in the full depth of Mareuil pinot and all the theatrics of partial barrel fermentation, ever a reliable and affordable go-to. Never has it looked as dashingly gorgeous as it does today. Radiating through its pretty, pale-straw hue, this is a fresh and lively expression of the delightful, deep red and black cherry fruits of pinot noir from the south-facing slopes of the Montagne de Reims. It captures the essence of Philipponnat in contrasting rich, ripe fruit with tension and poise. Ripe malic acidity is delightfully fine, tangy and impeccably integrated, underlined by finely structured chalk minerality. It lingers very long and pure, dancing with pristine, enticing red cherry purity.

Philipponnat Royale Réserve Non Dosé NV $$

94 points • 2013 BASE VINTAGE • DISGORGED SEPTEMBER 2017 • TASTED IN CHAMPAGNE

As above, with zero dosage

The absence of dosage is stark here, and this is a captivating demonstration of the significance of a touch of sweetness. Philipponnat's ripe-fruit generosity and clean precision stands confidently with no added sugar, though it's markedly more tense and austere, its red fruits diminished and its malic acidity heightened. With magnificent purity and tension, it upholds an acid line that will captivate champagne die-hards and challenge the uninitiated.

Philipponnat Royale Réserve Rosé Brut NV $$

94 points • 2013 BASE VINTAGE • DISGORGED SEPTEMBER 2017 • TASTED IN CHAMPAGNE

20% chardonnay, 75% pinot noir, 5% meunier; majority premier and grand crus; 5-7% red wine from Clos des Goisses in Mareuil-sur-Aÿ; aged 3 years on lees; 26% solera of reserves aged in barrels; partial malolactic fermentation; aged at least 3 years on lees; 9g/L dosage

Philipponnat's Rosé aspiration is freshness, and it's now entrusted to dark bottles for the first time, 'because it's impossible to educate retailers on lightstruck degradation in clear bottles!' explains international marketing and sales director Antoine de Boysson. The bright purity and gentle structure of Mareuil-sur-Aÿ pinot is well suited to rosé (as Billecart has also exemplified), and Philipponnat has always excelled with this blend. You would have to go all the way back to 2008 to find a release of such refined elegance as the 2013 base. A tiny dose of Clos des Goisses red wine is all it takes to stain it a beautiful medium salmon hue. The presence of pinot noir brings great depth of savoury spice and tomato over a core of red cherry and wild strawberry fruit. Chalk mineral structure is very fine and pronounced, in wonderful synergy with lively, focused acidity and fine-grained, well-toned tannins. A rosé of true greatness, presenting refined elegance with lingering persistence.

Philipponnat Grand Blanc Extra-Brut 2008 $$$

96 points • Disgorged March 2017 • Tasted in Champagne

Oger, Chouilly, Avize, Cramant, Trépail and Clos des Goisses; aged 8 years on lees; 50% fermented and aged in barrels with no malolactic fermentation, 50% in tanks with malolactic fermentation; 4.5g/L dosage

Described as 'a blanc de blancs made with a pinot noir mindset', the house deploys a component of Clos des Goisses to contrast the focus of the Côte des Blancs. The supernova vintage of 2008 crossed orbits with the ascending trajectory of starship Philipponnat, and the result was the dawning of a new age of Grand Blanc. The generosity of the house meets the tension of the season to commanding effect, delivering outstanding, succulent ripeness with the focused tension of inimitable 2008 malic acidity. Impeccable purity of generous white fruits evoke mirabelle plums and ripe white peaches, beautifully contrasting tense lemon and grapefruit. Breathtaking chalk minerality of heightened precision draws out a very long finish. For a house that prides itself on pinot, this is an epic Grand Blanc and the greatest I have ever tasted from Philipponnat. More precision, more tension, more generosity, more everything.

Philipponnat Sublime Réserve Sec 2005 $$

92 points • Disgorged January 2014 • Tasted in Champagne

100% chardonnay; majority grand & premier crus; partial malolactic fermentation; aged 8 years on lees; 30g/L dosage

Sweet vintage champagne of such maturity is rare (Deutz is the only other one, but just half this age) – so if sweet is your vibe, this is a great find. It is a cunning play indeed for Philipponnat to create a blanc de blancs from scratch purposely for this style, deploying the gentle phenolic grip of the season and strategically placed malic acidity to balance its sweetness. Sugar unites with the toasty complexity of age to wonderful toasted-meringue effect. A complex and sweet champagne, it lingers creamy and custardy, with honey and fruit mince spice.

Philipponnat Blanc de Noirs Extra-Brut 2012 $$

95 points • Disgorged May 2018 • Tasted in Champagne

100% pinot noir; mostly from Mareuil-sur-Aÿ, the balance from the Mailly Grand Cru coopérative, Avenay-Val-d'Or and Aÿ; 50% fermented and aged in barrels with no malolactic fermentation, 50% in vats with partial malolactic fermentation; aged 5 years on lees; 4.5g/L dosage; 40,793 bottles

Introducing the finest Philipponnat Blanc de Noirs since the house announced 'noir is the new black!' with the launch of the splendid 2008. It's both a grand testimony to the great 2012 harvest and a tremendous credit to the ever-ascending talent of the house in the precarious art of seamlessly marrying the texture of oak fermentation, the tension of bright malic acidity and the structure of fine, salty chalk minerality. Gorgeous strawberry and raspberry fruit showcase the understated presence and refined finesse of Mareuil, fragranced with delightfully fresh and delicate rose petal notes, and accented with hints of balsamic. It's at once gracefully dainty and confidently complete.

Philipponnat 1522 Grand Cru Extra-Brut 2008 $$$

96 points • Disgorged March 2018 • Tasted in Champagne

42% chardonnay from Le Mesnil-sur-Oger, 58% pinot from Le Léon in Aÿ; 50% fermented and aged in barrels with no malolactic fermentation, 50% in vats with partial malolactic; aged 8 years on lees; 4.25g/L dosage; 14,664 bottles

Commemorating the date of the first proof of the Philipponnats growing pinot noir in Le Léon in Aÿ, a monumental half millennium ago (almost!), 1522 unites pinot noir from the same plot with Le Mesnil chardonnay. This is a blend of grand proportions, the voluptuous curves of pinot noir amplified in the stature of Aÿ and the voluminous character of barrel fermentation. A little more chardonnay than usual might seem counterintuitive in a season of such tension, but the synergy it creates is thrilling. Power meets poise as the elegance of red cherry fruit purity of Aÿ contrasts the deep, yellow-fruits presence of Mesnil and the brioche complexity of bottle age. The tension of malic acidity furnishes a finish of great energy and endurance, rippling with pronounced chalk minerality to the lively rhythm of 2008. I can't be certain this is the best 1522 in 486 years, but it is far and away the greatest I've tasted.

Philipponnat 1522 Premier Cru Brut Rosé 2007 $$$$

90 points • Disgorged June 2016 • Tasted in Champagne

30% chardonnay from Le Mesnil-sur-Oger, 70% pinot noir from Le Léon in Aÿ; 8.5% pinot noir red wine from Clos des Goisses in Mareuil-sur-Aÿ; 50% fermented and aged in barrels with no malolactic fermentation, 50% in vats with partial malolactic; aged 8 years on lees; 4.25g/L dosage

I liked this cuvée on release two years ago, with its explosion of bright, characterful wild strawberry, red cherry and pink grapefruit declaring all the theatrics of Mareuil and Aÿ pinot noir. The show's over, unfortunately, and the same disgorgement with another couple of years under cork has toned to a medium salmon-copper hue. A little tired now, it's showing a touch of oxidation, with a savoury profile of tomato and balsamic over gentle, elegant red berry fruits and spice. The tannin grip of its youth has now mellowed, concluding with focused acidity, fine, salty chalk minerality and good persistence. Wait for the 2008 instead.

Philipponnat Clos des Goisses Extra-Brut 2009 $$$$$

94 points • Disgorged March 2018 • Tasted in Champagne

39% chardonnay, 61% pinot noir; 37% fermented and aged in oak barrels; no malolactic fermentation; aged 9 years on lees; 4.25g/L dosage; 19,805 bottles

For its lofty credentials (and price to match), Clos des Goisses should consistently rank in the highest echelons of Champagne. If sheer, booming power were the only criterion, it would have no equal. The house describes it as a 'big, Burgundian style of champagne!' To me, its thumping ripeness can be alarming, creating disconcerting phenolic coarseness, though in the more elegant vintages it finds an alluring harmony.

'2009 was a sunny solar vintage,' Charles Philipponnat recalls, 'with beautiful fruit much lower in acidity than 2006 and 2007, but the freshness is there thanks to the minerality. It reminds me of the 1989, but in the end it will be better than 1989 because our winemaking now is cleaner and better than it was then.'

Philipponnat is astute in rolling out its barrels to suit the season, pulling back from 73—75% oak fermentation in 2007 and 2008 to a restrained 37% in the presence of the 2009 harvest. With a gold tint to its medium straw hue, the grand power and volume of this ripe harvest make for a cuvée of thundering proportions. Generous, mature yellow fruits jostle with the roast nut character of barrel fermentation. This warm season furnished low levels of gentle malic acidity, hence its definition owes more to the fine chalk minerality of the site. It's inimitable Clos des Goisses of other-worldly dimensions.

Philipponnat Clos de Goisses Juste Rosé Extra-Brut 2007 $$$$$

96 points • Tasted in Champagne

Saignée of 45% chardonnay and 55% pinot noir; 40% vinified in oak barrels; no malolactic fermentation; 4.5g/L dosage; 2039 bottles

For Charles Philipponnat, creating rosé from Clos des Goisses is a delicate balance, so it is only released in exceptional years, and in roughly just one-tenth the volume of the blanc. 'The tricky part is getting good pinot for rosé, and this doesn't happen every year,' he explains. The plots he chooses tend to be from the top of the slope, in the same area as those for his Mareuil-sur-Aÿ single vineyard. 'The steeper slopes are ripe, but they also have more chalk, and so the wines are too hard and tight for rosé.' He uses a saignée rather than a blend, to enhance endurance.

The 2007 vintage gave birth to the most alluring and harmonious Clos des Goisses since 1996, and its pink companion rises to the same lofty ambition. All the depth and power of this fabled site swirls in a spiralling vortex of fig, prune, juicy peach, even pawpaw and toffee. Oak and age bolster this maelstrom with all manner of complexity of ginger cake, spice and dried nectarine. In length and line it is a sensation, pulled into disciplined line by focused malic acidity and the fine, salty chalk minerality of the top of the slope. This is benchmark rosé, a stark contrast to both Krug and Dom Pérignon, yet circling in the same deep end of the rosé pool.

Philipponnat Mareuil-sur-Aÿ Premier Cru Extra-Brut 2008 $$$$$

98 points • Disgorged September 2017 • Tasted in Champagne

100% pinot noir; three of the best parcels right at the top of Clos des Goisses, part of or adjacent to Clos des Goisses, exposed but less steep, with deeper topsoils and a higher clay component than further down the slope; 44% vinified in barrels without malolactic fermentation; 56% vinified in vats with partial malolactic fermentation; aged 8 years on lees; 4.5g/L dosage; 3339 bottles

Sitting above Clos des Goisses in every way, this is an awe-inspiring premier cru that walks all over virtually every grand cru blanc de noirs this year. The higher clay content and less accessible chalk at the top of the hill set a generosity in perfect harmony with the brilliant precision of the classic 2008 season. A full straw hue with a subtle salmon tint declares its rumbling potency, boring to a fruit depth of another order, satsuma plum, even blackberry, yet simultaneously soaring to breathtaking heights of epic 2008 malic thrust, exploding in a glittering shower of chalk minerality. Complexity lurks in its folds, dark fruit cake and fruit mince spice. In contrast of tension and generosity, in unrelenting persistence and in sheer, unnerving endurance, this is Clos des Goisses on another level. In line and length alone, it is singly the greatest Philipponnat I have ever tasted.

Mareuil-sur-Aÿ, winter 2013

PIERRE GIMONNET & FILS

(Pee-yair Zhi-moh-neh e Feess)

8/10

I RUE DE LA RÉPUBLIQUE 51530 CUIS
www.champagne-gimonnet.com

PG

CHAMPAGNE

Pierre Gimonnet & Fils

‘The difference between a good wine and an exceptional wine is only a question of very, very small details, but we must focus on every detail all of the time,’ declares Didier Gimonnet, who oversees his family’s glorious estate with his brother, Olivier. The champagnes of Pierre Gimonnet & Fils are intricately assembled by masterful hands exclusively from enviably positioned and painstakingly tended old vines. Every cuvée sings its aspiration of ‘precision, purity and minerality’, each speaking articulately of its place in the northern Côte des Blancs through expressive, chalky minerality, without one molecule of detail out of place. With high-strung tension, crystalline structure and rapier-sharp precision, these are blanc de blancs champagnes charged with an energy that will sustain them long indeed. They represent some of the best-value apéritif champagnes of all.

‘My father always told me the most important thing is to make wine, and after that to sell it at a reasonable price,’ Didier explains. From one of Champagne’s most intelligent and insightful growers, wines of such purity and fine-spun, mineral-laden precision should sell for much higher prices. Little wonder Gimonnet has experienced strong global demand in recent years, fully allocating its production of 250,000 bottles. There is not a champagne in this collection unworthy of your table again this year.

GRAND VINEYARDS

‘Our champagnes have a personality because of the vineyards they come from,’ Didier enunciates. ‘In Champagne, as everywhere, the most important thing is the origin of the grapes.’ The family owns a substantial estate of 28 hectares, most proudly located in the heart of each of their village’s terroirs, almost exclusively in the Côte des Blancs.

In a region afflicted with generally young vines, more than 80% of Gimonnet’s are now more than 30 years old, more than half are aged over 40 years, 80% of his grand crus are aged more than 45 years, and one hectare more than a century — incredible numbers for a region that typically replants every 35 years. Every bottle of Gimonnet comes exclusively from these vineyards; not a single grape is purchased from growers.

‘When you have great terroir, it is a child’s game to create a great blend,’ Didier says. Half of Gimonnet’s vineyards are located in its premier cru home village of Cuis, which he is frank in admitting is the black sheep of the Côte des Blancs, not a great terroir. ‘With less body and structure, Cuis does not have the character, body or structure of a grand cru, but it has higher acidity, giving us very fresh wines,’ Didier explains. ‘Without doubt, the best of our domaines are in Cramant. I compare Cramant with lace — it is precise and delicate, with an interesting, chalky minerality, and

it has a concentration but is not heavy.' He holds 5.5 glorious hectares in the village.

One hectare in the more stony soils of Oger contributes concentrated, spicy, smoky power and graphite minerality; two hectares in Vertus have less power, but more exotic tropical fruit character; while a substantial 5.5 hectares in Chouilly add a fruity elegance. A little pinot noir is derived from just half a hectare, shared between Aÿ and Mareuil-sur-Aÿ.

'Fruitiness, elegance, power and minerality can therefore be determined according to the villages that we use in each blend,' Didier clarifies. 'Our objective is to make wines of minerality, not of explosive fruit.'

Of Gimonnet's considerable 12 hectares of grand cru holdings, three-quarters are located in the prized heart of the mid-slopes of their villages.

'We do not inherit land from our parents, we borrow it from our children,' he quotes Antoine de Saint-Exupéry. 'In this spirit, we practise meticulous, reasoned viticulture. We are not idealogues, but quite simple pragmatists with commonsense. We respect the soil by limiting herbicides, planting grass on some parcels and tilling the soil on others. We use practically no fertilisers, in order to encourage the root system to go deeper into the chalk.'

UNCOMPROMISING MIXOLOGISTS

Some in Champagne suggest Didier's blends do not do justice to the greatness of his terroirs. He has only just begun to create thundering single-cru old-vine cuvées from the grand crus of Cramant, Chouilly and Oger, but only in tiny quantities, so as not to deprive Gimonnet of the powerful blending material that so eloquently lifts the mood of Cuis in all but the very first of his nine blends. He singles out the strength of Oger as an exception, making it tricky to blend without dominating.

'I created a single Oger cuvée, as I'm not clever enough to know how to blend all of it!' He defines the best terroirs as those that respect others in a blend. 'Champagne is a blend, and a grand terroir is one that can be blended without dominating,' says Didier, who has been dubbed a 'mixologist'. This blending is the key to the philosophy of the house. 'I am against monoterroir,' he declares, 'but I am adept at very polished blends that combine the qualities of different terroirs to produce complexities. When I present the house I always say I'm not a winemaker, just an interpreter of terroir. Making something good when one has good land is natural, but to make something exceptional is a degree above. This is what drives us.'

Gimonnet owns 12 grand cru vineyards, but none of his core cuvées can be labelled grand cru, 'because they're better balanced when blended with premier cru parcels to confer freshness of acidity and balance between concentration, finesse and elegance,' Didier explains. 'The blend is the highest ideal here, more than the sum of the parts.'

But there are always exceptions to prove the rule. 'Blending is always our philosophy because we prefer harmony to intensity, but we decided from 2012 to create a range of Special Club Single Terroir cuvées in limited quantities.' He explains, '2012 marked an extraordinary vintage year for our estate. Our grand crus were so impressive that we decided to continue the experiment that we had begun with Oger and create single-cru cuvées.' He repeated this in 2014, 2015 and 2016, all in tiny volumes of around 3000 bottles (his Special Club blend is typically 15–25,000 bottles) 'so as to maintain the quality of our traditional assemblages'.

His mantra is to produce the most balanced wines, not those that can be labelled to command the highest prices. A noble pursuit, rare in Champagne, and it begins in the vineyards.

METICULOUS ATTENTION TO PURITY

When I visited at the height of harvest 2014 I found Olivier in the vineyards and Didier on the forklift unloading grapes in the winery. They are both very hands-on, and have the help of only two others in the winery. 'It is very important for the quality for me to be here,' Didier says.

'The date of harvest is very, very important,' he maintains. 'Eighty percent of vinification is done in determining the harvest date! Just four days too early or too late and it will disrupt concentration, structure and elegance.'

He prizes minerality and freshness above concentration, so does not harvest at the maximum maturity, but at the optimum level of ripeness to give a good balance of alcohol potential and high acidity. To achieve this, yields are moderated to around 11–12 tonnes/hectare (equating to about 75hL/hectare), compared with a potential of 18–20 tonnes. Old vines naturally regulate yields, and he green-harvests in abundant vintages such as 2018. Chaptalisation is performed only when necessary, and in the mature 2015 vintage, only in Cuis.

The goal of every stage of vinification is to preserve purity, freshness and minerality with the utmost precision. Gimonnet's winery is a pristine declaration of this mandate, a bathroom-fresh environment of floor-to-ceiling tiles and gleaming stainless steel. 'It is like cooking,' Didier suggests. 'To create purity you must have the freshest ingredients.' He upholds this mantra stringently, and most years sells or distils at least one tank that isn't up to standard. 'My father always explained to us that the most important rule of blending is to only use what you like,' he says. He attributes the secret of their success to rigorous technical precision and artisinal work that he likens to that of a watchmaker.

Vinification is as simple as possible, 'so the expression is due only to the terroir and the maturity of the fruit'. With 90% of vineyards within four kilometres of the house, all grapes are pressed within six hours of harvest. Gimonnet presses more lightly than most, so of the little he harvests he extracts even less juice, but juice of finer quality. As at Billecart-Salmon and Pol Roger, the juice is clarified at 10°C for 24 hours prior to fermentation, a crucial procedure for the refined elegance of the style. Selected yeast is then added to achieve a rapid start to fermentation.

'My goal is to have the juice in fermentation less than two days after picking; this is very important for maintaining purity

Cuis, summer 2018

and freshness.' Fermentation and maturation take place only in temperature-controlled stainless steel tanks. 'Our grapes come from good terroirs, and we want no other taste than that of the fruit.' There are 40 parcels in the estate, and 40 tanks to permit every plot to be vinified separately, as has been the practice of his family since his father Michel first took over the business and started producing his own champagnes in 1955. His ancestors have been growing grapes in Cuis since 1750.

The tendency of Cuis chardonnay to oxidise quickly in tank dictates that reserve wines are instead kept on fine lees in magnums under crown seal, allowing them to mature and develop body, while retaining purity and freshness, without evolving too rapidly. An unusual and painstaking process, it takes six people to open 10,000 magnums a day.

Vintage cuvées comprise a much more significant part of the portfolio than in most houses, representing a substantial 30–40% of production.

Malolactic fermentation is employed in all wines to soften the high acidity of Cuis. A light dosage of 8g/L of sugar is used, as little as 5g/L in the vintage cuvées, and there is no impression of sweetness. 'Dosage is very important to avoid angular wines without introducing the taste of sugar,' Didier explains. He considers it crucial to oxidise the liquor before adding it to the bottle. 'It seems like nothing, but it makes a subtle difference to the taste.' He uses only a small amount of sulphur as a preservative, but sufficient to uphold freshness.

Timing of disgorgement is likewise given careful consideration, with every bottle freshly disgorged to order. Disgorgement dates and full details of each cuvée are printed on back labels as requested by importers in each market. 'The date of disgorgement is very important in champagne,' Didier points out. 'A cuvée is very different six months after disgorgement than it is two years after disgorgement.' More than half of Gimonnet's non-vintage cuvées are sealed with reliable Mytik DIAM closures, as his trials have found these to preserve freshness more reliably than natural cork.

In order to centralise production and provide more space for ageing, Gimonnet constructed an impressive new cellar on two levels in Cuis in 2017. This was prompted not by increasing production, but by a desire to age cuvées *sur pointe* (neck down) rather than *sur latte* (on their side). 'The ageing is slower *sur pointe*, but I need 40% more storage space,' he explains. He now has capacity to hold 1.6 million bottles, an enormous volume for an annual production of just 250,000.

Enviable vineyards and meticulous practices stir strong demand, and Gimonnet has been working to increase production to keep up, which is not as easy as it sounds. 'We don't want to be wine merchants by buying grapes to increase production,' he emphasises. 'We don't want to make volume, we want to make the quality that we like and then offer it on allocation. We therefore need to buy vineyards with the potential of our style. But there are not many vineyards on the market, and when they are they are too expensive.' Over the past decade, five hectares have been purchased in the Côte des Blancs to increase production by about 50,000 bottles.

Gimonnet's cuvées represent some of the best buys on the Côte des Blancs again this year, and two releases rank as the very finest to have ever emerged from this legendary grower.

PIERRE GIMONNET & FILS CUIS 1ER CRU BRUT NV $$

91 points • 2015 base • DISGORGED SEPTEMBER 2018 • TASTED IN CHAMPAGNE AND AUSTRALIA

Cuis; 9.3% 2014, 8.4% 2013, 6.3% 2012, 7% 2011, 2% 2010; reserves are the previous year's bend, aged in magnum to preserve freshness and the autolytic complexity of maturity, without the oxidation of ageing in tank; aged 2 years on lees; 5.5g/L dosage; DIAM; 139,564 bottles, 18,333 half-bottles and 3920 magnums

Didier Gimonnet's aspiration for his entry non-vintage is a cuvée with attack on the front, roundness in the middle and crispness on the end. This cuvée is his first priority. 'I can only produce other cuvées if I take what I need for the non-vintage first,' he says.

Gimonnet's Cuis is the quintessential apéritif, and one of the most pristine champagnes for its price. The north-facing elegance of this bright premier cru infuses freshness and purity of lemon, grapefruit and crunchy nashi pear. The ripe and structured 2015 base adds a hint of pineapple core and lends its grip of phenolic mouthfeel, yet this has been well moderated by Gimonnet's precision engineering, to let the fine salt chalk minerality of the village sing in harmony with crystalline acidity. Bottle age has built seamless texture without yet contributing secondary complexity, besides a fleeting glimpse of brioche. Dosage is well integrated with vibrant acidity, laying out a tense, bright and long finish. As ever, this is signature Cuis, classic Gimonnet and great value champagne.

PIERRE GIMONNET & FILS BRUT EXTRA 1ER CRU BLANC DE BLANCS NV $$

93 points • 2013 base • DISGORGED APRIL 2018 • TASTED IN CHAMPAGNE AND AUSTRALIA

Cuis with longer on lees and lower dosage; 6% 2012, 9% 2011, 10% 2010, 5% 2009; reserves are the previous year's bend, aged in magnum; aged more than 4 years on lees; 4g/L dosage; DIAM

I love how confidently Gimonnet's Cuis ages, and I purchased 24 magnums of 2008 base to pour at my 40th birthday in 2015! There is a rising trend among the top champagne houses to re-release their entry non-vintage cuvée with longer on lees, a bold statement of both integrity and endurance. What makes Gimonnet unique in this is to do so with such an affordable cuvée as its Cuis NV. In a grand statement of the credentials of its vineyards and ultra-attentive winemaking, its brand-new release is a serious cuvée that juxtaposes the crunchy lemon and nashi pear of cool, north-facing slopes with the roast almond, brioche, honey and mixed spice complexity of more than four years on lees, uniting seamlessly and lingering long on the finish. The energetic acidity and bright salt minerality of the village shine brilliantly, in all their stark purity, illuminated by low dosage. It would benefit from even longer still to show its full potential, or even a fraction more dosage to calm its tension.

PIERRE GIMONNET & FILS CUVÉE GASTRONOME 1ER CRU BLANC DE BLANCS 2014 $$

94 points • DISGORGED JULY 2018 • TASTED IN CHAMPAGNE AND AUSTRALIA

34.5% Cuis for signature vivacity and freshness, 28% Chouilly Mont Aigu (planted 1951 and 1991) for fruit and elegance, 18% Cramant for plumpness, 10% Oger for masculine structure and spicy minerality, 9.5% Vertus for exoticism; aged more than 3 years on lees; 5g/L dosage; cork; 28,543 bottles

The aspiration of Gastronome is to present the spirit, elegance, freshness and approachability of a non-vintage, with structure and body. The fruity depth and approachability of Chouilly Mont Aigu provides the core, balanced with the power of Cramant and Oger, the freshness of Cuis and a 'petite mousse' of 4.5 atmospheres for creaminess. This cuvée effortlessly transcends the challenges of the 2014 season, personifying its aspiration in purity, freshness and vivacity of lemon, grapefruit and crunchy nashi and beurre bosc pear. Even at five years of age, its dynamic freshness and youthful purity of fruit are everything, exemplifying the tension and crunch of the northern Côte des Blancs, with no suggestion of secondary complexity besides the most subtle hint of almond meal and the gentle mouthfeel of lees texture. Its acid line is at once ripe and integrated, and simultaneously tense and enduring, drawing out a very long finish that heightens the presence of prominent, mouth-filling, glittering, salty minerality. A great 2014, ready to pop as a refined apéritif right away, or to hide away for the medium-term.

PIERRE GIMONNET & FILS ROSÉ DE BLANCS IER CRU NV $$

93 points • 2016 BASE • DISGORGED 15 JULY 2018 • TASTED IN CHAMPAGNE AND AUSTRALIA

92% chardonnay, 8% pinot noir; 63% Cramant for plumpness, Chouilly Mont Aigu for fruit and elegance, and Oger for masculine structure and spicy minerality, 29% Cuis for signature vivacity and freshness, 8% Bouzy pinot noir red wine; aged 2 years on lees; 5.5g/L dosage; DIAM; 19,918 bottles

Gimonnet's cracking and cleverly named rosé is just 8% Bouzy red wine (not least because it costs him almost €15 a litre to buy!) blended with his vintage Gastronome cuvée – his blanc de blancs with the most body and power to handle the pinot. 'The aspiration is to elaborate a very refreshing rosé that upholds the identity of Gimonnet and of the Côte des Blancs,' Didier Gimonnet explains. Its popularity has taken him by surprise. 'I thought a blanc de blancs specialist like me would not sell more than 5% rosé, but this cuvée is now 7–8% of my sales, and Gastronome has halved in production accordingly.'

Charged with more than 50% grand cru chardonnay, the result upholds its mantra of sustaining the mouthfeel, persistence and surging bath-salts chalk minerality of the Côte des Blancs with great accomplishment, this year touched with a pale salmon-pink hue and the lightest reflections of white cherries, lemons, ruby grapefruit, red apples and strawberry hull. Delightfully restrained and refreshingly tense, it's more about crystalline precision and vibrant drive than flavour. One of the most refreshing apéritif rosés this year, serve it like a delicate blanc de blancs, not like a rosé. One bottle showed a subtle lack of freshness, lending a savoury tomato hint.

PIERRE GIMONNET & FILS OENOPHILE NON DOSÉ IER CRU BLANC DE BLANCS BRUT NATURE 2012 $$

93 points • DISGORGED OCTOBER 2018 • TASTED IN CHAMPAGNE AND AUSTRALIA

40% Cramant, 38.5% Chouilly (mostly Mont Aigu), 14% Cuis, 7.5% Oger; aged more than 5 years on lees; 2012 Fleuron with no dosage; cork; 15,750 bottles

Didier Gimonnet's sincerity is refreshing. 'I am not a lover of champagne without dosage, as dosage is part of the tradition of our region, and even 4–5g/L rounds out the wine. Wine without dosage is interesting when it's recently disgorged, but when I pull them out of the cellar 18 months later I always prefer the same wine with a little dosage to add complexity and balance.' Still, sales of his zero-dosage Oenophile are on the rise. This is not a dedicated blend, but chosen from the cellar each year according to which cuvée has the natural balance to stand best without dosage.

The great 2012 season upholds wonderful tension and confidence, slowly building subtle almond-meal and toast complexity, while upholding a whiff of grilled-toast reduction. Its grand cru credentials are proclaimed resoundingly in a core of fantastic fruit concentration, grand persistence, crystalline chalk minerality and crushed oyster shell structure. True to the lineage of this cuvée, all the unashamed grip and tension of grapefruit, lemon, apple and pear define an incisive, steely acid line, contrasted cunningly with fine, creamy lees texture and a very fine bead. The result is one of the greatest zero dosages to emerge from the distinguished Gimonnet cellars, a chiselled and highly sophisticated champagne, not for the uninitiated, but it will enthral oyster fanatics, and is certain to improve for many years to come.

PIERRE GIMONNET & FILS CUVÉE FLEURON 1ER CRU BLANC DE BLANCS 2010 $$

94 points • DISGORGED JULY 2018 • TASTED IN CHAMPAGNE AND AUSTRALIA

40.5% Cramant, 27% Chouilly (mostly Mont Aigu), 6% Oger, 16% Cuis, 10.5% Vertus; aged 7 years on lees; 5.5 atmospheres of pressure; 4.5g/L dosage; 33,680 bottles

'Fleuron' means 'best of', created when there was only one non-vintage and one vintage wine in the house. Today it is Gimonnet's signature vintage cuvée, a blend of the best parcels from each village, boasting almost three-quarters grand cru Côte des Blancs, a preposterous proportion for a wine of this price. Gimonnet's goal here is to capture the taste of the domaine and the spirit of the season in a single blend of complexity, more about structure and focus than the immediacy of Gastronome.

A complex and immediate take on this mandate, 2010 is a vintage that fast developed on its release three years ago into a medium-straw hue (bright by any standards, yet deep for Gimonnet) and grand complexity. Amazingly, it has since held its own magnificently. After three more years on lees, its subtle evolution for a fast-evolving vintage is testament to the endurance of this house and its terroirs. Its vivacious core of lemon and grapefruit remain, as does its progression into mixed spice, toast, ginger and honey, now adding vanilla, nougat and toasted marshmallow to the party. It presents integrity and persistence remarkable for this weaker harvest. The impact of salty grand cru minerality remains transfixed, defining a long finish of vibrant acid line, invisible dosage and subtle, well-handled phenolic grip. I admired it then years ago, and I love it even more now.

PIERRE GIMONNET & FILS SPECIAL CLUB GRANDS TERROIRS DE CHARDONNAY 2012 $$$

96 points • DISGORGED OCTOBER 2018 • TASTED IN CHAMPAGNE AND AUSTRALIA

60% Cramant for structure and minerality (vines over 40 years old, and 20% from 1911 and 1913); 30% Chouilly Mont Aigu planted 1951 for elegance; 10% Cuis for signature freshness; aged 5 years on lees; 4.5g/L dosage; cork; 21,516 bottles

Gimonnet's Special Club is a blend of the best of each vintage, with the aspiration of creating an elegant style that's greater than the sum of its parts. It's built on old vines of 40–100 years of age, from the best parcels of the domaine in the heart of the terroirs, relying on Cramant for structure, balanced with the silkiness of Chouilly Mont Aigu and the definition of Cuis. Didier Gimonnet considers 2012 greater even than 2008 and 2002, which is about as high as praise for any season could ever be.

His Special Club presents a grand and captivating contradiction, on the one hand desperately subtle and delicately understated, with tightly clenched apple, grapefruit, lemon and white peach compressed into an infinitesimal singularity, yet simultaneously rippling with grand cru depth, enduring persistence and seamless, mouth-evading presence that marks out the most dramatic and unwavering line. Over the two years since its release, further time on lees has begun to reveal subtle almond meal and vanilla nougat. The one detail that is not understated is the inimitable chalk mineral presence that defines its enviable positions in the great crus of the Côte des Blancs, captured in full magnificence thanks to Gimonnet precision, frothing and churning with salty, chalky, mouth-filling texture from start to very long finish. Time has not diminished its profound mineral signature, and its salty chalk manifesto is proclaimed today with greater conviction than ever. It is still but embarking on its odyssey, and is far from ready yet, with every detail in precisely the right place to blossom into breathtaking greatness in many, many years to come. It epitomises the essence of the northern Côte des Blancs with the pinpoint accuracy of Gimonnet.

PIERRE GIMONNET & FILS SPECIAL CLUB CRAMANT GRAND CRU 2012 $$$$

98 points • DISGORGED 17 APRIL 2018 • TASTED IN CHAMPAGNE AND AUSTRALIA

Cramant; more than 10 parcels in the heart of the terroir; old vines, 80% more than 50 years of age, and 1 hectare planted 1911 and 1913; no chaptalisation; aged 5 years on lees; 4.5g/L dosage; cork; 3013 bottles

Of its 28-hectare estate, Gimonnet owns an enviable 5.5 hectares in the heart of Cramant, spanning more than 10 vineyards. 'Without doubt, the best of our domaines are in Cramant,' Didier Gimonnet waxes. 'I compare Cramant with lace – it is precise and delicate, with an interesting, chalky minerality, and it has a concentration but is not heavy.' He claims 2012 is better even than 2002 and 2008, 'with a cool summer upholding dizzying acidity, and perfect conditions from mid-August producing generous sugar ripeness'. He harvested Cramant at an average of 9.5 tonne/hectare, 'nearly optimum for elegance and balance'.

The sheer stature of Cramant's greatest mid-slope sites is a grand and stark contrast to its neighbours of Chouilly and Cuis, and there is perhaps no more profound exemplification of this than Gimonnet. The grand old vines of the domaine's finest sites articulate the purity and chalk mineral definition of this village in cinematic high definition. The pinpoint clarity of super-fine, heightened, mouth-filling chalk minerality is all-encompassing, the defining signature of one of the greatest of all grand crus. Pristine, bright lemon and white peach fruit launches with profound theatrics of piercing purity, like white fireworks exploding in a black firmament. Line and length are undeviating, trailing with spectacular confidence and exacting determination, setting an impeccable juxtaposition between grand cru stature and Gimonnet precision. Brilliant nuances of vanilla, almond meal, marzipan and anise are just fleeting glimpses of six years on lees. A cuvée that will unravel slowly and effortlessly for decades to come, this is categorically the greatest Gimonnet I have tasted. And then along came Millésime de Collection 2008 in magnum...

PIERRE GIMONNET & FILS SPECIAL CLUB CHOUILLY GRAND CRU 2012 $$$$

96 points • DISGORGED 17 APRIL 2018 • TASTED IN CHAMPAGNE AND AUSTRALIA

Exclusively from 1.9 hectares of Chouilly Mont Aigu planted 1951; harvested at natural potential of 11.43 degrees; no chaptalisation; aged 4 years on lees; 4.5g/L dosage; cork; 3003 bottles

Gimonnet has long built its grandeur on some of the most enviably placed grand cru sites of the Côte des Blancs, and now, for the first time, the house has granted us a privileged insight into the untouched purity of the very greatest of these. The presence and generous confidence of Chouilly Mont Aigu are on grand display here, built around a compact yet dense core of golden delicious apple, lemon, white peach and beurre bosc pear, even suggestions of ginger and anise. Subtle complexity of honey biscuits hints at a little more development than the Cramant of the same season, yet it remains coiled and profoundly fresh, even at seven years of evolution. The deep-set, very salty and ultra-fine minerality tapped by the deep roots of these grand old vines is almost creamy by contrast with the spine of its neighbours, Cramant and Cuis. Yet it is a vector of focused purity, an impossible juxtaposition of power and ethereal elegance as only Chouilly can achieve, charged with a salivating energy that will sustain it effortlessly for decades.

PIERRE GIMONNET & FILS MILLÉSIME DE COLLECTION VIEILLES VIGNES DE CHARDONNAY 2008 $$$$$

98 points • DISGORGED 20 JULY 2018 • TASTED IN CHAMPAGNE AND AUSTRALIA EN MAGNUM

57% Cramant (35% of the vines planted in 1911 and 1913, and 10% more than 40 years old), 29% Chouilly (mostly Mont Aigu planted 1951), 12.5% Cuis Croix-Blanche planted in the 1960s, 1.5% Vertus; aged 9 years on lees; 4.5g/L dosage; cork; 3596 magnums

Didier Gimonnet's aspirations for Special Club are elegance and ageing potential, and his Millésime de Collection represents a later release of the greatest vintages, exclusively in magnums. So far, this collection has comprised only 2002, 2006 and 2008, with 2012 yet to come. His philosophy is to age magnums 10 years on lees.

Debuting in 2015 as the most stunning-value prestige cuvée I'd tasted in five years, Special Club 2008 is back for a breathtaking encore, to the tune of just 3596 magnums. Its jaw-droppingly affordable price aside, this cuvée astounded me with its utmost finesse and enduring stamina from the moment it first hit the ground, when I begged you not to touch a bottle for 10 years, and to keep one for at least 30 years. I have marvelled at its freeze-frame slow-motion evolution in bottles since, but there was no anticipating its profound immunity to the passage of time in glorious magnums: it seems as pristinely beach-fresh today as the moment its precious grapes left their grand old vines. My note was virtually unchanged in both of the previous two editions of this Guide, and, unfathomably, again today. In raw, youthful innocence, it's the definition of pinpoint purity, the epitome of introverted, tightly coiled restraint, revealing only the most subtle signs of its petals beginning to curl open. Beguiling transparency of pure acid drive propels an incredible finish that splashes long and strong with frothy, salty chalk minerality, somehow boring even deeper into its hallowed chalk bedrock in magnum than bottle. Brilliant white cherries and citrus still ring out in clear peals like church bells to an undercurrent of ever so slowly rising nuances of nougat, anise and now toasted brioche. A cuvée of effortless poise, unrelenting drive and breathtaking, scintillating, crystalline purity. Gimonnet's greatest achievement – at least until 2012.

PIERRE GIMONNET & FILS MILLÉSIME DE COLLECTION VIEILLES VIGNES DE CHARDONNAY 2006 $$$$$

94 points • DISGORGED 20 APRIL 2018 • TASTED IN CHAMPAGNE AND AUSTRALIA EN MAGNUM

65% Cramant (vines over 40 years old, and more than 30% from vines planted 1911 and 1913) for structure, minerality and laciness, 22.5% Chouilly (mostly Mont Aigu planted 1951) for elegance, 12.5% Cuis old vines for signature freshness; light chaptalisation; aged 11 years on lees; 5g/L dosage; cork; 3713 magnums

In the fanatically precise style of Gimonnet, the acid line and all-encompassing, salty chalk mineral structure of well-positioned sites throughout the Côte des Blancs spells out compelling longevity, even in a season as ripe and immediately approachable as 2006. Now a teenager, it has evolved gracefully to a medium to full straw hue and a complex place of honey, toast, gingernut biscuits, mixed spice, even notes of apricot, shedding primary pear fruit, while just beginning to show the tertiary complexity of a hint of green olives. There is a rich approachability to this release that reflects the exuberance of the season, making it right for drinking right away, yet upholding the poised balance and mouth-filling, salty chalk minerality that define Gimonnet. I wrote two years ago that this was a vintage to drink then, and it has since held its own confidently, though threatens to dry out on the finish in time to come.

PIERRE PAILLARD

(Pee-yair Peye-yarh)

—

2 RUE DU VINGTIÈME SIÈCLE 51150 BOUZY
www.champagne-pierre-paillard.com

CHAMPAGNE
PIERRE PAILLARD

DOMAINE À BOUZY - GRAND CRU

The Paillard family has been making champagne in Bouzy since 1768, and brothers Quentin and Antoine Paillard are the eighth generation to tend their family's privileged holdings of 11 hectares exclusively in the village. Chardonnay comprises a strong 40% of their vineyards, unusual for Bouzy, but smart for blending options, the balance of course pinot noir. Vines are tended sustainably, using their own organic compost, and completely shunning herbicides and insecticides. Grapes are picked at full maturity and treated with a minimalist approach in the winery, to fully express their terroirs. Each plot is vinified separately and aged for nine months in vats and barrels, and sulphur dioxide preservative is used sparingly, so malolactic fermentation is never blocked. Roman numerals are used cleverly to indicate base vintages on the front labels of non-vintage cuvées, and informative back labels detail cépage, vintages, disgorgement dates and dosage. An annual production of 90,000 bottles receives extra-brut dosages of just 2–4g/L, which in concert with low sulphur make for a tense and dry style that appreciates the flesh of a warm vintage.

PIERRE PAILLARD LES PARCELLES BOUZY GRAND CRU XIII EXTRA-BRUT NV $$

89 points • 2013 BASE VINTAGE • DISGORGED NOVEMBER 2017 • TASTED IN AUSTRALIA

30% chardonnay, 70% pinot; 22 estate plots in Bouzy; no oak; 14% 2012 & 6% 2004 reserves; 2.7g/L dosage; cork

Declaring the presence of Bouzy in a full straw hue and red apple and yellow plum fruit, this is a dry and tense style of firm phenolic grip and acid tension. A callow palate lacks the generosity for which this village is renowned, exacerbated by low dosage. True to the style of the house, this is a taut style that deploys both tight acidity and phenolic bitterness to create structure and tension.

PIERRE PAILLARD LES TERRES ROSES BOUZY GRAND CRU XIV ROSÉ EXTRA-BRUT NV $$$

88 points • 2014 BASE VINTAGE • DISGORGED JULY 2018 • TASTED IN AUSTRALIA

70% chardonnay, 30% pinot noir; Bouzy; 20% reserves; 5% Bouzy rouge; no oak; 1.8g/L dosage; cork

Pierre Paillard's rosé is unusual in its Bouzy chardonnay lead, with a subtle 5% Bouzy rouge lending a pale copper hue. It's a savoury and secondary style, reminiscent of sun-dried tomatoes, balsamic vinegar and tart redcurrants, with the nougat complexity of three years of lees age. The palate finishes dry and callow, with astringent phenolic grip, and would appreciate more primary fruit and dosage to build flesh and generosity.

PIERRE PAILLARD LES MOTTELETTES BOUZY GRAND CRU BLANC DE BLANCS EXTRA-BRUT 2013 $$$

89 points • DISGORGED JANUARY 2018 • TASTED IN AUSTRALIA

100% chardonnay; Bouzy single vineyard of 0.6 hectares planted 1961; 1.8g/L dosage; cork

A Bouzy blanc de blancs of savoury complexity, this is a style layered with charcuterie, pear, and all the mixed spice of Bouzy. The interplay of tart acidity and firm phenolic bite makes for a callow finish, lacking in the fruit lift of 2013 and the depth that characterises Bouzy. Strictly for champagne die-hards.

PIERRE PAILLARD LES MAILLERETTES BOUZY GRAND CRU BLANC DE NOIRS EXTRA-BRUT 2013 $$$

91 points • DISGORGED JANUARY 2018 • TASTED IN AUSTRALIA

100% pinot noir; Bouzy single vineyard of 0.36 hectares planted 1970; 2.7g/L dosage; cork

A medium straw with a blush tint heralds Bouzy pinot fragranced with red gala apples and a hint of rose hip. The palate leads out with morello cherries, raspberries, even a suggestion of musk sticks. For the promise with which it commences, it sadly closes short and a little callow, with grainy phenolic grip and bright acidity wanting for more flesh and generosity. Even 6g/L dosage could have helped.

PIERRE PAILLARD LES GOUTTES D'OR BOUZY BLANC COTEAUX CHAMPENOIS 2012 $$

91 points • TASTED IN AUSTRALIA

50% chardonnay, 50% pinot noir; Bouzy; cork

A classy and beautiful expression of Bouzy blanc that unites the pretty, bright lemon of chardonnay and the strawberry hull, white cherry and almost fig tension of pinot noir to compelling effect. Backward, pure, energetic and enduring, it's very youthful at seven years of age, driven by a tense line of vibrant yet ripe acidity, sensitively supported by the elegant vanilla notes of classy oak. The finish is a little attenuated today, but it has all of the tightly coiled potential to fan out and blossom for many years yet.

PIERRE PAILLARD LA GRANDE RÉCOLTE BOUZY GRAND CRU MILLÉSIME EXTRA-BRUT 2006 $$$

93 points • DISGORGED SEPTEMBER 2016 • TASTED IN AUSTRALIA

50% chardonnay, 50% pinot noir; Bouzy old vines; 2.6g/L dosage; aged 9 years on lees; cork

The tense and dry style of Pierre Paillard calls for the generosity of a ripe vintage and the calming influence of long lees age, uniting in 2006 to compelling effect. The magnitude of this wine is amplified three-fold, in the powerful grand cru of Bouzy, the ripe harvest of 2006, and the generosity of a full 13 years of age. The result is a full straw-yellow hue and a rich interplay of ripe fig, fresh pineapple, toffee, toasted brioche and preserved lemon. Ample, succulent and secondary, it leads out with the full breadth of ripe Bouzy, trailing into a long finish of chardonnay's lemon zest accents. Energetic acidity, salt minerality and phenolic tension unite to make for a dry finish, yet its fruit presence holds its own with confidence. One bottle was cork tainted.

Bouzy, harvest 2014

PIERRE PÉTERS

(Pee-yair Peh-tair)

7/10

26 RUE DES LOMBARDS 51190 LE MESNIL-SUR-OGER
www.champagne-peters.com

Pierre Péters
CHAMPAGNE
PROPRIÉTAIRE-RÉCOLTANT

Very few champagnes more eloquently articulate their terroirs than those of Pierre Péters. Many encounters with the young Rodolphe Péters, exploring the fruits of three decades, have left me mesmerised by the remarkable capacity of the chardonnay vine to extract the salty minerality of the Côte des Blancs's finest grand crus and preserve it in its wines for time eternal. This little estate, more than any other, has given me the realisation of another dimension to champagne, one in which minerality assumes a personality all of its own. And I have discovered Les Chétillons, the Le Montrachet of Le Mesnil-sur-Oger.

Celebrating its centenary, the Péters family has tended its vines in Le Mesnil-sur-Oger for six generations, and made its own champagne since 1919. Today, the estate is the privileged custodian of 20 hectares of chardonnay. Besides a small parcel in the Sézanne, every one of its 60 plots is well placed in the finest grand crus of the Côte des Blancs: Oger, Cramant, Avize and, most of all, Le Mesnil-sur-Oger.

ATTENTIVE VINEYARD CARE

Rodolphe Péters took control in 2008, but has been helping his father with the blending since 1994, and knows his vines as well as anyone in Champagne. I quickly discovered just how well when I first met him in late July 2011, four weeks before the earliest harvest in history, when he was about to depart for holidays.

'Everyone says I am a crazy man taking holidays until August 19, but I wrote in my book in May that we would begin harvest on August 23, 24 or 25 and I have not revised this since.' A remarkable insight in one of Champagne's most erratic years,

in which others extended their projections by as much as four weeks. 'That's crazy,' he says, 'but I spend more time than any of them in my land.'

Péters' vines are lavished some of the most attentive care in all of Champagne. 'I am reluctant to walk in the vines for fear of crushing the chalk,' he says. I have never heard this from any other grower, but there are few other places that enjoy such ready access to chalk, just 10–30 centimetres below the surface in Le Mesnil-sur-Oger. For this reason, deep roots to access the minerality of the chalk are not the priority for Péters.

'Minerality deep in the chalk is not accessible to the plants, but the interface between the topsoil and the deep soil is where the roots are able to find it,' he explains. The role of micro-organisms and worms in mixing the deeper soils and making this minerality available to the roots is crucial, and he works hard to keep the soil alive with organic material. Grass is planted in the mid-rows to provide competition for surface roots, forcing them down to the interface with the chalk.

He is adamant that he cannot keep his soils alive using certified organics. 'My philosophy is to follow the best procedures of the best of all philosophies,' he says, comparing the health of his vines with his own health, treating his allergies with a mixture of conventional medicine, vitamins and homeopathy. 'My first responsibility is to take care of my workers, the first people in contact with the chemicals I use – and by protecting them, I naturally take care of my customers, the vines and the environment.' His soil analyses have revealed high levels of copper sulphate from years of treatment by previous generations, detrimental to the soil, but permitted under biodynamics. He instead relies mainly on conventional treatments to protect his vineyards.

A natural balance is achieved in the vineyards, thanks to the regulating effect of old vines (averaging more than 30 years of age) and competition from grasses in the mid-rows. 'The fashion now is to say low yields and high maturity, but Champagne was not built on this – it was built on a comfortable balance of production to achieve the correct level of ripeness and acidity.' He considers pH, rather than acidity, to be the best indicator of balance, always aiming for low pH as a sign that he has captured the minerality of the soil.

Péters replants his vines using a *sélection massale* of vines cultivated from cuttings from his old vines, to preserve clonal diversity and resistance. He shares two nurseries with other like-minded estates like Louis Roederer, and evolves the selection according to the pressure of disease, changes in climate and the evolving taste of consumers. 'With changes in the climate, some clones are better suited to warm weather than others. A clone selected 30 years ago might not be compatible with the new environment, the new way in which we farm, and the new tastes of consumers,' he explains.

INNOVATIVE VINIFICATION

Péters' intuitive and adaptable approach in the vineyards extends to his winemaking, and he is constantly experimenting with different yeasts and fermentation techniques tweaked to the specific nuances of each vintage. The racy acidity of his cuvées has traditionally been softened by full malolactic fermentation, but since Rodolphe has been in command, he has selectively blocked malolactic in some tanks, particularly in low-acid seasons like 2017 and 2018. Typically he blocks malolactic fermentation in 15–25% of his parcels, but in 2018 it was 45%.

To preserve character and maintain freshness, Péters commissioned a new cuverie, to allow him to focus more attention on the finer details of vinification. 'You cannot keep your two feet still on the ground!' he grins. New computer-controlled presses provide more precise control and allow him to keep smaller blocks separate. He personally tastes the juice as it comes off the press, and makes the press cuts by taste, not by the authorised volumes.

He cultivates yeast strains from his own vineyards and uses these for a selection of his ferments (40% in 2018). 'We will never be 100% wild fermented, for the same reason that we will never be 100% malolactic fermentation,' he explains. Some of his plots match better with particular yeasts than others. He focuses on yeasts that draw our the chalky character of his terroirs, but suggests that he needs to be very attentive to keeping this in check. 'I want the impression of the fruitiness to be lower, but Le Mesnil is a very mineral terroir, and if the chalkiness is too much it is not enjoyable. I like a glass of excessive wine, but I don't like a bottle of excessive wine!'

He considers structure and freshness to be derived from a combination of minerality, acidity and 'pleasant bitterness' from lees contact, and hence keeps wines on gross lees for long periods after alcoholic fermentation. The presence of gross lees keeps the wines fresh, permitting a low level of sulphur dioxide as a preservative.

Péters stringently protects the juice from oxygen at all times, and ferments only in small stainless steel tanks under temperature control. His recent passion has been experimentation with different vessels for storing reserves. A new room with natural temperature control is dedicated to concrete tanks, which he describes as the 'opposite concept to eggs', designed to decrease movement inside and produce fresher, earthier and less fruity wines. He has always kept reserves in stainless steel and concrete, and has also introduced a large Croatian oak foudre, not for oak flavour, but for increasing the texture and creaminess of reserves. With two additional foudres commissioned in early 2015, he now maintains a balance of 50% reserves in stainless steel (for fruitiness), 30% in concrete (for earthiness) and 20% in foudres (for creaminess). 'If you can blend your wine from a diverse selection with subtle differences, at the end of the day, you make a better wine,' he upholds. 'You can even make a better single-vineyard wine by blending from the same terroir.'

FORGOTTEN RESERVE

Péters maintains a fantastic reserve, including half of his crop of Les Chétillons every harvest. He was concerned about the tendency of reserve wines to lose their freshness over time, necessitating use of the best wines as reserves, rather than in vintage and prestige cuvées. This led to a radical reinvention of the non-vintage blend in 1997. Every reserve wine, spanning 1988 to 1996, was blended into a modified solera which became the ongoing reserve, topped up every year except in 1999 and 2003; these were kept separate to preserve the purity of the reserve. Kept on fine lees in a stainless steel tank at 13–14°C, the reserve is kept lively through refreshing each year. I was amazed that in 2011 (a sample up to and including the 2010 vintage), a wine of such complexity could still retain such purity of grapefruit and preserved lemon.

This reserve solera embodies Péters' philosophy of keeping the memory of the estate alive in his Cuvée de Réserve Blanc de Blancs Brut NV, which claims a generous 40% reserve wine. His aim is to showcase the terroir of grand cru blanc de blancs, achieved with

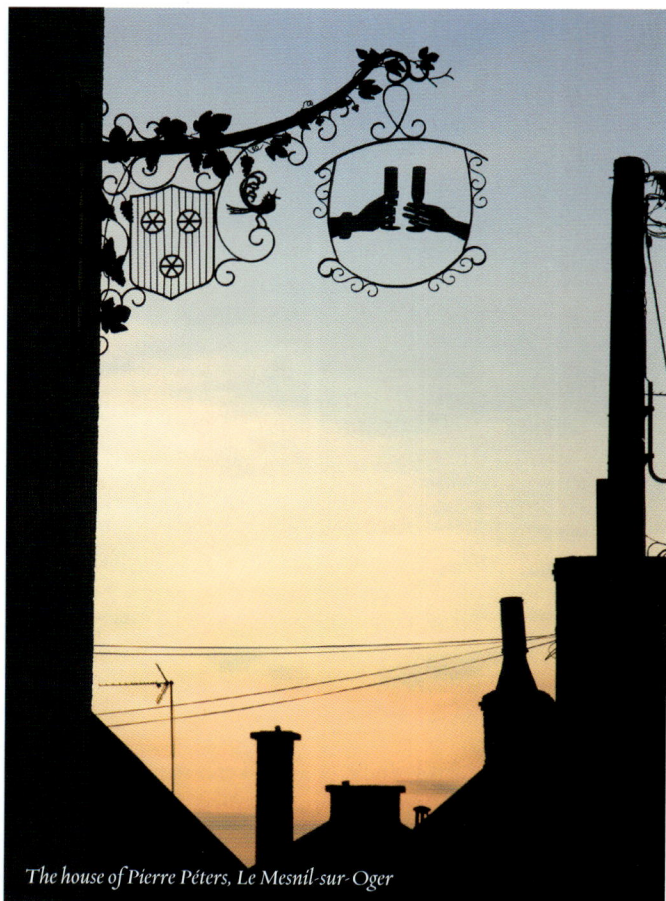

The house of Pierre Péters, Le Mesnil-sur-Oger

'The south-east-facing slope of Cramant is like the brown of fall, the perfect chardonnay, of similar profile to Le Mesnil, yet less cold. More lemony, with a creamy chalkiness and nuances reminiscent of vanilla, cinnamon, saffron, dried fruits and something dry, like dried flowers or cinnamon, that evokes autumn leaves falling before winter.

'I have parcels that really express each of these characters, and I focus on these for my vintage blend. If a harvest expresses more generosity of summer and autumn, it is released as a vintage wine, but if it has more of the austerity of winter and spring I blend it as a non-vintage extra brut,' says Péters.

THE 'LE MONTRACHET' OF LE MESNIL

On the southern edge of the village flanking the road to Vertus, the large vineyard of Les Chétillons is one of the finest sites for sparkling winegrowing in Le Mesnil-sur-Oger – and, indeed, anywhere on earth. Here the chalk is never more than 10 centimetres from the surface, so the vines are effectively rooted in pure chalk. In slope and exposition, Péters describes it as perfect – not too much and not too little.

The family has nurtured three plots in these calcareous soils since 1930, with vines now an impressive 52–73 years old. Each has been vinified separately and blended to produce a single-vintage wine since 1971.

Péters speaks of the minerality of Les Chétillons as crushed oyster shells, sea salt, and flavours of the ocean that laid down the chalk more than 70 million years ago. 'If you taste a stone in the vineyard, it is salty,' he explains, and it is this that infuses the mineral texture in his wines.

The mesmerising minerality of this extraordinary site remains steadfast in every old vintage I have tasted, right back to 1985. Through changes of season and winemaker, flavours evolve, intensity builds and bubbles fade, but the minerality remains transfixed. 'It is a stake, it stays for a very long time,' he declares. 'The best terroir will always be stronger than the best winemaker.'

Péters has trialled different closures since 2001, prompting a switch to DIAM for his non-vintage cuvées. 'If your wine has good structure, it has more resilience to shipping and storage under DIAM than the same wine under cork,' he says. 'When I taste my wine in very far markets like Japan or the west coast of the US, it still tastes like my wine when it is sealed with DIAM.' He currently reports 2–5% inconsistency in natural corks.

Every time I visit Péters he has a new cuvée to show me in his line of 11 labels (and counting). Such is the demand for his wines that he is not able to offer every cuvée in every market. He is very concerned that his annual production of 160,000 bottles is no longer able to meet the demand of his loyal customers.

'I try my best to purchase more vineyards, but another two hectares is nothing in terms of increasing production. And it will cost €3 million.'

Since 2014, a QR code on every bottle reveals the disgorgement date, base vintage and dosage.

60% of the current vintage from 50 plots spanning all of his Côte des Blancs estate vineyards, including Les Chétillons.

'The reserve is the key to the quality, making it easy to maintain consistency,' he says. It's a genius concept, and such is the class of the reserve that he has released it as its own cuvée, aptly named La Réserve Oubliée – 'the forgotten reserve'.

Cuvée de Réserve and Péters's vintage blend L'Esprit draw estate chardonnay from across the Côte des Blancs's grand crus. 'I like to think of each of the villages as a season, according to how they make me feel when I taste the vins clairs,' Péters explains.

'Le Mesnil-sur-Oger is the grey of winter for its sharp, stony minerality – austere and cold in character, with a cold sea breeze that gives the feeling of being in Normandy in winter.

'Oger is spring, for its elegant white flowers and white fruits, pear and pepper, the first white sunlight and the first blossoms of the fruit trees. Its amphitheatre concentrates the sunlight and provides warmth. It is very soft, feminine and delicate, giving you the feeling of spring after a long winter.

'Avize is all about the character of summer, more orange than yellow in its full-bodied, showy and developed chardonnay of rich, ripe grapefruit, orange and mandarin. Its terroir is less chalky and more graphite in its structure.

PIERRE PÉTERS CUVÉE DE RÉSERVE BLANC DE BLANCS GRAND CRU BRUT NV $$$

93 points • 2016 BASE VINTAGE • TASTED IN CHAMPAGNE
90 points • 2015 BASE VINTAGE • TASTED IN CHAMPAGNE
91 points • 2014 BASE VINTAGE • DISGORGED MARCH 2017 • TASTED IN AUSTRALIA

50% current vintage, 50% reserve solera of roughly 25 vintages from 1988 stored in stainless steel, concrete and Croatian oak foudres (full details under 'Forgotten Reserve' in introduction on page 471); Le Mesnil-sur-Oger, Oger, Cramant and Avize; partial malolactic fermentation; 6–7g/L dosage; DIAM

Rodolphe Péters did not expect 2016, a good vintage that he describes as balancing power and elegance, to hold such balance after 2012, 2013 and 2014. It shines in this blend with clarity, precision and excellent freshness of apple, pear, grapefruit and lemon. All the theatrics of his masterful reserve solera build out a backdrop layered with enticing brioche and mixed spice. Its fruit presence contrasts well-poised malic acid line, with the magnificent, frothing, salt mineral structure of Le Mesnil singing loud and clear. The 2015 base reflects three months of hot, dry summer in a dry style of bruised apple and pear amidst the dry extract of phenolic grip, though holds its poise and line on the finish, which Péters attributes to the refreshing chalk of his village. The phenolic dryness of the challenging 2014 vintage is not so pronounced, softened by the creamy texture of its deep reserve solera, and brightened by lemon freshness and crunchy nashi pear purity.

PIERRE PÉTERS GRANDE RÉSERVE BLANC DE BLANCS GRAND CRU BRUT NV $$$

91 points • 2015 BASE VINTAGE • DISGORGED DECEMBER 2018 • TASTED IN CHAMPAGNE

L'Esprit vintage blended with reserve solera of roughly 25 vintages from 1988 stored in stainless steel, concrete and Croatian oak foudres (full details page 471); grand cru Côte des Blancs; partial malolactic fermentation; 5.5g/L dosage

I was the first to taste Péters' new blend, which unites his vintage L'Esprit blend with his perpetual reserve and is blessed with a longer period on lees than his Cuvée de Réserve. The dry extract of 2015 makes for an apple- and pear-skin style of phenolic grip and long-lingering citrus vibrancy. Excellent salty mineral expression drives a finish of good persistence and confidence.

PIERRE PÉTERS BLANC DE BLANCS GRAND CRU EXTRA BRUT NV $$

96 points • 100% 2012 • DISGORGED DECEMBER 2016 AND DECEMBER 2018 • TASTED IN CHAMPAGNE AND AUSTRALIA

A blend of four vineyards, one each in Le Mesnil-sur-Oger, Avize, Oger and Cramant; 2g/L dosage

Rodolphe Péters releases his generous vintages as Millésime L'Esprit, and his austere vintages as Extra Brut NV. Confusingly, in some stages of the release cycle, he releases exactly the same wine under both labels, as he has done here. Buy the Extra Brut because it's generally 40% cheaper! For my tasting note, see Pierre Péters Cuvée Millésime L'Esprit Blanc de Blancs 2012 overleaf.

PIERRE PÉTERS RÉSERVE OUBLIÉE BLANC DE BLANCS BRUT GRAND CRU NV $$$$

94 points • 2012 BASE VINTAGE • TASTED IN CHAMPAGNE

Perpetual reserve solera of 23 vintages spanning 1988 to 2012, missing only the inferior 1999 and 2003; a selection of the best Croatian oak foudres, concrete and stainless steel tanks; 4g/L dosage from grape juice aged in a small barrel; aged under natural cork; DIAM closure

Few reserves can boast such ravishing integration, seamless internal harmony and sheer completeness, a credit to both the genius of this modified solera and the painstakingly tended vines that feed it. Rodolphe modestly points to the terroir as the inspiration and driver of its endurance. He upholds the 2012 base as the best yet and he's right. It sings with the freshness and dynamic tension of the *réserve perpétuelle*, charged with great energy and integrity. The salt minerality is super fine and deep set. Age has brought depth and presence in a deeply layered backdrop of spice, apple and almond. Its richness is profound, held in focus by the formidable presence of super-fine salt chalk mineral structure that draws out fantastic length and character.

PIERRE PÉTERS CUVÉE ROSÉ FOR ALBANE BRUT NV $$$

95 points • 2013 BASE VINTAGE • DISGORGED SEPTEMBER 2016 • TASTED IN AUSTRALIA

57% Le Mesnil-sur-Oger chardonnay blended with a saignée of 43% Cumières meunier; DIAM closure; 7-8g/L dosage

Fourteen years ago Péters discovered a rosé saignée of meunier by a grower in Damery and Cumières, and was intrigued to find it tasted more like pink grapefruit and apples than red berries – a style he felt would marry perfectly with the yellow citrus of a more fruity parcel of his Le Mesnil-sur-Oger chardonnay. Since this grower retired after the 2012 harvest, he has continued the style by trading for pinot noir with his friend Jean-Baptiste Geoffroy (page 267), the master of Cumières pinot noir rosé saignée, who has enjoyed the challenge of making a meunier saignée for Péters. It is named in honour of Péters' daughter.

Rosé made by blending chardonnay with a saignée is a fantastic method but fraught with challenge, and hence rare in Champagne, first attempted by Roederer, then Vilmart, and more recently by Philipponnat (Clos des Goisses), but Péters is the only one I know to have tried this daring recipe with meunier. I have long loved this cuvée and awaited the 2013 base with bated breath in anticipation of whether a change in meunier sourcing might disrupt its feng shui. Tasting it for the first time, I was astonished at how closely it follows in the footsteps of his stunning 2012. With a pretty, pale salmon hue and a subtle copper tint, this is a wonderfully characterful and lively rosé of pink pepper and red cherry fruit of impressive flavour more than aroma. The mid-palate bursts into a flourish of redcurrants, underlined exactingly with the delightful fine chalk minerality of Le Mesnil and magnificent fine, bright acid that coasts long through the finish. A beautiful Rosé for Albane that perfectly marries the disparate crus of Le Mesnil-sur-Oger and Cumières.

PIERRE PÉTERS BLANC DE BLANCS GRAND CRU BRUT MILLÉSIME L'ESPRIT DE 2014 $$$

94 points • TASTED IN CHAMPAGNE

A blend of four vineyards, one each in Le Mesnil-sur-Oger, Avize, Oger and Cramant; 4-5.5g/L dosage

Rodolphe Péters describes 2014 as another great vintage in succession, balancing the richness of 2012 with the energy of 2013. His vintage cuvée masterfully unites the four grand crus at the core of the Côte des Blancs, confidently led by Le Mesnil-sur-Oger. Shortly before its release, this vintage projected great poise and structure, layered with granny smith apple and pear fruit, tensioned with grapefruit. Showcasing the salty chalk minerality of Le Mesnil, it's a cuvée of focused restraint and consummate elegance that just needs time to uncoil.

PIERRE PÉTERS BLANC DE BLANCS GRAND CRU BRUT MILLÉSIME L'ESPRIT DE 2013
$$$

94 points • TASTED IN CHAMPAGNE

As for L'Esprit de 2014

One of my first defining impressions of the 2013 vintage was my first encounter with Cuvée de Réserve based on this harvest, when Rodolphe Péters announced that he loves its freshness and tension even more than the great 2012. His adoration of this late, cool season has in no way diminished since. 'The 2013 vintage is everything I like from Champagne,' he waxes. 'It has an electric character, with vibrations like we have not seen since 2008. This was the last vintage in which the phenolics had enough time to mature elegantly, so we did not have to pick with too much sugar. I make my picking decision by taste and not by chemistry, and the elegant citrus taste of the grapes is stuck in my mind. Mandarin flavours are the set for me, not grapefruit, orange or lime, but just a step riper than lemon.'

This is a beautifully pure expression of Le Mesnil, with lifted ripe-fruit notes of mandarin precisely as Rodolphe would have them. This ripe fruit definition brings presence and stature on the front and middle, coasting seamlessly into a finish of salt mineral tension and excellent length. Its acid line is fantastic, ripe yet high-energy, seamlessly entwined with the toasted brioche of bottle age. A gorgeous Pierre Péters and ready to drink right away.

PIERRE PÉTERS BLANC DE BLANCS GRAND CRU BRUT MILLÉSIME L'ESPRIT DE 2012
$$$

96 points • DISGORGED JANUARY 2017 • TASTED IN AUSTRALIA

As above; also released as Pierre Péters Blanc de Blancs Extra Brut NV (above); 3g/L dosage

'I was scared because it was a boring vintage and it was all too easy to farm, harvest, vinify and blend,' admits Rodolphe Péters. 'It should not be so easy, so I was worried that I had missed something! With no rot, it was a vintage of perfect maturity from sunny days and balance from cold nights, producing generous, well-balanced, refreshing and energetic wines. With structure and generosity, it will age forever; 2012 to me is the new 2002!'

A sneak preview announcement in the previous edition of this Guide heralded this as one of the great vintages in the lineage of L'Esprit. I loved this cuvée then, and it has since ascended to astonishing heights of purity and salt mineral tension like nothing I have ever seen from Péters outside of Les Chétillons itself. It still radiates with green tints to its glowing, bright straw hue. A grand statement of an outstanding season, its core of precise lemon and crunchy beurre bosc pear is underscored by a stunning chalk minerality, frothing and foaming with the sea salt that defines Le Mesnil. Culminating in a grand crescendo of phenomenal line and length, this is a Péters of the utmost precision, charged with scintillating, crystalline energy.

PIERRE PÉTERS LES CHÉTILLONS CUVÉE SPÉCIALE BLANC DE BLANCS BRUT 2012 $$$$

97 points • TASTED IN CHAMPAGNE

See intro above; 3 plots of vines aged 52-73 years, vinified separately; 75% malolactic fermentation; 4-5g/L dosage

Les Chétillons articulates its mineral birthplace with greater precision than I have tasted anywhere in Champagne outside the thundering single vineyards of Krug itself, and the great 2012 continues the hallowed legacy of the exhilarating 2008, 2007, 2004, 2002, 2000, 1996 and 1986. This exuberant season infuses a confident concentration and density all of its own, yet as ever this legendary place asserts its seamless, calm tension, drawn from its thundering depths of the earth through the arteries of distinguished old vines. The mineral signature of Les Chétillons is crystalline, like ground glass, yet impeccably creamy and enticing, permeating every corner of the palate with chalky sea salt and oyster-shell notes that heave and froth with the waves of the ocean that created this remarkable place more than 70 million years ago. Its length soars to spectacular heights, navigating undeterred for minutes, propelled by an acid line that shimmers like jet exhaust. Patience is mandatory, and while this vintage will be ready before the eternal 2008, anyone with the discipline to hold out at least another decade will be royally rewarded.

Pierre Péters L'Étonnant Monsieur Victor Edition Mk.10 $$$$$

94 points • 2010 base vintage • Tasted in Australia

As for L'Etonnant MK.12; aged 6 years on lees on natural cork; 4–5g/L dosage

Rodolphe Péters tirages this cuvée under natural cork, for more nutty flavours, more creamy texture and better integration of mousse. The 2010 season was a challenging one, and the first time where I see the reserve solera elevating Les Chétillons. The brightness and definitive salt mineral chalk tension of the site is underlined, amplified and filled out by the spice, almond meal complexity and beautifully nutty backdrop of its deep perpetual reserve. The result unites lemon citrus brightness with long-lingering almond meal complexity.

Heritage Pierre Péters Blanc de Blancs Grand Cru NV $$$$$

96 points • 2010 base vintage • Tasted in Champagne

19 vintages from 1921 to 2010, one-third 1921-1996, one-third 2002-2008; 1600 bottles

In celebration of the centenary of the domaine in 2019, Rodolphe Péters conceived to blend 19 vintages made by the four generations of the family. Together with his father, uncle and cousin, he chose one-third of the blend from vintages spanning 1921 to 1996, one-third 2002 to 2008 and the remaining third from 2010. The blend included their last three bottles of 1921, which he described as very high in sugar, tasting like madeira. The 1947 was reported to be the best component, undisgorged, and still clear and bright. The exercise of opening the oenothèque, tasting these old vintages, and assembling the blend, proved to be a special experience that drew the family together.

I know of no blend of anything, anywhere, spanning such a profound expanse of time. Too often, an untried recipe as bold as this yields nothing more than a token wine, awkwardly blended for disjointed sentimentalism before good sense or good taste. The first surprise here is that every one of 19 elements find their place in the whole. The oldest bring very deep, rumbling, tertiary complexity of green olives, cedar and deep-set spice, even a hint of prune. The middle years contribute dried fruits and roast nuts, and 2010 enlivens the mood with citrus, stone fruits and youthful acid drive. It is a rousing family reunion of dry, structural confidence and profound persistence that hovers, unchanging, for minutes. It saves its final surprise for last, a jubilant celebration of the timelessness of the chalk minerality of Les Mesnil, transfixed in time like an ice man. It is a stake, it does not move or change, even in a century.

PIPER-HEIDSIECK

(Pee-per E-dseek)

6/10

12 ALLÉE DU VIGNOBLE 51000 REIMS
www.piper-heidsieck.com

MAISON FONDÉE EN 1785

PIPER-HEIDSIECK

CHAMPAGNE

'In all of our wines, the idea is to let the fruit talk,' announces Piper-Heidsieck's new 31-year-old chef de cave, Émilien Boutillat. 'The pure expression of the fruit and the terroir are the aspirations.' Herein lies the essence of Champagne's eighth-largest house and its friendly and approachable style, distinguishing it from its smaller sister house of Charles Heidsieck, with whom it shares a unique coexistence. Piper-Heidsieck is enjoying a new lease on life since new ownership in 2011, with exciting new cuvées beginning to hit the ground. With the energetic Boutillat on board since October 2018, it's a brand-new day for Piper-Heidsieck. But it hasn't always been smooth sailing.

I first visited Piper-Heidsieck 17 years ago, and left more than a little bemused by its Disney-like automated tour. Thank goodness it is no more. Piper-Heidsieck has come a long way since then, transformed by champagne genius Daniel Thibault from an austere non-malolactic to a more appealing malolactic style, relying on meunier to bring roundness to the blend, and then ascending again in both quality and price under Thibault's friend and offsider, talented chef de cave Régis Camus.

The global financial crisis hit Piper and Charles Heidsieck hard, throwing the company into some €240 million of debt, and forcing it to lay off a quarter of its staff. Owner Rémy Cointreau sold the brand to French fashion-led luxury company Société Européenne de Participations Industrielles (EPI) in early 2011. President Christopher Descours named Régis Camus as one of the key reasons the company committed to the purchase.

Piper-Heidsieck and Charles Heidsieck (page 172) are made together in an impressive cuverie at Bezannes on the southern outskirts of Reims, using the same production methods, from essentially the same pool of vineyards and reserve wines.

'I want to stay in touch with the vineyards, as this link is very important to me,' says Boutillat, who was trained as both a winemaker and an agronomic engineer before working six years as chef de cave at Cattier and Armand de Brignac. 'We have strong partnerships with vine growers everywhere in Champagne,' he says, thanks to the legacy he has been left by Thibault and Camus. Some of Piper's growers have been supplying the house for five generations, and it is a sign of Camus' close relationships with them that he is godfather to their children and invited to their weddings.

'We don't have a lot of vineyards at Piper-Heidsieck, but we believe in working closely with our growers,' Boutillat emphasises. 'Piper-Heidsieck was the first to launch tastings of the *vins clairs* with the growers under Daniel Thibault, and I want to do more with this philosophy. We have a strong friendship and partnership with our growers, and we work with them to make our wines, sharing experiences and making the wines together. I believe strongly in this conversation and collaboration as the key, rather than building our own facilities. We bring our knowledge of winemaking and they bring their knowledge of the terroirs.'

Mareuil-sur-Aÿ lies at the juncture of the Côte des Blancs, Montagne de Reims and Vallée de la Marne.

Piper's deep roots in the Aube today are thanks to Camus, who was among the first chef de caves to source seriously from Champagne's most southerly district. 'He loves the pinot from Aube, as do I, because it is so different from the pinot here in the Marne,' Boutillat reveals. 'It is much more fruity, generous and powerful in the Aube, and more straight, structured, delicate and austere in the Marne. Our style at Piper is about elegance and generosity, so the combination of both is important.'

Boutillat is working closely with his growers to improve vineyard practices. 'Sustainable farming is one of the keys for us,' he says. 'We want to be more than organic. To focus on the soil and the biodiversity. Managing the vineyards differently is good for the environment and can make a huge difference to the quality of the grapes and the wines.'

Boutillat is in a privileged position to build on the tremendous work done before him by Camus and Thibault. Camus was nervous to fill Thibault's big shoes after his untimely death in 2002, but was determined to maintain his legacy in Charles Heidsieck and to take it further in revitalising Piper-Heidsieck. Since the mid-2000s, Charles and Piper have found their own separate lives in the selection of crus, styles and ages.

'It is all about the magic of the blend!' Camus explains. 'It is very important for me that the nuances of the wines speak so as to express the styles of the two different houses.' His goals for Piper are elegance and tenacity in a bright, fruity style, which he speaks of in terms of a floral register, a fruity register and a toasty register in each of the wines. 'I aim to evoke the first days of spring in Piper, with springtime flowers, sun, vegetal nuances, chlorophyll, fog and smoke.' The fruity register follows the floral register.

'Piper is all about apples, pears and citrus, like biting into a crunchy granny smith apple, with a nervousness, minerality and tension.' The vivacious, dynamic Piper style, with its lighter colour, is designed for warmer weather, to be poured at 6–8°C.

From an estate pool of some 60 hectares of vineyards, substantially supplemented by some 400 growers, some 15–20% of crus are upheld for Charles, about 30–40% as signature Piper and the remainder versatile according to the season. 'Many of the villages of the Côte des Bar, Les Riceys, Merville, and Sézanne for chardonnay are our classic Piper villages,' Camus points out. The house vinifies every cru separately.

'It could be perceived as a challenge to deal with both brands side by side, but we have transformed the challenge into an opportunity,' he explains. 'Allocating tanks is half the job of an architect and half the job of a banker!'

For him, the true measure of a house is the quality of its brut NV and he has worked hard to elevate Piper's Brut NV. In his frank and unpretentious manner he shares how much he had enjoyed Taittinger NV with friends.

'The NV wines are the real business for me,' he says. 'After that it's all about having fun! The vintage wines are the vacation photos of the season, signed by Piper or by Charles!'

Non-vintage wines are blends of all three champagne varieties. Pinot noir is the core of the blend, the 'vertebra' or 'DNA molecule' as Camus puts it; chardonnay contributes its dynamic liveliness ('It's me on Saturday night!'); and meunier its fruitiness, freshness, and 'we particularly like its crunchiness'.

Reserve wines represent about half of the harvest, comprising a strong percentage of Charles, and Piper as little as 6% and as much as 18%. 'I want to see just how far certain wines will go,' Camus explains. Most of his reserves are chardonnay and pinot noir, but he is proud to show off a tank of 2004 meunier from Verneuil of stunning freshness and vivacity. 'This breaks the absurd impression that meunier can't age!' Reserve wines are dedicated separately to Piper and Charles, and are stored in 300–500hL stainless steel tanks to guard their freshness, 'so we can use them whenever they're needed, frozen in time like an ice man!'

When he arrived, Boutillat was greatly indebted to Camus and Thibault for keeping such levels of reserves. 'We have a huge library of reserve wines!' he exclaimed. 'One of the biggest and best libraries of reserves in Champagne.'

Fermentation and maturation are performed exclusively in stainless steel. 'The only wood here is the boardwalk above the tanks!' he quips.

The modern Piper style relies on full malolactic fermentation for complexity and texture, but in increasingly warmer vintages, Boutillat is considering options to maintain freshness. He trialled blocking malolactic in some parcels in the ripe 2018 harvest, but emphasises that if he were to use these in his blends, it would only be very small percentages. 'To block malolactic, you either have to chill, which is expensive, or use sulphur dioxide as a preservative, and I prefer not to use so much, because it can hide aromas and make the wine more strict. But we are not closing any doors, and maybe we will use our trial without malolactic as reserve wines.'

To balance their vivacity, all cuvées used to be finished with a broad sweep of full dosage of 10–11g/L, but today this is much more carefully tweaked for each cuvée, as low as 4g/L and usually no more than 10g/L.

In 2017, Piper-Heidsieck launched its new Essentiel Cuvée Réservée, an impressive re-release of its Brut NV, blessed with more time on lees and less dosage. The label refreshingly features base vintage, reserves, dosage, time on lees and bottling and disgorgement dates. A stunning Essentiel Blanc de Blancs was introduced in 2019. This new range heralds an exciting new era for the house, the first fruits of President Christopher Descours' long-term vision to revitalise Piper-Heidsieck.

Régis Camus retired as chef de cave for Piper-Heidsieck in 2018, but remains on board to oversee its Rare cuvée.

Sales of 4 million bottles make Piper Champagne's eighth-largest house, and third-largest exporter, though a mere shadow of its scale at its historic peak of 13 million bottles, prior to its dark days under Rémy Cointreau. President Christopher Descours resolves to return the house to its former glory, and has sacrificed significant volume in this pursuit. 'His ambition is to return Piper-Heidsieck to where it was and where it deserves to be in the world of champagne,' says Benoît Collard, vice president of the house. 'We are not looking for high-volume growth, but a market position that reflects our brand quality and our identity.'

This has been a long and at times uncomfortable journey for Piper-Heidsieck, but value for money remains compelling, and quality is as buoyant as ever.

PIPER-HEIDSIECK CUVÉE BRUT NV $$

90 points • 2015 BASE VINTAGE • TASTED IN CHAMPAGNE

20% chardonnay, 50% pinot noir, 30% meunier from more than 100 villages; 15-20% reserves; 9-10g/L dosage

Fresh, lively, fruity and precise, Piper is a reliable champagne at a great price, and I recommend it all the time for weddings, parties, anything. Émilien Boutillat's aspiration for Piper's entry cuvée is 'complexity without being complicated', and he picks up where his predecessor Régis Camus confidently left off in fulfilling the mandate of the house to elevate this cuvée into a more serious, textural and complex offering, thanks to longer lees age, more reserves and a little more chardonnay in the blend.

Pinot takes the lead, defining the classic red apple profile that matches Piper's distinctive red label, backed with pear and the tang of grapefruit. The honeyed influence of lees age is enhanced with dosage, though there is less secondary development in this release, the base vintage having progressed four vintages over the past two years (four years on lees then, and three here). It finishes long and spicy, with just the right amount of acidity and crunch on the end. The dry grip and structure inherent to the warm 2015 season marks this release with a grippy apple-skin texture.

PIPER-HEIDSIECK ESSENTIEL CUVÉE RÉSERVÉE EXTRA BRUT NV $$

92 points • 2012 BASE VINTAGE • DISGORGED JUNE 2017 • TASTED IN CHAMPAGNE

25% chardonnay, 55% pinot, 25% meunier; 18% reserves; Piper-Heidsieck Brut aged 5 years on lees with 6g/L dosage

Some years ago, while tasting different lots of the Brut NV blend, one lot stood out as particularly special. Based on the splendid 2008 vintage, it was left in the cellar for an additional year and bottled as a new, more serious extension of the brand. The label refreshingly features base vintage, reserves, dosage, time on lees and bottling and disgorgement dates. Production of Essentiel grew from a small base in 2017 and has increased progressively each year.

A complex and characterful cuvée that leads out with Piper's signature red apple crunch and lemon freshness, and backs it with excellent complexity of brioche, toast and nougat. It coasts with good length and elegant refined acidity, true to the philosophy of the house. Fine salt minerality and seamlessly integrated dosage confirm a classy blend.

PIPER-HEIDSIECK ESSENTIEL BLANC DE BLANCS NV $$

94 points • 2013 BASE VINTAGE • DISGORGED OCTOBER 2017 • TASTED IN CHAMPAGNE

New release; almost 100% grand cru, mostly Côte des Blancs; aged 3.5 years on lees; 4g/L dosage

A shining beacon for the new era of Piper-Heidsieck, the philosophy of this spanking-new cuvée is restraint and precision, and it delivers both like this house has never done before. For a house forever led by pinot noir, blanc de blancs might seem a surprise, but the refreshing mood of Piper makes this an exciting addition to its portfolio, and the result thoroughly overdelivers on the expectation. It's a very refined and detailed style in a refreshing apéritif guise, reminiscent of crunchy beurre bosc pear and granny smith apple. Age has added impressive, subtle notes of almond nougat. Côte des Blancs takes a confident lead in fine salt minerality, in an elegant and refined finish of great length. From my very first taste, it leapt forth as one of my favourite cuvées of the house.

PIPER-HEIDSIECK ROSÉ SAUVAGE NV $$

93 points • 2012 BASE VINTAGE • TASTED IN CHAMPAGNE

15% chardonnay, 55% pinot noir, 30% meunier; Piper-Heidsieck Cuvée Brut with 25% pinot noir red wine, almost entirely from the Aube; 9.5g/L dosage

'It's a bit darker than most rosés in Champagne!' grins Émilien Boutillat, who is well familiar with making deep rosés for Armand de Brignac. 'For me, champagne rosé needs to be a rosé – I want to smell the difference!' He works closely with his growers in the Aube to make the red wines together. 'The Aube is very good for red wines, and if we are selective with the sites, pruning and ripeness, we can get some wonderful red wines of concentration without tannins,' he explains.

The house goes a little far in describing this as 'the most extravagant and audacious rosé in the world', but when it was first released in the early 2000s, it may well have been. Régis Camus resolved to create a distinctive rosé to contrast the Charles Heidsieck style, a wine of intense colour and dark fruit presence. That it is. In its full, unabashed crimson-red hue, it certainly floats far down the deep end of the champagne rosé pool. In colour, palate grip, concentration and food-matching dexterity, it's best considered part-way between champagne rosé and Coteaux Champenois rouge, and should be served in big red wine glasses, as they do at the house. Distinctive, inimitable, potent and rustic, this is a champagne rosé with a personality all of its own. There's sarsaparilla here, pepper and blood orange, too, wild strawberries, sweet herbs, orange rind and Piper's classic red apples. The very fine salt minerality of Champagne unites with super-fine tannins of one of the region's most generous doses of pinot noir red wine, concluding with persistence and integrity. Thank goodness its Barbie-pink label is no more, slipping into a far more suave and distinguished robe to match its mood. Try it with a big, spicy duck.

PIPER-HEIDSIECK CUVÉE SUBLIME DEMI-SEC NV $$

87 points • TASTED IN CHAMPAGNE

20% chardonnay, 50% pinot noir, 30% meunier; 35g/L dosage

I have admired the place to which Sublime has ascended for the past five years, its clean and pristine lines making it one of the more reliable performers in the oft-fraught demi-sec category. It's slipped a little in this release, with some firm astringency creeping into its structure. It nonetheless upholds citrus freshness amidst honeyed sweetness and layers of character in toasted brioche, nougat and butter. One bottle was cork affected.

PIPER-HEIDSIECK VINTAGE BRUT 2008 $$$

93 points • TASTED IN CHAMPAGNE

52% chardonnay, 48% pinot noir, from 20 villages, mostly grand and premier crus; 9g/L dosage

Piper Heidsieck's vintage philosophy is always an almost equal blend of chardonnay and pinot, to 'reflect the truth of the vintage and of Champagne' by sourcing from everywhere. The backward, primary fruit focus, bright acid line and salty chalk mineral prominence of 2008 frame a delightful contrast to the toasty, spicy, vanilla-accented bottle age of the Piper-Heidsieck style. Now at the end of its release cycle, subtle tertiary notes of flint and pipe smoke have begun to appear. It's poised to drink right away, at the perfect juncture between the vector of primary, crunchy almost-ripe red apples and lemons, and the arc of mature development, yet with the acid spine to hold its own for some years yet. It has built wonderful layers of secondary complexity while upholding endurance, persistence, poise and fine chalk mineral expression true to this stunning vintage.

PIPER-HEIDSIECK RARE MILLESIME 2002 $$$$

98 points • TASTED IN AUSTRALIA

70% chardonnay from Avize, Vertus, Verzy and Villers-Marmery; 30% pinot noir from Aÿ; first released in 2011; the eighth vintage since 1976; 11g/L dosage

This is indeed rare, the eighth vintage since 1976, and it keeps on coming, still current in the market eight years after release. And, my goodness, it continues to radiate more than its quota of sheer joy! I have tasted it dozens of times and I rated it 95 points between 2011 and 2013, 97 between 2015 and 2017, and both bottles I have tasted recently are the finest I have ever seen, one so stunningly fresh it looked like a magnum. It still glows in elegantly medium-straw hues, radiantly bright for 17 years of age. Enticing gunflint reductive notes continue to lead out, carrying with them a wonderfully complex yet compact and elegant array of succulent yellow stone fruits, basking in the fruity exuberance of 2002, now increasingly showing the complexity of glacé pear, with rising notes of molten wax, wood smoke and buttered toast. Lees age has built seamless, creamy, silky integration, having attained its lofty plateau, which it will continue to hold for some years yet. Its chalk minerality is fine, salty and definitive, uniting the finesse of the Côte des Blancs with the firmer definition of the Montagne. It epitomises the gentle, textural minerality, the buttery allure of long age, and the harmonious personality and magnificent persistence of chardonnay in this epic vintage. The place of calm satisfaction to which it has evolved is all-encompassing. There is harmony here, and peace, like the gentle misty haze before dawn. A place that makes you slow down, and begs you to stay.

POL ROGER

(Pol Roh-zheh)

9/10

1 Rue Winston Churchill 51200 Épernay
www.polroger.com

CHAMPAGNE
POL ROGER

Stepping into Pol Roger's production facility in Épernay is like entering a different world. 'We call this the kitchen,' introduced managing director Laurent d'Harcourt. This was not like any kitchen I'd ever seen. Immaculately polished stainless steel tanks perfectly reflected shiny white tiles and snow-white surfaces. It was as if we were entering a brain surgery unit or a NASA assembly room, and I had an uneasy feeling that I might be asked to don a body suit, lest I contaminate this precision machine with a single molecule of foreign material. I have been buying Pol Roger for decades, but it was not until that moment that everything about this celestial estate suddenly snapped into perfect focus. The champagnes that emerge from this extraterrestrial building are as desperately precise, intricately delicate and flawlessly pristine as its polished interior, revealing the manifesto that defines all that lies within. And Pol Roger is on the rise.

It hasn't always been this way. The disorganised regime of the 1990s was 'a mess', according to d'Harcourt. The pace of transformation amazes me every time I visit Pol Roger. Since chef de cave Dominique Petit joined the company in 1999, after 24 years at Krug, more than €15 million has been invested in upgrading the winemaking facilities alone.

And it never seems to stop. The stainless steel fermentation space was updated in 2001, 2004, 2008, 2010 and 2011, and now provides full capacity to vinify every parcel separately. New cold-settling and fermentation halls were installed in 2011, alongside six new tiny 2200-litre tanks. The cellar was extended, and the floors concreted to reduce vibrations from electric vehicles. More consistent and more precise disgorgement and dosage machines were also installed. In 2013, the old concrete tanks were refreshed, in 2014 a new cuverie for reserve wines was constructed, in 2015

a grand new reception room completed, in 2016 a state-of-the-art bottling line was commissioned, and the house is currently rebuilding to relocate the oldest section of its production facility. Even the address has changed, after the street was renamed. Pol Roger now proudly stands at 1 Rue Winston Churchill.

Pol Roger's investment is not primarily to increase production, but to improve quality and consistency. Having grown from 1.5 million bottles annually, the house has increased its sourcing to 200 hectares in recent years, and is producing close to its target of 2 million bottles. There is no immediate plan to increase further.

'Every year for the past 14 years we have seen results in the consistency of the wines from the work we are doing in the winery,' d'Harcourt explains. 'We have made a solid investment to ensure the family house remains secure in the family's hands into the 21st century.'

The pristine cuverie of Pol Roger

GRASSROOTS RELATIONSHIPS

In 2014, I was privileged to an even deeper insight into the internal workings of this incredible company. Laurent d'Harcourt granted my request to shadow him for a full day mid-harvest, and I was surprised by what I discovered from the moment I sat down in his car as we set off in the morning. There on his passenger seat was the full harvest data of the company, which he was personally tracking and updating daily. 'I have more than 70 presses where our growers and our own vineyards press, and I spend all of harvest doing miles and miles visiting them,' he revealed. 'For me it is most important to visit all of the growers and taste the fruit, as this is the ultimate opportunity to discover the harvest.' And these are not just flippant visits. 'Half of my visits are a breakfast, lunch or dinner. And sometimes two breakfasts a day!' Now *there's* a managing director who's engaged with the grass roots of his company. 'We have partnerships,' he explains, 'and we work with families for generation after generation.' It's dedication like this that sets Pol Roger apart.

Our first stop was Diebolt-Vallois, one of the finest growers in Cramant, where I witnessed some of the cleanest fruit I saw going into any press that vintage. Such was the demand for this famous grower that it sold its own wines on allocation, and yet it proudly supplied Pol Roger (as does Pierre Gimonnet in the next village, who is in the same situation). More than this, such was the pride of the Diebolt family in the partnership that its workers were proudly wearing Pol Roger t-shirts.

Pol Roger provides for an impressive 51% of its production from 90 hectares of estate vines. 'These holdings allow us to be more consistent over the long term,' clarifies d'Harcourt. The remainder is sourced exclusively from the Marne, and most importantly from Épernay and Chouilly, from long-term contracts under an arrangement that pays bonuses for quality. 'We are Pol Roger, we are not really growers,' d'Harcourt admits. 'Many of the growers from whom we source also care for vineyards that we own ourselves. They cultivate our vineyards, we press all the fruit and then give a portion back to them as payment.'

For some years, Pol Roger has been renewing its grower contracts to strengthen its sourcing in some grand crus, to enhance its capacity to make its Blanc de Blancs, Vintage and Sir Winston Churchill cuvées. The house already produces a higher proportion of vintage wines than virtually any other (in the order of 20%), and this only bolsters its position. In 2015 it produced the largest volume of Sir Winston Churchill ever.

EXACTING PRECISION

The rise of Pol Roger is very much a credit to the exacting precision of Dominique Petit, who transformed a disorganised regime with an attention to detail learnt at Krug. The house preference for stainless steel over concrete and oak barrels rests on judicious temperature control of its musts during clarification and vinification. Musts undergo a double cold-settling process at just 5°C, producing the most pristine juice – a process that

Petit's predecessor, James Coffinet, brought to Pol Roger from Billecart-Salmon. Held below 18°C, a cool primary fermentation is drawn out over 15 days, maintaining fruit freshness and aromatic definition. The house has succeeded in fermenting some tanks at 16°C, but isn't convinced there is any benefit compared with 18°C.

Pol Roger's reserves are held in concrete tanks for stability at a constant 11°C underground, without need for temperature control.

Secondary fermentation is likewise cool, thanks to Pol Roger's 7.5 kilometres of cellars, which are among the coolest (9–11°C) and deepest (up to 33 metres) in Épernay. Most of the bottles rest in the deepest parts of the cellar. This slow fermentation produces wines of great finesse, fine effervescence and enduring longevity. 'Greater precision in the first and second fermentations have enabled a trend towards lower dosage,' explains d'Harcourt. The house tests dosages between 6g/L and 9g/L, and has currently settled around 7g/L.

Everything in the cellar is done by hand by a team of no more than 10. Pol Roger boasts four of the remaining nine riddlers still working in Champagne, and is currently training a fifth. With each turning 50,000–60,000 bottles a day, it takes 4–5 weeks to riddle every bottle. Every bottle is touched 18–25 times before it leaves the house. Each is stacked in the cellar by hand, including every non-vintage wine – a painstaking process for a company with an incredible 9.5 million bottles in its care. 'Our neighbours think we are strange with such a huge inventory!' d'Harcourt exclaims.

Pol Roger doesn't disclose disgorgement dates, but the bottle code indicates the packaging date, shortly after disgorgement. The first digit denotes the year, and next three digits the day of the year

With such a regime of excellence in the vineyard and winery, and having been under the ownership of the same family since the house was founded in 1849, Pol Roger's success is no surprise. 'We have been selling every cuvée in every format under allocation for some years now,' d'Harcourt reveals. 'We could sell two or three times the volume in the UK, but we don't want to be too dependent on one market. We've been telling some markets to stop selling, particularly Blanc de Blancs and Sir Winston Churchill, because we don't have enough to send! We could increase our size, but we would lose our soul.'

That's a line you don't often hear from any medium-sized wine company in the current climate. And with ever-improving facilities every time I visit, this company is poised for even greater things to come.

In April 2018, Dominique Petit retired, after 19 years with the house, succeeded by 43-year-old Damien Cambres, who had worked alongside Petit for 18 months, following 20 years with coopératives in the region.

It certainly is a different world at Pol Roger.

Pol Roger Réserve Brut NV

94 points • 2014 base vintage • Tasted in Champagne
91 points • 2011 base vintage • Tasted in Champagne

A blend of the three champagne varieties in roughly equal proportions; 25% reserves from 2-4 years; 150 parcels from 30 crus; 42-54 months on lees in bottle (previously 36-48); 9g/L dosage; 1.3-1.6 million bottles

Pol Roger's famous 'White Foil' is an attractive and refreshing apéritif, and the 2014 base is as magnificent as ever, loaded with all the freshness of focused lemon, red apple and white peach. Around four years on lees has built a creaminess to its mouthfeel, without yet progressing into secondary complexity. It flows seamlessly into a long and zesty finish, heightened by excellent salt mineral texture. The company's investment in its facilities and fruit sources over the past two decades is now paying strong dividends, and individual parcel vinification preserves fantastic detail, showcasing its components with greater precision than ever. It projects fresher citrus fruit, more pronounced salt minerality and more seamless persistence – the most distinguished White Foil yet. The 2011 base suffers in the wake of this challenging season, upholding bright acidity and now presenting the almond-meal complexity of maturity, with a contracted dryness to the finish.

POL ROGER PURE EXTRA BRUT NV $$

93 points • 2014 base vintage • Tasted in Champagne

The three varieties in roughly equal balance; a different blend to Brut Réserve, with more floral and less acidic components; a blend of 30 crus; reserves from three vintages; aged 3 years on lees; zero dosage

In the past, Extra Brut was aged a year longer, but now that Réserve Brut has moved from three to four years on lees, Extra Brut has actually done the reverse, so as to maintain the right balance between acidity and drinkability. Extra Brut would typically come in a point ahead of Réserve Brut in my ratings. Now this, too, has flipped. The 2014 base delivers an Extra Brut of contrasts, juxtaposing the purity of crunchy grapefruit tang with the integration of biscuit and spice. Prominent, fine salt minerality draws out a crisp finish of clean, focused acid line and great persistence. One of five bottles I opened for a masterclass was corked.

POL ROGER RICH DEMI SEC NV $$

92 points • Tasted in Champagne

Réserve Brut with 34g/L dosage; very small production; 34g/L dosage

'If you have a good Brut, you can make a good Demi Sec,' declares Laurent d'Harcourt. His is one of the best. It's been eight years since I last tasted this cuvée, and its ascent has been marked, naturally in tune with that of Réserve Brut, on which it is based. True to the clean lines and pure finesse of Réserve Brut, this is a demi-sec of integrity and finesse, deepened to a medium straw-yellow hue, with the citrus, red apple, spice and vanilla of Réserve Brut sweetened with notes of boiled candy. It concludes with even balance of bright acidity, chalk minerality and succulent sweetness.

POL ROGER VINTAGE BRUT 2012 $$$

95 points • Disgorged 14 February 2019 • Tasted in Australia

40% chardonnay, 60% pinot noir; 20 grand and premier crus of the Montagne de Reims and the Côte des Blancs; 7g/L dosage; cork

This cuvée has been a mainstay of my personal champagne cellar longer than any other, and I still have many vintages since the early 1990s tucked away. The 2012 vintage is poised to go down among the great, enduring seasons for this regal house. Following the release of the sublime 2008, Pol Roger's Vintage Brut 2009 came and went (read on), the challenging 2010 and 2011 seasons were tactically and astutely side-stepped, and it is back on form in the energetic 2012 vintage. Pol Roger claims seven years on lees, but its first release that I am tasting at the beginning of its release cycle could not have been more than six – a short time in the lineage of Pol. The result is consequently youthful and vibrant, a celebration of crunchy strawberry hull, red apple and fresh lemon, with lees age lending subtle touches of almond nougat. Elegantly poised pinot noir takes its signature lead, confidently supported by the citrus cut and refined chalk mineral texture of chardonnay. All of the beguiling purity of Pol Roger is on grand display in this electric season, and it holds its own effortlessly on a very long finish of great line and drive. It has a grand future before it, and will only become more enticing over the coming decade.

Pol Roger Vintage Brut 2009 $$$

94 points • Disgorged 16 May 2018 • Tasted in Champagne and Australia

40% chardonnay, 60% pinot noir; 20 grand and premier crus in the Montagne de Reims and the Côte des Blancs; 7g/L dosage; cork

Pol's vintage blend is always led by 60% pinot noir, and in the powerfully ripe 2009 season it steps forward with particular gusto, bursting with black cherries and spice, even black fruit cake, ginger and honey. Ripe chardonnay swoops in with succulent white peach and pineapple. It's rich and immediate, yet remains ever true to the precision of Pol Roger definition, with crunchy grapefruit tang laying out an acid line, focused drive and lingering persistence to contain its confident exuberance. This is a powerful and full Pol Roger to drink while the 2008 and 2012 rest in the cellar.

Pol Roger Blanc de Blancs Brut 2012 $$$$

96 points • Disgorged 26 March 2018 • Tasted in Champagne

100% Côte des Blancs grand crus: Avize, Oiry, Chouilly, Cramant, Oger; 7g/L dosage

For a house once led by pinot noir, Pol Roger is increasingly focusing on chardonnay in its vintage wines, and recent vintages of its Blanc de Blancs demonstrate why. The 2012 proudly joins its greatest hits, alongside 2002 and 2008. This cuvée has been on allocation for some years, and the house has made the call to release 2012 after just five years on lees (2008 had a little under six years, 2006 had eight and 2002 had nine). Testimony to the molecular precision of Pol Roger's exacting regime, the propensity of this cuvée to age is astonishing, and the best vintages keep on escalating every time I come back to them. With a bright, medium straw hue, this is a thrilling blanc de blancs that sings with the finesse of the house in exacting purity and drive to contrast grand cru concentration. It delicately sets beautiful yellow peach and lemon fruit against a dizzying shard of pure acidity. The finish surges onward amid powerful, crashing waves of salt minerality that glide long and strong up an endless beach of glistening white purity.

Pol Roger Blanc de Blancs Brut 2009 $$$$

95 points • Disgorged May 2017 • Tasted in Champagne

100% Côte des Blancs grand crus: Avize, Oiry, Chouilly, Cramant, Oger; 7g/L dosage

It takes a house of both the finesse and fragrant delicacy and the fanatical discipline of Pol Roger to draw a beautifully refined blanc de blancs from the rich 2009 harvest in the powerful grand crus of the northern Côte des Blancs. The dainty lemon and crunchy nashi pear of its first venture into the stark light of day have now faded as its release cycle draws to a close, ushering in grand presence of apple, grapefruit, stone fruits and spice. A decade of maturity has massaged a creamy texture, drawing out magnificent character of marzipan, vanilla, even a hint of anise amidst classic toasted Parisienne baguette and roast almonds. It propagates with great persistence, sustained by the bright acidity of Pol Roger, even in such a warm vintage, energised by the frothing, salty, grand cru chalk minerality of the Côte des Blancs. A triumph of the season, commanding and yet refined, this is the vintage to drink over the next five years as we eagerly await the awakening of the sublime 2008 and the stunning 2012.

POL ROGER ROSÉ BRUT 2009 $$$$

94 points • Disgorged 27 July 2018 • Tasted in Champagne

30% chardonnay, 70% pinot noir; 20 premier and grand crus on the Montagne de Reims and Côte des Blancs; same base as Brut Vintage, with around 15% pinot noir red wine from Bouzy, Ambonnay and Cumières, purchased by the company 'because we are not good at vinifying red wine ourselves'; 7g/L dosage

Fifteen percent red wine is a generous addition for a house of the delicate elegance of Pol Roger, and the effect is a stark transformation of Vintage Brut into the most powerful cuvée of the house. When I'm pouring Pol all night, I reserve this cuvée for last. The style has slowly evolved into a deeper colour and more vinous and exuberant mood over the past decade, now taking on a full crimson copper hue. Thanks to exacting Pol Roger precision, its proportions are well managed, making for a delightfully fresh take on the ripe 2009 vintage. Pinot noir takes a confident lead, contributing elegant fragrance and succulent flesh and body within the strict and consummately controlled mood of Pol Roger. Characterful blood orange, raspberry and strawberry fruit linger with excellent persistence, structured with the subtle bite of orange rind bitterness. Tannins so fine they're virtually invisible mesh intricately with fine, salty chalk minerality, energised by bright acidity, conspiring to build the structural confidence to work with flexible dexterity amidst a wide plethora of cuisines on the table. One bottle was corked.

POL ROGER CUVÉE SIR WINSTON CHURCHILL 2008 $$$$$

99 points • Tasted in Champagne and Australia

Predominantly pinot noir (more than 60%), as Winston Churchill was a pinot drinker, the balance chardonnay, all from grand cru villages under vine at the time of Churchill; cold settled at 6°C; fermented below 18°C; full malolactic fermentation; secondary fermentation in the lowest part of the cellars (9°C); aged almost 10 years on lees; cork

Sir Winston is the distinguished gentleman of the prestige champagne world, and never has he looked more majestic than in 2008. The purity and finesse that define Pol Roger attain new heights in this scintillating season. Pinot noir assumes a commanding lead, without force or ambition, yet with a confidence this cuvée has not seen since 1996, and a grace that transcends even that epic season and every other in recent decades. Sir Winston captures the exuberance of the greatest pinot noir crus, and presents it with astonishing determination, exacting purity and pinpoint precision, eloquently articulating the tension of the finest intricacies of the 2008 season. It leads out with the most gorgeous white cherries, elevating in time to the full depth of black cherries and strawberries, flowing harmoniously into layers of almond nougat, vanilla and brioche, brimming with mixed spice, even suggestions of dark fruit cake. Its chalk mineral definition is a revelation of the highest order, surging with a deep infusion of super-fine, profoundly salty and deeply expressive chalk that rumbles to the very core of the greatest crus of the Côte des Blancs and the Montagne de Reims, embracing the palate, transfixing the senses and bringing the will to complete surrender. In seamless line and unwavering length, this is a Sir Winston like no other, revelling in the brilliance of 2008 acidity, which cunningly snaps its finish into strict control, undeviating focus and effortless, determined endurance. It is a vintage that simultaneously elevates Sir Winston to soaring heights of finesse and greater depths of complexity. Stunning now, it will age in slow motion for many decades, firming its place among the greatest of all time. True to the manner of Pol Roger, this is not a cuvée that will turn heads by flashy flamboyance or heightened exuberance, but by effortless poise and understated integrity. A tense vintage eloquently translated with peace, calm and harmony.

POL ROGER CUVÉE SIR WINSTON CHURCHILL 2006 $$$$$

96 points • TASTED IN CHAMPAGNE AND AUSTRALIA

As for Cuvée Sir Winston Churchill 2008

The blend of Sir Winston Churchill is a closely guarded secret. I ask d'Harcourt every time we taste a new vintage. 'I have not been drunk enough yet to tell you!' he replies. I'll keep working on it. Elusive details aside, Sir Winston steps up with a characterful presence in the powerful 2006 season, with pinot noir commanding a confident lead, freshened consummately by the definition and pristine purity of chardonnay. Time moves slowly in Pol Roger's deep, cold cellars, and it is only now that the tell-tale signs of maturity are beginning to emerge in layers of butter, spice, brioche and dried fruits, even hints of sweet pipe smoke. Age is declared more dramatically in gorgeously seamless and silky texture. The signature, salty chalk minerality of the greatest crus of the Côte des Blancs and Montagne de Reims lays out a finish of outstanding line and enduring length, with a bright acid line that defines the finesse of the house and promises short- to medium-term potential. A distinguished highlight of the season.

POL ROGER CUVÉE SIR WINSTON CHURCHILL 2004 $$$$$

98 points • TASTED IN CHAMPAGNE AND AUSTRALIA

As above

Sir Winston is looking particularly dignified and refined in 2004. I have adored this vintage since the glorious day of its release four years ago, and I am absolutely astonished by the pristine poise it has upheld today, at a full 15 years of age. The precision engineering of every detail of Pol Roger and the slow-motion evolution of its deep, cold cellars have long defined profound longevity, but only now are the full blessings of Pol's investments in its fruit and facilities becoming fully apparent. It's a marvellous juxtaposition between the bright, elegant refinement of classic Sir Winston demeanour and grand layers of complexity. It leads with the rhythm of pinot noir in layers of black cherries, strawberries and spice, gaining momentum in fruit mince spice and dark fruit cake. Entrancing freshness cascades into a torrent of impeccably refined acidity, swirling into a river of minerality that flows deep and swift all the way to the distant horizon. Effortless grace and youthful vigour lurk under that distinguished exterior.

POL ROGER CUVÉE SIR WINSTON CHURCHILL 1998

98 points • TASTED IN AUSTRALIA EN MAGNUM

As above; recent disgorgement

The slow-motion evolution that epitomises Pol Roger is redefined in glorious magnums. One of the great Winstons of the recent era, 1998 is evolving with exacting precision. At a full two decades of age, it's attained that magical moment when primary and secondary character marry to create a thrilling accord, upholding vibrant red fruits that ripple amidst layers of spice of immense complexity and seamless poise. Its mineral presence is profound and undeviating, and its freshness is stunning, and never more so than in magnum. Evidence of the great rewards of cellaring Winston for at least five years after release, and preferably ten.

POMMERY

(Poh-mer-ee)

---

5 PLACE DU GÉNÉRAL GOURAUD 51053 REIMS

www.pommery.com

CHAMPAGNE

POMMERY

À REIMS-FRANCE

With annual sales of close to 5 million bottles, Pommery is Champagne's seventh-largest house and the lead brand of the Vranken-Pommery Monopole group, recently overtaking Lanson-BCC to become Champagne's second-largest group after LVMH. Together with its sister houses of Vranken and Heidsieck & Co Monopole, total production exceeded 17 million bottles in 2019, sourced from the estate's 288 hectares and more than 1700 hectares of purchased fruit. The three houses remain quite distinct, with different chef de caves, production sites, philosophies and blends. 'Freshness, vivacity, fruit aromas and long length are the aspirations of Pommery, without being too strong,' was the aim of Thierry Gasco, chef de cave of 25 years.

Pommery has had a rough ride, falling victim to buy-out after buy-out over recent decades, the most recent in 2002, when it was sold by Moët & Chandon to Belgian entrepreneur Paul-François Vranken, minus all but 20 hectares of its exceptional vineyard holdings of 470 hectares, including more than 300 hectares of glorious grand crus. The inconsistency of its wines, particularly its non-vintage cuvées, is perhaps understandable in the context of this tumultuous history, though the house vigorously disputes this, and has recently claimed it made an agreement at the time with Bernard Arnault, chief executive of LVMH, to buy back 54 hectares, so as to protect and uphold the grand cru sourcing for its Louise prestige cuvée. Vranken was already in possession of 188 hectares of vineyards at the time and, to its credit, the house has now rebuilt its holdings to a respectable 288 hectares today, though only 40% in premier and grand cru villages. It also has management of a further 77 hectares under lease. The house has traditionally had strong sourcing in the Montagne de Reims, particularly in the northern and eastern crus from Ludes to Villers-Marmery.

Pommery claims to be the first house to have made a brut champagne, in 1874 when Madame Pommery gambled upon producing a dry style to suit the British palate (necessitating a change in the Champagne regulations, which mandated dosage at the time); the aspiration has been low levels of dosage ever since – though 10g/L in its Royal cuvées and 9g/L in its Apanage range are not particularly low by modern standards. There is no rule for dosage, and dosage trials are run on each cuvée for six months, aspiring for 'a good balance between sugar and tension, with a little subtle noble bitterness', explains chef de cave Thierry Gasco. All ferments are in stainless steel tanks, and no oak is used by the house. 'We are aiming for a very fresh and slightly reductive style,' he adds.

Pommery keeps its reserves in 300 stainless steel tanks, and holds its entire stock of around 20 million bottles at a stable, cold 10°C, 30 metres under its grand fairytale turrets in Reims, in 120 glorious crayères, which Madame Pommery acquired between 1868 and 1878 and connected with 18 kilometres of tunnels.

Pommery's chef de cave since 1992, Thierry Gasco retired in July 2017, succeeded by Clément Pierlot, vineyard director for the company since 2004, when he was just 24 years of age. Pierlot joined the Vranken tasting panel in 2010 and was responsible for oenological development since 2014, both in Champagne and in the company's sparkling project in England.

The grandson of a farmer, Pierlot resides among the growers in Aÿ. 'It is very important to me to remain in touch with the growers,' he emphasises. Sustainability is a high priority for him, and all Vranken vineyards are certified High Environmental Value. No herbicides are used across the company.

Vranken-Pommery Monopole is now the largest vineyard owner in Europe, with more than 2500 hectares of vines, close to three-quarters of which are in Camargue in the far south of France, and the remainder in Champagne, Provence and Portugal. It is the first champagne house to have released English sparkling, with significant plantings of some 55 hectares set to come online in the coming years.

The modern era of ever more attentive viticulture and vinification has heralded a new day for many of Champagne's biggest houses, most notably in a general refinement in entry non-vintage blends. Against this backdrop, the austerity of bitter phenolic structure that continues to mark the Pommery style is particularly pronounced. I hope its cuvées are now able to find a new life under Pierlot.

POMMERY BRUT ROYAL NV $$

86 points • 2013 BASE VINTAGE • DISGORGED 12 JUNE 2017 • TASTED IN AUSTRALIA

About one-third of each variety; a blend of about 40 crus; reserves by cru and variety as well as a proportion of the previous year's blend; aged 3 years on lees; 10g/L dosage; cork

Grapefruit, red apple and pear flavours are underlined by the toast and biscuit notes of lees age, accented with subtle reductive complexity. True to the impressive 2013 base vintage, this is a fresh expression of Brut Royal, concluding with lemon-accented acidity. It suffers from firm phenolic bite and disjointed, candied dosage on a short and grainy finish.

POMMERY BRUT ROSÉ ROYAL NV $$

84 points • 2015 BASE VINTAGE • DISGORGED 8 NOVEMBER 2018 • TASTED IN AUSTRALIA

About one-third of each variety; Brut Royal with 5% Bouzy red wine; a blend of about 40 crus; reserves by cru and variety as well as a proportion of the previous year's blend; aged 2.5 years on lees; 10g/L dosage; cork; 9% of production

A pretty, pale salmon hue infused by a dash of Bouzy rouge is true to Thierry Gasco's aspiration for this cuvée of not wanting to have 'a very pink colour'. He suggests that 'when you see a pale colour, you anticipate an elegant wine'. This is a firm and savoury style of bruised apple skin, crab apple and beurre bosc pear grit, lacking in fragrance and fruit lift, with a short finish completely overwhelmed by bitter phenolic austerity, amplified by the warm 2015 base vintage.

POMMERY ROYAL BLUE SKY SUR GLACE NV $$

86 points • 2014 BASE VINTAGE • DISGORGED 28 MARCH 2018 • TASTED IN AUSTRALIA

About one-third of each variety; a blend of about 40 crus; aged 3 years on lees; 38g/L dosage; cork

Sweetness is the focus here, and the defining character is of boiled sweets, which dominate over subtle lemon drops and red apple fruit and the understated beginnings of toasty complexity. It's a clean expression, and the sweetness flatters the phenolic grip of the Pommery style, concluding short and simple.

POMMERY BRUT APANAGE NV $$$

89 points • 2014 BASE VINTAGE • TASTED IN CHAMPAGNE

40% chardonnay; a blend of 17 crus; aged 4 years on lees; 9g/L doage

First released in 1996, Apanage is purposely a more gastronomic wine than Brut Royal, with a little more chardonnay in the blend, more honed sourcing – including a higher proportion of grand and premier crus – and another year longer on lees. The result is a little more of both fruit character and aged complexity. Apple and bruised pear fruit are underlined by firm grapefruit acidity and gentle phenolic bitterness. It carries subtle honey and brioche notes on a short finish, a little overwhelmed by phenolic structure.

POMMERY APANAGE BLANC DE BLANCS NV $$$

91 points • 2014 BASE VINTAGE • TASTED IN CHAMPAGNE

Côte des Blancs, Montagne de Reims and Reims; 20% reserves; 9g/L dosage

A brand-new cuvée in 2019, Clément Pierlot introduces the idea as 'a meeting between several terroirs' – a large base of 20–30% Côte des Blancs, supplemented with strong sourcing from the east- and north-east-facing crus of the Montagne de Reims for 'structure and originality', and a little from south-facing Montagne de Reims and even the company's Clos Pompadour in Reims. 'The idea is to have something both very fresh, in the style of the house, and also very open at four years of age,' Pierlot says. Reserves are selected from 3–4 years and include 1995 Cramant – 'just 1%, but very important for character'. The result is a very fresh style of lively lemon focus, with bright acidity and fine chalk mineral persistence. True to its brief, it concludes tense and lively, with well-integrated dosage. A touch of lemon-zest bite adds phenolic tension to the finish, meshing seamlessly with fine chalk minerality. A light style of balance and precision, if a little short.

POMMERY GRAND CRU ROYAL BRUT 2006 $$$

87 points • TASTED IN CHAMPAGNE

50% chardonnay from Avize, Cramant, Oger and a little Verzenay and Sillery; 50% pinot noir from Aÿ, Verzenay, and a little Sillery and Bouzy; 8g/L dosage

Clément Pierlot announces this as having formerly been the top cuvée of the house, and hence its prestige cuvée, before Louise was conceived 40 years ago. 'We are one of the only houses to have only grand crus in our vintage cuvée,' he claims. 'We like the idea of the synergy and opposition of the chardonnay and pinot noir of the Côte des Blancs and the Montagne de Reims,' creating an intentionally powerful style to contrast the elegance of Louise. This vintage has been in the market for a few years, and it has now shed the reductive character of its youth and put on a medium to full straw hue. It's faded a little, though upheld lime and lemon fruit on a short finish. Boiled-sweets dosage contrasts with the firm, astringent phenolic grip of this warm vintage.

POMMERY CUVÉE LOUISE EXTRA BRUT 2004 $$$$

93 points • TASTED IN CHAMPAGNE

68% chardonnay from Cramant and Avize, 32% pinot noir from Aÿ; a blend of 51 plots; fermented at 18°C to preserve freshness; 5g/L dosage

Louise is Pommery's blend of the finest plots of its best vintages. When Thierry Gasco commenced at Pommery in 1992, he made a selection of the best 85 plots on the mid-slopes of Avize and Cramant for chardonnay, and Aÿ for pinot noir, which Clément Pierlot describes as the crus most closely linked to Pommery. Aÿ was a difficult decision for Gasco, as Pommery is more closely aligned with the northern Montagne de Reims. Sourcing was upheld when Paul-François Vranken made an agreement with Bernard Arnault, chief executive of LVMH, to buy back the 54 hectares of grand crus dedicated to this cuvée when he acquired the house in 2002. Unusually, the selection for Louise is made a full three weeks before the harvest, and a second selection is made at the traditional point of blending post-fermentation. 'We are looking for the maturity of the grapes,' Gasco explains. His pre-selection is necesary for a special pressing that he considers very important for the best extraction. Just 1800 litres of juice is pressed from each 4000 kilograms of grapes, compared with the authorised 2550 litres. The 2004 features a little more chardonnay than the usual 60/40 blend.

Louise 2004 has been about for a few years now, and it upholds its youthful spirit of lemon freshness and the white peach, grapefruit, beurre bosc pear and golden delicious apple definition of ripe Avize and Cramant chardonnay, backed sensitively with the depth of Aÿ pinot noir. Bottle age has elevated layers of complexity reminiscent of honey, caramel and toast, layered with cream brûlée, gingernut biscuits and even toffee. A bright and energetic acid line accurately projects the character of the great 2004 season, charged with the fine, salty chalk minerality of Avize and Cramant. It's just started to slip from its magnificent peak, with its firm and tense finish now beginning to show the first signs of drying out.

POMMERY CUVÉE LOUISE BRUT NATURE 2004 $$$$

93 points • TASTED IN CHAMPAGNE

As above, with zero dosage

When Gasco conceived to follow Madame Pommery's lead in creating a zero-dosage cuvée, he chose to do so with his prestige cuvée, 'because it has the best representation of terroir'. Pierlot points out that with more sugar in the grapes today, thanks to climate change, dosage is no longer required for the grand crus in this blend.

A lesson in the disproportionate influence of dosage, the absence of just 5g/L (the equivalent of less than one-third of a teaspoon of sugar in a cup of coffee) has a profound effect, and no less so at a full 15 years of age than it had on first release a few years ago. More tense, dry and mineral, this is a cuvée that contrasts taut lemon juice of freshness and purity with the drying structure of salt minerality. Notes of crab apple and grapefruit lend bite to its firm and structured finish. An elegant Louise, true to 2004, this is a cuvée for champagne purists.

POMMERY CUVÉE LOUISE 1999 $$$$

93 points • TASTED IN AUSTRALIA

As per Extra Brut 2004 above

Six years on from its first release, the generosity of time has calmed the firm bite of warm-season phenolic bitterness, making for a cuvée now more about layered, honeyed, toasty maturity than it is about the lemon, grapefruit and apple of its youth. It upholds impressive character and speaks gently of the fine chalk mineral voice of Cramant, Avize and Aÿ . A hint of burnt-orange development suggests that it has now just edged past its prime.

POMMERY CUVÉE LOUISE ROSÉ 2004 $$$$$

91 points • TASTED IN CHAMPAGNE

Cuvée Louise Extra Brut 2004 (as above) with 5-6% Bouzy red wine; aged 12 years on lees; 5g/L dosage; 5000 bottles

Gasco and Pierlot seek just a little dribble of very elegant red wine, to bring a pale colour and add subtle fruit aromas, while upholding the elegance of Louise. The result is a case in point of how much impact just a little red wine can make – not so much in pale salmon-copper hue, but in lending a new personality while upholding the structure and mineral expression of Louise. By contrast to Louise blanc, this is a savoury and secondary style in both flavour and aroma, yet upholding lively vibrancy in chalk mineral structure and acidity. Notes of savoury spice and tomato accent a dry and astringent finish.

POMMERY LES CLOS POMPADOUR 2003 $$$$$

93 points • DISGORGED 2016 • TASTED IN CHAMPAGNE EN MAGNUM

75% chardonnay, 25% pinot noir, 5% meunier; single clos on the hill of La Butte Saint-Nicaise within Reims; full malolactic fermentation; 7-8g/L dosage; 3000 magnums

The extraordinary vineyard of La Clos Pompadour commands an enormous 25 hectares on the hill of La Butte Saint-Nicaise, directly behind the house of Pommery within Reims, not only making this the biggest vineyard within the city by an order of magnitude (Château Malakoff has just three hectares and Clos Lanson is but one hectare), but indeed, the biggest clos in all of Champagne. Madame Pommery planted the vines and built the wall directly atop her crayères in the mid-1800s, fraught with danger due to the risk of collapse. To this day, parts of the vineyard must be worked by horses, for fear of a tractor crashing dramatically to the bottom of a crayère! Horses have been employed for five years now, and falcons have been used for protection against a hungry local bird population.

Sitting just 25cm atop perfect chalk, this is a site protected by its walls and warmed by the city and it tends to be the first to be harvested, at a full ripeness of 11 degrees potential, and hence is not chaptalised. Thus, it was from this site that Madame Pommery made Champagne's first experimental brut nature in 1874. In recent times, the site was not considered worthy of standing alone, and so it was only when Paul-François Vranken took ownership in 2002 that the first Clos Pompadour was created. The Clos is planted to all three varieties, and the best fruit of the season is reserved for this cuvée (usually from the oldest vines, planted in the 1960s), in a blend that changes according to the vintage. It has been made every vintage since 2002, though there is a suggestion that perhaps not all will be released.

A season of extreme ripeness, with tiny yields of just three tonnes per hectare, the house was concerned for the freshness and acidity of this particularly warm site. At a full 16 years of age, it's held good freshness in magnum, all things considered. The full impact and grip of 2003 is on extravagant parade in bountiful layers of coffee, crab apples and bruised pear, morphing into all the secondary complexity of gingernut biscuits and honey. True to the season and the site, this is a firm and phenolic style, displaying some bitter lemon zest structure. It holds its poise, with tangy grapefruit acidity defining good line and length.

R. POUILLON & FILS

(R Poo-ee-oh e feess)

---

17 Rue d'Aÿ 51160 Mareuil-sur-Aÿ
champagne-pouillon.com

DOMAINE
R. POUILLON
& fils

The Pouillon family has been growing grapes for more than a century, and Fabrice Pouillon is the third generation since 1947 to produce his own wines. Holdings of six hectares are centred on his home in Mareuil-sur-Aÿ and the surrounding villages of Aÿ, Avenay-Val-d'Or, Mutigny, Tauxières-Mutry and Épernay, and Festigny in the Vallée de la Marne. Planted half to pinot noir, one-third to chardonnay and just one-sixth to meunier, his 36 parcels are picked at full ripeness and vinified and aged individually (for as long as 18 months — often too long) in oak barrels, foudres, terracotta and enamel-lined vats according to the terroir. Fabrice began conversion to organic viticulture in 2003 and today incorporates biodynamic principles, fertilising only with organic composts, planting cover crops in the mid-rows and ploughing alternate rows with his horse named Tango. Every cuvée is wild fermented, malolactic fermentation is completed, and ageing takes place in cool cellars at a depth of 15 metres. His cuvées present a powerful and ripe take on the Grande Vallée de la Marne, though unfortunately tend to speak more of wild fermentation, oak, and long oxidative maturation than they do of place or fruit — but they are capable of shining in great seasons like 2008.

R. POUILLON & FILS RÉSERVE BRUT NV $$$

84 points • 2015 BASE VINTAGE • 15% CHARDONNAY, 65% PINOT, 20% MEUNIER • 40% RESERVES • DISGORGED DECEMBER 2017 • 6.8G/L DOSAGE • TASTED IN AUSTRALIA

85 points • 2014 BASE VINTAGE • 15% CHARDONNAY, 70% PINOT, 15% MEUNIER • 30% RESERVES • DISGORGED DECEMBER 2016 • 6G/L DOSAGE • TASTED IN AUSTRALIA EN DEMI-BOUTEILLE

Mareuil-sur-Aÿ, Mutigny, Avenay-Val-d'Or, Épernay and Festigny; wild fermented 85% in enamelled tanks, 15% in old oak; reserves vinified in foudres; cork

With a full straw hue beginning to brown, this is a cuvée that speaks more of the dry dustiness and bitter almond character of wild fermentation and the firm phenolics of 2015 than it does of fruit character and integrity. The result is callow, short and hard. After a short time on lees, the 2014 base spent longer on cork in its little bottle than it did on lees. It's a savoury and developed style that lacks primary fruit definition, integrity and lift. Wild fermentation has built notes of charcuterie amidst bitter almond character more prominent than subtle strawberry fruit.

R.POUILLON & FILS LES TERRES FROIDES BRUT PREMIER CRU NV $$$$

86 points • 2015 BASE VINTAGE • DISGORGED MARCH 2018 • TASTED IN AUSTRALIA

100% chardonnay; lieu-dit Les Terres Froides in Tauxières; wild fermented and matured for 18 months in 60% old oak barrels and 40% enamelled tanks; 40% reserves, vinified in foudres; bottled April 2017; 5g/L dosage; cork

The tension of Tauxières chardonnay makes for a crunchy style of nashi pear, tart granny smith apple and fennel, even hops, on the verge of underripeness. Sadly, long maturation in tanks and barrels has built a dominant yeasty, lactic character that dulls fruit definition. It concludes short, astringent and bitter.

R.POUILLON & FILS ROSÉ BRUT PREMIER CRU NV $$$$

87 points • 2015 BASE VINTAGE • DISGORGED MARCH 2018 • TASTED IN AUSTRALIA

100% pinot; Mareuil-sur-Aÿ; macerated on skins for up to 12 hours before pressing; 80% wild fermented in enamelled tanks, 20% in old oak barrels; 20% 2014 reserves fermented and aged 12 months in barrels; 6g/L dosage; cork

A medium salmon crimson hue heralds a precocious rosé that leads out with raspberry jube and ripe, macerated strawberry fruit and pink grapefruit zest. Bottling in March following harvest helps to preserve freshness, though reserves aged in oak barrels for a year lend developed, savoury notes of tomato and paprika. Fine tannin structure is balanced with a lick of dosage. The finish is unfortunately contracted and hollow. It leads out with such promise and anticipation, which hurriedly vaporises.

R.POUILLON & FILS LES VALNONS BRUT NATURE AŸ GRAND CRU 2011 $$$$

84 points • DISGORGED APRIL 2018 • TASTED IN AUSTRALIA

100% chardonnay; lieu-dit Les Valnons in Aÿ; fully vinified and aged for 18 months in old oak barrels; 2g/L dosage; cork; 1512 bottles

The dry, dusty, fresh mushroom character of imperfect fruit in the wet and rot-infused 2011 harvest collides with the splintery oak and firm tannins of long barrel age, with no dosage to save it, making for a callow and austere cuvée devoid of fruit and flesh.

R.POUILLON & FILS CHEMIN DU BOIS MÉTHODE FABRICE POUILLON 2009 $$$$

85 points • DISGORGED SEPTEMBER 2017 • TASTED IN AUSTRALIA

100% pinot; lieu-dit Chemin du Bois in Mareuil-sur-Aÿ Premier Cru; wild fermented and aged in old oak barrels; no added sugar at chaptalisation, *prise de mousse* or dosage; tiraged under cork; zero dosage; cork; 1534 bottles

Making a champagne with no added sugar is relatively straightforward at chaptalisation and dosage, but more tricky at *prise de mousse*, because sweetness is required in order to create bubbles. Fabrice Pouillon solves this dilemma by keeping 15% of the juice unfermented in tank until spring, then blending it back in to initiate wild fermentation in bottle to produce the bubbles. A full gold hue with browning notes, this is a dry and oxidative style that clashes the roast walnuts of lees age with the chestnut grip of oak fermentation. Its dry astringency is heightened by oxidation, rendering the finish dry and callow, devoid of fruit lift, integrity and flesh. The subtle red berry fruits of Mareuil-sur-Aÿ are regrettably swamped by oak and oxidation.

R. POUILLON & FILS CHEMIN DU BOIS MÉTHODE FABRICE POUILLON 2008 $$$$

93 points • DISGORGED THIRD TRIMESTER OF 2016 • TASTED IN AUSTRALIA

As for the Chemin du Bois 2009 (above); harvested ripe at 12 degrees potential; 4g/L dosage of concentrated and rectified grape juice (MCR); 2313 bottles

Boasting a full straw hue with a golden tint, this is a powerful 2008 that ricochets with the exuberance of pinot noir and the spicy honey of barrel fermentation. It's a delightful and exact expression of Mareuil-sur-Aÿ picked at full ripeness, loaded with tangy mirabelle plums, morello cherries, blood oranges, even loquats. Oak has been sensitively played, upholding the precision of the variety, the village, the vineyard and the vintage. A taut blanc de noirs of balance and poise that celebrates the tension of ripe 2008 acidity, amplified by low dosage. One bottle showed some dry, biscuity development and grainy phenolic grip.

Mareuil-sur-Aÿ, harvest 2014

ROBERT MONCUIT

(Roh-beah Moh-kwee)

7/10

2 PLACE DE LA GARE 51190 LE MESNIL-SUR-OGER
www.champagnerobertmoncuit.com

ROBERT MONCUIT

The Moncuit family has been growing chardonnay in the grand cru of Le Mesnil-sur-Oger since 1889, and Robert Moncuit made his first champagne in the great vintage of 1928. Five generations later, his grandson Pierre Amillet has managed the estate since 2000, sustainably working the family's eight hectares of vineyards, located exclusively in the village and neighbouring Oger. Insecticides are shunned, as are herbicides, in favour of ploughing for weed control. Full maturity is the goal, and chaptalisation is completely avoided, except in the challenging seasons of 2001 and 2011. His are cuvées of low dosage that express mature fruit character with great freshness and the precise mineral tension that defines Le Mesnil-sur-Oger. His non-vintage cuvées are more precise than ever this year.

Amillet is sensitive, intuitive and attentive in the winery, pressing every plot separately to maximise his palette of options for blending. He is a master at long *élevage* in oak to build backbone and expression without sacrificing purity or imposing oak flavours.

Fermentation and maturation takes place in barrels and foudres according to the parcel (he has recently moved away from stainless steel, though in the high-yielding harvest of 2018 he resorted back to tanks when all of his barrels were full). He buys barrels after a minimum of four seasons at Henri Boillot in Burgundy, and in 2018 he purchased two new foudres which will hold his perpetual reserve (after a year of seasoning with tailles for distillation).

Bottling takes place in July, so as to facilitate long *élevage* of 8-9 months in barrels and foudres. Bottle age is likewise long, with every cuvée privileged to a minimum of three years maturation on lees, thanks to a stock of 300,000 bottles, which furnishes annual sales of 80,000. Disgorgement dates are printed on corks.

The family's holdings are magnificent, none more so than a 2.17 hectare parcel of the legendary Les Chétillons planted in 1956, and released as a single lieu-dit for the first time in the spectacular 2008 harvest. This family certainly has a knack of nailing the most sublime vintages for its new releases! Amillet bottles his vintage cuvée every year, though relying on vines only in two villages can make for strong variations between seasons.

Amillet is content with his compact portfolio of five cuvées. 'Lieux-dits are the fashion, but for me it is difficult and I only want to bottle two, Le Mesnil Chétillons and Oger Vozémieux, to show the difference between the villages,' he reveals. 'I do not want to make ten lieux-dits like some others. Champagne should be a blend.'

Pruning in Oger, winter 2013

ROBERT MONCUIT LES GRANDS BLANCS EXTRA BRUT NV $$

94 points • 2014 BASE VINTAGE • TASTED IN CHAMPAGNE

Le Mesnil-sur-Oger and Oger; 20% 2013 reserves; entirely fermented and aged 8 months in barriques; full malolactic fermentation; no fining or filtration; 33,000 bottles

Formerly named 'Grand Cru Brut', this cuvée has undergone a magnificent transformation inside and out, and the 2014 base represents a stunning starting point stronger than I have ever seen for Pierre Amillet's range. He has masterfully captured an excellent expression of Le Mesnil, celebrating the deep fingerprint of the village in fine, frothing salt minerality and dynamic acidity. His mandate of ripeness is exemplified in beautiful fruit character of pear and apple, tensioned with bright, pure lemon and grapefruit. Barrel fermentation builds texture without disrupting the purity and precision of Les Mesnil, making for a finish of impressive line and length.

ROBERT MONCUIT RÉSERVE PERPETUELLE BLANC DE BLANCS EXTRA-BRUT NV $$

94 points • 2014 BASE VINTAGE • DISGORGED FEBRUARY 2018 • TASTED IN CHAMPAGNE

Le Mesnil-sur-Oger; 50% perpetual reserve of every vintage since 2006, with 50% drawn each year and replaced with the new harvest; fermented and aged 8 months in barriques; 3g/L dosage

The energy and salt mineral drive of Le Mesnil are all consuming, laying out a very fine, mouth-filling texture and beautifully defined acid line. Almost ripe apricots, lemons and crunchy white peaches define a refreshingly pure apéritif style of great integity and excellent length. A stunning and exact potrait of Le Mesnil.

ROBERT MONCUIT BLANC DE BLANCS 2012 $$$

93 points • DISGORGED MAY 2017 • TASTED IN CHAMPAGNE

50-80-year-old vines; vinified in barriques; full malolactic fermentation; tiraged under cork; 3g/L dosage

The generous enthusiasm of 2012 sets the foundation for a style of character and presence, framed eloquently by the mineral purity of the Le Mesnil-sur-Oger, the ripe fruit mandate of Pierre Amillet and the precision of his art in the winery. He has captured the perfect moment of ripeness in apple and pear presence, backed by the grapefruit and lemon tension of the village. It euphorically unites great ripeness, grip, body and beautifully frothing chalk minerality.

ROBERT MONCUIT CHÉTILLONS BLANC DE BLANCS GRAND CRU 2012 $$$$

95 points • DISGORGED JANUARY 2018 • TASTED IN CHAMPAGNE

Single lieu-dit Chétillons in Le Mesnil-sur-Oger; fully vinified in barriques; full malolactic fermentation; tiraged under cork; 2.25g/L dosage

The thundering cru of Chétillons (see Pierre Péters, page 470) occupies a commanding 14 hectares on the southern edge of the village, and Pierre Amillet is privileged to a generous slice of more than two hectares. He describes 2012 as a very mature vintage, thanks to sunny months from April through July. He has presented this season to thrilling effect, a tightrope tension between the taut acidity and mineral structure of Le Mesnil, the body of fruit ripeness, and the creamy texture and toasty complexity of barrel fermentation. He has found the perfect moment of ripeness to juxtapose the generosity of apricot with the taut lemon and grapefruit of the village. The accessible chalk of Les Mesnil makes for a long, salty finish of very fine, mineral texture, illuminated by brilliant acidity. A wine of character and presence that in no way disrupt harmony or purity.

ROBERT MONCUIT VOZÉMIEUX BLANC DE BLANCS GRAND CRU 2010 $$$$

90 points • DISGORGED MARCH 2017 • TASTED IN CHAMPAGNE

Single lieu-dit Vozémieux in Oger; vinified in foudre; 1.12g/L dosage

Pierre Amillet's aspiration with his two lieux-dits is to contrast the diverse personalities of Le Mesnil-sur-Oger and neighbouring Oger. He has done so to profound effect. True to the exuberance of Oger, this is a generous cuvée of medium straw hue. This is not a village that typically ages long, and, true to form, it's ready to drink right away. Apricots and white peaches are the themes of this luscious style, carrying on with spice and honey and ginger. Its ripeness builds bite on the finish, which lends some firmness to the gravelly minerality of Oger, amplified in foudre.

ROBERT MONCUIT LE MESNIL SUR OGER COTEAUX CHAMPENOIS BLANC 2014 $$$

92 points • TASTED IN AUSTRALIA

100% chardonnay; Le Mesnil-sur-Oger; no oak; cork

True to the tension of Le Mesnil and the understated mood of 2014, this is a Coteaux Champenois blanc that proclaims the mineral stamp of this great terroir, yet presents a beautifully, indeed unexpectedly, creamy texture. It's a testament to Pierre Amillet's talent in nurturing his vineyards to impeccable ripeness, and then building lees texture in tank, without the fallback of oak here. The pure lemon line of Le Mesnil is the dashing hero, with a support team of beurre bosc pear, supported by the almond meal notes of lees maturity. The salty chalk minerality of Le Mesnil guides and elongates a finish of magnificent line and length. He has created a stunning Coteaux Champenois blanc with a long and confident future before it.

ROGER BRUN

(Roh-zheh Bruh)

6/10

1 Rue Henri IV 51160 Aÿ
www.champagne-roger-brun.com

CHAMPAGNE

ROGER BRUN

Brun is a famous name in Aÿ, where the family have been growers since the late 1700s, and three distinct houses in the village bear the name today: Edouard, René and Roger. Philippe Brun took the lead of his little house from his father Roger in 1999, and oversees production from 18 hectares of mostly growers spanning 15 villages across the Grande Vallée de la Marne around Épernay. Non-vintage cuvées are sourced from growers and fermented in stainless steel tanks, and vintage cuvées from estate vines in Aÿ and Avize, fermented in small, old oak barrels. Non-vintage cuvées receive full dosages of 11–12g/L, though vintage cuvées are much lower at 3–8g/L. Declaring the full magnitude of Aÿ, these are powerful cuvées that uphold graceful calm and class.

ROGER BRUN GRANDE RÉSERVE BRUT NV $$

92 points • TASTED IN AUSTRALIA EN MAGNUM

20% chardonnay, 60% pinot noir, 20% meunier; six villages around Épernay in the Grande Vallée de la Marne; roughly one-third reserves; vinified in stainless steel tanks; aged at least 2 years on lees; 12g/L dosage

A full straw hue proclaims the magnitude of Aÿ and the surrounding villages of the Grande Vallée de la Marne, while the palate showcases an even and harmonious synergy between the depth of mirabelle plum and white peach, the crunch of pear and apple and the tang of grapefruit. Hints of red cherries emerge in time, upholding grace and calm, heightened in a big bottle.

ROGER BRUN GRAND CRU CUVÉE DES SIRES MILLÉSIME 2013 $$$

94 points • TASTED IN AUSTRALIA

30% Avize chardonnay fermented in stainless steel tanks, 70% Aÿ pinot noir fermented in small, old oak barrels; 8g/L dosage; cork; this bottle was suspected to have been disgorged in mid-2017, but the youthfulness of the cork looks more like mid-2018

Built around its best parcels in Aÿ, this cuvée is claimed by the house to be 'well known in the village and not to be drunk in a dancer's shoe'. Duly noted. With a medium straw hue, it rejoices in the beauty of barrel-fermented Aÿ pinot noir with considerable confidence and class. A core of bright red cherry and raspberry fruit with black cherry depth articulates the fresh confidence that defines this great cru in the vibrant 2013 season, illuminated skilfully by a lemon flash of Avize chardonnay. Lees age has heightened the biscuity complexity and spicy undertones of barrel fermentation, which meld seamlessly with a long-lingering fruit profile and fine chalk minerality.

ROGER BRUN AŸ LA PELLE BLANC DE NOIRS MILLÉSIME 2012 $$$$

87 points • DISGORGED JANUARY 2017 • TASTED IN AUSTRALIA

100% pinot noir; single, south-facing plot La Pelle, the first of the house to ripen in Aÿ; fully fermented in small oak barriques; 3g/L dosage; cork; disgorgement date is declared on the front label

A full straw-yellow hue heralds a powerful blanc de noirs, sadly pushed too far in small oak barrels to the point of oxidation, devoid of fruit integrity and collapsing into a dry and astringent finish of coarse oak tannins and phenolic bitterness. Lees age has redeemed it slightly, lending biscuity, spicy, golden fruit cake complexity and creaminess to the structure. A second bottle was identical.

Aÿ, winter 2015

ROLAND CHAMPION

(Roh-lon Shohn-pee-yon)

6/10

16 Grande Rue 51530 Chouilly
www.champagne-roland-champion.com

CHAMPAGNE

Roland Champion

À CHOUILLY

The Champion family has been growing grapes in Chouilly since the 18th century, and André Champion started making his own champagnes in 1929. His untimely death elevated his eldest son Roland to head of the company at the age of sixteen, and he went on to expand the estate to 40 plots spanning a respectable 18 hectares, comprising 70% chardonnay in Chouilly, and 22% meunier and 8% pinot noir in Verneuil and neighbouring Vandières in the Vallée de la Marne. Today, Roland's son François and his children Carole, Ambroise, Clémence, Astrid and Félix sell the majority of their production 'sur latte' to négociants, leaving just 35,000 bottles to sell under their name. All are bottled under reliable DIAM closures. Vinification is conducted in stainless steel tanks, with full malolactic fermentation. The family has skilfully tamed the muscular nature of Chouilly in a characterful set of sensitively styled cuvées.

ROLAND CHAMPION CARTE BLANCHE GRAND CRU BLANC DE BLANCS NV $$

92 points • 2014 BASE VINTAGE • DISGORGED APRIL 2017 • TASTED IN AUSTRALIA

100% Chouilly chardonnay; 20% 2013 and 25% 2012 reserves; aged at least 2 years on lees; alcoholic and malolactic fermentations in temperature-controlled stainless steel tanks; 6g/L dosage; DIAM

The embodiment of Chouilly: luscious, juicy and rich, energised by the glassy chalk minerality of the village. It oozes with ripe white peach, fig, mixed spice and honey, nuanced with ginger and layers of buttery Parisian croissants, finishing with mineral focus and impressive line and length. Body, confidence and character are all rolled into its generous folds. A blanc de blancs ready for main-course fare.

ROLAND CHAMPION CARTE NOIRE GRAND CRU BLANC DE BLANCS 2008 $$

95 points • DISGORGED APRIL 2017 • TASTED IN AUSTRALIA

100% Chouilly chardonnay; aged 8 years on lees; alcoholic and malolactic fermentations in temperature-controlled stainless steel tanks; 5g/L dosage; DIAM

From the very first aroma, this wine transports one back to Chouilly, in all of its fleshy, juicy white peach, wild honey and fig personality. Its exuberant generosity is impeccably toned by the energy and tension of 2008, amplifying the fine-ground chalk minerality of the village to dizzying heights, drawing out a finish of hauntingly elongated persistence. Its acidity will hold it in the cellar for some years yet, but it's irresistibly enticing right away.

Chouilly, harvest 2014

RUINART

(Roo-ee-nar)

6/10

4 RUE DES CRAYÈRES 51100 REIMS

www.ruinart.com

Ruinart

LA PLUS ANCIENNE MAISON
DE CHAMPAGNE

Frédéric Panaïotis grew up between his grandparents' chardonnay vines in Champagne, and the variety remains close to his heart, making him very much at home as chef de cave at Ruinart since 2007. 'I'm glad somebody took the decision long ago to play with chardonnay at Ruinart!' he beams. The longest-established champagne house of all has an affinity with chardonnay's freshness, finesse and elegance, and all of its finest cuvées lead with this variety, even its prestige rosé. Without the might of Moët & Chandon, the brand impact of Veuve Clicquot or the cachet of Krug, Ruinart lurks as the low-profile member of the Louis Vuitton Moët Hennessy family. On Reims' famed Rue de Crayères, its premises hide behind the grand street presence of Pommery and Veuve Clicquot. This is just as Panaïotis would have it. 'In France we have a saying, if you live underground, you live happy!' he says. But on its performance, Ruinart has no need to lie low. Its cuvées are pure and pitch-perfect, singing with the crystalline precision of chardonnay.

Champagne is planted to just 30% chardonnay, and although it's on the rise, it remains the rarest of the region's three key varieties, yet the most sought-after and hence the hardest to acquire. Ruinart owns just 10% of its vineyards, including historic resources of 15 hectares of chardonnay in the grand crus of Sillery and Puisieulx on the eastern slopes of the Montagne de Reims, providing a richer and rounder style than the Côte des Blancs.

Sillery and Puisieulx are lesser-known grand crus that encompass vineyards at the bottom of the slopes between Mailly-Champagne and Verzenay, in a similar way that Oiry catches the lower edge of Chouilly and Cramant. Sillery is the only grand cru outside of the Côte des Blancs to boast more chardonnay than pinot. 'With east-facing slopes, it is perfect for chardonnay!' exclaims Panaïotis, who sources more from the village than any other house. He describes the style of chardonnay from Sillery and Puisieulx as so similar to

that of Verzenay and Verzy that he can't tell the difference.

'Our idea is to make a round, supple and easy-to-drink blanc de blancs that is approachable and ready to drink on release,' explains Panaïotis, who achieves his style by limiting the Côte des Blancs to 60% of his blends. 'Harmony and balance are super important, not too lean or focused.'

Long-term contracts with growers form the vast bulk of Ruinart's supplies, supplemented through vineyards acquired from Lanson and Joseph Perrier. This has enabled the house to increase its annual production from 1.4 million to 2.5–3 million bottles over the past two decades. 'Ruinart is in demand, so I'm getting all the chardonnay I can find!' Panaïotis exclaims. Annual growth today is under 5%.

To maintain the aromatic freshness and elegance of its fruit, the Ruinart house style is decisively reductive. 'We hate oxygen!'

he declares, describing his approach as the antithesis of Bollinger and Krug. A pneumatic press is used instead of a traditional champagne press, to guard the juice against oxidation, and inert nitrogen gas protects the wine at every stage of production. Vinification takes place only in stainless steel. 'We have absolutely no need of oak in any of our wines,' Panaïotis states.

Ruinart's cuvées often carry flattering hints of struck flint or gunpowder, remnants of reductive winemaking. 'My goal is to take reduction even further!' proclaims Panaïotis. 'The stinky white Burgundy thing, I just love it! Like Domaine Roulot, but they use oak. The question is how to do it without oak!'

To soften the austerity of young chardonnay, all cuvées undergo full malolactic fermentation, and non-vintage wines are balanced using respectable quantities of reserve wines. This makes for a style that permits refreshingly low dosages, declining admirably over recent years. The dosage is tweaked for successive disgorgements of Ruinart's prestige Dom Ruinart cuvée, typically lowering as the wine ages.

'For me, it's not a matter of numbers, but of balance,' Panaïotis explains.

After Panaïotis joined Ruinart in 2007, he recalls that 'it took a couple of years to figure out what was going on, and 2009 was the first year when I said, "Right, we can now start to do things! I don't think there's much I can do with the blanc de blancs or the rosé, but I can do things with R de Ruinart!"' This remains his aspiration a decade later. 'It is never finished!' he exclaimed recently. 'I would like to bring more freshness to R de Ruinart. It is a big volume, so not that easy to manoeuvre!'

Building freshness into all of the base wines is his priority, which he is achieving through tighter control of ferments and more frequent monitoring, three times daily. Reduction is monitored by plotting the pace of ferments. 'Not crazy temperatures!' he says. 'Too slow and it gives oxidation, too fast and it gives too much reduction.' He is also working to reduce flavours picked up during malolactic fermentation.

'We are aiming to make wines of more precision and purity, while upholding the smoothness and drinkability of the house,' is his aspiration. 'We are never finished, and we are still working on trying to bring everything up. And I am never satisfied! Happy but not satisfied!'

Ruinart's distinctive rounded bottles make riddling challenging, and the house relies exclusively on gyropalettes, which Panaïotis claims give a far better result. The clear glass of these bottles renders the wine susceptible to lightstruck degradation, making it vital to store them in the dark.

An informative website now discloses impressive detail on the *cépage*, crus and vinification of every cuvée. The disgorgement date is disclosed on the back labels of Dom Ruinart.

Ruinart has occupied its premises in Reims since 1768, and was the first in Champagne to use the 3rd-century Roman crayères (chalk mines) under the city to age its champagnes.

Its location on top of the hill makes its eight kilometres of cellars some of the deepest and most spectacular in the region, plunging to depths of up to 38 metres. These are the only cellars in Champagne classified as a national monument – a distinguished home for such graceful champagnes.

Ruinart's third-century Roman crayères

Ruinart R de Ruinart NV $$

90 points • 2015 base vintage • Tasted in Champagne and Australia

40% chardonnay, 49% pinot noir, 11% meunier; a blend of around 50 different crus, including a little Aube; full malolactic fermentation; 20-25% reserves; 8g/L dosage; cork; 60% of the production of the house, hence more than 1.5 million bottles

The red apple of pinot noir meets the grapefruit of chardonnay, set against a backdrop of spicy, toasty gingerbread lees complexity. On first release, this was a particularly pure and focused R de Ruinart, with subtle wisps of the struck-flint reduction of the house, something I've not seen in this cuvée in the past, which Frédéric Panaïotis puts down to the purity of the blend today. A year on, the phenolic grip of the warm 2015 season is beginning to sink its claws in as it sheds its primary freshness. Nonetheless, it upholds good acid drive and integrity.

Ruinart Blanc de Blancs NV $$$

91 points • 2015 base vintage • Tasted in Champagne and Australia

100% chardonnay; a blend of 20-25 crus, mostly premier crus from Côte des Blancs and Montagne de Reims, with Sézanne for maturity and the Massif de Saint-Thierry for freshness; 20-25% reserves; 7.5g/L dosage; cork

A crunchy, vivacious and youthful blend presents the fine chalk mineral texture, pale colour and pure lemon, apple and pear fruit of the Côte des Blancs, with a note of fennel suggesting fruit on the cusp of ripeness in this generous season. Signature struck-flint and smoky grilled toast reduction speak Ruinart. Montagne de Reims chardonnay is strategically deployed to provide body and mid-palate fleshiness, without diminishing the tension, line and salty chalk mineral structure of the Côte des Blancs. Bottle age has built subtle nougat and toasty, biscuity complexity. The phenolic grip, grainy coffee bean texture, pear skin bite and grapefruit bitterness inherent to the 2015 season make for a firm finish of dry-extract graininess. It concludes with well-balanced dosage and fresh, clean acidity.

Ruinart Rosé NV $$$

91 points • 2015 base vintage • Tasted in Australia

45% chardonnay from the Côte des Blancs and Montagne de Reims, 55% pinot noir from the Montagne de Reims and Vallée de la Marne; 20-25% 2014 and 2013 reserves; 16% pinot noir red wine; 8g/L dosage; cork; 20% of the production of the house, hence more than 500,000 bottles

Ruinart makes its red wines in-house. 'It's very critical to make red wine specifically for rosé, which is very different to making it for red wine,' says Frédéric Panaïotis. He uses red wines from reserves of the previous year, as a year of maturity helps with stability of colour. He has reduced the proportion of red wines from 18–19% to 16% over the past decade. 'In recent years we have had warmer vintages and hence more phenolics than in the past, so we need less red wine now,' he explains.

Ruinart's rosé is intentionally fresh, fruity, aromatic, approachable and full in colour. A light structure is the aspiration, but a strong inclusion of 18–19% red wine has traditionally infused a full-crimson hue, firm, fine tannin grip and a suggestion of bitterness to the finish. A little less red wine today makes for a medium crimson hue and subsequent relaxation in its structure. A large dose of chardonnay declares the house style of restraint and soft, chalk mineral mouthfeel, while pinot noir fulfils Panaïotis' aspiration for this blend of aromatic freshness, lending aromas and flavours of all shades of red: strawberries, pink grapefruit, pomegranate, guava and a savoury edge of pink pepper and tomato. Subtle notes of dry extract lend a hint of coffee to the finish and a gentle, fine tannin structure. It upholds good persistence, balancing chalk mineral structure with finely textured tannins, vibrant acidity and well-integrated dosage. A fresh, approachable and pretty Ruinart Rosé, ready to drink now.

RUINART DOM RUINART BLANC DE BLANCS BRUT 2007 $$$$$

96 points • DISGORGED 25 SEPTEMBER 2017, AND 2018 • TASTED IN CHAMPAGNE AND AUSTRALIA

100% grand cru chardonnay; 75% Côte des Blancs (Chouilly, Le Mesnil-sur-Oger, Oger and Avize), 25% northern Montagne de Reims (predominantly Sillery and Verzenay); aged more than 9 years on lees; 5g/L dosage; cork

The 2007 vintage was Frédéric Panaïotis' first at Ruinart. 'I was nervous!' he admits. 'This was not 2002 or 2004! And the vintage is more important than the guy who made it!' He recalls the season as a good year for chardonnay, dodging the botrytis that afflicted pinot and meunier. Picked at a potential alcohol of 9.6–9.7, he describes the ripeness as not particularly high, but phenologically ripe and still fresh. 'In 2007, the Montagne de Reims was even less ripe than the Côte des Blancs, so there is a little less Montagne de Reims in the blend, as it tends to show greener characters in the lesser years, so we rely more on villages like Chouilly for generosity.'

A Dom Ruinart of layered complexity, 2007 is a vintage that seamlessly unites tension with generosity. It leads forth with the signature, subtle gunsmoke reduction of the house, amidst a complex assemblage of exotic fruits reminiscent of star fruit. The slightly lower maturity of the season contrasts the generous ripeness of the 2006 before it, reflected in prominent lime fruit, green tea and fennel, described by Panaïotis as 'green flavours and vegetal, but in a nice way'. A decade on lees has blessed it with unctuous, silky and generous layers of brioche, melted butter, freshly whipped cream and roast brazil nuts. It unites focused acid line with silky, creamy structure and the heightened, fine salt minerality of the Côte des Blancs, making for a graceful and enduring finish of impressive line, length, concentration and character. A confident and alluring vintage for Dom Ruinart, ready to drink right away, yet holding good potential for the medium-term.

RUINART DOM RUINART BLANC DE BLANCS BRUT 2006 $$$$$

95 points • DISGORGED OCTOBER 2016 • TASTED IN CHAMPAGNE AND AUSTRALIA

69% Côte des Blancs (predominantly Chouilly, Le Mesnil-sur-Oger and Avize), 31% Montagne de Reims (predominantly Puisieulx and Sillery); 4.5g/L dosage

Frédéric Panaïotis describes 2006 as 'elliptical and large, with a savouriness thanks to a phenolic character that it requires so it doesn't look too flabby or soft, bringing an interesting bite and structure that keeps the wine alive. I'm not sure it will age for decades, like 2007, which will age better in my opinion.'

Dom Ruinart of power and presence like I have never seen before, this is a vintage brimming with peaches and white nectarines over a focused core of lemon fruit purity. It transposes the generosity of the season with definition and structure, thanks to well-balanced acidity and not inconsiderable support from the heightened chalk minerality of the Côte des Blancs. Struck-flint reduction inscribes the signature of the house, while time has built a silky texture and wonderful complexity of brioche and vanilla.

RUINART DOM RUINART ROSÉ BRUT 2004 $$$$$

95 points • DISGORGED FEBRUARY 2016 • TASTED IN CHAMPAGNE

Dom Ruinart Blanc de Blancs Brut 2004 with 19% Sillery red wine; aged 11 years on lees; 4.5g/L dosage

Panaïotis calls his Dom Ruinart Rosé 'blanc de blancs rosé', but the influence of 19% pinot noir red wine is profound, transforming its base Dom Ruinart 2004 into a copper-salmon thing almost beyond recognition. This is a deeply complex and characterful rosé of potpourri and spice that he looks for as part of the signature of the style. Reductive complexity of struck flint takes on a smoked paprika sensation here, while 15 years of maturity draws out savoury nuances of tomato and toast. It concludes gentle and complex, with very fine tannin structure melding seamlessly with its chalk mineral core.

RUINART DOM RUINART BLANC DE BLANCS BRUT 2004 $$$$$

98 points • DISGORGED AUGUST 2014 • TASTED IN AUSTRALIA

100% grand cru chardonnay; 69% Côte des Blancs (predominantly Chouilly, Avize and Le Mesnil-sur-Oger), 31% Montagne de Reims (Sillery, Puisieulx, Mailly-Champagne and Verzenay); aged 8 years on lees; 5.5g/L dosage

Ruinart's flagship blanc de blancs plays the high strings of the Côte des Blancs to the thick orchestral scoring of Montagne de Reims, filling out chardonnay's pitch-perfect freshness with layers of creamy generosity. I have adored the 2004 since the moment it first landed four years ago, when I announced that it promised two decades of potential in the cellar. It has been blessed immeasurably by another year on lees and three more on cork, possessing endurance and effortless confidence. Its vitality and an edginess are emphasised by brilliant, diamond-cut acidity, underscored by the nostalgic timbre of inimitable Côte des Blancs chalk minerality. A distinctive and enticing air of reductive character blows through in gunflint, grilled toast and white pepper, the signature of Ruinart and of chardonnay, while more than a decade in Ruinart's ancient chalk mines has deepened its voice with rising tones of nougat and toasty complexity. Its euphoric vigour and sheer stamina surpass even the masterpiece of 2002, promising decades of potential yet, though already drinking marvellously. Large glasses will be your best ally when it is finally time to awaken this sleeping beauty.

Ruinart, winter 2013

SALON

(Sah-loh)

5–7 Rue de la Brèche d'Oger 51190 Le Mesnil-sur-Oger
www.salondelamotte.com

CHAMPAGNE

S

SALON

Le Mesnil

There is only one Salon, and there has only ever been one. One wine of one variety from one vintage, sourced from one region (Côte de Blancs) and one village (Le Mesnil-sur-Oger). The romantic ideal ends abruptly here, however, because this is not a single-vineyard wine, nor an estate wine, nor even is it made at Salon or in Le Mesnil. The fruit of the single-hectare estate vineyard of Jardin de Salon was declassified until 2012 to its lower-tier sister house, Delamotte (page 191), because the vines were replanted in 2003. Salon is sourced from 15 hectares of vines of average age 35–40 years, and some older than 90, owned by 19 longstanding growers, all of whom sell their fruit only to Salon. Winemaking is handled by the owner of both houses, Laurent-Perrier.

The minute scale of this operation sinks in as I absorb it from the homely tasting room in the house in Le Mesnil-sur-Oger. The windows frame the Jardin vineyard stretching up the gentle slope just outside. Directly below, a decade of future releases lie waiting in the small cellar, though most lie in warehouses off-site. There are only 10 employees: six in the cellar and four in the office. Production is typically just 50,000–60,000 bottles, and only in worthy vintages. There is no non-vintage wine, so production is limited to the finest years, of which the current release, 2007, is just the 41st since 1905.

It was in that year that Eugène-Aimé Salon created Champagne's first blanc de blancs, originally only for personal consumption. To this day it remains among the most celebrated and most expensive. Of the original vineyards from which Eugène-Aimé purchased, all but two are still part of Salon's sourcing. The philosophy from the start was to build a champagne that could age, with every element

of its production honed towards this goal. The first pressing is used exclusively, fermented in stainless steel under temperature control. Its natural acidity is upheld by blocking malolactic fermentation, distinguishing it from Delamotte. Aged for an average of 10 years before release, the timing for each vintage is determined according to when it is ready. Riddling is performed by hand, and bottles are disgorged according to when they are released. This usually equates to four to six disgorgements across two years of release. Dosage is tweaked for each disgorgement, typically 5–6g/L.

Salon is usually among the last houses to release its vintage cuvée, and even at this age, it is far from its peak. 'Whenever I produce a vintage I say, "This is not for me or for my children, but for my grandchildren",' declares Salon Delamotte president Didier Depond, who considers the perfect time to drink Salon to be after 20 years.

'It takes 20 years to truly define a great wine,' he suggests. 'We are always very surprised by the potential of Salons opened from the '70s, '60s and even '50s.'

Depond is afforded the freedom to manage the house independently, and feels no pressure to increase volumes, in spite of limited supply and high demand.

'It's difficult to increase the volume because the vineyards are limited,' he points out. 'And it would be a disaster to increase the number of vintages we release.' A noble stance at a time when some houses appear set on churning out flagship champagnes in lesser seasons.

The house released five vintages from the first decade of the new millennium, not far above its longstanding average of just under four per decade. It upholds 1996, 2002 and 2008 to be the finest vintages for long ageing. The 2008 will be followed by 2012. Sadly, only 10,000 magnums of 2008 will be released, and only in timber boxed sets with four other vintages, making this aspirational release all the more unobtainable.

Salon is an undisputed legend of Champagne, possessing astonishing longevity, and its scarcity and reputation will continue to drive its price ever upwards. But is it everything today that it once was? In tasting after tasting, I am increasingly left contemplating whether Salon possesses the same sublime polish, purity and persistence that once set it apart among the greatest of all blanc de blancs.

My ratings for Salon spanning the first decade of the 2000s have consistently been a point behind those of equivalent vintages of the 1990s. This is why my overall rating for the house has dropped again this year. This has happened to coincide with progressive and substantial price rises.

Meanwhile, the blanc de blanc landscape is on the move. Wine for wine, vintage for vintage, Taittinger Comte de Champagne is consistently one or two points ahead of Salon in every vintage in the 2000s to date, and this was not the case in the 1990s. Other blanc de blancs have arisen that now frequently eclipse Salon, including Charles Heidsieck Blanc des Millénaires, Pierre Péters Les Chétillons, Billecart Cuvée Louis and Deutz Amour de Deutz. None of these have experienced spiralling price rises like Salon. Le Mesnil-sur-Oger is every bit deserving of extreme pricing and is capable of trumping every other blanc de blancs – Krug Clos du Mesnil has proven both points on countless occasions.

In May 2019, Laurent Perrier announced the appointment of Dominique Demarville as Michel Fauconnet's successor, effective from the beginning of 2020. Demarville has spent the past quarter of a century transforming the pinot-led houses of Mumm and then Veuve Clicquot. It will be more than a decade before we have the opportunity to judge whether his talents transfer equally to chardonnay. But I have a very good feeling.

Salon corks are coded with a letter to indicate the semester, and an inverted number for the year of disgorgement, so A81 is the first trimester of 2018.

Salon's quaint cellars under Le Mesnil-sur-Oger.

SALON 'S' LE MESNIL BLANC DE BLANCS BRUT 2007 $$$$$

96 points • DISGORGED JULY 2018 • TASTED IN AUSTRALIA

19 parcels from Le Mesnil-sur-Oger; 5g/L dosage; cork

A medium straw hue at 12 years of age, this is a vibrant Salon that captures the cool, coiled mood of 2007 in a bright flash of lemon, lime, crunchy granny smith apple, even hints of fennel. The grand cru magnitude of Le Mesnil infuses magnificent confidence of beautifully determined line and length, structured with the inimitable, salty and super-fine chalk minerality that reverberates with the voice of the village. Its malic acidity froths and churns in unison with its minerality, having already found a seamless harmony with the creamy texture of a full decade on lees. An effortless Salon of lighter-than-life airiness and exacting refinement, uncharacteristically approachable in its youth, though vibrantly youthful in every detail, promising a long life, even if not demanding it in the manner of the greatest Salons. It concludes with good line and length, though not in the echelons of the true greats.

SALON 'S' LE MESNIL BLANC DE BLANCS BRUT 2006 $$$$$

96 points • TASTED IN CHAMPAGNE AND AUSTRALIA

19 parcels from Le Mesnil-sur-Oger; 4g/L dosage; less than 60,000 bottles

My first encounter with Salon 2006 was at the maison on the day of its global release. While this cuvée tends to pick up a little colour as it develops across its release cycle, it is characteristically a brilliant, pale straw hue when it first emerges from the darkness of a decade in the deep, blinking, into the stark light of day. Hence a suggestion of yellow to its hue immediately signals the magnitude of the season and the proportions of this release. This is a Salon of immense exotic complexity, nuanced with the spicy mandarin, succulent persimmon and juicy white peach of fully ripe chardonnay, the caramel of more than a decade of age, even an unexpected note of dark chocolate, surrounding a core of golden delicious apple and grapefruit. True to the ripeness of 2006, it is creamy, soft and engaging, with gentle saline mineral structure highlighted by softly integrated acidity. Without the acid drive or energy of a great Salon, the malic level is evidently low in this warm season. A very fine bead sets off a long finish, marked by a subtle touch of warm-season phenolic grip. A fresh and lively take on a ripe vintage, this is a Salon for early consumption, though it will benefit from another five years to evolve.

SALON 'S' LE MESNIL BLANC DE BLANCS BRUT 1997 $$$$$

97 points • ORIGINAL DISGORGEMENT, PROBABLY AROUND 2007 • TASTED IN CHAMPAGNE
97 points • DISGORGED 2018 • TASTED IN CHAMPAGNE

The talent of Salon to desperately cling to incisive youthfulness is electrifying, and no more astonishing than in seasons that in their own merits are not otherwise flattered by the passage of time. This is a release that utterly transcends its season. The rounded integration of the warm 1997 season produced a maturity of fruit that made for a more accessible Salon from the outset, yet acidity on par with 1996 has infused it with astonishing accomplishment in the cellar. Its evolution since I first tasted it for the inaugural edition of the Guide in 2010 is unparalleled by any other champagne from this unheralded season. It has now attained a wonderful place of transcendental complexity, rolling with brioche, vanilla, toasted coconut, cream and slowly rising spice. In bottles disgorged for the original release, tertiary complexity of subtle pipe smoke is beginning, while recently disgorged bottles uphold preserved lemon tang and glacé apricot exotics. At a glorious 22 years of age, its heightened malic acidity has found integration and balance, while vibrantly driving an energetic finish, caressed by a silky, creamy mouthfeel and permeated by omnipresent Le Mesnil chalk minerality. It lingers very long, pure and lively, coiled with great potential that promises to continue to unravel for many years yet.

Taittinger

(Tet-ahn-zhay)

7/10

9 PLACE SAINT-NICAISE 51100 REIMS
www.taittinger.com

CHAMPAGNE
TAITTINGER
Reims

'My grandfather gave me a book when I was five years old,' Pierre-Emmanuel Taittinger recalls. 'In the dedication he wrote, "To my grandson, who will one day be an entrepreneur and be the guardian of the family tradition."' Little did he know how true his prophecy would prove to be, and just what it would take to achieve. In these days of corporate takeovers, it's a gutsy commitment to buy back the family business. When most of the heirs voted to cash in and Taittinger was sold in 2005, Pierre-Emmanuel launched a fierce, year-long buy-back for his branch of the family, to the tune of €550 million, with the help of family friends and French bank Crédit Agricole. The family has since built up its stake in the company to almost half, with the remainder mostly in the hands of its friends. Annual sales of 6.5 million bottles rank Taittinger as Champagne's sixth-largest house.

The fulfilment of his grandfather's prediction returned Taittinger to its place among the last big independent, family-owned houses that uphold the family name not only on the label, but in their management. Pierre-Emmanuel remains president of the company, his dynamic son, Clovis, is deputy managing director, and his delightful daughter, Vitalie, is marketing and communications director. The board and family are involved in each cuvée's tastings. 'My father leads the tasting, but it is a collective decision,' says Clovis.

It's a compelling story of fighting for the family business in the middle of one of the biggest corporate jungles anywhere in the wine world. It took Pierre-Emmanuel years to bring his buy-back to fruition, and it was not until 2008 that it was complete. More than a decade later, the final releases from the beginning of the new era are yet to emerge from the hallowed caverns of Taittinger, and the portfolio has never looked more refined.

NATURAL VITICULTURE
Taittinger's 288 hectares of vineyard holdings, predominantly in the Montagne de Reims and Côte des Blancs, provide for 45% of the company's annual production, with recent growth of around 7% each year. This makes it the third-largest vineyard owner in Champagne and the largest family owner. Its own vines comprise 48% pinot (primarily in Ambonnay, Mailly-Champagne, Rilly-la-Montagne and the Côte des Bar), 37% chardonnay (most notably in Cramant, Avize, Chouilly, Oger and Le Mesnil-sur-Oger) and 15% meunier (in the Vallée de la Marne and the Massif de Saint-Thierry). Chardonnay plays a

Hautvillers, winter 2013

significant role in the house style, sourced predominantly from the Côte des Blancs.

An increasingly eco-friendly approach is taken in the vines, with a reduction in the use of pesticides and elimination of herbicides. 'We are aiming to use half the usual dose of chemicals,' outlines Taittinger's young and talented managing director, Damien Le Sueur, 'and in 2010 we used less than six treatments across all our vineyards.'

The house is not seeking organic certification, to retain the flexibility to use full doses when difficult seasons dictate. 'Our philosophy is to be sustainable and to add less and less products in the vineyards, but we are not dogmatic about an organic approach,' he clarifies. A 35-hectare vineyard on the edge of Reims in Murigny has been worked organically for 5–6 years, out of respect for nearby residents and a hospital.

Natural treatments remain the preference across the estate, and attention has been given to trellising to provide ventilation to balanced canopies. Grasses are planted in the mid-rows of 80% of estate vineyards, believed to be an unprecedented proportion for an estate of this size, and ploughing is used for weed control.

Seven hectares are ploughed by horse, 'not for marketing, but to maintain the traditional work of the past'.

Le Sueur reports that these initiatives over the past 10–15 years have decreased yields to less than 11 tonnes per hectare. Green harvesting to limit yields is only used when necessary, such as in the high-yielding year of 2004, when as much as 40% of fruit was dropped in some vineyards.

Taittinger employs 700–800 pickers and is purposeful in paying them by the hour, not by volume, which is rare in Champagne. 'It is more difficult to demand quality if we pay by volume, so we never do that,' explains Le Sueur. 'We explain to them what we want in terms of quality and tell them to be selective.'

Taittinger prizes its growers and takes an approach of building good relationships rather than supervising quality. 'To us, they are not just a number; a personal relationship is important,' says Le Sueur. 'It's about long-term relationships, of remaining loyal and maintaining confidence.' Pierre-Emmanuel Taittinger is actively involved during the harvests and visits all of Taittinger's press houses. 'They are proud to see him, as they appreciate the image of Taittinger and the family involvement.'

ATTENTIVE VINIFICATION

At the time of the family buy-back, the decision was made to work only with the finest juices, using around 10% of the tailles of chardonnay only in the Brut Réserve NV and Brut Prestige Rosé NV, and only the first pressing in the other cuvées. 'We only use the tailles from chardonnay, because the tailles of the black grapes are too heavy,' Le Sueur explains. 'Too much of the tailles in the blend makes them too strong and mature, but we want to produce very fine and accurate wines.' Excess tailles are exchanged for the cuvées of other houses.

In the winery, fermentation is conducted in tanks below 18°C to preserve freshness. Malolactic fermentation is allowed to complete on all cuvées, crucial for softening these chardonnay-led styles. 'I say we work with four varieties: chardonnay, pinot noir, meunier and time!' says Le Sueur, emphasising the importance of maturity in allowing these nervy styles to develop. Non-vintage wines are aged on lees for at least three years, Prélude Grand Crus Brut NV for a minimum of five years, vintage wines for longer again, and the flagship Comtes de Champagne eight years or more (the current vintage is 2007).

Such long ageing necessitates large cellar stocks. Taittinger ages 3 million bottles of Comtes de Champagne at 9–10°C in its breathtaking four kilometres of galleries under its headquarters in Reims, including a section of fourth-century Roman crayères. Its remaining stores of some 23 million bottles are kept in a facility in town. This tremendous stock facilitates an average of more than 4.5 years on lees, a massive duration for any house.

For Le Sueur, the key to maintaining quality, even at such a large scale of production, lies in the details. 'We have to be extremely focused on quality, to adapt continually and to question our practices every day,' he emphasises. 'Details, details details!'

Taittinger bottles under natural cork, since it hasn't found its cuvées evolve in the same way under DIAM. Since mid-2014, all cuvées except Comtes de Champagne have boasted a QR code; unfortunately this does not reveal bottling or disgorgement dates, but simply links to the website, where you can find PDFs with basic details for each cuvée.

COMTES DE CHAMPAGNE

Taittinger's flagship Comtes de Champagne holds an enviable position among the very finest blanc de blancs. It is sourced principally from Avize and Le Mesnil-sur-Oger, and to a lesser extent from Oger, Chouilly, Cramant, Vertus and Bergères-lès-Vertus.

'We are lucky to work with a huge quantity of wines from the Côte des Blancs, allowing us to choose the best samples for Comtes de Champagne each year,' explains cellar master Loïc Dupont. 'We look for the vats that represent the typicity of each cru, to build the expression of the vintage. Avize brings elegance, finesse and balance, Le Mesnil-sur-Oger contributes body and a subtle reduction akin to grilled bread, Chouilly delivers roundness, Cramant grilled almonds, and Oger elegant citrus.' Just 5% is aged for four months in oak barrels, one-third new, and the rest up to four years old – not for strength, but to bring subtle notes of toast and brioche to the delicacy of chardonnay.

Taittinger's depth of reach into the Côte des Blancs grand crus has made Comtes de Champagne one of Champagne's most consistent blanc de blancs, and every even-numbered vintage since 1996 has been nothing short of transcendental.

The Taittinger family tradition remains as alive and well as ever, and continues to post new records, thanks to the daring of Pierre-Emmanuel, his children, and their loyal, talented team.

I congratulated Pierre-Emmanuel recently on all he has achieved. He grinned warmly and exclaimed, 'I have a very good team!'

TAITTINGER BRUT RÉSERVE NV $$

92 points • 2015 BASE VINTAGE • DISGORGED SEPTEMBER 2018 • TASTED IN AUSTRALIA
92 points • 2014 BASE VINTAGE • DISGORGED MID-2018 • TASTED IN CHAMPAGNE

40% chardonnay, 35% pinot noir, 25% meunier; from 35-45 crus; 20% grand crus, half in reserves and half in chardonnay tailles; 30% reserves, aged 2.5-3.5 years on lees; 8-9g/L dosage; cork

Taittinger always prepares its Brut Réserve blend first, and only if the vintage is deemed of sufficient quality are its other cuvées assembled. This philosophy, together with a generous inclusion of reserves and long lees age, has produced another impressively poised rendition. With a bright, pale straw hue, this is a lively and crunchy apéritif style that magnificently juxtaposes the vibrancy of chardonnay with the complexity and texture of maturity on lees. It sings with the apple, pear, lemon zest and grapefruit vivacity of chardonnay, the crunchy red apple and tangy strawberry hull of pinot and, in the 2014 base, ever more prominent roast almonds, gingernut biscuits and vanilla nougat of bottle age. The 2015 base is a clean and vital style of subtle lees-derived complexity, retaining impressively bright focus for its warm season. This is a refreshing apéritif of persistence, poise, intricately integrated dosage and lively acid line, basking in the glory of the fine chalk mineral structure of great chardonnay crus.

TAITTINGER CUVÉE PRESTIGE BRUT NV $$

91 points • 2015 BASE VINTAGE • DISGORGED JULY 2018 • TASTED IN AUSTRALIA

40% chardonnay, 60% pinot noir and meunier; a blend of almost 50 crus; aged 2.5 years on lees; 9g/L dosage; cork

Prestige is a blend designed for on-premise venues. Announcing its extended maturity in a medium straw hue and bitter almond complexity, this is a style led by the apple, pear and grapefruit of chardonnay, beginning to become gently toasty. Chardonnay carries a fine and vibrant acid line, which melds with understated dosage on a dry finish, accented by fine chalk mineral texture. It's a clean, fresh and appealing apéritif.

TAITTINGER PRESTIGE ROSÉ BRUT NV $$$

92 points • 2014 BASE • DISGORGED AUGUST 2017 • TASTED IN CHAMPAGNE AND AUSTRALIA

30% chardonnay, 55% pinot noir and meunier, 13-14% pinot noir red wine, mostly from the Montagne de Reims and Les Riceys (including 20% reserve red wines); 9g/L dosage; cork

A traditional inclusion of 15% red wine has made Taittinger Rosé a fruity style. 'We are looking for more freshness, more brilliance, more easy-drinking appeal and less heaviness,' says Damien Le Sueur, who has decreased the red wine inclusion slightly in the 2014 base, and down to 12% in subsequent releases, as he has observed that there is 'a huge difference' between 12% and 14%. 'We have been tasting year after year to find the best red wines for the blend, and in the blends to come we are using more wines of the harvest and less reserve reds – only 5%, compared with 20% today.

With a medium salmon crimson hue, Taittinger's rosé leads out with layers of toasty, biscuity, roast almond complexity of maturity, underscored with the macerated red berries, pomegranates, crunchy red delicious apples and cracked pink pepper of pinot noir. The fine chalk minerality and lemon cut of chardonnay meld with fine-ground tannins, harmonised by well-integrated dosage. The aspiration of the house for its rosé is structure and a little touch of tannins, and this blend meets the brief with flair. A rosé of confident structure, it will step up to the proteins of pink meats. A bottle tasted at the house showed more fruit fragrance than in Australia, leaping out of the glass with candied raspberry and fresh strawberry flamboyance, though the palate was consistent.

TAITTINGER NOCTURNE SEC NV $$

91 points • 2010 BASE VINTAGE • DISGORGED MARCH 2016 • TASTED IN AUSTRALIA

40% chardonnay, 30% pinot noir, 30% meunier; Brut Réserve, aged 4 years on lees, with 17.5g/L dosage of cane sugar; cork

Nocturne deserves more respect than its flamboyant 'city lights' livery might suggest. The recipe is a more mature and slightly sweeter version of Brut Réserve – not too cloying, and not a 'leftovers' cuvée of rotten fruit and too much tailles, as sweet champagnes all too often tend to be. By comparison, this is well made and fruity, with a yellow fleck to its medium straw hue and layers of apricot tart, baked peach and pineapple fruit, upholding some of the glittering lemon freshness of chardonnay that defines Taittinger. The dosage lends boiled-sweets notes, which meld with the honey and roast almonds of maturity. It's not too sweet, particularly when served well chilled. It holds good persistence, balanced acidity and fine chalk mineral poise. Turn down the lights, crank up the volume and give it a swing! One bottle was faintly corked.

TAITTINGER PRÉLUDE GRAND CRUS BRUT NV $$$

95 points • 100% 2014 VINTAGE • TASTED IN CHAMPAGNE
95 points • 100% 2013 VINTAGE • DISGORGED DECEMBER 2017 • TASTED IN AUSTRALIA

50% chardonnay from Avize, Le Mesnil-sur-Oger, Oger and a little Chouilly; 50% pinot noir, half from Mailly-Champagne and half from Ambonnay, Verzenay and Verzy; 100% single vintage, though not communicated; aged 3.5 years on lees; 9g/L dosage; cork

Taittinger selects its grand cru parcels for Prélude to show the characters of their crus, rather than the mood of the vintage, looking for elegance, finesse, delicacy and structure, reserving those with more power for its Comtes de Champagne Rosé. 'This is purposely a cuvée of finesse and subtlety,' says Damien Le Sueur. It is always entirely from a single year, though disappointingly its vintage is never declared, 'as we don't aim to show the vintage effect'. Le Sueur describes the vision as the opposite to Bollinger (who contrast warm south-facing pinot with cool, north-facing chardonnay). 'We are looking for a fresh, easy-drinking style, so we source from the cooler pinot crus of Ambonnay, Verzenay, Verzy and, most of all, Mailly-Champagne, the signature of the structure of the wine,' he says. Taittinger is privileged to large holdings in Mailly-Champagne. 'We are big fans of this cooler village, and we love its structure and freshness – a pinot of chardonnay freshness yet pinot structure.'

True to its aspirations, 2014 Prélude is a cuvée of tension, focus and energy, with lifted struck-flint and grilled-toast reduction over a core of lemon, crunchy red apple and grapefruit freshness. The pure chalk of its grand cru sites defines a style of frothing salt minerality of prominent, lingering texture. Age has built subtle Parisian pâtisserie character, evoking freshly baked baguettes and brioche. It delivers presence and character on the front, and carries a long and focused finish of mineral tension and character. Classy, terroir-infused, and precise.

Prélude 2013 exudes a tightrope tension between power and precision: a medium, bright straw hue and flavours of apple, beurre bosc pear, fennel and fig, accented by a flattering hint of struck-flint reduction. The toasty complexity of long lees age is a signature of Taittinger, pronounced here, in an enticing overlay of almond nougat, buttered toast, candied lemon rind and fruit mince spice. Tangy, enduring acid line melds evenly with creamy, toffeed dosage. The chalk mineral definition of its dignified crus is pronounced, a confident sea of swelling, frothing salt-infused texture that brings freshness, vivacity and character to its very long, even and toasty conclusion.

TAITTINGER FOLIES DE LA MARQUETTERIE BRUT NV $$

93 points • 100% 2014 VINTAGE • TASTED IN CHAMPAGNE

45% chardonnay (35% from Pierry and 10% from Trépail), 55% pinot noir (50% from Verzenay and 5% from Pierry); 30% vinified in oak foudres (10% Verzenay pinot and 20% Pierry chardonnay); harvested at full ripeness of 11.2-11.3 degrees potential; 100% 2014, though not communicated; 40,000 bottles

Taittinger's first single-estate wine was formerly also a single-vineyard wine, blended from parcels surrounding its Château de la Marquetterie in Pierry, just south of Épernay. With yields reduced to just half of Champagne's average, it was always a particularly rounded and rich style. This site is now supplemented with vineyards of more than 45 years of age from the family holdings of 'beautiful parcels, to try to refine the style and enlarge the vision of the wine', in Damien Le Sueur's words. Not to increase the volume, 'but to be more selective of our many tiny vinifications'. He is frank in admitting that they knew they had better pinot in other villages than in Pierry. 'The cuvée had a lot of density, so the idea was to increase its freshness with chardonnay from Trépail and fresh pinot noir from Verzenay.'

The body and intensity of low-yielding vines harvested at full ripeness in Pierry remains the mood here, astutely tempered with the fresh tension of Verzenay pinot noir. The result is characterful, spice-laden and crunchy, with the presence and grip of pear and red apple and fig fruit and notes of pâtisserie, set against a backdrop of gentle salt mineral texture and the subtle phenolic grip of ripe fruit. It lives up to its aspiration of presenting the elegant Taittinger style within a mood of riper fruit of deeper character and the presence of old-vine concentration. It lingers with good persistence and the creamy mouthfeel of fermentation in oak foudres.

Three million bottles of Comtes de Champagne lie in Taittinger's fourth-century Roman crayères under Reims.

TAITTINGER BRUT MILLÉSIMÉ 2013 $$$

93 points • TASTED IN CHAMPAGNE

50% chardonnay from Avize, Le Mesnil-sur-Oger, Oger, Vertus, Bergères-lès Vertus, Villers-Marmery and Trépail; 50% pinot noir, mostly from Ambonnay, and also from Mailly-Champagne and Verzenay, with a little from Écueil, Sacy and Hautvillers; 70% grand cru, 30% premier cru

By contrast to its philosophy of parcel selection for Prélude, to show the characters of the crus rather than the mood of the vintage, Taittinger selects parcels for its Brut Millésime according to their vintage typicity. It's always a 50/50 blend of chardonnay and pinot. 'We play with more approachable parcels in this cuvée,' explains Damien Le Sueur, 'with more fireworks to communicate a clear vision of the vintage!'

Le Sueur describes 2013 as 'a beautiful and fresh vintage'. He has presented a particularly strong take on the season in his vintage cuvée, leading out with the personality of chardonnay in a richer and fuller style to contrast the mineral tension of Prélude. It's filled with apple, fig and preserved lemon fruit, layered with biscuity complexity. The finish coasts on salt mineral structure, accented with subtle spice and a touch of dry grip.

TAITTINGER BRUT MILLÉSIMÉ 2012 $$$

93 points • DISGORGED SEPTEMBER 2017 • TASTED IN AUSTRALIA

50% Côte des Blancs chardonnay, 50% Montagne de Reims and Grande Vallée de la Marne pinot noir; 70% grand cru, 30% premier cru; 15 villages, selected for their vintage typicity; 9g/L dosage; cork

The bright and lively 2012 season has found a place of harmonious appeal at seven years of age, evenly uniting crunch with complexity, and supporting it with vibrant acid line, fine, glassy, grand cru chalk minerality and seamlessly integrated dosage. The crunchy pear and apple fruit of chardonnay meets the understated, cool strawberry-hull tang and mixed spice of pinot noir and the toasted brioche depth of lees age. It concludes long, even, bright and engaging. One bottle was dramatically cork tainted.

TAITTINGER COMTES DE CHAMPAGNE GRANDS CRUS BLANC DE BLANCS 2007 $$$$

98 points • DISGORGED JANUARY 2018 • TASTED IN CHAMPAGNE AND AUSTRALIA

100% grand cru Côte des Blancs chardonnay; 60% Avize and Le Mesnil-sur-Oger, the pillars of Comtes, for structure and finesse, then Chouilly for body and strength, Oger and a little less than 10% Cramant; 5% from Chouilly aged (not fermented) for 6 months in young oak barrels (new, with one-third renewed each year) to add body and subtle burnt-vanilla and coconut character; 9g/L dosage

'It is the blade of the sword of the story of Taittinger!' exclaims Damien Le Sueur of the 2007 vintage. 'Exactly the idea that I have for Comtes in terms of finesse. After the freshness of 2004, the density and maturity of 2005 and the balance of 2006, the 2007 vintage is all about chalk structure and finesse more than freshness.' He arrived at Taittinger in January 2007 and his first question of Pierre-Emmanuel Taittinger was why 'Grands Crus' was not on the label. He agreed immediately, but was not able to action this for the vintages in the cellar at the time, since the documentation was not retained to show the traceability for every vat in the blends. Hence, 'Grands Crus' appears on the label for the first time from 2007.

After the might of 2005 and 2006, there is a pretty elegance, exacting purity and beguiling freshness to 2007 that I find thrillingly compelling, and it's captured in pinpoint detail in this enchanting Comtes. The theme of radiant freshness of lemon blossom and fragrant finesse of apple of its first release two years ago has been upheld, deepened into delightful notes of brioche, marzipan, nougat, vanilla cream and almond. The grilled-toast reduction of chardonnay presents a delightfully complexing nuance, as does the creamy texture of lees age, both amplified by the toasty, biscuity, nutty touch of a little barrel maturation. The chalk mineral signature of Comtes rumbles magnificently with the ancient geology of the finest grand crus of the Côte des Blancs. Still pale and bright straw in hue with a green tint at 12 years of age, this is my style of Comtes. In line and length, it is pristine, determined, undeviating and captivating. It upholds an air of eloquent confidence, effortless harmony and graceful beauty. Turn down the lights and the music and pour it for the one you love most.

TAITTINGER COMTES DE CHAMPAGNE BLANC DE BLANCS 2006 $$$$

97 points • TASTED IN AUSTRALIA

As above

In grand testament to Taittinger's profound reach into the Côte des Blancs' most enduring grand crus, the poise and stamina of Comtes even in the warm and ready 2006 season is nothing short of staggering. The lemon, lime, grapefruit, crunchy apple, pear and pineapple of its youth have softened further as bottle complexity of toast, roasted almonds and nougat builds in layers of complexity and richness. Nuances of grilled toast and brioche are considered by the house to be signatures of the season. The ripe, supple succulence of the vintage furnishes a fleshy mid-palate of immediate allure, making this a Comtes to enjoy while the 2002, 2004 and 2008 continue to evolve, though there is no immediate haste here. Not even the finest detail in its epic line and length has been shed since its release two years ago. Its textural presence is mouth-embracing, permeating every crevice, masterfully uniting very fine phenolic grip with delightfully delicate, frothing salt minerality that bores to the very core of the finest chalkfields of the Côte des Blancs.

Taittinger Comtes de Champagne Blanc de Blancs 2005 $$$$

96 points • Tasted in Australia

As per 2007 (opposite)

'It was harder to make Comtes de Champagne in 2005, as the still wines were more mature and more dried-out right from the start, and these are the same characters we see in the wine now,' responded Damien Le Sueur, when I queried the decision to release Comtes in this challenging season. I found its dry extract, dusty, bitter almond character and the grip of 2005 pronounced on release in 2013, interrupting the otherwise seamless flow of the finish. I was impressed at how admirably the wine had grown into itself by 2015, but never has it looked more impressive than it does today. At a full 14 years of age, it holds its head high, with stunning poise. The grilled toast reductive signature of the house is impressively prominent amidst the toasty, smoky, nutty, honeyed complexity of maturity. Its primary citrus, apple and pear spectrum has progressed to a secondary, spicy complexity. This is a Comtes of flamboyant intensity and masculine strength, rejoicing in the texture of lees age, at once soft and creamy, chewy and full. It's got the grit to age for many more seasons yet. One bottle was slightly cork tainted.

Taittinger Comtes de Champagne Rosé 2007 $$$$$

92 points • Tasted in Champagne

30% chardonnay from Avize, Oger, Le Mesnil-sur-Oger and a little Chouilly; 70% pinot noir from Ambonnay, Verzenay, Mailly-Champagne and a little Bouzy; 12% Bouzy rouge; no oak; less than 10% of the volume of Comtes Blanc de Blancs

If the philosophy of Comtes Blanc de Blancs is that of restraint, the aim of its extroverted rosé sister is of aromatic explosiveness and energy. Previously released younger than the blanc, the house has discovered how magnificently the rosé ages, and now the releases coincide, with the aim of releasing the rosé even later in future. I have always found the bombastic personality of this cuvée at odds with the elegant chardonnay focus of the house, and it is pleasing to learn that future releases will ultimately evolve to the chardonnay-led style that defines Taittinger.

At 12 years of age, the new release of Comtes Rosé beams a bright, full crimson hue with a copper tint. This is a distinctive vintage for this cuvée, a complex and savoury style of green herbal notes reminiscent of Campari, green capsicum and tomato leaf, that give the impression of underripe fruit. Tart acidity and fine tannin structure takes a green astringency. It concludes with good persistence, supported by fine chalk minerality and the supple texture of a decade on lees.

Taittinger Comtes de Champagne Rosé 2006 $$$$$

93 points • Tasted in Champagne

30% chardonnay from Avize, Le Mesnil-sur-Oger, Oger and Chouilly; 70% pinot noir from Ambonnay, Mailly-Champagne, Verzy and Verzenay; 12.5% red wine from Bouzy; no oak; less than 10% of the production of Comtes de Champagne

The finesse and grace of this release seem at odds with its brief and its full crimson copper hue, particularly in the warmth of the 2006 vintage, which possesses a latent power that continues to unravel four years after its release. The primary red fruits of its youth have now faded into a rich and savoury style that showcases the mature personality of pinot noir in roast tomato, truffles, game and forest floor. It's tangy and tart, yet savoury and secondary, with a long mineral finish driven by prominent bath-salts chalk texture. The firm fine tannins of its early days have been enveloped by the softly creamy mouthfeel of maturity, lingering on a persistent finish.

Tarlant

(Tahr-lohn)

(7/10)

Rue de la Coopérative 51480 Oeuilly

www.tarlant.com

CHAMPAGNE
TARLANT
VIGNERONS DEPUIS 1687

'Our goal is to express the personality of our unique place,' declares young Benoît Tarlant, and there are few in Champagne who have gone to greater lengths to do so. Within six years of taking the lead at his family estate in 1999, he had eliminated dosage in 80% of his annual production of 120,000–130,000 bottles, no mean feat for less than noble terroirs on the cool, north-facing slopes of the Marne, in a house that preserves tension with malic acidity. 'I am not a cane sugar or beet sugar maker, I produce grapes!' he declares. His is an intuitive and sensitive approach that dares to ride the cutting edge of practice in the vineyard and the winery. 'There are no rules — it depends on the grapes!' he exclaims. A unique display of dried herbs in a corner of the winery celebrates a regime of cover crops and treatments that he dubs 'herbal therapy'. Fermentation is conducted mostly in barrels, some tanks and even small clay amphorae. 'The goal is not the method, the goal is to make great wine,' he sums up, exemplified in a large range of champagnes energised by malic acidity and characterised by the creamy generosity of ripe fruit, barrel fermentation, liberal use of reserve wines and long ageing. Against all odds, the wines of Benoît Tarlant are now the finest they have ever been, and unequalled from his part of the Vallée de la Marne. His Zero is one of Champagne's best brut natures.

Benoît Tarlant has deservedly won himself quite some respect in recent years, not least among the movers and shakers within Champagne itself. 'Benoît Tarlant proves that you can be extremely successful, even if you are in the middle of nowhere,' Jacquesson's Jean-Hervé Chiquet mentioned to me recently.

His family has tended its vines in the Vallée de la Marne since 1687, made its own wine since the 1870s, and champagne since 1929. Today, the family is one of the most distinguished growers in its village of Oeuilly.

'Our priority is to take care of the vines and make our wines,' says Tarlant, who has relished the opportunity to mark his own print

on the estate while working alongside his grandfather Georges, his parents Jean-Mary and Micheline, and his sister Mélanie.

HERBAL THERAPY
Mostly on the southern side of the river, Tarlant's north-facing sites require meticulous attention, and even the use of a tractor winch to haul equipment up the rows of the steepest vineyards in the village. North- and east-facing slopes are prized for retention of acidity, particularly in meunier.

Tarlant took me to the edge of the vines on the eastern side of the village. 'The Marne Valley is defined by the river, cutting

like a knife and making many soil types,' he explained, pointing out six different soil varieties between us and the river, less than 800 metres away. 'Our job is to keep the character of each vineyard.' Tarlant's almost 14 hectares are spread across 57 plots, mostly in Oeuilly and neighbouring Boursault, and to the west in Saint-Agnan and Celles-lès-Condé. Each plot is vinified separately, and in tasting an extensive range of 2012 *vins clairs* with him, I was impressed at how accurately each exemplified its distinctive mineral expression and flavour profile.

Most of these vineyards were planted by his family and boast an average age of 34 years. The estate has had opportunity to increase slightly as the contracts on his grandfather's vineyards end, though only one hectare has been gained in this way in recent years. Tarlant credits chalk in the soil for a diversity of grape selection.

'This area is best suited to black grapes, as chardonnay is quite rustic,' he points out, explaining his breakdown of 50% pinot noir, 30% chardonnay, 15% meunier and 5% petit meslier, arbane and pinot blanc. He has recently doubled his holdings of the three old Champagne varieties by grafting sites where he couldn't achieve ripeness in pinot noir. In these days of warmer vintages, lower acidities and consequently higher pHs, he is impressed with his 16-year-old petit meslier vines. 'We are getting 13 degrees potential alcohol with a pH of 2.8, which is crazy!' he exclaims.

Tarlant prizes the diversity of his plots, but admits it's a challenge to manage so many distinct sites using techniques sympathetic to organic practices. Three hectares are managed biodynamically, some organically, neither certified; the remainder rely on his ingenious regime of 'herbal therapy'. A wide range of herbs are planted in the vineyards, including oregano, which he harvests for pizzas and salads. Small concoctions are made from the plants and sprayed on the vines to protect against fungus attacks. He says 2012 was a good year to practise. 'We only lost 30% of fruit in our vineyards with herbal therapy, but 40% with organics and 50% with biodynamics.'

INTUITIVE WINEMAKING

The goal is to harvest ripe, tasty grapes with balanced acidity. To this end, malolactic fermentation is completely blocked. 'I think malolactic is an industry mistake from the 1960s and 1970s,' Tarlant suggests. 'Traditionally, the majority of champagne was without malolactic fermentation. It makes sense to me to show the wine naturally, with its natural acidity.'

Intensity, precision and presence of texture are his priorities. Since 2007, he has employed a new Coquart press to minimise

oxidation. Every transfer in the winery is performed by gravity. The traditional champagne pressing regime is taken one step further, by carefully splitting the juice from the first pressing into two separate components, and the tailles into two components. 'I hate pre-blending, so we vinify every parcel separately,' he explains. 'We should respect the origin of the place here in Champagne as much as they do in Burgundy.'

In recent years, Tarlant has progressed from two-thirds to three-quarters of the harvest fermented in Burgundian barrels, one-eighth in clay amphorae and one-eighth in temperature-controlled stainless steel tanks, to preserve vitality. All of his ferments are with wild yeast, without additions of enzymes or bentonite for clarification or stabilisation.

Inspired by friends in Italy, Tarlant experimented with ageing in four 200-litre clay amphorae in 2012, for greater oxygen exchange than in barrels, though he's quick to point out he doesn't want to make orange wines. In 2018, he buried new clay *qvevri* ('my fifth-generation Georgian amphorae!'), and believes he's the first in Champagne to do so. 'I have no prejudices, I am still experimenting,' he says. 'We are making champagne a spiritual wine, and we are connecting with the soil and with history by fermenting in clay with no yeast or sulphite – if it weren't for Georgia we would not be making wines in Champagne! It is culturally important for us.'

As he proudly drew the first results from his amphorae to show me in early January 2019, he exclaimed, 'It is a new landscape in clay! More texture and a new aftertaste.' I was amazed at the purity of his 2018 chardonnay and especially his 2018 pinot, bright in colour, lifted and pretty, with beautifully resolved tannins – great potential for Coteaux Champenois, though at the time he was uncertain of exactly how he would utilise them.

Barrels are always purchased new and now average 10 years of age, with the oldest now 32 years. 'I'm not a big fan of new barrels, but as a non-malolactic cellar, I don't want to bring the wolf into the sheep pen!' Benoît exclaims, in reference to the risk of introducing malolactic and other bugs from used barrels. Parcels fermented in new barrels are always blended. 'I prefer older barrels, but after long ageing of 7–10 years, the impact of a well-managed new barrel is not so scary!'

Bâtonnage is used to help finish fermentation and to build texture. 'I love working with barrels, so the wines can breathe and not look so monolithic,' he says. Reserve wines are aged in oak casks, and he incorporates at least three vintages in his Zero Brut, which he considers crucial for this style. Long bottle ageing is also critical in this process. Non-vintage wines are typically matured at least 3.5 years in bottle, and vintage wines around 10 years in deep cellars dug progressively since the seventeenth century, up to 30 metres below the slope of the hill under his house.

'When I was young, I wanted to hurry the disgorgement, but my grandfather taught me to wait six years by showing me the profound texture and character that developed as the wine breathed over time. I don't want to show a wine until it reveals its personality.'

ZERO DOSAGE

Tarlant's ultimate goal is to make zero-dosage champagne. 'We don't need to add sugar to Chablis, so why do we need to do it with champagne?' He aims to pick grapes ripe when he can. 'We must always reach the prettiest maturity, not the highest maturity, so adding sugar should not be a question.' The point is not zero dosage, but to create wine of flavour and atmosphere. He chaptalises when he has to and uses low dosages of less than 6g/L in cuvées that require it, though he doesn't enjoy adding dosage.

His father had been making Zero Brut since the early 1980s, long before zero dosage was the rage in Champagne. 'Back then you could count on one hand all the people making this style,' Tarlant points out. 'I'm scared that it's becoming trendy now.'

It took him six years to build Tarlant Zero to the major cuvée of the estate, now representing around 100,000 bottles annually – a monumental feat for one of Champagne's better composed examples of this challenging style. He has also elevated Rosé Zero to the main rosé of the house.

'There are perhaps four or five zero-dosage rosés now, but when I began in 2000 it was a no-man's land, and I had no one else's wines to look at,' he says. He made six trials of pinot noir and meunier, each with skin contact, blended from red and white wines and blended with chardonnay.

'The question with zero-dosage rosé was how to get acid and tannin to live together. I found the skin-contact wines too angular in their tannin expression, so I prefer to blend.'

Tarlant chose chardonnay blended with pinot noir red wine, but the evolution continues. The current dilemma is an attempt to build greater persistence using white wine from black grapes – a challenge because even white pinot noir contributes tannins.

Tarlant's single-vineyard wines are characterful expressions of his diverse terroirs. 'I'm not here to make single vineyards, but sometimes the taste of the samples makes it irresistible!' he exclaims. 'The first year I experienced real taste, explosiveness and length in single parcels was 2003.'

He recently added a new building to extend the winery, not to increase production but to provide space to work with his 57 plots and a portfolio now spanning 13 cuvées. All have boasted informative back labels since 2000, detailing terroirs, cépages, vintages, disgorgement and bottling dates and dosages.

Benoît Tarlant epitomises what greatness can be achieved even at the far extremes of Champagne. For wines of such integrity and beauty to be drawn out of lesser terroirs, without the polishing potential of dosage, the security of normal levels of sulphur, even with the unlikely inclusion of amphora-fermented components, is not only unexpected, it's downright remarkable. As he pushes ever further into these extremes, it's an incredible testament to his daring courage and his steep learning curve of experience that his cuvées become not more 'worked' or more edgy, but more pure, more silky and more enticing. Against all odds, the wines of Benoît Tarlant are now the finest they have ever been and unequalled from his part of the Vallée de la Marne.

Tarlant Zero Brut Nature NV $$

94 points • 2012 base vintage • Tasted in Champagne
93 points • 2011 base vintage • Disgorged early 2018 • Tasted in Champagne

Roughly one-third of each of the three varieties (a little more chardonnay in the 2011 base due to dusty rot in the black grapes); Vallée de la Marne; vines more than 25 years of age; no malolactic fermentation; 40% reserves of 2010, 2009 and 2008 (in both 2011 and 2012 base vintages); aged 6 years on lees; zero dosage; ~100,000 bottles

Benoît Tarlant has sensitively honed every stage of viticulture and production to foster balance in his Zero, aiming for an accuracy, purity and directness that he likens to playing darts. Flavour, not austerity, is his priority here, with ripe fruit, three reserve vintages and extremely long bottle ageing creating balance and presence.

He describes 2012 as a 'wonderful vintage of depth, length and purity – I really feel the vibrancy of the 2008 base once more!' and the result is the best Zero he has made yet. Glowing with a beautiful medium yellow-straw hue, it's a wonderful contrast between crisp lemon, crunchy golden delicious apple and exotic notes of white nectarine. This is a delightfully complex and characterful Zero that exudes succulent texture of wonderfully ripe fruit complexity, held in poised tension thanks to beautifully integrated malic acidity, defining sensational line and length.

Tarlant admits that 2011 was a real challenge. 'We have an expression that you have to cut one arm off to be able to walk, but in 2011 we had to cut off two arms and half a leg! The selection had to be dramatic, as it was a very dusty, green vintage. To make a brut nature, you cannot make something average. You have to be strong with the choice, even if you lose some potential production, so you can be relaxed and not stressed five or six years later when you disgorge it!' His stringent selection has completely transformed this tough season, and his Zero stands in stark contrast to the austerity of so many others. Flying in the face of its recipe, this is a paradoxically rich, ripe and confident Zero, layered with honey, wonderfully succulent complexity of white peach, baked apple and quince, and deep maturity of roast nuts. It's rounded out beautifully with the creamy texture of barrel fermentation that creates a finish of even, flowing persistence.

Tarlant Rosé Zero Brut Nature NV $$

93 points • 2013 base vintage • Disgorged mid-2018 • Tasted in Champagne

50% chardonnay, 36% pinot noir, 14% meunier; Vallée de la Marne; 13-14% red wine; 2012 reserves; no malolactic fermentation; aged 4.5 years on lees; zero dosage

Tarlant blends one-third white wine of pinot noir with pinot red wine, and adds young-vine pinot and one or two barrels of red meunier for 'redness' character without tannin. 'The duality of pinot noir red wine and white wine define this cuvée, and if this doesn't work in a vintage then I don't make it,' he says.

One of Champagne's very first zero-dosage rosés remains one of the best. A very pretty medium salmon crimson is paler than usual, in spite of a full addition of 13–14% red wine. Delightful strawberry and red cherry fruit integrity is underlined by the roast nuts and toasty complexity of long age. An alluringly creamy and silky texture is thanks first to natural maturity in the grapes, second to a carefully handled oxidative approach in barrels, and finally to a long life on lees. An outstanding Rosé Zero of line, length and integrity.

Commanding a spectacular position on the southern bank of the Marne adjacent to Oeuilly, Château de Boursault was the final residence of Madame (Veuve) Clicquot Ponsardin.

TARLANT BAM! BLANC ARBANE MESLIER NV $$$$

93 points • 2011 BASE VINTAGE • TASTED IN CHAMPAGNE

48% petit meslier, 26% pinot blanc, 26% arbane; 50% reserve of the previous BAM! (2010, 2009, 2008 and 2007), which Tarlant refers to as a 'perpetual blend' as it is not made like a solera; zero dosage

Benoît Tarlant's learnings with the old Champagne varieties in the vineyard and the cellar have united to elevate BAM! to a benchmark of these varieties in the region, and never more impressive than in the 2011 base (now there's something I've never said before!). The first release back in 2013 was more than challenging, and it's improved out of sight since. 'BAM!' was the codename in the cellar and it stuck, 'because the wine used to be more strict and acid and it was a big smash!' Tarlant recalls. Depth of reserves and time on lees has transformed the style into a much more civilised blend today. It captures the personality of its varieties in exotic notes of star fruit and honeydew, with a faintly herbaceous edge and lingering mixed spice complexity. Structurally, it confidently walks a carefully strung tightrope between bright yet ripe malic acidity, wonderfully creamy, buttery texture, the tension of grapefruit and the subtle phenolic bitterness of crab apple. It concludes with great length and integrity that fly in the face of a more than daring recipe, uniting the grip and personality of its varieties with the ever more silky and creamy style that Tarlant has perfected.

TARLANT CUVÉE LOUIS NV $$$$

95 points • 2003 base vintage • Disgorged October 2018 • Tasted in Champagne

50% chardonnay, 50% pinot noir; single-vineyard Oeuilly near the Marne river with vines of average age 69 years; fermented and aged in old oak barrels with regular lees stirring; no malolactic fermentation; 40% 2002 reserves; aged 14.5 years on lees; zero dosage

Tarlant's original and chalkiest vineyard, 'Les Crayons', is closest to the cooling influence of the Marne, the quintessential expression of Oeuilly, ripening slowly to yield grapes of the highest maturity and highest acidity in the estate. He released the 2003 base before the 2002, which he says is still too strict. 'I loved 2003,' he discloses, 'not for the quantity, but the challenge to achieve richness, structure and full body was fun!' His blend unites 'a classy and wonderful year like 2002' with 'the wild thing of 2003!'

The wine rises to its grand credentials, a radiant and monumental expression of the profound generosity of 2003 and the grand depth of decades of maturity. A glowing, full straw-yellow hue with a hint of copper declares its depth and age. It's a wonderfully rich and characterful cuvée that contrasts the ripeness of its unique site with the freshness of cool malic acidity. Exuding sensational complexity and integrity, it has attained a compelling place where the primary fruit of white peach, grilled pineapple, persimmon and lemon meets the toasty, spicy, honeyed, fruit mince spice complexity of lees age, just beginning to take on a faintly tertiary profile of green olive. The phenolic texture and grip of 2003 is well encompassed into the generosity of the wine and the creamy and silky texture of the house. A masterfully crafted cuvée that captures the richness, power, purity, tension and length of its historic site on the Marne.

TARLANT L'ETINCELANTE PRESTIGE MILLÉSIME 2002 $$$$$

95 points • Disgorged September 2018 • Tasted in Champagne

57% chardonnay, 29% pinot noir, 14% meunier; three chardonnay vineyards, two pinot and one meunier; aged 15.5 years on lees; zero dosage

'My first year at the domaine was 1999, but 2002 was my first fireworks year, the first year when everything I received was wonderful!' Benoît Tarlant beams. He has waited an incredible 17 years to unveil what he rightfully considers to be one of his finest wines, making this what must be the very last cuvée in Champagne to be unleashed from this celebrated season. He appropriately named it 'L'Etincelante' – 'the sparkling one'.

A mesmerising display of characterful personality transcends terroirs not renowned for their longevity, a towering showpiece for the ripe approach and textured mood that define Tarlant. Glowing, radiant white peach and succulent grilled pineapple are met by a rumbling upsurging of layered spice and honey on buttered toast. True to the Tarlant signature, its silky creaminess is seamlessly integrated with ripe malic acidity. Very fine and salty mineral texture draws out a very long, fine and honed finish. This is one of Tarlant's greatest achievements year. L'Etincelante, indeed.

Morning mist veils Ville-Dommange during harvest 2017.

THIÉNOT

(Tea-e-noh)

---

4 RUE JOSEPH-CUGNOT 51500 TAISSY
www.thienot.com

CHAMPAGNE THIÉNOT

REIMS.FRANCE

Since establishing his eponymous house in Taissy just out of Reims in 1985, former broker Alain Thiénot has acquired a formidable empire encompassing champagne houses Canard-Duchêne, Joseph Perrier and Marie Stuart, and several Bordeaux châteaux. This small house of 350,000 bottles annually remains a family affair, and is the proud custodian of 27 hectares of estate vineyards in the Montagne de Reims, Côte des Blancs and Sézanne, supplying an impressive three-quarters of its needs. Use of oak has been abandoned in the hope of better expressing each cuvée's terroir. Cuvées are long aged for a minimum of four years and prestige wines as long as 11 years. The house today is managed by his son Stanislas and daughter Garance. The Thiénot style is marked by the bitterness of phenolic grip, more apparent in pinot and meunier in its current set of cuvées.

THIÉNOT BRUT NV $$

86 points • 2013 BASE VINTAGE • DISGORGED MARCH 2019 • TASTED IN AUSTRALIA

40% chardonnay, 50% pinot noie, 10% meunier; Sermiers, Aÿ, Avenay-Val-d'Or, Verzenay, Mailly-Champagne, Vertus, Avize, Bergères-lès-Vertus; 30% 2012 and 2010 reserves; no oak; aged 5 years on lees; 5g/L dosage; cork

A simple cuvée of primary apple and pear fruit, bolstered by the gingernut biscuit complexity of five years lees age. Candied dosage lends a boiled-sweets dominance surprising for a published level of just 5g/L. It concludes short, with firm phenolic grip.

THIÉNOT BRUT ROSÉ NV $$

87 points • 2013 BASE VINTAGE • DISGORGED APRIL 2018 • TASTED IN AUSTRALIA

60% chardonnay, 35% pinot noir, 5% meunier; Sézanne, Vertus, Nogent l'Abbesse, Bassuet, Sermiers, Aÿ; 20% 2012 reserves; no oak; aged 4 years on lees; 8g/L dosage; DIAM

A medium salmon copper hue heralds a savoury rosé of fading strawberry, raspberry and red apple fruits, contrasting oxidative development that imparts notes of tomato and paprika. The finish collides phenolic grip with candied dosage.

Thiénot Blanc de Blancs NV $$

90 points • 2014 base vintage • Disgorged November 2018 • Tasted in Australia

100% chardonnay; Avize, Villers-Marmery, Vertus, Vitryat; no oak; aged 3.5 years on lees; 8g/L dosage; cork

A light blanc de blancs of lemon, apple and pear fruit, touched by the vanilla and almond notes of lees age and an attractive wisp of reductive matchstick complexity. It's delicate, if a little dilute and short, though shows good freshness and structure of vibrant acidity, fine salt minerality and well-balanced dosage. Phenolics exhibit the best management of the Thiénot line-up this year. One bottle was corked.

Thiénot Vintage 2008 $$$

89 points • Disgorged April 2018 • Tasted in Australia

40% chardonnay, 40% pinot noir, 20% meunier; Avize, Cuis, Bassuet, Hautvillers, Rilly-la-Montagne, Aÿ; no oak; aged 9 years on lees; 10g/L dosage; DIAM

I introduced Thiénot Vintage as an unusually ready-to-drink 2008 on release two years ago, and it has sadly already passed its peak. A particularly developed and secondary take on the vintage, it's now layered with toasty, buttery complexity evolving into imperfect notes of charcuterie and bruised pear. The energetic acidity of the season is toned by the creamy softness of lees age, interrupted by the bitter grip and grainy structure of phenolic coarseness. It upholds a finish of good persistence, guided by the acid drive of 2008.

Thiénot Cuvée Stanislas Blanc de Blancs 2007 $$$$

90 points • Disgorged October 2018 • Tasted in Australia

100% chardonnay; Avize, Oger, Cramant, Bassuet; no oak; aged 10.5 years on lees; 7g/L dosage; DIAM

Following in the mould of the 2006, this is a cuvée of deep lees age, built around the silky, creamy, butteriness of maturity. The tension of chardonnay cuts through in grapefruit and pear on the finish, with taut acidity clashing with soft maturity. This interplay is interrupted by the grip of firm phenolic structure, lending a rising bitterness which makes for a touch of astringency on the finish. A note of reduction lends a subtle vegetal overtone which dissipates with air.

Thiénot Cuvée Garance Blanc de Rouges 2010 $$$$

89 points • Disgorged October 2018 • Tasted in Australia

100% pinot; Aÿ, Cumières, Rilly-la-Montagne, Les Riceys; no oak; aged 7.5 years on lees; cork

A full straw yellow hue contrasts the pale colour of the 2008 before it, and in spite of its lesser season, its fruit is better defined, too. It's a spicy style of red apple and beurre bosc pear, underlined like the 2008 by the biscuity complexity of lees age. The finish balances bright acid line with well-integrated dosage, but the mark of bitter phenolic grip is intense, making for a grainy and astringent close.

Thiénot x Penfolds

(Tea-e-noh Pen-folds)

———

4 Rue Joseph-Cugnot 51500 Taissy
www.penfolds.com

CHAMPAGNE THIÉNOT × Penfolds®

To celebrate its 175th birthday in 2019, the historic and iconic Australian still and fortified winemaker of Penfolds launched a new foray into champagne in partnership with the house of Thiénot (page 528). 'The sentiment is to make the best wine we can in Champagne and to work collaboratively and proactively with the Thiénot family,' announced Penfolds Chief Winemaker, Peter Gago.

Long world famous for many of South Australia's most legendary red wines, not least Grange itself, Penfolds releases frequently rate at the top of my Australian tastings ever year. Its new venture into champagne, however, is a very different undertaking.

Buyer's own brand cuvées have long been commonplace across the champagne landscape, but for a region that has fought vigorously for more than a century to protect its appellation exclusivity, an association with a brand so intrinsically and famously associated with wines from elsewhere is fraught with bureaucratic complications. The company spent AUD$14,000 on negotiations around the label alone.

Thiénot x Penfolds cuvées rightfully bear the Thiénot name first and foremost. Back labels succinctly and accurately declare 'Champagne Thiénot Cuvée Selected by Penfolds'.

Gago selected the cuvées from Thiénot tirage stock, from grapes originally sourced from Thiénot growers. He made the decision on when they would be disgorged, and had involvement with the dosage liqueur, which was aged in Penfolds Yattarna Chardonnay barrels. Front labels display disgorgement dates.

The wines are thus fundamentally and intrinsically Thiénot more than they are Penfolds, carrying the DNA of Thiénot and the finishing touches of Penfolds. The Thiénot house style is marked by the bitterness of phenolic grip, more apparent in the black grapes than in chardonnay in its own cuvées this year, and the same style naturally defines the Thiénot x Penfolds cuvées.

The big question is, do Thiénot cuvées justify Penfolds prices?

The choice of Thiénot as its partner is puzzling for a concept that aspires to 'aim for the top end', as Gago puts it, perhaps owing to Penfolds' longstanding relationship with Thiénot France as its French distributor. 'Why not Richard Geoffroy, Vincent Chaperon or Olivier Krug, all good friends?' he asks, referring to two of his favourite luxury champagnes in Dom Pérignon and Krug, and then answers his own question, 'But they are LVMH.'

This is 'quite courageous and controversial' admits Gago, 'but it's not unpatriotic. It's what we will be doing for the next 175 years. This is a celebration of our 175th and also a nod to the future.'

A self-confessed champagne nut, it was in fact his 'addiction' to champagne that led Peter Gago to study winemaking, before commencing his first role at Penfolds as sparkling winemaker in 1989. 'In future, I would like to be more involved in the production from the start,' he says. This would certainly be a crucial first step in creating a champagne that is truly Penfolds.

Thiénot x Penfolds Chardonnay Pinot Noir Cuvée Vintage 2012 $$$$

90 points • Disgorged 15 October 2018 • Tasted in Australia

50% chardonnay (25% Vertus, 15% Le Mesnil-sur-Oger and 10% Cramant), 50% pinot noir (15% Verzenay, 15% Tauxières-Mutry, 10% Aÿ, 5% Cumières, 5% Avenay-Val-d'Or); dosage liqueur aged in Penfolds Yattarna Chardonnay barrels; full malolactic fermentation; 2.4g/L dosage added, and with residual it totals 4g/L; cork

Source from distinguished grand and premier cru villages of the Côte des Blancs and Montagne de Reims, this is a spicy and complex expression of the great season of 2012, uniting the red apple and strawberry fruit of pinot noir with the grapefruit zest of chardonnay, underlined by the gingernut biscuit complexity of five years of lees age. It concludes with impressive persistence, energised by the bright acidity of the season, well balanced with neatly integrated dosage. Phenolic grip intrinsic to the Thiénot style lends a firm bite and bitterness, which detract from the finish.

Thiénot x Penfolds Blanc de Blancs Grand Cru Avize Vintage 2012 $$$$$

90 points • Tasted in Australia

100% Avize chardonnay; single vineyard of 0.40 hectares, planted in the late 1960s and early 1970s; no malolactic fermentation; 1.2g/L dosage added, and with residual it totals 2g/L; less than 4000 bottles; cork

A tense style that captures the chalky, salty mood of Avize with full malic tension and firm, bitter phenolic bite on the finish. It concludes with good persistence and a reductive note of struck flint that lends a note of vegetal character to the nose and palate.

Thiénot x Penfolds Blanc de Noirs Grand Cru Aÿ Vintage 2012 $$$$$

89 points • Tasted in Australia

100% Aÿ pinot noir; single vineyard Chambre aux Loups of 1 hectare, with east-south-east exposure; 100% malolactic fermentation; 4g/L dosage; less than 10,000 bottles; cork

A tense and focused blanc de noirs of crunchy redcurrant fruit and chewy red apple-skin grip. It captures the spicy mood of Aÿ in dark cherry fruit and mixed spice. The firmly structured, bitter phenolic grip of Thiénot collides with firm acidity. It looks awkward at the moment and screams out for time to find harmony.

Mutigny, harvest 2014

ULYSSE COLLIN

(Oo-lees Kohl-la)

6/10

21 RUE DES VIGNERONS 51270 CONGY

CHAMPAGNE

Ulysse Collin

CONGY

Nestled into the gentle slopes between the Côte des Blancs and the Sézannais, west of Bergères-lès-Vertus, the district of the Val du Petit Morin is little known, yet holds important potential for the future of Champagne, according to young grower Olivier Collin. From his village of Congy in the heart of the region, his cuvées mount the most compelling evidence for the potential of the area. Unusually, Collin's little production of just 60,000 bottles is exclusively single varietal, single vineyard and non-vintage, with each cuvée expressing the deeply characterful and distinctly mineral-driven personality of his unique terroirs.

It was after working with Anselme Selosse that Olivier Collin was inspired to reclaim a portion of his family's vines to produce his first vintage in 2004. 'My family has been in Congy for two centuries, and I came back to create a new adventure!' he exclaims.

He has since re-established the family winery and cellar and reclaimed 8.7 hectares in the village, neighbouring Vert-la-Gravelle and nearby Barbonne-Fayel, planted to chardonnay and pinot noir.

Midway between Épernay and Sézanne, the warm, south-facing slopes of Congy in the Val du Petit Morin are among the first to begin harvest in Champagne. 'We are not part of the Sézannais or the Côte des Blancs here,' Collin points out. 'We have our own particularity that falls in between.' He was active in campaigning for the area to receive its own appellation, which was granted in 2018.

The soils here vary from clay to limestone, with chalk only as close as 1.5 metres below the surface. 'We have good chalk here, and it is the source of our most interesting wines,' Collin reveals. 'When we have 3–5 metre deep clay, we have less personality in the wines.'

He upholds the distinctive saltiness of his wines as the most particular character of the area, and is fascinated by deposits of flint in the chalk, though suggests it will take time to ascertain the impact these have on his wines.

Collin's aspiration is to capture the personality of his unique terroirs. 'I don't want to produce heavy wines,' he says. 'I want good maturity, but we are in Champagne, so I want to produce fresh wines. After 10 years, they will become much more round, so they need to be fine but not sharp to begin.'

To this end, Collin aims to harvest at 10.5 degrees potential on average, sometimes as high as 11.2, but never higher, for fear of losing definition. His vines are privileged to be between 30 and 60 years of age.

His family vineyards had been leased to larger houses before Collin returned to the estate, and he found 'the viticulture was not up to standard'. It took him some years to get the vineyards back on track, to the point that he was comfortable to put the names of the sites on his cuvées for the first time.

His vines and are tended using a combination of organic and conventional practices, applying organic compost, ploughing and avoiding pesticides. 'We are 80% organic, but I don't like copper sulphate as a fungicide, so I don't use it,' he explains. In 2012, he attempted a 100% organic regime in his Les Enfers vineyard, but lost the entire crop.

Winemaking is likewise natural within sensible reason, relying on wild yeasts to complete very long fermentations exclusively

in barrels and old casks, mostly of around five years of age. Malolactic fermentation may proceed in part, though not by design. 'When the wine decides to go through malolactic, it goes through malolactic!' he exclaims.

Sulphur dioxide is used as a preservative to facilitate long ageing, and all cuvées are kept on gross lees for an unusually long period of 23 months. Reserves are stored in barrels five metres underground, and stainless steel tanks are used only for blending.

Collin's first two harvests of 2004 and 2005 were bottled as vintage cuvées ('because I had no choice!') and since this time he has worked to increase reserves, to an impressive 80% today, which he upholds as very important for building complexity in his blends. Dosages are minuscule, between 1.7 and 2.4g/L. Back labels declare base vintages and disgorgement dates.

With a wide grin, the jovial and extroverted Olivier Collin is a master of characterful cuvées that have sparked great fascination in terroirs hitherto unknown to champagne lovers.

Ulysse Collin Les Pierrières Blanc de Blancs NV $$$$

92 points • 2014 base vintage • Disgorged March 2018 • Tasted in Australia

100% chardonnay; Les Pierrières lieu-dit of 1.2 hectares with south-east exposition in Vert la Gravelle, Coteaux du Petit Morin; 50% 2013 reserves; wild fermented and matured for 11 months in old oak casks; unfined and unfiltered; aged 3 years on lees; 1.7g/L dosage

Ulysse Collin's Les Pierrières in the nearby village of Vert la Gravelle is a chalky site with between just 10 centimetres and 50 centimetres of topsoil, and he suggests 90% of the roots are in the chalk. Resonating deeply with the fine, salty chalk minerality of the village, this is a complex and spicy style that unites the generosity of golden delicious apple with layers of spice. Wild barrel ferment brings subtle notes of charcuterie, while lees age makes for a creamy mouthfeel. A characterful and well-crafted cuvée of impressive length, personality and lovely texture. Set off with minuscule dosage, it's the ultimate oyster match.

Olivier Collin, champion of the Val du Petit Morin between the Côte des Blancs and Sézanne.

ULYSSE COLLIN LES ENFERS BLANC DE BLANCS NV $$$$

91 points • 2013 BASE VINTAGE • DISGORGED MARCH 2018 • TASTED IN AUSTRALIA

100% chardonnay; Les Enfers lieu-dit of easterly exposure in Congy, Coteaux du Petit Morin; 100% 2013 vintage, though labelled as non-vintage; 40-year-old vines; aged 4 years on lees

With one metre of iron-rich clay topsoils over limestone, Olivier Collin describes Les Enfers as being more 'shouldered' than Les Pierrières. It boldly lives up to the expectation in a deep, full straw-yellow hue and powerful intensity of golden fruit cake, fig and toffee. For all of its proportions, it finds tension, freshness and focus in a cut of grapefruit crunch, layers of grapefruit-pith texture and the pronounced salt chalk minerality of Congy, concluding with impressive length.

ULYSSE COLLIN LES MAILLONS BLANC DE NOIRS NV $$$$

92 points • 2014 BASE VINTAGE • DISGORGED MARCH 2018 • TASTED IN AUSTRALIA

100% pinot noir; Les Maillons lieu-dit in Barbonne-Fayel, Côte de Sézanne; wild fermented and aged for 7 months in 3–6-year-old barrels and foudres; 50% 2013 reserves; 2.4g/L dosage; 20,000 bottles

Collin farms 2.5 hectares of the six-hectare Les Maillons vineyard, planted in 1971 on an east-facing, iron-rich clay slope in the Sézanne, 35 kilometres from his home in Congy. From it he produces the largest volume of any of his cuvées, and he suspects it might rank as the biggest single-vineyard production in all of Champagne. A little warmer in Sézanne than Congy, he achieves an impressive average ripeness of 11 degrees potential. He describes this as a 'semi-oxidative style, so as to drink consistently for a decade, without any further oxidation'. True to its ripe aspirations, this is a blanc de noirs of full straw-yellow hue, in a rich and powerful style that ripples with pineapple and golden delicious apple, concluding in crunchy, bitey, crab apple grip. Pinot exerts its flesh and body to full effect in this muscular and characterful style, with tension upheld thanks to the grainy, salty minerality of the Sézanne.

ULYSSE COLLIN LES MAILLONS ROSÉ DE SAIGNÉE NV $$$$

91 points • 100% 2014 BASE VINTAGE • DISGORGED MARCH 2018 • TASTED IN AUSTRALIA

100% pinot noir; Les Maillons lieu-dit in Barbonne-Fayel, Côte de Sézanne; 45-year-old vines; cropped at less than 50hL/ha; macerated 24–36 hours, depending on phenolic maturity; 20% of stems retained and layered in the ferment; fully fermented and matured 1 year in barrels; 2.4g/L dosage

Olivier Collin's aim is freshness in rosé, and he finds rosé reserves too fragile and rapid in their evolution, hence his rosé is a single vintage, though labelled as non-vintage, as it's sometimes released too early to be a vintage. He describes saignée rosé as the hardest style of champagne to make, and 2014 as one of his most difficult vintages. Maceration is varied from one to three days, according to the harvest. 'If it's too quick or too long, we could lose a lot of character,' he explains. 'And when I drain the saignée, I have four hours before it finishes draining, so I need to anticipate it.' He nailed the colour again in 2014, a throbbing, bright, medium crimson hue, heralding a pinot noir saignée loaded with presence and character. This fruity style captures the blood orange personality of pinot noir with notes of plum pudding and bitter orange zest. Fine tannin structure unites with the grainy salt minerality of the Côte de Sézanne. Collin suggests drinking it with pigeon.

VADIN-PLATEAU

(Vah-duh Pla-toh)

---

12 Rue de la Coopérative 51480 Cumières
champagnevadinplateau.com

CHAMPAGNE
VADIN-PLATEAU

The Plateau family has been growing grapes in the premier cru village of Cumières on the south-facing slopes of the Grande Vallée de la Marne since 1785, and producing its own champagnes since 1958. The family estate now encompasses seven hectares exclusively on south- and south-east-facing slopes spanning seven crus: Cumières and its surrounding villages of Hautvillers, Damery, Venteuil and Aÿ, Pourcy in the middle of the Montagne de Reims, and as far-flung as Château-Thierry. Planted to 44% meunier, 39% pinot noir and 17% chardonnay, vineyard soils are tilled and chemical treatments are minimised. Ninth-generation grower Yann Vadin ferments variously in temperature-controlled stainless steel tanks, oak barrels or, since 2011, oval clay tubs, according to the village, variety and plot. His bold cuvées reflect the generosity of ripe, well-exposed fruit, sadly afflicted with oxidation. Back labels declare cépage, dosage and crus.

VADIN-PLATEAU CHÊNE LA BUTTE PREMIER CRU DOSAGE ZÉRO 2013 $$$$

86 points • TASTED IN AUSTRALIA

100% Cumières chardonnay; single vineyard Chêne la Butte; aged 4 years on lees; zero dosage; cork; 550 bottles

A powerful blanc de blancs that captures the exuberance of ripe, spicy chardonnay in Cumières in an oxidative style of bruised apple and pear fruit. Some aldehyde lends austerity to the finish, accentuated by zero dosage, concluding assertive and attenuated.

Vadin-Plateau Les Oubliées Autre Cru Dosage Zéro NV $$$

85 points • 2007 base vintage • Tasted in Australia

100% Damery meunier; 20% reserve solera dating since 1987; aged 9 years on lees; cork; 1500 bottles

Long lees age and a deep solera conspire to create a toasty, biscuity style with gingernut notes, lacking freshness and vitality. It displays advanced, oxidative development in notes of burnt toffee, concluding dry and tense.

Vadin-Plateau Bois des Jots Premier Cru Dosage Zéro 2013 $$$

Tasted in Australia

100% Cumières pinot; single vineyard Bois des Jots; aged 4 years on lees; zero dosage; cork; 450 bottles

Cork-tainted. No back-up bottle supplied.

Rilly-la-Montagne pinot noir, harvest 2014

VAUVERSIN

(Vooh-veh-sah)

———

9 BIS RUE DE FLAVIGNY 51190 OGER
www.champagne-vauversin.fr

CHAMPAGNE
VAUVERSIN
à OGER

The Vauversin family has been growing chardonnay in the grand cru of Oger since 1640, and bottling its own champagnes since 1929. Fifteen generations later, Laurent Vauversin has worked alongside his father Bruno to tend their small estate of just 3.15 hectares in the village organically since 2011, capturing the characterful and fast-maturing flamboyance of Oger, taken to its full extreme in ripe fruit, wild fermented in oak barrels. Malolactic fermentation is blocked selectively to suit the cuvée. Disgorgement dates and dosages are printed on back labels.

VAUVERSIN ORIGINAL GRAND CRU BLANC DE BLANCS BRUT NV $$

88 points • 2015 BASE VINTAGE • DISGORGED OCTOBER 2018 • TASTED IN AUSTRALIA

Oger; 36% reserves; wild fermented in oak barrels; unfiltered; 5g/L dosage; cork

The exuberant and ripe presence of Oger is met head-on, confidently and unashamedly by the toasty, roast nut and chocolate personality of oak, making for a powerful and characterful style with a creaminess that surpasses its youthfulness. The succulent, yellow-fruit ripeness of the village is countered by the fine grip of oak tannins. It concludes long and spicy, even faintly tropical.

VAUVERSIN ORPAIR GRAND CRU BLANC DE BLANCS EXTRA BRUT NV $$

92 points • 2013 BASE VINTAGE • DISGORGED SEPTEMBER 2018 • TASTED IN AUSTRALIA

100% chardonnay; two plots, Chênets and Gallois in Oger; harvested at high ripeness, wild fermented and matured exclusively in old barrels; unfiltered; no malolactic fermentation; 4g/L dosage; cork

Oger is never wanting for presence or impact, and the full fanfare of ripe fruit and 100% oak fermentation take it to its full extreme. For all of its exuberance, it showcases the experience of fifteen generations in the village in well-executed polish. The succulent, buttery creaminess of ripeness and barrel ferment is nicely gauged, complemented but never dominated by the vanilla custard and spice of oak. It lingers long with the gliding, impeccably ripe malic acidity of this strong season.

Vauversin Grand Cru Extra Brut Millésime 2014 $$$

91 points • Disgorged December 2018 • Tasted in Australia

100% chardonnay; two plots planted in 1952 in Oger; wild fermented in oak barrels; unfiltered; zero dosage; cork

This is a young and tense expression of Oger that really needs time to come together, quite a contrast to the flamboyance of the 2010 vintage that I reviewed two years ago. Nuances of star fruit and lime reflect lower ripeness levels in this difficult season, making for a tense finish of firm acid cut. It holds with integrity, persistence and line, reflecting the craftsmanship of this longstanding estate. A youthful and coiled style with great potential, it will appreciate a few years to unwind and soften, and will improve confidently over the coming decade and beyond.

Oger, harvest 2014

VAZART-COQUART & FILS

(Vah-zah Kho-khar e Feess)

7/10

6 RUE DES PARTELAINES 51530 CHOUILLY
www.champagnevazartcoquart.com

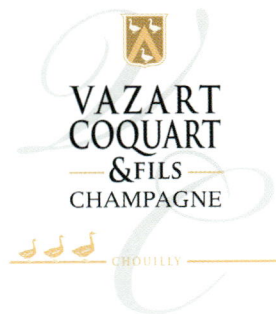

**VAZART
COQUART
&FILS
CHAMPAGNE**

The Vazart family has sold champagne from its 11 hectares of estate vineyards exclusively in the Côte des Blancs grand cru of Chouilly for more than 60 years. Tall in stature and in warmth, Jean-Pierre Vazart is a gentleman with a broad smile and an acute attention to the finest details in his vineyards and winery. Since he took charge of the estate almost 25 years ago, he has meticulously crafted a ripe fruit style in every cuvée that articulates the quintessential expression of Chouilly terroir. 'With soils like these, how could I do anything less?' he says graciously.

The story of Chouilly is all about the robust character and mineral expression of chardonnay, which makes up 94% of Vazart-Coquart's 30 plots of organic vines, averaging more than 30 years of age. 'My father has the récoltant-manipulant's mind, wanting to make everything himself, so after a few years of buying red wine, he hid some plantings of pinot noir in a lesser-known part of Chouilly,' reveals Vazart. Chouilly pinot noir was approved as grand cru in 2009. 'Next time I plant it, it will be on the road so everyone can see it!' he grins.

Perfectly ripe fruit is Vazart's goal, with a target of 10.5–11 degrees of potential, as he finds 11.5 too rich. 'I do all I can to avoid chaptalisation!' he declares. Fruit maturity is achieved through limiting yields by green harvesting and cultivating grasses between the rows.

Vazart ploughs his vineyards to encourage deeper root penetration. He achieved High Environmental Value certification in 2012, followed by Viticulture Durable en Champagne certification. In 2017, he commenced full conversion to organic viticulture, because he wanted 'something to oblige me to stop using herbicides', but more importantly, 'because I want to leave something good for my daughter if she would like to follow me. A few years ago, I said I would never be organic, but now I will never say, "No!" I changed because of my organic friends.'

In 2016, he trialled one-quarter of his plots organically. 'And it was the worst year for mildew, but we saved the harvest, even for the organic grapes. I talked a lot with my organic guru friends, Eric Rodez (page 246) and Erick De Sousa (page 185) and both said, "It is difficult, but you saved your harvest, so what are you waiting for?!" So I said, "OK, let's go!"'

Conversion to organics has come at a cost to Vazart. 'If we were not organic in 2018, we could have had the same yields as 2004, but because we were organic, we had 30% less,' he disclosed.

Chardonnay harvest 2017

He is expecting to make his first certified organic cuvée in 2020, to be released in 2025 or 2026. 'Becoming organic is our focus, not certification on the label,' he clarifies.

For him, bringing his non-vintage wines up to organic certification is more challenging than it is for most, because reserve wines are stored as a perpetual blend in a 20,000-litre tank. Encompassing every vintage back to 1982, it's one of the oldest soleras in Champagne, held fresh at 12°C. Each year 40% is taken as 'the backbone' for Brut Réserve NV, Extra Brut NV, Rosé and for dosage liqueurs, and replenished with the current harvest. The solera is given priority over vintage cuvées and receives the estate's highest-potential fruit. 'My only regret is that it will never be organic,' he says

His 11 hectares yield more than he can make in his small winery and cellars, so he sells everything surplus to his 65,000-bottle requirements to Veuve Clicquot. 'Of course, the best parcels are for me, but they know what they buy!' he smiles. Veuve Clicquot chef de cave Dominique Demarville is a friend of Vazart's from school, and he enjoys a very flexible contract. 'If I have a small harvest, I can sell them less, and if I have a big harvest, they buy everything I don't need.' It doesn't get any better than that.

Vazart's aspiration in the winery is to preserve the character of his grapes, so he uses stainless steel vats 'for their neutrality' rather than oak barrels, and cultured yeasts rather than wild. Malolactic fermentation was traditionally carried to completion, and deep reserve stocks are employed to soften the robust character of Chouilly.

Vazart's production was spread across two premises on opposite sides of the village, which he integrated into an impressive, pristine and cleverly conceived new facility in 2016. With every detail carefully thought out in classic Vazart manner, his new winery has transformed his winemaking on five key levels. The traditional vertical press was replaced with a new horizontal press for gentler treatment of the fruit. Forty tiny new tanks were installed to enable most plots to be vinified separately (giving rise to new single-plot cuvées in his portfolio), and temperature control was added to these tanks. Disgorgement is completed in the same facility, rather than transferring backwards and forwards across the village.

Finally, temperature-controlled fermenters facilitated the opportunity for him to selectively block malolactic fermentation parcel by parcel, and in 2016 he put two-thirds of his ferments through malolactic, in 2017 one-third and in 2018 none. 'I think we might need to block malolactic more often, but I will never say, "I will always do it this way",' he clarifies. 'The question is always, "Is the wine balanced, or not?"'

He has also experimented with vinification in a terracotta egg fermenter, giving rise to a new cuvée, L'Aventure. 'We have compared fermentation with stainless steel and in just two to three months, the difference is huge!' he exclaims. 'Stainless steel is always sharp and needs time, but terracotta opens very quickly.'

Vazart's new facility provides capacity for 200,000 bottles. His current stock of 150,000 furnishes annual sales of 65,000. All the details of every cuvée, including bottling and disgorgement dates, are clearly printed in-house on back labels in gold ink.

Jean-Pierre Vazart knows his craft intimately, and his fanatical attention to detail and sensible and sensitive approach make him one of the most attentive growers in Chouilly. The first fruits of his new facility have begun to emerge, and they look more precise and terroir-driven than ever.

Vazart-Coquart & Fils Brut Réserve Blanc de Blancs Chouilly Grand Cru NV $$

93 points • 2015 BASE VINTAGE • DISGORGED SEPTEMBER 2018 • TASTED IN CHAMPAGNE

100% Chouilly chardonnay; 5% 2014, 5% 2013 and 25% solera of every vintage since 1982; aged 2.5 years on lees; 6.5g/L dosage; 50% of production, 30–35,000 bottles

The embodiment of the great Jean-Pierre Vazart himself, his lead cuvée is impeccably crafted and uncomplicated, a quintessential apéritif champagne that declares the signature of Chouilly and the precision of blanc de blancs. His ripe fruit mandate sings in the mature 2015 season in white peach, fig, even a dash of the exoticism of apricots, finding harmonious tension with bright acidity and the classic, finessing structure of fine Chouilly chalk minerality. To express such commanding chalk mineral precision in his entry blend is a true triumph, lingering very long, salty and precise.

Vazart-Coquart & Fils Extra Brut Blanc de Blancs Chouilly Grand Cru NV $$

94 points • 2014 BASE VINTAGE • DISGORGED JULY 2018 • TASTED IN CHAMPAGNE

Brut Réserve with 3.5 years on lees and 3.5g/L dosage

Jean-Pierre Vazart created Extra Brut and Zéro from his Brut Réserve a decade ago. Reflective of his acute attention to detail, he begins dosage trials from zero for each blend. His Extra Brut is one of the few in Champagne that is able to present the cuvée of the house with balance and poise with lower dosage. It's signature Chouilly, succulent, yellow-fruited and wonderfully generous, holding impeccable tension, thanks to fine acidity and heightened chalk mineral texture amplified by low dosage. Another year on lees has blessed it with a hint of malt and vanilla. A brilliant Vazart, very long, poised and profoundly, frothingly, sea salt mineral.

Vazart-Coquart & Fils Brut Zéro Blanc de Blancs Chouilly Grand Cru NV $$

91 points • 2011 BASE VINTAGE • DISGORGED JULY 2018 • TASTED IN CHAMPAGNE

Brut Réserve with 6 years on lees and zero dosage

Maturity on lees has always been Jean-Pierre Vazart's goal for his Zéro, and now he aspires to increase time post-disgorgement, possible thanks to his new facility. Lees age has built a creamy and textured style that presents the dry grip of 2011 with flattering appeal, though there is no fully escaping the bite and grit of this challenging season, especially without the massaging help of dosage. Creamy, biscuity and vanilla-accented, it lingers with good length and dry salt minerality.

Vazart-Coquart & Fils La Cerisiere Par Vazart-Coquart Blanc de Blancs Chouilly Grand Cru 2016

95 points • DISGORGED MID-2018 • TASTED IN CHAMPAGNE

100% Chouilly chardonnay; single, tiny lieu-dit La Cerisiere; no malolactic fermentation; tiraged under crown cap; still some years from release; this sample zero dosage, though final release may have a tiny dosage; 1500 bottles

The micro-vinification of Jean-Pierre Vazart's new facility opened up the possibility for single-site cuvées for the first time in 2016, and a sneak preview revealed two very exciting wines in the pipeline. This is a blanc de blancs of tension and drive that magnificently captures the body and succulent allure of Chouilly with layers of white peach and spice, held in fine tension by the cut of malic acidity. Still only partway through its life on lees, it has already amassed lovely notes of vanilla and crème brûlée. Seamless and dynamic, a very long finish is driven by the energy of malic acidity and terrific chalk minerality of heightened chalk presence which Jean-Pierre says is enhanced by deep roots, thanks to no herbicides.

Vazart-Coquart & Fils L'Aventure Blanc de Blancs Chouilly Grand Cru 2015

95 points • Tasted in Champagne

100% chardonnay; a 'very good' single site in the middle of Chouilly; vinified in terracotta egg fermenter; tiraged under cork; still some years from release; no malolactic fermentation; this sample zero dosage, though final release may have perhaps 3g/L dosage; less than 1000 bottles

Chouilly of magnificent body and succulence, capturing all the theatrics of this village. Generous white nectarine and white peach is layered with spice, hints of vanilla and crunchy apple and pear. It's creamy and silky and yet crunchy and energetic, thanks to the tension of beautifully ripe malic acidity. Its salty mineral personality is magnificent, lingering long, frothing and fine, with great tension and all the character of the sea.

Vazart-Coquart & Fils Grand Bouquet Blanc de Blancs Chouilly Brut 2012 $$

94 points • Disgorged July 2018 • Tasted in Champagne

100% Chouilly chardonnay; tiraged under crown cap; 6g/L dosage

A powerfully characterful and exuberant blanc de blancs that defines the succulent generosity of Chouilly and underlines it precisely with gently supportive acidity and the deep, fine, salty mineral texture of the village, frothing and bubbling on a very long, sea salt tail. Fruit presence is elevated to another level by the great 2012 vintage, and salt minerality rises and looms confidently to meet it, finding a wonderful harmony in these two extremes. An impressive vintage to drink in the next two years.

Vazart-Coquart & Fils Special Club Brut Blanc de Blancs Chouilly Grand Cru 2010 $$$

94 points • Disgorged October 2018 • Tasted in Champagne

100% Chouilly chardonnay; tiraged under cork; 3.5g/L dosage

Grand Bouquet is tiraged on crown cap, and the same wine tiraged on cork is Special Club, because 'after ageing they are completely different, of course!' That they are. It takes Jean-Pierre Vazart half a day to disgorge 500 bottles (tasting every one for cork taint), the same time it takes to disgorge 3000 in crown cap. He has coaxed a splendid result from the lesser 2010 season, a Chouilly of tension and presence, if not the generosity or exuberance of his greatest Special Clubs. It is centred on a core of grapefruit and pear of excellent focus and integrity, with a subtle hint of coffee bean. The salt minerality of Chouilly reigns supreme, very fine and confidently structured, heightening the poise and grip of a very long finish.

Vazart-Coquart & Fils 82/13 Blanc de Blancs Grand Cru Extra Brut NV $$$$

94 points • 2013 base vintage • Disgorged June 2018 • Tasted in Champagne

100% Chouilly chardonnay; 60% solera of every vintage since 1982; 1g/L dosage; 1300 bottles

Jean-Pierre Vazart describes his solera like a mille-feuille vanilla custard slice of 1000 layers. 'Since the beginning of my career, it was simply a tool to make the Brut NV, but my father and I decided to show it alone for the first time with the 2012 base' (hence labelled 82/12), 'and now with the 2013.'

The complexity of 32 vintages in one bottle is intoxicatingly profound, but even from the vortex of this swirling maelstrom, the churning, sea salt minerality of Chouilly bursts through triumphant and all-conquering, imposing a finesse and deep-set mineral structure that define start, middle and end. Fruit and secondary character unite seamlessly, with deep spice, dried peach, ripe white nectarine, fig and nuances of brioche, even fruit mince spice. For such an incredible recipe, its freshness and precision are disarming and thrilling in equal measure. A blanc de blancs of profound length and character, it will age effortlessly for decades.

Chouilly, winter 2013

VEUVE CLICQUOT

(Verv Khlee-kho)

7/10

1 PLACE DES DROITS DE L'HOMME 51100 REIMS
www.veuve-clicquot.com

Veuve Clicquot

■ REIMS FRANCE ■

Dramatic developments are underway in the bellows of Veuve Clicquot that are bubbling to the surface with increasing vigour. Its characterful, full-bodied, pinot-focused wines are more refined every time I look, an astounding feat for a house with a dizzying annual production somewhere in the vicinity of 20 million bottles, ranking a confident number two by volume behind Moët & Chandon in Louis Vuitton–Moët Hennessy's (LVMH's) champagne kingdom. Even Clicquot's conspicuous 'Yellow Label' non-vintage, in its inimitable, trademark, mango-orange livery, is looking trim and fit today, having lost its curvaceous sweetness of its darker days – quite a workout for a cuvée that alone now likely accounts for a whopping 17 million bottles every year. Its vintage wines are where Veuve Clicquot really steps up. For an operation of such a grand scale, the consistency of Veuve Clicquot is unrivalled in all of Champagne.

'Veuve Clicquot is a big house where we have a big responsibility to maintain the style, but every day we work to improve the quality,' chef de cave Dominique Demarville explains as he shows me through one of his two expansive wineries in Reims. With a glimmer in his eye he announces, 'The winery is like a kitchen where we can experiment!'

Then he thrusts open a gigantic door to reveal a grand spectacle of proportions I have never witnessed anywhere in Champagne. Oak barrels. Huge oak barrels. New foudres of 5000 litres and 7500 litres. Lots of them. I know of winemakers proud to show off just one of these beauties. And here, hidden in an enormous warehouse somewhere in the depths of Veuve Clicquot, are 36 of them, lined up in all of their towering magnificence of intricately crafted French oak, perfectly interconnected with arteries of polished stainless steel.

These 240,000 litres of oak-fermented wine – a tiny drop in the ocean of Clicquot – now comprise just 10–15% of its vintage wines, and 1–3% of non-vintage cuvées. Leading me around the room to sample from his battalion of barrels, Demarville is as excited as a kid with a room full of new toys. 'Sometimes my team tells me I'm too involved in what I'm doing, but I work with my heart and not my head,' he confesses as he pours me an Oger chardonnay of which he's particularly proud. 'Barrel fermentation offers the chance to improve without changing the Clicquot style,' he explains. 'To add some spice!'

PROGRESSIVE TRANSFORMATION

It's a subtle twist, but it typifies the evolution that is slowly transforming one of Champagne's biggest players, leaving no stage of production untouched, revolutionising vineyards, vinification,

and most notably its regimes of malolactic fermentation, reserves and dosage. 'The Veuve Clicquot style is about richness, but also about brightness: strong and full-bodied and at the same time fresh,' Demarville clarifies.

'I am aiming to build more freshness, vibrancy and brightness into the wines, as Veuve Clicquot had a reputation of being full and heavy when I started,' he discloses. 'People are looking for a more refined style, so this is our goal, even in the wake of climate change.'

It's in brightness and freshness that he has most demonstrably refined these wines since taking the helm in 2006, at just 39 years of age. This has not been an easy time to drive such evolution. 'With climate change, we are seeing vintages which are more and more diverse,' he reveals. 'Managing reserves is the most important part of my job, and this is why I sometimes need to say I will not declare a vintage.' Since 2000, the house has declared just seven vintages: 2002, 2004, 2006, 2008, 2012, 2015 and 2018 (and no Vintage Brut in 2006 or La Grande Dame in 2002). The current vintage of 2012 represents just the 66th vintage release of the house since Madame Clicquot created what is believed to be the first recorded vintage champagne in 1810.

Demarville remains confident about the future. 'So many things have happened in Champagne over the past century, and we will adapt again. We will adjust our winegrowing and winemaking to ensure we can continue to make champagnes of elegance and minerality.'

PRIVILEGED VINEYARD RESOURCES

'Everything starts in the vineyard!' Demarville declares, and, for Clicquot, this represents a substantial and enviably positioned resource of now 393 hectares of estate vines, including a wealth of premier and especially grand crus, providing for 20% of its needs, with a further 122 hectares supplied by LVMH vineyards, boosting the total to 26%. The remainder is sourced from 1200 growers with an average of less than one hectare each. Many have supplied fruit to no other company for some generations. Top price is paid when the quality warrants it.

'The challenge for my team every year is to create a higher level of quality and consistency, even at a very high level of production,' Demarville declares. 'Management of the grape supply and ensuring that we get the best grapes is our focus.' Every year, he cancels one or two grower contracts. 'I prefer to stop contracts that do not work with growers who are not doing a great job.'

One famous grower-producer in Ambonnay, who has trouble supplying demand for its own cuvées, and hence wants to keep as much of its fruit as it can, still sells to Veuve Clicquot because the company provides great support and expertise for managing its vineyards. 'Not every house is like this, but Clicquot is very good,' they revealed. Last year, the company created a new association to encourage its young growers.

Clicquot's own vineyards are planted to almost 50% chardonnay – a high proportion in Champagne, particularly for a house in which every cuvée is led by pinot noir. It has strong holdings in

Oger, Le Mesnil-sur-Oger, Vertus and Villers-Marmery. The Montagne de Reims has been the focus for Clicquot historically, and it is the proud custodian of some of the finest sites for pinot noir in Verzy, Verzenay and Bouzy. These form the core of La Grande Dame. 'Our goal is to showcase what we can do in the vineyards,' Demarville reveals. The 2008 La Grande Dame is 95% pinot noir and 2012 will be 90%. The house is also privileged to strong representation in Aÿ, Ville-Dommange and Saint-Thierry.

I was privileged to an inside perspective at Clicquot, shadowing Demarville on four different days during harvest 2014, visiting growers and experiencing his press centre in Verzy and red winemaking facility in Bouzy. 'Most of my job during harvest is to go all over Champagne and taste and smell what is different in every terroir, because every village is different from one year to the next,' he explains. I was astounded by his dedication: over the three weeks of harvest, he visits every one of 300 press centres across Champagne and 15–20% of his vineyards to engage with his growers. 'Motivation, motivation, motivation!' He works long days from 6am every morning and spends 80% of his time in the vineyards, including in the Côte des Bar, where the house sources 15% of its needs. 'I have a dream,' Demarville announces. 'I hope that one day in Champagne we will pay for grapes according to quality, not according to volume and vineyard designation.'

EXEMPLAR OF SUSTAINABILITY

Clicquot is working to enhance quality by reducing use of herbicides, and has planted grasses in the mid-rows of 95% of its vineyards to encourage deeper roots. Of its estate holdings, 200 hectares are certified sustainable, with a goal of 300 hectares in 2020. 'We are changing our view about grape-growing and what we're doing with the growers,' Demarville says. 'We are more aware of what happens in the soil, of how to follow the ripening of the grapes, and we are tasting the grapes more and more during the ripening season. This all helps to increase the quality of our wines.'

Outside of harvest, Demarville spends more than one-third of his year in the vineyards, the part of his job he loves the most. 'Champagne is a wine, and you can't make a good wine without understanding what happens in the vineyards. I believe that in the future, viticulture will make all the difference. Environmentally friendly sustainability will help us to achieve a higher expression of terroir.'

Demarville's goal is to encourage deeper roots to draw out more precise terroir character by implementing an organic approach to the soils, herbicide-free and using only organic fertilisers in all estate and grower vineyards by 2020. 'Not to be organic for the sake of organics, but for the sake of the quality of the soil and the life in the soil, which is crucial in viticulture,' he emphasises. He admits that chemicals are sometimes necessary in protecting against disease and pests. 'I believe the ideal for us for the future is to use organic, chemical and biodynamic philosophies in perfect balance.'

Louis Roederer chef de cave Jean-Baptiste Lécaillon names Veuve Clicquot as the other house that is moving fastest towards organics.

Dominique Demarville

'As far as the vineyards are concerned, Clicquot is doing a very good job,' he observes. As chef de cave of a major house, Demarville considers it his responsibility to be an exemplar for sustainability. He has already achieved his goal of eradicating all herbicides from estate vineyards, and is tackling fungicides for botrytis.

'Mildew and oïdium are the next challenges, and I believe within ten years we will be able to do away with chemical treatments for these also,' he postulates. 'We are pushing our suppliers to follow these trends.'

The house pays bonuses to its sustainable growers and has employed a team of three, dedicated to teaching sustainable practices and helping their growers. 'The first step is sustainable viticulture for all of our growers, and I hope that we can achieve this within 10 years,' Demarville says. 'We are making good progress.'

Veuve Clicquot reported zero botrytis in its own vineyards in the extreme-rot year of 2017, and puts this down to its eradication of herbicides and to planting of grasses in the mid-rows. But Demarville admits that he would have lost 50–70% of his crop by May 2018 if he didn't use chemical fungicides.

EVOLUTIONARY WINEMAKING

'Our terroir is crucial in our approach, and this is why we vinify cru by cru and variety by variety, even though we blend at the end,' Demarville reveals.

Veuve Clicquot has trialled earlier harvesting and other means of retaining acidity. 'In the wake of climate change we must manage not only what happens in the vineyards, but also the winery,' Demarville clarifies. He has traditionally allowed every parcel to complete malolactic fermentation, but since 2007 has

experimented with blocking malolactic in some parcels destined for his reserves and vintage cuvées. 'About 10–15 percent without malolactic fermentation will likely help our wines, without changing the style,' he suggests.

In recent vintages he has blocked malolactic in just one percent of his ferments, but in the warm 2018 he increased this to a record 10 percent, by blocking malolactic in all ferments in his wineries in Verzy and Bouzy. 'Honestly, if I need to do it again, I will,' he declared. 'Having 10 percent without malolactic or even 20 percent will not change the style, but will bring what we need in freshness, especially in years that are very hot.'

This has created a dilemma in maintaining consistency, since malolactic fermentation also contributes texture. The introduction of Demarville's prized foudres in 2007 may prove to be the answer, providing the texture of barrel fermentation and maturation (for one year), without oak flavour, to a house style that has traditionally relied on stainless steel tanks. 'The foudres bring complexity, creaminess and broad shoulders,' he observed at the end of his eleventh vintage with his foudres.

He stepped up the regime in 2012 – a vintage of 'amazing acidity' – by blocking malolactic fermentation in half the foudres. These *vins clairs* looked incredible at just a few months of age, but the real proof came in the launch of the spellbinding 2008 vintage. He added six more foudres in 2017, and the goal is to double the number to 70 within five to six years.

The threat of more extreme vintages in the wake of climate change has also bolstered Demarville's resolve to increase his stocks of reserve wines. 'Look at four recent harvests – 2008 was exceptional, with high acidity and lots of structure; 2009

was ripe, with low acidity; 2010 was dilute, and 2011 was very inconsistent. 'If you don't have sufficient stocks of reserve wines, you can't make great non-vintage champagne,' he points out. On average, Yellow Label Brut Non-Vintage receives 35 percent reserve wines, increasing every year, and the 2017 base boasted 49 percent and the 2012 a phenomenal 55 percent.

'We have been increasing the level of reserve wines to increase both the consistency and the complexity in our blends,' he explains. 'Our style of lots of body, complexity and richness needs a lot of reserve wines.' Clicquot holds the biggest collection of reserve wines in Champagne besides Krug, currently comprised of 17 vintages. These are amazing wines, and at a full 31 years of maturity, a 1988 Cramant was ravishingly concentrated and complex, with allusions of white chocolate yet such insane energy that it could live another decade still. Clicquot holds the equivalent of an entire year of production in 450 different reserve wines, each of which is tasted twice every year, and allocated before it begins to decline. All are held fresh on lees without filtration in stainless steel and concrete vats cooled to 12–13°C.

Demarville points out that it's easier to control and refine wine in stainless steel tanks with temperature control, than under oak without temperature control. 'We are able to be more precise with our blending now, which has enabled us to reduce levels of dosage,' he says. 'We are not reducing dosage due to climate change, but because we have better control in the winery. Over the past 40 years we have been able to build greater purity and precision and so reduce dosage gradually.'

It's a flattering trend for Clicquot, embodied most emphatically in Yellow Label Brut Non-Vintage, which was candied and sweet with 12g/L dosage a decade ago, now much more refreshing at 9–10g/L. Demarville has resisted the 'low-dosage lobby', as he calls it. 'We have a different vision in that the final sensation of sugar is affected not only by quantity, but by time in the cellar after disgorgement. Our vintage wine is released a year after disgorgement, so the impact of the sugar is diminished.'

Dominique deploys 10 percent of premier tailles in his non-vintage cuvées, half from chardonnay and half from red grapes, for 'suppleness, fruitiness, harmony and positive bitterness'.

Rosé is an increasingly important style for Clicquot, having grown from five to eight percent of sales in recent years, with forecasts that this will double (and a strong precedent in Moët & Chandon, which grew rosé from 3 percent to 20 percent in less than 20 years). 'Our demand for rosé has been amazing!' he exclaims. 'It's growing as a category so much faster than white champagne, fuelled by incredible improvements in the style over the past five or six years. It's eight percent of sales today, but in 10 or 20 years it will be 20 percent, for sure!'

Ten hectares of estate pinot noir vines are allocated to red wine production for rosé in Bouzy alone, green harvested to reduce yields by 30–40 percent, and picked at high maturity. Clicquot also sources from 'top' growers in Bouzy and Ambonnay, and in 2012, for the first time, signed a contract with direct suppliers dedicated to red wines, to grow production. The house operates a state-of-the-art winery dedicated to red wine production in Bouzy, Demarville has created a new room for red wine storage in Reims, and a red wine facility was recently constructed in the Aube. When he showed me through his Bouzy facility I was stunned at its pristine cleanliness mid-vintage. Samples of red wine ferments displayed breathtaking violet and rose petal aromatics, culminating in one of the most profound Champagne red wines I've ever tasted. From the earth-shaking Clos Colin parcel on the mid-slope of Bouzy, there is complexity and depth that I have only ever seen in grand cru red Burgundy. It's fittingly reserved for La Grande Dame Rosé.

Until now. In the warm 2018 season, he doubled his production of red wine, and kept 12 barrels of Clos Colin aside as a potential Coteaux Champenois, alongside 15 barrels of an incredibly powerful Coteaux Champenois blanc of 12 degrees natural ripeness.

After much anticipation, I'm delighted Clicquot has introduced QR codes on its Extra Brut Extra Old, Cave Privées and La Grande Dame, revealing blends, crus and dosages. The back labels of these cuvées disclose disgorgement dates. QR codes across the rest of the range provide only the dosage and a rough indication of the blend and the number of crus.

Veuve Clicquot has plans to grow slowly, expecting to outgrow its facilities on Rue des Crayères in Reims within the next few years, and aspiring to ultimately increase capacity from 20 to 30 million bottles. To this end, a massive new €280 million facility commenced production in 2017 on a 44 hectare site on the road from Reims to Châlons, with the hope that it will be ready for vintage 2020. 'If the market is asking for more bottles, we will produce more,' Demarville reveals. 'And it is also a good opportunity for us to improve our logistics and efficiency. We are trialling many things in winemaking today, so we have the answers to design our new facility with new technologies for blending, bottling and disgorging.' The goal is to transfer the full production from the historic site in Reims to the new facility within 10 to 12 years.

The lack of pretence and big-company 'spin' of Dominique Demarville is refreshing in the world of corporate champagne. I greatly respect what this man has achieved in his short time. There are few in Champagne who could seamlessly refine a house as enormous as this. The 2008 base Yellow Label was his first blend, and the finest I have seen.

'It is because 2008 is an amazing year!' Demarville responds with unassuming humility. 'And I am very fortunate to have a talented and passionate team.'

In May 2019, Demarville announced his departure from Veuve Clicquot, to take up the position of chef de cave at Laurent-Perrier, Salon, Delamotte and De Castellane, effective from the beginning of 2020. He is the first of Veuve Clicquot's six chef de caves not to retire in the position. Having already transformed Mumm before Veuve Clicquot, it seems there is yet more to come from this dynamic and talented spirit.

Veuve Clicquot Yellow Label Brut NV $$

91 points • 2014 BASE VINTAGE • 36.7% RESERVES FROM 2013 TO 2004 AND 2002 • DISGORGED NOVEMBER 2017 • TASTED IN AUSTRALIA

92 points • 2013 BASE • RESERVES FROM 2012, 11, 10, 08, 07, 06 AND 02 • TASTED IN AUSTRALIA

28% chardonnay, 52% pinot noir, 20% meunier; 50-60 crus; aged 2.5 years on lees; 9-10g/L dosage; cork; 85% of production, hence some 17 million bottles

It takes Demarville and his team four months of daily tastings to make Yellow Label, tasting some 1100 different base wines and reserves, and selecting 400–500 to make up the final blend. Their expertise is reflected in a gentle trajectory of refinement over recent years, and it's as confident as ever today. This is a release that flies the flag of the Veuve Clicquot style in presenting the bright freshness of pinot noir amidst the depth of deep reserves. In step with Demarville's aspiration, the 2014 base is as lively as I've seen it, leading out with tangy strawberry hull and morello cherries, energised by a focused line of vibrant lemon acidity, closing with the aged complexity of gingernut biscuits, bread and roast almonds. Its full dosage is well subsumed by its bright acid line, holding medium length on the finish. Not only a triumph for its sheer magnitude of production, this is a compellingly crafted cuvée and a fine drink. The 2013 base is even more confident in its pretty, bright red cherries and red plums, well supported by brioche complexity.

Veuve Clicquot Rosé NV $$$

92 points • 2014 BASE VINTAGE • DISGORGED JUNE 2017 • TASTED IN AUSTRALIA

28-33% chardonnay, 50-55% pinot noir, 15-20% meunier; 50-60 crus; 5-6 vintages of reserves; Yellow Label with 13% pinot noir red wine; 10g/L dosage; cork

This is a lesson in just what a difference 12% red wine can make in a blend, particularly in the hands of one of the finest red wine outfits in all of Champagne. In its pretty medium salmon guise, this is an elegant, refined and pretty rosé, in an appealingly fruit-focused style of raspberries, red cherries and strawberries. A reductive overtone lends a note of balsamic complexity. True to the Veuve mandate, pinot noir takes a confident lead in a fleshy and full mid-palate which coasts into a long finish of accurate line. This is a particularly vibrant blend in which lively red fruit presence is the champion, and lees age has contributed more in texture than secondary complexity. Tannins are impeccably handled, leaving energetic acidity to define the structure, uninterrupted by well-integrated dosage, making for another particularly refined and distinguished Clicquot Rosé.

Veuve Clicquot Extra Brut Extra Old 2 NV $$

94 points • TASTED IN CHAMPAGNE

27% chardonnay, 45% pinot noir, 28% meunier; a blend of reserves, comprising 3.5% 2012, 59% 2010, 7% 2009, 18.5% 2008, 2.5% 2006, 1% 1999, 6% 1998 and 1.7% 1990; 20 crus spanning Montagne de Reims, Côte des Bar, Côte des Blancs, Vallée de la Marne, Vallée de l'Ardre and Massif de Saint-Theirry; 3g/L dosage

The official line is that this exciting new cuvée was inspired, first, by Veuve Clicquot's desire to produce its first extra brut (besides Cave Privée) and second, to communicate the philosophy of Yellow Label, from which it draws its components. To me, this cuvée bears a far more profound message, for it is composed exclusively from six vintages of Clicquot's remarkable reserves, and reverberates with their full depth of rumbling complexity and startling energy. 'With this cuvée, I want to show that the reserve wines age on their lees, and also that one percent of a very old wine can make such a difference,' Dominique Demarville declares.

Extra Brut Extra Old Mark II somehow possesses even more complexity than the first (see overleaf), and more freshness, too – astonishing for its age. Dried fruits and spice are layered with the biscuity character of deep, deep age, persisting with great length, drive and glittering, salty minerality.

Veuve Clicquot Extra Brut Extra Old NV $$

93 points • Disgorged June 2017 • Tasted in Champagne and Australia

27% chardonnay, 47% pinot noir, 26% meunier; a blend of reserves comprising 50% 2010, 42% 2009 and 2008, 5% 2006, 2% 1996 and 1% 1998; aged 3 years in tanks and foudres on lees, and 3 years in bottle on lees; bottled November 2013; low pressure of 4.5 atmospheres; 3g/L dosage; cork; small production of less than 1% of Yellow Label, hence fewer than 200,000 bottles

I have been privileged to taste key components from each vintage of this blend, and have been repeatedly stunned by their youthfulness and stamina. Together, they offer the first ever release to showcase the astonishing depth and confidence of Clicquot's reserves. This is a cuvée that unites depth and complexity with tension, albeit without the freshness of young base material. It contrasts layers of apple, pear and red berry fruits with the lemon brightness of chardonnay and all the biscuity, spicy, toasty, almond, walnut and sweet pâtisserie fanfare of a plethora of layers of age. Focused acidity marries with fine salt minerality and a well-gauged bite of phenolic grip to define a long finish of well-engineered confidence. It's a cuvée that will rise confidently in the presence of white-meat protein.

Veuve Clicquot Vintage 2012 $$

93 points • Tasted in Champagne

34% chardonnay, 51% pinot noir, 15% meunier; 11% vinified in oak foudres; 8g/L dosage

Dominique Demarville admires the 2012 season for bringing the full-bodied style that he is looking for in his vintage cuvée, with greater complexity than 2008. He vinified 11 percent in foudres to bring structure to the signature crispness and brightness of the harvest.

Veuve Clicquot's vintage cuvées sing to the melodies of their seasons, and its 66th release plays a much deeper tune than the 2008 before it, while confidently hitting pitch-perfect high notes. It's layered with a panoply of citrus, stone fruits and red berries, to a rich backing track of lees-derived toasted brioche and spice. A subtle note of bitter grip and firm texture in its newly disgorged guise are well massaged by the fine, supple texture of more foudre-fermented components than ever. Long-lingering acidity and fine chalk minerality mark out a finish of excellent line and persistence. This is a vintage to drink while the euphoric soprano of 2008 contemplates its eternal endurance backstage.

Veuve Clicquot Vintage Rosé 2012 $$$

94 points • Tasted in Champagne

34% chardonnay, 51% pinot noir, 15% meunier; Veuve Clicquot Vintage 2012 with 15% red wines from Bouzy; 8g/L dosage in this pre-release sample, and it might be 9g/L in the final release 'to make it more precise'

It's in Clicquot's red wine facilities that I've encountered some of the most transcendental red wines in all of Champagne, visible to the world only through the window of its rosé blends. Fifteen percent Bouzy rouge transforms its Vintage 2012 into a medium salmon crimson hue. The voice of pinot noir speaks with depth and vibrancy, wafting seamlessly with rose petal fragrance and swimming in layers of strawberries, raspberries and red cherries, accented with notes of pink pepper. The true mastery of red winemaking in Champagne is tannin texture, and this wine is a case study in how it's done: so subtly that it does nothing to interrupt the profound, salty chalk minerality of a great season, yet with the confidence to hold a finish of great length and allure. Another impressive vintage in the line of greatest hits of this rosé specialist. Kudos to Dominique Demarville for skipping the dreary 2009, 2010 and 2011 vintages. If only more houses had the same quality imperative.

VEUVE CLICQUOT CAVE PRIVÉE BRUT 1989 $$$$$

95 points • DISGORGED 2010 • TASTED IN CHAMPAGNE EN MAGNUM

33% chardonnay, 67% pinot noir; a blend of 25 grand and premier crus; aged 20 years on lees and 8 on cork; 4g/L dosage; 7000 bottles

Veuve Clicquot has the resourcefulness to set aside a respectable allocation of every vintage release for its late-disgorged Cave Privée, a remarkable collection of 700,000 bottles of a depth and magnitude that must be unmatched in all of Champagne. A bold venture, not least because vintages that don't age well will never surface. Demarville considers 1989 to be one of the best harvests of the last 30 years, with a ripe concentration that sustains it in spite of lower acidity, a combination that he likens to 2018. I've been privileged to taste this cuvée many times over the past six years, and it just began to fade around 2016, but this is the first time I've seen it in magnum, and it predictably holds a poise and confidence that trumps those tiring bottles. A dashingly handsome expression of the secondary development of a rich and powerful season, it brims with glacé fruits, pineapple, persimmon, honey, fruit mince spice, dried nectarine and baked apple. A hint of sweet pipe smoke is a sure sign that tertiary complexity is blossoming. The ripeness of the season lingers in fine phenolic grip, but it is fresh acidity that defines the poise and persistence of a finish that shows no suggestion of tiring any time soon. Ah, magnums!

VEUVE CLICQUOT CAVE PRIVÉE BRUT 1980 $$$$$

94 points • TASTED IN CHAMPAGNE

By no means a famous year in Champagne – so much so that I do not believe I have ever, in fact, tasted it – 1980 was a low-yielding vintage, harvested in October with a high level of acidity. This is a bottle that has stood the test of four decades with confidence, presenting a panorama of fig, baked peach, dried nectarine and spice. A dry and structured finish suggests it's reaching the close of its life, yet it upholds fantastic persistence.

VEUVE CLICQUOT CAVE PRIVÉE ROSÉ 1979 $$$$$

99 points • TASTED IN CHAMPAGNE

33% chardonnay, 61% pinot noir, 6% meunier; a blend of 22 grand and premier crus; 19% red wine from Bouzy; 4g/L dosage; 1700 bottles

The 1979 has proven to be the most enduring vintage of the 1970s, and according to Dominique Demarville, it was a harvest of elegance and finesse, yielding a good volume after the very small 1978. It happened to be privileged to the highest proportion of red wine of any Clicquot vintage (19%). This serves to draw out its Burgundian-like pinot noir personality, even at a dignified 40 years of age. This cuvée has graced every edition of this guide for the past six years, and my most recent encounter resoundingly trumps them all.

If its gorgeous crimson sunburst hue is a testimony to the mesmeric longevity of 1979, then its primary aromas and flavours are nothing short of spellbinding. Wild strawberries and cranberries still abound, remarkably perfumed and fragrant, in the ultimate conjunction of primary, secondary and tertiary. A lifetime of gathered complexity has led it to an enchanting place, wafting with extraordinary fragrance straight from the hallowed depths of great old Burgundy: sweet pipe smoke, smouldering white truffles, *sous bois* and musk. Line and length of undeviating confidence burst through four decades of grand maturity, deeply implanted in impeccably pronounced chalk mineral definition. A legendary showpiece for Veuve Clicquot's fabled mastery with rosé, it's a towering monument to its ability to blossom in grand old age, with no suggestion of crumbling on any side.

Veuve Clicquot La Grande Dame 2008 $$$$

97 points • Disgorged January 2018 • Tasted in Champagne and Australia

8% chardonnay from Le Mesnil-sur-Oger, 92% pinot noir (37% Verzy, 23% Bouzy, 14% Verzenay, 14% Aÿ, 4% Ambonnay); 60–70% estate vineyards; aged 9 years on lees; 6g/L dosage; cork

Dominique Demarville's first vintage leaps forth with 92 percent pinot, the highest proportion in La Grande Dame yet (it's normally more like 60 percent). 'The idea is that it will now always be more than 90 percent,' he reveals. 'Pinot noir is the signature of Veuve Clicquot, and now La Grande Dame really presents the style of the house, as the only prestige cuvée with this level of pinot. This cuvée aims to show the mandate of the house, that pinot noir has a beautiful elegance, finesse and delicacy, yet with creaminess and silkiness.' It lives up to this aspiration with effortless conviction, its evolution inside the bottle matched with a brand-new label.

For such a strong pinot noir presence, its bright, pale straw hue even at 11 years of age is refreshing. The focus and tension of 2008 is built with the body and richness of pinot noir to spectacular effect, uniting the freshness of a core of more than 50 percent Verzy and Verzenay with the intensity of Bouzy and Ambonnay, and the toning restraint of a touch of Le Mesnil chardonnay. This combination tactically builds restraint, crunch and energy in this tense season, screaming out for a long time to tame and calm. Red apple, cranberry and morello cherry fruit meet notes of cracked pepper, lifted with nuances of musk and rose petal, with a whiff of reductive tension quickly dissipating, underlined by complexity of nougat, brioche and wild honey, even a hint of truffle unexpected in such desperate youth. Structurally, it unites all of the enduring potential of its thundering crus with the tension and energy of this legendary season, colliding high-tensile acidity with deep, fine, powdery chalk minerality and just the right level of phenolic bite to bring its finish into stark focus. This is a La Grande Dame that has been intricately engineered by a master for the long-haul, with decades of potential unravelling before it. If you must dip in now, give it plenty of time to uncoil in a large glass. Better to first wait at least a decade.

Veuve Clicquot La Grande Dame 2006 $$$$

96 points • Disgorged February 2016 • Tasted in Australia

47% chardonnay, predominantly from Avize, Oger and Le Mesnil-sur-Oger; 53% pinot noir, largely from Verzy and Verzenay, with a touch of Bouzy, Ambonnay and Aÿ; 8g/L dosage

In response to the generous, rounded, supple 2006 season, Demarville's predecessor, Jacques Péters, increased the share of chardonnay in his final La Grande Dame. Demarville confessed to some nervousness at launching the 2006 after the calibre of the linear and refined 2004. Bookended by the enduring energy of 2004 and 2008, this release certainly stands in stark contrast, and it's the vintage to enjoy while its siblings rest in the cellar. That said, if anything, it's gained in integrity and poise over the two years since its release. Pinot noir has arisen to wonderful effect, showcasing the north-eastern slopes of the Montagne in spicy, peppery tension, heightened by struck-match reduction. A citrus zest liveliness to its acidity continues to uphold its focused, tangy finish, enlivened with fine chalk mineral structure. It propagates with admirable energy, endurance and persistence for its warm season, reinforced in a bright medium-straw radiance. Two of four bottles opened for a dinner were corked.

VEUVE CLICQUOT LA GRANDE DAME BRUT ROSÉ 2008 $$$$$

97 points • DISGORGED MAY 2017 • TASTED IN CHAMPAGNE AND AUSTRALIA

8% chardonnay from Le Mesnil-sur-Oger, 92% pinot noir (37% Verzy, 23% Bouzy, 14% Verzenay, 14% Aÿ, 4% Ambonnay); 60–70% estate vineyards; La Grande Dame with 14% Clos Colin Bouzy pinot noir red wine; aged 8 years on lees; 6g/L dosage; cork

Clicquot's Vintage Rosé's ideal is for the grapes to speak, and La Grande Dame Rosé's mandate is for the soil to speak. And speak it does, like never before in 2008, with an avalanche of tumbling fury of chalk minerality that melds so seamlessly with very fine, impeccably managed tannins that it's impossible to detect where one finishes and the other starts. Clos Colin delivers a red wine of folkloric magnificence, building a medium salmon copper tint. This is a rosé of enormous energy and potential, bolting a grand body of pinot noir lines and curves to a rigid chassis of tremendous endurance. It swoops and dives with the wonderful fragrance of pinot noir in notes of rose hip, pink pepper, granny smith apple, tangy morello cherry, crunchy strawberry hull and fresh pomegranate, true to the perfumed and understated mood of the northern Montagne de Reims. Hints of grilled-toast reductive complexity lead out, underscoring hints of anise. So lively and primary is it that there are no hints of secondary development yet, with just one bottle hinting at but the briefest air of French pâtisserie. The enduring acid line of this great season marks out a finish of high-tensile definition, epitomising the energy and poise of the glorious, bracingly cool slopes of Verzy and Verzenay, playing pinot's most operatic soprano notes, underlined by the heightened, ultra-fine, chalky minerality of six of the most enduring grand crus. A cuvée of great line, length and enduring potential, it's set to go down among the longest-lived rosés of the modern era. Demanding at least another decade to show its full flare, it will reward those with the stamina to wait until at least 2028, and promises to power on for many decades beyond. One bottle was corked.

Oger, summer 2011

VEUVE FOURNY & FILS

(Verv Fawny e Feess)

6/10

5 RUE DU MESNIL 51130 VERTUS
www.champagne-veuve-fourny.com

CHAMPAGNE
Vve FOURNY & FILS
une Famille, un Clos, un Premier Cru

When a tiny plot on pure chalk in the coveted 'Le Mont Ferré' hillsides of the northern end of Vertus towards Le Mesnil-sur-Oger came up for sale in the summer of 2011, offers poured in from big houses, but the grower chose the brothers Emmanuel and Charles-Henry Fourny as its new custodians. The offer was indicative of the respect with which the young fifth-generation growers manage some of the finest terroirs in Vertus. Their location on Rue du Mesnil on the northern edge of Vertus is a clue to their success, creating a style of purity, precision and freshness that captures the more mineral side of the premier cru village from vineyards neighbouring the grand cru of Le Mesnil-sur-Oger itself.

When I first visited just four weeks before the scheduled start of vintage 2011, Rue du Mesnil was completely closed off. Veuve Fourny's winery was totally gutted and swarming with construction workers. Emmanuel Fourny emerged from an early-morning meeting with his builders.

'We are grateful for the cooler weather,' he said, 'because there's no chance our new winery would be ready for an early vintage!'

It was the beginning of a grand new era for a family who has tended vineyards at the southern end of the Côte des Blancs since 1856 and made its own champagne since 1931. Theirs is one of the most expressive champagnes of the character of their beloved village of Vertus.

VINEYARD FOCUS

Veuve Fourny's focus remains resolutely and exclusively on Vertus, apart from a small parcel in Cramant, contributing just 7% of production, and a few plots in Le Mesnil-sur-Oger and Oger recently added to their sourcing, all of which are blended into their non-vintage cuvées. 'I like to express the terroir of Vertus and show that you can have a lot of expression with just one village,' says Emmanuel, who has a self-confessed obsession with purity and precision.

The sunny, south-east-oriented slopes of Vertus are a great part of the Côte des Blancs for Emmanuel to bottle his vision. 'Vertus gives us better expression of fruit than the neighbouring grand crus of Le Mesnil-sur-Oger and Oger,' he explains. 'The chardonnay

Emmanuel Fourny ferments one-quarter of his harvest in small, old oak barrels.

here has more of a pinot noir richness to it, which enables us to create blends exclusively from chardonnay that can be complete.'

The brothers are now harvesting riper than in the past, aiming for 10.4–10.5 degrees potential, completely eliminating the need for chaptalisation since 2014, but increasingly picking on flavour rather than sugar ripeness. In 2015 they started harvest five days after the rest of the village, achieving an average of 10.8 degrees potential, and in 2018 they were the last to harvest, along with Larmandier-Bernier. 'To have real phenolic maturity this year, we had to wait until we hit 11.6 or 11.7 degrees of sugar, and rosé de saignée was 12.8!' exclaimed Emmanuel. 'I am convinced that the riper you pick the grapes, the more pronounced the minerality.'

This is evolving the house style towards the riper, more exotic fruit spectrum of Vertus, resembling notes of ripe oranges, while upholding freshness and mineral focus. 'We used to think that we should not harvest too ripe, so as to keep acidity, but now we see that we can move from ripeness to mineral freshness, which upholds stability.'

The east-facing slopes of the village nurture chardonnay of fresh definition, while its warmer south-facing aspects are among the only vineyards of the Côte des Blancs planted to pinot noir, leading the brothers to dub Vertus 'the paradox of the Côte des Blancs'. They own 8.7 hectares, predominantly on the mineral hillside of 'Le Mont Ferré' on the border of Le Mesnil-sur-Oger, where thin soils bless vines with easy access to chalk, and an east and south-east aspect imparts greater fruit expression and 'strictness' than the more rounded style of south-facing slopes.

They manage a further 3.6 hectares of family vines now owned by their cousins, supplemented with almost eight hectares managed according to an organic philosophy, most of which were originally part of the family estate. The Fournys work closely with their growers, whom they describe as 'small, serious and interested in separation of plots for precision winemaking'. These are mostly young growers and friends, who are invited back to taste their plots after vinification. In all, the brothers manage the vineyards and harvests for a sizeable 60% of the grapes they purchase. A total of 20 hectares provides for an annual production of 200,000 bottles.

Estate vines now average a hefty 45–48 years of age, with some up to 65 years. 'Vines over 30 years transform the minerality of the chalk into the salty minerality of the wine, which we feel is very important,' Emmanuel explains. 'We can compare vines to people: at less than 35 years of age, they have vivacity and tension, and after 35 years, minerality and character are the themes.' The oldest vines are replaced individually, rather than replanting vineyards *en masse*, a very different philosophy to past generations. 'My mother said we had to replant every 20 years, but we keep our vines as long as we can.' To meet increasing demand for rosé (a relatively new venture and already 12–13% of production), the brothers are currently looking to purchase more pinot noir vineyards in Vertus, and are searching for vines planted in the 1950s and 1960s.

Such old vines ensure that yields are very low for Champagne, averaging just 50–56hL/hectare, barely more than half of Champagne's average, 'to produce a balance in our wines'. Green harvests are conducted in high-yielding years like 2004, when 30% of the crop was dropped.

Veuve Fourny balances a resolute commitment to the environment with a realistic awareness of the limitations of viticulture in a climate as marginal as this. Vineyard practice is essentially organic, with the exception of sprays, which are used when necessary. Grasses are cultivated in the mid-rows of one-third of vineyards, another third is cultivated to bare soil, and herbicide has been completely eradicated since 2016. In vineyards too steep to plough, they are currently trialling new technology to burn weeds with steam. Insect breeding is controlled using pheromones, and canopy management is used instead of chemicals to control botrytis. Since 2017, they have worked with a specialist to create their own compost in place of fertiliser.

Phosphonate has been adopted to fight mildew in the vineyards in place of copper sulphate. Certified organic in Germany and Switzerland, the brothers consider this to be better for the vineyards. 'We like the organic philosophy, but we don't want to sacrifice our grapes to mildew,' Emmanuel says, referring to a trial they conducted shortly after returning to the family estate in the mid-1990s. Synthetic chemicals were forsaken in two parcels, but the wild spread of mildew necessitated weekly sprayings with copper sulphate – permitted under biodynamics, despite its toxicity and detrimental effect on the soil and vine growth. Much of the crop was lost and they returned to non-toxic synthetic products at the time.

On the same site as the house on Rue du Mesnil, Clos Faubourg Notre-Dame is a tiny plot of less than one-third of one hectare, believed to be the smallest clos in Champagne. Originally one of four clos of the monks of the Abbaye Notre-Dame in Vertus, it was purchased by the brothers' grandfather in 1931, but it was only in 1993 that Emmanuel and Charles-Henry proposed to their mother that the vineyard be bottled separately, with commercial production commencing in 1996.

With just 40 centimetres of soil before the chalk, they consider it a good plot, 'not better, but different, holding its freshness as a long-ageing style'. Its microclimate is protected by the enclosure. This plot is the source of their flagship cuvée. The brothers' grandmother built a house on part of the clos in 1965, which they removed in 2012 after she passed away. They have replanted this part of the vineyard to chardonnay, though won't use the fruit in this wine until the vines have reached 12 years of age.

MINIMAL-INTERVENTION WINEMAKING

A flexible and intuitive approach in the winery facilitates adaptability according to every vintage and parcel, with malolactic fermentation, barrels, foudres and small tanks deployed selectively to suit. The brothers are excited about the potential of their new winemaking facility to capture greater detail from every parcel. Previously, the press house was in a different location to the winery. Tanks and winemaking equipment that had gradually amassed over the years were not well suited to small-batch winemaking, so they boldly sold it all and created the new winery from scratch. A huge investment for a small company, and all the more impressive with no imperative to increase production.

Charles-Henry was initially sceptical about the outlay, preferring to see the investment poured into more vineyards, but he was impressed with the outcome, enabling them to separate every single parcel for the first time. 'The new winery is completely adaptive to the size of the plots, giving us greater precision in the details,' he said. 'It will help us make a more precise expression of each place, so you can expect our wines to be finer.'

The now 76 plots from which the brothers source are quite distinct, and are kept separate in 72 distinct ferments. They showed me 2012 *vins clairs* that revealed that even parcels just 150 metres apart can show significant diversity. These can now be kept separate for the first time, thanks to a small press that runs 24 hours a day during vintage, and tanks to keep 20 blends, compared with just 12 previously. In 2018, they purchased a new press so as to uphold single-parcel vinification and to permit timely pressing as parcels arrive in increasingly warmer vintages. The hot seasons of 2015, 2017 and 2018 prompted them to plan a new room to cool the grapes on arrival.

Such is the diversity of their plots that Emmanuel quips, 'We need to add another 's' to Vertus! Our village is so large that we cut it into three parts to set three different dates for harvest!' The result is a total of nine cuvées, the largest portfolio in Vertus besides Duval-Leroy, though single-vineyard wines are not the aspiration, with two notable exceptions.

Fourny's philosophy of respect and minimal intervention in the vineyards applies equally in the winery, an insulated building built from stone from northern Burgundy and wood from the nearby Vosges. Glass is utilised to capture natural light, all waste water is recycled on the gardens, and a natural cooling system pulls air in when it's cooler outside.

To preserve purity, only the first pressings are used, and the tailles are sold. Vintage wines are unfiltered, as are non-vintage wines since the 2012 base. Freshness is preserved through cool ferments of 15–16°C. They now use half the sulphur dioxide preservative of the past, but never so low that wines are at risk from oxidation, with wines held on lees for protection. Minimal sulphur is used at harvest, none during vinification, and they are considering adopting jetting to eradicate sulphur addition at disgorgement. To further inhibit oxidation, barrels are topped weekly rather than monthly.

Malolactic fermentation is blocked selectively by chilling to 8°C, so as to maintain tension in each cuvée, with an average of about 80% of parcels completing malolactic, though in the warm 2015 and 2018 seasons, this was decreased to around 65%. Wines are aged on lees with bâtonnage for 6–8 months after primary fermentation, and aged in bottle between 2.5 and 9 years. The purity of the house style permits refreshingly low dosages, and all cuvées are extra brut, never more than 6g/L, dosed with

concentrated grape liqueur (MCR) rather than sugar, 'to preserve the pure expression of the wine'.

Emmanuel learnt the craft of barrel fermentation with bâtonnage in Burgundy, and this has been a key element of the house style since he commenced in 1990. 'I don't like oxidative champagne, so I don't want to be extremist with wood,' he says. The goal is not to impart the taste of wood, but rather to create fresh, focused and textured wines. 'We do not want oak barrels to bring anything to the wine, but to enhance the characters and salty taste of the minerality. Micro-oxygenation in barrels vaccinates the wines against oxidation for the future, thus maintaining freshness and elegance for many years after disgorgement.'

Barrels are purchased from Marc Collin in Burgundy after 3–4 harvests and used for ageing a rich resource of some 200 reserve wines. A preference is given to small, 208-litre barrels to keep small plots separate and provide a balance of surface area and volume. Across the estate, 25% of parcels are fermented in old barrels of now 7–25 years of age, and most cuvées are blended with more citrus-accented parcels from tanks.

Since 2014, a new 4000-litre foudre has been purchased each year for fermenting and storing reserve wines for Grande Reserve NV and Blanc de Blancs NV, with an aim to avoid oxidation and maintain freshness better than small barrels. Reserves are held on lees for complexity and texture.

This thoughtful approach produces wines that display sensitive oak influence, imparting great resilience and long-ageing potential.

Since 2004, all Veuve Fourny wines have been sealed with Mytik DIAM closures. A ten-year trial of DIAM and natural cork revealed DIAM-sealed bottles to be identically consistent and fresh, with pure fruit, while those under natural cork were more evolved, some were oxidised and 'each bottle had its own personality'. The letter of reply when a corked bottle is returned has not been sent out once since the change was made. Emmanuel refers to natural cork as 'Russian roulette' and regards DIAM as a revolution, crucial for upholding the freshness and purity of the house.

Back labels have been updated to feature impressive detail, including disgorgement date, terroirs, *cépage*, vinification, assemblage, dosage and even the type of cork. The website is likewise informative. 'More and more people consider champagne like they do table wine,' Charles-Henry explains. 'Our customers keep champagne in their cellars and need to keep track of it.'

Demand for Veuve Fourny has put supply on allocation in every market. The hope is to increase the bottle age of Grande Réserve and Blanc de Blancs from 2–2.5 years to 3 years, but this will take a decade to achieve, as these cuvées comprise 60% of production.

There is no goal to increase production, for the time being, anyway, even with increased vineyard resources in recent years. 'Our goal is to grow the quality, not the volume, continuing to focus on the vineyards and the winery,' says Emmanuel. 'It depends on whether your goal in life is money or pleasure. My goal is to be able to host tastings and dinners in Japan and Australia and for people to say, "Your wines are wonderful!" That's the goal for me.'

It's a goal the brothers are capably translating into the bottle. The pristine champagnes of Veuve Fourny encapsulate their aspiration of purity, precision and freshness.

VEUVE FOURNY & FILS GRANDE RÉSERVE BRUT PREMIER CRU NV $$

91 points • 2015 BASE VINTAGE • TASTED IN CHAMPAGNE AND AUSTRALIA

80% chardonnay, 20% pinot noir; 90% Vertus, 10% Cramant and Oger; 40% reserves from 2014, 2013 and 2012 with 3-4% solera; 40% aged in small oak barrels on lees; 6g/L dosage; DIAM

The 2015 vintage makes for a particularly bold take on Fourny's Grande Réserve, the dusty, coffee bean, dry-extract grip of this warm season heightened by the small oak maturation of a generous inclusion of reserves. A touch of pinot noir lends harmonious depth and breadth, bringing flesh, body and red apple and strawberry fruit to a focused core of crunchy apple, pear and zesty lemon and grapefruit purity of Vertus chardonnay, with the generosity of orange reflective of ripe fruit in a warm vintage. Oak-aged reserves lend a subtle backdrop of almond meal and spicy complexity, but most of all creaminess to its textural mouthfeel. The pronounced, fine, salty chalk minerality of the Le Mesnil edge of Vertus melds seamlessly with a little phenolic bite on a long finish.

VEUVE FOURNY & FILS BLANC DE BLANCS PREMIER CRU BRUT NV $$

92 points • 2015 BASE • DISGORGED APRIL 2018 • TASTED IN CHAMPAGNE AND AUSTRALIA

100% chardonnay, predominantly from 1950s vines in Fourny's best terroir of Le Mont Ferré in Vertus; 20% 2014, 2013 and 2012 reserves and a little solera; 75% vinified in stainless steel vats, and 25% in small oak barrels on lees; 6g/L dosage; DIAM

This is a cuvée that reaches deep into the mineral hillside of Le Mont Ferré in its elegance and mouth-embracing chalk mineral completeness, thanks to the privileged position of this plot on the border of Le Mesnil-sur-Oger. Fourny's mandate of purity and precision shimmers in a pale straw hue and spicy wild lemon, tangy grapefruit and crunchy apple of soap-powder brightness. There are nuances of fennel and star fruit along the way, true to the expressive, exotic personality of Vertus, lending a little more body and depth in the ripe 2015 season. This vintage possesses some of the dry-extract grip and green capsicum characters of mature phenolics that also marked the 2005 season, appearing subtly on the finish. A little oak vinification coaxes out understated nuances of ginger, biscuits, nougat, even fig, coffee and chocolate, without disturbing purity or drive. A characterful take on the identity of Vertus, and as persistent, reliable and affordable as ever.

VEUVE FOURNY & FILS BLANC DE BLANCS PREMIER CRU BRUT NATURE NV $$

91 points • 2015 BASE VINTAGE • DISGORGED JUNE 2018 • TASTED IN AUSTRALIA

100% chardonnay; 20% reserves from 2014, 2013 and 2012; predominantly from 1950s vines in Fourny's best terroir of Le Mont Ferré with a south orientation, harvested later with higher concentration; 20% aged in small oak barrels on lees; 80% malolactic fermentation; zero added dosage, though residual yields 2.5g/L sweetness; DIAM

The Fourny brothers unite south-facing plots of vines of more than 50 years of age to provide ripeness and concentration that does not call for dosage. An ever heightened precision of viticulture and vinification elevates Veuve Fourny with each passing year, on stark display without the safety net of dosage, and serves to create a compelling Brut Nature, even in the warm and boldly structured vintage of 2015. It upholds the pinpoint lemon juice, grapefruit, crunchy granny smith apple and pear signature of this cuvée, with the exotic notes of mandarin and tangelo of a warm season, bolstered eloquently by the biscuity, spicy complexity of a touch of oak-barrel vinification. Its old-vine-tapped minerality is a revelation, defining a mouthfeel of pronounced and inimitable salt-infused chalk texture that lingers amidst vibrant lemon juice acidity, holding the presence and integrity to balance the phenolic bite and grip of 2015 on the finish, accentuated by malic acidity and zero dosage.

VEUVE FOURNY & FILS ROSÉ PREMIER CRU BRUT NV $$

89 points • 2015 BASE • DISGORGED MARCH 2018 • TASTED IN CHAMPAGNE AND AUSTRALIA

50% chardonnay and 50% pinot noir from different plots predominantly in Vertus; 30% reserves from 2014, 2013 and 2012 aged in oak barrels; 15% pinot noir red wine aged 1 year in barrel on lees; 6g/L dosage; DIAM

Rosés are a relatively new adventure for the Fourny brothers, and already their three new pink cuvées comprise a strong 12–13% of production. Their entry NV is typically a light apéritif style of medium salmon crimson hue, with 50% chardonnay 'for freshness and citrus true to the spirit of the house'. The ripe fruit character and structural presence of the warm 2015 harvest on the south-facing slopes of Vertus has made for a particularly bold release. Filled with red gala apples, crab apples and fennel, it collides the dry-extract grip, bitter phenolic bite and dried coffee bean and tobacco of the season with fine pinot noir tannins, tense, bright acidity and the pronounced salt minerality of the far north of Vertus. The result is an astringent style of structural firmness.

VEUVE FOURNY & FILS MONTS DE VERTUS BLANC DE BLANCS PREMIER CRU EXTRA-BRUT 2012 $$$

95 points • DISGORGED JULY 2017 • TASTED IN CHAMPAGNE AND AUSTRALIA

100% chardonnay; Monts de Vertus lieu-dit near Le Mesnil-sur-Oger, east-facing mid-slope on thin topsoils over pure chalk; estate vines more than 60 years of age; vinified in stainless steel vats; aged 4 years on lees; 3g/L dosage; DIAM

Under the command of old vines, the chalk soils of Le Mont Ferré hark more to the mineral structure of the thundering grand crus to their north than to the more fruity premier crus further south in Vertus, and the strength of strong, salt-infused mineral texture is pronounced. Emmanuel Fourny likens 2012 to 2002 and 2008, and believes it will be better than 2002. Whether this will hold universally is yet to be seen, but it is certain for this little estate, whose progress in its vines and wines over this decade has been striking, and 2012 marked the first great harvest following the construction of its all new winemaking facility.

This cuvée seamlessly unites the vibrant fresh lemon, nectarine, even fig, pear, succulent white peach and crunchy golden delicious apple of ripe fruit from the northern edge of Vertus with the biscuits, vanilla, almond nougat, wild honey and brioche of lees age. The finish evenly, harmoniously and gloriously unites a line of vibrant 2012 acidity with wonderful persistence and that inimitable salt chalk minerality tapped by majestic old vines. Leading out with great presence and concentration, and concluding with energy and drive, this is one of the greatest vintages for Fourny yet.

VEUVE FOURNY & FILS MONTS DE VERTUS BLANC DE BLANCS PREMIER CRU EXTRA-BRUT 2011 $$$

89 points • TASTED IN CHAMPAGNE

As above; aged at least 5 years on lees; 3g/L dosage; DIAM

I don't expect there will be a lot of vintage cuvées unleashed from the harrowing 2011 harvest, marked as it is by the dry, dusty, coarse finish of imperfect fruit. Fourny's attention in the vines and the cuverie has produced a pretty good result under the circumstances, with the generosity of their later-harvest priority producing a fleshy mid-palate that goes some way towards alleviating the dry, earthy, phenolic grip, grainy structure and mushroom notes of the season. Seven years of maturity has built layers of toasty, biscuity, honeyed complexity that carry well on the finish, though a few more years of age since I tasted it last have done nothing to resolve its woes.

VEUVE FOURNY & FILS CUVÉE R BLANC DE BLANCS EXTRA-BRUT VERTUS PREMIER CRU NV $$$.

93 points • 2013 BASE • DISGORGED MARCH 2018 • TASTED IN CHAMPAGNE AND AUSTRALIA
94 points • 2012 BASE VINTAGE • TASTED IN CHAMPAGNE

100% chardonnay; predominantly Vertus lieu-dit Les Barilliers; vines of more than 60 years of age; 50% base vintage (aged 8 months in old oak), and 50% of the previous vintage (aged 18 months in old oak); fully fermented and aged with bâtonnage in small oak barrels of 4-15 years of age; 4 years on lees; 3g/L dosage; DIAM

The honed restraint of Fourny's pristine fruit, meeting the ravishing complexity of old oak, makes for quite a display in the presence of swirling, tossing minerality. Fermentation in old oak barrels amplifies umami, even a hint of seaweed, and bath-salts minerality drawn from thin soils by grand old vines in the north of Vertus near Le Mesnil-sur-Oger. Carefully crafted old oak cranks things up a notch from Fourny's other non-vintage cuvées, with creamy texture and deep, ripe fruit presence of figs, baked apples, just-picked nectarines and blood oranges, underlined by the ginger, honey, coffee, mocha, high-cocoa dark chocolate and roast hazelnuts of barrel work. For all its presence and flesh, it finishes with great tension of vibrant acidity and lemon zest crunch inherent in the bright 2013 and 2012 harvests. This makes for an impressive R of dynamic presence and great energy, sustained confidently by the salty chalk minerality of northern Vertus. The 2012 base marks the first R of 100% chardonnay, a particularly toasty, buttery and generous blend that transcends its 50% inclusion of 2011.

VEUVE FOURNY & FILS ROSÉ VINOTHÈQUE PREMIER CRU EXTRA-BRUT 2011 $$

91 points • TASTED IN CHAMPAGNE

50% pinot noir and 50% chardonnay from Vertus lieux-dits Les Barilliers and Les Gilottes, largely south facing; vines more than 50 years of age; 15% pinot noir red wine; vinified in oak casks; 3–4g/L dosage; DIAM

Fourny's first-release vintage rosé has been kicking around for a couple of years now, and it's evolved to a medium to full salmon hue, while admirably upholding its youthful, pretty red cherry and strawberry fruit, pink pepper and spice. A glorious full, bright salmon hue heralds a complex, spicy and savoury rosé that contrasts the flavour and bitter texture of crab apple with exuberant red fruit exoticism. The result is quintessential northern Vertus, at once refreshing, bright, exuberant and deeply chalk mineral, though it hasn't escaped the dry, dusty, bitter phenolic finish that marks the 2011 harvest. It's elegant and fine, with subtle tannin grip on the finish.

VEUVE FOURNY & FILS ROSÉ VINOTHÈQUE VERTUS PREMIER CRU MV12 EXTRA-BRUT NV $$$

95 points • 2012 BASE • DISGORGED JANUARY 2018 • TASTED IN CHAMPAGNE AND AUSTRALIA

50% chardonnay, 50% pinot noir; predominantly Vertus; 95% 2012 with 5% 2011, 2010 and 2009 reserves; blended pinot noir red wine; largely matured in old oak barrels; 3g/L dosage; DIAM

The brothers Fourny have fast ascended in the world of rosé after a relatively recent start, and MV12 is their crowning glory. A pretty, bright, medium salmon hue heralds an elegant and energetic style. The juxtaposition of elegantly vibrant fruit presence of tangy morello cherries, pretty wild strawberries, oranges and pomegranates with the tension of bright acid cut and pronounced salt minerality is captivating and engaging. Nuances of star anise and sarsaparilla root lend elegant complexity without for a moment disturbing its electric focus and magnificent brightness. Tannins are finely structured and meld confidently with pronounced, fine chalk minerality of articulate expression that dances on a long finish. It carries with outstanding length, energised by a fine line of focused morello cherry acidity. Subtly deployed oak-aged reserves lend a complex backdrop of high-cocoa dark chocolate and coffee. One bottle in Australia was slightly lacking in freshness, more savoury and secondary than in Champagne, showing nuances of fresh tomato.

VEUVE FOURNY & FILS ROSÉ LES ROUGESMONTS EXTRA BRUT PREMIER CRU NV $$$

95 points • 2013 BASE VINTAGE • TASTED IN CHAMPAGNE

100% pinot noir; 100% 2013; single plot Les Rougesmonts, east-facing Vertus, with a dramatic slope of 47 degrees; saignée maceration for 48 hours; vinified in vats (no oak); 3g/L dosage; DIAM

The aspiration here is ripeness with balance and without too much tannin. 'For me, tannin and bubbles is war – you cannot have this combination!' declares Emmanuel. The juice is taken off the skins the moment they feel the sensation of tannin in the mouth. It's released as non-vintage to permit the flexibility to release early if required. 'For us, rosé saignée is better at a young age, to uphold its fruitiness.' Rougesmonts means 'red clay', which sits above pure chalk in this dramatic site. The perfect name for a distinguished rosé.

The result resoundingly and spectacularly fits the aspiration, a pretty and beautifully expressive rosé of medium crimson pink hue. I adored the 2012 and I love the 2013 equally, a gorgeously fragrant thing that celebrates ripe Vertus pinot noir from a slope as extreme as the very Clos des Goisses itself. Rose petals waft over ravishing red cherries, redcurrants and pink pepper of stunning purity. It's all laced together with refreshing acidity, bright and vibrant, underlined by fine, salty chalk mineral texture that melds seamlessly and compellingly with the fine, supple tannins of pinot noir maceration. A characterful wine, true to the expression of a very special place

VEUVE FOURNY & FILS ROSÉ LES MONTS DE VERTUS PREMIER CRU EXTRA BRUT NV

$$$

91 points • 100% 2015 VINTAGE • TASTED IN CHAMPAGNE

100% pinot noir; predominantly Les Rougesmonts (see opposite) blended with Monts de Vertus; 100% 2015; saignée; no oak; DIAM

Relatively new to the rosé game, the Fourny brothers are ever experimenting, and five different rosé cuvées in this Guide are reflective of their journey, though only three are listed in their current portfolio. This one is a blend, because 'we discovered that by blending Monts de Vertus with Rougesmonts, the result was greater than Rougesmonts alone'. It's 100% 2015, but the desire is to release it young, without the mandated three-year lees age requirement for a vintage cuvée.

The warm 2015 season presents a very different mood to the precision of 2013 and 2012 on the dramatic slope of Les Rougesmonts. The colour is stepped up to a full crimson, and the frame is stiffened to a rigid structural grip of tannin tension, reflecting the phenolic grip of the vintage, all the more pronounced without the softening influence of oak or long lees age. Its fruit profile has evolved, too, with red fruits and pomegranate becoming subtly more savoury, hinting at tomato. The pronounced salt minerality of Vertus triumphs on the finish.

VEUVE FOURNY & FILS CLOS FAUBOURG NOTRE-DAME BLANC DE BLANCS EXTRA BRUT VERTUS PREMIER CRU 2009 $$$$

95 points • DISGORGED JANUARY 2018 • TASTED IN CHAMPAGNE AND AUSTRALIA

Clos Faubourg Notre-Dame monopole (see introduction page 555); planted 1951; 0.29 hectares; 100% chardonnay; fully vinified and aged 7 months on lees in oak barrels of 5–6 years of age; full malolactic fermentation; aged 8 years on lees; 3g/L dosage; DIAM; released before 2008, because 2009 is 'more mature, from a sunny year'

Following the legacy of the great 2006, Clos Notre-Dame shines in the warm seasons, lending generosity and approachability to the eternal longevity which the Fourny brothers infuse into their flagship. Upholding a vibrant medium straw hue impressive for this warm season at a decade of age, it reverberates with the full exoticism of Vertus in kiwi fruit, star fruit, fresh fig, ripe peach, glacé orange and preserved lemon. The body and intensity of the Clos is pronounced in its fruits even as young *vins clairs*, and after full fermentation in barrels and a decade in bottle it grows into a wonderfully powerful and exuberant thing of crème brûlée, vanilla and custard. For all of its flamboyance, its pure, prominent, searing acid line is more pronounced and vibrant than ever, drawing out a finish of profound proportions, heightened at every moment by soft, creamy, salivating chalk minerality. Its chalk defines its scaffolding more than its oak support, which furnishes an eloquently supportive backdrop of roast hazelnut, high-cocoa dark chocolate and coffee. The result is a cuvée of effortless integrity that transcends both its season and its little plot in the village, and one of the finest vintages for Clos Notre Dame yet. It's off the scale in amplified proportions by every measure and screams out for time – decades – to mellow.

VEUVE FOURNY & FILS CLOS FAUBOURG NOTRE-DAME BLANC DE BLANCS EXTRA BRUT VERTUS PREMIER CRU 2007 $$$$

94 points • TASTED IN CHAMPAGNE

As above

The energy and tension of Vertus chardonnay in 2007 is elevated to an all new stratosphere in Clos Notre-Dame, in a deeply spicy and buttery cuvée that rumbles with an undercurrent of oak in toasty, nutty personality. The ripe fruit mandate of the house expresses the exoticism of Vertus in spicy blood-orange exuberance. It begs for time for its fruit and oak to find balance, and possesses the enduring acid drive and fine salt mineral structure to go the distance. A cuvée of great length, characterful personality and grand longevity.

VEUVE FOURNY & FILS CLOS FAUBOURG NOTRE-DAME BLANC DE BLANCS EXTRA BRUT VERTUS PREMIER CRU 2000

96 points • TASTED IN CHAMPAGNE

As above

Unleashed on the world at a full decade of age, Clos Notre-Dame demands at least another decade again before it even begins to hit its prime – if not two decades – or three. When I first tasted the 2000 on its release in 2011, I was amazed at such a taut and honed expression of this generous vintage, and I wrote in this Guide at the time that it will 'age long and slow, appreciating the softening effect of time.' Since that time, the prime of life has come and gone for most from this fast-maturing season. Meanwhile, Clos Notre-Dame projects transcendental tension and focus, carrying the full grandeur of the season and honing it with vitality and energy impossible for this vintage. In astonishment, I asked Emmanuel Fourny how he got so much acidity, surely by blocking malolactic fermentation? 'No,' he responded, 'It is the Clos.' Its chalk minerality is all-encompassing, salty, intense and enduring, holding a finish of profound line and length. Clos Notre-Dame is set to go down among the longest-lived wines of the vintage. Children of 2000, reserve this one for your 40th.c

Chardonnay in flower in Villers-Marmery, summer 2016

VILMART & CIE

(Viil-mar e See)

(7/10)

5 RUE DES GRAVIÈRES 51500 RILLY-LA-MONTAGNE
www.champagnevilmart.com

CHAMPAGNE

Vilmart & Cie

Depuis 1890

In the heart of the village of Rilly-la-Montagne, a stained-glass window handcrafted by René Champs hangs proud in the reception room of Vilmart & Cie. In five scenes of vivid colour and geometric intricacy, the hands-on attention to detail of Vilmart is depicted in hand pruning, tilling the soil with a hoe, hand picking, pressing, and vinification in large and small oak barrels. It's a fitting tribute to the champagnes of this lauded grower, which faithfully reflect every element of their painstaking production in seamlessly interlocking detail and slightly larger-than-life colour.

'My philosophy is to make wine first and bubbles and effervescence second,' fifth-generation grower Laurent Champs explains.

On the northern slopes of the Montagne de Reims, the leading grower of Rilly-la-Montagne has set a pace decades ahead of his time, followed by eco-friendly growers everywhere. Painstakingly tended family vineyards, confident but masterful use of oak and an absence of malolactic fermentation make for full and vinous wines that uphold great purity and fine-drawn detail.

The Vilmarts have tended vines in their premier cru village since 1890, and their wines today are sourced exclusively from 11 hectares of family-owned vines in the village and neighbouring Villers-Allerand, spread across just 12 large plots. 'For the area of my vineyards, I should have 90 plots!' he says. Old vines make for low yields, and his estate boasts a majority of vines 40–45 years of age, with an average of 35 years The oldest vines are now 60 years, reserved for Coeur de Cuvée and Blanc de Blancs.

The estate is planted almost exclusively to chardonnay (60%) and pinot noir (37%), with just 3% meunier. 'Vilmart is a paradox with so much chardonnay in a village planted to 80% pinot noir and meunier!' Champs points out. In a village long famous for

its pinot noir, it's Vilmart's chardonnay-led cuvées that shine brightest, thanks to chalk just 40 centimetres below the surface. 'Chardonnay in Rilly-la-Montagne has a good balance between fruitiness, roundness and a minerality more open and less direct than the Côte des Blancs,' he explains.

A pioneer of eco-friendly viticulture, Vilmart's 12 plots have been organic since 1968, with grasses cultivated in mid-rows. 'I try to respect the soil, the environment and the people as much as I can,' he says. Such is the attention to detail here that soils between the rows of vines have been tilled with a hand hoe for five generations, and no chemical fertilisers, herbicides or pesticides are used. 'My father was organic since 1970, but it was too complex, so I try to balance the philosophies of different methods. I am not convinced that one regime is the answer, so I try to adapt to the seasons, which change dramatically here!'

The great-great-grandson of Désiré Vilmart, the founder of the estate, Laurent Champs has carefully refined vinification since his arrival in 1990. 'When I was just 24, my father gave me the keys to the estate, and I have tried to respect his tradition, while aspiring to build precision every year,' he explains. 'My wines have

something to say to you, and hence the winemaking is different to classic winemaking.'

Everything is fed by gravity, and after traditional Coquart pressing and 24 hours settling, all juices are sent straight to oak for fermentation and ageing for 10 months, non-vintage wines in 35–40-year-old foudres of 2200–5000 litres (for micro-oxygenation without oak flavour), and vintage wines in 225-litre Burgundy barrels and 600-litre demi-muids.

Barrels are purchased from Meursault after just one use, and recycled until they are six years old. 'Fifteen years ago we were treated like dinosaurs for using barrels, but now it is very trendy in Champagne!' says Champs. Malolactic fermentation is completely blocked in all cuvées.

Of champagne's practitioners who make full use of oak without malolactic fermentation, the wines of Laurent Champs are among the most seamless and well integrated. 'Wood is a good servant, but a bad master!' he points out. 'It is only there to draw out the flavours of the vintage. I like wines of creamy softness, silky, yet still fresh.' His wines meet this aspiration with resounding precision. These are cuvées of freshness, elegance and richness, articulating the salty minerality of the northern Montagne with unusual clarity, while utilising the creamy texture of oak fermentation to integrate malic acidity, blessing young cuvées with a harmonious approachability while upholding ageworthy endurance.

In 2018, Champs' daughter Morgane joined him, the fifth generation to carry on the legacy of this lauded estate.

Their cuvées are set off with stunning labels, and disgorgement dates and blends are printed on the back of every bottle. The website features technical sheets for each cuvée.

VILMART & CIE GRANDE RÉSERVE BRUT PREMIER CRU NV $$

93 points • 2015 BASE VINTAGE • DISGORGED JUNE 2017 • TASTED IN AUSTRALIA

30% chardonnay, 70% pinot noir; Rilly-la-Montagne and Villers-Allerand; 2014 reserves; fermented and aged 10 months in large oak foudres; no malolactic fermentation; 9g/L dosage

Grand Réserve and Rubis are Vilmart's only cuvées led by pinot noir, and they never hit quite the high notes of the other cuvées. That said, this is the best Grande Réserve in five years, a well-crafted, harmonious and seamless cuvée of layered complexity of yellow fruits of all kinds. Excellent tension of grapefruit and lemon contrasts with the ripeness of spicy white peach. Large oak-foudre fermentation integrates the tension of malic acidity and the prominent chalk minerality of the northern slopes of the Montagne de Reims with the wonderfully creamy texture and toasty, spicy expansiveness of old oak. It's a compelling accord, concluding with definition and freshness.

VILMART & CIE COEUR DE CUVÉE PREMIER CRU 2010 $$$$

95 points • DISGORGED DECEMBER 2016 • TASTED IN AUSTRALIA

80% chardonnay, 20% pinot; from Vilmart's oldest vines of 60 years of age, yielding under 45hL/hectare, less than half of Champagne's average; only the heart of the pressing, 1400L, instead of 2050L; fermented and matured 10 months in 228L barriques of 1–4 years of age; no malolactic fermentation; aged 6 years on lees; 7g/L dosage

'From the heart of the vines, the heart of the press and the heart of the maker,' says Laurent Champs of his Coeur de Cuvée. From his best plots on the Montagne de Reims, with south-south-east exposure on the most exposed chalk, he obtains the highest maturity. 'And hence we are pushing the winemaking more.' Taking just the heart of the cuvée, 1400 litres, rather than the permitted 2050 litres, yields juice of increased concentration and expression.

A wonderfully spicy cuvée that unites tension with power, this is a masterful testimony to Laurent Champs' wizardry, and a terrific result for a season he describes as 'not an easy vintage'. The complexity and presence here are pronounced, packed with golden fruit cake, fig, dried fruits and spice. Such exuberance is drawn decisively yet effortlessly by the honed precision of malic acidity, at once tense, yet impeccably ripe and never for a moment austere. Its persistence is a marvel, drawn out long and even by fine chalk minerality and that delightful acidity. Season in, season out, the consistency that Champs upholds with this cuvée is something to behold, and I have greatly admired every release for the past decade. That he can maintain his own lofty benchmark even in 2010 is a mighty achievement indeed.

VILMART & CIE GRAND CELLIER BRUT PREMIER CRU NV $$$

95 points • 2014 BASE VINTAGE • DISGORGED DECEMBER 2016 • TASTED IN AUSTRALIA

70% chardonnay, 30% pinot noir; 2013 and 2012 reserves; fermented and aged 10 months in large oak foudres; no malolactic fermentation; 8g/L dosage

Laurent Champs describes Grand Cellier as 'audacious and elegant', expressive of the fresh citrus notes and saltiness of Rilly chardonnay. It rises magnificently to the expectation, confidently chardonnay-led in its stunning brightness of white citrus and depth of ripe white peach. Champs is a master of marrying pristine fruit, enduring malic acid drive, soothing oak texture and the salty chalk minerality of Rilly-la-Montagne, and this release is a shining exemplar of his skill. A delightfully even and gracious finish lingers long and true, laced with nuances of vanilla and spice.

VILMART & CIE GRAND CELLIER D'OR BRUT PREMIER CRU 2012 $$$$

94 points • DISGORGED NOVEMBER 2016 • TASTED IN AUSTRALIA

80% chardonnay, 20% pinot noir; fermented and aged 10 months in 228-litre barriques of 4–6 years of age; no malolactic fermentation; aged 3.5 years on lees; 7g/L dosage

Laurent Champs unites two vineyards in Grand Cellier d'Or, with chalk just 25 centimetres from the surface, tapped by the deep roots of 50-year-old vines. He describes 2012 as a very ripe vintage in Rilly-la-Montagne. The result is a powerful cuvée of grand cru white Burgundian magnitude, finding tension and balance thanks to well-integrated, ripe malic acidity. In spite of its considerable proportions, it strikes masterful seamlessness, with intense grapefruit and white peach uniting with all the toasty, spicy complexity of barrel fermentation, finding cunning balance on a long finish.

Rilly-la-Montagne, winter 2013

VILMART & CIE CUVÉE RUBIS PREMIER CRU BRUT NV $$$$

94 points • 2014 BASE VINTAGE • DISGORGED DECEMBER 2016 • TASTED IN AUSTRALIA

10% chardonnay, 90% pinot noir; 13-14% red wine; 2013 reserves; fermented and aged 10 months in large oak foudres; red wines aged in 600-litre demi-muids; no malolactic fermentation; 9g/L dosage

Rubis has classically represented a savoury and structured take on northern Montagne pinot, but Laurent Champs has refined it into a magnificently elegant style, and never has it looked more graceful. A pretty medium salmon hue heralds a delightfully expressive and characterful rosé of pristine wild strawberry and red cherry fruit. The deep roots of old vines embedded in pure chalk lay out a spectacular backdrop of fine sea salt minerality. Malic acidity is tactically played to create brightness and tension, driving a grand finale of undeterred persistence and exacting line.

VILMART & CIE GRAND CELLIER RUBIS PREMIER CRU BRUT 2011 $$$$

93 points • DISGORGED APRIL 2016 • TASTED IN AUSTRALIA

40% chardonnay, 60% pinot noir; 45-year-old vines; 60% pinot noir saignée maceration blended with chardonnay just before bottling; fermented and aged 10 months in 228L barriques; no malolactic fermentation; 8g/L dosage

Stating diplomatically that '2011 was not a very famous vintage', Laurent Champs made the astute call to harvest six days later than others in his village, tactically dodging the underripeness that marks this harrowing season, yielding the fruitiness he was looking for in his pinot noir saignée, which he blended with chardonnay for 'elegance, expression and to moderate pinot's fruitiness'.

Champs' decision to pick late saved the harvest, providing a presence of fruit to moderate the structural tension of the season, making for an impressive 2011. With a pretty medium salmon copper hue, this is a powerfully toasty, nutty and creamy style of roast peanuts and spice, with a core of ripe strawberry fruit underscored by a finely structured tannin profile.

Yvonne Seier Christensen

(Ee-von Zay-er Cri-sten-sehn)

lescinqfilles.com

C H A M P A G N E
YVONNE SEIER CHRISTENSEN

V

Les Cinq Filles

Swiss entrepreneur Yvonne Christensen has recently established her own virtual champagne brand Les Cinq Fils, calling on friends from across the region to each create one of a portfolio of five cuvées. The house is officially registered as a 'Marque d' Acheteur' (buyer's own brand), though she emphasises that this is not simply a brand that buys finished wines, as she upholds personal involvement in the winemaking decisions, from purchasing of the juice after the harvest, to blending and disgorgement. Aspirations of luxury and a price tag to match are more than ambitious for a virtual brand, but the first two cuvées to be released are sound, and certainly demonstrate that there is some potential in this model, albeit naturally dependent upon quality fruit in the right hands. The house unfortunately does not wish to communicate the winemakers, but these are easily ascertained from the fine print on the label 'Elaboré par...' as the récoltants of JM Labruyère in Verzenay, and the famous biodynamic family of Fleury in Couteron in the Aube, though there is a suggestion that these might change for future releases. There is clearly some impressive fruit in play here, and some skill in the way these cuvées have been assembled, albeit made to a brief that would be improved with some relaxation (particularly in regard to low dosage). Nonetheless, a promising result for a first release, with the potential for some refinement in future, assuming continuity of fruit sources and makers can be secured. Christensen is currently awaiting planning permission to build her own winery and hopes to take on more of the winemaking process.

Yvonne Seier Christensen V Les Cinq Filles Blanc de Blancs Grand Cru Zéro Dosage NV $$$$

91 points • 2009 BASE VINTAGE • DISGORGED JUNE 2018 • TASTED IN AUSTRALIA

100% Verzenay chardonnay; made by JM Labruyère; full malolactic fermentation; zero dosage; cork

Blanc de blancs is unusual in Verzenay, but récoltant JM Labruyère who makes this cuvée includes 30% chardonnay in his own blends and also elaborates his own blanc de blancs. True to the ripe 2009 season and the mood of this pinot noir cru, this is a particularly structured blanc de blancs of full straw hue. It's a tense and bony style of beurre bosc pear and lemon fruit, lacking in aroma and flesh (which a little dosage would have gone a long way in lifting). Eight years on lees has built subtle almond meal complexity and enhanced palate texture. The fine salt minerality of Verzenay is prominent, meeting fresh, lemony acidity and grainy phenolic grip on a dry and tense finish. A cuvée of character and definition, well assembled from noble fruit, though it's not for the uninitiated.

Yvonne Seier Christensen V Les Cinq Filles Rosé Extra Brut Biodynamic NV $$$$

90 points • 2012 base vintage • Disgorged November 2018 • Tasted in Australia

100% Aube pinot noir; lieu-dit Valverot in Courteron; 28-year-old biodynamic vines; saignée, made by Fleury; fermented in stainless steel tanks; full malolactic fermentation; aged 5 years on lees; 3g/L dosage; cork

Yvonne Christensen has astutely called upon the saignée experts of the Fleurys in Couteron to craft this cuvée. With a full crimson hue, this is a bold and flamboyant rosé, brimming with cracked pink pepper, watermelon, poached strawberries, fresh raspberries and a hint of Campari. The juiciness of Aube pinot noir, the vibrant acidity of 2012 and the firm grip of fine tannin structure collide in full force, making for an exuberant style of sufficiently confident scale to tame cuisine of even Peking-duck proportions. For its vivacious start, its fruit dissipates rapidly on the finish, disappearing in a cage of fine tannins.

Verzenay, summer 2018

Montaigu Lodge, Chouilly, harvest 2014

EPILOGUE

BEAUTY

Of all the mysteries of wine, it is its ability to articulate the subtleties of the place that gave it birth that I find most enchanting of all. The challenge of unravelling the most complex wine style in the world is my greatest thrill, and it is my hope and wish that you have caught a glimpse of the stories of the places, seasons, processes and people that make every bottle of champagne sparkle like no other.

If a champagne's ability to reflect its place and time is remarkable, the possibility of capturing the very personality and even the mood of its maker is truly astonishing.

In the ancient cellars of Louis Roederer deep under Reims, chef de cave Jean-Baptiste Lécaillon often reflects on the slow passage of time and how it has shaped Champagne into what it has become today. 'I have read all the archives of the house on every vintage since 1832,' he shares. 'You can only create a vision for the future if you dig deep into your roots. Only when you know where you have come from can you build something.'

His oenothèque is a living memory of that history, preserving the story of every season for time immemorial. 'You can taste history, and really see what happened,' he says. 'The wines tell the stories of the years and what people were thinking when they made them.

'Why was 1947 the vintage of the century in Champagne? And why were 1945, 1949 and 1952 so great? Why so many top vintages in the forties and fifties? Two possibilities. Perhaps the climate, warming due to carbon dioxide from the war? But maybe, more importantly, the people who made those wines made them with lots of joy. It was post-war and they were happy to have the opportunity to reconstruct. The Second World War was so horrible in Champagne, so human nature tried to compensate with a wish to make life beautiful. It was the same for the First World War in 1914 and 1921. I think that is why those wines are so beautiful.'

Champagne is born of strife. Rooted in austere, stark white stone and grappling for survival in the most harrowing wine-growing climate on the planet, champagne is the toughest wine on earth to grow. It is the most complex, time-consuming and costly of all beverages to create, fashioned by resilient survivors and raised in ancient cellars that provided refuge through wars over two millennia. Yet in the ultimate juxtaposition, champagne transcends cultures and creeds as the universal, uncontested symbol of celebration, of hope, of unity and of peace.

After two decades in wine, the past 10 years have embedded me ever deeper in the enthralling world that is Champagne. I return multiple times every year on my own and during harvest with my little tour groups, and every word and picture in this book bears testimony to my deepening relationship with the region and its people. It's no accident that this book is more than double the size of every edition before it, now almost the length of five novels.

But for me, sharing champagne must be more than just words on a page. My annual Taste Champagne events are now in three countries, and every week of the year I am honoured to host tastings and dinners to share the stories of the greatest beverage on earth.

Australia is about as far from Champagne as it is possible to live, and I make it my aspiration not only to get under the surface of the region itself, but to embed myself in the wider place of champagne across the vast and volatile world of wine. My annual free downloads on the state of play of champagne present detailed trawls through the performance and trends of champagne in the key markets of the world.

Compiling this edition is more than just an assemblage of hundreds of visits and thousands of tastings over the past two years. For each chapter and house, I reflect back on everything I have written in the past five editions. It is quite astonishing just how far Champagne has progressed in the nine years, since my first Champagne Guide.

In a quiet moment of reflection after completing this book, I am left with a deep sense of admiration for where Champagne has come in recent years and tremendous anticipation for where it is heading. There will always be much work still to be done, but I am convinced that for the first time in decades the region is finally headed on the right track. There is a sense of unity among its key players, large and small, defined by a practical sense of purpose and resolve in the vines, the wines and the marketing like I have never seen in Champagne. Even in these volatile days of climatic, economic and political upheaval, I have a new and ever rising sensation that the champagnes we will be drinking in 10 years and 20 years will be even greater than they are today.

'We know that the wines we are making today will drink in 60 years time,' reflects Lécaillon. 'We know that the wines will survive us.'

One day his successors will discover his creations in the oenothèque and contemplate the world that gave them birth, and what joy and what beauty brought them to life. Santé!

INDEX

RISE TO THE TOP

Champagnes tasted but not reviewed in the Guide are featured without page numbers.

Back-vintage champagnes not currently available are listed without indication of price.

The Champagne Guide Master Index of all cuvées in all six editions to date is a free download from www.TysonStelzer.com

Art in the cellar of Perrier-Jouët, deep under Épernay.

Pol Roger Cuvée Sir Winston Churchill 1998, 490
Ruinart Dom Ruinart Blanc de Blancs Brut 2004, $$$$$, 509
Taittinger Comtes de Champagne Grand Crus Blanc de Blancs 2007, $$$$, 520

97 POINTS

Billecart-Salmon Cuvée Elisabeth Salmon Brut Rosé 2007, $$$$$, 133
Billecart-Salmon Vintage 2008, $$$, 132
Bollinger La Grande Année Brut 2007, $$$$, 146
Bollinger R.D. Extra Brut 2004, $$$$$, 147
Charles Heidsieck Millésime Vintage Rosé 2006, 177
Deutz Amour de Deutz Brut Millésime 2009, $$$$, 203
Deutz Amour de Deutz Rosé Millésime Brut 2009, $$$$, 203
Deutz Hommage à William Deutz La Côte Glacière Pinot Noir Parcelle D'Aÿ Brut 2012, $$$$, 204
Deutz Hommage à William Deutz Parcelles d'Aÿ Brut 2010, $$$$, 204
Dom Pérignon P2 Rosé Brut 1996, $$$$$, 221
Dom Pérignon Vintage Brut 2008, $$$$, 216
Dom Pérignon Vintage Brut 2004, 217
Duval-Leroy Femme de Champagne NV, $$$$, 236
Egly-Ouriet Brut Grand Cru Millésime 2009, $$$$, 241
Egly-Ouriet Brut Rosé Grand Cru NV, $$$$, 240
Egly-Ouriet Coteaux Champenois Ambaonnay Rouge Cuvée des Grands Côtes 2015, $$$$, 242
Jacquesson Dizy Corne Bautray Extra Brut Recolte 2008, $$$$$, 312
Jacquesson Vauzelle Terme Recolte 2008, $$$$$, 311
Krug Grande Cuvée 158ème Édition Brut NV, 329
Krug Grande Cuvée 163ème Édition Brut NV, 329
Krug Grande Cuvée 166ème Édition Brut NV, $$$$$, 328
Krug Rosé 22ème Édition Brut NV, $$$$$, 329
Louis Roederer Brut Vintage 1988, 389
Louis Roederer Cristal Rosé 2009, $$$$$, 396
Louis Roederer Cristal Rosé 2002, $$$$$, 397
Pierre Péters Les Chétillons Cuvée Special Blanc de Blancs Brut 2012, $$$$, 475
Salon 'S' Le Mesnil Blanc de Blancs Brut 1997, $$$$$, 513
Taittinger Comtes de Champagne Blanc de Blancs 2006, $$$$, 520
Veuve Clicquot La Grande Dame 2008, $$$$, 551
Veuve Clicquot La Grande Dame Brut Rosé 2008, $$$$$, 552

96 POINTS

Agrapart & Fils Mineral Blanc de Blancs Extra Brut 2012, $$$$, 84
André Clouet Le Clos 2008, $$$$$, 96
Billecart-Salmon Blanc de Blancs Grand Cru Brut NV, $$$, 131
Billecart-Salmon Cuvée Louis Blanc de Blancs Brut 2006, $$$$$, 133
Bollinger La Grande Année Brut 2005, $$$$, 146
Bollinger La Grande Année Rosé 2007, $$$$, 146
Bollinger Rosé Brut NV, $$$, 145
Bollinger Special Cuvée Brut NV, $$, 144
Bollinger Vieilles Vignes Françaises Blanc de Noirs 2010, $$$$$, 149
Bruno Paillard Assemblage Brut 2008, $$$$, 158
Camille Savès Grand Cru Cuvée Prestige Bouzy NV, $$, 160

Charles Heidsieck Blanc des Millénaires 1983, 179
Charles Heidsieck Brut Réserve NV, $$$, 175
Charles Heidsieck Rosé Réserve NV, $$$$, 175
De Sousa Cuvée des Caudalies Grand Cru Millésime Extra Brut 2008, $$$$$, 190
Deutz Brut Millésimé 2013, $$, 201
Deutz Brut Rosé Millésimé 2013, $$, 202
Deutz Cuvée William Deutz Brut Millésime 2009, $$$$, 202
Deutz Cuvée William Deutz Brut Millésime 2007, $$$$, 203
Diebolt-Vallois Blanc de Blancs Prestige NV, $$, 210
Diebolt-Vallois Fleur de Passion 2010, $$$$, 211
Dom Pérignon P2 Brut 2000, $$$$$, 218
Dom Pérignon Rosé Brut 2006, $$$$$, 220
Dom Pérignon Rosé Brut 2003, $$$$, 220
Egly-Ouriet Brut Grand Cru Millésime 2007, $$$$, 242
Egly-Ouriet Brut Tradition Grand Cru NV, $$$$, 239
Egly-Ouriet Grand Cru Extra Brut VP Vieillissement Prolongé NV, $$$$, 240
Eric Rodez Cuvée des Grands Vintages Ambonnay Grand Cru Brut NV, $$$, 249
Eric Rodez Les Beurys & Les Secs Ambonnay Pinot Noir 2008, $$$$, 250
Eric Rodez Les Fournettes Ambonnay Pinot Noir 2009, $$$$, 250
Franck Bonville 1976, 256
Gosset Celebris Vintage Extra Brut 2007, $$$$, 278
Henriot Millésime 2008, $$$$, 290
J. Lassalle Special Club Premier Cru Brut Rosé 2012, $$$$$, 295
Jacquesson Avize Champ Cain Extra Brut Recolte 2008, $$$$$, 312
Lanson Gold Label Brut Vintage 2008, $$, 352
Larmandier-Bernier Vieille Vigne du Levant Grand Cru 2008, $$$$, 359
Laurent-Perrier Grand Siècle NV, $$$$, 366
Louis Roederer Blanc de Blancs 1998, 390
Louis Roederer Brut Vintage 2008, $$$, 388
Louis Roederer Cristal 2009, $$$$$, 393
Louis Roederer Cristal 1993, 395
Louis Roederer Rosé 2013, $$$$, 391
Louis Roederer Rosé 1996, 392
Mailly Grand Cru Exception Blanche Blanc de Blancs 2007, $$$$, 401
Marc Hébrart Mes Favorites Vieilles Vignes NV, $$, 404
Perrier-Jouët Belle Epoque 2008, $$$$, 447
Philipponnat 1522 Grand Cru Extra-Brut 2008, $$$, 457
Philipponnat Clos de Goisses Juste Rosé Extra Brut 2007, $$$$$, 458
Philipponnat Grand Blanc Extra Brut 2008, $$$, 456
Pierre Gimonnet & Fils Special Club Chouilly Grand Cru 2012, $$$$, 465
Pierre Gimonnet & Fils Special Club Grands Terroirs de Chardonnay 2012, $$$, 464
Pierre Péters Blanc de Blancs Grand Cru Brut Millésime L'Esprit de 2012, $$$, 475
Pierre Péters Blanc de Blancs Grand Cru Extra Brut NV, $$, 473
Pierre Péters Heritage Pierre Péters Blanc de Blancs Grand Cru NV, $$$$$, 478
Pierre Péters L'Etonnant Monsieur Victor Edition MK.12, $$$$$, 477

Pierre Péters Montjolys Cuvée Spéciale Blanc de Blancs Brut 2012, $$$$$, 477
Pol Roger Blanc de Blancs Brut 2012, $$$$, 488
Pol Roger Cuvée Sir Winston Churchill 2006, $$$$$, 490
Ruinart Dom Ruinart Blanc de Blancs Brut 2007, $$$$$, 509
Salon 'S' Le Mesnil Blanc de Blancs Brut 2007, $$$$$, 513
Salon 'S' Le Mesnil Blanc de Blancs Brut 2006, $$$$$, 513
Taittinger Comtes de Champagne Blanc de Blancs 2005, $$$$, 521
Veuve Clicquot La Grande Dame 2006, 551
Veuve Fourny & Fils Clos Faubourg Notre-Dame Blanc de Blancs Extra Brut Vertus Premier Cru 2000, 561

95 POINTS

Agrapart & Fils Terroirs Grand Cru Blanc de Blancs Extra Brut NV, $$$, 84
Alfred Gratien Brut Rosé NV, $$, 90
Alfred Gratien Cuvée Paradis Brut Rosé 2007, $$$$, 92
Alfred Gratien 1975, 92
André Clouet Dream Collection Vintage 2008, $$$, 96
André Clouet Versailles Diamant Coteaux Champenois 2015, 96
Bérêche & Fils Le Cran Ludes Premier Cru 2010, $$$$, 120
Billecart-Salmon Brut Réserve NV, $$, 130
Billecart-Salmon Cuvée Nicolas François Brut 2006, $$$$$, 134
Billecart-Salmon Rosé Brut NV, $$$, 132
Billecart-Salmon Vintage 2007, $$$, 133
Billecart-Salmon Le Clos Saint-Hilaire Brut 1999, $$$$$, 135
Bruno Paillard Blanc de Blancs Grand Cru NV, $$$, 157
Bruno Paillard N.P.U. NEC Plus Ultra 2002, $$$$$, 158
Camille Savès Cuvée Anaïs Jolicoeur Brut Grand Cru Bouzy 2012, $$$$, 162
Charles Heidsieck Blanc de Blancs NV, $$$, 176
Charles Heidsieck Millésime Vintage Brut 2006, $$$$, 176
Charles Heidsieck Mis en Cave 1990 NV, 179
De Sousa Cuvée des Caudalies Brut Rosé NV, $$$$, 190
De Sousa Cuvée Umami Grand Cru 2009, $$$$, 189
De Sousa Grand Cru Réserve Brut Blanc de Blancs NV, $$, 188
Dehours & Fils La Croix Joly Lieu-dit Extra Brut 2009, $$$$
Delamotte Blanc de Blancs 2008, $$$$, 193
Delamotte Collection Blanc de Blancs 1999, $$$$$, 193
Deutz Blanc de Blancs Brut 2013, $$$, 200
Deutz Brut Millésimé 2012, $$, 201
Devaux D Millésimé 2008, $$$, 208
Dom Pérignon Rosé Brut 2005, $$$$$, 220
Dom Pérignon Vintage Brut 2006, $$$$, 217
Dumangin J Fils Le Vintage Extra-Brut 2004, $$$, 225
Egly-Ouriet Les Vignes de Vrigny Premier Cru Brut NV, $$$, 239
Gaston Chiquet Or Premier Cru Brut 2008, $$$, 264
Gosset Celebris Rosé 2007, $$$$$, 278

Pierre Péters Blanc de Blancs Grand Cru Brut
    Millésime L'Esprit de 2013, $$$, 475
Pierre Péters Les Chétillons Cuvée Special Blanc
    de Blancs Brut 2011, $$$$, 476
Pierre Péters L'Étonnant Monsieur Victor
    Edition Mk 10 , $$$$$, 478
Pierre Péters Réserve Oubliée Blanc de Blancs
    Brut Grand Cru NV, $$$$, 474
Piper-Heidsieck Essentiel Blanc de Blancs NV,
    $$, 482
Pol Roger Brut Réserve NV, $$, 486
Pol Roger Rosé Brut 2009, $$$$, 489
Pol Roger Vintage Brut 2009, $$$, 488
Robert Moncuit Les Grands Blancs Extra Brut
    NV, $$, 500
Robert Moncuit Réserve Perpetuelle Blanc de
    Blancs Extra Brut NV, $$, 500
Roger Brun Grand Cru Cuvée Des Sires
    Millésime 2013, $$$, 503
Tarlant Zero Brut Nature NV, $$, 525
Vazart-Coquart et Fils 82/13 Blanc de Blancs
    Grand Cru Extra Brut NV, $$$$, 543
Vazart-Coquart et Fils Extra Brut Blanc de
    Blancs Chouilly Grand Cru NV, $$, 541
Vazart-Coquart et Fils Grand Bouquet Blanc de
    Blancs Chouilly Brut 2012, $$, 542
Vazart-Coquart et Fils Special Club Brut Blanc
    de Blancs Chouilly Grand Cru 2010, $$$, 542
Veuve Clicquot Cave Privée Brut 1980, $$$$$, 550
Veuve Clicquot Extra Brut Extra Old 2 NV, $$, 548
Veuve Clicquot Vintage Rosé 2012, $$$, 549
Veuve Fourny & Fils Clos Faubourg Notre-Dame
    Blanc de Blancs Extra Brut Vertus Premier
    Cru 2007, $$$$, 560
Veuve Fourny & Fils Cuvée R Blanc de Blancs
    Extra Brut Vertus Premier Cru NV, $$$, 558
Vilmart & Cie Cuvée Rubis Premier Cru Brut
    NV, $$$$, 565
Vilmart & Cie Grand Cellier d'Or Brut Premier
    Cru 2012, $$$$, 564

93 POINTS
Alfred Gratien Brut NV, $$, 90
Alfred Gratien Cuvée Paradis 2009, $$$$, 91
André Clouet Dream Collection Vintage 2009,
    $$$, 95
André Clouet Versailles Ruby Coteaux
    Champenois 2015, 96
André Clouet 1994, 96
André Heucq Héritage Millésime 2012, $$$, 100
Apollonis Monodie Meunier Vieilles Vignes
    Extra Brut 2008, $$, 102
AR Lenoble Les Aventures Grand Cru Blanc de
    Blancs Chouilly NV, $$$$, 106
AR Lenoble Premier Cru Blanc de Noirs Bisseuil
    Vintage 2012, $$$$, 106
Armand de Brignac Blanc de Noirs Assemblage
    One NV, $$$$$, 109
Ayala Blanc de Blancs 2010, $$$, 112
Ayala Cuvée Perle d'Ayala Brut Millésime 2006,
    $$$$, 112
Bérêche & Fils Campania Remensis Rosé 2014,
    $$$, 120
Bérêche & Fils Rilly-La-Montagne 2014, $$$$, 120
Billecart-Salmon Extra Brut NV, $$, 130
Boizel Grand Vintage 2008, $$$, 138
Boizel Joyau de France Rosé 2007, $$$$, 138
Bruno Paillard Blanc de Blancs Extra Brut 2006,
    $$$$, 158
Bruno Paillard Rosé Première Cuvée NV, $$$, 157

Camille Savès Grand Cru Bouzy 2011, $$$, 162
Cattier Clos du Moulin Brut Premier Cru NV,
    $$$$, 168
Charles Heidsieck Millésime Vintage Brut 2005, 177
Comtes de Dampierre Family Réserve Blanc de
    Blancs Grand Cru Brut 2007, $$$$, 183
Delavenne Père & Fils Grand Cru Brut Tradition
    NV, $$, 194
Denis Salomon Rosé de Saignée NV, $$
Deutz Brut Millésimé 2014, $$, 201
Devaux Cuvée D NV, $$, 207
Diebolt-Vallois Millésimé 2011, $$, 211
Dom Pérignon Vintage Brut 2003, 218
Dumangin J Fils Hippolyte Blanc de Pinot Noir
    Brut Nature 2000, $$$$, 226
Dumangin J Fils Le Vintage Extra-Brut 2002, 226
Duménil 'Les Pêcherines' Prestige Vieilles
    Vignes Premier Cru NV, $$, 228
Duménil Millésimé Premier Cru 2007, $$, 228
Eric Rodez Pinot Noir Brut 2006, $$$$, 250
Fleury Boléro Extra Brut 2006, $$$, 253
Franck Bonville Grand Cru Blanc de Blancs Pur
    Avize 2012, $$$, 256
Franck Bonville Grand Cru Blanc de Blancs Pur
    Oger 2012, $$$, 256
Franck Bonville Grand Cru Extra Brut Blanc de
    Blancs Vintage 2012, $$, 256
Franck Bonville Grand Cru Rosé NV, $$$, 255
Gaston Chiquet Blanc de Blancs D'Aÿ Grand
    Cru Brut 2014, $$, 264
Geoffroy Empriente Millésimé Brut Premier Cru
    2012, $$, 271
Gosset Grand Blanc de Meunier Extra-Brut NV,
    $$$$, 277
Henriot Brut Rosé NV, $$$, 288
J. Lassalle Preference Premier Cru NV, $$, 293
J.L. Vergnon Eloquence Grand Cru Blanc de
    Blancs Extra Brut NV, $$, 300
J.L. Vergnon Resonance Blanc de Blancs Grand
    Cru Extra Brut 2009, $$$$, 302
Jacquesson Cuvée 737 Dégorgement Tardif Extra
    Brut NV, $$$$, 311
Jacquesson Cuvée 741 Extra Brut NV, $$, 311
Jerome Prevost La Closerie Fac-simile LC14 NV,
    $$$$$, 318
Jerome Prevost La Closerie Fac-simile LC15 NV,
    $$$$$, 317
Jerome Prevost La Closerie les Béguines LC15
    NV, $$$$, 317
JmSélèque Solessence Nature 7 Villages NV,
    $$, 321
José Michel & Fils Special Club 2010, $$$, 323
L. Bénard-Pitois Brut Millésimé Premier Cru
    2008, $$$, 338
L. Bénard-Pitois Rosé LB Brut NV, $$, 337
Laherte Frères Les Vignes d'Autrefois Extra Brut
    2013, $$$$, 342
Lanson Noble Cuvée Brut Rosé NV, $$$$, 353
Larmandier-Bernier Les Chemins d'Avize Grand
    Cru 2012, $$$$, 359
Larmandier-Bernier Special Club Vertus 1994, 360
Larmandier-Bernier Terre de Vertus Premier
    Cru 2013, $$$, 358
Larmandier-Bernier Vieille Vigne du Levant
    Grand Cru 2009, $$$$, 359
Laurenti Grande Cuvée Brut NV, $$, 361
Le Brun de Neuville Authentique Par
    Champagne Brut Assemblage NV, $$, 368
Le Brun de Neuville Authentique Par
    Champagne Brut Blanc de Blancs NV, $$, 368

Le Brun de Neuville Lady de N Cuvée Clovis
    Brut NV, $$$, 369
Le Mesnil Sublime Blanc de Blancs Grand Cru
    2012, $$$, 374
Louis Roederer Blanc de Blancs 2011, $$$$, 389
Louis Roederer Blanc de Blancs 1978
Mailly Grand Cru L'Intemporelle Rosé 2010,
    $$$$, 401
Mailly Grand Cru Magnum Collection
    Millésimé 1998, $$$$$, 401
Mailly Grand Cru Rosé de Mailly Brut NV,
    $$, 400
Mumm RSRV Blanc de Blancs Brut Grand Cru
    2013, $$$$, 420
Nicolas Maillart Chaillots Gillis Écueil Premier
    Cru 2012, $$$, 427
Nicolas Maillart Franc de Pied Écueil Premier
    Cru 2012, $$$$, 428
Palmer & Co Blanc de Blancs NV, $$$, 431
Pascal Agrapart Exp. 14 Brut Nature À Avize
    Grand Cru Blanc de Blancs NV, $$$$$, 85
Pascal Doquet Le Mesnil-sur-Oger Grand Cru
    Coeur de Terroir 2006, $$$$, 437
Paul Bara Bouzy Grand Millésimé Brut 2012,
    $$, 439
Paul Bara Bouzy Réserve Brut NV, $$, 439
Paul Déthune Blanc de Noirs Brut NV, $$$, 443
Paul Déthune Extra Brut NV, $$, 442
Paul Déthune Millésime 2008, $$$$, 443
Pierre Gimonnet & Fils Brut Extra 1er Cru Blanc
    de Blancs NV, $$, 462
Pierre Gimonnet & Fils Oenophile Non Dosé 1er
    Cru Blanc de Blancs Brut Nature 2012, $$, 463
Pierre Gimonnet & Fils Rosé de Blancs 1er Cru
    NV, $$, 463
Pierre Paillard La Grande Récolte Bouzy Grand
    Cru Millésime Extra Brut 2006, $$$, 469
Pierre Péters Cuvée de Réserve Blanc de Blancs
    Grand Cru Brut NV, $$$$, 473
Pierre Péters L'Etonnant Monsieur Victor
    Edition MK.11, $$$$$, 477
Pierre Péters Les Chétillons Cuvée Special Blanc
    de Blancs Brut 2010, $$$$, 476
Piper-Heidsieck Rosé Sauvage NV, $$, 482
Piper-Heidsieck Vintage Brut 2008, $$$, 483
Pol Roger Pure Extra Brut NV, $$, 487
Pommery Cuvée Louise Brut Nature 2004,
    $$$$, 494
Pommery Cuvée Louise Extra Brut 2004, $$$$, 494
Pommery Le Clos Pompadour 2003, $$$$$, 495
Pommery Louise 1999, $$$$, 494
R.Pouillon & Fils Chemin du Bois Méthode
    Fabrice Pouillon 2008, $$$$, 498
Robert Moncuit Blanc de Blancs 2012, $$$, 501
Taittinger Brut Millésimé 2013, $$$, 519
Taittinger Brut Millésimé 2012, $$$, 519
Taittinger Comtes de Champagne Rosé 2006,
    $$$$$, 521
Taittinger Folies de la Marquetterie Brut NV,
    $$, 518
Tarlant BAM! Blanc Arbane Meslier NV, $$$$, 526
Tarlant Rosé Zero Brut Nature NV, $$, 525
Vazart-Coquart et Fils Brut Réserve Blanc de
    Blancs Chouilly Grand Cru NV, $$, 541
Veuve Clicquot Extra Brut Extra Old NV, $$, 549
Veuve Clicquot Vintage 2012, $$, 549
Vilmart & Cie Grand Cellier Rubis Premier Cru
    Brut 2011, $$$$, 565
Vilmart & Cie Grande Réserve Brut Premier Cru
    NV, $$, 563

Mailly Grand Cru Blanc de Pinot Noir Brut NV, $$, 399

Moët & Chandon Grand Vintage Extra Brut 2012, $$$, 410

Mumm Cuvée Lalou Vintage 2006, $$$$$, 421

Palmer & Co Blanc de Noirs NV, $$, 431

Palmer & Co Brut Réserve NV, $$, 430

Pascal Agrapart Complantée Extra Brut À Avize Grand Cru NV, $$$, 84

Perrier-Jouët Grand Brut NV, $$, 445

Philippe Fourrier Blanc de Noirs NV, $$, 448

Pierre Gimonnet & Fils Cuis 1er Cru Brut NV, $$, 462

Pierre Paillard Les Gouttes d'Or Bouzy Blanc Coteaux Champenois 2012, $$, 468

Pierre Paillard Les Maillerettes Bouzy Grand Cru Blanc de Noirs Extra Brut 2013, $$$, 468

Pierre Péters Grande Réserve Blanc de Blancs Grand Cru Brut NV, $$$, 473

Pommery Apanage Blanc de Blancs NV, $$$, 493

Pommery Louise Rosé 2004, $$$$$, 495

Ruinart Blanc de Blancs NV, $$$, 508

Ruinart Rosé NV, $$$, 508

Taittinger Cuvée Prestige Brut NV, $$, 517

Taittinger Nocturne Sec NV, $$, 517

Ulysse Collin Les Enfers Blanc de Blancs NV, $$$$, 534

Ulysse Collin Les Maillons Rosé de Saignée NV, $$$$, 534

Vauversin Grand Cru Extra Brut Millésime 2014, $$$, 538

Vazart-Coquart et Fils Brut Zero Blanc de Blancs Chouilly Grand Cru NV, $$, 541

Veuve Fourny & Fils Blanc de Blancs Premier Cru Brut Nature NV, $$, 557

Veuve Fourny & Fils Grande Réserve Brut Premier Cru NV, $$, 556

Veuve Fourny & Fils Rosé Les Monts de Vertus Premier Cru Extra Brut NV, $$$, 560

Veuve Fourny & Fils Rosé Vinothèque Premier Cru Extra-Brut 2011, $$, 559

Yvonne Seier Christensen V Les Cinq Filles Blanc de Blancs Grand Cru Zero Dosage NV, $$$$, 566

90 POINTS

Alexandre Bonnet Blanc de Noirs Brut NV, $$, 87

André Clouet Dream Collection Vintage 2005, $$$, 96

André Heucq Héritage Blanc de Meunier Brut Nature NV, $$, 99

Ayala Brut Majeur NV, $$, 111

Ayala Brut Nature NV, $$, 111

Bérêche & Fils Les Beaux Regards Ludes Premier Cru 2014, $$$, 119

Bernard Remy Grand Cru NV, $$, 122

Besserat de Bellefon Blanc de Noirs NV, $$$, 124

Boizel Blanc de Blancs NV, $$$, 137

Boizel Blanc de Noirs NV, $$$, 137

Bourgeois-Diaz Cuvée M 100% Meunier NV, $$$, 152

Canard-Duchêne Millésime Vintage 2012, $$, 165

Cattier Brut Premier Cru NV, $$, 167

Charles Dufour Blanc Gourmand Coteaux Champenois 2010, $$, 171

Devaux Cuvée Rosée NV, $$, 207

Diebolt-Vallois Blanc de Blancs NV, $$, 210

Duval-Leroy Blanc de Blancs Grand Cru Brut NV, $$$, 233

Duval-Leroy Bouzy Grand Cru Extra Brut 2007, $$$$, 235

Duval-Leroy Petit Meslier Extra Brut 2007, $$$$, 234

Emmanuel Brochet Les Hauts Meuniers Extra Brut 2009, $$$$$, 245

Eric Rodez Pinot Noir 2005, $$$$, 250

Gardet Brut Premier Cru Blanc de Noirs NV, $$, 260

Gardet Extra-Brut Millésime 2012, $$, 260

Geoffroy Coteaux Champenois Cumières Rouge Pinot Noir 2012, $$$, 273

Geoffroy Meunier Millésimé 2013, $$$$, 270

Geoffroy Terre Millésimé Extra Brut Premier Cru 2000, 273

Georges Laval Garennes Extra Brut NV, $$$

Hatt et Söner Grande Cuvée Premier Cru Blanc de Blancs Brut Nature 2010, $$$, 280

Henri Giraud Esprit Nature NV, $$, 284

J.L. Vergnon Murmure Brut Nature Premier Cru Blanc de Blancs NV, $$, 300

Jacquart Brut Mosaïque NV, $$, 304

Jeeper Brut Premier Cru NV, $$$$, 314

José Michel & Fils Blanc de Blancs Brut 2008, $$, 323

L. Bénard-Pitois Carte Blanche Premier Cru Brut NV, $$, 336

Laherte Frères Rosé Meunier Extra Brut NV, $$

Lanson Extra Age Brut Rosé NV, $$$$, 351

Lanson Vin Biologique Green Label Organic Brut NV, $$, 350

Larmandier-Bernier Latitude Blanc de Blancs Extra Brut NV, $$, 357

Larmandier-Bernier Vertus Rouge Premier Cru Coteaux Champenois 2012, $$$$, 360

Le Brun de Neuville Blanc de Blancs Brut NV, $$, 367

Leclerc Briant Millésime Brut 2007, $$$$, 378

Mailly Grand Cru Délice NV, $$, 400

Moët & Chandon Grand Vintage Extra Brut 2009, $$$, 411

Mumm Brut Millésime 2012, $$$, 419

Mumm RSRV Rosé Foujita Brut NV, $$$$, 421

Nicolas Maillart Mont Martin Premier Cru 2015, $$$, 427

Pascal Doquet Horizon Blanc de Blancs NV, $$, 436

Perrier-Jouët Belle Epoque Rosé 2010, $$$$$, 447

Philippe Fourrier Cuvée Prestige NV, $$, 449

Philippe Glavier La Grace d'Alphaël Blanc de Blancs Grand Cru Zero NV, $$, 451

Philipponnat 1522 Premier Cru Brut Rosé 2007, $$$$, 457

Piper-Heidsieck Brut Cuvée NV, $$, 481

Robert Moncuit Vozémieux Blanc de Blancs Grand Cru 2010, $$$$, 501

Ruinart R de Ruinart NV, $$, 508

Thiénot Blanc de Blancs NV, $$, 529

Thiénot Cuvée Stanislas Blanc de Blancs 2007, $$$$, 529

Thiénot x Penfolds Blanc de Blancs Grand Cru Avize Vintage 2012, $$$$$, 531

Thiénot x Penfolds Chardonnay Pinot Noir Cuvee Vintage 2012, $$$$, 531

Yvonne Seier Christensen V Les Cinq Filles Rosé Extra Brut Biodynamic NV, $$$$, 567

89 POINTS

Alexandre Bonnet Grande Réserve Brut NV, $$, 86

Alexandre Bonnet Harmonie de Blancs Brut NV, $$, 87

Alexandre Bonnet Perle Rosée Brut NV, $$, 87

André Heucq Héritage Assemblage NV, $$, 99

Armand de Brignac Brut Gold NV, $$$$$, 108

Armand de Brignac Demi-Sec NV, $$$$$, 109

Ayala Rosé Majeur Brut NV, $$, 112

Bérêche & Fils Rive Gauche 2014, $$$, 119

Bernard Remy Blanc de Blancs Brut NV, $$, 121

Besserat de Bellefon Extra Brut NV, $$$, 124

Boizel Joyau de France Chardonnay 2007, $$$$, 138

Bruno Paillard Dosage Zero NV, $$$, 156

Cattier Brut Millésime Premier Cru 2009, $$, 168

Charles de Cazanove Brut Tradition Père et Fils Millésime 2007, $$, 170

Collet Brut Art Déco Premier Cru NV, $$, 180

Delavenne Père & Fils Grand Cru Brut Nature NV, $$,

Domaine La Borderie Les Devoix Coteaux Champenois Rouge 2015, $$

Dumangin J Fils Achille Blanc de Pinot Meunier Brut Nature 2000, $$$$, 226

Dumangin J Fils Le Vintage 2006, $$$, 225

Duménil 'Amour de Cuvee' Blanc de Noirs NV, $$, 229

Duval-Leroy Brut Réserve NV, $$, 232

Duval-Leroy Clos des Bouveries Brut 2003, $$$, 235

Gardet Brut Tradition NV, $$, 258

Gardet Prestige Charles Gardet Brut Millésime 2004, $$$, 261

Gardet Prestige Charles Gardet Rosé de Saignée Millésime Brut 2008, $$$, 261

Geoffroy Volupte Brut Premier Cru Millésimé 2011, $$$, 271

Henri Abelé Brut Millésimé 2006, $$$, 282

Hubert Soreau Le Clos l'abbe Chardonnay Brut NV, $$$$

J. Vignier Les Longues Verges Brut Grand Cru NV, $$$, 297

Jacquart Rosé Mosaïque NV, $$$, 304

Jeeper Brut Grand Cru NV, $$$$$, 314

L. Bénard-Pitois Laurent Bénard Blanc de Noirs Extra Brut Vendange 2011, 338

L. Bénard-Pitois Rosé Premier Cru NV, $$, 336

Laherte Frères Blanc de Blancs Brut Nature NV, $$, 341

Laherte Frères Extra-Brut Ultradition NV, $$, 341

Laherte Frères Les 7 Solera 05-13 NV, $$$$, 343

Laherte Frères Les Empreintes NV, $$, 342

Laurent-Perrier La Cuvée Brut NV, $$, 364

Le Brun de Neuville Grand Vintage Brut 2008, $$$, 369

Le Brun de Neuville Tendre Rosé Brut NV, $$, 368

Le Brun Servenay X.B. 3.2 Rosé Ultime Réserve Privée Extra Brut NV, $$$, 373

Lombard Brut Nature Grand Cru NV, $$, 381

Lombard Brut Nature Grand Cru Millésime 2008, $$$$, 382

Lombard Extra Brut Premier Cru NV, $$, 380

Mailly Grand Cru L'Intemporelle Brut 2011, $$$$, 400

Moutard Père et Fils Cépage Arbane 2012, $$$$, 414

Mouzon-Leroux L'Atavique Tradition Verzy Grand Cru NV, $$, 415

Nicolas Feuillatte Palmes d'Or Brut Vintage 2006, $$$$, 423

Nicolas Feuillatte Réserve Exclusive Rosé NV, $$, 423

Pascal Doquet Anthocyanes Premier Cru Rosé NV, $$, 436

Mutigny, harvest 2014

GLOSSARY

ACIDITY A crucial element that gives champagne its tangy freshness, vitality and life, and a sharp, clean taste on the finish.

AGRAFE
A large metal 'staple' to secure the cork during second fermentation and bottle ageing. Historically, used prior to the invention of capsules, and retained today by some houses and growers.

APÉRITIF
A drink used to get the tastebuds humming before a meal (champagne, naturally!).

ASSEMBLAGE
The process of blending a wine (see page 54).

AUTOLYSIS The breakdown of dead yeast cells during ageing on lees, improving mouthfeel and contributing biscuity, bready characters (see page 55).

BALTHAZAR 12-litre bottle (usually filled with champagne fermented in standard bottles or magnums). Be sure to have help on hand to pour it (and drink it!).

BARRIQUE
Small oak barrel of 225-litre capacity.

BÂTONNAGE
Stirring of the lees in barrel or tank.

BEAD Bubbles. The best champagne always has tiny bubbles, the product of the finest juice fermented in cold cellars.

BIODYNAMICS An intensive viticultural regime of extreme organics, eschewing chemical treatments and seeking a harmonious ecosystem.

BLANC DE BLANCS Literally translates as 'white from white'. White champagne made exclusively from white grapes, usually chardonnay, but may also include arbane, petit meslier, pinot blanc and/or pinot gris.

BLANC DE NOIRS Literally 'white from black'. White champagne made exclusively from the dark-skinned grapes pinot noir and/or meunier. This is achieved by gentle pressing to remove the juice from the skins before any colour leaches out.

BRETTANOMYCES 'Brett' is a barrel yeast infection, considered a spoilage character in champagne. It may develop further in bottle, manifesting itself as characters of boiled hot dog, antiseptic, horse stable, barnyard, animal or sweaty saddle, adding a metallic bite to the palate and contracting the finish.

BRUT Raw/dry, containing less than 12g/L sugar (formerly less than 15g/L sugar).

BRUT NATURE OR BRUT ZÉRO
No added sugar (less than 3g/L sugar).

CAPSULE Crown cap.

CARBON DIOXIDE The gaseous by-product of fermentation that is responsible for the bubbles in sparkling wine.

CAVE Cellar.

CÉPAGE Grape variety or blend of varieties.

CHAMPAGNE Wine from the region of the same name in north-east France. Champagne with a capital 'C' refers to the region; with a lower-case 'c' to the wine. French law prohibits the name for sparkling wines grown elsewhere.

CHAPTALISATION The addition of sugar (yes, this is legal in France) or concentrated grape juice to increase the alcohol strength of the wine (see page 54).

CHEF DE CAVE The 'chief' or 'chef' in the cellar (champagne winemaker).

CIVC Formerly 'Comité Interprofessionnel du Vin de Champagne', now 'Comité Champagne', a semi-public agency of the French government to represent the growers and houses in overseeing the production, distribution, promotion and research of champagne.

CLOS Historically a walled vineyard, though the walls may no longer exist.

COEUR DE LA CUVÉE
'Heart of the cuvée', the middle of the pressing, yielding the best juice.

COOPÉRATIVE DE MANIPULATION (CM)
A co-op of growers who produce champagne under their own brand.

CORKED Cork taint is an all too common wine fault resulting from the presence of 2,4,6 trichloroanisole (TCA) in natural cork. It imparts an off-putting, mouldy, 'wet cardboard' or 'wet dog' character, suppressing fruit and shortening the length of finish (see page 75).

CORK TAINT See 'corked'.

COTEAUX CHAMPENOIS
Champagne released as still wine, mostly red; typically made in tiny quantities, and mostly by smaller producers.

CRAYÈRES Roman chalk pits, now gloriously atmospheric cellars under Reims.

CRÉMANT Formerly used to describe slightly less fizzy champagnes (2–3 atmospheres of pressure), but no longer permitted on champagne, and instead often used for French sparkling wines produced outside of Champagne. Not to be confused with the village of Cramant in the Côte des Blancs. Mumm's de Cramant cuvée is both crémant (in the traditional sense) and exclusively sourced from Cramant.

CROWN CAP A metal seal like a beer cap, used to seal a champagne bottle during second fermentation and lees ageing.

CRU A commune, village, vineyard or officially classified 'growth'.

CUVÉE The first pressing of the grapes (2050 litres from 4000 kilograms of grapes), yielding the best juice. Also refers to an individual blend or style.

CUVERIE Tank room.

DÉBOURBAGE Literally 'de-sludging' to settling the solids from the must prior to fermentation (see page 54).

DÉBOURBAGE À FROID
Cold settling to clarify the juice, as practised by Billecart-Salmon, Pol Roger and others.

DÉGORGEMENT Disgorgement.

DEGREES POTENTIAL The ripeness at which grapes are picked, which determines the alcohol content of the finished wine.

DEMI-MUID Large oak barrel of 500–600-litre capacity.

DEMI-SEC Half-dry or medium-dry (32–50g/L sugar).

DIAM Mytik DIAM is a brand of champagne closure made by Oeneo, moulded from fragments of cork which have been treated to extract cork taint. Its reliable performance has made it an increasingly popular choice for champagne in recent years (see page 75).

DISGORGEMENT Removal of a frozen plug of sediment from the neck of the bottle (see page 55).

DOSAGE The final addition to top up the bottle, usually a mixture of wine and sugar syrup called *liqueur d'expédition* or *liqueur de dosage*. A dosage of 8–10g/L of sugar is typical in champagne (see page 55).

DOUX SWEET 50+ g/L sugar (Coca-Cola is 150g/L).

ÉCHELLE DES CRUS 'Ladder of growths', Champagne's crude classification of vineyards by village, expressed as a percentage.

ÉLEVAGE The process of 'bringing up' a wine, encompassing all cellar operations between fermentation and bottling.

EXTRA BRUT Extra raw/dry (less than 6g/L sugar).

EXTRA DRY OR EXTRA SEC Off dry (12–17g/L sugar).

FERMENTATION The conversion of sugar to alcohol by the action of yeasts. Carbonic gas is produced as a by-product.

FLUTE Narrow champagne glass.

FOUDRE Very large oak cask, typically with a capacity between 2000 litres and 12,000 litres.

GRAND CRU The highest vineyard classification. In Champagne, a classification is crudely applied to a village and all the vineyards within its bounds acquire the same classification. Seventeen villages are classified as grand cru.

GRANDES MARQUES An obsolete, self-imposed term for the big champagne brands. Still used informally.

GREY IMPORTS See 'Parallel imports'.

GROWER-PRODUCER A champagne producer who makes wines from fruit grown only on his or her own vineyards; 5% of fruit is permitted to be purchased. Olivier Krug defines a grower champagne as one made from your garden.

GYROPALETTE A large mechanised crate to automatically riddle champagne bottles.

INOCULATE To seed a ferment with yeast.

JÉROBOAM A 3-litre bottle, previously typically filled with champagne fermented in standard bottles or magnums. However, it is now a legal requirement that it must be made in its own bottle from first bottling.

LATE DISGORGEMENT A champagne that has been matured on its lees for an extended period.

LEES Sediment that settles in the bottom of a tank, barrel or bottle, primarily dead yeast cells.

LIEU-DIT Individually named plot or vineyard site.

LIGHTSTRUCK The degradation of wine exposed to ultraviolet light. Sparkling wines in clear bottles are most susceptible.

LIQUEUR D'EXPÉDITION The final addition to top up the bottle, usually a mixture of wine and sugar syrup.

LIQUEUR DE DOSAGE See 'Liqueur d'expédition'.

LIQUEUR DE TIRAGE A mixture of sugar and wine or concentrated grape juice added immediately prior to bottling, to produce the secondary fermentation in bottle (see page 55).

LUTTE RAISONNÉE Literally 'reasoned struggle', a middle ground between conventional viticulture and organic farming, reducing the use of herbicides and pesticides while retaining the right to employ them in times of need. Often a sensible approach in Champagne's erratic climate.

MACERATION Soaking of red grape skins in their juice in the production of red or rosé wine (see page 55).

MAGNUM A 1.5-litre bottle. According to the Champenois, the perfect size for two, when one is not drinking.

MAISON House.

MALIC ACID A naturally occurring acid in grapes and other fruits, particularly green apples. It is most pronounced in grapes in cold climates and is responsible for champagne's searing acidity, which is usually softened through malolactic fermentation.

MALOLACTIC FERMENTATION 'Malo' is the conversion of stronger malic (green apple) acid to softer lactic (dairy) acid (see page 54).

MARQUE D'ACHETEUR (MA) Buyer's own brand. An 'own label' owned by a supermarket or merchant.

MÉTHODE CHAMPENOISE An obsolete term for the traditional method of sparkling wine–making, now 'Méthode Traditionnelle' or 'Méthode Classique'.

MÉTHODE TRADITIONNELLE The official name for the traditional method of sparkling wine–making, in which the second fermentation occurs in the bottle in which the wine is sold.

METHUSELAH A 6-litre bottle, usually filled with champagne fermented in standard bottles or magnums.

MILLÉSIME Vintage.

MINERALITY The texture and mouthfeel of a wine derived from its soil.

MOUSSE See 'Bead'.

MCR (MOÛT CONCENTRÉ RECTIFIÉ) Concentrated and rectified grape must, used by some houses as an alternative to cane or beet sugar to sweeten dosage.

MUSELET Wire cage to hold a champagne cork in the bottle.

NEBUCHADNEZZAR A 15-litre bottle, usually filled with champagne fermented in standard bottles or magnums. Do not attempt while home alone!

NÉGOCIANT-MANIPULANT (NM) Champagne producer who purchases grapes and/or unfinished wines. A négociant may also include up to 95% estate grown fruit.

NON-VINTAGE (NV) A champagne containing wine from more than one vintage.

OENOTHÈQUE Literally a wine library or shop. Sometimes used to refer to bottles held back for extended ageing.

OÏDIUM Powdery mildew, a fungal disease that can have a devastating effect on grape crops.

ORGANICS A viticultural regime that avoids the use of any synthetic pesticides, herbicides, fungicides or other treatments. Copper is permitted, though criticised in some circles for a toxicity higher than that of some synthetic products.

OXIDISED A wine that has reacted with oxygen. At its most extreme, oxidation can produce browning in colour, loss of primary fruit, a general flattening of flavours, a shortening of the length of finish, or even a vinegar or bitter taste.

PARALLEL IMPORTS Champagne brought into a country by parties other than the usual agent, typically via a third-party country. Good for keeping pricing competitive, but can become problematic if transportation or storage are compromised.

pH The level of acid strength of a wine expressed as a number. Low pH equates to high acidity; 7 is neutral.

PHENOLICS A grape compound responsible for astringency and bitterness in the back palate. It is particularly rich in stems, seeds and skins, and especially prevalent in champagnes from warm vintages such as 2003 and 2005.

PIÈCE Small oak barrel of 205-litre capacity in Champagne (228 litres in Burgundy).

POIGNETTAGE The vigorous shaking of the bottle after corking to mix the wine and liqueur. It can also refer to the old practice of shaking the bottle by hand to stir up the lees and enhance autolytic flavours, rarely used today, though still upheld by De Sousa and Dumangin J. Fils.

PREMIER CRU The second highest vineyard classification, awarded to 41 villages. In Champagne, a classification is crudely applied to a village, and all the vineyards within its bounds acquire the same classification.

PRESTIGE CUVÉE The flagship champagne or champagnes of a brand, typically the most expensive. Olivier Krug says it should be defined as one that can age.

PRISE DE MOUSSE The second fermentation that creates the bubbles (see page 55).

PUPITRE Hand-riddling rack.

RATAFIA A beverage of unfermented grape juice, typically from later press cuts, fortified with grape brandy spirit.

RÉCOLTANT-COOPÉRATEUR (RC) Champagne grower selling wine under his/her own brand, made by his/her cooperative.

RÉCOLTANT-MANIPULANT (RM) Champagne grower who makes wine from estate fruit; 5% of grapes may also be purchased to supplement production.

REDUCTIVE A wine made or aged with limited contact with oxygen may develop reductive characters, hydrogen sulphide notes akin to struck flint, burnt match and gunpowder. At their extreme, these can manifest themselves as objectionable notes of rubber, rotten eggs, garlic, onion or cooked cabbage.

REHOBOAM A 4.5-litre bottle, usually filled with champagne fermented in standard bottles or magnums.

REMUAGE The riddling process (see page 55).

RESERVE WINES Wines held in the cellar for future blending in a non-vintage cuvée (see page 54). Usually aged in tanks, although sometimes kept in barrels or bottles.

RETROUSSE Separation and redistribution of the cake of grape skins, stems and seeds between each pressing in a traditional vertical press.

RIDDLING The process of moving the lees sediment into the neck of the bottle prior to disgorgement, either by hand or by gyropalette (see page 55).

SABRAGE A technique for opening a champagne bottle with a sabre. Practice is recommended prior to attempting this in public. Not recommended for fear of wastage and glass shards in your flute (see pate 75).

SAIGNÉE A technique in which rosé is made by 'bleeding' off juice from just-crushed pinot noir or meunier grapes after a short maceration (soaking) on skins prior to fermentation (see page 55).

SALMANAZAR A 9-litre bottle, usually filled with champagne fermented in standard bottles or magnums.

SEC Dryish (17–32g/L sugar).

SOLERA A system of fractional blending using wines of different ages, with the bottled wine drawn from the last stage. Also used in Champagne to refer to a simplified system of perpetual blending, in which successive vintages are added to a single tank.

STALE Lacking in fruit freshness.

SUR LATTES See 'vins sur lattes'.

SUR POINTE The storing of bottles neck down, between riddling and disgorgement. Sometimes also used for long-term storage of undisgorged bottles. With the lees settled in the neck, it is believed the wine stays fresher for longer.

TAILLES Coarser, inferior juice that flows last from the press.

TCA See 'Corked'.

TERROIR A catch-all term for anything that defines the character of a vineyard – soil, micro-climate, altitude, aspect, exposure, slope, drainage, and even the hands that tend it.

TIRAGE Bottling of the blended wine with an addition of sugar and yeast, so as to provoke the second fermentation in bottle (see page 55).

TUN Large oak barrel, typically around 1000 litres in volume.

VENDANGE Vintage or harvest.

VIEILLES VIGNES Old vines.

VIGNERON Vine grower.

VIN CLAIR Still base wine that has undergone its primary fermentation and (potentially) malolactic fermentation, but not its secondary fermentation.

VINS SUR LATTES Champagne bottles laid on their side, having undergone second fermentation, but yet to be riddled. Also refers to the legal but shady practice by which champagne houses purchase finished but yet to be disgorged champagne made by another producer, to then market under their own label.

VINTAGE Wine from a single year. To be released as a vintage cuvée, a champagne must spend a minimum of three years on lees.

ZERO DOSAGE No sweetness is added during the final addition to top up the bottle (see page 55).

Charles Heidsieck's third-century Roman crayères

AUTHOR THANKS

I owe a great debt of gratitude to hundreds of champagne houses and their agents for their hospitality and generosity in inviting me into their homes, cellars, tasting rooms and vineyards, sending samples and offering the privilege of discovering their stories and their wines. A project of this magnitude is only possible with a cast of thousands. Here are just 260 of the many to whom I owe a special thanks.

Charlotte Agard-Derolez, Nathalie Agrapart, Pascal Agrapart, Daniel Airoldi, Pierre Amillet, Ricardo Antunes, Axelle Araud, Sylvie Arvois, Tyler Austin, Godefroy Baijot, Danielle Bailly, Frédéric Baiocco, Chantale Bara, Stephane Barlerin, Sam Barry, Kiron Barui, Laurent Bénard, Michelle Bénard-Louis, Raphaël Bérêche, Vivien Bernard, Philippe-Alexandre Bernatchez, Katy Beurton, Will Bolton, David Bone, Olivier Bonville, Christelle Bosser, Alison Bouchet-Maugran, Emilien Boutillat, Justine Boxler, Emmanuel Brochet, Béatrice Brossier, Cyril Brun, Nat Burch, David Burkitt, Audrey Campos, Régis Camus, Antoine Caparros, Pierre Casenave, Alexandre Cattier, Jean-Jacques Cattier, Laurent Champs, Morgane Champs, Vincent Chaperon, Alexandre Chartogne, Paméla Cherrier, Louis Cheval-Gatinois, Sandrine Chiono-Veisse, Jean-Hervé Chiquet, Nicolas Chiquet, Audrey Clisson, Marie-Laure Clouet, Jean Francois Clouet (JFC), Johann Cochut, Olivier Collin, Dominic Coulton, Sophie Couvreur, Julien Craeye, François Crémière, Catherine Curie, Antrim Dalton, Gisella D'Ambra, Hervé Dantan, Christian Darquier, Evelyne Dauvergne, Nicole Daven, Georgia De Biasi, Antoine de Boysson, Guy De Rivoire, Charlotte De Sousa, Odilon de Varine, Conrad Dean, Magda Debiec, Constance Delaire, Sébastien Delaire, Dominique Demarville, François Demouy, Eleonore Denieau, Didier Depond, Caroline Desaulle, Hervé Deschamps, Gilles Descôtes, Pierre Déthune, Sophie Déthune, Pierre Alexandre Dhainaut, Laurent d'Harcourt, Odile Didier, Isabelle Diebolt, David Donald, Laure Doquet, Pascal Doquet, Leigh Dryden, Peter Dubourdieu, Anais Dubourg, Stéphanie Ducloux, Nathalie Dufour, Gilles Dumangin, Marie Dupas, Marie-Albane d'Utruy, Francis Egly, Tim Evans, Margaux Falala, Laurent Fédou, Samuel Ferjou, Tessa Flores, Charles-Henry Fourny, Emmanuel Fourny, Mathilde Fourrier, Inge Fransen, Tiffany Frapart, Laurent Fresnet, Peter Gago, Emmanuel Gantet, Mim Gardiner, Lauren Gatley, Jean-Baptiste Geoffroy, Axel Gillery, Didier Gimonnet, Jean-Noël Girard, Benoît Gouez, Julian Goût, Sandy Grant, Christine Hauberdon, Amy Hayes, Anne-Sophie Hennique, Brune Hilde, Katri Hilden, Joseph Ho, Anton Hobbs, Victoria Hogan, Christian Holthausen, Vincent House, Ildi Ireland, Nicolas Jaeger, Brian Jo, Tiffany Johnson, Thomas Jorez, Mathias Kahn, Tierney Kelman, Jesper Kjaersgaard, Olivier Krug, Gabriella Kuiters, Sophie Kutten, Jérôme Lafouge, Benoît Lahaye, Aurélien Laherte, Jean Marc Lallier-Deutz, Arthur Larmandier, Pierre Larmandier, Sophie Larmandier, Jemma Lawrence, Gauthier Le Brun, Damien Le Sueur, Jean-Baptiste Lécailllon, Ian Leckie, Stuart Leece, Sylviane Lemaire, Stephen Leroux, Rachel Linard, Thommas Linnrose, Sandrine Logette-Jardin, Thomas Lombard, Alicia Lor, Cécile Lorson, Justine Lyons, Erwin Magat, Nicolas Maillart, Baptiste Marchal, Magalie Maréchal, Tim McGie, Sally McGill, Tess McLachlan, Ed Merrison, Sabine Mignon, Marie-Charlotte Mignucci, Marion Milesi-Costa, Xavier Millard, Claire Moreau, Jeff Morgenthal, Maud Moussy, Julie Murez, Bruce Nancarrow, Sebastian Nickel, Angelica Nohra, Megan Nunn, Ernie O'Rourke, Cam O'Keefe, Alice Paillard, Marie Pamart, Frederic Panaiotis, Mario Panzarino, Toby Parker, Jo Pearson, Rodolphe Péters, Lorène Petiau, Jean-Jacques Peyre, Charles Philipponnat, Charles-Antoine Picart, Clément Pierlot, Maxime Pinon, Eliza Pithers, Maddie Polson, Pierre Pommarede, Tom Portet, Mathieu Pouchan, Jérôme Prévost, Victor Pugatschew, Matthew Quirk, Louise Raisin, David Reberger, Christophe Rebut, Jean-Pierre Redont, Myriam Renard, Sandrine Renard, Thibault Renard, Amanda Richard, Raymond Ringeval, Anthony Rocher, Eric Rodez, Antoine Roland-Billecart, Jody Rolfe, Florent Roques-Boizel, Angus Ross, Fabrice Rosset, Alex Rougeot, Branca Salaverry, Claire Sarazin, Hervé Savès, David Seymour, Chris Sheehy, Nesh Simic, Michelle Slater, Elsa Source, Gary Steel, Huon Stelzer, Linden Stelzer, Rachael Stelzer, Vaughn Stelzer, David Stredwick, Clovis Taittinger, Vitalie Taittinger, Benoît Tarlant, Laurence Tellier, Angéline Templier, Jenny Tracey, Kaitlyn Tremblay, Craig Underhill, Helen Underhill, Laurent Vauversin, Jean-Pierre Vazart, Gauthier Vecten, Clément Vergnon, Remi Vervier, Amandine Volhuer, Nathalie Vranken, Matthew Wallace, Patrick Walsh, Rob Walters, Danika Windrim, Jon Yarnall, Neville Yates, Thibaut Le Mailloux, John Noble.

Research and production of this book are entirely self-funded, including all travel and accommodation in Champagne.

TYSON STELZER was named The International Wine & Spirit Competition Communicator of the Year 2015, The Wine Communicators of Australia Australian Wine Communicator of the Year 2015 and 2013, and The International Champagne Writer of the Year 2011 in The Louis Roederer International Wine Writers' Awards.

He is the author of 16 wine books and a regular contributor to many magazines. Tyson is a contributor to Jancis Robinson's *The Oxford Companion to Wine*, 3rd edition. He is the host of the television series *People of the Vines* and the *Taste Champagne* event series. He founded the *Teen Rescue Foundation* to address teen alcohol abuse.

As an international speaker, he has presented at wine events in 12 countries. He is a regular judge and chairman at wine shows throughout Australia and is a co-creator with UK wine writer Matthew Jukes of *The Great Australian Red Competition* and *The Great New Zealand Pinot Noir Classification*. Tyson personally hosts intimate champagne tours.

He was the winner of the Best Digital Wine Book in Australia 2017, Digital Wine Communicator of the Year 2015, Best Wine Book of the Year 2014, Best French Wine Book in Australia 2014, Best Trade or Technical Writer of the Year 2013 and the Award for Best Food and Wine Writing 2008.

Tyson is 44 years of age and lives in Brisbane with his wife Rachael and sons Linden, Huon and Vaughn.